The **Gun Digest** Book Of

SPORTING CLAYS

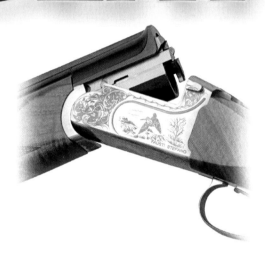

RICK SAPP

©2005 Gun Digest Books
Published by

Gun Digest Books
An imprint of F+W Publications

700 East State Street • Iola, WI 54990-0001
715-445-2214 • 888-457-2873

Our toll-free number to place an order or obtain
a free catalog is (800) 258-0929.

Library of Congress Catalog Number: 2004097728
ISBN: 0-87349-940-9

Cover Photos Courtesy of U.S. Repeating Arms Co.
and Remington Arms Company, Inc.

Designed by Paul Birling
Edited by Kevin Michalowski

Printed in United States of America

ABOUT THE AUTHOR

One of the best-rounded figures in outdoor sports literature, **Rick Sapp** has been blessed with the opportunity to shoot, hunt and fish across the United States. He has taken trophy bears with a bow and arrow, pulled walleye through holes in the ice of frozen Minnesota lakes, tossed his cookies over the side of fishing boats on the Gulf of Mexico, and missed spectacularly easy shots on skeet station no. 7.

Growing up on an island off the coast of Florida, Rick loved nothing better than tying a BB gun on the handle bars of his bicycle and pedaling to remote and romantic hammocks, sand dunes and swamps, to stalk bears, re-create Civil War battles or even fight alongside Superman and Roy Rogers. A veteran of the shooting, hunting, and outdoor trades industry, Sapp has a breadth of interests and expertise that is equaled by few and exceeded by none. Today, Rick's driving passion is to understand and write about the spirit of the shooting sports and the outdoor adventure.

DEDICATION

It is not often, when one reaches *un certain age*, that we have the opportunity to extend ourselves deeply into a field of knowledge, into an activity, that truly expands our horizons. I suppose that if I took up mountain climbing or undersea exploration, they would have the same broadening effect that sporting clays has done for me.

I have never taken sporting clays too seriously, approaching it as a tune up for bird hunting or something to do with the neighbors on a Sunday afternoon when we were all bored with the barbecue grill.

What I discovered was a pastime or leisure activity that I could easily become passionate about. It involved excercise for the brain and body. It required mastering a new skill and, even at my relatively low level of achievement, had a nice competitive edge. I like that.

With the grateful appreciation to all of the individuals and companies that have helped me prepare this book, with their ideas, their photos and their products.

Rick Sapp
Gainsville Florida
May 2005

The **Gun Digest**® Book Of

SPORTING CLAYS
- 3rd Edition

TABLE OF CONTENTS

1
Chapter

AN INTRODUCTION TO SPORTING CLAYS:
KING OF THE SHOTGUN GAMES

Sporting clays is a game that one plays with a shotgun and a box of shells. Disks called "pigeons" or "birds," or simply "clays," are thrown by machine and players try to shoot them while they are in the air. You can tell when you hit one because they break in flight. Hit one squarely and they virtually evaporate in front of your eyes. That is exciting … especially when your good friend, who is next in line to shoot, misses entirely!

SPORTING CLAYS COMES OF AGE

Clay shooting has been around for a long time and both trap and skeet, which have enormous followings, predate sporting clays. In America, trap shooting was documented in the mid-19th century. Competitors shot at live pigeons released from a box or "trap." It slowly evolved through a series of target styles, including glass balls, to become the highly structured game it is today. (You may still be able to find live pigeon shooting events in the United States and around the world, but because of pressure from a changing society, these events have virtually gone underground.)

Skeet began in the United States about 80 years ago when shotgunners who were bird hunters tried to develop a more field-realistic alternative to trap shooting. It derived its name in a quintessential American way. According to documented legend, Gertrude Hurbutt of Dayton, Montana, entered the name "skeet," a derivative of a Scandinavian word for "shoot," in a magazine-sponsored contest and won $100 when it was chosen for the new game. In those days, skeet was shot in a 360-degree circle. For obvious reasons, that structure did not last and skeet was soon changed to the 180-degree semi-circle it is today.

Both trap and skeet evolved as games that would make participants better wingshooters. They still have this function, but there is apparently some natural human impulse to keep score, to challenge and compete, that has turned these venerable shooting games quite rigid and unvarying. The birds are thrown in order in predictable directions at fixed speeds and angles. With practice and some coaching, even an average shooter can reasonably expect to score a perfect round.

Photo courtesy of South Dakota Tourism.

Shotgun sports such as sporting clays, skeet and trap began with a desire by wingshooters to be more proficient with their guns. While skeet is an American original, trap and sporting clays were essentially imports from Great Britain.

Sporting clays has its roots in England. The game spread to the US by-and-large in the '70s and grew quietly in the '80s as shotgunners slowly discovered how much fun it could be to break out of the mold of skeet and trap and have fun with a shotgun again. Of course, it took 10 to 20 years for range owners and entrepreneurs to realize that if they built courses, people would come and shoot.

Although it is now legal to shoot with a shouldered gun in sporting clays competition, at most informal AND competitive shoots, participants will still begin with their gun below the armpit ... as sporting clays were intended to be shot!

Dr. Henry Rodeffer and sons shot together at WW Sporting Clays in Baldwin, Florida. It may be a cliché, but the family that enjoys shooting together is ... well, ahead of the game in our pressurized achievement-oriented society.

Enterprising course builders may have been the key to sporting clays' rising popularity in the decades of the '80s and '90s and perhaps they still are. Trap and skeet were established games, whereas sporting clays was still a gamble in the early days. It is difficult to shoehorn a good clays course into a corner of an established range, so a rising interest in sporting clays shooting required an investment in land. It also required an investment in trap machines and course design. At today's prices, a new, top-of-the-line Pro-Matic SuperSporter for throwing standard, midi and mini clays costs $2495. You need a dozen or so to set up a good clays course. Then, there is insurance and business licenses and a ton of government forms and a cooperative agreement with an area shooting club to develop leagues.

A lot of things had to come together to grow sporting clays. Magazines like Sporting Clays and organizations such as the National Sporting Clays Association (the NSCA) sprouted in the '80s and began to standardize some of the elements of competitive shooting. National championships were organized and the Americans eventually integrated some of the competitive aspects of their game with other shooters around the world in the Federation Internationale de Tir aux Armes Sportives de Chasse or FITASC. Sporting clays was on a roll and growing in popularity. It has not stopped.

TO COMPETE ... OR NOT

There is a strain in the sporting clays game, which you will soon-enough encounter if you enjoy the shooting, and that is the concern with keeping score. In a sense, all shooting formats – trap, skeet and sporting – began as a way to tune-up for wingshooting, hunting wild game birds. It is in the nature of things, however, that the games took on a life of their own, and many people began shooting not so they could hunt better – unfortunately, relatively few Americans have an opportunity to hunt much these days – but shooting for the sheer pleasure of busting clay birds. It is perfectly understandable. People pick up a shotgun for many reasons and bird-hunting opportunities are not evenly distributed around the United States. In the Southeast, hunting native quail has become a rich man's game. In the Northeast, put-and-take programs for shooting released pheasants attract huge crowds. In the Midwest and West, apparently natural grouse and pheasant cycles often determine whether birds are available, even to a dedicated hunter and his or her dog. And across the Unites States and Canada, waterfowl migrations – governed for many years now by international treaties – are heavily regulated to maintain breeding populations as well as places for them to breed.

Most people initially come to shotgun games from a hunting background. When they find they can spend more enjoyable days on the range shooting clays in one year than they can shoot grouse or quail in a lifetime, many choose to enter extend their fun by entering competitions.

Occasional shooting for the sheer fun of it may be the soul of sporting clays or perhaps that designation should be saved for tournament shooting. Competing to see who shoots the best is surely not new. Men and women have most certainly challenged one another since the dawn of the spear or the bow and arrow or maybe even before that, as we know that among the Yanomamo Indians of South America, men engage in public chest-pounding duels with their fists and forearms. Competition builds intensity and focus. It demands a level of attention not found among shooters who unlimber their 12-gauge shotgun a few times a year.

Whether or not you choose to participate in sporting clays competitions depends on your own motivations, but many shooters say that competition keeps them sharp. In a way, it provides that additional personal incentive or a perspective that helps them define themselves outside the nest of family and work or retirement. Competing requires a different mindset than the casual, "Oh, shucks. I missed that one again," approach of the once- or twice-a-year shooter.

Should you choose to compete, there is no limit to the opportunity to travel except your desire, dedication, ability and finances. If you are good enough, however, your shooting and positive attitude will attract sponsors that will help you defray expenses. The World FITASC Championships in Signes, France, featured international competition as rugged as the mountainous terrain.

Competing means shooting for score. If this idea troubles you, if you are a freewheeling wingshooter who disdains counting things in your "free time," just remember that hunters have bag limits. When you sit down for a beer at the local rod and gun club, it is the scattergunner who regularly comes in with a limit that is acclaimed as the superlative hunter and shooter. Competition strengthens your shooting and, I believe, makes everything about your shotgun game sharper, crisper and cleaner.

Shooting registered targets sounds a bit formidable, but it is essentially no different than shooting non-registered targets. It only means that you are writing down your scores at NSCA-sanctioned events (and almost any true sporting clays event in the United States will be so sanctioned) and sending them to the NSCA, of which you have become a member (www.mynsca.com), for classification. "Classification" only means that you are competing against individuals at your own ability level.

When you start shooting clays, you will be learning the game and will not be expected to start at the top of the heap and compete with the pros. As you begin to be comfortable with the varied target presentations, and with shooting while a lot of people are standing around watching, you gain experience and ability and move up in classification and status from E to D and so on.

Like a road race, if you are a runner, everyone's time or score is listed on a sheet from the fastest to the slowest. In addition then, after a shoot, people are grouped secondly by experience and ability or by special category: Ladies (women), Sub-Junior (under 14 years of age), Junior (under 18), Veteran (55 through 64) and Super-Veteran (65 and over). The bigger the shoot, the more categories there will be (and the greater your chance of winning something). This system gives you many opportunities to measure your ability against all other shooters and within your own particular age and experience class. (Of course, in the manner of rule-book-bound organizations, the NSCA goes a bit further to complicate classification by instituting a system of "punches." It is like having a floating average in school. Anyway, as a novice shooter, it should not overly concern you. The only individuals who truly worry about "punches" are those with secretarial duties.)

The final word about whether to compete or not may be to pay attention to your own interests. If you are a hunter, use a few rounds of sporting clays to warm up for the season. Shooting these unexpected clays will make you a better hunter. If you only shoot for fun, clays are all of that. If you are an A-type personality, who chafes because you are not the first in every line, then certainly, competition should be on your agenda.

THE SHOOTING COURSE

It is almost a joke to say "the shooting course" when you write about sporting clays, because the game's emphasis is on varied rather than highly repetitive shooting. This is different from trap and skeet or the doubles and international versions of those games. In both of those older games, you stand in the open and you know exactly where the bird will emerge and when, after you call "Pull!" In those games, clay targets are thrown at precise, prescribed angles, heights and speeds. The fun of sporting clays is that all of this goes out the window and pulling the trigger once again becomes an adventure.

Sporting clays course designers emphasize diverse target presentations. You may not even see where the target launcher, the trap, is positioned. Say "Pull!" and a bird appears, somewhere. Because its appearance and

The glory of sporting clays is that if you can imagine a shot, some course designer has already incorporated it into a station.

Photo courtesy of Quail Creek.

Unless you shoot totally for fun and do not care how many targets you break, you will benefit from professional shooting instruction. In this photo from Callaway Gun Club in Georgia, the instructor works to correct this novice shooter's form, stance and gun movement.

flight are unanticipated (at least at first), the round target seems to fly faster and the time you have to shoot is shorter, and this of course may be an illusion.

In actual practice, it is not quite so bad, because when your group or squad appears at a station, the trapper will get everyone's attention and throw a complete set of birds. If you are a novice, and it is not a registered shoot where there is a strict rotation, someone else will usually shoot first. This gives you a second chance to see where the targets emerge and how they fly. Thus, you have an opportunity to decide, before you step into the shooting cage, where to shoot each one and perhaps what choke or type of shell to use.

When it is your turn to shoot, step into the designated shooting stand and load your gun, keeping the barrel pointing downrange and away from everyone. You may be shooting downward into a ravine; there is a famous shot like that at Cherokee Rose, south of Atlanta. You may be shooting over water; there is a beautiful over-the-lake presentation at Claythorne Lodge in Kansas. Perhaps the bird will fly high and fast through a shroud of oaks; there are several targets like this at the small Turkey Run course north of Gainesville, Florida.

In sporting clays, if you can imagine a shot, a course designer has probably beaten you to it and installed

it somewhere. With shooting courses in as different locations as the arid Southwest and the swamps of south Florida (unfortunately, the host club for the Caribbean Cup near Miami recently closed), you can find shooting in any environment. Clubs in Canada and New York and Minnesota hold fun shoots in the dead of winter. With hundreds of courses in all 50 U.S. states and throughout the populated zones of Canada, there is certainly an event being held or a course open for drop-in shooting near you at any time of year.

There has been a movement of late to make courses easier to shoot. The conventional wisdom for a dozen years was to make shooting more challenging, meaning more difficult. Longer shots. More extreme angles. Faster birds. Apparently, this has driven more potential clays enthusiasts away from the sport than it has gained in advocates. Today, it is not unusual to find two or more routes available at a clays course, a challenging route and one that is more forgiving for novice and intermediate shooters. At the Bobwhite Hill Ranch in North Little Rock, for example, there are four courses graded by difficulty from easy to expert.

As a novice, during your first outings you may be nervous that you did not hit anything or will be embarrassed by your shooting. I certainly was and the first few times I shot a complete round, I broke the least birds – by a considerable margin. As I became more involved and took a few hours of instruction, watched a few tapes and read a few books, I got better.

On the subject of instruction, tapes and books, there are dozens of excellent opportunities available. In our chapter on "Coaches, Classes and Shooting Schools," you can find instructional information. For a first book, I recommend Bob Knopf's *Wing & Clay Shooting Made Easy*. As far as tapes and CDs are concerned, there are dozens available for wing and clay shooting, but these are a few that I have studied: "The World of Wing & Clay Shooting" with Michael Murphy and Ed Scherer; "The Art of Shooting Flying: A Lesson in the Key Points of Instinctive Wingshooting" with Bryan Bilinski and Tom Huggler; and a three-volume set from Gil and Vicki Ash of Optimum Shotgun Performance Shooting School, "How to Practice and Understanding the Move," "14 Tips to Better Shotgunning" and "Strategy & How to Play the Game." Of course, there are many good tapes, books and CDs offered for clays and those from skeet and trap masters will also help tremendously.

I find that many (or maybe most) instructors teach essentially the same techniques and fundamentals. Some types of presentations or perhaps the instructor's personalities (or my mood that day) make all the difference in what I hear, retain and am able to use later on a course.

A day of sporting clays shooting will normally consist of presentations for 50 or 100 birds. Serious shooters often precede walking a course with a warm-up of 25 birds on a 5-Stand (more about 5-Stand later).

HIT THESE PITCHES OUT OF THE PARK

After you become accustomed to the weird presentations a course can throw at you, you soon realize there are only a few truly unique shots. Now, the question immediately arises whether you should shoot from a pre-mounted gun position … just because you now can do so. Personally, I feel that a pre-mounted gun goes against the grain of sporting clays' original purpose, which was to present the joy and surprises of a complete day of wingshooting with crossing mallards, springing teal, woodcock springing up and away, and maybe a grouse thundering through the brush in any direction, perhaps right over your head. Nevertheless, unless a club specifies otherwise, this is your choice.

First, most shots will cross in front of you, usually at an angle, but either left-to-right or right-to-left. This is like middle skeet positions three, four and five, and those stations are good spots to practice. Do not set your body and feet to break the bird as soon as it emerges from a skeet house, high or low. Imagine that you are on a clays field and you cannot see the trap. Set up so that you and your feet are facing close to the skeet "eight post," that visible stake in the center of the field that all skeet birds fly over when they exit the high and low houses. Your break point is just to the right (high house

birds) or left (low house birds) of center. Remember to swing through these birds. Do not stop your swing when you pull the trigger. Practice shooting birds from both houses and then practice doubles. (It does not count if you hit both with one shot!)

The harder the crossing shot the more you will turn your body from the ankles, from your foundation, and the more difficult it becomes to achieve good follow-through. The tendency will be to lift your cheek off the stock and look up. Remember that no tennis player or baseball player stops their swing immediately upon contact, and neither should you (of course, they do not have doubles to worry about, either). Good follow-through is essential, so keep your cheek tight against the comb as you swing. With a clay target, a kill means that you only have to knock off a "visible piece." You do not have to make the disk evaporate in a puff of dust. Both count equally.

Master the straightaway and you are well on your way to excelling at sporting clays. The straightaway looks easy, but it is a deceptive shot because the angle can fool you. Birds flying away from you probably are not on a perpendicular line as you are not above the trap, so as viewed from your shooting position, they will have an angle – two angles – plus a curve and changing speed. Straightaway shots fly out angling, sometimes

Checking for your name in a list is half of the fun and excitement of competition. The "leader board" is always a gathering spot and place to talk about results, stations and the mechanics of shooting.

Crossing shots over water are always more fun than standard crossing shots through the trees. Remember that you have time, and resist the impulse to rush your shots.

The straightaway shot – outgoing or incoming – can be deceptive because it is moving in two directions and slowing down as you get the muzzle to the break point. This is a straightaway shot beside the tower at SteelClay in Iowa.

imperceptibly, to the left or right; they rise to their apogee and then descend. A disk's maximum speed is immediately following launch; from that point until it hits the ground about 60 yards away, it loses speed. You certainly want to get on these birds before they begin their descent, otherwise the distance becomes great and even the speed of the shot cannot normally overcome the trouble your mental computer has determining a break point.

Skeet stations one and seven or perhaps an hour on the trap range will help you judge the angles and speeds of straightaways. In trap, birds fly almost directly away from you. If you stand at the beginning positions, the 16-yard line, with success you can gradually work your way back to 27-yard shots. You will probably not see many shots exactly like a trap set-up in sporting clays, with birds launched from a trap machine directly in front of the shooting line, but this is excellent practice for straightaway shooting, as standard birds have the same dynamic.

In skeet positions one and seven, you are standing next to the traps. At position one, the bird flies out above your head from the high house and, as all skeet shots do, over the "eight post" that you can mark forward of your position. You can also shoot low house birds from here as well, and such a bird simulates a low crossing shot. Then, at position seven, the low house bird is thrown out almost at your elbow, so a right-hand shooter positions himself to take this bird smoothly and easily, but without a rush. There is plenty of time with your normally fluid shooting fundamentals to get on these birds and break them.

If you choose to call for simultaneous doubles, high and low birds at the same time, take the bird going away from you first and then swing back on the bird that is crossing because, to a point, the longer it is in the air, the closer to you it gets. Once you groove the shots from skeet stations one and seven, you should never miss them again.

This is also a good time to practice overcoming any basic shotgunning form errors. One in particular that is seen on every course from expert shooters as well as from beginners is the tendency to begin mounting the gun before the muzzle moves toward the break point. The shot preparation sequence is: pick up the bird with your eyes and, never taking your eyes off it, begin a smooth muzzle swing toward the point you are going to break the bird and then mount the gun smoothly and without hurrying. Some shotgun experts say you should watch the flying disk so closely that you can read the lettering.

Now, imagine quail flushing or dove streaking over your head. An incoming bird should be an easy shot with an open choke in any gauge gun, and with proper shooting technique, it is. Unfortunately, finding a place to practice this presentation is more difficult. Neither skeet nor trap offers such shots, as those are all straightaways and crossers. The game of Crazy Quail is good practice, because although you know where the trap is set, you do not know where the bird is going to fly. It could as easily fly over your head as straight away, depending on the program or the whim of the trapper.

Another option is to set up your own portable trap in a vacant field, perhaps with a friend. Of course, the safety of the person launching the target is crucial, but this can be a relatively easy way to learn this shot if you are conscientious about safety. An adjustable Trius 1-Step is a good example of a trap that you and a buddy could operate for practicing this shot. Except for the mount and mainspring, the 1-Step comes pre-assembled, sets up fast and operates easily and without much maintenance. The beauty of this trap is that one person can throw a bird up to 70 yards and shoot at the same time … just not incomers! This foot-operated trap costs about $120.

On a sporting clays course, the tendency with incoming shots is to begin the mounting and aiming sequence too early. This is the time to take an extra moment, pick up the speeding bird with your eyes and then with your muzzle. Finally, your smooth, rapid mount will be on the bird, and you can swing through it, obliterating the visual image, by pulling the trigger at this time. Vapor. Many shooters feel they must see a bird to shoot it. They have trouble with the idea that it is actually obscured by the barrel and they want to pull their head away to peek around the comb as they shoot. This error will normally cause you to miss the bird. You must trust that your open choke will nail it as you follow through.

No discussion of standard shots would be complete without a mention of the running rabbit. Now, here is something you will not see in skeet or trap or even in Crazy Quail. On a normal sporting clays course you will have to shoot it once and perhaps twice or in combination with a crosser or flushing grouse as a report doubles.

The running rabbit is a target thrown so that it bounces along the ground and you must shoot it there, during the high, low and unpredictable bouncing. Although sporting clays began as a bird-hunter's game, and there is a general aversion to shooting birds on the ground, you must think of this clay as a rabbit. Indeed, the clay disk will probably even have a rabbit image molded on the surface.

Clays thrown for the rabbit station are specially constructed, thicker, heavier and tougher than standard clays, even though they are the same 110-mm (about 4-1/4 inches) diameter. Do not even imagine this is a clay to shoot in the air, unless some bump or stick on the ground causes it to jump unexpectedly high. If the range manager is especially devious, he will show you a slender angle from a trap next to your stand, which makes the rabbit even harder to break, because even though all you must show is a "visible piece," the edges of a rabbit disk are much tougher than standard disks. This presentation requires a durable target because it is usually thrown into the ground with enough force to bounce along for 20 or 30 yards and the impact would shatter a standard, concave disk.

Because it is bounding and running irregularly, the rabbit is an easy target to shoot behind. Most shotgunners begin with their muzzle beneath the anticipated course and swing through it. Watching the clay disk only, you will fire when your gun barrel moves smoothly through and obliterates the sight picture.

Sporting clays course designers are fond of giving you unusual shooting applications such as on platforms raised over swamp water as this shot from south Florida demonstrates.

As with golf, on this station you will never score by leaving your ball short of the cup. You will never break a clay by shooting behind it. Therefore, even if your lead is not perfect, you may still break clays with flyers (pellets that are outside the main pattern) if you are out in front.

To the uninitiated, tower shots look intimidating, and depending upon their angle or height, they can be tough. A 50- or 100-foot tower, positioned behind or to the side of your shooting position, with a trap or even two on a platform are part of the unexpected thrill of sporting clays. For a major event, clubs will often rent elevated articulating arms to raise traps off the ground where permanent towers are either unavailable or perhaps illegal. Targets may be of any size or color except the rabbit: standard, mini, midi or even battue. Now, this is different from any other clay target game!

Your shot distance on a tower bird, representing doves and ducks, may be from 20 to 50 yards. Although its height will give you a good look at it, you need to get on this bird quickly if it is outgoing, as the height plus the distance can more often than not cause you to shoot behind it.

If you encounter an incoming tower shot, you need not rush. Give the shot time to develop and come to you. It will, and this will make your job easier. As the bird comes toward you, the surface will become flatter, more open and, you might say, more receptive to your shot pattern. Swing through this bird and trigger your shot as soon as your barrel passes the leading edge and obscures the disk.

One of the easiest running rabbit presentations may be the straightaway such as this shot at Turkey Run, Alachua, Florida. Do not rush. Move your muzzle with the rabbit and pull the trigger when the clay disappears beneath your barrel.

A "Fur & Feather" station, such as this marker indicates, lies ahead at WW Sporting Clays in Baldwin, Florida. It announces that you will shortly have an opportunity to bust one running rabbit and perhaps a crossing duck.

TYPES OF TARGETS

You may face six or seven types of targets on a sporting clays course, including standard, midi, mini, battue and rabbit. These targets are technically not clay, but a baked petroleum pitch (residue from the distillation of coal or wood tar). A number of biodegradable targets have recently appeared for environmentally sensitive shooting sites. White Flyer notes, for instance, that its biodegradable targets will biodegrade at least 95 percent within two years depending on moisture (and heat). White insists that its pitch and its biodegradable targets are sized, weighted, and shaped to fly the same. The only difference is that when pitch targets are powdered, the powder is black, whereas the powder used on biodegradable targets is a grayish-white.

The standard, domed and ribbed target is approximately 110 mm (4-1/4 inches) in diameter. It is the same bird used for skeet and trap shooting, so its flight characteristics have been proven millions of times on thousands of courses and ranges.

The midi uses the same domed and ribbed design as a standard target, but it is only 90 mm in diameter. Because it is just a smaller standard bird, it catches any breeze and rises or falls about the same as a 110, but this of course also makes it harder to hit. Your depth perception can fool you on this bird, because you will expect that it is farther away than it is, especially if it is thrown with a standard as a pair.

The author waits for a bird from one of the magnificent towers at Cherokee Rose south of Atlanta, Georgia. Pick the bird up with your eye before you begin to move the gun.

Photo courtesy of Wimpy's Wobble Trap Assn.

When is the best time of year to shoot? Pennsylvania's Terry Lampman says, "Any time you can, even in the snow and ice!"

The mini is a tiny saucer, also domed and ribbed like a standard or a midi, but it is only 60 mm in diameter. Shooting at a mini has been described as like shooting at an aspirin traveling at the speed of sound … and it is so small that it can be hard to pick up against a leafy background of sun and shade. The tiny mini can easily slip through any hole in a pattern, so a choke that provides a dense, even shot cloud can be beneficial here.

At 110 mm, the battue is a flat, slender disk, which flies like a rock and breaks about as easily. Many course designers like to throw a battue so that when you first see it and are inclined to shoot, you will only see its slender, whirling 3/8-inch edge. A battue can be tough to see or hit as a single, but it is often thrown as a pair of hard crossers, making it doubly hard. The battue's saving grace is it will usually turn in flight as it begins to slow and this action gives you a shot at its flat side. This is referred to as "development," but to wait for it to present a full circle is fatal, because by the time it develops that far, it is falling away from the shooter. So, there is a relatively narrow window of opportunity to break this bird.

Finally, there is the rabbit target. The running rabbit requires a special mold for the ground shot. It is a 110-mm clay that is designed to be thrown at and to bounce along the ground. It is designed to be tough, and it is. You will often see rabbit clays as the first of a "Fur and Feather" presentation, doubles with a crossing standard.

The presentation of rocket and flash targets is rare on many clays courses. Both are 110 mm diameter, but the rocket is heavier than a standard bird and therefore maintains its velocity over a greater distance; this can fool you if you do not take notice early. Flash targets are prepared with a little pouch of powder on the underside or top so that when they are hit and disintegrate, they truly look like they have exploded. Flash targets are often seen in a shoot-off or a televised match because the experience is more visual than with standard birds.

SHOOTING SINGLES AND DOUBLES

You will see four types of shots during a day of sporting clays shooting: singles, simultaneous doubles, following doubles and report doubles. In sporting clays, these birds can go or come from just about anywhere including right beside the shooting box, from a high tower, or a trap placed in a bunker at the edge of a pond.

Fortunately, two elements of clay shooting will help you make a mental shot plan and decide how to orient your body position when you step into the box. First, the shots are numbered and printed on a sheet of paper at each station. You can walk up and read what your shot options may be: a crossing single, a simultaneous pair, a springing teal and a report pair, for instance. The second thing that gives you an edge before you shoot is that the trapper will show you each sequence before the first person steps in the box. Usually, everyone in the squad will simulate shooting with his or her outstretched finger pointing at and following the arc of each pull. (It is illegal to point with your shotgun unless you are in the box shooting.)

A single is just that, one bird at a time. The special feature of sporting clays however, which we have emphasized throughout this chapter, is that this target may appear from and go almost anywhere, although few will come overhead at you because of crowd safety.

A report pair is two sequential targets; the second bird is launched at the sound of the gun firing at the first target.

A following pair is also two sequential targets. In this presentation, however, the trapper has discretion when to pull the second bird after the first is launched. Usually, only a second, or perhaps two, elapse between the first and second birds.

A simultaneous pair is two targets launched concurrently. Depending upon the difficulty of each individual shot, this may present an extreme challenge or it may sound more difficult than it actually turns out.

Professional shotgun instructor Gil Ash of OSP Shooting Schools says to wait for a target to turn slightly in the air and present its underneath cupped side, which it will do, rather than try to take it on its edge, a much smaller target.

When you step into a sporting clays box, you will have seen "show birds," a complete set of the birds that will be thrown at the station. So make a shot plan before you load your shells and call for a bird, and then shoot your plan.

A NOTE ABOUT "SHOT PLANNING"

When you step into a sporting clays box, you will have seen the birds in the air from launch to the point they become impossible to shoot, perhaps because they hit the ground or their flight takes them past the sides of your shooting cage or they disappear into the trees. You will also have been able to read a posted sign that spells out the target sequence.

How you plan to shoot them is primarily a question for simultaneous doubles. When you see them thrown as "show birds," make a mental shot plan – decide in what order to shoot them and at what spot to break them – and then execute your plan. Usually, you will shoot the bird that is going to be most difficult first, but this is not always the case.

What happens when you see a simultaneous pair and you become convinced that you cannot hit one of them? This should not happen, of course, but if you come to this decision, you can use your two shells to make sure you get a visible piece from the one you are certain you can hit.

What happens when you take your first shot, at a bird you break 99 times out of a hundred, and miss? Should you stay on the first bird and shoot it again or should you always switch to the second bird? If you have fired at a bird and missed, you have acquired and tracked it, so you know its speed and trajectory. Perhaps you should keep

your composure, stay with it, and make your second shot count rather than move quickly to acquire the second bird, which, by this time (unless it is an incomer), is almost always going to be a more difficult shot … and is becoming more difficult at the rate of about 60 fps.

Questions like this are the beginning of your shot plan. When you step into the cage or box or up to the shooting line, you should have made a decision about which bird to shoot first, where you can break them smoothly and what to do if you miss the first shot in a doubles presentation. Remember that even in a tournament, missing is not the end of the world (almost no one will break them all), and if, as a novice shooter, you look on this as a fun, personal challenge, you will end up with a better feeling at the end of the day whether you place first or last in your class.

FORM FOLLOWS FUNCTION

Whereas in skeet and trap, your stance, posture, gun hold and target break points have been worked out almost scientifically so that people often shoot perfect scores, a perfect score is rarely shot on a sporting clays course, even at the professional level. It happens, but it is rare, and especially in FITASC, the international game.

These days, you have a choice of holding your gun in a low or below-the-armpit position, or pre-shouldered. If you begin in the low position, you have an extra set of mechanical difficulties to face, but you will be shooting the game as it was originally intended. However you choose to shoot, if you secure a smooth, consistent gun mount, you will be more likely to have the gun shoot where you are looking. (And, yes, you can shoot one target from low mount and the next one pre-shouldered – your choice.)

Unlike trap and skeet shooting, in which scattergunners adopt some of the most uncomfortable-looking, corkscrew-like stances, sporting clays shooters are much more relaxed and "normal." Most instructors recommend an open stance with the feet about shoulder-width apart and a little forward momentum, or more weight on the leading than the trailing foot. Exactly how much more weight forward is a matter of individual discretion and comfort. No

A shot at doubles, especially low crossing doubles, will make you believe you must shoot a little faster than normal. Have a shot plan: "If I miss the first, will I stay on it for a second shot or will I automatically move toward the second bird?"

A shoot in the snow at La Roue du Roy in Hemmingford, Quebec, will awaken you to the possibilities of enjoying sporting clays year round. Fall asleep here and you can wake up with frozen toes!

rifleman's stance – weight centered more over the back foot – will do in shotgun shooting.

Orienting your body position toward a break point or kill zone for each target is easy in singles, but accommodations must be made for doubles. This is why paying attention is crucial when the trapper shows you the birds after your squad arrives at a new station. You can see where you will best be able to break birds with minimum gun and body movement. With two birds in the air, or a second bird flying as soon as you shoot, you must not be shuffling your feet. You must set up so that your swing accommodates both flight patterns; hence, the need for an upright, fluid stance. If you find that you are consistently shooting behind a bird, you may want to adjust the point at which you first see it. New shooters tend to twist back too far toward the trap and this allows the bird to get ahead of them.

A note about gripping the forend of your shotgun is appropriate here. Most novice shooters grip the forend as they would a rifle, their thumb on one side and their fingers bunched together on the opposite side. In shotgunning, coaches teach you to aim or align the pointing finger of the hand on the forend with the barrel. This rotates your arm slightly outward and, for most people, makes swinging the gun more fluid. Whereas effective rifle shooting is a point-to-point action, effective shotgunning is a fluid movement that must mesh the speed of the target with the speed of the shot, and the fluid movement of your body and the gun brings it all together.

CONSIDER THE LEAD

Fine, consider the lead. Not "lead" as the majority element in your shotgun shell, but lead as in the way you see a target and the way you want to shoot it. Shooting a stationary target, you simply align the beads on top of the sight rail and pull the trigger. Shooting a moving target, you must ignore the beads. Focusing on the target, bring the gun crisply to your cheek and estimate where, in front of the moving clay disk, you must shoot to have an 1150-fps load of shot hit a 60-fps bird. The distance ahead of a disk you shoot is "lead" and it is one of the most difficult aspects of learning to shoot well. Essentially, close shots require little or no lead; distant shots require up to 6 feet of lead.

Some shooters use what is called a "sustained lead." The gun muzzle starts ahead of the bird and never gets behind it. Once ahead, gun and target speed are matched while the shooter seeks a precise lead before triggering the shot.

Folks who shoot sustained lead are already familiar with shooting games, however, perhaps from skeet, and can tell you that you should pull the trigger when your gun is 3 feet in front of a certain clay presentation. That is almost impossible for a newcomer to clay shooting to visualize because a dot is moving across a blank space and there are no referents. Not only that, but unlike skeet, on a clay course, every shot is slightly different in angle, distance and even speed.

I have written elsewhere that the "fast swing" technique is almost invariably the one that can bring sporting clays newcomers the fastest success. Here, you begin with the gun behind the bird and swing quickly through it, thereby moving the gun faster than the target is moving. As your muzzle overtakes the target, you trigger the shot when the correct amount of lead opens. With this shooting technique, the gun tracks the bird's direction and this almost certainly allows you to get on the bird faster and more accurately, especially on windy days when the target may make unexpected movements or when the target's path is not as invariably predictable as it is in skeet.

As you gain experience and confidence, your game will no doubt encompass some combination of both of these two dominant lead-shooting techniques.

Take a focused look at the show birds and make a good shot plan, because specialist course and station designers like Mike Davey are working hard to fool your shooting ... and to help you have an enjoyable, but challenging sporting clays experience.

2
Chapter

FOR WOMEN ONLY

Sporting clays events promote a friendly competitive atmosphere, but these women a took back seat to no one at the 2004 Seminole Cup near Orlando, Florida (from left to right): South Carolina's Teresa Knight; Connecticut's Gayle Campbell; New Jersey's Ashleigh Hafley; Lisa Dirska (left in photo) and Dorothy LaMarra.

"Women are natural multi-taskers," says internationally regarded shotgun instructor Chris Batha. "Women listen better than men and coach-up better. They seem to learn more from my lessons."

I WAS MY HUSBAND'S DOG

During an interview in the mid '80s, Ohio's Ann Clark told me that she was "her husband's dog." I have never forgotten it. Some of today's great female shotgun champions like Casey Atkinson may be shocked to hear of such treatment, but Clark's statement illustrates the changes in the shooting sports and in American society in general, since Clark's first husband taught her to hunt birds and shoot a shotgun in the '50s. Such a manner of treating the "weaker half" may not have been too far from the norm in those days. Nevertheless, the petite, but redoubtable Ms. Clark went on fame – if perhaps not fortune – as an archery champion and celebrity, but she never forgot her own war between the sexes, of which she was a scarred, but wiser veteran.

WOMEN LISTEN BETTER THAN MEN

Women have a few issues in the shotgun sports, but competing with men on an equal footing is not one of them. Women compete equally; their scores in head-to-head competition are just not as high as the highest men's scores.

Here is an example chosen at random. When it comes to scoring, typical shoots end like the 2004 Kansas State Shoot held at the marvelous Claythorne Lodge in Columbus (www.claythorne.com). Deborah Cole Richter was Kansas State High Overall (HOA) Lady resident shooter with a 142 score; Ms. Richter is a B-class shooter. The resident HOA championship was won by Derrick

World Champion Jon Kruger (green rain slicker) waits his turn as World Champion Junior Women's Olympic Skeet shooter Haley Dunn shoots at "The Bridge" station at SteelClays Shooting Sports in Iowa.

Mein with a 173. Linda Joy, a Masters class shooter, shot the top non-resident lady score of 152, well below HOA Will Fennell's 183 non-resident open score.

Is this score differential between men and women real and if so is it important?

Internationally regarded shotgun instructor Chris Batha says the difference is real, but that it is perhaps not very important. Women are shaped differently from men from the inside-out and, maybe from the outside-in as well. What this means is that biologically (physiologically, really) and culturally, women and men are different.

23

Premier shooting instructor Chris Batha believes that there are cultural reasons as well as physical reasons why women often need extra coaching to perform at their peak in sporting clays ... but once they arrive, nothing can hold them back, he says.

Shooting a Beretta DT10 with 32-inch barrels, Casey Atkinson of Cherokee Rose, south of Atlanta, won the individual bronze medal in the Ladies Division at the World FITASC Championships in Provence, France, in June 2004.

"Women move differently than men," Batha says, "and this is obvious when they run and throw. Generally speaking, their skeletal frame and muscular structure have evolved to accomplish tasks that do not require the mass that even desk-bound men attain."

Curiously, women also have more eye dominance problems than men (although this does not extend to the color spectrum where a far higher percentage of men than women are color blind in the red-blue spectrum). Whereas 80 percent of men have dominant eyes that match their dominant hands (right-handers are overwhelmingly right-eye-dominant, for instance), 80 percent of women experience something other than straightforward eye dominance. They are center-dominant (neither eye is dominant), or eye dominance may actually fluctuate or they may be cross-dominant, Batha says.

Batha readily admits that based on absolute scores the best men shotgunners will beat the best women "nine out of ten times." He notes that this is true in most athletic competitions including golf and tennis. "There are no women who make it in the NBA or are good enough baseball players to stick in the major leagues." On the other hand, there are thousands of excellent women shooters who would beat most men in any type of shotgun competition.

Nevertheless, there are not only physical reasons for this sex-typed difference; there are cultural reasons

as well. "Talk to some of the HOA champion men and they tell you that they were raised with slingshots and BB guns in their hands, and their daddies bought them a 22 rifle before they were big enough to pick it up. You won't find many women who give that kind of personal testimony."

Not being exposed to firearms or the attitude that firearms are acceptable tools and toys, albeit dangerous, in society at an early age, women never catch up. They are bombarded with anti-gun propaganda designed to hook their mothering and nesting instincts, and it is usually later in life that women are introduced to firearms by boyfriends or husbands. By then, most men have a head start of a couple dozen years.

Batha thinks something in the brain may be responsible, too. "Women are natural multi-taskers," he says, "whereas men tend to be able to focus all of their energy on one thing at a time for long periods.

Photo courtesy of Quail Creek Plantation.

There are numerous small changes to a standard, off-the-rack shotgun that can make shooting more comfortable for a woman. Marty Fajen believes, for instance, that a smaller grip and one with less pronounced pistol-grip curvature generally fits women's smaller hands a little better.

Perhaps this relates to the nerve structure in the brain, but women do not generally seem to me to be as single-minded as men."

This highly acclaimed shooting instructor says he sees the difference between men and women when he gives lessons. "Women listen better," he says, and they actually "coach-up" better and seem to learn more from what he tells them.

Apparently, men tend to only half-listen to the opening parts of any instruction about gun handling and safety and stance and follow-through. They have handled firearms for years and do not come to his clinics with a tentative attitude about guns. Men approach guns confidently, perhaps with a bit of a "what-can-you-teach-me-that-I-don't-already-know" attitude.

"Women come to a shooting lesson willing to listen to everything, and with an open mind," Batha says, "whereas men usually say something like, 'I need help with the 40-yard springing teal. It's eating my lunch.'"

Often, it helps to separate husbands and wives in a class or to have them attend different sessions. Frequently, wives have had some coaching from their husbands and, given the dynamics of a relationship, this coaching may be spot-on or … quite otherwise. Sometimes women who have experienced their husband's pressure to perform well, for whatever reason, find that it is a relief not to have the man

looking over their shoulders and they can learn at their own speed. On the other side, the husbands sometimes feel pressure to show that they know all the basics, that they are only present to pick up some technical pointers or to help the "little woman."

Consequently, Batha works hard during the first half of his lessons to help women overcome their apprehension about shooting, to become comfortable with a shotgun and to be at home with the basics. "Women are slower initially, but they often then surpass their husbands in a clinic."

I DON'T HAVE A THING TO WEAR

It should be obvious that women are shaped differently than men and that their clothes need to be formed and fitted to suit their special frames. But it has not always been obvious, at least not in the commercial sense of helping women outfit to hunt or for the shooting line.

Ohio's "girls with guns," JoAnn Mizek and Cindy McCrory have developed a clothing line especially for women named MizMac Designs, after themselves. Avid shooters for a dozen years, Mizek and McCrory are more interested in the fun of the game and the fellowship of shooting – our own "amusement and amazement" Mizek says – than their scores.

MizMac Designs has developed a clothing line specifically fitted to women's dimensions. Their "Perfect Fit" ladies shooting vest has an over-the-shoulder pad, bust side adjustments, waist side adjustments and a six-snap back adjustment.

"For years we were frustrated that we had to buy men's clothing to shoot in," Mizek says. "The problem was that nothing fit us properly. The shoulder pads were usually too large for most women, for example. So in 2002, Cindy and I began talking about developing and marketing a line of clothing just for women. A year later, we introduced our first apparel items: socks, visors and several types of short sleeve and sleeveless cotton shirts. We are expanding now into shooting vests and gloves. Basically, whatever women need. We have sizes from small through 3-X and our garment work is excellent and very competitively priced."

But was the development of MizMac only a trendy ploy to exploit the growing and politically correct market for lady shooters? Better not suggest that to Mizek, who shoots a 12-gauge over/under Browning 425, or to McCrory when you see her with her Beretta 686 12-gauge over/under.

"We got into business for the same reasons men get into business, to make a profit and maybe have a little fun," Mizek says. "Women generally get treated very well at clubs, clinics and shoots in the United States. It is rare that we face any unfriendly behavior. Let's face it. Women can compete successfully with men in any shotgun sport. Our clothing line just helps them do it by appealing to some of the things men look down on, like proper fit, for one! And yes, we pay attention to fashion and color, but coordinate them with essential function, the smooth handling of a shotgun."

Mizek and McCrory have a couple suggestions for women entering the great world of shotgunning. "Go to a club or clinic or sporting goods store and find a certified instructor," Mizek says, "rather than rely on your husband to teach you. An instructor will make sure you start with a gun that fits and will show you how to check for your dominant eye. Husbands … they get excited and want

their wives to succeed. They will hand you a gun that is too heavy and too long and load it with shells that are too powerful. Then, when the recoil knocks their wife down, they tell them it was their stance that was wrong. No, we would urge women to find a certified instructor and also not to buy the first gun they use; to try several different guns before they buy one."

MizMac relies on print advertising in Sporting Clays magazine, personal appearances at major competitions such as the ATA Grand American World Trapshooting Championships in Vandalia, word-of-mouth and their Internet site at www.mizmac.com.

FITTING & SHOOTING TIPS FOR WOMEN

1 Cast-off toe of the buttstock. Professional shotgun fitters like Michael Murphy suggest that women often prefer some cast-off at toe, some relief from having the toe of the buttstock grind into their chest. With a heavier build-up of muscle in front of the shoulder, men's physiques absorb the pounding of recoil better than women's and this means that a straight buttstock is more acceptable to men. Women often prefer some additional cast-off at the toe.

2 A higher comb and more drop at heel. Chris Batha says women tend to listen better to men, especially to his emphasis on the fundamentals. He did not say that men were necessarily "know-it-alls," only that much of what he has to say is new to women

The winner's circle at the Gene Sears Open at Silverleaf Shotgun Sports near Guthrie, Oklahoma, in May 2004.

In identical conditions, the difference in recoil between a semi-automatic and an over/under is measurable; however, it is very small. Carol Taylor shoots Cherokee Rose, south of Atlanta. ("Shoulder pads are for sissies," Carol said ... no, just kidding!)

Women largely shoot as well as men in trap, skeet and sporting clays. Generally, however, because of their smaller, lighter frames, they may prefer lighter guns and lighter loads.

The conclusion is that women listen to his suggestions and learn to bring the stock to their cheek, not their cheek down to the stock. With factory-produced guns, this means they need more cast-off at the comb and he teaches them to raise the gun properly, not "rubberneck" it.

3 Additional cast-off and better fitting grip. Marty Fajen also believes that women benefit from small changes in the stock to accommodate such physical differences as eyes closer together in the face, smaller hands and weaker grips. Because women's eyes tend to be set closer together in their face, she says, and they need more cast-off to properly center their master eye over the rib. When it comes to gripping the pistol-grip-style stock, women's smaller hands mean certain adjustments will make shooting more comfortable and more successful as well. A fitted palm swell helps position their hand on the grip; a more slender grip and one that is less dramatically curved, gunslinger style, helps bring women's fingers more easily to the trigger; and perhaps a more slender forend, rather than the beefy style found on most factory guns, gives women more control with their leading hand.

4 Choose a lighter gun. While it is customary for new shooters to begin with a gun that weighs more than 8 pounds, an hour of sporting clays shooting can become more fatiguing for women than men. Women

27

It is customary to start new shooters with a lightweight BB gun. Florida 10-year-old Ryan Gridley found that the heavy GAMO Hunter was too large for his grip and preferred beginning with a smaller Daisy.

can put their shopping gene to good use by looking around for a lighter gun. Another possibility is to move from the 12-gauge to a 20-gauge, which can save 5 or 6 critical ounces. Scores indicate that shooters who know what they are doing lose very little when they make such a move. It helps to also have padding over the top of the off-shoulder because, whether they have a break-barrel over/under or simply hold their semi-auto by the barrel, over the mile of a sporting clays course, the awkward weight and feel of carrying the gun when they are not shooting can be stunningly exhausting – for men as well.

5   Shoot lighter loads. Reduced recoil loads are available that should please most shooters who are sensitive to recoil, and this includes both experienced champions and inexperienced newcomers. Sensitivity to recoil is not sex-linked. It happens just as frequently to men as to women. An option that many shooters feel is every bit as effective is to switch from full 1 1/8-ounce 12-gauge loads to 1-ounce loads or even to lighter 24-gram (0.85-ounce) international loads. For relatively close shots to 35 and perhaps even to 40 yards, these lighter loads should be effective for most shooters. At 40 yards or beyond, however, you might want to keep a few 1 1/8-ounce shells in the cart for backup.

6   Semi-auto vs. over/under. It is something of a commonly held myth in shotgun circles that semi-autos deliver less felt recoil than over/unders. Outfitted with the proper recoil-reducing devices and a properly padded vest, an over/under will not pound your shoulder any more than a semi. The reason that so many women are started on semi-autos may lie in the fact that a good semi-auto generally costs less than a good over/under. Uncertain whether the women in their lives will like shooting or not, there is a temptation to spend less on a beginner gun. This, of course, can be self-defeating. Poor equipment will perform poorly and even beginners recognize hand-me-downs or cheap gear when they see it. Good equipment delivered with confidence and respect may earn a shooting partner for life.

A NOTE ABOUT MAKING NEWCOMERS FEEL WELCOME

Introducing a new person to sporting clays, whatever their age, requires that we be especially sensitive to the noise, the recoil … and perhaps most especially to their feelings.

Man or woman, a newcomer to any of the shotgun sports is going to be nervous near a shooting station. Certainly, they need very good (not just adequate) eye and ear protection, but they also need a guide who is aware that the anti-gun movement in America has made shooting something of a dark art, and the longer someone waits or is kept away from trying it, the more difficult the experience becomes. Because of societal pressure today, it is a great and praiseworthy accomplishment to help someone, who has not been raised with firearms accepted in the household, learn to shoot.

There is no "best time" to introduce someone to shotgun shooting. If you are careful to make an event safe and fun, control the noise and give newcomers personal attention, you can perhaps start them as early as a few years old. Here, Ina Thormalen, the daughter of Floyd "Wimpy" Lampman, who invented Wimpy's Wobble Trap, shows her daughter Jacklynn around the wobble trap course.

The best approach is a slow, gentle immersion, making the shooting experience safe and fun, and moving at the newcomer's own pace. A newcomer often feels more comfortable if a friend learns with them, if they go through basic firearms safety or take an introductory lesson in shotgun shooting alongside an acquaintance that is also at their level of knowledge and ability. Men may be willing to jump in blind (for reasons we have discussed earlier in this chapter), but women and young people do find safety in numbers.

Go slow with the technical details, too. Newbies can suffer as much from too much attention as from too little. Insertion into a squad of friendly, but competent, shooters can be an overwhelming experience. Not only will the novice shoot poorly compared to the others, but he or she will also receive lots of bewildering coaching that can best be delivered, retained and practiced one-on-one.

And of course, if you attempt to start someone with hand-me-down equipment and your old shooting clothing, expect that most people will sense that you are not serious, that you do not value their time and the quality of their experience. If you are serious, get them fitted for a new shooting vest or help them choose their own shooting glasses. The cost-benefit ratio will balance the dollars you spend with a positive shooting experience.

Unless you are the exceptional parent or friend, your new shooter will learn more, faster with a lesson from a certified coach. Remember how strained and difficult it became when your dad tried to teach you to drive? The same applies to shooting. A professional will not take it personally when a student fails to hear or to learn and put everything into practice right away.

3
Chapter

OTHER EXCITING SHOTGUN GAMES

TRAP

You can shoot trap for fun or your can shoot official, registered targets in a manner approved by the Amateur Trapshooting Association (www.shootata.com).

A regulation trap field consists of a single launcher located in a trap house and partially buried in the ground. Sixteen yards behind the trap house are five shooting positions, spaced three yards apart in a semi-circle. The most common and the easiest trap game, is called "16-Yard Trap," and it is shot from these five positions.

From each of the 16-yard positions, a lane, marked in yardage increments, leads backward to 27 yards behind the trap house. "Handicap Trap" is shot from these yardage markers after one establishes an official ATA yardage handicap.

The trap machine launches clay disks at unknown angles for each station. Clays fly within 17.14 degrees right or left of the trap center, which is directly in front of shooting position three. These oscillating traps use interrupters to break up patterns and prevent the shooter from "reading the trap" or guessing the angle of flight before shooting. Thus, the shooter is never quite certain where – within the prescribed angles – the bird will fly.

Standard 4-1/4 by 1 1/8-inch (110 mm) round clay targets are used and may be any of a number of colors including orange, black or yellow. The pre-set trajectory places birds between 8 and 10 feet above the ground at 10 feet in front of the trap and propels them to a distance between 49 and 51 yards from the trap house. Peak speeds are juts in excess of 40 mph. These measurements are standard everywhere you shoot trap.

The most popular trap event is 16-Yard shooting, and in tournaments, shooters compete based on previous scores and known ability. Previous scores generally require a shooter to have engaged about 500 registered

Shooting wobble trap from the 16-yard trap line in Pennsylvania. In front of the shooters is Floyd "Wimpy" Lampman's ¾-line for Wimpy's Wobble Trap.

targets, and a simple percentage of those targets broken will be his or her average.

Serious trap competitors shoot the 12-gauge, the largest gauge the ATA allows. Smaller gauges are often shot in separate events.

Allowable ammunition in a trap shoot is strict. You may use lead, steel, bismuth or other composite non-toxic shot materials, but not loads containing nickel or copper. The ATA specifies allowable ammo by size – nothing larger than 7-1/2s – and by maximum speed and shot charge: 1290 fps with 1-1/8 ounces, 1325 with 1 ounce and 1350 with 7/8-ounce. Some shooters use lighter, 1-ounce 12-gauge loads to reduce recoil, reserving maximum loads for handicap rounds and the second shot in a doubles match.

A trapper is loading the launcher with clay birds while the trap squad takes a break in the background. Novice trap shooters begin at a semi-circular set of five stations that are 16 yards behind the partially sunken trap house. As their skill improves, shooters may move backward and shoot from handicap positions as far as 27 yards behind the launcher.

Bunker trap or international trap is very different from the standard version shot in the United States. American trap uses one machine in front of the 16-yard line whereas the international game, shown in this photo, buries 15 separate launchers in the long, low trap house. Clays thrown from the international bunker tend to be faster and more extreme in angle.

A round of regular trap consists of 25 shots and a trap "squad" may contain up to five shooters, each taking one of the five stations. The shooter on station one shoots first. Once he has fired, the shooter on station two calls for a bird, with the remaining shooters calling for birds in turn. This rotation is repeated until each shooter has fired five rounds from his station.

After everyone has shot five rounds, the puller/scorer calls "Change," followed by a quick rundown of the number of birds each contestant has hit at that station. Shooters move in a clockwise manner, station one to station two; the shooter on five rotates to one. Then, the shooter who is now on station two, begins the next round. This person is the designated first shooter for each new round and at each new station.

Guns may not be loaded until every shooter is on his station and the leadoff shooter has called for his first bird. Knowledgeable shooters load their gun, but do not snap it closed, with only one round at a time and only when the shooter two positions ahead of them calls for a bird. When moving between stations, the gun must be unloaded and the action open.

Typically, scorers shout "Lost" to denote a miss. To score a hit, the shooter must knock a visible piece off the target.

Trap is fast-paced. Of all the shotgun games, a 16-Yard round is usually completed in 15 minutes. Trap shooters get used to the fast pace and a slow shooter or one who continually questions the scorer's calls disrupts the game.

Coaching in any shotgun game will help with other games. You will see trap- and skeet-type shots in sporting clays and the fundamentals of stance are roughly the same. Now, sporting clays even authorizes a pre-mounted gun!

Courteous trap shooters fall into the squad's shooting rhythm. When you take your position, you should be ready to shoot and have the shells in your pocket.

Keeping a squad's rhythm is not solely for convenience. A herky-jerky squad disrupts a shooter's concentration and lowers his score. In trap, the shooters around you can exert a positive or negative influence on your performance without conscious effort.

Photo courtesy of Joe Potosky, The Lost Target www.lostarget.com.

Trap shooting at Underhill Rod & Gun Club in Westford, Vermont.

WOBBLE TRAP

Trap shooters playing this game will experience a significantly greater challenge than on a conventional trap field. Since the '60s when it was introduced, wobble trap has used oscillating devices on the trap throwers to both vary the angle AND the height of the bird over the ground. Alternatively, special wobble trap machines with vertical and horizontal travel such as the Beomat MT 400 may be installed.

For singles shooting, regulation ATA traps are set to throw birds precisely between 17.14 degrees left and right of center; precisely between 8 and 10 feet high when 10 feet forward of "Point B;" and to remain in the air from 49 to 51 yards. Period. For doubles shooting, the parameters are essentially the same: 34.28 degrees total, between 8 and 12 feet high and to remain in the air and land between 44 and 52 yards.

You can forget all these angles and distances when you shoot wobble trap. You do expect that birds will fly out from the trap house away from you, but since targets are not certifiable for ATA registration, the trap may be placed almost anywhere in front of you along a centerline.

Incidentally, the Pennsylvania-based Wimpy's Wobble Trap Association, founded in 1998 by Floyd "Wimpy" Lampman, offers a unique variation on wobble trap shooting. Originally a dairy farmer who liked to shoot, Lampman built his game around 16-Yard 22-degree trap shooting and wrote his own official rulebook. He also invented 3/4-deck shooting, which is only 35 feet

Floyd "Wimpy" Lampman (left) altered the basic game of wobble trap shooting by moving shooters closer to the trap. Wimpy's daughter Ina Thormalen (right) administers shoots at affiliated clubs with her sister, Terry Lampman.

from the trap house, and included it in his association's registered target presentations along with the standard 16 yards (48 feet).

At this time, 13 clubs are affiliated with Wimpy in five states (California, Delaware, Illinois, New York, Pennsylvania, South Carolina and Washington) and Canada. Wimpy's daughters, Ina Thormahlen and Terry Lampman are co-presidents of the association (www.wimpyswobbletrap.com) and say that they are happy to discuss their dad's great game with any club.

Shooting from a pre-shouldered gun mount, the gunner on skeet station six is waiting to call for a bird from the low house. The bird will be thrown at an upward angle from a trap arm positioned 3 feet above the ground inside the house.

SKEET

Originally developed as a bird-hunter's game requiring a low gun position, skeet has evolved into a formal competitive event and winning is very tough because the winners rarely miss. In the first national championship match held in 1927, the winning team missed eight targets out of 125. Missing eight targets out of 1000 today would embarrass a master shooter. Nevertheless, everyone begins skeet with a single bird.

A skeet field is laid out in a semi-circle with trap houses located at opposite sides. The trap house on the left, the "high house," launches its bird 10 feet above the ground at a slight upward angle. Birds speed out of the trap house on the right, the "low house," at a more abrupt upward angle from 3 feet above the ground.

Skeet launchers are fixed in position and throw the bird to the exact same spot every time. There is not even the variation one finds in trap shooting. When properly regulated, they launch birds at about 42 to 45 mph. These birds must travel between 58 and 62 yards through the air, landing at a predetermined spot under "no wind conditions."

Seven shooting stations are set in a semi-circle. Station one is directly under the high house, with the following stations moved precisely 26 feet, 8-3/8 inches to the right of the previous station. Thus, station seven is directly beside the low house and station eight is centered in the field, midway between the two trap houses.

Ten feet forward of station eight is a white stake, called the "Eight Post." Launchers send birds directly over the top of this stake. Thus, the speed and flight path of skeet birds are fixed. You know precisely where they come from, where they go, how fast they travel and when they are launched. Shooting positions are fixed and each shooter sees the same speed and angle of each bird.

Each shooting position presents a different angle, but once you learn the proper lead and technique for each station, you have all the information you need to break every target consistently. Work it out in Maine and it works precisely the same way in Moscow. After that, it is simply a matter of biomechanics.

The shooting format for standard or American skeet is simple. A squad of up to five shooters starts at station one and works around the field to station eight. At stations one, two, six and seven, each shooter gets four targets: a single bird from the high house, a single from the low house and a set of doubles (high- and low-house birds launched simultaneously). Shooting singles, the high-house target always comes first. In doubles, the outgoing target must be shot first; then the shooter swings back to pick up the incoming bird. At stations three, four, five and eight, the shooter will get only a single target from each house, taking the high house bird first.

Competitive skeet is a four-gauge event. In a registered match, the 12-gauge event is open to all gauges 12 or smaller, using shot loads not exceeding 1-1/8 ounces. The 20-gauge event is for guns 20-gauge or smaller, with a shot charge not to exceed 7/8-ounce. The

Photo courtesy of Nemacolin.

Regardless of the shooting game you try – skeet, trap, sporting clays, Hélice or something new – the fundamentals of successful shotgunning are the same: bring the gun to you and keep your cheek firmly on the comb.

28-gauge event can be shot with the 28 or the 410 and a maximum 3/4-ounce shot load. The 410 event requires the 410 with no more than 1/2-ounce shot. No shot smaller than #9 may be used.

Inexperienced shooters do not compete head-to-head with experts. Skeet's classification system pits shooters against others of similar ability. You may establish a classification after as few as a couple hundred targets.

A round of skeet is 24 birds/25 shots, but you should have an extra half-dozen shells because it is possible to break both birds during a doubles presentation with one shot. In this case, you have to shoot again. You can also get a broken bird flying out of a house in doubles and not be able to stop shooting in time. "No birds" are also re-shot. Nothing is more irritating to those waiting their turn to shoot by the way than to have a shooter run off for more shells.

A skeet squad can be as many as five shooters. The reason for limiting it to five is that many trap machines do not hold enough birds for any more people than that.

Skeet guns are never loaded until the shooter steps onto the shooting pad for his turn. Otherwise, the gun must be visibly unloaded. This is common sense and it both guarantees that the gun is unable to fire and lets other squad members confirm that at a glance.

The governing body for skeet competition in America is the National Skeet Shooting Association (NSSA). You will find a full copy of their current rules on line at www.mynssa.com.

MODERN SKEET

Ken Gagnon essentially invented modern skeet in 1993. The game is a variation on traditional skeet, using Gagnon's oscillating mechanism to vary the height and angle of a clay bird. Modern skeet adds a little surprise to the highly regimented game of skeet because the shooter does not know in advance quite how the bird will be presented.

"Modern skeet simulates a windy day," the garrulous Rhode Island waterfowl hunter and manufacturer of rubber Quack decoys says. "While birds still fly over the eight-post, you can't anticipate whether they will be five feet off the ground or 45 feet."

Although he is right-handed and blind in his right eye, Gagnon began shooting skeet in the 1960s. When he switched to shooting left-eyed and from the left-hand side, the former state champion eventually became so proficient at breaking targets that he came within a few birds of making the U.S. Olympic skeet team in 1976.

Gagnon coached his son, daughter and former spouse, Ken, Heidi and Liz, to be state champions, so he understands what he is saying when he insists that shooting modern skeet teaches someone to be a better shooter. "Modern skeet is a great training aid," he says, "but they do not qualify for registered targets for NSSA purposes."

Some ranges have added doubles to the modern skeet experience. For these shoot presentations, you will see a combination of true and report pairs on the standard skeet stations (with an occasional single from high house on station eight).

Quack Decoy's Ken Gagnon developed and actively promotes Modern Skeet, which gives shooters a more diverse shooting program than standard skeet. Gagnon mounts his traps on a patented oscillating platform and the results are surprisingly refreshing for those who are accustomed to the rigid shooting of skeet and trap.

Today, there are around 275 of Ken Gagnon's Quack Modern Skeet Oscillators being used on courses around the United States. The cost to equip a lightweight pair of traps is $1495 while the cost of retrofitting a heavy-duty pair is $1950 (www.quackdecoys.com).

5-STAND SPORTING

5-Stand is sporting clays in a box. Or, rather, in five boxes. When you arrive at a range and see five tall cages of wood or PVC pipe or old fence rail standing alone in a field and practically side-by-side, you know the owners have a 5-Stand.

When sporting clays began to take off in the United States during the '80s, most ranges had already used their available space for multiple trap and skeet fields and sometimes for a special "fun event" like Crazy Quail. Then again, the new sporting clay courses wanted an alternative to shoot but rarely wanted to be burdened with the rigid formality of a registered trap or skeet set-up. So 5-Stand was invented as a mini-sporting course that could serve both as a stand-alone game and as a true warm-up for the long walk required by sporting clays. Today, 5-Stand set-ups are found at most sporting clays courses and at many trap and skeet ranges as well. A large sporting clays tournament will have 5-Stand competition with all gauges.

5-Stand was conceived by a Scotsman named Ray Foreman to fit on a regulation skeet field. He used the high and low skeet houses plus four to six additional traps to throw the same presentations one would see

5-Stand shooting at Birds Landing, California. A round of 25 birds at this fully automated facility costs just $8.

One of the better games for handicap shooters may be 5-Stand Sporting. The necessity to move from station to station is restricted to a short distance and yet the shot presentations are varied and interesting.

5-Stand sporting is an excellent place to pack a lot of sporting clays instruction into a small place. There are plenty of different types of shots in a small space.

on a full sporting clays course: crossing, looping up, straight in-straight out-straight up, running rabbit, dove tower, a variety of doubles and so on. Today, however, 5-Stand set-ups are as about as varied and difficult as an individual field chooses to make them and few are as wide open as a skeet range.

5-Stand is named for its five shooting stations (or cages). These may be lined up in a straight line so that they almost touch or may be as much as a dozen feet apart. (The NSCA recommends a 5-yard separation between stations for tournaments and shooting registered targets.) Remember that the idea of 5-Stand is to maximize, within a very small space, a course's ability to present a variety of targets. Although launchers are often visible (or their numbers are visible) from each station, rotating shooters will get a different angle and mix of birds, both singles and doubles.

Foreman's design called for two true pairs and a single for each station. He wanted the origin of the targets to be unknown, but his original concept is usually modified at each course depending on the philosophy of the owner or the layout of the property. In addition, shooters usually ask to "see the birds," just like on a full sporting clays course. A round of 5-Stand is always 25 birds and when a shooter steps into the stand, he or she will see and may continually refer to a written "menu" of shots, in order of their presentation, posted on the stand. (This formality was recommended by the NSCA so that 5-Stand fun can be shot for registered competition.) This, of course, takes some of the fun and surprise out of the event.

Because 5-Stand was conceived as a space-saving alternative to a complete sporting clays layout, there is a tendency for birds to converge in the middle of the venue. Understanding this will help you decide on a break point for your series of birds.

Planning your shot means getting a good look at each presentation. Because birds and angles are limited in 5-Stand and because you have a written "menu" at each station, you should be able to make a decision about the best shot sequence quickly. Generally, this means shooting the lower or faster bird first, the bird flying away, and then, using good muzzle management, swinging smoothly onto the higher or arcing bird that is now reaching its zenith, with a smooth follow-through.

As 5-Stand is usually shot within a very confined area and shot fall is also confined, it makes for a visually appealing spectator sport. Consequently, many charity and celebrity shoots use it for moneymaking purposes.

NSCA 5-Stand rules specifically outline the official registered game, although there is a move afoot to replace 5-Stand with European Compak Sporting. NSCA 5-Stand shooting specifies six to eight numbered traps, a tower not less than 12 feet in height, rabbit and vertical shots and a menu card at each station. No choke tubes may be changed after a round has begun.

The 5-Stand sporting set-up at Kansas' Flint Oak shooting resort is covered and looks out on numbered, but hidden traps. Flint Oak hosted the 2004 FITASC 5-Stand, which will now, by agreement with the NSCA, become the FITASC Compak.

COMPAK SPORTING

Compak Sporting from FITASC allows all the usual targets from international sporting games to be used in a competition that can be shot in a very small area. It is similar to 5-Stand Sporting. It might be good to shoot a few rounds of this at first opportunity since the NSCA is rapidly moving in its direction and away from the homegrown 5-Stand game.

Compak is also set on a skeet range and uses four firing stations: skeet stations three, four, five and six. In addition to the high- and low-house birds, four extra traps are used, three spread in front of the houses and a tower behind the semi-circle. All target presentations are encouraged, including running rabbit and vertical springing teal.

A single round is 25 shots and shooters change firing points every sequence of targets in a round. Both singles and doubles are thrown when the shooter calls with their gun out of their shoulder.

An open-choked gun is most suitable for Compak, as most targets will be broken at relatively close range. Shooters usually discover that a sporting load of #8s is the most versatile load. For the 2004 World Championships in San Antonio in May, during the changeover from 5-Stand Sporting to Compak Sporting, loads were limited to 1-ounce.

At www.clayshooting.co.uk, the web designers suggest an obvious idea – that beginners watch other shooters before they shoot Compak Sporting for the first time, because making a mental note of target sequence, angle and direction is advantageous. On the other hand, they note that "shooting from a cage confines your angle of fire, and as the targets come from many differing angles, it can be easy to get carried away and bang your barrels on the cage. Obviously, this is not good for your gun, so it is best to keep a cool head."

And scoring? For a beginner to hit 50 percent in his or her first Compak outing would be superb. Expect to hit fewer than that unless you have 5-Stand or clay course experience. Experts should score about as they do in 5-Stand or on a full sporting clays course, 80 to 95 percent.

CRAZY QUAIL

I shot Crazy Quail with co-workers from the U.S. Fish & Wildlife Service in Minnesota in about 1981. I could not hit a thing in the game then and am barely more accomplished now, but even that first game was huge fun.

If you are ready for a shotgun challenge, Crazy Quail is it! And you ought to try it before some organization of suits begins making rules and regulations for keeping score and specifying arcs of flight and angles and loads and protests. In 1981, a blackpowder smoothbore shooter accompanied us, which meant we waited – for him to load and then for the smoke to clear – and certainly today a National Crazy Quail Association would prohibit that in its rush to hurry shooters along. So, shoot now or forever hold your peace about this great little game.

Crazy Quail is designed to imitate the flush of a covey of frightened wild bobwhites. If your English pointer scatters them, these diminutive birds are likely to fly in any direction, even right over your head. Consequently, the single buried trap – usually manually operated – in front of the shooting position rotates to throw standard birds in a 360-degree circle. And you, the shooter, will never know where the next bird is going to fly when you call for it, because it is not patterned and there is no shooter's "menu" printed at the station to guide you like there is in 5-Stand. Birds may fly directly away from you or directly over your head. A devious trapper or one whose tip was small on the former round, may throw report pairs or even true pairs.

I specified "buried" because obviously the safety of the trapper is as critical in this game as that of the shooter and spectators. Consequently, the trap and operator will be both buried and protected by a low, hard-packed tapered dirt berm or some other protective device impervious to a careless shot.

Much about this game is up to the discretion of the range operator. A round may consist of 10 to 25 thrown birds. A trap like David Whiteside's Crazy Quail SuperFlyer may be buried anywhere from 15 to 25 yards in front of the shooter's position. Because they must come out of a pit, clay flight angles are usually about 50 or 60 degrees.

Designed originally to encourage television, Make-A-Break is a tough, winner-take-all game designed to give shooters long and difficult shots.

MAKE-A-BREAK

In the early '90s, everyone affiliated with the shooting sports industry believed that if they could just get their sport on television – archery, trap and skeet, hunting, fishing – they could expose millions of people to the thrill of shooting and interest them enough to try pulling a trigger, releasing a bow string and buying more gear. After all, TNN (The Nashville Network) and The Outdoor Network and Outdoor Life channel seemed to offer new opportunities to market shooting events.

The idea of attracting millions by television and video rather than the thousands who read books and magazines was extremely appealing. Of course, it did not turn out to be that easy. After a couple of decades of working with the electronic venues, we still by-and-large "preach to the choir." Shooters watch shooting shows. Non-hunters watch sitcoms. We do not argue politics or religion with the relatives.

Make-A-Break was designed to make breaking clay targets more enjoyable for people who watch from their living room. Because it is a head-to-head competitive event, with excited winners advancing to a final shoot-off and sorrowful losers dropping out, the game has the potential for intense competition and more excitement than an hour of shooting around a hot and dusty sporting clays course.

Make-A-Break is shot from a single station with eight automatic traps. Often, two shooters compete at the same time, and hence, there are two No. 1 traps. The No. 1 traps are set close to throw a bird away from the station, count for one point and are always shot first. The other traps, set at progressively greater distance with harder angles, are shot in sequence. Each competitor shoots 10 report doubles during a round. A broken No. 1 target scores one point; a broken No. 7, the most difficult shot on the course, typically scores seven points although individual course designers can alter the basic scheme on an event-by-event basis.

Make-A-Break requires skill with the gun and, if you are to advance through a crowd to the finals, some quick thinking and perhaps a bit of gambling. In follow-up rounds leading to the final shoot-off, there are options for bonus pairs and the gamble of selecting birds that are more difficult over targets one may be comfortable shooting. A competitor who is behind in the score may call for more difficult birds in order to catch up, but risks losing everything if he misses. The shooter in the lead must choose between protecting his or her lead with a safe shot … or padding it by attempting something difficult. The top score wins. Everyone else goes home a loser.

In March 2004, Hunter's Pointe Sporting Clays in Washington, North Carolina, held the 2004 East Coast Sporting Clays Championship. With a 200-bird main event, the club guaranteed a $13,000 cash payout including $1200 and a trophy to high overall. Concurrently, it held a Make-A-Break fun shoot with a $15 entry fee that paid out $800 to the winner after a final shoot-off under the lights on Saturday night.

Hélice shooting in the great out-of-doors. Hélice is a prestigious, stand-alone sport that falls under the umbrella of FITASC.

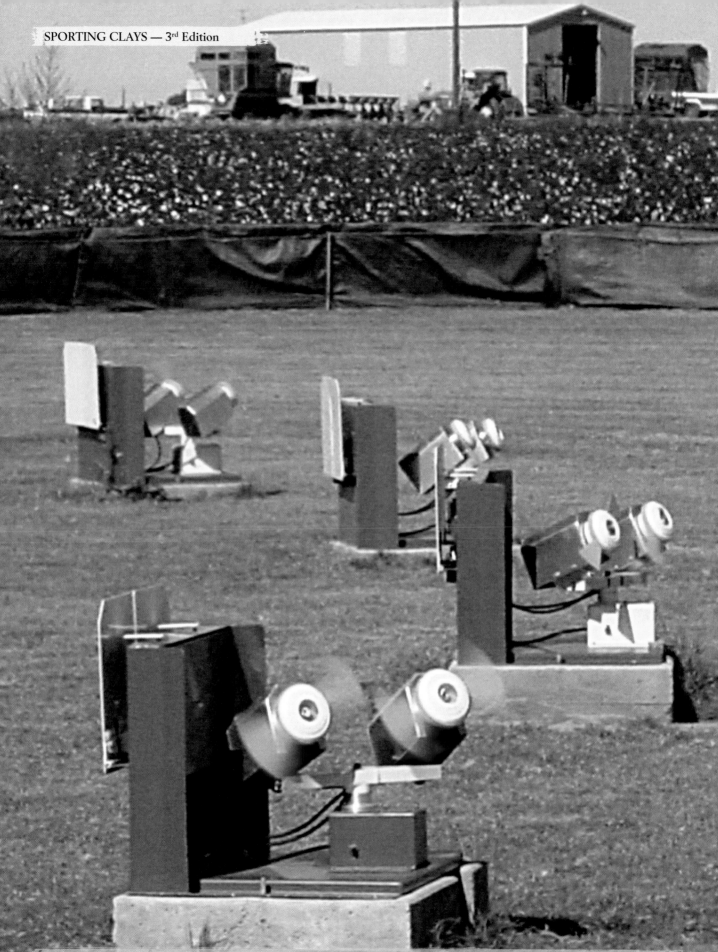

Hélice launchers spin targets directly away from the shooter in a random pattern and order. Organized Hélice shooting in the United States is governed by the U.S. Hélice Association.

HÉLICE *(ZZ BIRD OR ELECTROCIBLES)*

When hand-held, battery-operated calculators were introduced 40 years ago, the cost (in '60s dollars) seemed prohibitive. While they were relatively large and performed only the basic mathematical functions, they seemed exotic. The same scenario unfolded with desktop computers. For shotgunners, ZZ Bird or Hélice is that way today. There is interest, but caution, because the game is new and it is expensive. Nevertheless, the shooting is fun, innovative and different enough to hang around and slowly gain converts.

Tom Veatch wears many hats. He is proprietor of an Ohio shooting club and sales representative and distributor of Wells Hélice Equipment (www.helice.us). According to him, Europeans already shoot millions of Hélice targets each year and the game is making rapid inroads in the United States.

"Hélice isn't a side-game or novelty," he says. "It is a prestigious, stand-alone sport that falls under the FITASC umbrella. Hélice is more challenging than the live pigeon shooting it is designed to replace. Where it has been introduced, Hélice is an accepted improvement over live birds. The flight of plastic Hélice targets is unpredictable and outstanding. There are no political repercussions from the animal-rights crowd, either. FITASC's World Cup competition circuit now offers some of the most exciting and shooting available anywhere."

The US Hélice Association (USHA, www.ushelice.com) sanctions Hélice shoots in America, awarding points for shooters seeking to be Team USA members and earn paid trips to the Hélice World Championships. The USHA notes that shooting its plastic target is not intended to replace clay games. Hélice was designed to replicate and replace shooting "Box Pigeon" or live birds.

Hélice is shot from a single station. Depending on a shooter's earned or observed handicap, it may be as close as 27 meters (or as distant as 30 meters depending on your handicap) from a semi-circle of five, seven or nine green boxes containing 110-volt Hélice throwing machines, spaced an equal distance apart.

"All shooters shall begin shooting from 27 meters and slide back one meter each time that five (for seven box rings) or three (for five box rings) consecutive targets are scored 'good.' Maximum slide shall be to the 30 meter mark," says the USHA.

Hélice targets are spun or thrown away from the shooter in a random pattern and order. This differs from the highly regulated pattern of trap and skeet and to a great degree from sporting clays as well since it is impossible to guess the sequence and there is no menu. No bird is thrown for general viewing before a shooter steps to the shooting stand, either. The USHA recommends, perhaps for obvious reasons relating to visibility, that they be thrown in a north or northeasterly direction.

A Hélice is a two-piece target. The orange or red body with two angled wings has a white snap-on cap, which is called the "witness." The object in Hélice is to hit the

Helice is shot from a single station, one shooter at a time. Shooters have two shots to separate the witness from the wings and have the reusable witness fall between the first semi-circle of throwing machines and a second semi-circle 21 meters beyond, usually marked by a low, white fence.

spinning target and cause the witness to separate from the body and wings. To count for a score, the witness must fall between the first semi-circle of throwing machines and a second semi-circle 21 meters beyond the throwing machines, that is usually marked with a low, white fence.

Unlike a clay disk, there is no such thing as a "visible piece." The two parts of a Hélice target are reusable until they become visibly damaged. (This sometimes happens after one shot if the orange wings are broken.)

The USHA specifies that Hélice targets measure 28 cm (11 inches) from wingtip to wingtip. The snap-on white witness in the center is 10.4 cm wide and the lightweight target weighs a maximum of 70 grams. The wings must be built of a material fragile to impact (usually polystyrene) while the witness is specifically not fragile (50% polyethylene) and hence reusable. Throwing machines or "Hélice traps" adjust from zero to 10,000 rpm.

Hélice traps are not universally standard and present or spin targets in different manners. As long as the targets it throws will perform within FITASC rules, any Hélice trap is allowed in a sanctioned match. Thus, in competition, you may shoot Spanish machines and Spanish targets in Spain, Italian in Italy and French in France. The best advice is to do a little research – perhaps on the Internet before heading off to a match – to give yourself the best awareness of the types of presentation you will see. An hour of research may well be worth a target or two.

The sequence of commands in Hélice also differs from conventional clay shooting. When participants are called to shoot, they advance to the shooting station with their gun empty. They load and call "Ready" when the range is declared clear. The operator then responds with "Ready." The shooter calls "Pull" and the target is thrown instantly by an automatic voice-activated system such as the Canterbury Voice Release (www.cvr.co.nz).

Another difference between Hélice and more formalized clay target shooting is that any safe preliminary gun hold is allowed. Shooters may wait with their gun down or with it fully shouldered. On stand, they must stand within a marked space and fire during the target's acceleration phase.

Hélice rules state that a 12 gauge is the largest gun allowed. No scoring credit is given for using a smaller gauge. The maximum size lead shot used is American #7-1/2 (European #7). The maximum shot load is 1-1/4 ounces (36 grams) and you need all of it for Hélice.

A Hélice gunner has two shots to separate the witness from the wings and have the reusable witness fall between the semi-circles.

USHA gives a range operator some latitude to develop his or her shoot format, but generally 25 or 30 targets a day make up a program. Shooters move on and off the stand as individuals. There is no squad rotation, so your shooting day can easily be over in an hour. In a seven-machine competition, each shooter shoots five single birds one after the other.

Major Hélice competitions are frequently 2- to 3-day events and are often held at a range near some "destination" such as Las Vegas or Reno or Dallas. Although each day consists of only a 25- or 30-target main match, shorter 10- or 15-target events or "races" often follow these matches.

Tom Veatch says that one of the exciting aspects of Hélice is that shooters from all major disciplines are usually present. Champions from skeet, trap, sporting clays and even Olympic competition regularly attend Hélice shoots. They are surprised to learn that HOA often goes to the person who breaks 86 out of 90, rather than 100 out of 100 plus a shoot-off, as is common elsewhere.

Depending on your finances, the short shooting day may be fine, because Hélice is expensive. Given the flexibility (and many would argue the necessity) of a venue to charge a little more to pay for the new computerized infrastructure, say $3.00 per bird, a round of 30 targets might well cost $90.00 plus options and ammo.

The "Summer Hélice Championship" at Veatch Gun Club in Bladensburg, Ohio, charged $125 per day with a "mandatory option" of $75 to the Lewis Class prize purse. A shooter at a 3-day event may thus pay $600 or more, but according to Veatch, the HOA winner can take home between $4000 and $6000, significantly higher even than HOA at a "Big Blast" sporting clays shoot. And the Lewis Class money is available, too.

Why is Hélice so expensive compared to shooting a clay game?

Hélice differs in numerous ways from the clay sports and target cost is one of them. Hélice supporters say the difference is not as bad as it appears, however, because Hélice competitions and even practice sessions require far fewer targets to be shot. Where a full day of sporting clays may be 100 to 200 targets, a full day of Hélice may only be 25 to 30. Additionally, the base cost of the Hélice is higher due to their more complex design and non-polluting injection molded plastic components. Clay targets cost 5 to 7 cents each. Hélice targets cost between 70 cents and $1.00 each!

CHOKES AND LOADS FOR Hélice

Hélice is most successfully shot with comparatively tight chokes and powerful cartridges because a "visible piece" does not count. The white "witness" must physically separate from its red-orange carrier and wings. Shots are taken between 32 and 47 yards and an on-edge target presents a shallow (3.25 cm) profile. Light Modified or Modified will be the most open choke you want to use and then only for your first shot. When shooting a semi-automatic, .025 to .030 choke constriction is about right, and with a double barrel a Modified and/or even a Full setup should be adequate.

MISCELLANEOUS GAMES

DUCK FLUSH

This simulated hunting game is designed to give you the feeling of shooting from a Mississippi duck blind when the central flyway is healthy and a lot of birds are moving! It is fast. Three hunters shooting simultaneously, as fast as they can load and shoot, have a chance to hit as many as 75 birds in 3 minutes. There is no time to talk or plan strategy or develop the give-and-take of a normal blind in the marsh on a cold, wet day. The duck flush forecast calls for shooting and more shooting! The Willows shooting range at The Grand Casino in Tunica, Mississippi, calls "Duck Flush" a great team-building experience!

There are many variations on this basic game. Most of them are reserved for conservation and charitable fund-raising events because the idea is to have fun rather than to keep score. A typical two-man flush event may be shot on skeet, trap or even wobble trap fields. Often in these events, partners will have time to plan their approach. They can divide the field in half, or shoot targets only from particular traps or have one partner shoot until he or she is out of shells, whereupon the second takes over and shoots until he or she is out of shells. As one person points and fires, the other reloads.

DOVE TOWER

A high tower over a skeet field is a sure sign that the club occasionally offers a Dove Tower shoot. Because this is not a nationally regulated shooting event, course owners are free to set up stands, develop shot presentations and make rules as they see fit. From one event to the next then, the organization can be quite dissimilar with the exception of two items:

• Dove hunters and, indeed, most shotgunners, universally seem to enjoy the challenge of breaking birds from traps set on towers.

• Course designers do typically apply their rules fairly across the shooting register.

Dove Tower, as it is played at clubs like Cherokee Rose, south of Atlanta, is fast and exciting. Its game often consists of 25 to 50 targets per round with shooters firing multiple times at each station.

It could be ducks or dove, but a high crossing shot presents this problem: By the time you begin moving on the bird, it will be decelerating and as you begin to measure your lead, it will also be losing altitude. Unless the birds are close, this is a tough shot. If you are shooting a pair, you must approach the station with a shot plan and then shoot your plan.

The high tower at Flint Oak near Fall River, Kansas. Imagine streaming dove or high passing ducks and geese.

FITASC SHOOTING

Most shotgun games began as a way to prepare for field shooting. Flushing pheasants flapping straight away. Woodcock, dropping their worms and fluttering skyward out of the brambles. Grouse thundering away through the quakies. Even teal launching vertically from a pond while your anxious Labrador whines and shakes in excitement. Skeet, trap, 5-Stand and sporting clays are all imitations of field shooting.

It constantly surprises me, who only has to check the regulations to see what is open, then throw my gear in the truck, that with the exception of skeet, our games began in Europe. "Old Europe" at that! Adding insult to supposed injury, the Europeans believe that the American versions of these games are easy and need to be stouter, toughened up for international competition. This sentiment seems to be universally held, and it is as true in the difference between our "English sporting" clays versus the FITASC version as it is in 16-Yard trap versus Bunker or International trap. Or perhaps so it only appears …

What is FITASC?

"FITASC" stands for *Federation Internationale de Tir aux Armes Sportives de Chasse.* Headquartered in Paris, FITASC is a worldwide cooperative association of shooters – working together through licensed committees that represent their countries – who have banded together for purposes of international competition. They have established rules to standardize the international game so that a shotgunner in Phoenix, Arizona, can compete fair-and-square against a shotgunner from Delhi, India, or Lima, Peru.

FITASC governs four games: *Parcours de Chasse* (hunter's sporting clays), *Compak* Sporting (the international version of 5-Stand), Hélice (ZZ Bird, which simulates live pigeon flight) and Universal Trench. (Universal Trench is a compact form of International Trap with five traps throwing targets at varying angles and heights. A shooter attempts to hit five randomly thrown targets at each of its five stations). FITASC is no longer affiliated with live pigeon shooting.

FITASC sporting or Parcours de Chasse shooting is commonly held to be a little more difficult than what we normally shoot in the United States, which is a version of "English sporting." All competitors - English or FITASC - shoot the same, standardized clays, but FITASC shooters must begin in the low-gun position. Low gun is optional in NSCA or English sporting in the United States.

Although FITASC is a little more difficult to shoot well, the techniques of shooting, the fundamentals of stance, gun hold, focus and lead remain the same.

The rules for FITASC allow shells filled with 1 1/4-ounce shot, but guns must not be moved from the low-gun position until the speeding clay becomes visible to the shooter. In the United States, range operators often use a "Hula Hoop" to mark the shooter's station.

In the United States, FITASC shooting is essentially *Parcours de Chasse*. Our style of "English sporting" is only shot in the United States and England. The NSCA is a FITASC member and is exclusively licensed to govern and conduct *Parcours de Chasse* and *Compak* shooting in the United States.

Annual World Championships are held in each discipline. In 2003, the United States hosted the world *Parcours de Chasse* championship at the beautiful Claythorne Lodge in Columbus, Kansas. Team USA won that event. Then, in 2004, 20-year old Minnesotan Gregg Wolf won the Open Class gold medal at the 26th Annual FITASC Sporting Clays World championship in Signes, France. It appears that we Americans have "caught up!"

FITASC has a president (currently J.F. Palinkas of South Africa) and a vice president to represent each continent: Africa, Australia, Europe and the Americas (north and south together).

Hal DuPont of Vero Beach, Florida, represents the Americas. Because he is a Krieghoff distributor, travels to competitions 35 weekends a year and shoots all of the shotgun games regularly, DuPont is essentially a full-time shotgunner. "I've been doing this for 42 years," he says, "but the job of FITASC vice president is new for me. My main goal is to convince other countries in our hemisphere to join FITASC and then to help them set up their national *Grand Prix* championships. We've gotten Mexico, Canada and Venezuela to join and are working on Chile, Columbia, Ecuador and Argentina. It boils down to some pride of nationalism and besides, joining only costs $400." Apparently becoming a member of FITASC is what is called a "no-brainer."

Shooting instructor Chris Batha uses this hoop as a teaching device, but it is similar to shooting inside the usual hoops you see on FITASC *parcours de chasse*.

DuPont, who has shot on the U.S. international team and pays for his own travel and time as team manager, says FITASC shooting is growing around the world, in part because it is challenging and in part because it is fun. "It's a great game. The chance FITASC offers to get a second shot at a singles target appeals to the ego," he says. "Lots of good shooters don't believe they can possibly miss if they get two shots."

The NSCA recently approved merging our 5-Stand-style competition with FITASC *Compak* Sporting. The layout changes are relatively minor, but this allows international shooters to compete with consistent rules and venues. This "may improve opportunities to have a form of sporting clays included in future Olympic competition," the NSCA says.

WHO SHOOTS FITASC?

Millions of shotgunners abroad and thousands of NSCA members in the United States compete in one of the four FITASC games, breaking millions of targets a year. Although shooters from America and Britain normally face "English sporting" at local clubs and tournaments, FITASC is gaining in popularity. Most other countries, Mexico to Madagascar, only shoot FITASC, so if you dream about conquering the shotgun world, you will have to shoot the world's game and that means FITASC sporting.

FITASC shooters are considered more advanced than average and they have influenced the development and acceptance of the game in the United States and extended it around the world. Consequently, shooting has become, if anything, more difficult as it has become more widely accepted. At big shoots, the NSCA reports that FITASC events are the first to fill and always have a waiting list.

WHAT IS SHOOTING FITASC LIKE?

"English sporting" entered the United States quietly in the 1970s and began attracting admirers in the '80s. It is often reported that sporting clays developed in England to help gunners prepare for high pheasants and rough shooting. In the United States, people originally thought of sporting clays as an effective method to tune up for bird hunting. After all, as shot, it was more realistic than skeet or trap because the shot sequence began with the gun down and it incorporated all types of target sizes and presentations.

As the U.S. version of English sporting developed during the past 25 years, it took on distinctive patterns. While English clays flew perhaps a little faster, a little further and a little straighter, U.S. shooters were accustomed to birds in difficult set-ups (crossing shots between two trees with a quick, narrow sight window, for instance). U.S. birds were thrown with curls and drops and often at closer range than English birds.

Avid shooters now say there may not any longer be much difference in English sporting games presented on either shore of the Atlantic. The English Clay Pigeon Shooting Association (CPSA) changed its regulations to allow an "any gun" mounting position just as the U.S. interest was developing. The NSCA soon followed with what it calls a "free gun mount." Nevertheless, while most shooters begin without the gun on their shoulder, occasional newcomers find that it is easier to shoot a pre-mounted gun.

At first then, it was a shock for U.S. clay champions to shoot FITASC. FITASC was "different" and a perception gradually took hold that FITASC shots were more difficult than standard English sporting or 5-Stand. This perception is maintained to this day among average shooters and professionals alike. You occasionally hear a difficult shot referred to as a "FITASC bird."

The perception that FITASC shooting is more difficult

Will Farrell shoots a FITASC event in Florida.

and somehow requires that someone be an elite shooter to enjoy it, begins in a couple technicalities. First, more than half of thrown FITASC birds are singles and you can take two shots at them. "Why," shooters ask, "would you need two shots for singles unless they were more difficult?" Secondly, a low gun position is required and is strictly monitored.

Whether there is or is not a difference in the quality of the English sporting game and the FITASC game, there are two types of FITASC venues, an older and a newer variety. Each has its proponents … and detractors.

The older FITASC set-up places three stands around four to five traps. Gunners moved from station to station in an arc or even in a full circle around the traps. Thus, each station presented differing target angles and directions even though the traps did not change position. Because the same traps served all of the shooting stations on a *parcours*, only one squad shot at a time. Another squad on the course would present a safety hazard, but because FITASC demands that participants move through the shooting expeditiously, squads had to be ready when their turn came. Staging areas thus became a place for the squad to gather and get nervous together. The obvious disadvantage of this older-style shooting was scheduling. Shoots had to be small because few people could shoot at any one time.

Shooting the running rabbit in FITASC *parcours de chasse* competition at Rochester Brooks Gun Club, Rochester, New York.

FITASC shooting at *La Roue du Roy* in Hemmingford, Quebec, Canada.

In the <u>new</u> variation of FITASC *parcours de chasse* shooting, each station is self-contained with its own dedicated traps, just like what we are accustomed to in English sporting. Everyone shoots with their squad and moves in the flow of squads to subsequent stations. Every stand is thus occupied and more people can shoot the course. There is a downside, however. The new version takes up to four times the number of traps, space and referees, so it is only cost effective at big shoots where lots of shooters gather.

FITASC MECHANICS

A FITASC squad consists of six competitors who shoot in a fixed rotation beginning with a single on stand one. Each shooter gets two shots to break their singles. When everyone has shot the singles, the number two individual in the rotation steps up and starts the doubles.

When the squad moves to the next stand, competitor number three begins the singles, number four begins the doubles and so on. You may usually count on four singles and two doubles on each stand with an extra single thrown in somewhere on the course to bring the total birds to 25, a complete *parcours*.

In this manner, in each round of 25 targets, each person eventually leads the shooting once in the singles and once in the doubles.

Shooting positions on a FITASC course are marked with 1-meter circles or squares on the ground. FITASC does not use a cage like in English sporting.

To lead off, the first person steps into the shooting

position. The referee will ask for everyone's attention and then show the 4-5 singles targets. Unless simultaneous or following pairs are part of the menu, this is the only time targets are shown, although if a squad member was obviously distracted, the referee may decide to throw a bird for a second look. This is the time to begin paying attention, because in FITASC shooting, your ability to read or "groove" a station will be much less than in English sporting.

Why is FITASC so strict about showing birds? Apparently, the thought is that report pairs are essentially two singles thrown one after the other. Simultaneous or rafale pairs, however, are a new presentation. (Rafale doubles are two targets thrown from the same trap on the same trajectory, a following pair. These may be shot in any order.)

So, the shooting ritual is as follows: step into the position, re-check the printed menu (traps are identified left-to-right with capital letters, A-B-C-D), set your feet, load the gun with two shells, close the gun and point to the spot you want to begin moving the muzzle. Remember that you get two shots at a single so take your time; should you miss, use your second shot to score a "visible piece." Then, even if you only shoot once and break the bird, unload your gun before you move to turn. FITASC referees have a reputation for being sticklers for the details.

Another detail to which U.S. shooters must become accustomed is the required low gun position. Unlike in English sporting, this is not just a casual suggestion. It is a rule and it is enforced. Here is how the FITASC rule reads:

A.5. (1.05) SHOOTING POSITION – The shooter will adopt the ready position, i.e. standing with both feet within the limits of the shooting stand, with the heel of the gun touching the body under a horizontal line marked on the shooter's jacket. This line will be indicated by a tape of contrasting color fixed to the jacket by some permanent means. The horizontal line shall be located 25 cm (9.85") below an imaginary line drawn over the top of the shoulders over their axis. The shooter will maintain this position with the gun not pre-mounted until the target(s) are in sight.

To position your "low-gun" line, measure from the middle top of your shoulder down 25 cm or 9.85 inches. The line should be at least 2 cm (about 3/4 inch) wide. You may not move the gun until the target is visible – not when you hear the trap throw it – or you may either have to re-shoot with a warning or even take a "lost bird" if the referee has any reason to be annoyed with you. If you are caught beginning to shoulder your gun before the bird is clearly in the air, think of it like being a baseball pitcher caught in a balk, a false move toward home plate when he is actually throwing to first base. You may get one warning per layout you are penalized and have targets taken away.

The sub-clause to the low-gun rule is that the butt must touch your body on or below the line. The purpose of the line, of course, is not to interfere with raising your gun. The line helps the referee and prevents the shooter from "dry-swinging," swinging the gun in the arc of the target's flight to practice the movement before actually shooting. This prevents firing by accident, too. FITASC referees are very strict about dry-swinging and prevent it altogether.

Pairs are always more interesting than singles. Perhaps this is because they are naturally more challenging, but in FITASC, a double killed with one shot counts as two kills. Doubles present two scenarios to think about before you step into the shooter's circle. If the first bird is broken when it flies out of the trap you may not score, even if you shoot and break it or the second bird. That is a "do-over." If the second bird is broken, you "establish" the first as dead or lost before re-shooting the second.

Loads of 1-1/4 ounces are allowed in FITASC shooting. Remington's Express Extra Long Range loads are available in all gauges in #7-1/2. The 12- and 20-gauge shells are also available in #9 for an ultra-close shot.

Many experienced shooters recommend that you set up more for the second target than the first. On the other hand, if you miss bird one, you may want to shoot a second time at it if the second bird is more difficult. You have a split second to decide.

FITASC rules specify guns and loads. A 12-gauge or smaller with a barrel length minimum of 66 cm (26 inches) is prescribed. Shot is not to exceed 36 grams (1-1/4 ounces) and sizes between 2.0 and 2.5 mm or American #7, #8, #8-1/2 and #9.

Reloaded shells and shells with spreaders or disperser wads are <u>not</u> allowed on FITASC venues. (Since many Americans who shoot are often reloaders and one of the main reason is the affordability of reloads compared to factory ammunition, this rule will initially come as a special surprise.)

It is acceptable to change guns, chokes or barrels between stations or while waiting for your turn as long as it does not delay the shooting. No changes are allowed once a shooter has entered the shooting box, perhaps because FITASC rules state that you only have 20 seconds to get ready between targets.

5
Chapter

PATTERN, PRACTICE AND CLEAN

As with any firearm, having the bullet or the shot go where you want it to go, and arrive when you want it to, is the trick that separates the money-winning competitors from the also-rans. Even if you are not planning to compete seriously and only want to have fun, you want to be sure your shotgun hits where you are aiming. Part of the process of accomplishing this is called "patterning" and it can be as easy or as complex as you make it.

Shotguns shoot single projectiles called slugs, or multiple, small round Bbs, called shot or pellets, and the latter are, of course, what you use to shoot sporting clays (or trap or skeet, for that matter). You want to provide a pattern of shot traveling at about 1000 fps that will intersect precisely with a clay disk traveling significantly slower than that, maybe 40 mph or around 60 fps.

Patterning is the effort involved in understanding how your shot disperses or spreads out from your muzzle. Every shotgun will have a characteristic pattern, but its particular pattern also depends on the size of the bore (the gauge), the constriction or choke at the muzzle and on the specific load of the shell. A Full choke has a much different signature than an Improved Cylinder choke; a 1 1/8-ounce load of Clever's Mirage brand #7-1/2 will pattern differently than its own #8 or #9 or from equivalent shells in Federal's Premium Gold line.

Ideally, you want a uniform pattern of shot to cover the break point, the area you expect the clay bird to be flying when you smash it. Because the bird is moving, and you are swinging the shotgun, and the air may be still or windy, your pattern will never be precisely uniform or precisely consistent. Still, you would like to be sure that your pattern does not leave a huge gap through which birds can squeeze unscathed.

Here is a method that many people in the shooting sports industry, both shooters and manufacturers,

If there is no sporting clays course near you or there is no event in which you can spend all weekend participating, shooting any shotgun discipline - trap, skeet, or wobble trap - will help keep you sharp.

suggest you use to begin patterning. With your gun, chokes and loads at your favorite range, step off 40 yards from your target. You want a large sheet of paper, which can be tacked between two uprights. I suggest you draw a dot that you can see from the firing line in the middle of the paper, and also a mark to differentiate the top from the bottom. This gives you an aiming point and an orientation when you take the paper down for study after shooting. Now, select a choke and a load and fire carefully at the dot.

Retrieve the paper and draw a 30-inch circle around the largest concentration of pellets. The number of pellets inside the circle divided by the total number of pellets in the load gives you a percentage. At 40 yards, it is about standard to expect that your Full choke (.040-inch constriction) will put 60 to 70 percent of its pellets

World Champion Casey Atkinson (with a Beretta) and Shayla Royal (with a Daisy BB gun) practice shooting tower targets in front of the Cherokee Rose clubhouse in Gay, Georgia. Most professionals believe that it is better to concentrate on tough shots until you "groove them" rather than to shoot complete rounds and expect to improve.

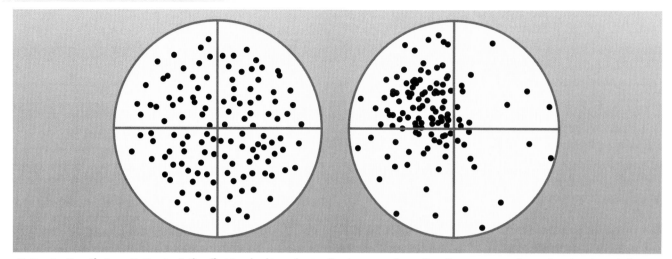

Patterning Your Shotgun - Patterning is the effort involved in understanding how your shot pellets disperse or spread out when shot through the muzzle of your gun. In the pattern on the left, an even distribution of pellets prevents clays or quail from squeezing through any holes in your shot pattern. It gives you the best possibility of hitting what you are shooting at.

If you shoot a pattern that results in something like the diagram on the right, however, there is a good chance that you may miss shots that you should be making with a more even distribution of pellets. You can often remedy an uneven pattern by experimenting with chokes and loads, or the off-kilter pattern may be a gun-fit problem. In the worst case, you will need to take your shotgun to a professional gunsmith for examination.

inside a 30-inch circle. A Modified choke (at .020-inch, half the constriction of a Full choke) should ordinarily place 55 to 60 percent inside and an Improved Cylinder (.010-inch constriction) about 45 percent. Most students of shotgunning recommend that you fire three shots with each gun/choke/load and take an average for better statistical verification.

A small problem with this is that with factory ammunition, you can only "guesstimate" the number of shot pellets in a load. A 1 1/8-ounce of #8 may or may not contain 462 pellets, for example. The only way to know for certain is to load your own.

Theoretically, you want to pattern your shotgun with the chokes and loads that you will use on a sporting clays course. A long shot with #7-1/2 at 45 yards perhaps with a Full choke and perhaps a True Cylinder with #8-1/2 at skeet range or about 15 yards. (Sporting clays courses normally limit your choice of loads to a maximum of 1-1/8 ounces of #7-1/2, #8 or #9 size shot.)

Whether you buy store ammo or load your own, you want to shoot multiple brands, loads and perhaps even different powder types to find the combination that consistently gives you the greatest percentage of shot inside that circle. That is what patterning is all about and what

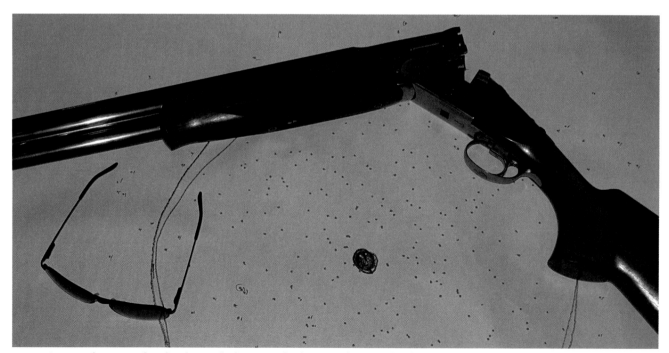

Patterning your shotgun need not be a huge or frightening task. A big piece of paper and a place to shoot is the beginning. Even a newspaper can be used if you tape a few sheets together.

makes it both fun and immensely aggravating, because the more you work to perfect your loads with your gun, the more variables you will discover in your gun, your loads, the weather and in your own shooting form.

Now, here is a little practical patterning test that I have seen written about numerous times, but have not personally tried. Even if it does not work, though, it should be fun, so maybe one day I will try it. Perhaps an open choke and loads of #7-1/2 would be right. (This patterning test ties into the chapter about gun fitting where you will learn about such terms as "cast-off.")

1 Use a big sheet of paper, the size you use to pattern your gun. Alternatively, use a bed sheet, an *old* bed sheet.

2 Paint a black dot in the middle of the sheet and then measure 16 yards precisely from your eyes (not from the muzzle) to the hanging sheet.

3 Now, get ready just like you would at a sporting clays station. Good form. Balanced. A deep cleansing breath, raise the gun and fire at the black dot without stopping to aim.

4 Shoot at the dot three or four times. By now, you are truly tearing up the sheet or the paper. Remember. No aiming, and certainly no "quick mount." Just smooth, rapid shooting with your very best form. If you follow this prescription, all of your shots should be sub-consciously guided so that they will build a consistent pattern.

5 When the range is clear, take your sheet down. Ignore the black dot for the moment and find the *center of your pattern*. This is eyeball technology, not science, so go ahead and slap a ruler on the sheet to measure the distance between the spot you determine to be the center of your pattern and the center of your black dot. Besides showing where your gun patterns with your specific load and choke, this measurement is supposed to tell you, in inches, how your stock fits in increments of 1/16 inch.

6 Remember that you shot at exactly 16 yards so every inch that your actual pattern center is off from the center of the black dot means 1/16 inch at your eyes and the stock.

7 Now, think how sights work. Archery, rifle or shotgun, the principle is the same. Move your sight(s) in the direction you want to move the projectile impact. If the eyeballed center of your pattern is dead on, congratulations! That probably will not happen, though. If you are shooting high, you might move your front beads higher, which lowers the muzzle.

8 Say, for instance, that your pattern is centered about 2 inches high and 3 inches to the left of the black dot's center. Figure that you can bring the pattern down those 2 inches by lowering the comb of your stock 2/16 of an inch at the position your cheek rests against it. You can move the pattern to the right 3 inches then by moving the stock 3/16 inch to the right: in other words, adding more "cast-off."

9 Do you want to put the center of your shot directly on the center of the target? That would seem logical, but this is actually an arguable point in sporting clays (and in other clay shooting games). Some shooters argue that for sporting clays you want a perfectly even distribution of pellets around the center of your target, with 50 percent above it and 50 percent below it. Others are adamant that you divide your target into quarters and, by counting and adjusting the comb, work toward placing 60 percent of your shot above the dot and 40 percent below it. There is no solid evidence that either will be adopted by every shooter or that either can be scientifically proven to be the best pattern distribution, but keep in mind that your objective is to shoot in front of, not behind, a disk. Therefore, it is entirely your choice.

PRACTICE MAKES PERFECT

A CHAMPIONSHIP PROFILE

In October of 2003, Wendell Cherry bought a new home in Red Boiling Springs, Tennessee, and moved in with Anne, his wife and bride of 13 years. However, such is the life of a shotgun professional, a persistent All-American and in-demand coach that he was only home 23 days out of the whole year. Twenty-three days is not enough time to unpack the boxes, much less fire-up the barbecue grill where he and Anne cook their favorite meals, Cherry admits.

U.S. sporting clays champion Wendell Cherry, who hails from Red Boiling Springs, Tennessee, believes it may now be more difficult than ever to entice people away from indoor entertainments to try action-packed games like shotgun shooting.

Wendell Cherry says some people seem to be naturally competitive. You have to have some "fire in the belly" to be a champion he says.

In the past year, Cherry has also coached hundreds of shotgun athletes … and couch potatoes. Nevertheless, he still had time to win the 2003 U.S. Open and place High Overall at the Angle Port Open, the Kruger Cup and the Homestead Cup (English sporting and FITASC courses). Because of his terrific shooting, he was invited to be a member of Team USA for English sporting and FITASC competition, a team that eventually won the gold medal at the World Championships in Texas.

Without slowing down, Cherry came back to Team USA in 2004 as the FITASC captain. His team proceeded to win the World Compak Championship in San Antonio where he took the individual silver medal. He is an NSCA first-team All-American (Open class) again for 2004, too. The man simply does not slow down and has been called the "Tiger Woods of the shotgun sports."

Perhaps Anne, who accompanies her husband on many trips, ought to think about turning that barbecue grill into a planter.

Wendell Cherry grew up around guns and has carried one to hunt with since he was 8 years old. All the men in his family hunted and they shot well.

"I think the outdoor life was natural in those days," he says. "We didn't have all the distractions that are available now: wide-screen TVs with a hundred channels, video games and the Internet. When we were bored, we went outside and found something to do. I think that today, when kids get bored, they go inside."

As a youngster, Cherry's first love was music, and so when he appeared on the stage of the Grand Ole Opry as lead guitar for "The Four Guys" at only 17 years of age, he was hooked … or seduced. Big time. By 21, he was touring the United States and Europe playing country music.

When he finally married, the bright lights began to lose some of their brilliance and appeal, though. Twenty-two years on the road can wear even a strong man down.

One day in 1995, returning home from a rare, but unsuccessful quail hunt, Cherry dropped by a sporting clays course near Nashville. "Grinders Switch" (now closed) had a spirited reputation for befuddling even the best shooters with difficult shot presentations on a dramatically vertical course. When he broke 83 clay pigeons that first day with his 870 pump, Cherry realized he had gotten more shooting in one afternoon than he would get in a whole season hunting wild quail. Since then, he has not gone a week without unlimbering his shotgun and breaking the hearts of hundreds and sometimes thousands of clay birds.

Although he loved shooting and perhaps wanted to spend more time at home, making the transition from in-demand lead guitar to in-demand shotgun professional took years of planning and discussion, and more than a few thousand practice birds. By 2001, however, he was winning tournaments regularly and was ready to make his move.

In 2002, Wendell and Anne Cherry took on the shotgun world headfirst: Wendell as a competitor and coach, Anne as his office manager. Almost immediately, they realized their circle of friends was going to change. Gone were the sequins, cowboy hats and nights of wild applause. Now, they surrounded themselves with friends in caps and jeans on bright sunny days. The nature of their friends changed as well, but the intensity, the focus of effort and the hectic travel schedule remained the same. Remember the 23 days at home in 2003? *Plus ça change*, say the French, *plus ça reste le meme*. The more things change, the more they stay the same.

Competition was not new for Wendell Cherry. What could be more competitive than those few places on stage accompanying a touring country music vocalist? After all, he had been a competitor his entire life, beginning with baseball and football as a kid and continuing into the quail fields where out-shooting his adult mentors became a hunger for the young buck.

"I believe that some people are naturally competitive," he says, "and you need some fire in your belly to win. A lot of people are physically capable of achieving the very highest levels of shooting, but there are only a few who are mentally capable. Only a few who can actually do it. I can teach someone how to shoot at that level and give them some insights – from my experience – about the kind of intensity it takes, but they have to find winning inside them."

According to Cherry, winning may be instinctive for some people. Perhaps it is even buried in their genetic code, like being the "alpha male" in a pack. Who is to say that organized sports, team or individual, do not work the same way? Or perhaps winning in sporting clays is just luck. Perhaps someone's hand-eye coordination is especially acute; future baseball Hall of Fame member Kirby Puckett once said in the middle of a hitting streak that the 93-mph baseball floating toward him looked like a big fat pumpkin and all he had to do was meet it with his bat. He said he could see the laces turn!

Whatever the fundamental truth of that claim, Wendell Cherry believes that almost everyone can learn to win. It is a spirit, an intensity plus the correct mechanics. Winning is focus and some people understand that and have it or can sometimes develop it … and some do not and never could.

"I can watch people get out of their cars and pretty much tell you how well they are going to shoot," he says.

Cherry believes the intensity world champion George Digweed brings to the game is a good example of what he means when he talks about focus. "George may – or may not – be the most technically proficient man to ever handle a shotgun," Cherry says. "I tend to think he isn't, but he has something that is exceptionally rare. He is intensely focused and very competitive. He doesn't talk to people around him much during competition. There's no chitchatting with George. And his wife, Kate, is always there to run interference for him. That's what I mean by focus. He's got it."

Focus is something a person can learn however, and it is one of the things Cherry concentrates on with students in his Peak Performance Shooting School sessions. "You can teach focus," he says, "but nothing stirs the spirit, fuels the fire more than success. Once a focused competitor gets a taste of winning, there's no stopping him – or her!"

It is a long way from main stage at the Grand Ole Opry to a hot, buggy sporting clays course, but Cherry says he enjoys the teaching and the shooting. His opportunity to learn came in the forests and fields around his childhood home near the Tennessee-Kentucky state line. Very little acreage was posted in those days and besides, his family knew everybody and the quail were wild and free. Today, he laments the fact that these beautiful native game birds are all but gone from their natural range and blames loss of habitat and modern farming practices – the practices, not the farmers themselves – of cleaning out fence-lines and plowing from centerline to centerline, which leaves no room or cover for wildlife.

"This is a sad state of affairs," Cherry says, "but it brings me students. People don't have access to fields and birds … or free time … like when I was a kid, so when they find out how much fun breaking clay birds is, they look for someone to take them to the next level, from breaking 45 birds a round to 85 birds a round. My job is to help them learn the tools required to achieve."

When he began to get serious about competition, Cherry recalls, he knew he needed to practice and learn a progressive series of mental and physical techniques, but there was no map for getting from "A" to "B." He was never sure what to do next. That is why he gives homework to the students who attend his shooting schools: gun-mounting skills, foot position, practice for particular shots and bird presentations.

"About half of the students who come to me for instruction truly *get it*," he says, "which is sad because I teach them all the same way, use the same methods. But I find that only about half really have the desire to do the hard work to improve. That's the difference. The will or the determination they bring to the instruction I give."

And what is the number one problem newcomers to sporting clays bring to the course? "It would have to be mounting their gun too fast," he says, "taking their eye off the target and looking down at the gun barrel. Mounting a shotgun is a matter of trust, trusting the shot and your preparation."

Cherry says he challenges each class. "I'm willing to teach you," he tells them, before he asks, "but are you willing to do the work to learn?"

For his own practice, Cherry shoots what he calls "The Grid," and it has become a much-written-about regimen. It is not a shooting routine he necessarily recommends to his students, though, for obvious reasons.

A small question, but one you will need to face if you become serious about shooting any shotgun game–do you practice with cheap ammo, do you reload or shoot the very best in practice? FITASC *parcours de chasse* shooting does not allow you to shoot reloads. In the words of a famous football coach, "You play like you practice."

"I believe that for most of us, effective, successful shooting is a matter of discipline," he says. "Disciplined practice carries over to disciplined competition, or disciplined shooting for game birds for that matter."

To complete "The Grid," Cherry shoots 10 targets each from 20, 30, 40 and 50 yards. "If I miss," he says, "I go back to the beginning and shoot it all over again, even if it is the final bird. It is hard work, and it takes discipline and concentration. When I lose any confidence or lose a few birds I think I should have broken, I go to The Grid." It is like therapy for a shotgunner.

Shooting The Grid, Cherry believes, burns the sight picture of every presentation into his mind. Still, in spite of the success The Grid has helped him achieve, Cherry admits he has privately grown to hate the routine.

Today, this much-in-demand instructor and competitor is both an All-American shooter and an All-American teacher as well. Three of his students are members of the 2004 NSCA All-American shooting team: Matt Treece (Oklahoma), Hub Johnson (Kentucky) and Jamie Riggs (Tennessee). Many of his students do the work and earn 20-plus NSCA punches in a year's time, quickly moving up the class ladder.

When he enters a shoot, Wendell Cherry can be seen with a Perazzi MX 2000 over/under. The top barrel is choked Full at .0034, and the bottom barrel is choked Improved Modified at .0028. His choice of shell is Lyalvale Express, 1-1/8 ounces of #7-1/2 shot, and he uses this load exclusively, even on the short-distance birds where some would switch to #8s or even #9s.

You can learn more about Wendell Cherry's Peak Performance Shooting School at www.wendellcherry.net. "My coaching will involve you in a complete program to improve your shooting and your ability to compete," he writes on this site. "You will learn the best technique for your sport, how to practice CORRECTLY and how to compete to the best of your ability. You will not leave your session with no idea of where to go from there; you will have 'homework' to keep you moving forward between sessions. My success and that of my students prove that with good technique, hard work and the will to win, success is obtainable."

Photo courtesy Silverleaf Shotgun Sports.

Keeping your shotgun clean is an essential part of shooting sporting clays. It is easy for crud to build up in the barrel and in the action. A routine cleaning only takes a few minutes of conscientious effort.

NOW, CLEAN YOUR GUN!

What happens when you pull the trigger of a loaded shotgun? A barrel camera might record an intense flash followed by a thundering explosion, which is really an extremely intense burn, the result of combining a tiny spark and a tightly compressed ounce of highly combustible gunpowder. The aftermath leaves a nasty mess of charred debris scattered up your barrel.

A conscientious shotgunner takes care of his guns meticulously. This means performing routine maintenance. It is easy and is not time-consuming. Unless you have a serious malfunction, just a couple minutes of effort performed religiously will insure that your shotgun performs as expected when you take it out of its case.

THE BORE

The bore of your shotgun should be kept exceptionally clean. There is very good news here for frequent shooters, too, because the more you shoot, and the more you scrub and clean the bore, the smoother and shinier it becomes.

When you begin to clean your shotgun, remember that the choke threads, both male and female, must be thoroughly cleaned and given a light coating of oil before you insert them again. If your shotgun uses screw-in chokes, never fire it without a choke in place.

Unless you clean your bore religiously, you run the risk of metal corrosion from moisture build-up and of jamming due to the build-up of fouling in the action. This will eventually affect your accuracy, cause jamming and shorten your gun's useful life. Of course, powder

59

Gun Scrubber is a solvent and degreaser from Birchwood Casey that comes in an aerosol spray. It will remove all types of dirt, grease and grime and should soften powder residue so that it can be brushed and cleaned with a rag or a patch. It is non-flammable and harmless to metal surfaces. A 16-ounce can is $9.60.

and plastic residue, and tiny irregularities in the barrel cannot be seen without a bore scope. Fear not, however. You have corrosion whether you can see it or not. By the time you can see a scratch or a marred surface finish with your naked eye, it has already become a problem.

Water condensing inside your gun's barrel and action is a huge problem. If you shoot in the rain, it is obvious you must clean and dry your gun, but what is not so obvious is when you are shooting outside on a cold day and then take your gun into the clubhouse. The temperature changes and condensation immediately forms on all metal surfaces, inside the gun and out. Moisture from any source immediately causes rust to begin forming. For this reason, the first rule of gun care is to wipe and dry your gun right away … especially if you are shooting or hunting near salt water. Miles away from the ocean, salt spray can be deadly to a fine metal finish.

We have heard shooters complain, "I can't understand it. I cleaned it and oiled it before I put it away. Now, look at it! It's a @#$#*~* mess!" Perhaps they only intended to store the gun for a few months and things got out of hand. Years later, when they got around to shooting again, they pulled the gun out and it was loaded with heavy spots of corrosion! Storing a gun for an extended period requires some special care.

It is important that a stored gun be kept in a clean, dry and, need we say, safe place. To store your gun for any significant period, you would like to have a temperature- and humidity-controlled environment, just like your best cigars. Even though you cleaned it before

putting it away, a gun should be stripped and cleaned periodically … even if it is not being handled or fired. This is required because leftover oils from fingerprints and normal moisture inside the case around the gun cannot be 100 percent removed.

YOUR TOOLS AND MATERIALS

New guns, especially guns that are still in their original box, usually have a light coating of grease on all the metal parts. Greasing a gun keeps it from corroding while it waits for a new home. This grease, however, will slow your new gun's action, and you should remove it with a clean rag and light coating of solvent.

If you are like most gun owners, you will religiously clean your new gun after use for the first year or so. After that, care and cleaning falls in the, "I'll rake leaves or fix the leaky sink and then do it," category. Every day you put it off, the job becomes more necessary.

1. Be absolutely certain that the gun is not loaded. It sounds so simple, but every year, people are killed and permanently maimed by "empty" guns. Even a dove load, an ounce of #8s, can make a vegetable out of you … a blind vegetable at that.

2. Remember that the first principle of gun cleaning is to run the rods, cleaning swabs and brushes from the receiver to the muzzle. Always. Never shove them in the opposite direction or pull them back through. For over/under owners, this is easier than for semi-automatics, which must be partially disassembled for a complete cleaning. (You will be tempted to clean semi-autos from muzzle to breech. After all, it is quicker and easier that way. You must resist this impulse because you can irreparably harm the finely machined lining of your barrel.)

As you run patches and brushes through the bore, do not allow the rod to scrape against the bore if you can help it. Many people have said that firearms record their history inside their barrels as much as on the softer stock. This is why prospective buyers look down the barrel of a firearm before making an offer. An experienced eye can estimate the method of cleaning and the number of shots made through the barrel. If you allow the tip of the rod or the rod itself to carelessly scrape along the inside of the barrel, you leave scratches, which serve as centers of crud build-up. These spots can only be removed by a competent gunsmith.

Your first step is to run a patch past the forcing cone, through the barrel, then past the choke and out the crown or muzzle. Soak this patch or swab it with solvent, not so much that it will pool, but enough that it will swab 360 degrees of barrel. This lubricates the bore and prevents sand or dirt from scratching the muzzle end of the barrel because it is picked up on the patch and carried out. Too much solvent and it will drip into the trigger mechanism and cause a slow trigger response, perhaps even delayed firing. Solvent can also damage the stock finish.

Hoppe's sells a fine-looking cleaning kit for those moments between shoots (or when you have let your gun lie unattended for a few months) when your shotgun needs a more extensive cleaning. It includes an instructional brochure, cleaning mat, general scrubber, bore light (requires two AAA batteries), solvent, gun oil, and rigid cleaning rod with various tips. Everything is packed in a lightweight cedar box.

3 Following this swabbing, run dry patches through the barrel until you absorb the solvent. Then use a brush. Select something perhaps a little oversized to clean the forcing cone and the barrel, especially if you have enlarged, backbored barrels.

Another caution is to never run the bore brush through the barrel before using a lubricated patch. This would almost certainly cause damage. Any dirt or sand in the muzzle end would adhere to the bristles on the brush. Then, when you brought the brush through the forcing cone, the dirt would be deposited in the chamber and forcing cone, places that are remarkably clean, even following a shot. This is the equivalent of cleaning in the wrong direction (muzzle to breech).

Always spray the brush clean with a solvent like Birchwood Casey's Gun Scrubber Solvent/ Degreaser after you use it. This Solvent/Degreaser is environmentally safe and dries rapidly, leaving metal clean and free of film or grease. Fouled solvent left on the brush is messy and can weaken its bristles. In addition, if the brush is used dirty, when you are trying to clean your gun the next time, it can easily cause more harm than good.

4 Now, if you notice miniscule lead or plastic fouling inside the barrel, you will probably see scratches, too. These scratches may be caused when the cleaning rod – with either a patch or a brush on the end – is moved back and forth on the false assumption that this is the proper way to remove built-up grit and lead fouling. It also means that abrasive dirt from the muzzle was brought back into the chamber and forcing cone. (Conventional tools do not clean the wider-diameter forcing cone very well.) Do not forget. You are not scrubbing pots and pans in the kitchen. Run patches and brushes one way only, from receiver to muzzle.

Speaking of brushes, never reverse their direction while they are inside the bore, as this bends the bristles on the brush. It is the equivalent of bending a wire back and forth until it breaks. While a brush may not be significant, you will ruin it if you reverse it while it is inside the bore, and this will not help your cleaning effort.

Most abrasions, caused by dirt pulled backwards down the barrel, are invisible on casual inspection. Scratches allow tiny lead and plastic fragments to adhere to crevices in the bore's steel and, depending on their depth and the hardness of the eventual deposit, they become resistant to cleaning. Your pattern suffers. If you clean the chamber and forcing cone by working only in the direction the shot is fired, they and the bore should never be scratched.

Otis' flexible steel cleaning rod allows you to perform daily swabbing of your semi-auto without disassembly.

Just open the action as you would to insert a shell, and pull the flexible steel rod with lubricant-soaked patch attached down the barrel, pulling it out the muzzle. This quick cleaning, while not necessarily complete, is quite good and takes under a minute.

Shotgunners who are casual about cleaning want to simply turn a patch over and re-use it. You may be able to get away with turning it over depending on how you

Whether you shoot a gas gun or a stack-barrel, clean from chamber to muzzle with brushes and patches. This ensures that you do not push crud into the more delicate mechanisms of the action.

Photo courtesy of Otis.

fold it and how dirty the swab is, but swabs are cheap. Why risk using it a second time? The abrasive material adhering to it, the stuff you want to remove, will certainly scratch the forcing cone and bore at the breech. This will cause lead and plastic buildup and defeat the purpose of the cleaning.

Use a chamber-cleaning rod with oversized bore brush to clean the chamber and the choke tube threads, male and female. It is desirable to clean the barrel first before changing the choke. This keeps dirt out of the threads. If you find the choke tube does not screw in or out easily, do not force it. A local gunsmith can help you remove it and then you should clean and lubricate the threads carefully. If you force a choke tube into place, a bulged barrel or shattered choke could result. When you have cleaned the threads, immediately reinsert the choke tube.

5 After cleaning the bore, apply a small amount of lubricating or gun oil to a clean patch and run it through. Your barrel will now be clean, lightly lubricated and ready, once again, to give you peak performance.

FINISHING THE JOB

The action and trigger can be cleaned with solvent and scrubbed lightly with a brush. A fast-drying spray solvent works well unless you are sure you can disassemble your gun and then reassemble it correctly. Very few shooters are able to do this, especially with a semi-auto. Some parts of the action just cannot be easily cleaned or disassembled by occasional shooters.

(Check your gun's Owner's Manual and "exploded parts list" before performing anything more than routine disassembly. Just like your car engine, if there is one part left over, it will not operate properly or for long.)

After spraying and brushing, using solvents and degreasers, wipe your gun clean and apply a light coating of gun oil. Apply this oil lightly, but thoroughly.

The last thing to do is wipe the outer metal surfaces to remove fingerprints or runny drips of solvent or oil. A clean cloth or even a clean patch with a light coating of Hoppe's No. 9 is fine.

When shooting in damp conditions, several manufacturers offer specialty gun cloths with ingredients that drive out moisture, lubricate and help prevent rust. It is an excellent idea to carry several in your case to wipe down the barrel right after shooting. Birchwood Casey's convenient and disposable Sheath Take-Alongs, for example, are small individual cloths, impregnated with Sheath Rust Preventive and sealed in a foil packet for compact carrying. A 12-pack of these costs less than $6.

What about the stock and forearm? Unless they are synthetic, these pieces are usually walnut and even though shooters are usually careful of their own and other shooters' guns, it is easy to bump the metal edges of a gun rack or scratch against the tailgate of your pickup. A spot application of stock finish followed by an oiling and a good rubdown with a clean cloth should once again bring out the gun stock's luster and original brilliance.

A small cleaning kit such as this one from Otis – and a rarely used, but indispensable "wad knocker" – will help you avoid numerous problems when shooting any shotgun discipline. Many shotgunners believe cleaning is an arduous chore and put it off ... and put it off ... whereas five minutes will make a terrific difference in your gun's long-term function.

Shooting in damp conditions and especially near the ocean requires that you clean your shotgun more frequently to prevent the build-up of corrosive particles in the bore and on the outside of the barrel.

Photo courtesy of Birds Landing, California.

6
Chapter

COACHES, CLASSES AND SHOOTING SCHOOLS

Lessons are for kids, right? We buy piano lessons for our daughter, tennis lessons for our son. In fact, we went to baseball camp one summer when we were kids. Lessons are for kids. Not so fast, my friend.

Every professional performer – from football players to viola players – has a coach. Think about it. Every baseball team has a full-time batting coach. Tiny Olympic gymnasts and petulant professional ice skaters have personal coaches. Professional domestic partners employ marriage counselors. If you want to get better

at shooting a shotgun, you too will avail yourself of the services of a professional coach and/or attend a shooting school.

To step up in your ability to consistently hit what you are shooting at with a shotgun load, your best – and most people would argue, your most cost-effective – action is to participate in a course of instruction. Whether it lasts one hour or is a complete three-day weekend (a shotgun camp), you are virtually guaranteed to shoot better when it is over than before it began.

Lessons are for kids, right? Right! And adults, too!

Every coach, class and instructional book or CD says that the ability to focus on a single task is vitally important in moving from "very good" to championship status.

Most sporting clays courses, trap and skeet clubs and even local rod and gun clubs have shooting training available from NSCA- or NSSA-certified instructors who are members or residents of your area. In case there is not an organized class, program or certified instructor near where you live, your best bet for good, low-cost instruction near your home is to check with other clubs in your area. Generally, an NSCA-certified instructor is going to charge about $50 to $75 an hour for personal instruction and they will offer small group instruction for a little less.

To supplement personal instruction, which can be pricey (an 8-hour day of one-on-one with Lanny Bassham, who teaches "mental management," for example, is $3000 – although this is certainly on the high side), there are dozens of books and videos available to help your shooting game. These are priced reasonably and you get to hear and watch as true champions talk about their practice routines and demonstrate exercises, discuss their mental and physical approach, and their execution. Jon Kruger, Gil and Vicki Ash, George Digweed, Marty Fischer, Andy Duffy and Michael McIntosh have books and tapes available at reasonable prices over the Internet or through notices and advertising in *Sporting Clays* and other shotgun magazines.

Shooting a shotgun proficiently, whether it is in skeet or trap or sporting clays, takes the same type of technical proficiency and mental toughness. So, just because a tape is offered, for example, by trapshooting champion Kay Ohye, it does not mean you cannot learn from it. You definitely can! Almost any time you spend thinking about your game, questioning and practicing your technique is good – except when you step up to the line. At that point, it is time to let all of your work become automatic.

Once you have learned what you can from the local instructors – and only you will know – you may want to try one of the nationally advertised and recognized programs. We discussed shooting schools and instruction with the popular Gil Ash, highlighting the method he and his wife, Vicki, promote at their OSP Shooting School.

OPTIMUM SHOTGUN PERFORMANCE SHOOTING SCHOOL

"Eventually, success and failure become more a matter of attitude than anything else," Gil Ash writes. The saying is an "Ash Attitude" and it epitomizes the approach to shooting success that Gil and Vicki, his wife, have preached since they leapt into full-time teaching 10 years ago.

Today, Gil and Vicki Ash may be the most celebrated shotgun instructors in America. These avid bird hunters began shooting sporting clays in 1982. Before that, they shot skeet. Like many of us, when a sporting clays range opened not far from his house, Gil thought he would try the game. The fun and variety of the game hooked him badly.

"I found out right away that sporting clays lends itself to people who are competitive and like a challenge," Gil says. "Sporting clays is different from skeet and trap in that no two courses – and a course will often change from week to week – are alike. Every time you shoot them, skeet and trap are the same, but in sporting clays the target presentations are varied and challenging."

Gil speaks rapidly, as if he has so much information he wants to give you that there is not possibly enough time in one clinic. He describes himself as on the creative edge, the "left-brain team," while his wife, Vicki, is more analytical and practices right-brain thinking. Good balance.

"Vicki and I approach problems and arrive at solutions differently," Gil says. "In a way, we are opposites and we learn things differently."

Gil says that he and Vicki "don't teach like other instructors. We don't try to teach you lead and don't care what pointing technique you use or where you put your shot string in relation to the bird. We don't teach – well, we do, but only as technique, not as a fundamental approach to clays that you need to master – particular

Gil and Vicki Ash of Optimum Shotgun Performance Shooting School are among the elite shotgun instructors in the world.

For the individual who is not quite ready for a round of personal instruction, there are plenty of books, tapes and CDs available from qualified instructors.

target presentations. Our objective is to show you why you miss and then teach you what to do about it. We can do that because we understand the eye-brain connection and how your brain interprets what your eyes see."

A program of "teaching success" sounds like marketing hype, but Gil says success is dependent on your eye-brain messages and on your physical coordination. Shooting 2 feet behind a flying bird is probably a symptom, not a cause.

"People must learn to turn off their analytical brain after they master the mechanics, and let their athletic brain execute the shot. Like in golf. First, you understand the mechanics; then, you practice and groove your swing. When you step onto a tee or into the shooting box at a meet, you can't be running through a mental checklist and execute the shot precisely."

Is their approach just a shotgun version of the popular cliché "men are from Mars, women are from Venus" or does it mean they understand effective teaching? Gil insists that men and women see things very differently. Of course, that transcends the shooting realm, but it applies there as well.

Gil believes they are the first instructors to come right out and say that women perceive lead differently than men. Women tend to "see" lead as inches at the muzzle. Men tend to perceive lead in the conventional sense, perhaps because shooting has been a male-dominated sport, as feet in the air in front of a flying target.

"Only one or two of the thousands of women we have taught," Gil says, "see lead as feet in front of the target. On the other hand, one out of a hundred or so

men see lead as inches at the muzzle. We believe and teach that this is a symptom of the difference in the way men and women see the world, and so we try to adapt our shooting instruction to take advantage of it."

Have any World Champions attended OSP clinics? As far as Gil knows, no, but thousands of former students report they are now shooting better than ever.

"The biggest component in the making of a World Champion," Gil says, "is not the coach – although everyone benefits from professional coaching – but a person's attitude, commitment, financial backing and, to a lesser extent, their equipment. If your objective is to be a World Champion, expect that it will take you 5 focused and dedicated years. A good coach may cut that pathway a little shorter or may not, depending on the student. You will take 3 years to reach the 60 to 70 percent level, another year-and-a-half to shoot 80 percent and finally, another year to reach the 90 percent bird-busting stage. But unless you are a natural – and there are some naturals out there – this takes extreme commitment. But this desire and the follow-through have to be number one in your life, in front of work or children or even your family and love life."

When should the average person take lessons? "Anytime you become dissatisfied with your current level of competence is the time to do something about it," Gil says.

Gil Ash warns that when people finish an OSP class, they often expect to begin busting clays at a record pace … and that usually does not happen. An instructor can set you up to feel good about a clinic – and then fail in the long run – if he or she teaches the easy shots. This is not the way to truly improve, however.

Gil Ash of OSP has a philosophy of teaching the solution rather than the problem. "Vicki and I try to show our students how to diagnose and correct errors in their own form," he says, "which we believe is of greater long-term value than teaching the specifics of lead on a given presentation."

After finishing an OSP class, he says, the student will understand how to improve, why he missed and will understand his weaknesses and how to go about remedying those weaknesses. "We don't teach the problem," he says, "we show the way to a sound solution. On average, a student must practice what we teach for a couple weeks to see an improvement in their game. Physiologists have documented that it takes 2500 to 3000 repetitions to make your neurons rearrange and begin firing in the correct order."

Are there any emerging trends in clay shooting? In the mid-1980s, Gil says, a long target was 25 yards; now it is 45 yards. Moving the birds farther from the shooting cage pushes people to be better, but it discourages some, too. In the '90s, there was a movement to make shooting more difficult with long distance shots, tricky angles and obstacles, but course owners soon found that they lost a lot of weekend shooters. Making it hard for the professionals was fine, but the average person wanted to go out and bust some birds and have fun and not feel bad about themselves when they were done.

According to Gil, three to four million people shot sporting clays last year. They are doing this instead of golf ... perhaps because it is less frustrating than golf. "I believe that 90 percent of them are interested in a fun 2 1/2-hour walk where they can go make noise and break things," he says. "Smart range owners help average folks enjoy shooting. They may give them a challenge, but they send them home feeling good. I believe that less than 1000 people actually travel consistently and truly worry about their shooting. After all, there are only 17,000 or so NSCA members in the U.S."

Gil believes the trick for a range owner is to have targets close enough and easy enough for weekend shooters, but that still cause them to miss occasionally and think, "I can do this!"

For more information about Optimum Shotgun Performance Shooting Schools, look up www.ospschool.com or www.74ranch.com or call (800) 838-7533/(281) 346-0888. Clinics normally run from 9:00 a.m. to 5:00 p.m. for 3 days and may be attended as 1-, 2- or 3-day events, as each has a particular focus. Clinics include class instruction on mechanics and enough field shooting to define and solve problems. Some 150 to 300 targets will normally be shot per student. Fees range from $275 to $475 per person per day, depending on the location and the package offered by the host club.

ADDITIONAL SHOOTING INSTRUCTION PROGRAMS

CLAY SPORTS TRAINING

This is the site of national champion Wendell Cherry's shooting training program. "My method has been developed through countless hours of study, practice, determination and experience. My coaching emphasizes the importance of discipline in these areas. I incorporate sound fundamentals, efficiency of gun movement, visual focus and mental commitment into a technique that works ... and works consistently. My system has evolved over the years through shooting with and against the best in the world. It is learnable and fosters success and self-confidence. If you are willing to put in the time and effort, it will improve your shooting and your scores." Contact Wendell Cherry's Clay Sports Training, 4963 Clay Co. Hwy., Red Boiling Springs, TN 37105 (931) 258-3707 www.wendellcherry.net.

ELITE

Bobby Fowler, Jr. is a World Champion and this sets him apart, he says, from the average instructor. His aggressive approach to breaking clay is epitomized by his answer to the following question: "When I get to the last station, I tend to fall apart. How do I stay focused and keep myself in the game?" Bobby says that many times when shooters are in good standing on their last station they get into a "try not to miss it" mode instead of trying to hit the target. It is the "prevent defense" of sporting clays. When you are trying not to miss, you surely will. The reason for this is that you have just put a negative thought into your head, making yourself believe (sub-consciously) that you will miss the bird. Instead of trying not to miss, think about how you will approach the bird in order to hit the target (a positive thought). Negative thinking can cost you your game. Always stay aggressive and think in positive terms. Contact Elite Shooting School, 14231 Jaubert Ct., Sugar Land, TX 77478 (281) 313-3309 www.eliteshooting.com

MENTAL MANAGEMENT

As children, we became familiar with the Little Engine Who Could, or the idea of believing in ourselves and adjusting our mental attitude to succeed (*The Power of Positive Thinking?*). There are numerous books and tapes available about the results you can achieve with a shotgun if you just believe and have a positive mental attitude. All of this, of course, is a variation on the build a ballpark in an Iowa cornfield idea: "Build it and they will come." Assuming there is something to this idea and the author believes there is – but only after you understand the mechanics and can make the basic movements and shots – the books, CDs, videos and tapes by former Olympic champion Lanny Bassham are an example of some of the most widely publicized motivational programming for shotgunning, air rifle and now, archery. "The purpose of such a course [of study] is to improve the performance of an individual by improving one's self image and the ability to use the pressure of competition to one's advantage."

Contact Lanny Bassham Mental Management System, 2509 Dartmouth Dr., Flower Mound, TX 75022 (800) 879-5079 www.mentalmanagement.com.

MIDWEST ACCELERATED

The host facility in the Ozarks has three sporting clays courses and various other shooting events: trap, skeet, 5-Stand and wobble trap. Instruction packages include instructor fees, new shells and targets. The basic 4-hour program features 350 targets and costs $450. A 3-day course of private instruction (3 hours in the morning and afternoon) is $1950 and involves 1800 targets. Based at Ozark Shooters and just 11 miles north of Branson, Missouri, Midwest is open 362 days a year. Contact Midwest Accelerated Shooting School, 759 U.S. Hwy. 65, Walnut Shade, MO 65771 (417) 443-3093 www.ozarkshooters.com

PARAGON

Dan Schindler is an NSCA Level III instructor, member of the English Guild of Shooting Instructors and clay course designer. He learned gun fitting from Peter and Wendy Crabtree at the West London Shooting School. "Feather or clay, there is a proper, step-by-step approach to every successful shot. Paragon coaching organizes your approach to that shot, making it easier to understand. That knowledge is your most important shooting tool." Contact Paragon, P.O. Box 1276, Flat Rock, NC 28731 (828) 693-6600 www.paragonschool.com

SPORTS PERFORMANCE

The CD offered by Sports Performance and scripted by hypno-therapist Kay Hall, advertises this statement: "We work with the most critical inches in any game, the inches between your ears." Obviously, their work is cut out for them.

Sports Performance figures you have said the following or something like it many times: "If I could just put all of my good shots together in one round, it would be great!"

Their answer is that through a series of imaging,

visualization and relaxation techniques, their Performance CD will "consistently and comfortably [help you] exhibit [use] the skills you have already learned." They do this by identifying and then banishing the mental issues, fears, doubts and uncertainties that harm your game, and replacing them with self-confidence by reinforcing the positive communication between your conscious mind and your sub-conscious mind.

Shooting for maximum performance relies on the idea that you can achieve peak results only when your mind and your body are working skillfully and almost thoughtlessly together. The Sports Performance CD is designed to help you break your maximum number of targets by maximizing your mental game. Kay Hall advises, up front, that training your body to do the biomechanical part of shooting is separate from what you will achieve by using the CD. Nevertheless, using the relaxation techniques on the CD can help you become a better sporting clays shooter no matter what your classification. It is almost a shooting sports meditation.

Hall says she has worked with many athletes and "weekend warriors" and the audio tracks on these CDs should be played just before you step up to shoot. Version 2 of the Sports Performance CD features "more work in the area of recovering from missed clays," in "positive concentration" (which must be regained immediately on a sporting clays course) and in relaxation techniques. As you practice these skills, Hall says, you will get better. The central idea is to help you stay "in the zone" even if you miss.

Although Sports Performance is an audio-only CD, it offers what is called "guided imagery" through a program of deep relaxation. Therefore, Sports Performance warns that you should not listen to their CD while driving or operating equipment. The cost is $29.99 from www.sports-performance.biz

Shooting instruction at the 5-Stand on the island of Lanai in the Hawaiian Islands. Most shooters will testify that taking lessons cut years off their learning curve, but instructors say they only give their students the basics and the personal attention. It is then up to you, the student, to put their lessons into practice.

Even the highest-paid athletes retain personal instructors to help them perform at the top of their game. If the very best - in tennis or skating or shotgunning - benefit from coaching, how much more will those of us who are weekend shooters excel if we take lessons - and then take them to heart!

10 ADDITIONAL CLINICS, SCHOOLS AND COURSES OF INSTRUCTION

1 Custom Shooting Sports, Inc., 6970 Somers-Gratis Rd., Camden, OH 45311 (937) 787-3352 [NSCA Level III shooting coach Jim Arnold and psychologist Dr. Dennis Schneider: Summer home Mad River Sportsman's Club, Ohio and winter home Bray's Island Plantation, SC.]

2 Chris Batha Shooting School, 43 Pinckney Colony Rd., Bluffton, SC 29909 (866) 254-2406 www.chrisbatha.com [Senior instructor and gunfitter for London gunmaker E.J. Churchill with more than 30 years of wing and clay competition experience. Teaches Churchill instinctive style of shooting.]

3 Pete Blakely Shooting School, Dallas Gun Club, P.O. Box 292848/3601 I-35 South, Lewisville, TX 75067 (972) 462-0043 www.dallasgunclub.com [Experienced in Britain and United States at highest levels of coaching, Blakely teaches "intuitive judgment" shotgunning to help his students build a repertoire of shot pictures, by mastering the elements of a shot that are under their control.]

4 Fieldsport Wingshooting Schools, 3313 W. South Airport Rd., Traverse City, MI 4964 (213) 933-0767 www.fieldsportltd.com [The instructor team of Bryan Bilinski, Michael McIntosh and Chris Batha teach all shotgun fundamentals and give gunfitting analysis.]

5 Griffin & Howe, 33 Claremont Rd., Bernardsville, NJ 07924 (908) 766-2287 www.griffinhowe.com [Lars Magnusson, managing director, learned at the West London Shooting School, home of James Purdy & Sons. Locations in NY and NJ or traveling to work with advanced or beginning shotgun.]

6 Jon Kruger Shooting Enterprises, 21166 Quail Ridge Ln., Sunman, IN 47041 (812) 926-4999 www.quailridgeclub.com [Hugely successful competitor Jon Kruger, host of the annual Kruger Classic, and a team of instructors are available.]

7 Michael Murphy & Sons Shooting Schools, 6400 SW Hunter Rd., Augusta, KS 67010 (316) 775-2137 www.murphyshotguns.com [Personal instruction and shooting development by Michael Murphy and national champion sporting clays shooter Gary Phillips. Two-day courses at Augusta facility or around the United States. Gun fitting, repair and sales available.]

8 Orvis Shooting Schools, Historic Rt. 7A, Manchester, VT 05254 (800) 235-9763/(802) 362-3622 www.orvis.com [Classic shooting school setting in Sandanona, NY or Mays Pond, FL with NSCA-certified instructors at all levels; gun rental available. Teaches "Old English" method of shooting.]

9 The Shooting School (WRA Services), 1665 Steller Ct., Excelsior, MN 55331 (800) 742-7053/(952) 474-0240 [Two- or 3-day sessions are held at various gun clubs across the United States. Small

The NSCA offers four levels of instructor certification - Youth, Level I, II and III - but writes that there are "no advanced shooting techniques, just advanced application of the basics."

classes, 4:1 or less, include unlimited targets and school equipment.]

10 West London Shooting School, West End Rd., Northolt UB5 6RA United Kingdom 011-44-20-8845-1377 www.shootingschool.co.uk [The classic shotgun shooting school against which all others are measured. This school has been in business for more than 100 years.]

A NOTE ABOUT NSCA CERTIFICATION

The National Sporting Clays Association (NSCA) offers three levels of instructor certification and a separate youth certification. Typically, an instructor holding a Level III certificate will charge more per hour because he or she will have had additional training beyond the basics required for Levels I or II. You should also expect that the higher the level instructor you work with, the greater the level of insight they will bring to your shooting challenges and questions.

Shooting instruction is a very personal time, however. Not every instructor will mesh with every student in the same way that not every marriage will succeed. Personality conflicts can easily arise. Just imagine the tension when you attempt to teach a spouse to shoot or algebra to your high-school-age student. One size does not fit all.

You should also understand that the ability to shoot successfully at a very high level does not necessarily mean that a person has insights into why he or she is successful and can convey those insights successfully to someone else. Because the act of shooting successfully at the highest level – whether it is a shotgun, a 22 rifle or a bow and arrow – must become mechanical, the champion must turn off their analytical brain and enter a zone of thoughtlessness or what students of Zen philosophy aptly refer to as "the gateless gate." In other words, the ability to do something well is not the same as the ability to teach others to do something well. Master archery instructor Bernie Pellerite (*Idiot Proof Archery*) has found this to be the case with many top bow-and-arrow competitors – that they do not have a clue why they are so good.

For more information about NSCA instructor requirements and a schedule of courses, you may visit their Internet site and view instructional materials at www.mynsca.com/forms. Included here is an overview of requirements for youth certification and to progress from Level I through Level III.

YOUTH COACH:

NSCA youth coaches are qualified to teach proven, sound techniques to the beginning youth shooter. The course is approximately 25 percent classroom and 75 percent hands-on training, shooting and teaching exercises over 2 full days. This course, and all NSCA Level courses, cover safety, gun mount (eye dominance, mount and fit), stance, target selection, shooting methods, stance, general shotgun knowledge and teaching, plus interpersonal skills. The emphasis at each level is continuing refinement of technique and communication. Registration is $350 and students are responsible for their own gun, approximately 250 shells and a percentage of course materials and instructor fees.

LEVEL I:

A 3-day course of classroom instruction and hands-on shooting. This course is designed for individuals who wish to "teach orthodox NSCA shooting methods to beginner or novice students." Participants must be 18, pass a written test and demonstrate good shooting skills. Registration is $500 and students are responsible for their own gun, approximately 250 shells and a percentage of course materials and instructor fees.

LEVEL II:

The NSCA says that a "high level of expertise is required for the Level II course with an emphasis on diagnostics and communication skills." The Level II course is a 4-day course of classroom instruction and hands-on shooting. "A sound knowledge of the fundamentals is vital as well as the realization that there are no advanced shooting techniques, just advanced application of the basics." Requires a Level I certification, 12 months of teaching at Level I and more than 200 hours of work with paying clients. Participants must pass a written test upon completion of the course. Registration is $750 and students are responsible for their own gun, approximately 250 shells and a percentage of course materials and instructor fees.

LEVEL III:

You must have been a Level II instructor for 2 years, have completed a minimum of 1500 hours of paid Level II instruction and the cost is $1500 for a 5-day course involving 3 days of refresher training and 2 days of evaluation.

7
Chapter

GUNS FOR CLAYS

Sporting clay shooting has only been available in the United States since about 1980, but even so, it has quickly become a divided camp. First, there are those who shoot it because it is just good fun and a great way to be outside perhaps before the waterfowl or grouse or snipe seasons open. Clay shooting is an excellent tune-up for hunting, as a good sporting course will faithfully replicate the flight patterns you see from your butt or walking behind your dog. A second group consists of people who shoot sporting clays competitively and are more concerned with their score than with any carry-over of learned skills into the hunting season.

Consequently, the guns one uses or sees on a course are very much dependent on the camp with which the shooters are primarily (or loosely) affiliated. Hunters will take their camouflaged pump guns and semi-automatics, perhaps even side-by-sides, to a day of shooting, while competitors will be much more likely to shoot specialized over/unders or semi-autos … and God forbid the stock should become scratched!

As with any generalization, many (perhaps most) shooters do not fit these too-neat categories. Many avid competitors are just as avid wingshooters, for instance.

Nevertheless, it is my observation that his prized Perazzi MX8 is not the gun the average waterfowl hunter will put in his flat-bottom boat on a blustery day when the ducks and geese are flying low through the mist. The Remington 1100 semi-auto with a black synthetic stock or a camouflaged Mossberg 835 Ulti-Mag pump are the guns of choice on those days.

While any shotgun will do to shoot sporting games, one predominantly finds over/unders and semi-autos at the stands because they handle doubles more easily than pumps. As a shotgun's pump mechanism is manipulated for a second shot, even if it is exceptionally smooth and the shooter works it with astounding ease, there are about 8 inches of hand and arm movement involving the forearm and internal mechanisms that cannot help but misalign your shot and disturb your concentration, if only briefly.

Therefore, the guns we are primarily going to concentrate on in this chapter are those that are either specifically designated for sporting clay shooting or which fit our general guidelines for a fine clay gun. Additional shotguns suitable for sporting and competition purposes are included in the listing found in Appendix II.

In America, we tend to think of our gun as a utilitarian tool. This is not the case in Europe or around the sporting world, where a fine gun is a luxury item that can be used for generations.

Art courtesy of Sturm, Ruger & Co.

In Self Defense! Many if not most sporting clays shooters were hunters before they took to the relatively tame, but only slightly less intense, cart paths of competition. With the exception perhaps of a brush with death, almost all of the elements and emotions of a hunt - surprise, elation, disappointment - can be found on a sporting clays course if you dedicate yourself to being the very best that you can be.

BOXLOCK VERSUS SIDELOCK

You will occasionally hear a debate about the best type of shotgun action for double-barrel guns, and it focuses on two terms, "boxlock" versus "sidelock." These are two distinctive types of shotgun actions, two manners of building the firing mechanism, the parts that connect your finger to the shell. The boxlock is preferred

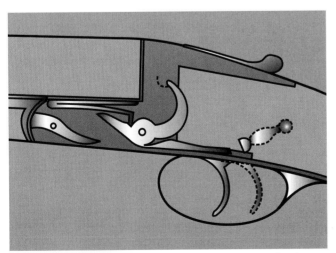

Inside Your Gun - A good shotgun should work reliably with only occasional routine maintenance. Although the interior of a gun may appear intimidating, and a high-quality gun is a work of art, the above schematic shows the basics of a boxlock shotgun's interior (as opposed to the older-style sidelock).

among manufacturers building double guns today, perhaps because it is simpler, more reliable and has fewer moving parts.

Sidelocks came first and were direct descendants of the firing mechanisms of flintlock and percussion-lock shotguns. These guns had external hammers and the evolving hammerless guns became sidelocks. The mainspring, sear, tumbler and hammer were built onto on a plate that formed one side of the action of a shotgun.

The boxlock-action shotgun was developed by Anson and Deeley in Great Britain in the 1870s. This type of action carries the triggers, sears, hammers and all the miscellaneous springs within the body of the action. There were no protruding hammers. The Anson and Deeley mechanism eventually proved to be simpler than the sidelock, using the leverage of the opening barrels to cock the internal hammers. Even original boxlocks had fewer moving parts than sidelocks by half!

Some shotgun aficionados believe that sidelocks offer cleaner trigger pull than boxlocks. Sidelock actions, they argue, have traditionally been easier to remove and clean. Nevertheless, they do not provide detectable benefits for modern shooters.

Boxlock guns are generally more robust and they seldom fail. Sidelocks, on the other hand, are notorious for suffering broken leaf mainsprings at critical moments. Although repair is relatively simple, it none-the-less takes a few minutes and can hold up a squad unnecessarily.

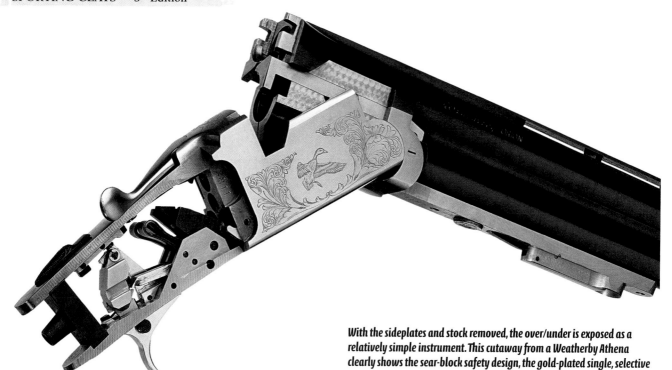

With the sideplates and stock removed, the over/under is exposed as a relatively simple instrument. This cutaway from a Weatherby Athena clearly shows the sear-block safety design, the gold-plated single, selective inertia trigger and the automatic ejectors in place on the barrels.

THE MANUFACTURERS AND *(Some of)* THEIR GUNS

Our review of shotguns begins with basic models that are suitable for sporting clay competition and suggests prices, the peculiarities of and specifications for each gun, as well as some of the well-accepted options. For popular gun manufacturers that do not produce specific competition guns, we have looked for guns that you will see at the shooting stations, if not in competition, in the hands of hunters who are tuning up for the bird season or are just having fun. After all, it was not competition, but hunting and fun that were the original purpose for sporting clays.

However, defending ourselves from carelessness and the manufacturers from rancorous commentary that their guns do not meet the specifications as presented, it is necessary to note that details of gun models change faster than a rock star's popularity. In fact, printed gun specifications, especially from the smaller or more exotic manufacturers – at least to us Americans, but this applies specifically to European companies – are often subject to interpretation as various printed materials – catalogs, flyers and sales sheets – and their Internet sites occasionally give conflicting data. Of course, many of the Internet sites are translations into English by native speakers of other languages and this causes certain minor errors in "the lingo," you might say. (Imagine how tasked you might feel if you were required to translate bore specifications into Italian, Spanish or Japanese!)

Then, too, there exists a world of different styles and legal difficulties and whatnot. There is the European metric-to-American foot-pound conversion that renders some measurements statistically imprecise. Quite a few

During a major, well-advertised competition, there is a tendency for semi-autos and over/unders to balance roughly in numbers. Semi-autos tend to be shot by individuals who have less time and money invested in shooting, whereas the over/under is usually the gun of choice for the more experienced competitor.

of the European manufacturers use dozens of catalog pages to show off wonderfully engraved sideplates with American movie stars or Old West scenes, but fail to give basic information about their guns.

And, finally, because each company has a different philosophy and positions itself uniquely in the marketplace, informational materials are often not easy to compare. Every effort, including discussions with the original manufacturer or his importing agent where possible, has been taken to ensure the accuracy and quality of the data. Prices quoted are at full "suggested retail" which, unless you place an order via the Internet or simply do not care about price, will invariably be higher than you will find at your local gun dealer. Therefore, the following information should only be used as a general guide. Again, additional shotguns suitable for sporting and competition purposes are included in the listing found in Appendix II.

Spanish gun manufacturing centers in the northern Basque region around Eibar, as Italian shotgun manufacturers cluster around Brescia, in the north of that country. AYA has been building side-by-sides for more than 90 years and has now entered the over/under market. Expect to see more of these fine, but medium-priced, guns on clay courses in the future.

ATA [www.ataarms.com]

ATA shotguns are imported from Istanbul, Turkey, for American hunters who are working within a budget. Nevertheless, in the right hands, several models would certainly score well on the shooting line. The ATA catalog notes, by the way, that the company has been producing scatterguns for more than 40 years. ATA advertises that its semi-autos and pumps are some of the lightest in weight of any on the market today.

Model: ATA Companion

Gauge and Action: 12- and 20-gauge semi-automatic

Chamber: 3-inch

Barrels: 24-, 26- and 28-inch blued barrels with ventilated rib and front bead

Chokes: Skeet, Improved Cylinder, Modified, Improved Modified and Full

Stock and Forend: Walnut with black ventilated recoil pad

Grip: Pistol grip

Standard Measurements: 48 inches long with a 28-inch barrel

Weight: 6-1/4 pounds (12-gauge) or 5-1/2 pounds (20-gauge)

Suggested Retail Price: Less than $1000

Note: This shotgun also comes in several camo patterns and with a black synthetic stock and forend. The upgraded version, with a chrome-polished receiver that features a number of engraving options, is the Centurion. Available shims allow change of drop and cast of any type stock.

AYA [www.aya-fineguns.com]

Pronouncing this Spanish manufacturer's name, *Aguirre y Aranzaba*, will cause most English speakers to bite their tongue, but you know these fine shotguns simply as AYA. They are built in Eibar, in Spain's northernmost Basque Country, and

the company has been building guns for 90 years. Sales, they say, approximate a million guns by now, mostly side-by-sides.

Like so many of the European guns, the way an instrument looks is as important as, or perhaps more so, than how it shoots, even though the action and mechanics of the lower-priced and higher-priced models are practically the same. The higher price may be many thousands of dollars or Euros higher because of wood stocks grained with more "character" plus beautiful engraving and gold inlays. AYA gunmakers ask for an 8-month (or greater) leeway to build one of their shotguns to your precise specifications for length of pull, drop, palm swell and cast on/off, but you may be able to find a used gun available right now on the Internet.

Model: AYA Excelsior

Gauge and Action: 12- and 20-gauge over/under

Chamber: 3-inch

Trigger Assembly: Custom-built (single or double triggers, selective or non-selective); with or without automatic ejectors

Barrels: 28-, 29-, 30- and 32-inch barrels

Chokes: Fixed or screw-in chokes to order

Stock and Forend: Sporting, skeet or trap walnut stocks and forend

Grip: Pistol grip

Standard Measurements: To order

Weight: About 7-3/4 pounds

Suggested Retail Price: Expect to pay about $4495. (A 7.88-pound AYA MD-6 over/under 12 gauge with 30-inch barrels and 14 7/8-inch length of pull, vented top and middle rib with "Rose and Scroll" engraving was $6095 from New England Custom Gun Service [www.newenglandcustomgun.com] in April 2004.) Delivery of a new, special-order gun takes 5 to 6 months.

The Super Sport is equipped with Benelli's latest low-recoil technology. This gun is also available with a walnut stock as the Sport II. Both 12-gauge guns have a 3-inch chamber and are factory ported to reduce muzzle jump.

The Benelli Montefeltro autoloader has a grooved receiver top that effectively extends the sighting plane for fast, consistent target acquisition.

BENELLI USA [www.benelliusa.com]

Benelli is a 34-year-old Italian manufacturer with a factory in Urbino. Benelli USA, headquartered in Accokeek, Maryland, also imports Franchi shotguns and Uberti classic guns. Best known perhaps for turkey-hunting guns, slug guns, and military and police arms, Benelli recommends its 12-gauge SuperSport and Sport II autoloaders as high-performance competition shotguns.

Model: Benelli SuperSport

Gauge and Action: 12-gauge semi-automatic

Chamber: 3-inch

Barrels: Factory ported 28- or 30-inch hammer-forged steel barrels, topped with a high-visibility red bar sight on the tapered (10 to 8 mm), stepped rib. Cryogenically treated, barrels are frozen to −300 degrees Fahrenheit. (Benelli says this changes the steel at its molecular level, evening out the "grain structure" for a smoother bore surface that will resist fouling.)

Chokes: Five extended chokes: C, IC, M, IM, F. (Longer chokes, Benelli writes, allow a more gradual constriction of the shot charge, and this reduces pattern-destroying pellet deformation.)

Stock and Forend: "ComforTech" carbon-fiber stock and forearm with distinctive imprint checkering in the pistol grip and a soft, gel comb insert that mounts against a shooter's cheek to reduce shock. The stock is split diagonally from the heel of the buttstock to a point just behind the pistol grip. Eleven synthetic "recoil-absorbing chevrons" fill the contoured holes in both sides of the stock.

Grip: Pistol grip

Standard Measurements: 51-1/2 inches long with 30-inch barrel. Length of pull is 14 inches with the short buttpad, 14-3/8 inches with the standard pad. Drop at comb is 1-5/8 inches and drop at heel is 2-1/4 inches. (Specifications are adjustable with a shim kit.)

Weight: 8 pounds

Features: Modern trigger-guard design allows 1/3 more room for fingers and gloves.

Suggested Retail Price: $1600

Note: The $1430 Benelli Sport II is built with a satin walnut stock and fore-grip, and with 28- or 30-inch barrels. Other specifications for the Sport II are identical to the SuperSport.

BERETTA [www.berettausa.com or www.beretta.com]

"In 1526, practically five centuries ago, Mastro Bartolomeo Beretta (1490 – 1565/68) of Gardone received 296 ducats as payment for 185 arquebus barrels sold to the Arsenal of Venice."

Headquartered in 75,000 square meters of manufacturing, warehousing, shipping, and research and development facilities in Milan, Italy, this remarkable firearms manufacturer has been a family-owned-and-controlled corporation for 500 years. That, in itself, plus the dozens of gold Olympic medals won by Beretta shooters, is a noteworthy … no, an astonishing achievement!

Today you see quite a few Berettas at sporting clay shooting stands because the company offers a superior selection of fine, tested guns at a variety of price levels.

Model: Beretta Teknys Gold Sporting

Gauge and Action: 12- or 20-gauge semi-automatic

Chamber: 3-inch

Trigger Assembly: Gold-plated trigger. Distinctively engraved receiver with blue enamel inserts.

Barrels: 28- or 30-inch overbored barrels with long forcing cones and interchangeable flat, floating 3/8- to 5/16-inch ribs. Red fiber-optic front sight.

Chokes: Five extended chokes

Stock and Forend: Select, oiled walnut. The 12-gauge Teknys is fitted with a tubular 8 1/2-ounce stock recoil reducer. Urika stocks accept the recoil reducer as an option.

Grip: Pistol grip

Standard Measurements: 1 1/3-inch drop at comb; 2 1/3-inch drop at heel

Weight: 7.9 pounds (12-gauge); 6.6 pounds (20-gauge).

Features: Molded, hard-sided polypropylene case for takedown gun, chokes and cleaning supplies. Supplied spacers allow altering drop, cast and length of pull.

Suggested Retail Price: $1653 (catalog) or $1820 (Internet)

Note: The Urika Gold Sporting semi-auto with white front bead sells for about $300 less.

If you use sporting clays to tune up for bird season, there is no reason you cannot shoot a reasonable round – perhaps even an excellent round – with your hunting gun. The Beretta Urika Max-4 12 gauge has a 28-inch barrel and retails for slightly more than $1100.

The Beretta DT10 Trident L Sporting is available with 28-, 30- or 32-inch barrels and has a $6383 suggested retail price.

Bernardelli's fine Mega Silver semi-automatic weighs in under 7 pounds.

BERETTA

Model: Beretta DT10 Trident L

Gauge and Action: 12-gauge over/under

Chamber: 3-inch

Trigger Assembly: Gold-plated, single selective trigger adjusts for length of pull. Field-removable trigger group. Rich floral engraving.

Barrels: 28-, 30- or 32-inch barrels with ventilated top and side ribs. 3/8 x 5/16-inch flat, top rib. Aiming points are a front white dot and a mid-rib bead.

Chokes: Five extended chokes

Stock and Forend: Highly select walnut and Schnabel forend

Grip: Pistol grip with palm swell

Standard Measurements: 1 1/2-inch drop at comb; 2 1/3-inch drop at heel.

Weight: 8 pounds

Features: Molded, hard-sided polypropylene case for takedown gun, chokes and cleaning supplies. Can be ordered with left-hand cast, palm swell and trigger shoe.

Suggested Retail Price: $7797 (catalog); $8580 (Internet)

Note: The EELL Diamond Pigeon Sporting is available in all gauges for $6207 (Internet price of $6830). After that, Beretta steps its over/under line down gradually. Expect to pay $3485 (Internet $4325) for the Gold E Sporting 12 gauge with adjustable stock and between $2547 and $4892 for the Pigeon-grade sporting guns; but in this class, you have a selection of 12, 20, and 28 gauges, and even 410 bore! The 687 EL Gold Pigeon II Sporting Combo ($5720 catalog, $5380 Internet) gives you 30-inch barrels in 28 gauge and 410 bore. Beretta's Model 686 comes in at $2008 ($2210 Internet) in 12 or 20 gauge. At $1856 ($2040 Internet), the new 686 White Onyx Sporting is only available in 12 gauge, but it nevertheless includes a walnut stock and forend, five chokes and a fitted, hard-sided case.

BERNARDELLI [www.bernardelli.com]

The Bernardelli name has been associated with firearms production in Italy since the 1600s. The modern Bernardelli factory is in Brescia where it produces shotguns, handguns, rifles and combination shotgun-rifle guns under its own name and for other manufacturers as well.

Model: Bernardelli Pull Skeet-Parcours

Gauge and Action: 12-gauge over/under

Chamber: 3-inch

Trigger Assembly: Single selective trigger

Barrel: 28-inch (710-mm) high-strength blued steel alloy with ventilated rib and front bead sight

Chokes: Five

Stock and Forend: Oil-finished walnut, Schnabel forend and leather-faced recoil pad.

Grip: Pistol grip

Weight: 7.6 pounds

Suggested Retail Price: N/A at time of publication

Model: Bernardelli Mega Silver

Gauge and Action: 12-gauge semi-automatic

Chamber: 3-inch

Trigger Assembly: Gold-plated trigger

Barrel: 24-, 26- or 28-inch high-strength blued steel alloy with ventilated rib and front bead sight

Chokes: Three

Stock and Forend: Oil-finished walnut

Grip: Pistol grip

Weight: 6.8 pounds

Features: Silvered, engraved receiver and anti-shock ABS shipping case

Suggested Retail Price: $1500

The Browning Citori 525 Sporting in any gauge has long been a respected performer in sporting clays circles. All models have a "comfortable right-hand palm swell," and an adjustable comb is available on the 12- and 20-gauge guns.

BROWNING [www.browning.com]

Browning offers one of the broadest shotgun lines in the world, so a shooter should have no trouble finding an over/under, semi-auto or pump that can be shot expertly for any clay game and can be very nicely tubed for sub-gauge shooting as well. This company in Morgan, Utah, offers various models in all four gauges – 12, 20, 28 and 410 – that shoot well enough to put you in contention on the leader boards and then will be suitable for a few shots at your favorite game birds as well. Browning offers every possible feature in one of its shotguns, from guns specifically for rugged waterfowl hunters like the $668 BPS 12-gauge pump in Mossy Oak Shadow Grass to the finely engraved Citori 525 Golden Clays that lists for $4429 in its 28-gauge and 410 models.

Model: Browning Cynergy Sporting

Gauge and Action: 12-gauge over/under

Chamber: 2 3/4-inch

Trigger Assembly: Low-profile silver-nitride engraved receiver with chrome-plated chamber. Mechanical trigger. Three interchangeable gold trigger shoes to fine-tune length of pull.

Barrels: 28-, 30- or 32-inch backbored and ported barrels are ventilated top and side. HiViz fiber-optic front sight and white mid bead. Tapered 5/16- to 7/16-inch rib.

Chokes: F, M, IC

Stock and Forend: Walnut stock and forearm or black, weather-resistant composite with grip-enhancing rubber over-moldings. Both types of stock feature the new Inflex Recoil Pad system.

Grip: Pistol grip

Standard Measurements: 47 inches long with 30-inch barrels. Drop at comb 1-9/16 inches; drop at heel 2-3/8 inches. Composite stock features integrated adjustability for drop of comb and heel.

Weight: 8 pounds

Features: All Browning firearms are shipped with an appropriate lock.

Suggested Retail Price: $2690

Model: Browning XS Sporting

Gauge and Action: 12- or 20-gauge over/under

Chamber: 2 3/4-inch

Trigger Assembly: Silver-nitride engraved receiver with chrome-plated chamber. Mechanical trigger. Three interchangeable gold trigger shoes to fine tune length of pull.

Barrels: 28-, 30- or 32-inch factory-ported barrels. (Browning offers a 30-inch non-ported barrel for this model.) 12-gauge gun has a tapered 3/8- to 1/2-inch rib (straight 3/8 inch in 20 gauge). HiViz fiber-optic front sight and mid-point bead.

Chokes: M, IC, S

Stock and Forend: Walnut with Schnabel forearm. Ventilated top and side ribs.

Grip: Pistol grip with right-hand palm swell

Standard Measurements: 47-1/2 inches long with 30-inch barrel, any gauge. 14 3/4-inch length of pull, 1 1/2-inch drop at comb, 2 1/4-inch drop at heel (7/16-inch and 2 3/16-inch, respectively, in 20 gauge).

Weight: 7-8 pounds depending on gauge and barrel length

Suggested Retail Price: $2400

Note: The related Citori XS Pro-Comp features a fully adjustable comb and buttplate, with GraCoil recoil-reduction system. Features moveable (or removable) forward weights. Citori 525 Golden Clays ($4236 to $4429) is available with high-grade walnut stock and forearm, plus intricate engraving with 24-karat gold inlay in all four gauges.

Model: Browning Gold Sporting Clays

Gauge and Action: 12-gauge semi-automatic

Chamber: 2 3/4-inch

Trigger Assembly: Three interchangeable gold trigger shoes to fine-tune length of pull

Barrels: Ported 28- or 30-inch barrel with 1/4-inch ventilated rib, mid-point bead and HiViz fiber-optic sight

Chokes: M, IC, S

Stock and Forend: Walnut. Shim-adjustable stock moves comb 1/8 inch up or down.

Grip: Pistol grip

Standard Measurements: 50-1/2 inches with 30-inch barrel. 14 1/4-inch length of pull, 1 1/2-inch drop at comb, 1 3/4-inch drop at heel.

Weight: 7 1/2 to 8 pounds

Features: Browning Gold Sporting Clays shotguns include two interchangeable gas pistons for optimal performance with light or heavy loads. They can be switched in minutes without tools.

Suggested Retail Price: $1033

Note: The 12-gauge Gold Ladies Sporting Clays ($966) is built to smaller overall dimensions (13 1/2-inch length of pull and 47-3/8 inches long with a 28-inch barrel). The receiver of the Gold "Golden Clays" Sporting Clays 12-gauge ($1596) depicts a game bird transitioning into a clay bird on a polished silver-nitride receiver.

The new Cynergy Sporting is equipped with Browning's interchangeable Inflex Recoil Pad.

The Gold Sporting Clays 12 gauge from Browning comes with ported barrels and adjustable shims to move the comb over a range of 1/8 inch down and 1/8 inch up.

The Charles Daly Superior II Sport over/under with gold-plated single selective triggers and selective automatic ejectors is built specifically for this American importer in Italy and Spain.

Side-by-sides from Charles Daly, custom built in Italy and Spain, have barrels that are bored from solid steel bars and brazed with silver alloy.

CENTURY [www.centuryarms.com]

From its offices located in Boca Raton, Florida, Century International imports inexpensive Khan shotguns from Turkey. Over/unders are in the Arthemis line, while the semi-autos are the Centurions.

Model: Khan Arthemis
Gauge and Action: 12-gauge over/under
Chamber: 3-inch
Trigger Assembly: Single selective trigger with gold inlay in the receiver
Barrels: Chrome-lined 28-inch barrels are machined 4140 steel. Ventilated 10-mm top rib. Solid side rib.
Chokes: Five
Stock and Forend: Walnut with Monte Carlo stock and Schnabel-style forend
Grip: Pistol grip
Standard Measurements: 45 inches long
Weight: 7-1/3 pounds
Suggested Retail Price: $399

CHARLES DALY [www.charlesdaly.com]

"Charles Daly" is not a manufacturer. This Harrisburg, Pennsylvania, firm imports fine 12-gauge over/unders and side-by-sides from Italy and Spain, and semi-automatics and pump-action guns from Turkey. Under one corporate moniker or another – it has been owned by K.B.I. since 1996 – it has, in fact, been importing firearms since the 1870s!

Model: Charles Daly Superior II Sport
Gauge and Action: 12-gauge over/under
Chamber: 3-inch
Trigger Assembly: Gold-plated single selective triggers and selective automatic ejectors. Silver receiver.
Barrels: 28- or 30-inch ported, blued barrels are internally honed, chromed and polished for lead or steel. Ventilated, 10-mm rib, mid bead and red fiber-optic aiming post. Solid mid-rib.
Chokes: Five multi-chokes
Stock and Forend: High-gloss walnut
Grip: Pistol grip
Approximate Measurements: 46-7/8 inches long with 30-inch barrel. Length of pull 14 inches, 1-3/8 inches drop at comb, 1-7/8 inches drop at heel.
Weight: 7-1/2 pounds
Features: Gold-inlaid clay bird in flight in sideplates.
Suggested Retail Price: $1589

Model: Charles Daly Superior Hunter
Gauge and Action: 12-gauge side-by-side
Chamber: 3-inch
Trigger Assembly: Gold-plated single selective trigger. Anson & Deeley actions. Automatic ejectors.
Barrels: 26- or 28-inch blued barrels.
Chokes: Five multi-chokes
Stock and Forend: High-gloss walnut with splinter forends
Grip: Pistol grip
Suggested Retail Price: $1599
Note: Also available in 20 and 28 gauges and 410

Turkish-built semi-autos like the Charles Daly Superior II Sport are available in 12, 20 and 28 gauges.

EAA imports the Baikal IZH27 from Russia. It is available in every gauge and comes with chrome-lined barrels and a cast-off stock.

Available in 12 or 20 gauge, the FAIR Master Sporting comes with 28-, 30- or 32-inch barrels.

CHARLES DALY

Model: Charles Daly Superior II Sport
Gauge and Action: 12-gauge semi-automatic
Chamber: 3-inch
Trigger Assembly: Gold-plated trigger
Barrels: 28- or 30-inch factory ported barrels are internally honed and polished. 10-mm ventilated rib with brass mid bead and red fiber-optic front sight.
Chokes: F, M, IC
Stock and Forend: High-gloss walnut
Grip: Pistol grip
Suggested Retail Price: $599
Note: Superior II semi-autos are also available in 12-, 20- and 28-gauge field versions.

DIAMOND [www.diamondguns.com]

Diamond imported shotguns is a division of ADCO Sales, in Woburn, Massachusetts. You may be familiar with the 20-year old ADCO name from its well-advertised red dot sight. Modestly priced, gold-engraved Diamond semi-autos are occasionally seen on sporting clays shooting stands, now that this exciting clay game is rapidly becoming extraordinarily popular. At this time, Diamond imports 12- and 20-gauge semi-autos and pumps, but the company says that 28s and 410s are on the way.

Model: Diamond Gold Series
Gauge and Action: 12-gauge semi-automatic
Chamber: 2 3/4- or 3-inch
Barrels: 28-inch, chrome-lined blued stainless barrel with vented rib and front bead sight
Chokes: Three
Stock and Forend: Turkish walnut (also available in black matte synthetic stock)
Grip: Pistol grip

Weight: 7-1/2 pounds
Features: Gold engraving on blued receiver
Suggested Retail Price: $549

EAA [www.eaacorp.com]

Headquartered in Sharpes, Florida, EAA (European American Armory) imports a wide variety of shotguns, pistols and rifles. "If you want an eyebrow-raising label," President John Bernkrant says, "a big name, a wall hanger, a fancy catalog, or a fancy carry case, buy the competition's gun." The EAA philosophy is to provide excellent value for a safe, good-quality, reliable gun. Today, two basic models are available through EAA for sporting clays shooting, the Russian-built Baikal IZH27 Sporting and the Baikal MP233 Sporting.

Model: Baikal IZH27 Sporting
Gauge and Action: 12-, 16-, 20-, 28-gauge and 410-bore over/under
Chamber: 3-inch with machined steel receiver
Trigger Assembly: Gold-plated, single selective trigger in a polished nickel receiver. Selective ejectors.
Barrels: Ported 29 1/2-inch hammer-forged and chrome-lined barrels with solid side rib and ventilated top rib. White front aiming point and mid-rib bead.
Chokes: IC, M, F
Stock and Forend: Walnut with cast-off and rubber butt pad
Grip: Pistol grip with right-hand palm swell
Standard Measurements: 45-1/2 inches long with 14 1/2-inch length of pull, and drops of 1.5 inches at comb and 2.5 inches at heel
Weight: 7.4 pounds
Suggested Retail Price: $629
Note: Stock and size dimensions of the 20 gauge are identical to the 12-gauge gun. The Baikal MP233 Sporting lists for $899.

Fausti Stefano's Classic Series, both field and sporting models, are imported through Traditions. The field gun usually retails for less than $1000 while the Sporting Clays editions, featuring higher-grade walnut stocks and extended choke tubes, cost more than $1000.

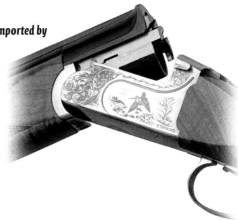

Close-up of Fausti Stefano Real 16, which is imported by Traditions of Connecticut.

FAIR [www.fair.it]

As the United States is increasingly incorporated into the European economy, you can expect to see more Italian guns on the shooting line ... guns other than the established and well-advertised Perazzi or Beretta models. In business since 1971, FAIR is the acronym for *Fabbrica Armi Isidoro Rizzini,* located in Brescia, Italy. Today, FAIR produces guns that it designates specifically for trap or for skeet and six models for sporting clays.

Model: FAIR Master Sporting

Gauge and Action: 12- and 20-gauge over/under

Chamber: 3-inch

Trigger Assembly: Gold-plated single selective trigger and automatic ejectors. Fret-worked top lever.

Barrels: 28-, 30- and 32-inch chrome-lined barrels with solid side rib. Ventilated top rib with red, fiber-optic front sight. Top rib has central sighting groove with checkered flanks. 12-gauge rib is 11 mm; 20-gauge rib is 9 mm.

Chokes: Interchangeable, knurled extended Technichokes

Stock and Forend: Walnut with rubber ventilated recoil pad. Optional adjustable stock.

Grip: Pistol grip

Weight: 7.8 pounds (12 gauge)

Suggested Retail Price: Although the price range in current U.S. dollars is sometimes difficult to establish with guns made outside the United States and imported on a limited basis, a slightly used but similar Model 702 20 gauge with 28-inch barrels in a condition rated "98 percent" by Cabela's was recently selling for $2495 through the Cabela's Internet site at www.cabelas.com.

FAUSTI STEFANO [www.faustistefanoarms.com]

This Italian company has been "operating in the shotgun field" near Brescia for 50 years and leadership is now headed from Fausti to his three daughters, Giovanna, Barbara and Eelna! Two models of sporting guns are available with slightly different parts (beavertail versus Schnabel forend, for instance) and accessories.

Model: Fausti Stefano Primatist De Luxe

Gauge and Action: 12- and 20-gauge over/under

Chamber: 2 3/4- to 3-inch

Trigger Assembly: Chrome-plated, checkered, single selective triggers and automatic ejectors

Barrels: 26-, 28- or 30-inch blued barrels with lengthened forcing cone and ventilated 10-mm top and side ribs. Bright red front aiming point.

Chokes: Fixed or interchangeable

Stock and Forend: Oil-finished walnut with Schnabel forend and thin coral buttpad

Grip: Pistol grip

Standard Measurements: Custom dimensions and adjustable stocks are available.

Features: Chrome-plated receiver with gold inlays. Hard plastic protective case.

Suggested Retail Price: $1659

The Franchi Alcione 612 Sporting semi-auto can be found with a suggested retail price of less than $1000.

Franchi's Alcione SL Sport over/under features ported, overbored barrels and comes with a set of extended chokes.

FRANCHI [www.franchiusa.com]

Although the Franchi name was first associated with firearms in about 1868, these fine Italian guns only began showing up in the United States after World War II. Today, Franchi is part of the Benelli USA business family (Beretta Holdings) with Uberti classic reproductions and Stoeger. Franchi produces more than 22,000 shotguns a year with 60 percent in the semi-auto family, 40 percent over/unders.

Model: Franchi Alcione 612 Sporting
Gauge and Action: 12-gauge semi-automatic
Chamber: 3-inch
Trigger Assembly: Gold-plated trigger
Barrels: 30-inch ported, overbored barrel. 4-inch extended forcing cone. Mid bead and white front sight. Chrome lined and proofed for steel shot.
Chokes: Extended, knurled chokes: IC, M, F.
Stock and Forend: Select walnut
Grip: Pistol grip. Buttstock of synthetic stock is designed to accept an optional mercury recoil reducer.
Standard Measurements: Overall length is 51 inches. Length of pull is 14-1/4 inches. Drop at comb is 1-1/2 inches and drop at heel is 2-1/2 inches.
Weight: 7.1 pounds
Features: Supplied with custom-fitting hard case, cleaning kit and kit of shims that fit between buttstock and receiver to allow the owner to customize cast and drop.
Suggested Retail Price: $975
Note: Franchi recommends a minimum 1 1/8-ounce, 3-dram load for reliable cycling. This basic semi-auto is available in 20 gauge as the 620 with 24-, 26- and 28-inch barrels for $675.

Model: Franchi Alcione SL Sport
Gauge and Action: 12-gauge over/under
Chamber: 2 3/4-inch
Trigger Assembly: Gold-plated mechanical trigger
Barrels: 30-inch ported, overbored and ventilated (top and side) barrels. 4-inch extended forcing cone. Chrome lined and proofed for steel shot. Mid bead and high visibility white front sight.
Chokes: Extended, knurled chokes: IC, M, F
Stock and Forend: A-Grade walnut
Grip: Pistol grip
Standard Measurements: 47 inches long, 14 1/4-inch length of pull, 2 1/4-inch drop at heel and 1 3/8-inch drop at heel.
Weight: 7.7 pounds
Features: Custom-fitting hard case and cleaning kit. Patented slip recoil pad. Interchangeable 20-gauge barrel set is available.
Suggested Retail Price: $1650
Note: Also available in left-hand model with cast-on in the buttstock.

GRIFFIN & HOWE [www.griffinhowe.com]

In 1910, after reading Theodore Roosevelt's *African Game Trails,* a New York cabinetmaker named Seymour Griffin bought a Springfield rifle and a fine chunk of French walnut. He proceeded to whittle and shape a custom stock and within a few months was building custom stocks for others as well. In 1923, he was introduced to James Howe, a machinist at the Franklin Arsenal in Philadelphia, and a rifle manufacturing enterprise coalesced around the two men. Four months later, Howe abandoned the fledgling company, which was eventually purchased by Abercrombie and Fitch. Over the years, Griffin & Howe guns were used by Ernest Hemingway, Robert Ruark and Dwight Eisenhower. Today, under new ownership, the company is headquartered in Bernardsville, New Jersey.

Model: Griffin & Howe Claremont Sporting
Gauge and Action: 12-gauge over/under boxlock
Chamber: 2 3/4-inch
Trigger Assembly: Removable for cleaning. Selective or non-selective gold-plated trigger.
Barrels: 30-inch with tapered and ventilated 10-mm top rib and ventilated side rib
Chokes: Five
Stock and Forend: European walnut
Grip: Pistol grip
Standard Measurements: 15-inch length of pull. Drop at comb 1 3/8 inches and at heel 2 3/8 inches.

Relatively new to U.S. sporting clays venues, Italian Caesar Guerini shotguns are available at a medium price range in either 12 or 20 gauge.

Many experts believe that the best way to start young people in the shooting sports is with a lightweight BB gun like the classic Daisy Red Ryder.

Weight: 8 pounds

Suggested Retail Price: Standard grade with hand-engraved fine scroll, $8750; Extra Finish with full coverage, large acanthus scroll, $11,500; full coverage, large scroll Lusso grade $18,000.

Note: This gun is manufactured in Italy.

CAESAR GUERINI/GUERINI USA

[www.caesarguerini.com]

Guerini is a relatively new name on the U.S. sporting scene, but its headquarters location is not. Brescia, Italy, like the Basque Country of northern Spain, has a long tradition of gun manufacturing.

Model: Guerini Summit Sporting

Gauge and Action: 12- or 20-gauge over/under

Chamber: 3-inch

Trigger Assembly: Single selective, gold-plated adjustable (up to 1/2 inch) trigger. Automatic ejectors.

Barrels: Ventilated 28-, 30-, 32- and 34-inch glossy blued barrels with 5-inch forcing cones. 10-mm ventilated top rib with "self-centering" track and two beads. Barrels and chambers are chrome-lined with lengthened forcing cones.

Chokes: "Crowned Conical Parallel" competition extended screw-in chokes have conical-parallel interior design, crowned muzzle and polished interior

Stock and Forend: Oiled Circassian walnut stock and Schnabel-style forearm. Soft rubber recoil pad.

Grip: Pistol grip with right-hand palm swell.

Standard Measurements: Stocks are 14-3/4 inches long to allow for custom fitting. Drop at comb and heel are approximately 1-1/3 and 2 inches, respectively.

Weight: About 7-1/2 pounds

Features: Lifetime warranty. Lockable, fitted hard case.

Balanced approximately one centimeter in front of the hinge pin for increased stability in the hand.

Suggested Retail Price: $2650

Note: The Magnus Sporting ($3395) features upgraded wood and sidelock-style receiver instead of a boxlock. The receiver is embellished with fine scroll engraving including gold inset game birds. The new 20-/28-gauge Guerini combo set features 32-inch barrels.

HUGLU [http://hugluarmsco.com]

"In their tiny village high in the mountains of Toros in Huglu there are no restaurants, coffee houses or hotels, but there is a shotgun clay target range." Huglu – Turkey. With hunting over/unders, side-by-sides, semi-autos and a few cowboy-action long guns in their line-up, Huglu's guns are distributed in the US by Armsco of Des Plaines, Illinois.

Model: Huglu English Sporter

Gauge and Action: 12-gauge over/under

Chamber: 2 3/4-inch

Trigger Assembly: Single trigger with blued receiver. Automatic ejectors.

Barrels: 28-, 30- or 32-inch lightweight, overbored (to .736), polished blued barrels. Ventilated side rib and 10-mm top rib with front and mid-rib sighting beads.

Chokes: 10 (ten) included

Stock and Forend: Walnut with Schnabel forend. 4-way adjustable comb.

Grip: Pistol grip with palm swell

Standard Measurements: 14 3/4-inch length of pull with 1 1/2-inch drop at comb and 2 1/4-inch drop at heel

Weight: 8 pounds

Suggested Retail Price: $1899

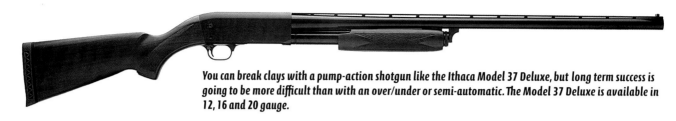

You can break clays with a pump-action shotgun like the Ithaca Model 37 Deluxe, but long term success is going to be more difficult than with an over/under or semi-automatic. The Model 37 Deluxe is available in 12, 16 and 20 gauge.

ITHACA [www.ithacagun.com]

Located in King's Ferry, in the midst of New York's beautiful finger lake country, Ithaca Gun began manufacturing 126 years ago. Although the company has gone through numerous evolutions since then, its pump guns are still made entirely in the United States.

Ithaca produces relatively inexpensive pump shotguns, but, of course, the words "relatively" and "inexpensive" depend on the context. A Model 37 High Grade pump, Ithaca's top-of-the-line gun, can be ordered with a custom fit stock and engraved receiver. The price starts at $1185. The Deluxe Vent Rib, on the other hand, runs less than $618 off the retail shelf. For a hunter on a budget, either of these guns should give years of shooting enjoyment for live or clay pigeons with a minimum of maintenance.

Of course, sporting clays was developed as a hunter's game. If you are a hunter, there is no better place to learn the fundamentals of effective shooting than on a sporting clays course. Nearly every shot you will see in the field is replicated there. So, the fact that pump shotguns are not "competition-grade" should not at all deter you from grabbing your Ithaca Model 37 and taking your best shot at clay pigeons.

If you should become seriously interested in competition, you will then want to consider finding an over/under or a semi-auto, as they eliminate the fore-and-back arm movement required to eject a spent hull and position a new shell for firing at a doubles presentation. Until then, enjoy your pump as a fine, low-maintenance and very-little-can-go-wrong shooting tool.

Model: Ithaca Model 37 Deluxe

Gauge and Action: 12-, 16- and 20-gauge pump

Chamber: 3-inch (12 and 20 gauge), 2 3/4-inch (16 gauge)

Barrels: 24-, 26- and 28-inch interchangeable blued barrels with ventilated rib and Raybar fiber-optic front sight

Chokes: IC, M, F flush-mount tubes. Proofed for steel shot.

Stock and Forend: Deluxe walnut with sprayed lacquer finish

Grip: Pistol grip

Standard Measurements: 14-inch length of pull, 1 1/2-inch drop at comb, 2 1/4-inch drop at heel. 49 inches long with 28-inch barrel.

Weight: 7+ pounds

Features: Brown recoil pad

Suggested Retail Price: $618

KEMEN USA [www.fieldsportltd.com]

Manufactured in Elgoibar, in the Basque region of northern Spain, Armas Kemen shotguns have been imported to the United States for 15 years. The factory employs a small workforce and produces a limited number of guns each year. Kemen has an excellent name for quality, particularly on the European continent, where it is better known than it is in North America.

The Kemen reputation is based on producing a high-quality and highly individualized product. These shotguns do not fall in the one-size-fits-all mold and are custom-built following a complimentary gunfitting.

Kemen shotguns are imported from Spain by Fieldsport in Traverse City, Michigan, and are delivered in a hard-sided case. Their Internet site sells consignment Kemens.

To purchase a new Kemen over/under or side-by-side shotgun, you should complete a "Kemen Custom Order Work Sheet," which allows you to specify such individual preferences and measurements as: mid-rib (ventilated, solid or none), point of impact for each barrel (% high/% low), comb (Monte Carlo or normal), palm swell, length of pull and, of course, quality of engraving.

Model: Kemen KM-4

Gauge and Action: 12-, 20- or 28-gauge boxlock over/under

Chamber: 3-inch

Trigger Assembly: Drop-out, trigger assembly. Single, non-selective adjustable trigger.

Barrels: Barrels come in three lengths: 27-5/8 inches with flat rib but without mid-rib; 30 inches with flat and ventilated mid-rib; and 32 inches with step 3-mm (or 10-mm) rib and ventilated mid-rib.

Chokes: Five flush-mount Briley chokes

Stock and Forend: High-grade walnut with palm swell built to customer's specifications. Includes Kick-eez or Pachmayr recoil pad. Beavertail, Field, Schnabel or Suprema forends.

Grip: Full- or semi-pistol grip

Standard Measurements: Length of pull is 14-9/16 inches

Weight: 8 pounds

Suggested Retail Price: The cost of a new KM-4 depend on the extras and quality of engraving, ranging from a base price of $7995. (In July 2004, the Fieldsport Internet site offered a slightly used 12-gauge Kemen Extra Gold B over/under with gold bird inlays and 28-inch barrels for $16,500.) Kemens are delivered in a special carrying case. For 2004, Kemen announced a new 12-gauge Peregrine Sporter with 34-inch barrels.

Is the semi-automatic or the over/under a better all-around shotgun? Although the over/under has become the elite sporting clays gun, the semi-automatic may very well be the best gun type for all-around shooting and hunting tasks.

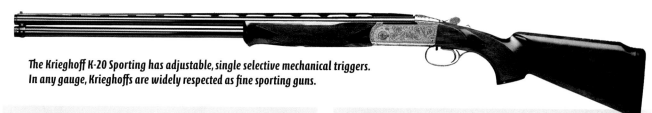

The Krieghoff K-20 Sporting has adjustable, single selective mechanical triggers. In any gauge, Krieghoffs are widely respected as fine sporting guns.

KEMEN USA

Model: Kemen Imperial Sporting

Gauge and Action: 12-gauge side-by-side

Chamber: 3-inch

Trigger Assembly: Drop-out, trigger assembly. Single, selective adjustable trigger.

Barrels: Barrels come in lengths from 28 to 31-1/2 inches. Two types are available, center-fire or off-center (60/40 or 65/35), with tapered or cylindrical bore.

Chokes: Five removable Briley chokes

Stock and Forend: Walnut. Forends can be beavertail or slender.

Grip: Four styles available: semi-pistol, pistol, straight English or swan-neck English.

Weight: 8+ pounds

Features: Comes with extra firing pins and springs

Suggested Retail Price: $11,595 (standard with blued receiver, fixed chokes)

Note: Side-by-sides are a new line of guns from Kemen.

KIMBER [www.kimberamerica.com]

The Augusta shotgun is manufactured for Kimber in Brescia, Italy.

Model: Kimber Augusta Sporting

Gauge and Action: 12-gauge over/under

Chamber: 2 3/4- or 3-inch.

Trigger Assembly: Unbreakable coil-spring trigger system and inertia cocking. Adjustable trigger.

Barrels: 28.4-, 30- or 32-inch barrels with polished blue finish. Ventilated 11x8-mm flattop and side with front HiViz bead sight. Tri-alloy steel barrels have long forcing cones and are backbored to .736.

Chokes: Six-tube set and wrench are included.

Stock and Forend: Satin- or gloss-finished walnut. Schnabel forend.

Grip: Pistol grip with "robust" palm swell.

Standard Measurements: 2.4-inch drop at heel and 1.5-inch drop at comb. Length of pull is 14.7 inches.

Weight: 7-3/4 pounds

Features: Includes lockable, hard-sided case and 1-inch black Pachmayr Decelerator recoil pad.

Suggested Retail Price: $5676

KRIEGHOFF [www.krieghoff.com]

Krieghoff International is headquartered in Ulm, a city on the Danube River in south Germany. U.S. offices are in Ottsville, Pennsylvania.

Krieghoff was founded in 1886 and today is known as one of the premier shotgun manufacturers in the world. While the K-80 12 gauge and the new K-20 sub-gauge are the primary guns recognized in the United States, Krieghoff builds many guns only for the European market.

"The challenge of sporting clays," Krieghoff writes, "lies in the fact that you start with a dismounted gun and shoot at a nearly infinite variety of targets. Whether you are on an English sporting course or a FITASC parcours, the game requires a fine balance between the well-honed instincts of a good wing shot and the controlled, measured performance of a clay target veteran."

Model: Krieghoff K-80 Sporting

Gauge and Action: 12-gauge over/under

Chamber: 3-inch

Trigger Assembly: Single selective trigger is adjustable for length of pull. Trigger weight is 3-1/2 to 4 pounds.

Barrels: 28-, 30- or 32-inch available in traditional blued, brilliant coin or classic case-colored finish. Two rib configurations – tapered flat (12 to 8 mm) or 8 mm – with white pearl front and metal center bead. Point of impact of bottom barrel can be raised or lowered in relation to the top barrel by changing the barrel hanger. Eight different barrel hangers available for barrels with choke tubes.

Chokes: S, IC (2), M, IM

Stock and Forend: Satin-finished walnut. Schnabel forend.

Grip: Pistol grip

Standard Measurements: 14 3/8-inch length of pull, 1 5/8-inch drop at comb and drop at heel is 2-1/4 to 2-3/4 inches.

Weight: 8-3/4 pounds

Features: Available with a host of options and adjustments for personal preferences including complete competition tube sets.

Suggested Retail Price: A standard grade K-80 Sporting with five choke tubes cost $8595 from duPont/Krieghoff, Vero Beach, Florida, in July 2004.

Note: Comes with fitted aluminum case with slots for extra barrels. The K-80 was introduced in 1980 and is available today as a single-barrel gun, an over/under or in a combo-pack. Krieghoff's theory was to make one receiver work with numerous combinations of barrels and stocks. This way, a single high-quality, hand-engraved receiver could, with the simple attachment of a different barrel and/or stock combination, shoot any competition game or go to the field for pheasants or woodcock. Your receiver could thus handle anything from a 410-bore over/under in the morning and a 34-inch "unsingle" barrel in the afternoon.

Model: Krieghoff K-20 Sporting

Gauge and Action: 20-gauge over/under

Chamber: 3-inch

Krieghoff's K-80 can be purchased with your choice of a number of scenes engraved on the receiver. The scene on this gun, from Krieghoff's "Patriot Series," features America's redoubtable Molly Pitcher at the battle of Breed's (Bunker) Hill.

Trigger Assembly: Single selective mechanical trigger is adjustable for finger length. Trigger pull is 3-1/2 to 4 pounds.

Barrels: 28- or 32-inch barrels available in traditional blued, brilliant coin or classic case-colored finish. Two rib configurations – tapered flat (12 to 8 mm) or 8 mm – with white pearl front and metal center bead. Point of impact of bottom barrel can be raised or lowered in relation to top barrel by changing the barrel hanger. Eight different barrel hangers available for barrels with choke tubes.

Chokes: Five

Stock and Forend: Satin-finished walnut. Schnabel forend.

Grip: Pistol grip

Standard Measurements: Approximately 14 3/8-inch length of pull, 1 5/8-inch drop at comb, 2 1/4- to 2 3/4-inch drop at heel.

Weight: 7-1/2 pounds

Features: Many options, additional barrels and fitted tube sets available.

Suggested Retail Price: $8595

Note: Comes with fitted aluminum case with slots for extra barrels. The K-20 with 3-barrel set (20, 28 and 410), five chokes per barrel and 3-barrel case is $16,105.00.

Virtually all metal surfaces on expensive guns such as the Krieghoff K-20 are engraved. This fine 20-gauge gun costs about $8595, and you may purchase it in a number of custom configurations.

LANBER [www.lanber.net]

Lanber has been in business for 40 years, first producing fine side-by-sides and then over/unders. By the '80s, Lanber was producing semi-autos as well. Today, Lanber builds about 15,000 shotguns a year in a modern 3000-sq/m facility in the Basque Country of Spain, but these guns still remain relatively rare in the United States. (Lanber recently discontinued production of side-by-sides.)

Model: Lanber 2097

Gauge and Action: 12 gauge over/under

Chamber: 2 3/4- or 3-inch

Trigger Assembly: Gold-plated single selective trigger. Automatic ejectors.

Barrels: 28- or 30-inch blued and vented barrels. White dot aiming point on raised, ventilated rib.

Chokes: Five

Stock and Forend: Oil-finished walnut with Schnabel forend

Grip: Pistol grip

Standard Measurements: 44-1/2 inches with 14 3/8-inch length of pull, 1 3/8-inch drop at comb, and 2 1/8-inch drop at heel

Weight: 7.7 pounds

Features: Rubber buttpad with hardened surface for smooth mounting

Suggested Retail Price: $1485 plus shipping from Fisher Firearms, Australia (July 2004)

Note: Other Lanber 12-gauge guns such as the Models 2088, 2089, 2098 and 2099 come with 28- or 30-inch barrels. The elevated, ventilated rib is topped with a red bead aiming point and Lanber opens the spaces between the barrels as much or more than most other manufacturers. Length of pull is 14.6 inches.

The Republic of Turkey has entered the arms race with multiple semi-automatic and over/under shotguns, plus many semi-automatic pistols built by Sarsilmaz. Find out more about these guns at www.sarsilmaz.com.

Pump-action guns are not seen in clay competition unless they are separated on their own venue, but the Mossberg 500 series will break clays and kill ducks and doves, too.

MAROCCHI [www.maroochi.it]

Stefano Marocchi opened his workshop north of Brescia, Italy, in 1926 and eventually won notice among gunmakers for a CO2-powered rifle. Today, the third and fourth generations of Marocchis are working in the expanded company headquarters and manufacturing facility in Sarezzo.

Model: Marocchi Model 99

Gauge and Action: 12-gauge over/under

Chamber: 2 3/4-inch

Trigger Assembly: Single selective adjustable trigger

Barrels: 28-, 30- or 32-inch barrels. Ventilated top and side ribs with red front fiber-optic aiming point and mid-point bead.

Chokes: Model 99 Grade I, five extended chokes; Grade III, five flush-mounted chokes

Stock and Forend: Walnut. Grade III features Schnabel forend.

Grip: Pistol grip

Standard Measurements: 14 3/4-inch length of pull, 1 1/2-inch drop at comb and 2-inch drop at heel

Weight: 8 pounds

Features: Model 99 Grade I has a silvered receiver. Grade III is fully engraved with game scenes embellished with gold inlay.

Suggested Retail Price: Grade I $2995 and Grade III $4595

Note: Spare barrel assembly is $1600, wood upgrade to "fancy" is $700, custom-fitted stock is $530 and adjustable comb $235. Purchase of a Model 99 qualifies you to join the Marocchi Club.

MERKEL [www.gsifirearms.com]

Merkel traces its roots to metalworkers in 1535 in Suhl, Germany. "In 1989," the catalog and Internet site agree, "the Merkel brothers founded a gun factory which was the first to manufacture over and under guns in an industrial way." Today, Merkel exports over/unders, side-by-sides and rifles to the United States through gun distributor GSI Firearms in Trussville, Alabama.

Model: Merkel 2000EL Sporter

Gauge and Action: 12-, 20- and 28-gauge over/under

Chamber: 3-inch (28 gauge is 2 3/4-inch)

Trigger Assembly: Single, selective trigger. Automatic ejectors can be changed to extractors by the shooter.

Barrels: 30-inch (12 and 20 gauges) or 28-inch (20 and 28 gauges) barrels with solid top and side ribs. White front aiming point.

Chokes: S, IC

Stock and Forend: Oil-finished luxury-grade walnut and 3-piece forearm.

Grip: English or pistol grip

Weight: 7 pounds (12 gauge) or 6.4 pounds (20 and 28 gauges)

Features: Comes in fitted luggage case

Suggested Retail Price: $6495

Note: A Merkel can be custom-built.

Model: Merkel Model 147E

Gauge and Action: 12- and 20-gauge side-by-side

Chamber: 3-inch

Trigger Assembly: Single selective or double trigger. Automatic ejectors.

Barrels: 30- (12 gauge), 28- (12 or 20 gauges) or 26 3/4-inch (20 gauge) barrels. Cold, hammer-forged steel with solid sighting rib.

Chokes: 30-inch barrels, S and IC. Other barrels, IC and M.

Stock and Forend: Oil-finished walnut

Grip: English or pistol grip

Weight: 6.8 pounds (12 gauge); 5.9 pounds (20 gauge)

Features: Includes fitted luggage case

Suggested Retail Price: $4495

Note: Hunting and game-scene engraving on receiver.

Perazzi shotguns come in almost any configuration and may be built with any custom detail or fitting specification. Of course, you will pay top price for these world-class Italian shotguns.

O.F. MOSSBERG & SONS [www.mossberg.com]

Pump and gas-operated guns from this Connecticut company are not commonly found in competition, but fortunately, breaking targets is not all about competition. If a beat-up, but reliable, Mossberg camo hunter accompanies you to the field for turkeys or pheasants or ducks, you ought to take it to a sporting clays venue for a couple rounds before the season opens. You will be pleasantly surprised at the results from guns from America's oldest family-owned-and-operated firearms manufacturer.

Model: Mossberg 500 Field

Gauge and Action: 12- or 20-gauge pump

Chamber: 3-inch

Barrels: 12 gauge, 28-inch; 20 gauge, 26-inch. Interchangeable blued barrels with vented rib topped with twin bead sights. Factory ported on select models.

Chokes: C, M, F – rated for any load.

Stock and Forend: Honey-satin finished wood or black synthetic with cut checkering. Includes rubber recoil pad.

Grip: Pistol grip

Standard Measurements: 47-1/2 inches long. Length of pull is 13-7/8 inches. 1 1/2-inch drop at comb; 2 3/8-inch drop at heel.

Weight: 7-1/2 pounds

Features: This rugged hunting shotgun is available in numerous configurations including a slug gun, several camo patterns and a combo-barrel set. The Mossberg Bantam 500 is produced with a short 13-inch length of pull and 22-inch barrels for young and small-frame shooters. The Bantam 500 is available in 12 or 20 gauge.

Suggested Retail Price: $316

Note: The 500 is available in at least 17 models including 410 bore. A gun lock is included.

PERAZZI [www.perazzi.it]

On the sporting clays courses of the world, English and FITASC, this high-grade gunmaker from Brescia, Italy, enjoys a true world-class reputation. The balance, reliability and handling qualities of a Perazzi are legendary and make it – arguably – the most sought-after over/under shotgun in the world.

Brescia sits at the foothills of the Alps, but at the pinnacle of world shotgun manufacturing. Not bad for a company with only 100 employees producing less than a dozen shotguns a day. And Perazzi is not even 50 years old! This manufacturer builds expensive guns in single-barrel, double-barrel and combo sets. Options include adjustable-impact ribs, adjustable stocks and a wide variety of barrel and choke options.

Close-up of the exquisite detail engraving on Perazzi guns.

Whether it is the Number One shotgun brand name in the world or not, Perazzi offers what amounts to total custom fitting in their basic over/under sporting clay models (all three in 12 or 20 gauge), the MX8 ($10,841), MX12 ($10,841) and MX2000S ($12,167). Prices quoted are for a smoothbore with minimal engraving and are essentially base cost. Upgrading to "SC3"-grade engraving, for instance, for the MX8 quickly raises the price to $18,394 and moving farther upward in design and execution, including gold inlays, can bring the cost to $31,275; it can eventually step it up to $100,449.

Model: Perazzi MX8

Gauge and Action: 12- and 20-gauge over/under

Chamber: 2 3/4-inch

Trigger Assembly: Trigger group is detachable for easier cleaning. Gold-plated, single selective trigger with flat or coil springs.

Barrels: Each gun is available with a number of different rib configurations and barrels in the unusual lengths of 27-9/16, 28-3/8, 29-1/2, 31-1/2 and 34 inches. The 12-gauge fixed-rib is tapered 7/16 to 9/32 inches with half-ventilated side ribs. The 20-gauge rib is 1/16 inch narrower.

Chokes: Seven interchangeable or fixed chokes in one or both barrels

Stock and Forend: The custom-made stock and Beavertail forend are superior-grade walnut. Buttstocks are interchangeable for a wide range of pull lengths, drop at comb and heel, with cast-on or cast-off, or straight comb with sloping, field pistol grip or Monte Carlo stock.

Grip: Pistol grip

Standard Measurements: Critical dimensions are customized to the purchaser

Weight: All Perazzi custom-made guns differ slightly in weight and balance, but that is simple to change, since all have interchangeable custom stocks.

Note: If you consider purchasing a high-end Perazzi, you may want to make an appointment to travel to Brescia for personal measurements and fitting!

Although very little can happen with over/unders or side-by-sides, when something does go wrong, it can be serious. This woman finished the round with a semi-automatic.

This is Remington's popular 1100 semi-auto in its 28-gauge version, which was new for 2004. The 1100 is one of the most popular and user-friendly shotguns ever produced, but like a lot of American shotguns, its barrel is a little short for the best sporting shooting. The 1100 Sporting 12 and 20 gauges are available with 28-inch barrels while the 410 and new 28 have 27-inch barrels.

Remington says its Model 332 over/under is an update of Remington's premier field-shooting classic built to today's standards. It features a slender pistol grip on the stock and deep finger grooves in the forend.

POLI [www.intred.it/poli or www.colegun.com]

The number of small, but exclusive, gun manufacturers in the world is growing almost faster than **Gun Digest** can keep up with them, but all in all, this is a good thing. Cole Gunsmithing in Harpswell, Maine, is the exclusive U.S. importer for the **Armi F.lli Poli** (loosely, Poli and Sons Arms) line of side-by-side shotguns, which date from 1966. The Poli plant is located about 20 miles northeast of Brescia in Gardone in the foothills of the Italian Alps.

Model: Poli Opal Sporting
Gauge and Action: 12-gauge side-by-side
Chamber: 3-inch
Trigger Assembly: Single, non-selective gold-plated trigger and manual extractor
Barrels: 30-inch overbored barrels with long forcing cones
Chokes: Five Mobil choke screw-in tubes (.733)
Stock and Forend: Brierwood or walnut with splinter-style forend
Grip: Pistol grip with right-hand palm swell or English
Weight: 8 pounds
Suggested Retail Price: Starts at $4395
Note: According to Cole Gunsmithing, the Opal Sporting was designed for clay shooting. This gun is also available with double triggers and 32-inch barrels. Other gauges can be manufactured on request.

REMINGTON [www.remington.com]

Remington traces its manufacturing roots to one Eliphalet Remington, who believed he could build a better rifle and, at his father's forge in Ilion Gulch, New York, proceeded to do just that.

Today, Remington's principal firearms plant is still in Ilion, although a newer plant was built in Mayfield, Kentucky, and affiliated smaller companies in Remington's substantial corporate orbit are scattered around the United States. The headquarters of this company, one of the oldest continuously operating manufacturers in the country, is now in Madison, North Carolina. Of course, Remington's rolling ambassador, Dale Earnhardt, Jr., and the #8 Budweiser stock car appear on NASCAR circuits virtually everywhere.

Model: Remington Model 1100 Sporting
Gauge and Action: 12-gauge semi-automatic
Chamber: 2 3/4-inch
Trigger Assembly: Gold-plated trigger. Assembly drops out easily for cleaning.
Barrels: 28-inch barrel with ventilated rib, ivory front bead and steel mid bead. Barrel and receiver are blued and polished.
Chokes: Four extended chokes – S, IC, LM, M
Stock and Forend: High-gloss walnut with sporting-clays-style recoil pad
Grip: Pistol grip
Standard Measurements: 49 inches long. Length of pull 14-3/16 inches. Drop at comb 1-1/2 inches; drop at heel 2-1/4 inches.
Weight: 8 pounds
Suggested Retail Price: $868
Note: The popular 1100 Sporting is also available in 20 and 28 gauges and 410-bore with otherwise similar specifications. Remington says its auto-loading 410 is the only auto-loading 410 on the market. Left-handers who enjoy the softer recoil of a semi-auto and prefer the Remington brand may want to try the Model 11-87 Premier Left-Hand ($809): 3-inch chamber, 28-inch barrel, walnut stock and forend, and three choke tubes.

Model: Remington Model 332
Gauge and Action: 12-gauge over/under
Chamber: 3-inch
Trigger Assembly: Blued, mechanical trigger and automatic ejectors
Barrels: 26-, 28- or 30-inch chrome-moly-steel barrels with 8-mm ventilated rib, ivory front bead and steel mid bead. Barrels and receiver are blued and polished.
Chokes: IC, M, F
Stock and Forend: High-gloss walnut
Grip: Pistol grip
Standard Measurements: 47-1/4 inches long with 30-inch barrels. 14-3/16 inches length of pull, 1 7/16-inch drop at comb and 2 1/8-inch drop at heel.
Weight: 8 pounds
Suggested Retail Price: $1624
Note: Designed as a field gun, the 332 will bust targets with the best of the more expensive guns, especially with the 30-inch barrel.

The Rizzini Artemis Deluxe is available in all gauges including 16 and 410 bore with fixed or interchangeable chokes.

The Rizzini custom shop provides customers with the opportunity to have shotguns tailored to their specific requirements without, they say, "the long time delay normally associated with custom guns."

Rizzini's adjustable comb has a true 360-degree capability by allowing adjustment of the actual pitch of the comb.

RIZZINI [www.rizziniusa.com]

Like many quality manufacturers, most Rizzini over/under hunting shotguns can be used successfully on clay targets. Still, Rizzini has been building over/unders for almost 40 years and five are specifically designated for sporting clays. Rizzini shotguns are imported through Rizzini USA in Harpswell, Maine. A high-end (Artemis EL) and a standard-grade (Premier Sporting) over/under have been selected to show the diversity of the Rizzini shotgun line.

Model: Rizzini Artemis EL

Gauge and Action: Over/unders in 12, 16, 20 and 28 gauges and 410-bore

Chamber: 2 3/4- to 3-inch

Trigger Assembly: Single-selective adjustable trigger and automatic ejectors

Barrels: 26-, 28- and 29.5-inch glossy-blued barrels with chrome-lined bores. Full side ribs; conical, hand-checkered top rib, which is solid or vented.

Chokes: Fixed or interchangeable (five extended chokes)

Stock and Forend: Varnish-finished extra-select Turkish walnut with Schnabel forend.

Grip: Prince of Wales pistol grip stock

Weight and Measurements: Built to personal dimensions. Approximately 7 pounds.

Features: Rizzini makes numerous Premium Grade options available. Highly polished coin finish with sideplates, hand-engraved English scroll and game scene. Limited lifetime warranty.

Suggested Retail Price: $17,470

Note: Comes in richly apportioned leather case with cleaning accessories.

Model: Rizzini Premier Sporting

Gauge and Action: 12-gauge over/under

Chamber: 2 3/4-inch/3-inch

Trigger Assembly: Single selective trigger with adjustable length of pull. Automatic ejectors.

Barrels: 28-, 29-, 30.5- or 32-inch chrome-lined, glossy blued barrels. Ventilated side and 10-mm top rib.

Chokes: Fixed or interchangeable (five extended chokes)

Stock and Forend: Oil-finished select walnut

Grip: Pistol grip with palm swell

Standard Measurements: 14.6-inch stock with 1 1/2-inch drop at comb and 2 1/8-inch drop at heel.

Weight: 7-1/4 pounds

Suggested Retail Price: The Premier comes in several grades and starts at $3000.

Note: Comes in hard-sided plastic case with cleaning supplies. Optional adjustable comb ($280) gives 360-degree adjustability. Also available in 20 gauge.

RUGER [www.ruger.com]

Sturm, Ruger, "Arms Makers For Responsible Citizens," is headquartered in Southport, Connecticut. Begun after World War II by William Ruger and Alexander Sturm, the company says it is now "the nation's largest firearms manufacturer." It has produced over/under shotguns for more than 25 years and recently began building a line of Gold Label side-by-sides also.

Today, Sturm, Ruger is the only company that actually builds rifles, pistols, revolvers and shotguns in the United States. Ruger guns and other industrial casting products are manufactured in New Hampshire and Arizona. More than 1200 people are employed by Ruger, which estimates that it has sold more than 21 million guns.

Model: Ruger Red Label

Gauge and Action: 12-, 20- and 28-gauge over/under (a 410 tube set is available for the 28 gauge for $550)

The Ruger Red Label is known on courses throughout North America as a tested over/under that will deliver superb shooting performance. This is the 12 gauge with engraved, silver-polished receiver and blued barrels. Suggested retail is $1725.

The new Ruger 12-gauge Gold Label side-by-side made its debut in 2004. It is available with a straight or a pistol grip for $1950. "At last," Ruger says, "there is an American-made side-by-side in production that can compete with the finest European and British handcrafted double shotguns."

Chamber: 12 and 20 gauge, 3-inch; 28 gauge, 2 3/4-inch

Barrels: Back-bored hammer-forged, blued steel. 26, 28 or 30 inches for 12 and 20 gauges; 26 or 28 inches for the 28 gauge. The dovetail, free-floating rib has a single gold bead aiming point. (The 30-inch barrel, designed specifically for sporting clay shooters, has a second, mid-rib gold bead but no barrel filler strips.)

Chokes: Five steel-shot compatible chokes: IC, S1, S2, M, F. Additional blued and stainless chokes ($39.30) available in most gauges.

Stock and Forend: Premium-grade American walnut

Grip: Pistol grip or straight

Standard Measurements: 47 inches long with 30-inch barrels. Length of pull is 14 1/8 inches. Drop at comb is 1-1/2 inches; drop at heel is 2-1/2 inches.

Weight: 6-8 pounds

Features: Shipped with shell ejectors, which can be deactivated to manually remove shells, a feature preferred by reloaders. Add $180 for factory engraving (pistol-grip stocks only). Includes 10-inch yellow cable lock.

Suggested Retail Price: $1545

Note: A 12-gauge Red Label, also $1545, is available with a black all-weather stock, pistol grip and stainless steel barrels.

Model: Ruger Gold Label

Gauge and Action: 12-gauge side-by-side

Chamber: 3-inch

Barrels: Blued, hammer-forged 28-inch barrels with relieved forcing cones. Matte steel rib and gold bead front sight.

Chokes: Five steel-shot compatible chokes: IC, S1, S2, M, F. Additional blued and stainless chokes ($39.30) available in most gauges.

Stock and Forend: AAA premium-grade American walnut

Grip: Pistol grip or straight

Standard Measurements: 45 inches long with a 14 1/8-inch length of pull. Drop at comb is 1-1/2 inches; drop at heel 2-1/4 inches.

Weight: 6-1/3 pounds.

Features: Small, rugged Dickson-style selective ejectors

Suggested Retail Price: $1950

SKB [www.skbshotguns.com]

The initials "SKB" were derived from the Japanese family name Sakaba by simply dropping the vowels. This family, which has some roots in samurai culture, then formed their firearms company in the Ibaraki province of Japan (north and east of Tokyo on the Pacific coast) in 1855.

SKB says mastering sporting clays requires a shotgun that provides a responsive fit, is well balanced between the shooters hands, has a smooth swing, fast sighting plane and crisp trigger for fast target acquisition, and hard-hitting patterns without producing shooter fatigue.

Model: SKB 85TSS

Gauge and Action: 12-, 20-, 28-gauge and 410 bore over/under boxlocks

Chamber: 3-inch (12, 20, 28) or 2 3/4-inch (28)

Trigger Assembly: Inertia (12, 20) or mechanical (28, 410). Trigger group is non-removable. Automatic ejectors.

Barrels: 28-, 30- and 32-inch .735 backbored barrels are available for the 12 gauge. (28- and 30-inch barrels for the 20, 28 and 410). All barrels and chambers are chrome-lined. Lengthened forcing cones on all barrels. Ventilated top and side ribs (12 mm in 12 and 20; 8.5 mm in 28 and 410) with nickel center post and Hi-Viz competition sights. Optional Pigeon Porting ($200) is available for the 12 gauge.

Chokes: Briley IC, S1, S2, M for the 12 or IC, M, S (20, 28, 410)

Stock and Forend: Walnut with matte polyurethane finish and Schnabel forend. Optional adjustable comb stocks are about $200. Upgraded stocks for $400.

Grip: Pistol grip with ambidextrous palm swells

Standard Measurements: Length of pull 14-1/2 inches, drop at comb 1-5/8 inches, drop at heel 1-5/8 inches

Weight: 7-9/16 pounds for the 410 (28-inch barrels) to 8-9/16 pounds for the 12 gauge (32-inch barrels)

Features: Pachmayr buttpad

Suggested Retail Price: $1949

Note: The 85TSS is available in 18 models and has multi-gauge sets in eight models. Multi-gauge barrel sets are available.

SKB's 85TSS over/unders are available in 18 models and the sporting clays multi-gauge sets are available in eight models. The three-barrel multi-gauge set delivers consistent weight, balance and feel. The 20, 28 and 410 are fitted with individual forends.

Stoeger's Model 2000 12-gauge semi-auto features chrome-lined barrels and uses Benelli's inertia-recoil operating system. The price is under $500.

The Condor Supreme over/under from Stoeger features a single selective trigger and automatic ejectors. The price is under $500.

Traditions has begun importing over/under and side-by-side shotguns from Italy, both Fausti Stefano and Emilio Rizzini. Pictured is the Rizzini Gold Wing III Silver with automatic ejectors, screw-in chokes and a single trigger. It is available in 12 gauge with 28-inch barrels, a 3-inch chamber and suggested retail price of $2289.

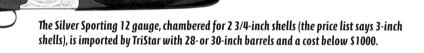

The Silver Sporting 12 gauge, chambered for 2 3/4-inch shells (the price list says 3-inch shells), is imported by TriStar with 28- or 30-inch barrels and a cost below $1000.

STOEGER [www.stoegerindustries.com]

You associate the name Stoeger with a fine shotgun, true, but it is also a publisher of outdoor books and is allied with imported guns from Benelli, Franchi and Uberti (classic firearms reproductions). The Stoeger company began in New York's tough "Hell's Kitchen" district in 1924 when Austrian immigrant and gun dealer Alexander Stoeger published his first catalog. Today, Stoeger is part of Beretta Holdings, Ltd.

Model: Stoeger Model 2000
Gauge and Action: 12-gauge semi-automatic
Chamber: 3-inch
Barrels: Chrome-lined 26-, 28- or 30-inch barrels are proofed for steel shot. Ventilated rib is topped with a white bar aiming point.
Chokes: C, IC, M, F and XF.
Stock and Forend: Satin-finished walnut stock and forend

Grip: Pistol grip
Standard Measurements: 51-1/4 inches long with a 30-inch barrel. 14 1/2-inch length of pull.
Weight: 7+ pounds
Features: Uses Benelli's inertia-recoil operating system with operating and moving parts entirely contained within the receiver.
Suggested Retail Price: $435
Note: Stoeger sells a slightly lighter synthetic stock for the Model 2000 ($420.00) with either 26- or 28-inch barrels.

Model: Stoeger Condor Supreme
Gauge and Action: 12- or 20-gauge over/under
Chamber: 3-inch
Trigger Assembly: Single selective trigger and automatic ejectors
Barrels: 26- and 28-inch barrels. Stoeger produces a

Built in Finland and imported by TriStar, the 512SC Sporting is built in youth and ladies sizes.

24-inch barrel for the 20 gauge. Barrels are topped with a ventilated rib, mid bead and red bar sight.

Chokes: IC, M
Stock and Forend: Walnut
Grip: Pistol grip
Standard Measurements: 44 inches long with 28-inch barrel. 14 1/2-inch length of pull.
Weight: 7.4 pounds
Suggested Retail Price: $500

TRADITIONS [www.traditionsfirearms.com]

Although we typically think of Traditions Performance Firearms in Old Saybrook, Connecticut, as a muzzleloader company, they have recently begun importing a new line of over/under and side-by-side shotguns made by Fausti Stefano of Brescia, Italy: "… all the features of the high-dollar manufacturers at a reasonable price."

Model: Fausti Sporting Clay
Gauge and Action: 12- and 20-gauge over/under
Chamber: 3-inch
Trigger Assembly: Single selective trigger. Automatic ejectors.
Barrels: 28- or 30-inch chrome-lined, ported blued barrels with ventilated 3/8-inch top and side rib. Red front sight.
Chokes: S, IC, M, F extended chokes
Stock and Forend: Walnut with Schnabel forend. (Grade II is standard and Grade III is upgraded walnut.)
Grip: Pistol grip
Standard Measurements: Length of pull 14-1/2 inches, drop at comb 1-1/2 inches and drop at heel 2-1/4 inches.
Weight: About 8 pounds
Suggested Retail Price: Grade II $1259 (12 gauge only) – Grade III $1659 (12 gauge) and $1859 (20 gauge)
Note: Grade III guns are wrapped in a velvet gun sock and delivered in a hard-molded takedown case.

TRISTAR [www.tristarsportingarms.com]

Tristar in North Kansas City, Missouri, imports firearms and accessories from the European community – shotguns, rifles, pistols and replica guns. Here are two examples of their offerings.

Model: Breda Mira Sporting (Brescia, Italy)
Gauge and Action: 12-gauge semi-automatic
Chamber: 3-inch
Trigger Assembly: Lightweight polymer trigger guard
Barrels: 30-inch blued barrel with 10-mm ventilated top rib and red fiber-optic front sight
Chokes: Five
Stock and Forend: High-gloss walnut

Grip: Pistol grip
Standard Measurements: Length of pull 14-1/4 inches, drop at comb 1-3/8 inches, drop at heel 2-3/8 inches
Weight: 7 pounds
Features: Spacers included to alter drop of stock and length of pull
Suggested Retail Price: $950

Model: Valmet 512SC Sporting (Finland)
Gauge and Action: 12-gauge over/under
Chamber: 3-inch
Trigger Assembly: Gold-plated trigger with automatic ejectors
Barrels: 28-, 30- and 32-inch backbored, chrome-lined blued barrels. Ventilated top rib is 11 mm wide with luminous red front sight bead and brass mid-point bead. Ventilated side rib.
Chokes: IC, S, M, IM, F
Stock and Forend: Walnut
Grip: Pistol grip
Standard Measurements: 14-3/8 inches long, 1 3/8-inch drop at comb, 2 3/8-inch drop at heel.
Weight: 7.4 pounds
Suggested Retail Price: $1160

TULA [http://toz.vpk.ru]

Perhaps it is some perverse pleasure in a former adversary clawing its way toward the community of nations, but "JSC Tulsky oruzheiny zavod" deserves a mention. After all, it was founded by Peter the Great 300 years ago and has produced everything from flintlock pistols to machine guns, anti-tank guns to sporting shotguns. "For the space of a long time of its history, the activity of [Tula Ordinance] was, is and will be of much benefit to Russia," the Internet site notes. Tula thinks of all of its shotguns (over/unders and semi-autos) as hunting guns.

Model: Tula TO3-120-12-1E
Gauge and Action: 12-gauge over/under
Trigger Assembly: Single selective trigger
Barrels: 28- or 30-inch barrels with solid side rib. Ventilated top rib with front bead.
Chokes: Three
Stock and Forend: Walnut or beech
Grip: Pistol grip
Standard Measurements: 46-1/2 inches long
Weight: 7.5 pounds
Features: Barrel and stock swivels for optional sling
Suggested Retail Price: This has not yet been established, but expect it to be $500 or less.
Note: A much more expensive "Souvenir Version" of this gun is available with a fantastically carved and inlaid stock and forearm.

The Weatherby SAS Sporting Clays 12 gauge is available with 28- or 30-inch barrels. Like Ruger, Weatherby has not yet embraced the longer 32- and 34-inch production barrels for its semi-autos that are becoming popular on clays courses.

When you close the action of a Weatherby SSC, Super Sporting Clays, you hear a solid, comfortable sound that reminds you of slamming the door on a Mercedes Benz S600 sedan. Superb shooting will feel like slipping into soft leather with surround-sound and a ride that is smooth, fast and quiet.

VERONA [www.docteropticsusa.com]

BC Outdoors, a subsidiary of PMC/El Dorado Cartridge, imports Verona shotguns from Italy. BC Outdoors is part of the Docter Sports Optics family with PMC ammunition.

Model: Verona LX980CS-12 Top Competition Sporting
Gauge and Action: 12-gauge over/under
Chamber: 2 3/4-inch
Trigger Assembly: Removable assembly allows easy adjustment. Gold-plated trigger.
Barrels: 30-inch ported barrels with ventilated side and top (11 mm) ribs, luminous red front fiber-optic sight and mid-rib bead.
Chokes: Five extended Briley chokes – C, IC, M, IM, F
Stock and Forend: Oil-finished walnut with black rubber recoil pad
Grip: Pistol grip with palm swell
Weight: 7-1/2 pounds
Features: Deluxe, padded and compartmentalized leather case
Suggested Retail Price: $1130
Note: Lifetime limited warranty. In Gold Series, this gun is available in 12 or 20 gauge for an additional $350.

Model: Verona SX801GI-12 Competition Sporting
Gauge and Action: 12-gauge semi-automatic
Chamber: 2 3/4-inches
Trigger Assembly: Gold-plated trigger
Barrels: 28- or 30-inch ported barrel with extended forcing cone and ventilated 9-mm top rib with green fluorescent HiViz front sight
Chokes: Four TruLock External chokes – C, IC, M, IM
Stock and Forend: Oil-finished walnut Monte Carlo Stock and forend with black rubber ventilated recoil pad
Grip: Pistol grip
Weight: 6-3/4 pounds
Suggested Retail Price: $1020
Note: Semi-autos are made for Verona by Bernardelli, both in Italy.

WEATHERBY [www.weatherby.com]

Founded in the 1940s, Weatherby is headquartered in California. Its over/unders are manufactured in Japan and its semi-automatic shotguns are imported from Italy. The semi-autos feature self-compensating gas systems to reduce felt recoil and an oversized Delta safety button on the rear of the trigger guard for what Weatherby calls "fast, easy access."

Model: Weatherby SAS
Gauge and Action: 12-gauge semi-automatic
Chamber: 3-inch
Trigger Assembly: Drops out for easy cleaning
Barrels: 28- or 30-inch chrome-lined, back-bored (to .735) barrels to improve shot pattern, reduce recoil and curb fatigue. Factory-ported barrels with long forcing cones to minimize recoil and shot deformation. Ventilated top rib with mid-point and front aiming beads.
Chokes: Five extended steel Briley Integral Multi-Choke tubes: IC, M, F, SCI, SCII
Stock and Forend: Checkered walnut. Includes shim spacer system to help fit the stock to your body. (Available with custom cast-on, cast-off and drop at comb and heel.)
Grip: Pistol grip
Standard Measurements: 14 1/4-inch length of pull, drop at comb 1-1/2 inches, drop at heel 2-1/4 inches. Length with a 30-inch barrel is 50 inches.
Weight: 7 to 7-3/4 pounds depending on density of the walnut
Features: Self-compensating gas system for reduced recoil and increased load versatility.
Suggested Retail Price: $849

Model: Weatherby Orion Super Sporting Clays (SSC)
Gauge and Action: 12-gauge over/under
Chamber: 3-inch
Trigger Assembly: Gold-plated, adjustable trigger for corrosion protection
Barrels: 28-, 30- or 32-inch ported and back-bored (to .735) barrels. Monobloc construction with lengthened forcing cone. Wide, 12-mm competition grooved rib with mid-bead, side vents and white front sight.
Chokes: Screw-in, interchangeable Briley multi-choke system. Chokes certified for steel shot only through

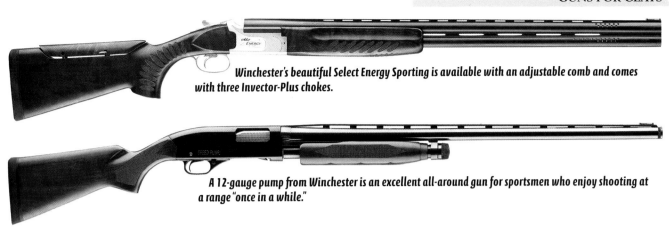

Winchester's beautiful Select Energy Sporting is available with an adjustable comb and comes with three Invector-Plus chokes.

A 12-gauge pump from Winchester is an excellent all-around gun for sportsmen who enjoy shooting at a range "once in a while."

Modified. 28- and 30-inch barrels come with S, IC, SCI, SCII, M.

Stock and Forend: Cast-off from top to bottom of the butt (3 to 6 mm). Satin, oil-finished walnut stock with a target-style pistol grip and Schnabel forearm. A longer buttstock fitted with a Pachmayr Decelerator recoil pad allows the stock to be cut to fit your exact length-of-pull requirements.

Grip: Pistol grip

Standard Measurements: 49 inches long with 32-inch barrel. Length of pull 14-3/4 inches; drop at heel 2-1/4 inches and drop at comb 1-1/2 inches.

Weight: 8 pounds

Features: Automatic ejectors

Suggested Retail Price: $2059

Note: The Orion is available in various 20- and 28-gauge field-grade models. Weatherby offers multi-barrel sets and handsome custom cases with individual compartments for barrels, buttstock, choke tubes and accessories.

WINCHESTER [www.winchesterguns.com]

With deep roots in the firearms and traditions of the "Old West," Winchester is one of the premier names in U.S. history. Today, it is a division of U.S. Repeating Arms in Morgan, Utah, and its incorporation into the Olin Corporation would most certainly be applauded by its founder, Oliver Winchester, who was an energetic businessman and gun enthusiast of the 1800s. Today, Winchester firearms are alive and well with a highly competitive line of rifles and shotguns.

Model: Winchester Select Energy Sporting

Gauge and Action: 12-gauge over/under

Chamber: 2 3/4-inch

Trigger Assembly: Adjustable trigger shoe

Barrels: 28-, 30- or 32-inch ported and vented barrels with wide, tapering runway rib, mid-rib bead and TruGlo front fiber-optic aiming point

Chokes: Three Invector-Plus chokes: F, M, IC

Stock and Forend: Walnut stock and forend with distinctive oval checkering. Comb adjusts 1 1/4-3/4 inches vertically and left-to-right for cast-on/cast-off.

Grip: Pistol grip with slight right-hand palm swell

Standard Measurements: 47-3/4 inches long with 30-inch barrels. Length of pull is 14-5/8 inches; drop at comb 1-1/2

inches; drop at heel 2 inches.

Weight: 7-5/8 pounds

Features: Back-bored barrels optional. Made in Belgium.

Suggested Retail Price: $2030 with adjustable comb, $1871 without

Model: Winchester Super X2

Gauge and Action: 12-gauge semi-automatic

Chamber: 3-inch magnum (includes two easily changed gas pistons for load versatility)

Barrels: 28- or 30-inch barrels with raised, vented rib and mid-point and front bead aiming points

Chokes: Five Invector-Plus chokes: S, IC, M, IM, F

Stock and Forend: Walnut

Grip: Pistol grip

Standard Measurements: With 30-inch barrel is 51 inches long. Length of pull is 14 3/8 inches; drop at comb 1-1/2 inches; drop at heel 2 3/8 inches.

Weight: 8-1/4 pounds

Features: Includes shim spacers to adjust drop and cast. Made in Europe.

Suggested Retail Price: $959 (Signature Red is $976)

Note: The unique Super X2 Signature Red Sporting comes with a fantastically dyed red walnut stock and forearm. Winchester Dura-Touch Armor Coating protects the finish.

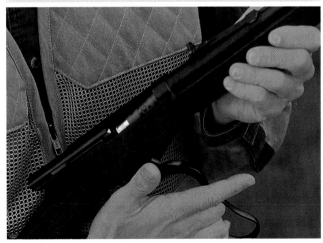

Winchester's Model 9410 Packer Compact 410 bore is excellent for small hands when hunting for small game and upland birds where shooting can be close.

8
Chapter

CHOOSING YOUR SHOTGUN

Sporting clays began as a hunter's game, a way to sharpen the shooting skills used to kill wild birds. Then again, skeet and trap began the same way. Only later, after the suits began to shoot them, did these games become institutionalized. Suddenly, there were committees that adopted rules and policies and charged special admission prices. Before they became rigid and people were AA- or B-class shooters or professionals who won money having fun, they were like Robert Redford wisecracking to Paul Newman in *Butch Cassidy and the Sundance Kid*, "What? Rules in a knife fight?" Good movie from 1969. Good news today. Sporting clays has not been entirely taken over yet, and you can still toss the kids in their pajamas and sneakers in the station wagon to shoot a round with a pump gun and have a ball.

If your shooting goal is to improve your skill in a duck blind or in the woods for grouse or out on the prairie for quail, then you should shoot your hunting gun for sporting clays. There is no better way to learn what to expect from a gun and any combination of chokes and loads than by actually putting it all to the test on the relatively controlled chaos of a clays course. If you go to the range with a semi-auto and then take a pump-gun hunting, you are going to miss some birds because you will forget to jack in a fresh shell. (It has happened to me.) "Uh oh," you will think. "Misfire." If you shoot clays with an over/under and take a semi-auto to the dove field, count on forgetting at least once or twice that you have more than two shells available.

If, however, you intend to pursue sporting clays both for the sheer fun of busting round birds or for the challenge of quality competition, you will very quickly discover that there are only two shotgun types that will, under normal conditions, take you into the winner's circle. These would be gas-operated semi-automatics and over/unders. This is not a knock on pumps or side-by-side doubles, just a statement of fact.

You can shoot sporting clays with any type shotgun, and you will see all kinds on a fun or recreational day at your local course: pumps, side-by-sides, semi-autos, over/unders and even antique guns.

SIDE-BY-SIDES

There is a small but active group of side-by-side sporting clays shooters, though, and this is good. After all, the side-by-side is often considered the "classic shotgun."

Unfortunately, side-by-sides are rarely found in the High Overall Shooter's hands when they are pitted against over/unders and gas guns. Side-by-side doubles such as a fine Merkel Model 47E ($3795) can be lively handling smoothbores. They can get off two rounds very reliably. Unfortunately, the broad sighting plane offered by the twin barrels has essentially been proven to give less precise leads on targets traveling on a largely horizontal plane, and that includes most flying game targets, too. Side-by-side barrels cover a lot of space through which a clay pigeon either is flying or will soon fly. Consequently, side-by-side shooters host their own events or shoot within the side-by-side-only category in separate events during major sporting clays competitions.

Sporting clays champion Tre Sides shows well-balanced form as he swings his long-barreled over/under for the second shot on doubles.

A wild South Dakota pheasant takes off in a wild flutter of wings and dry grass and for a moment, your heart takes off with it. Then you settle down, your eye follows the target, your gun comes to your cheek and the muzzle finds a sight picture and just the right amount of lead.

The essential difficulty with a pump-action shotgun is that moving a new shell into position to fire and expelling the hull requires 4 inches of forward and backward movement - 8 inches of gun parts, hand and arm movement. On singles, that is not an issue, but on simultaneous doubles, it can be fatal.

PUMP GUNS

Unfortunately, there is no Vintager-type organization for pump guns, and these guns are usually not found in a tournament setting, although there are occasionally side-events for pump gunners to compete against other pump gunners. Why this gun seems to work so well in the field or among police agencies, but has so few defenders on the sporting clays scene is a bit curious since clay shooting was organized by hunters for hunters[1].

To excel in clay competition, a shooter needs a gun that will reliably fire two shots while allowing total concentration on the target. Pump guns, such as the tough Ithaca Deluxe Model 37 12 gauge (#M37DV287 $618) with 26-inch barrel, which are excellent performers in thick grouse habitat, require the shooter to manually eject the spent cartridge and chamber the second round.

Few experienced scattergunners can jack in a fresh round and blow out gnats' eyes at 25 yards. Exhibition shooter Tom Knapp, however, who travels for Benelli and Federal Cartridge, is one who can. Knapp has been making a good living demonstrating his abilities with fast-action pump guns for years. On the full clay range, however, even the fastest shot will miss a couple of targets more per round with a pump than they would with a gas gun or an over/under. The reason, of course, is that there is 4 inches of back and then 4 inches of forward hand movement for the second shot – or there is on my Winchester 1300 – and that is debilitating when your concentration needs to be on the leading edge of the bird and you only have a second to move, point and fire.

That requirement for quick, accurate movement leaves us with semi-automatic gas guns and over/unders,

and the debate over the relative merits of each of these type actions can be a lengthy one. Both guns have their defenders … and their detractors.

CONSIDER RECOIL

Whether you are pulling the trigger on a pistol, rifle, muzzleloader or shotgun, recoil is an uncomfortable but inescapable result. It is one of the two biggest reasons – the other is cost and we will review that later in this chapter – shooters select a gas-operated semi-auto in preference to an over/under. The gas gun is universally believed to have less felt recoil. That statement is probably true if you are comparing factory guns right out of the box.

When a gas-operated semi-auto fires, a small amount of propellant gas is bled off through one or more small holes drilled in the barrel. The gas operates a piston in the forend that mechanically forces the bolt to the rear. An extractor mounted on the bolt grips the rim of the fired shell to pull it out of the chamber as the bolt recoils. When the bolt has drawn the shell back far enough to strike a fixed piece of metal called the ejector, the shell automatically kicks out of the gun. While all of that is going on, a new shell releases from the tubular magazine onto the shell carrier below the bolt. As the bolt moves forward under spring pressure, the carrier rises to position the shell and the bolt rams it into the chamber for the next shot.

That is a lot of mechanical "stuff" going on at one time and here is how it relates to recoil.

Actual recoil depends on the weight of the gun and the power of the shell. Obviously then, an 8-pound 12-gauge gun firing a 2 3/4-dram, 1 1/8-ounce load will have less recoil than the same gun firing a 3 1/4-dram, 1 1/4-ounce shell.

It is not necessary to shoot 1-1/8 ounces through a 12-gauge to play or compete in sporting clays. Not only do small gauges deliver less recoil, but courses usually offer events specifically for 28-gauge and 410 shooting.

The gas gun does not necessarily reduce the actual reaction from the exploding powder. What it does is retard it, give it multiple internal tasks that bleed off energy and spread it over a longer period. This makes a gas gun feel like it is a softer kicking gun. You get a shove instead of the sharp rap produced by a fixed-breech over/under of the same mass weight firing the same load.

In spite of the obvious mechanical differences in the semi-auto and the over/under, guns are highly individualistic, as are shooters. Some over/unders will bang you with less recoil than some semi-autos, and different shooters will react differently depending on their body's form. If it seems that I am straddling the fence and not answering the question directly, how can this be so?

The reason is the difference between *actual* recoil (which can be measured in foot pounds of energy, the amount of energy required to *raise* a one pound object one foot) and *perceived* or "felt" recoil, which is how our bodies react to the impact of recoil. The latter – what you get as opposed to what you are told – is the more important of the two, and it depends on several factors including how well the gun fits the shooter and what impact-absorbing material is present between the shooter and the gun stock.

Think of the pounding you take from recoil in this manner: A heavyweight boxer delivers a solid left hook to your jaw with his naked hand. This blow would injure you and perhaps the boxer's own hand severely. Now, if that boxer is wearing a regulation, padded 16-ounce glove, he will only knock you down and give you a massive headache. He will escape unhurt. Nevertheless, the actual, measured foot-pounds of energy (kinetic energy = $1/2$ mass x velocity^2) in the punch would be the same.

That is the case with my friend and fellow Floridian Chris Christian's Ruger Red Label semi-automatic. It was fitted precisely to him by shotgun specialist Jack West and has a thick KickEeze recoil pad and a padded comb. His Franchi over/under has a KickEeze pad as well, but no padded comb. Chris says that to him, the Franchi feels slightly softer on firing, but the Ruger still feels better over the long run. The subject of recoil is a personal issue.

Any unaltered out-of-the-box shotgun – gas operated, over/under, side-by-side or pump – can have its felt recoil reduced noticeably by selective use of fitting, practice on proper shooting form and the use of after-market recoil-reducing products. Nevertheless, the gas gun typically wins on the question of felt recoil. However, that should not be the only reason for selecting one type over another. Each can be made to shoot soft enough that practically any shooter can enjoy them.

A side-by-side such as this Stoeger Uplander Supreme (suggested retail price $445 for a 12 or 20 gauge) is a beautiful and traditional field gun, but unless you shoot in a special side-by-side event, it will not usually stand up against the over/unders and semi-autos on a tough sporting course.

A pump-action shotgun like this 12-gauge Ithaca Classic with a 28-inch barrel will break clays, just like it will bring down ducks and dove, but it is a rare gun type on a sporting course.

BALANCE AND HANDLING

Shooting coaches will generally tell you that over/unders have an advantage in this comparative category. Two barrels extending beyond the forend give more forward weight than the single barrel on a gas gun. This promotes a smoother swing (and one that is more difficult to stop once it is started, too). As a result, targets are splashed more often because follow-through is more effective.

The way the weight of the gun is distributed determines the balance and handling qualities of any shotgun. A bit more muzzle weight allows the gun to swing more smoothly. If there is more weight in the butt, the gun may mount quicker, but it can be a little more "whippy" or loose on the swing, like a steering wheel with too much "play." Over/unders tend to have a bit more muzzle weight and thus swing a bit more forcefully and positively.

Many shooters alter the balance of their gas guns to give them the same swing characteristics of an over/under.

There are several ways to add more muzzle weight to a semi-auto. You can fill an empty shotshell with shot, crimp it, seal it with duct tape, and stick it in the forward portion of the magazine in place of the wooden plug that is already there. A 12-gauge shell full of shot will weigh 2-1/2 to 3 ounces. This weight will lie forward of your leading hand and will promote a smoother swing. If you have a standard, five-shell magazine, you can add up to three of these weights and even customize each for your preferred balance.

Breako makes do-it-yourself interchangeable all-gauge counterweights that will fit both semi-auto and over/under barrels. The simple, universal clamp-and-weight system can be positioned anywhere along the free length of a barrel's underside, thus allowing you to customize balance points. Mark the spot on your barrel and Breako says you can use their counterweight system on your rifles and pistols also. It is easy to attach and remove. The set includes a 2 1/4-inch aluminum clamp,

Indoor shooting ranges are often not set up for shotguns, but in the northern states, where winter weather often makes outdoor shooting unbearable, a winter league or even instruction can carry you through the bleak months of snow and ice.

three weights (4, 6 and 8 ounces) and four adapters (12, 16, 20 and 410). It costs $66.65 from Brownells.

If these solutions seem inelegant, you can ask a local gunsmith for options and advice.

What if the opposite is true and the muzzle feels too heavy? In that case, stick one or more of your shot-filled shells in the bolthole in the buttstock. It does not get any easier than that.

You can also change the balance and handling qualities of an over/under, although this is a rarer complaint. Just add weight where you need it. Several products now on the market make that easy. Like the Breako interchangeable barrel weights mentioned earlier, the Barrel Buddy from Meadow Industries attaches to the underside of the barrel and gives you the option of adding up to 8 ounces of weight. It cannot easily be used with a semi-auto (and certainly not with a pump)

One argument against gas-operated semi-autos on the sporting clays range is that chokes may not be changed during your time on the shooting stand and each station will give you at least one doubles presentation, often a close shot and a long shot. This can be overcome by a selection of loads, but you must remember to insert them in proper order in the chamber.

because it prevents the forend from sliding off the gun in the normal manner during takedown, but it works well for over/unders. Buttstock weight can always be added via shotshells (fired and shot-filled, *not* live shells) in the bolthole of the stock.

These days, few shooters need to change the balance of their gas gun, as many manufacturers are adding more muzzle weight to the newer specialized semi-autos.

In short, if you do not like the way a gun balances when it comes from the factory, you do not have to accept it as is. It is so easy to change that the discussion of balance and handling between the two gun types essentially becomes moot. So, in the category of balance and handling, we should consider that over/unders and gas operated semi-autos tie in shooter benefit, with neither inherently conferring an advantage or disadvantage over the other.

THE ONE CHOKE SYNDROME

You only have one choke available at a time when you shoot a gas-operated semi-auto. If you shoot an over/under, however, you have a choice of two chokes. Many shooters will tell you that this is a major advantage of a stack-barrel gun. There is some truth in this, but perhaps not as much as one might at first suppose.

There are a number of clay target games where having only one choke is not considered a handicap. American skeet, ATA 16-Yard trap and handicap trap come immediately to mind. Every target is going to be broken within one relatively narrow range, and one choke is going to serve you just fine.

The ability to shoot different chokes is often given as a reason for the over/under's popularity in sporting

Titanium chokes from Trulock are lighter than comparable steel chokes: extended, knurled and notched, each choke has a unique color to make them easy to identify. They are ideal for "long-barreled sporting clays guns," says George Trulock. Only one choke is available at a time when you shoot a semi-auto. Choose wisely and expect to vary your loads to compensate for distance and angle.

clays, but it is rare to find a station where the shots vary more than 10 yards in range. Regardless of whether they are singles, report pairs, true pairs, following pairs or simultaneous pairs, once you have an idea of the range you will be shooting, you can usually find one choke that is right for both birds.

That said, a FITASC station occasionally presents a shot array at wildly varying ranges. In FITASC, when you step up to a shooting station – which may be a cement pad or nothing more than a plastic HulaHoop held in place with a stake – your chokes and loads must be ready. You must shoot whatever is presented with the choke or chokes that are in the gun. You cannot change once you step up to shoot. You may get a target at 15 yards and the next may be at 50, and this is part of the challenge. Shooting FITASC, it helps to have the versatility of two choke tubes, but it is possible to make one choke serve multiple tasks.

But how do you make one choke do the work of two? This is easily accomplished by changing the loads in your shells. Many shooters have learned – incorrectly – that if they want the proper pattern for the range encountered, they must put the proper choke tube in the gun. This is not true. You can vary the pattern performance of your gun by simply changing shells.

Here is something to think about. In clay target games, we do not give targets a grade. All it takes to score a kill is to knock the famous "visible piece" off the target, and for the scorer to see it. A target that is centered well in your shot string and dramatically reduced to powder counts not one bit more than one that is merely chipped by a flyer.

If your load gives you that visible piece, no matter how small it may be (as long as it is visible), who cares what your actual pattern looks like?

A growing number of shooters are doing more shell changing than choke tube changing, even if they shoot an over/under, which naturally gives them the option.

For example, you are facing a Fur & Feathers shot with a racing rabbit target that crosses about 15 yards in front of you followed by a quartering away aerial target that could most effectively be broken at around 25 yards. Ideally, following the charts, you would use a straight Cylinder choke for the rabbit and an Improved Cylinder for the pheasant.

The other option is to shoot them both with the Improved Cylinder or even a Skeet 1 choke simply by using a quick-opening load of #9s in the first barrel (for the 15-yard rabbit) and a 1 1/8-ounce load of hard, target-grade #8s in the second barrel for the more distant aerial opportunity. The first load could be an inexpensive promotional load with soft shot, a spreader reload using one of the Ballistic Products wads designed for that, or perhaps a less expensive shell from the Remington Gun Club line, a GC12L. Quick-opening shells will give you as large a pattern as you are going to get at 15 yards, regardless of the choke constriction in your gun. The second load of hard #8s provides plenty of pattern density and individual pellet target-breaking power for the longer shot, even if you blow them out of a straight Cylinder choke. For this shot, you might want the higher-grade Remington Premier STS12L shot.

To take an extreme example, think of a FITASC shot where you might have one target thrown at a bit under 20 yards and a second at a little over 45. You could choke Skeet 1 in the first barrel with a load of #9s, and slip a Full choke in the second barrel with a load of #7-1/2s. Shooting a single choke, however, you can accomplish the same thing with a Full or Improved Modified choke (you have to choke for the longer bird) and then effectively open the barrel to Skeet 1 by using a fast-opening load for the closer bird. A spreader-type load usually opens a Full choke to about Improved Cylinder, and a Modified choke to about Skeet 1. (Of course, in the heat of competition, trying to study the show-birds and watch the first shooters tackle them and taking a sip of water and adjusting your cap, you can easily forget in what order to put the shells in the gun!)

You can make more subtle modifications by altering the velocity and even the hardness of the shot. Soft shot at high velocity usually patterns one complete choke wider than the tube you are using. Hard, target-grade shot at moderate velocity often patterns a full choke tighter.

Not many sporting clays ranges throw shots beyond 40 yards unless it is a shoot-off or a special Make-A-Break fun event, and a shooter with a single barrel gun can break just as many birds as a shooter with the finest over/under. When you encounter a target thrown at greater distance, choke for it, and use a spreader load to open your pattern for the closer shot.

The usefulness of spreader loads is one reason that a gas-gun shooter is not at a disadvantage because the gun offers only one choke at a time.

We have so far covered the three most commonly discussed reasons for making a selection of either an over/under or a semi-automatic. With a few simple after-market alterations, it seems that there is little true difference between their performances on a clay course … at least so far. Now, let us get down to the differences you may experience in the field.

Compared to fixed-breech over/unders, semi-automatics have a relatively poor record when reliability is considered.

RELIABILITY

You can never be HOA or the finest wingshooter in your group of friends with an unreliable gun. In fact, if you want to see grown men and women break down into cursing, stomping, hair-pulling tantrums, just wait for their semi-auto to blow a fuse in the middle of the big game. The reliability factor is ultimately important in all shotgun competition and the over/under wins in this category without question. No argument. At best, a gas-gun shooter's semi-auto can be *as reliable as an over/under* and that is saying a lot.

In some game formats, if you cannot fire on the target *for any reason*, you lose it. Other games give you a certain number of "alibis" and allow you to call for targets again. Even then, there is a limit beyond which you lose targets.

A gun malfunction can devastate your rhythm and your confidence. It will immediately and negatively affect your performance. Count on it. It is very difficult for your subconscious mind to perform the multitude of tasks required to break targets if it is wondering if the gun will go off! And it does wonder. A gun malfunction early in a round or in the key later stages of a match almost certainly will cause you to miss subsequent targets even if the malfunction never recurs.

A semi-automatic gas gun will never be as reliable as a fixed-breech over/under because of the number of moving parts and mechanical operations required for it to operate successfully. That is the biggest single reason why top competitors show a marked preference for stack-barrel guns, for the Beretta White Onyx Sporting rather than the comparably priced Teknys Sporting (both retail under $2000). If you can jam a shell in the barrel and snap the action closed, the firing pin will strike the primer when you pull the trigger. Then, if the shell is any good, it will go off. This is not necessarily the case with gas guns. They can work perfectly at one station and fail at the next without warning!

Gas guns requires near-perfect ammunition, and the power level of the powder inside the shell must be sufficient to operate the action, yet not so powerful that it generates too much gas energy. Too much energy will cycle the action too fast and result in a failure to feed a second shell properly. This problem can show up with light target loads or some of the new, reduced or managed recoil loads.

Reloaders must be certain to build every shell as perfectly as if it came straight from the factory. A worn, slightly out of round, or poorly crimped reload may fail to feed and fire in a gas gun. Chances are that if that shell will slide into the chamber, it will operate just fine in an over/under.

Perhaps the number one problem with semi-autos is routine cleaning. It should not be a problem, but in the hectic pace of the 21st century, it is. And cleaning a gun is about as far from sexy as a gun can get. You must keep gas guns scrupulously clean if you expect them to even approach stack-barrel reliability.

For ease of cleaning and maintenance, an over/under beats a semi-automatic by almost every measure.

EASE OF MAINTENANCE

Unhook the forend, open the action, dismount the barrels, brush them out and reassemble. Congratulations. You have just cleaned your over/under. A light lubrication of the ejector/extractor arms and the barrel hinge, and your gun is again ready to kill pheasants or shoot another 100-bird round of clays.

Semi-automatics are far more tedious. First, remove the forend and slide the barrel out of the receiver, taking care not to lose any of the little O-rings found in most gas-operated systems. Then take the piston off and lay out all the attendant parts … and you are still not done. Smart shooters also remove the retaining pins that hold the trigger/shell carrier group in place. (You should have a "drift punch" and small hammer to avoid damaging this pin. You do have one, right?) Now, for truly detailed cleaning, remove the bolt.

Now that you have disassembled the gun, here are some potential problem areas:

1 The trigger/shell carrier. Flush it with something like Outer's Crud Cutter and allow it to dry. Spray the assembly lightly with Break-Free or any similar lube before reassembling. The reason this part must be cleaned is that unburned powder flakes do occasionally work their way into crevices and this can tie up the shell carrier. Some powders are notorious for this. When that happens, your gun becomes a single shot. It is a common problem and an area many shooters neglect.

2 You will scrub the barrel, naturally, but that does not finish that job. Pay particular attention to the gas ports, which, when clogged with carbon, can reduce gas flow and cause a feed malfunction. You also need to remove the plastic fouling from the chamber. This fouling is left by the outer surface of the shell itself from heat generated upon firing. If it is allowed to build up, it will seriously impede the gun's ability to feed and extract shells. Standard bore cleaning solvents and brushes do not remove it. Use a bore brush wrapped with 0000 steel wool. Once you scrub the chamber, leave it slick and dry! Oil in the chamber contributes to both feeding and extracting malfunctions.

3 Follow the manufacturer's instructions for cleaning the gas system. Some have certain lubrication "do's and don'ts." Remember to add some light lube to the action bars and the channels they ride in within the receiver. This is another area where unburned powder can cause the gun to foul and operate outside ideal performance standards.

That will handle routine cleaning. Every 10,000 rounds or so, you should take the gun to a certified gunsmith for a thorough strip down and tank dunk cleaning.

Considering all of this, is it any surprise that most fine shooters who fire 10,000 to 30,000 rounds per year prefer over/unders?

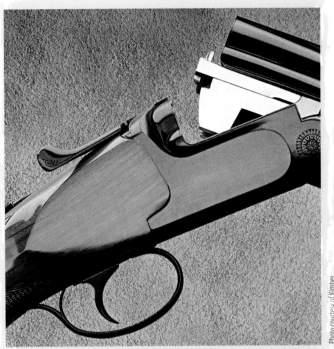

Photo courtesy of Kimber.

When overall durability and even ease of cleaning are considered, the over/under has the edge over the semi-auto, which has more moving parts that must work synchronously.

DURABILITY

At the risk of offending the pros who consistently win with new gas guns, the finest and most expensive gas-operated semi-auto made will not even come close to the lifespan of even a moderately priced (but well-made) over/under.

No one can predict how many rounds each type gun will handle before it is ready for the scrap heap. Far too many variables are involved. The very best competition gas-gun shooters replace their guns every year though and have one or more backup guns on hand.

This area looks like another win for the over/under.

EASE OF REPAIR

As a rule, a gas gun is easier to repair than an over/under. This is certainly true if you are shooting a well-known model that has been around for a few years, a gun like the Remington 1100 or the various Winchesters. You can certainly find parts and service at your local gunsmith. He knows what small parts routinely break – the rubber seals, for instance – or wear out and keeps them in stock. Because gas guns are all designed for modern mass production methods with parts-interchangeability, replacing parts is easy.

When over/unders need repairs, they can be much more complex. Generally, it is best to send them back to the factory than to work on them locally. If the gun is an American-made model with solid repair facilities, turn-around time can be relatively quick, but you should still expect to be without your gun from four to six weeks. If you have an expensive European model, repair time can stretch to many months.

On the plus side, over/unders seldom require minor repairs. When a well-made gun needs fixing, it is generally after a lot of shooting, more than most shooters who are also hunters will do in two or three lifetimes!

When all is said and done … ease of repair is almost certainly a plus for the gas gun.

USE OF RELOADS

The over/under comes out on top here, for reasons that have already been mentioned. Another factor that comes into play, however, is that over/unders are easier on shells and you can generally squeeze a few more reloads per hull from them. Their mechanism does not ram the empties around and then toss them on the ground. If your over/under is equipped with extractors, you simply pluck the hulls out of the chambers and stick them in your pocket. That can be especially important if you are shooting on a range whose policy is, "When a shell hits the ground, it becomes the property of the club." If your over/under has ejectors, you are in the same position as the semi-autos – shells on the ground – unless you are careful and wear a glove to remove the hot shells.

Since most serious competitive shooters are reloaders, the category of reloaded shells must be considered a strong point in favor of the over/under.

COST

The second most influential reason (and some would suggest it is really the primary reason) shooters choose semi-autos rather than over/unders is that they cost less than a good-quality stackbarrel. The cost difference can be a significant factor for shooters on a budget, but that is something each shooter must decide. In some cases, though, that difference can be deceiving.

There are quite a few budget-priced over/unders on the market, but they must be made with parts that are not the highest quality possible. In order to buy an over/under with the quality needed to be a top competitive gun, you are looking at a suggested retail price of at least several thousand dollars. A smart shopper can generally save a few hundred dollars if he looks for the best "street price" or perhaps finds a gun that is being sold by someone "trading up."

Quality gas guns like the Remington 1100, Browning Gold, Verona 692 Gold ($1765) and the Beretta Teknys models have a retail price that is several hundred dollars less than a comparable over/under. The "street price" philosophy also applies to them. (See for instance www.ozarkguns.com.)

If you are thinking of entering serious competition, the total difference in price of $800 to $1000 may not be worth the potential long-term inconvenience of the gas gun. That price difference is, after all, only about the equivalent of five to seven cases of shotshells. Over the lifetime of a good shotgun, it amounts to very little. When

you are talking about a gun you may want to keep, shoot and possibly even invest a bit of money in for custom fitting and after-market upgrades, that difference becomes a lot smaller. You are only talking about a few months supply of shells as the price difference on a quality gun you may well pass on to your children.

On the other hand … the difference between a moderately priced over/under and a very expensive gun is often the quality of the engraving. This is particularly true with European guns. Catalogs from manufacturers like Perazzi from Italy or AYA from Spain appear to spend more time showing and discussing the engraving options than they do the shooting characteristics of the individual gun. Engraving and gold inlays are the primary difference between a moderately priced European gun and one that is super expensive, and since the interest in sporting clays shooting began to grow in the '90s, American manufacturers have begun copying this fashion.

Over/unders also hold their value. If you decide you want to change guns after 20,000 or so rounds, you will get a much greater percentage of your original purchase price back if the gun you are selling is a well-made over/under that has been cared for properly.

Try selling a gas gun that has gone 20,000 rounds and most knowledgeable shooters will not even look at it.

"STATUS" AND SUMMARY

The final, almost imperceptible quality separating semi-autos from over/unders is one that most shooters will not discuss or may even deny. The over/under has the advantage in status.

A shooter wielding an Ithaca pump or a Winchester semi-auto may be able out-perform a shooter with a Krieghoff, but when everyone returns to the clubhouse, it is the beautifully engraved K-80 that people want to look at, to heft to their shoulder and swing on an imaginary target. (They think, "If it was me shooting this

Over/Under vs. Semi-Automatic: A Quick Comparison

CHARACTERISTIC	OVER/UNDER	SEMI-AUTO
Recoil	Loser	Winner
Balance and Handling	Tie	Tie
Choke Versatility	Winner	Loser
Reliability	Winner	Loser
Ease of Maintenance	Winner	Loser
Durability	Winner	Loser
Ease of Repair	Loser	Winner
Use of Reloads	Winner	Loser
Cost	Loser	Winner
Resale Value	Winner	Loser
Status Value	Winner	Loser
Clay-Breaking Ability	Tie	Tie

gun …") The Ithaca and Remington may be excellent guns, but they are not as relatively exotic as the German gun, and they certainly cost a lot less. Head to the range with a new Perazzi, even the cheapest in the line, and all your shooting buddies will "oooh and ahhhh" over it. If you were carrying a new camo Mossberg, they might not turn their head. What is the old saying about familiarity?

These last are the real reasons why over/unders dominate competitive clay target games.

This is certainly not meant to denigrate gas guns. With the exception of reliability, when it comes to busting clay targets, they do hold their own with the over/unders.

FOOTNOTES

[1] Lest you feel that I am unduly harsh estimating the pump shotgun, I do claim to own a Winchester Model 1300 12 gauge, and I have shot skeet, trap and sporting clays, 5-Stand and wobble trap with this gun … although not exceptionally well. On the other hand, a cynic might observe that I have not shot these games exceptionally well (unless having fun is considered "exceptionally well") with any type shotgun.

To the pump gun's credit, a Minnesota deputy sheriff once told me that when police cornered criminals in a building, they would surround the place with bright light and armed deputies. Then, they would move as close as was safe and hold a bullhorn next to the action of a pump shotgun. As often as not, when they broadcast the sound of an officer jacking a new shell into the gun's chamber, the criminal would throw down his weapon and come out with his arms raised. "The sound of buckshot loading in a pump shotgun is highly recognizable and very convincing," the deputy said.

THE TEACHER

Brad Varney is a Maine shooting coach and the owner of Varney's Clay Sports in Richmond. Brad guarantees (or your money back!) that you will shoot better after you attend his "Have Gun – Will Teach" shooting school. He says that every gun has its pluses and its minuses, but it is not the gun that makes the shooter. It is the shooter in a sense that makes the gun. A good shooter will shoot an average gun well, but a poor shooter cannot find a seat in the house even with a gold-plated Perazzi.

"People choose a semi-auto for one primary reason," Varney claims. "Recoil. Without doing something drastic, you just can't make a fixed-breech gun shoot as soft and as pleasant as a semi-auto."

For some shooters, with a tolerance to pain, the Rocky Marciano and Mike Tyson types, nothing hurts them. For everyone else, however, recoil is the enemy. If you shoot enough, you will eventually develop a flinch because you will automatically anticipate your gun's recoil.

"Many serious trap shooters flinch," Varney said. "They shoot a lot of shells quickly and sometimes they get so bad that they can't pull the trigger at all. Many of them install a release trigger to try to fool their subconscious. This will work for a while, but why get yourself into that difficulty in the first place? The softer recoil of a semi-auto can definitely minimize flinching."

Varney agrees that you can get away with not cleaning pumps or over/unders after every outing, but a semi-auto has to be cleaned regularly.

"A lot of people bring their gas guns to me and say they just quit working," he says. "I ask them if they clean it regularly and they always say they do. They wipe them off and maybe run a patch through the barrel. Well, that's enough with an over/under maybe, but not with a semi-auto. Those have to be taken apart and cleaned thoroughly."

Varney is quick to smother the thought that he is a gunsmith. "I know how to clean a gun, especially a gun in the Remington family of guns," he says. "I sometimes replace a part that has broken, but Rich Cole of Cole's Gunsmithing in Harpswell [Maine: www.colegun.com] does all my repair work. I always recommend him to my students and customers. I believe he's the most knowledgeable person in the Unites States in regards to Beretta firearms."

In addition, he says, parts of a gas gun's action do occasionally break. "I was at a shoot just recently and had a gas seal break, but fortunately," he says, "I knew this might happen and had some spares with me so it was easy to fix."

Varney says he rarely has someone shooting an over/under have mechanical problems with their gun. "They are pretty reliable. Side-by-sides, too. Under normal circumstances, not much can go wrong."

Varney's Clay Sports does get some side-by-side shooters and the problem they experience is with eye dominance. The wider sighting plane causes the eyes to fight each other for dominance, Varney says, and any time the side-by-side barrels obscure your vision, the other eye wants to take over. Obviously, this can be confusing.

As an NESCA (New England Sporting Clays Association) instructor, Varney says that most guys with field experience shooting birds adapt easily to sporting clays. "Better than the other way around. Clay hunters, especially trap and skeet shooters, even the very good ones, can have a difficult time in the brush shooting woodcock and grouse."

Varney, who was 62 at the time of the interview, has been shooting shotguns for more than a half century and has been teaching, in one form or another, since 1965. He has won many state skeet championships. To keep up with current trends and to deepen his historical understanding of clay target shooting, he is an avid reader.

"I swear by the Remington 1100 and 11-87," he says. "They are inexpensive and functional semi-autos. They are relatively easy to repair, so I use them for lessons, too. I believe there have been more championships won and more birds killed with the 1100 than with any other gun in history. You can take an 1100 off the shelf and shoot pretty well. I suppose it is the gun I talk about most in the book I am writing about wingshooting in Maine. That book, by the way, could go to press in 2005."

The magnificence of the guns seen at Vintagers events may only be rivaled by the Edwardian dress of the participants.

A fine-quality vintage shotgun can be a thing of great pleasure and value. Briley and others offer muzzle-to-butt gunsmithing services to help you refurbish an older gun and then keep it in top shape.

THE VINTAGERS
Order of Edwardian Gunners

If you enjoy shooting the side-by-side, you may want to contact The Vintagers, The Order of Edwardian Gunners, Inc. The mission of this not-for-profit corporation is to provide an opportunity for the use, appreciation and collection of side-by-side shotguns and rifles from the so-called "Vintage Years" of 1880-1914. The group's philosophy is to provide a shooting experience for "gentlemen and gentlewomen" who appreciate the guns, attire and habits of that special age.

The Vintagers organized in 1994 when four friends who loved both side-by-side shotguns and the game of sporting clays recognized that the emphasis on score discouraged the use of fine side-by-side game guns at sporting clay events. In response, they set up special shoots for these classic guns that emphasized fun targets, vintage attire (hence the name "Vintagers"), fine dining and good fellowship. Ray Poudrier, the president and one of the original four founders, worked tirelessly, "70 to 80 hours a week for over a year," he says, to make the first World Side-By-Side Championship and Exhibition happen in 1997.

Originally, Vintager events were not scored because the organizers believed that keeping score detracted from their dual purpose of fun and fellowship. That is no longer true for every Vintager event and some are held specifically for the challenge of keeping score and "winning."

Membership in Vintagers is open to anyone who shares the group's enthusiasm for side-by-sides, new or old ... with a light dose of "dressing in period costume." Mostly, Poudrier says, potential members need the right "frame of mind," and by that he means that they wish to associate in the easy company of others who enjoy shotgunning, but do not make keeping score the goal of their comradeship.

Members are invited to all shooting and social events promoted by the Order of Edwardian Gunners and its chartered affiliates, about 14 at the time of this writing with a total paid membership of around 600. Members in good standing receive a periodic newsletter, which may contain historic double-gun information, news and information from Vintager headquarters, an updated calendar of events and member-classified ads. Members also receive free admission to national and regional Vintager expositions.

A note regarding the special clothing and accessories, which, The Vintagers say "shall be appropriate to the English Sportsman of the period and their guests." This has a re-enactor's flavor similar to the Civil War buffs who dress in Federal and Confederate costumes of the 1860s and act out great battles of that era.

The 2004 Vintage Cup Side-By-Side World Championships were scheduled for the beautiful Orvis course at Sandanona in Millbrook, New York, on September 16 through 19. Numerous

italia series 1.tif> Several manufacturers offer new and replica guns that are welcome at Vintagers events. The Bernardelli Italia Series offers handsomely engraved side-by-sides with articulated double triggers.

manufacturers exhibited and provided support for Vintagers. Poudrier mentioned Merkel, Krieghoff, Ruger and the magazine *Shooting Sportsman.*

You may contact The Vintagers at 29 Pond Rd., Hawley, MA 01339 Telephone (413) 339-5347 or (www.vintagers.org). Annual membership is $60.00 (individual) or $100.00 for a couple.

"THE VINTAGE CUP: A DISTAFF PRIMER"
by Kathryn Barth

When my husband, Mike, said we should spend our 2002 vacation at The Vintage Cup, I was not enthusiastic until I realized that Victorian- or Edwardian-period attire was encouraged. Because I love "dress up," I got excited and coming up with appropriate outfits looked like a fun challenge.

A wealth of information about the 1880 to 1910 era exists on the Internet. We didn't need to dress in period attire, only to look like it. E-Bay was a great resource for studying authentic period clothing because sellers feature detailed photos.

I began haunting thrift shops. In the late 1970s, there was a revival of the romantic look. An old bolero jacket had leg-o-mutton sleeves. Gunne Sax dresses and blouses had high necklines, long sleeves and loads of lace. A floor-length, seven-panel black skirt had a perfect silhouette; so what if it was polyester instead of silk faille? Coupled with a bugle-beaded belt from an estate sale, the look was right.

Vintage Cup day one featured rifle events, so I wore my "Out of Africa" costume: a tweed jacket, khaki skirt, safari-style pith helmet, long-strapped leather bag worn bandoleer-style, brown gloves and a pair of laced boots.

Evening events allow ladies to go all out. Used bridesmaid outfits, floor-length taffeta gowns with puffed sleeves, faux bustles and lots of beading look appropriate. Modern broomstick lace dresses, often priced under $20 at discount dress stores, can work as well. I wore a dress by Nostalgia, added a ribbon sash, matching choker and hat embellished with more ribbon and silk flowers.

It is easy to create inexpensive period hats. By decorating a cheap, wide-brim straw hat with ribbons, lace, silk flowers, artificial fruits and feathers, you capture the Edwardian look. It's almost impossible to do too much to a hat of this era. Craft and fabric stores are good sources of raw materials. Using monofilament such as 3X fly-fishing tippet works well when sewing things to hats because the thread doesn't show.

Accessories are easy to find because of teenage trends: costume jewelry including chandelier earrings, beaded necklaces and marcasite pieces that replicate the Edwardian style. Beaded and drawstring purses have a vintage look and thrift shops often carry affordable gloves with interesting cutwork that look terrific.

It was great to dress up and take on the persona of an Edwardian lady. We had such a good time that we returned for the 2003 Vintage Cup. This time I had six outfits for the four days! I also made two pair of breeks for Mike by cutting off and cuffing trousers from thrift shops, dying a vest for him, and making a pocket watch chain and fob out of an old necklace. We had more fun the second time than the first, and we didn't think that was possible.

© Vintagers (Used with permission)

The trapper flintlock blackpowder pistols from Traditions are a little early for the Vintagers era perhaps, but they would fit right in at a rendezvous of American pioneers, hatchet throwers and early 1800s re-enactors.

9
Chapter

AMMUNITION:

LOAD 'EM UP FOR SPORTING CLAYS

Photo courtesy of Quail Creek.

There is no single load that is perfect for every shot in sporting clays. Couple multiple load options with a variety of chokes and you should be able to develop a superior pattern for any shot at any distance.

NSCA All-American Wendell Cherry shoots #7 1/2s, exclusively. No matter what the presentation or angle or type of target, he sticks with this single Lyalvale load. The top barrel of his Perazzi MX 2000 is choked Full and the bottom barrel choked Improved Modified. Wendell kicks butt with this load combo even when others in his squad may be shooting #8 1/2s and changing chokes like mad. It works for him, but it may not work for everyone.

Unlike other shotgun games, there is no single load that is perfect for sporting clays – in any gauge – because the game is so varied. Whether you are shooting our conventional English sporting or the supposedly more difficult international FITASC, 5-Stand or Compak Sporting, you have a diversity of loads and shells available to do the job. Millions of skeet shooters swear by their 1-1/8 ounces of #9, about 650 round pellets per 12-gauge load. The occasional shooter will chamber an #8-1/2 for the second shot in skeet doubles if he or she is just a touch slow or methodical getting on the bird. Trap shooters typically rely on loads of #8s (461 round pellets) for the closer birds and #7 1/2s (about 393 pellets) for those that get out beyond 40 yards. Registered trap targets and trap tournaments are regulated by velocity for 12 and 20 gauges: 1290 fps for a 1 1/8-ounce load or 1325 fps for 1-ounce and 1350 for a 7/8-ounce load.

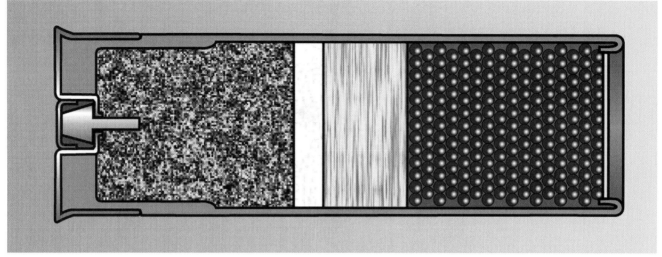

Your Cartridge - The shotgun shell has evolved gradually from muzzleloader days. Its components are designed to be a one-piece shot rocket and all parts, from the primer to the crimp, must work efficiently for superior shooting. Today, most wads and shells are plastic, while the powder is a highly evolved propellant that burns at a controlled rate.

In trap and skeet, you know where a bird is coming from and where it is going. Precisely. Sporting clays is different. Every course sets its traps to give you the same seven basic shot presentations – running rabbit, crossing left-to-right and right-to-left, springing teal, straight-away, high incomer and looping bird or chondelle – and yet they are all different. This is why sporting clays is occasionally referred to as "golf with a shotgun," most certainly referring to the diversity of opportunity one encounters on a course. Except for the loud "bang" after one pulls the trigger, the description is appropriate. No other shotgun game matches the mixed bag of shots, speeds, distances and angles one sees in sporting clays.

The variety of possible loads is one reason that some sporting shooters end up with pockets full of shells. "Oops, I thought I put the #9s in the left pocket and the #8s in the right pocket and the #7-1/2s in my …. Aargh! Where are the #7-1/2s?" Your #9s may still have enough concentrated BBs in its shot string, but not enough dynamic energy left to break a 50-yard crossing shot, but for a quick 15-yarder, the #7-1/2s are not normally the best load either. So, what this all means is that with courses often a mile long, this option for shell diversity becomes a boon to bag and cart manufacturers.

Here is how the NSCA regulates your shooting for competition. A 12 gauge, the maximum size officially allowed, may not have more than 1-1/8 ounces of shot; a 20 gauge no more than 7/8 ounce; a 28 gauge, 3/4 ounce; and a 410 shell is to be no more than 2-1/2 inches in length with 1/2 ounce of shot. The smallest lead shot allowed is #9 (diameter 0.08 inch) while the largest is a #7-1/2 (0.095-inch). The smallest steel shot allowed is #9 (nominal diameter of 0.08 inch) while the largest is #6 (0.110 inch). Reloads are fine unless specified and publicized otherwise at a particular shoot. Plated shot is permitted. (European standard sizes differ slightly from American standard sizes.)

For FITASC shooting, ammo specifications are slightly different. First, no reloaded shells or spreader loads are allowed in competition. No barrel shorter than 26 inches long, no gauge larger than 12 and no shell loaded with more than 1-1/4 ounces of shot (36 grams) are permitted. FITASC specifies shells with pellets from 2.0 to 2.5 mm in diameter, which roughly corresponds to the American sizes from #7 to #10 (which is darn near birdshot).

Some shooters tame the load selection problem caused by widely varying distances to their target with a variety of chokes. With the diversity of loads and chokes, there is no reason that the well-prepared shotgunner cannot cover with an effective string of shot any bird thrown. Using combinations of chokes and loads, the variety of patterns you can throw at a bird, while not infinite, is practically endless.

With enough practice, you will find what works best for you and your gun. That may be carrying multiple loads or multiple chokes or, like Wendell Cherry, you may settle on one particular, simple combination that works best for you on all targets. Because most shotguns use single triggers today but have a switch that allows the shooter to choose which barrel fires first, one's options are even more extensive as barrels are typically choked differently.

This all becomes important on a shooting venue. For our normal "English sporting" events, the NSCA specifies that barrels and chokes may only be changed "between stations." In other words, you cannot proceed to your stand, see the birds and then step out and change chokes. In NSCA 5-Stand, you may not change chokes "once a round has begun," presumably after the first shot has been fired by a member of your squad. In this regard, FITASC is slightly more liberal than the American rules, as changing chokes or barrels "is allowed during the same round, between two stands or between single or double targets." Internationally, the emphasis is on a level playing field and a smooth, speedy game.

TAKING THE SHORT-RANGE SHOT

Ten- to 20-yard shots are not at all uncommon on a sporting clay course, and the running rabbit will certainly cross within that range. You will not get to pull the trigger on a bird under 10 or 12 yards unless you are very fast at the mechanical skills of mounting, finding your lead, aiming and executing the shot, or shoot from the now-legal, pre-mounted position.

For short range shooting, one normally takes shots within skeet range, which gives the parameters needed to choose an effective shell and choke. Perhaps you could shoot any legal shell at such short range, #7 1/2s to #9s, but the close distance pretty well dictates that little will be gained by using any shot size other than #9. The 12 gauge is allowed a maximum of 1-1/8 ounces of shot, with the 20 gauge carrying 7/8 ounce, the 28 holding 3/4 ounce and the 410 only 1/2 ounce.

[Although shotgunners seem to be rediscovering the 16 gauge and manufacturers are responding to that renewal of interest, sporting clay rules from the NSCA do not mention the gauge. Then again, this handy-sized smoothbore is also ignored by skeet, trap and international rules committees. Nevertheless, for this chapter we will make an effort to pinpoint opportunities for 16-gauge use and identify ammo for it.]

Since #9 shot will reliably break any target inside 25 yards, it has become the almost universal choice for close-range shooting. With a pellet count of about 585 pellets per ounce (Winchester standard shot size), that gives a 1 1/8-ounce 12-gauge load a pellet count of over 650 chunks of lead. The 20-gauge shell packs 510, while the 28 gauge and 410 load 435 and 292, respectively. This means a 3/4-ounce #9 load for a 28 gauge is sending quite a few more pellets to do the job than say Wendell Cherry's 1 1/8-ounce load of Lyalvale #7 1/2s, which carries only 390.

The close shots that may bedevil #9s are those that a shooter allows to fly out to 25 yards and the course manager's deviously planned, on-edge running rabbits. Although the rabbit target is the same diameter as a standard 108-110-mm clay, the pitch is molded sturdier, especially at the edges to give it the strength to bounce and roll across a shooting lane without fracturing. Rabbits are also thinner or show about half the profile compared to a standard clay, 13 mm versus 25 mm. This will not matter on a clay thrown perpendicularly, but if it is thrown at an angle away from the shooting stand so that you see less of its flat surface, you may want to choose a larger shot size to cope with the bird's greater density.

For close shots, you want a pattern that opens quickly, overwhelming the flying bird with pellets. Nothing feels better or looks more impressive than to have a bird vaporize before your eyes. So for most of us, #9s with an open choke is still the favorite choice, as it delivers the highest pellet count per shell.

"I'm shooting behind them? Are you sure?" Sometimes the short-range crossing shots can be the most difficult. The 10- to 20-yard hard crosser can surprise you if you are not prepared to move your gun quickly, but smoothly, to your shoulder. If the butt pad hangs on your vest for a split second, consider it a miss.

Few things are more satisfying than saving money. It is the allure of discount marts. Good or bad, saving money sort of defines us as Americans. Before you get to the point of feeling a financial pinch from spending on your shooting habit, try building your own shotshells. You can save money, become more fully engaged in the sport, and you will take pride in the success of your shells and your chosen formulas.

It is often argued that for close shooting, soft, cheap shot is just fine. These are the 1-ounce loads marked "Dove & Quail" that you find by the ton at your local mass merchant before each bird season opens. Referred to as "promotional loads," these shells are not packed with the precision-formed pellets found in high-end and more expensive target loads. Typically, the pellets will be soft, but fast enough. The resulting pellet deformation during their trip through the barrel actually helps fill in a pattern that is generally regarded as "loose" by the industry. And that is just right for what you are trying to accomplish at short range, out perhaps to 25 yards.

KILLING INTERMEDIATE AND "HAIL MARY" BIRDS

Intermediate distance is one thing for one shooter and something different for another. Nevertheless, although there is no precise moment where a flying clay disk switches from one category to another, intermediate birds are usually thought of as 25- to 35- or 40-yard targets. Think of them as falling just beyond the extended range for skeet, but about normal for trap or wobble trap. In fact, most of the birds you will see on a well-maintained sporting course fall within this range, and shells to accommodate your desire to powder them are easy to find.

Loads for trap shooting are absolutely appropriate here. Within this yardage, your 1-1/8 ounces of #8 (or even #7-1/2) BBs are the go-to load. At the close end of the range or even out to 35-40 yards, if you place your swarm of pellets around it effectively, a 1-ounce load of #8-1/2s will probably work just fine. They should at least have plenty of target-breaking power to 35 yards. On the longer shots, you should switch to #8s, which will be your friend to 40 yards with their increased number of pellets.

Beyond 40 yards, our Alabama All-American Wendell Cherry's preferred load of 3-dram #7-1/2s are most certainly correct for us recreational shooters. These are often called "heavy trap loads." On the closer side, a 2 3/4-dram load of #7-1/2s will work fine, too. Many manufacturers specify ultra-hard shot in fast cartridges for these ranges, which means pellets with relatively high antimony[1] content.

Because 45-yarders are difficult shots to make without a lot of focused practice, there is continuing discussion among shotgunners about the best load for long-range birds. Many argue that with proper shooting technique and practice estimating lead, the standard 2 3/4-dram, 1 1/8-ounce, #7-1/2 load will do just fine. Others recommend stepping up to a faster international trap load, some of which appear to be in the 1400-plus-fps class measured at the muzzle with down-range or

Beyond 40 yards, All-American Wendell Cherry's preferred load of 3-dram, #7-1/2s may be the best-all-around load. These are often called "heavy trap loads."

Floyd "Wimpy" Lampman developed Wimpy's Wobble Trap, essentially registering wobble trap scores taken both from the 16-yard trap line (48 feet) and from the "3/4-Deck" at 35 feet from the trap house. Several dozen clubs around the United States participate and sell Wimpy's own brand of ammo.

"observed velocities" falling to near 1200 fps. Although the international load only has 24 grams of #7-1/2 shot (about 7/8 ounce), they often use special shotcups and plated pellets for tight patterns, even at long range. A cloud of fast-moving pellets with a relatively short shot string helps cut down the long leads required for shots out to extreme distances.

Acclaimed student of shotshell performance, Tom Roster, says that when comparing loads, velocities and shell effectiveness for any task, it is important to remember that all measurements are not the same. American manufacturers tend to report shot velocity 3 feet in front of the muzzle. This is called "instrumental velocity," and it is simply an agreed-upon point at which the chronograph is set-up. European manufacturers, however, often give velocities at the actual muzzle. The difference, Roster reports, can be as much as 100 fps!

When it comes to breaking "Hail Mary" targets, the most effective shells may be those with nickel-plated shot. These, however, are significantly more expensive than shells with lead shot, but you will not need many of them in a round and a couple boxes could last all year unless you shoot a game like Make-A-Break, which specializes in frustrating shooters by setting up long, difficult target presentations. When you need it, plated shot is well worth the extra cost.

Once you begin shooting shotgun games, you need to consider a specialized pouch, bag or box to carry your shells. Otherwise, you run the risk of looking like a newbie or a downright goober ... and who wants that?

FACTORY AMMUNITION
Baschieri & Pellagri

Settimio Baschieri and Guido Pellagri began working together in 1885 to develop a smokeless powder, and they accomplished their task within a year. They founded an independent company 5 years later. Curiously, the first military use of smokeless powder came during the Boer War (1899-1902) when the British, spurred by multi-millionaire developer Cecil Rhodes, invaded the independent state of South Africa. The Dutch resident farmers, called the Boers, had imported German firearms and Italian smokeless ammunition and gave the Brits a rather huge surprise before their families were herded into concentration camps and their small armies overwhelmed.

Now, 115 years after the founders began working together, Baschieri & Pellagri (www.baschieri-pellagri. com) sells a small, but well-thought-of line of ammo for 12, 20 and 28 gauges in #7-1/2, #8 and #9. B&P claim to be Italy's only producer of powders.

Clay Cartridge Co.

It's not the largest company in business, but UEE/ Clay (www.claycartridge.com) is well represented in competition with 12-, 20- and 28-gauge shells. Clay manufactures all components of its shotshells (called integrated production) and loads its shells as well. U.S. offices are in Camden, SC.

Clay Cartridge offers two lines of shells, its Competition (12, 20, 28) and Premium (12-gauge high-base only) loads. The 12-gauge Competition loads are available with #7-1/2, #8 and #8-1/2 shot in 1 1/8-ounce or reduced-recoil 1-ounce grams equivalent; 20 and 28 gauges are only #8. There is a 1 3/16-ounce load of #7-1/2s designated for FITASC competition in the Premium line.

Clever

Clever is imported from Verona, Italy, (www.clevervr. com) and its numerous shotshell sizes and loads are quickly becoming one of the staple shells seen at big tournaments, either English sporting or FITASC. Clever's Mirage brand offers 12-gauge 2 3/4-inch loads in #7-1/2, #8 and #9 shot in 24 (7/8 ounce), 28 (1 ounce) and 32 (1-1/8 ounces) grams. At this time, they have one load of 20-gauge 2 3/4-inch shells in 7/8 and 1 ounce.

Clever notes that it produced 12 million shotshells its first year in business, 1960. Today, it markets more than 10 times that number.

Eley Hawk

Eley Hawk is an old manufacturing name in England, but new to U.S. shooting. Eley (www.eleyhawkltd.com) says it is capable of producing "well in excess of 10,000 cartridges per hour" at their factory in Minworth, Sutton Coldfield, England.

When you get involved in competition, you realize there are many types of shells other than the ones you buy cheap at the local *BoxMart*. Take time to study these shells, because they may very well pattern better than what you are shooting, and you may even be able to find reloading specifications for them.

Eley has eight lines of clay target cartridges, each designed in a slightly different configuration: Eley First (an entry-level cartridge ideal for the price-conscious shooter), Eley Blues (a low-recoil club cartridge), Eley Superb Competition (a fast low-recoil high-antimony magnum shot for distance), Eley VIP (ultra-hard professional-caliber shot), Eley VIP Sporting (a "fine fiber wad cartridge" for speed and low recoil) and Eley Competition Trap (20 gauge). Several European manufacturers, and Eley is one of them, list the percentage of antimony in each load selection and the type of wad, plastic or "fibre," something not found in American catalogs.

There is not an #8-1/2 in the Eley line-up, but there are plenty of #9s. The 2-3/4 Eley Superb with 16-mm head and plastic wad has 5 percent antimony in its 1 1/8-ounce loads of #7, #7-1/2 and #8. Muzzle velocity is 1450 fps while "observed velocity" is 1130 fps.

Eley does not chart 28 or 410, but does have a few selections for 2 3/4-chambered 20-gauge guns in 3/4- and 7/8-ounce loads. These #7-1/2, #8 and #9, 3-percent antimony shot loads are called Competition Trap or CT shells.

The 12-gauge Eley Superb Competition, chambered in a 2 3/4-inch shell, offers a 1 1/8-ounce load of #7, #7-1/2 or #8. The wad is plastic and the "head" measures

16 mm. With 5 percent antimony, this hard shot has a muzzle velocity of 1450 fps and an "observed velocity" of 1130 fps. Eley says the VIP is designed for "smooth recoil and unrivalled speed."

Estate

Estate Cartridge (www.estatecartridge.com) is a division of Federal Cartridge in Anoka, Minnesota. Their 12-gauge #GTL12 and 20-gauge #GTL20 Game and Target Load is their inexpensive line of shells in #7-1/2, #8 and #9 with a hardness that Estate rates as "magnum." The 12-gauge shell uses 3-1/4 drams for 1290 fps with 1 ounce of shot. The 20-gauge shell uses 2-1/2 drams for 1210 fps with 7/8 ounce. (This load is also available in #6.)

Estate is a division of Federal Cartridge. Shells in this line are available in all standard sporting loads plus a 1 1/4-ounce FITASC and 7/8-ounce reduced-recoil 12-gauge load.

The Estate Competition Target and Flyer loads offer #7-1/2, #8, #8-1/2 and #9 in 2 3/4-inch shells. This line has a couple of "Mighty Light" loads for shooters who are sensitive to recoil, offering a 12-gauge shell with 7/8 ounce at 1250 fps and a 20-gauge shell at 3/4 ounce (21 grams) for 1220 fps. The three Competition Flyer loads are packed with 1-1/4 ounces of shot for FITASC shooting.

Estate has seven Super Sport Target 2 3/4-inch shells, six for the 12 gauge and one for the 20. They rate this shot hardness as "extra hard" and offer three 1 1/8-ounce and three 1-ounce loads, each with different speed ratings and power powders.

Federal Cartridge

Minnesota-based Federal Cartridge (www.federalcartridge.com) has been making at least one of everything since about 1916. It was purchased by ATK (Alliant Techsystems) in 2001 and today manufactures loads for every size smoothbore: 10, 12, 16, 20, 28 and 410.

For effective short-range shooting, you can find a Federal load of #9s or #8-1/2s in all competitive gauges: 12, 20, 28 and 410.

In the 12-gauge shell, there is much to choose from in the Premium Gold and Top Gun lines. A standard 2-3/4 offering such as T116 will give you 1200 fps with 1-1/8 ounces of #9, but to save your shoulder, you might want to drop down to a 1-ounce load in T113 or T175, both of which, at 1180 fps, are plenty fast. For #8-1/2, look to Federal's T113 (1-ounce, 1180 fps) or T114 (1 1/8-ounce, 1100 fps: an Extra Lite, shoulder-saving load).

Federal has a shell for each sub-gauge in Premium Gold. The 2-3/4 T206 for 20-gauge guns loads 7/8 ounce of #8s or #9s at 1200 fps. (This shell is also offered in the Top Gun Target line as the new TG20 at 1210 fps.) The 2-3/4 T280 for the 28 gauge is 3/4 ounce of #8-1/2 or #9 at 1230 fps. The 2-3/4 T412 for the 410 is 1/2 ounce of #8-1/2 or #9 at 1230 fps.

For longer-range clay busting, look for shells in standard trap sizes, #7-1/2 and #8. Federal has a dozen cartridge possibilities in its Premium Gold Medal Target line and three in the Top Gun Target line. Shot speeds range from 1145 fps to 1235 fps for a couple of special, long-range "handicap trap" loads that are designed to reach out effectively from the 27-yard line.

Federal maintains its paper shells, due perhaps to continuing demand from reloaders: N119 (24-gram, #7-1/2), T117 (1 1/8-ounce, #7-1/2, #8, #9), T118 (1 1/8-ounce, #7-1/2, #8, #9), T171 (1 1/8-ounce, #7-1/2, #8), T171 (Low Recoil: 1 1/8-ounce, #7-1/2, #8) and T175 (1 1/8-ounce, #7-1/2, #8, #9).

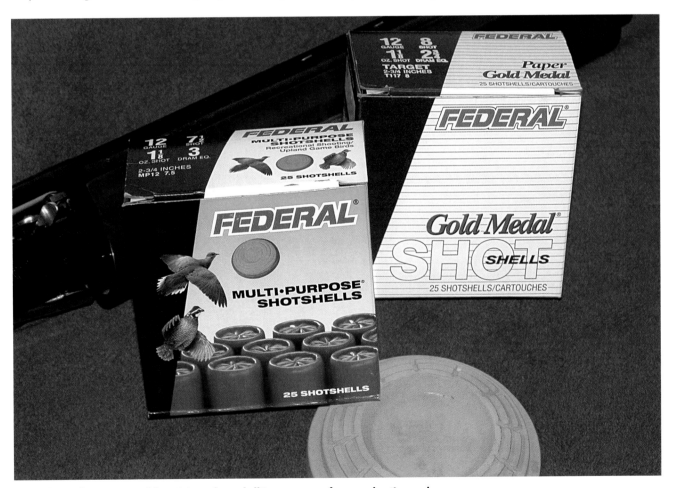

Federal Cartridge, now part of the ATK Group, has a shell in every gauge for every shooting need.

Fiocchi

Manufactured in Ozark, Missouri, since 1986 and in Italy since 1876, Fiocchi (www.fiocchiusa.com) has a range of hard, uniform shot designed with functional, one-piece plastic wads.

Fiocchi's sub-gauge loads are very specific. The 2 3/4-inch 20-gauge load uses 7/8 ounce of #7-1/2, #8 or #9 high-antimony lead pellets, while the 28 and 410 come in #8 and #9 only. All three loads achieve 1200 fps.

In 12 gauge, there are a dozen possibilities. In 1-ounce 2-3/4 high-antimony lead loads, Fiocchi offers four shells graduated in velocity from light to heavy. These are the 12TL Target Light (1150 fps, 2 3/4-dram in #7-1/2, #8, #8-1/2, #9), 12TH Target Heavy (1200 fps, 3-dram in #7-1/2, #8, #8-1/2), 12TX Little Rino (1250 fps, "handicap load" in #7-1/2, #8, #8-1/2) and 12CRSR Crusher (1300 fps, "maximum load" in #7-1/2, #8, #8-1/2, #9). With minor differences, the same type shell progression is available in 1 1/8-ounce loads.

Fiocchi specifies four 12-gauge, 2 3/4-inch lead loads for "the high volume and discriminating shooter." The 12MS3 holds 3 drams and 1 ounce of shot in #7-1/2, #8 and #9 for 1250 fps. Their 12MS118 lowers the powder to 2-3/4 drams, but raises the shot to 1-1/8 ounces with a resultant speed of 1150 fps.

Two "low recoil trap loads" in #7-1/2 and #8 use high-antimony content lead and are suitable for longer-range shots. The 2-3/4 drams achieves 1140 fps with 1-1/8 ounces of shot, while the 3-dram load achieves 1185 fps.

Hull Cartridge

It is curious how large enterprises often begin from odd sources, how it is not so much inspiration, but, as Thomas Edison is reported to have said, perspiration that achieves great results. Hull Cartridge has its roots in 1924 when England's Sydney Bontoft was peddling calcium carbide to manufacturers to generate acetylene gas for welding and to farmers for lighting. On touring the farms, he "realized there was a demand for shotshells" and so added them to his line. "Seeing the possibilities of expansion, he commenced the manufacture of loaded shotshells," the Hull Internet site claims. In 1947, Hull Cartridge was formed. Perspiration AND inspiration.

Hull Cartridge (www.hullcartridge.co.uk) is located in Kingston-upon-Hull, England. Their Sovereign High Performance and Pro One 12-gauge 2 3/4-inch competition loads are most widely known in the United States. These shells contain 5-percent antimony and are rated above 1500 fps (although that rating is probably measured at the muzzle rather than 3 feet in front of the muzzle as is the U.S. custom). In the Sovereign line, you will find shells in #7-1/2, #8 and #9 loaded variously in 7/8, 1 and 1-1/8 ounces. The Pro One line is similar, and the Pro One DTL300 is specifically designed as a reduced-recoil alternative at 1400 fps.

Kent Cartridge

Kent Cartridge of Ontario, Canada, has absorbed the Activ and Gamebore lines of shotgun shells. Kent offers excellent 12-gauge loads in full 1 1/8-ounce and reduced-recoil 1-ounce loads. Its 20-gauge shells are a full ounce or reduced to 7/8 ounce to minimize recoil with scarcely a difference in effectiveness.

Established in 1996, Kent Cartridge of Ontario, Canada, has already purchased Activ (West Virginia) and Gamebore (England) (www.kentgamebore.com). Kent was founded to develop a "non-toxic shotshell to equal or exceed high-quality lead shot for waterfowl." Their Tungsten Matrix shot contains, Kent says, the "only true alternative to lead." Nevertheless, it is the lead in their Diamond Shot All Purpose line that is specifically designed for clay shooting.

Kent's 2 3/4-inch Diamond Shot is available with #8 and #9 shot, but only in 12 and 20 gauges. Their new 12-gauge K122GT32 in #7-1/2, #8 and #9 is loaded at 1-1/8 ounces and 2-3/4 drams. At 1145 fps, it is sufficient for short-range shooting. Dropping down 1/8 ounce to the K122GT28 in all sizes will raise your speed to 1200 fps and give your shooting shoulder a small rest. In 20 gauge, both 1-ounce (#6, #7-1/2, #8) and 7/8-ounce (#7-1/2, #8, #9) shells are offered with 2-1/2 drams.

The Kent 12-gauge line of 2 3/4-inch All Purpose shells offers several shot sizes (#7-1/2, #8, #9), ounces of shot (1, 1-1/8) and drams (2-3/4, 3). Velocities (in fps) range from 1145 (1-1/8 ounces, 2-3/4 drams) to 1290 (1 ounce, 3-1/4 drams).

PMC (Precision Made Cartridges)

Headquartered in Nevada, PMC (www.pmcammo.com) does not currently offer an #8-1/2 shell, but they have plenty of #8 and #9. Their Field & Target Specific loads are offered in a Bronze Line and all gauges are covered.

For the 12 gauge, PMC's FT128 #8s and FT129 #9s are chronographed at 1230 fps with 1-1/8 ounces of lead and a 3-ounce dram of powder. PMC achieves their "High Velocity" loads by reducing the amount of shot from 1-1/8 to 1 ounce. This bumps up rated speeds to 1250 fps.

If you are shooting a 20 gauge, you have a choice of #7-1/2, #8 and #9 shells at 1230 fps. All are loaded with 7/8 ounce and 2-1/2 drams. The 28 gauge and 410 are equally served at 1220 fps in #7-1/2, #8 and #9 in the FT loads. (In their Gold line, PMC really loads up their sub-gauges with shot and powder. For instance, their HV419 for 410 is 3 inches long and carries 1-1/16 ounces of #9, shooting 1135 fps.)

According to PMC, their DymaFlex one-piece plastic wad flexes and cushions your shot on firing, and its integral shot cup completely encloses and protects shot from deformation during its trip through the barrel. The result is shot that flies true for better, denser patterns.

Remington

Some names are synonymous with America's shooting heritage and Madison, North Carolina's Remington Arms (www.remington.com) is certainly one of them. Remington's lineup for the shotgun is extensive in its Premier STS (Skeet-Trap-Sporting) and economical Gun Club lines.

The economy Gun Club line has three 12-gauge 2 3/4-inch shells. The 2 3/4-inch GC12L has 2-3/4 drams and 1-1/8 ounces of #7-1/2, #8 or #9 for 1145-fps shots. The GC121 is loaded with 1 ounce of #8 and boosts velocity to 1185 fps. Finally, the GC12 is hyped to 3 drams in #7-1/2 and #8 for a 1200-fps shot string. They offer one option for the 20 gauge: GC20, 7/8 ounce, 2-1/2 drams, 1200 fps. Remington says the Gun Club line allows many shooters to get "acceptable reloading life while stretching their shooting dollar."

The Premier STS line is available for all gauges with extra-hard, target-quality shot. In 12-gauge loads, you can buy it in standard, low-recoil and handicap versions in #7-1/2 and #8, but only occasionally in #8-1/2 and #9. Rated velocities measured at 3 feet from the muzzle

Remington's Sport Loads are economical, multi-purpose shells. They are built with premium Power Piston wads and plastic, Uni-body hulls. Loaded with #8 shot - 1 ounce for the 12 gauge and 7/8 ounce for the 20 - these loads are ideal for field and for all clay shooting games.

range from 1100 fps (STS12LR) in a light, 2-3/4 drams, to the Premier STS International (STS12IT) at 1325 fps with 7/8 ounce of #7-1/2 or #8-1/2 and 3-1/4 drams! Remington says its STS is the "most reloadable shell you can shoot."

In sub-gauges, Remington has several loads for the 20, 28 and 410. The 2-3/4 STS20LR is packed with 2-1/2 drams and 7/8 ounce of #8 or #9 at 1135 fps. The 20-gauge STS20H shell has an ounce of #9 and spits shot out at 1200 fps. In 28-gauge shells, look for #8 (STS28SC) or #9 (STS28), each at 1200 fps with 3/4 ounce of shot and 2 drams. For the 410, Remington's 1200 fps offerings are in #8-1/2 and #9 with 1/2 ounce of lead and a powder charge labeled "maximum."

Rio Ammunition

Headquartered in Houston, Rio (www.rioammo.com) imports shotshells from Álava, Spain. Rio's 2 3/4-inch 12-gauge #9 skeet loads with 2 3/4 drams (1210 fps) are fine for short distance clays. Load #24 has 7/8 ounce, Load #28 has 1 ounce and Load #32 (1150 fps) has 1-1/8 ounces. Loads in #8-1/2 are not available, but #8s are plentiful. Rio says their standard target loads feature a 3-percent antimony alloy while their top target loads have 5 percent.

The "Top Trap" #32 is rated at 1250 fps for longer-distance shooting. Top Trap/Sporting rounds are mixed with a 5-percent antimony alloy rather than the standard 3 percent.

A 2 3/4-inch load is available for smaller gauges as well in #7-1/2, #8 and #9. The 20 gauge is loaded with 7/8 ounce (1250 fps), the 28-gauge with 3/4 ounce (1300 fps) and the 410 with 1/2 ounce (1200 fps).

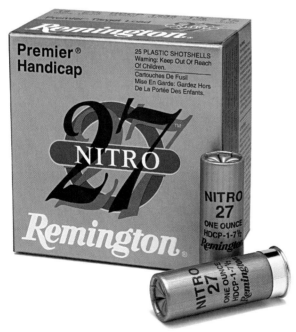

Remington's 12-gauge Premier Nitro 27 is designed for long-yardage shots in trap or clays. It is available in 2 3/4-inch shells with 1-1/8 ounces of #7-1/2 or #8 at 1235 fps or a reduced-recoil 1-ounce load of #7-1/2 or #8 at 1290 fps.

Winchester

This Alton, Illinois, company (www.winchester.com) has been building shotshells since 1886. Today, the Winchester/Olin Double A (AA) high-strength and economical Super-Target (TRGT) loads are standard at any shooting line.

While many of the 12-gauge AA loads are offered in #9, the company does not at this time offer any #9s in its economical Super-Target line. You can choose AA SuperSports, but the hotter powder and speedier shot (1300 fps minimum) is not necessarily a short-range asset. There is no special reason that a single designated shell, the AAL12 Xtra-Lite in either 1 ounce of #8-1/2 or #9, should not be a fine load, however, for short-range challenges. At 1180 fps, it is fast enough, and it will be easier on the shoulder than the AA12 (1145 fps), which carries 1-1/8 ounces of shot.

Winchester has easy-to-remember designations for its sub-gauge shells, which are all rated at 1200 fps. The 2-3/4 AA20 for 20-gauge guns loads 2-1/2 drams equivalent with 7/8 ounce of #9. The 2-3/4 AA28 packs 2 ounces of powder with 3/4 ounce of #8 or #9. The 2-1/2 AA41 packs the maximum powder charge and 1/2 ounce of #9s.

Winchester's AA hard-shot target loads were introduced about 40 years ago and the suggested retail price is about $7.90 per box of 25 shells or 32 cents per shot for the more common loads. Shells with the "HS" or high-strength designation are "superbly reloadable," Winchester says. All of the standard loads are present in the AA line from a 2 3/4-inch shell as straightforward as the AA127 with 2-3/4 drams and 1-1/8 ounces of #7-1/2 shot (1145 fps) to a fast 1350-fps load and 7/8 dram international load.

In the 1 1/8-ounce Super-Target 12-gauge shotshell line, Winchester has designed two value-priced shells in #7-1/2 and #8. The 3-dram shells are rated at 1200 fps while the 2-3/4s are rated at 1145 fps. Super-Target shotshells are designed for "high-volume, cost-conscious shooters" who do NOT want to reload. Suggested retail price is $5.70 per box or 23 cents per shell.

Wolf

Wolf Performance Ammunition (www.wolfammo.com) based in Anaheim, California, imports rifle, pistol, rimfire and shotshell ammunition. The shotshells have recently come from Spain's S.A.G.A. in Lerida (see www.globalshot.com).

For much of my summer sporting clay shooting during the development of this book, I relied on Wolf's "Target Sport Shotshells," 1-1/8 ounces of #7 1/2s, and a Weatherby SSC Orion over/under. With a muzzle velocity of 1360 fps, these Spanish shells feature high antimony content for good clay-breaking ability at a distance.

Although Wolf does not import #8 1/2s, they have several alternate loads for short-range shooting. In the Target Sport series, their designated 1360-fps 2 3/4-inch sporting clays shell only comes with 1-1/8 ounces of #7-1/2 or #8. Smaller, #9 shot is available with a slower-burning powder in a separate load that yields 1145 fps. A softer-shooting 1-ounce load is also available.

All sub-gauge loads are available in #8 and #9 for the 20 and 28 gauges. For the 410 or 36-gauge, Wolf offers loads of #9 (2 1/2-inch, 1/2-ounce, 1200 fps) and #7-1/2 (3-inch, 11/16-ounce, 1135 fps).

Some Wolf shells in early 2003 used roll crimps rather than the more standard star-crimps to seal their ends. As roll crimps tend to make the unfired shell slightly longer, some confusion arose about their actual length and a few shotgunners reported that they could not fully load field ammo, as the slightly longer shells took up more room in the tube magazine. Remember that shotshell length, 2 3/4- or 3-inch or whatever, is a measure of a fired hull, not the unfired hull. My latest Wolf 12-gauge Target Sport 2 3/4-inch shells with 1-1/8 ounces of #8s used conventional star crimps, and unfired, they measured 2-1/4 inches long.

FOOTNOTES

[1] A note about *antimony:* Known since ancient times, antimony (chemical symbol Sb) is today used in varying amounts from 3 to perhaps 7 percent to harden and increase the mechanical strength of lead shot. Antimony is produced as a by-product of reducing "stibnite" with iron scrap. About half the antimony used in the United States is recovered from lead-based battery scrap metal. It is toxic as an airborne fume.

According to the Sporting Arms and Ammunition Manufacturers Institute (SAAMI), the word "hard," as applied to lead shot, means that the pellets must have only 1/2 percent or more of antimony. Of course, this is a voluntary guideline and may or may not be followed in fact, or even in advertising, by shot producers. To be truly hard, lead shot in sporting clays sizes needs at least 6-percent antimony content.

Curiously, the more antimony you add to make harder and harder shot, the more difficult the manufacturing process becomes, and the less you can be guaranteed true, round spherical shot. If you cut open a shell and find that the shot rolls straight and uniform across the table or your kitchen counter, you can probably assume A.) that it is round and B.) that it is a relatively soft shot with little or no antimony content.

THE RIGHT FIT FOR THE JOB

"A fitted gun is one that points exactly where your eyes are looking when all you do is raise it to your cheek without moving your head." Michael McIntosh

Even expensive guns must be fitted to the owner. Once you learn the fundamentals, if you are a serious shotgunner, you will make two decisions: find a good instructor who can help you achieve the level of shooting that will make you happy and take your shotgun to a gunfitting specialist for those small things that separate champions from ordinary competitors.

ELEMENTS OF A GOOD CLAYS GUN

Hmmmm. Is it possible for you (or anyone) to pick up any shotgun and expect to shoot well with it? Like a car, perhaps – just get in and drive without giving it a second thought? But even in a car, before you turn on the ignition and pull away from the curb, you first adjust the mirrors and seats, maybe move the steering wheel up and down, back and forth, and pump the brakes a couple times. Then you set the radio to your favorite music station, yell at the kids and, almost as an after-thought, put it in gear.

To shoot sporting clays well, you need a gun that is sized and fit to your frame. Now, almost any shotgun will do to bust a few pigeons, but to bust a lot of them, you either need to be very good or you need to be lucky with a good gun. Sporting clays is a tough game. Targets and angles are not standardized. Unlike skeet and trap, which after a few years you can almost shoot in your sleep – okay, perhaps that is not quite true, but you can certainly predict the angle, speed and path of every target – sporting is a challenge for the very best shooters in the world and to break a perfect round is almost unheard-of.

Everyone who shoots more than a couple rounds a month is concerned about the effects of recoil. Apparently, it is something we are aware of both consciously and sub-consciously. Consequently, every shooter has a recoil pad on the butt of his or her shotgun along with a thin, absorbent pad on their shirt or vest to help absorb or distribute recoil. Recoil can

A proper fitting will probably set your gun up with an adjustable comb and a shock-absorbing recoil pad. Neither is expensive and both will put you on a bird faster because they help you solve fitting difficulties.

quickly cause flinching and that causes missing. Flinch is a form of target panic, which is caused by anticipating the shot, being aware that the recoil is coming as soon as you pull the trigger.

Therefore, even though many venues today allow a pre-mounted gun – a bad error in judgment by the NSCA rules committees, in my humble opinion (caused by bean counters, people who want to count targets more than they want to have fun or learn to be a better shot) – most sporting clays are still shot with the gun butt clearly visible below the armpit. Thus, a recoil pad needs to slide up smoothly when you bring it to your shoulder. It must not hang up on your clothing and must not cause any fumbling or bumbling when the bird is in the air. Otherwise, you will miss. Period. Your gun must snap to your shoulder as crisply and mechanically as you can train yourself to move it.

Looking over the barrel, most shooters want a relatively flat-shooting gun, one that patterns 50/50 – half of your lead shot above the target and half below it, with an even distribution of pellets to each side. This percentage above and below is arguable in sporting clays, some shooters preferring a 60/40 shot profile. The reasons for the apparently unbalanced pattern are: A. we predominantly shoot at rising targets and B. most misses are behind a flying bird. Therefore, many students of the game argue it is generally better to have more shot pellets above and ahead of a bird … than below and behind!

Nevertheless, this is still different from trap for instance, where by general agreement something in the neighborhood of a 60/40 or even 65/35 ratio is preferred. You can work this out for your own shooting form and gun at the patterning board. If you cannot learn to instinctively adjust your point of aim and follow-through to achieve a best shooting ratio – and during the pressure to perform, most of us cannot – you can take your shooting iron to a gunsmith for comb or rib adjustment.

Most new guns come with a front bead sight and a mid-rib brass bead and these are easily removed and changed. The bead-sight arrangement is highly individual. Some shooters never consider changing the rib and bead. Others take the manufacturer's beads off immediately and replace them with one of a variety of aftermarket products.

Some very competent gunners prefer a no-bead rib or a stepped rib, arguing that if the gun is properly fit to your eyes and frame, all you need to do is see the target over or along the flat sighting plane of the rib. Look at the target and teach your body to follow suit is their contention. Looking at your beads is only a distraction, something to worry about at the very moment your subconscious mind should be free. "Are the beads properly aligned for the shot?" is not a question you should be asking when you are ready to pull the trigger.

This left-handed shotgunner appears to be standing squarely on both feet and scrunched over his stock. This shooting stance is not one that a coach would recommend unless the shooter has some physical difficulty that would prevent him from adopting a weight forward stance and bringing the stock and comb to his cheek, rather than bringing his cheek (and shoulders and back) to the stock.

These days, there is a shift back to long barrels for sporting clays, barrels in the 32- and even 34-inch range. Gun fitters argue that longer barrels give you a better "feel" for your swing and that the increased moment of weight actually helps you follow through. The argument about barrel length once centered around between-the-hands balance. A gun with a shorter barrel is lighter and faster to swing. It was argued that it consequently has a balance point nearer your eye and will therefore swing faster and more true to your sight picture. Whether you shoot gas guns or over/unders, it is now recognized that the extra weight forward and having the balance point farther out toward your leading, balancing hand is a good thing.

A ported barrel helps reduce muzzle jump. This means you are going to be able to get back on track for a second shot more efficiently if your barrel has a dozen or so small holes drilled to vent gases backward, than if your barrel is not ported. The positioning of the ports is in the neighborhood of 4 inches from the muzzle, which is sufficient distance from the chamber so that almost all of the powder burns before it reaches these tiny exhaust ports.

[The Weatherby Orion Sporting over/under, which I shot during the summer I worked on this book, is machined with 22 ports per 32-inch barrel, 11 on either side. Ports begin about 2-1/4 inches back from the muzzle and 3/4 inch behind the supplied, flush-mounted screw-in chokes. The ports in the top barrel are aligned in two rows – six on top, five on bottom. The ports in the bottom barrel are aligned in a single, straight row.]

Combine barrel porting with today's emphasis on custom trigger and barrel work – back-boring, lengthened forcing cones and longer chokes (which we discuss more thoroughly in the barrel chapter) – and you begin to move toward the complete, modern sporting clays shotgun: solid, but not heavy in the hand; smooth to swing and fast to react; and reliable if kept only modestly clean.

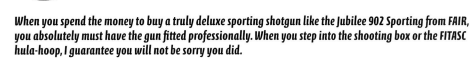

When you spend the money to buy a truly deluxe sporting shotgun like the Jubilee 902 Sporting from FAIR, you absolutely must have the gun fitted professionally. When you step into the shooting box or the FITASC hula-hoop, I guarantee you will not be sorry you did.

At the tip of your barrel, you may want extended, knurled chokes with their identifying names printed on the extended end. Because you occasionally change chokes (and loads) to adjust for different shot presentations on a sporting clays course, they should be easy to remove without tools. After all, you only want them finger tight. And to have to memorize a code … one slot for Full, two slots for … naah. Buy chokes that help you get the job done faster and easier, not chokes that give you something else to think about in the middle of a course.

FIRST THINGS FIRST: YOUR DOMINANT EYE

Just as we write, brush our teeth or eat with a fork right-handed or left-handed, we also have a dominant eye. It is sometimes referred to as our *master eye*. For most, hand and eye dominance are same-sided, but sometimes a right-handed person will have a dominant left eye and vice versa. This is an especially important concept in shooting. Hand-eye coordination is simplified if your dominant eye matches your dominant hand, but you can shoot your way to a World Championship with any combination by making a few adjustments … and without having a radical cross-over stock that is offset so far it places your off-hand (but dominant) eye on top of the rib.

There are two ways to determine your dominant eye:

Method One: Point your index finger at a distant object with both eyes open. Now, close your left eye. If your finger still appears to be pointing at the object, you most certainly have a dominant right eye. If your finger appears to shift to the side when you close your left eye, you probably have a dominant left eye. For confirmation, point again with both eyes open and then close your right eye. If, while you are looking with your left eye only, your finger still points at the object, you can feel certain that your left eye is dominant.

Method Two: An optional method that many people find less optically confusing uses both hands at the same time. First, place your hands together at arm's length from your eyes, palms facing out so you are viewing the backs of your hands. Now, touch the tips of your thumbs and forefingers and swivel your hands together so that the "V" between your thumbs and your forefingers forms a hole. Pick out some object on the far side of the room and center it in the hole. Slowly move your hands together so the hole becomes smaller and smaller and, while you are doing this, bring your hands and the hole back to your face. You should end up with the hole circumscribed by your hands in front of your dominant eye.

Finding your dominant eye may be step one in developing good shooting form. Effective shotgunning requires that you keep both eyes open, but your dominant eye needs to look straight down the barrel. The same visual techniques apply to shotguns and to archery.

There are two easy ways to find your dominant eye. One is a finger-pointing method and a second, the one illustrated in this picture, may be less visually confusing. This two-hand method focuses on an object across the room and by forming a small "O" using both hands, brings the "O" back to your face and your dominant eye.

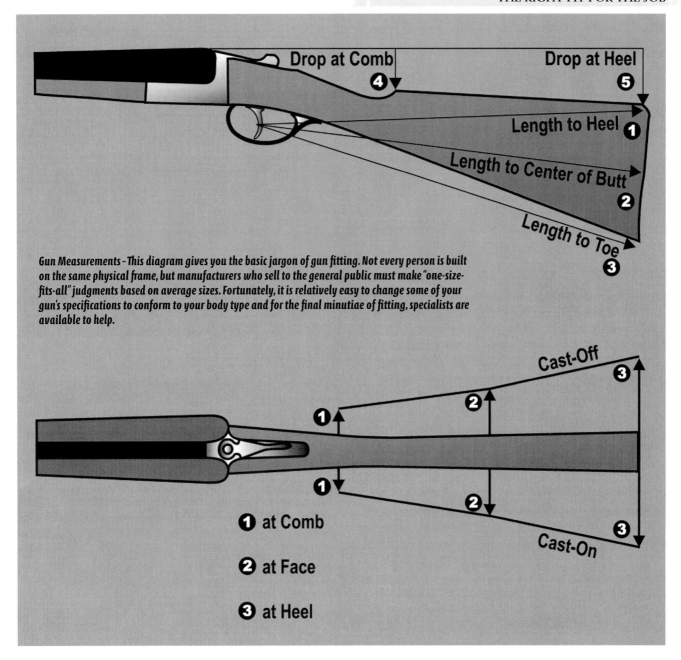

Gun Measurements – *This diagram gives you the basic jargon of gun fitting. Not every person is built on the same physical frame, but manufacturers who sell to the general public must make "one-size-fits-all" judgments based on average sizes. Fortunately, it is relatively easy to change some of your gun's specifications to conform to your body type and for the final minutiae of fitting, specialists are available to help.*

If you shoot a shotgun most effectively with both eyes open, pointing, not aiming, why should the concept of dominant eye be important? You have two eyes and the center of your pupils is about 2-1/2 to 3 inches apart depending on the width of your face. If you think about it, only one of those eyes is going to center itself in the middle of the 8- to 10-mm rib that runs the length of your shotgun barrel. The other eye simply tags along to help improve your depth perception; a handy concept for shooting moving targets at unknown distances, which is what sporting clays is all about.

This is the first element of proper fit. Everything else depends on aligning your dominant eye with the sighting plane of the rib. "Everything else" meaning making the stock of the gun conform to your physique, rather than making your physique conform to the stock.

"EVERYTHING ELSE"

Here is why fitting the gun to your body and not vice versa is important. A Browning Gold Sporting Clays semi-automatic comes with a nice walnut stock in these dimensions: 50-1/2 inches long with a 30-inch barrel, 14 1/4-inch length of pull, 1 1/2-inch drop at comb and 1 3/4-inch drop at heel. Since the general shooting public's sensibility has been raised about proper gun fitting, Browning includes a set of shims to adjust the height of the comb up or down 1/8 inch. Not only that, but the lady's version is built for smaller frames: 47-3/8 inches long with a 28-inch barrel and 13 1/2-inch length of pull.

Gun manufacturers like Browning who sell to the mass market understand that every man is not 5 feet 8 inches tall with a medium build. They know that every woman is not 5 feet 6 inches and 135 pounds. Some

Photo at *La Roue du Roy*, Hemmingford, Quebec courtesy Joe Potosky, The Lost Target www.lostarget.com.

Overall gun length matters when you bring a shotgun to your shoulder and cheek. For best shooting, you must smoothly and quickly bring a shotgun to full mount without having it snag on your shirt or shooting vest.

of us are tall and gaunt, while others are short and fat. Nonetheless, to keep the base price of a good-quality gun in the reasonable range – a new Browning Gold Sporting Clays semi-auto retails for about $1000 – gunmakers adopt reasonably average building standards, recognizing that as you become more proficient, you will make gun-fit adjustments for your frame. You will want to make their gun fit you, and as you step up to a finer and more expensive gun, this will become more important.

Length

The length of the shotgun is one of the least-understood measurements. It is the most obvious, however. What is most properly called length should perhaps be thought of as "length of pull," the distance from the trigger to the center of the buttstock, because even if a shotgun were 100 inches long, it would not necessarily matter as long as it fit well into your hands. (The only problem with a 100-inch gun being that the weight forward would prevent you from pointing it accurately, but if you ever got it swinging, watch out!)

Length matters when you raise a gun to your shoulder. You must smoothly and quickly bring a shotgun to full mount without having it snag on your shirt or shooting vest. You want the stock to cradle comfortably in the crease in your cheek; and you do not want to have your

cheek touching the base of your thumb. The gunstock must be long enough, overall, so that you do not curl your shoulder forward to meet it. It should simultaneously and comfortably nestle against your cheek and your shoulder without your having to scrunch around sideways, or tighten your elbow awkwardly, or lay your face at an extreme angle across the stock.

Your correct length of pull is probably somewhere within or near the comfort zone that manufacturers figure is between 14 and 14-1/2 inches. If you are taller than about 6 feet, you may want a little more distance there, perhaps an inch more, and it is relatively cheap and easy to add length to the buttstock with an extended recoil pad and some shims. If you are shorter than 5-1/2 feet, it is almost as easy to cut the stock to a shorter length, but before you cut the stock, remember the carpenter's rule: "Measure Twice. Cut Once."

A variety of adjustable pads are on the market and can be purchased from a local gunsmith, with or without installation, or direct from Brownells. The aluminum and rubber SpeedLock Adjustable Butt Plate, for instance, gives you full, four-way adjustment (1 3/4-inch length of pull; 3/4-inch drop at heel; up to 3 inches of comb adjustability; and 180-degree angle-of-stock rotation). The kit includes a black Pachmayr Presentation recoil pad and costs $144.95 plus shipping from Brownells.

Benelli says that the southpaw has been "the forgotten man of the shooting world." Their 12-gauge Montefeltro tosses the hull away from the left-hander's face and the safety button is conveniently placed on the rear of the trigger guard for the left hand.

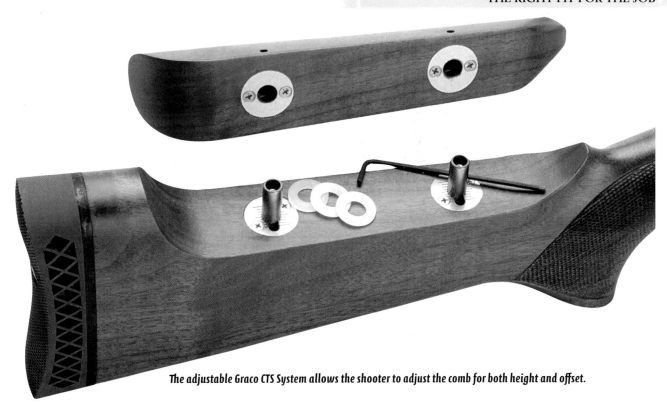

The adjustable Graco CTS System allows the shooter to adjust the comb for both height and offset.

Drop

If you lay a level on top of the sighting plane of your shotgun and carefully slide it toward the buttstock – or else lay the gun upside down on a flat table top, although to do this you must remove the bead sights – you can measure your gun's drop. Drop at comb is the vertical distance from the level to the peak of the comb. Drop at heel is the distance from the level to the tip of the buttstock.

Drop is a measure of the distance from the center of your dominant eye's pupil, which is on a plane with the sighting rib, to the "V" in your cheek where the stock nestles. It also measures the distance to the top of your shoulder, which in gun terms should be level with the top of the stock.

Quite a few sporting clays-class guns today are available with an adjustable-comb option. The Marocchi Model 99 (Grade I at $2995), for instance, offers a custom-fitted stock for an extra $530 and adjustable comb for $235. Otherwise, you can outfit your gun with a number of aftermarket items such as a Leather Lace-On Cheekpiece from Brauer Brothers ($22.50) for instant comb-height adjustment.

Cast

This is a term for angling the stock away from a line drawn from front to back of your gun through the center of the rib. You can think of cast as either "off" or "on." Cast-off angles the stock away from right-handers. Cast-on angles the stock away from left-handers.

It is relatively easy to make an educated guess about whether the cast is correct on a gun. Bring it smoothly and firmly, un-self-consciously if possible, to your cheek and shoulder. Now, ask yourself honestly if your dominant eye is looking straight down the rib without having to twist your head. If it is, the gun is about right. If not, chances are that you must still twist or rotate your head slightly over the top of the stock for proper eye alignment. In this case, your stock needs additional angle of cast.

A good gunsmith, one who can repair a trigger or lighten a spring, may not always be a good woodworker, and if adjusting the cast of your gun involves removing wood or making any fundamental alteration, you want to locate a specialist. Stocks can be permanently altered by removing wood from the side of the comb your cheek touches or by adding a permanent bend by heating it in a special stock-bending jig. This is not something you can do in the kitchen.

SKB 85TSS sporting clays 12-gauge guns are fitted with a 12-mm ventilated stepped rib. This rib has five center channel grooves bordered by two raised, matted surfaces. Sub-gauge guns are fitted with a smaller, 8.5-mm ventilated step rib.

Michael Murphy of Michael Murphy & Sons demonstrates how a professional fitter can alter stock measurements to your individual specifications.

When your dominant eye looks along the center of the rib, with your other eye open for depth perception and distance estimation, you have the ideal gun hold position. Now, ignore the beads and keep the clay in your mental shot picture.

Pitch

If you remember the straight line we drew from the front to the back of the gun along the rib or top of the barrel and stretch it out further in space, it will help us measure the angle of pitch. Pitch is the angle at which the butt of your gun is cut, compared to this straight line. You would ideally like the butt to fit snugly against your shoulder, but women usually prefer greater pitch to accommodate the structure of their chest.

Pitch can make a difference in whether you shoot high or low. If only the heel - the top part of the butt - naturally touches your shoulder, you will certainly shoot low because you will try to square the butt with your chest. If only the toe - the bottom part of the butt - naturally touches your shoulder, you will tend to shoot high for the same reason, just with opposite results.

A second way to measure pitch is to stand it flat on the floor with the receiver just touching the wall. If the muzzle stands away from the wall, this is called angle of pitch down. If the muzzle is flush with the wall, the pitch is zero or neutral. If the muzzle touches the wall, the butt is square on the floor and the receiver stands out from the wall, this is called negative pitch.

Most professional gun fitters, men like Michael Murphy in Kansas, say there is no reason to spend too much time taking the measurements of novice shooters. Although they can do it just as easily with a beginner as with a national champion, the shooter's technique must be firm before the fine points of fitting are going to work to their best advantage. It is a nice way to say that if you are only busting 40 out of 100 birds on a mile-long course, you have bigger things to worry about than 1/16 of an inch of cast-on or -off.

This is not to say that custom fitting is not important, just that the fundamentals come first: stance, raising the gun to your cheek bone, eye on the flying target, and good, clean follow-through. For a novice, time in the shooter's box or even a few hours of one-on-one coaching are more important than detailed and intricate fitting measurements. If you are a novice and can combine a good shooter's school weekend with a custom fitting, so much the better, but at this stage of your game, the individualized instruction is the most critical factor in moving your shooting to a higher level.

Michael Murphy of Michael Murphy & Sons says, "Shooters should regard a custom fitting as a complete physical, and have their stance, mount, weight distribution and eye dominance checked as part of the process. There are a lot of targets missed by one foot … and the one foot is that leading boot on the ground."

Having a custom gun such as the Spanish AYA built costs more than any gun off the rack and takes more time for your gun to be processed, by hand, at the custom shop. This can often take up to six months as the gunmakers work to build a stock and perhaps the rib or trigger to your personal dimensions and specifications.

11
Chapter

ALL ABOUT YOUR BARREL

A shotgun barrel is made in four basic sections. Your shot shell is seated in the *chamber*, which is physically connected with the forcing cone and the bore. When you pull the trigger and the shell's powder ignites almost explosively, the shot cup (wad) and the shot are shoved into the *forcing cone*. This is a short, conical section that necks the barrel bore down in size from the chamber (which accommodates the entire shell) to the bore (which must only accept what is inside the shell). Next comes the barrel *bore* itself, by far the longest section and the section in which the powder completes its burn.

Finally, toward the muzzle is the short *choke* section, which is responsible for shaping the shot pattern and helping separate the wad from the shot. Of course, not all shotguns in the past had a choke, or else were built with a fixed choke, and some had very short forcing cones, but those days are probably gone forever. In this chapter, we will spend most of our time discussing replaceable chokes and choke tubes since that is the current passion among competitive shotgunners.

A FEW BARREL IDEAS AND BARREL ISSUES

The Forcing Cone

The "forcing cone" is immediately in front of the chamber. It is a relatively short conical section of the barrel, which gradually tapers the barrel from the end of the chamber to the barrel diameter. The chamber holds the entire shell, but fires only what is inside the shell – the smaller-in-diameter shotcup and its load of pellets – into the bore. A shell that extends past the chamber will open into the forcing cone and thus the crimps will be destroyed. This will ruin your pattern, render the shell unusable for reloads and probably significantly increase felt recoil.

Today, it is thought that longer forcing cones are better for allowing your shot to transition from the shell to the bore. This means that there is also a better transition to the open air and your patterns are denser and more consistent. A longer forcing cone may also help reduce felt recoil, but whether this is true or not, the standard today is to move away from the older 1/2- to 5/8-inch forcing cone toward a tapered barrel section that is as much as 2 to 3 inches in length.

Backboring

A "backbored" or "overbored" barrel is nothing more than one that is larger than published SAAMI standards. A backbored 12 gauge, by standard open to .729 inches in diameter, may be backbored to .740. It is theorized that a wider open barrel allows the shot to travel more cleanly, with less deformity, down the length of the barrel. This should result in better patterning at any distance and shorten the length of your shot string.

With backbored barrels, your choke selection may need to be altered. A standard Modified constriction in a 12 gauge of .020 would give a .740 backbored barrel a diameter of .720 or only a constriction of .009. Small difference perhaps, but worth spending time at the patterning board before you are surprised at doubles with a springing teal and a crossing target to take at 40 yards!

"Over-boring is definitely a good thing," says Briley's Cliff Moller, "because it results in more even shot distribution, less recoil and more open patterns. Overall, this means better performance. As far as taming recoil is concerned, it is on a par with proper stock fit, porting and lengthening the forcing cone."

Keith Anderson at Anderson Custom Shotguns says that the purpose of lengthening forcing cones and backboring barrels is to reduce the friction of shot and wad passage after the powder ignites. Reducing turbulence in a barrel improves performance, Anderson says, but some shotguns will benefit from it and some will not. Before you rush to have the interior of your gun's barrel altered, it is best to have the gun professionally evaluated. This could save you hundreds of dollars and a lot of aggravation.

The breech on this Remington Model 332 over/under leads to a 3-inch chamber and immediately to the forcing cone. To load a breechloader, you insert a self-contained cartridge directly into the barrel's chamber.

Chrome-lined Barrels

Numerous shotguns have chromed barrels. The theory of a chromed barrel is based on two concepts:

• The thin chrome lining provides a slicker surface for your ejecta - the shot and wad - and therefore promotes full acceleration.

• The chrome resists pitting and is easier to keep clean.

Gunmaker Jack Rowe, a specialist in the repair of fine English shotguns and sporting arms, says that chroming a shotgun barrel is pointless. "Unlike a rifle barrel," Rowe says, "a shotgun barrel does not physically touch your shot, whether it is lead or steel, as it streams forward after you pull the trigger. The barrel is only in contact with the plastic wad or shot cup, which is very soft. How can there be any wear? I remember a shotgun that Eley in England said had a million rounds shot through it – or some other incredibly large number if not a million – and there was so little wear on the barrel that they estimated wear at less than one-thousandths – .001 inch – after all that shooting."

Rowe believes that chromed barrels are not needed and perhaps appeal to the vanity of the gun owner rather than provide any appreciable benefit. "Oh, it might help prevent corrosion if you don't keep your barrel quite clean," he says, "but today's barrel steel is very hard. It was in the old days when primer fouling caused corrosion that a chrome lining might have been useful, but not today. Today's primers and powders burn much cleaner."

Porting

Barrel porting in the forend of the bore is more a method for reducing muzzle jump than it is for reducing felt recoil, although there are those who believe that it does both, and it certainly increases the report of the shot as it enters your ear. This is why barrel porting is found on the most sophisticated guns and on many extended chokes as well. There are those who believe porting promotes pellet velocity and pattern integration by, in essence, "grabbing" the wad as it goes by and slowing it down. (Perhaps this idea is based on a vacuum principle of fluid dynamics, but it remains a theory rather than a proven fact.)

Porting may also have the effect of reducing in-barrel resistance to a shot. As the propellant burns and forces the wad and shot down the barrel, the air in the barrel is displaced very rapidly. Without porting, the resisting column of air in the barrel ahead of the shot must travel all the way to the end of the muzzle before exiting, but a ported barrel will have the effect of reducing that resistance by allowing air to escape before it reaches the muzzle.

Most manufacturers offer ported barrels, but if your shotgun is not ported and you are interested in a worthy aftermarket solution to muzzle jump, numerous quality gunsmiths can make this modification for you. Joe Morales at Rhino drills his patterned round, diagonal holes so that gas will blow backward toward the shooter. Mag-na-port's Pro-Porting is similar.

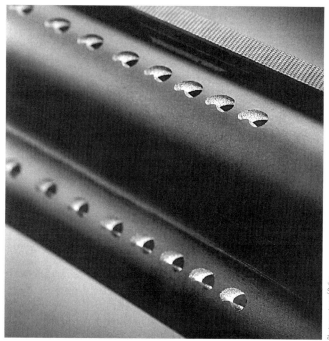

Photo courtesy of Briley.

Barrel porting reduces muzzle jump, thus allowing you to move toward a second shot more easily.

Barrel Length

Just a few years ago, 28- or 30-inch barrels were in vogue on sporting courses, perhaps because they were advertised as lighter, faster and easier to swing. Nevertheless, the pendulum is swinging back rapidly toward 32- and even 34-inch barrels.

Although shorter barrels are lighter, there is considerable feeling that longer barrels give you the heft needed to "feel" your shotgun's movement through its proper arc. Longer and heavier barrels, advocates argue, are easier to swing smoothly through a shot and onto a second bird. Longer barrels offer a longer sighting plane; provide a longer tube to constrict and channel burning powder, thus achieving 100-percent propulsion from your load; and help with a good, smooth follow-through.

An SKB monobloc is cut from a forged steel ingot. It contains two locking lugs that engage the crossbolt, two integral shoulder lugs and a base lug which interlocks with the receiver as the action is closed. Barrel tubes are seated and soldered into the monobloc to ensure correct point of impact for both the top and bottom barrel. Each side of the monobloc is precisely cut for a single-piece ejector and the pivot seat. The finished barrel group rotates at the pivot seat on two trunnions mounted through the sides of the receiver.

American Standard Bore, Chamber & Choke+ Dimensions in Inches (With English Choke Equivalents in Parentheses)

Gauge	Chamber Length	Standard Bore ID	Cylinder (True Cylinder)	SK1 (Imp Cyl)	Imp Cyl (1/4)	SK2	Mod (1/2)	Imp Mod (3/4)	Full (Full)	Xtra Full
10	2.875-3.5	.775	.000	-	-	-	.030	.035	.045	-
12	2.750-3.5	.729	.000	.005	.009	.015	.020	.025	.035	.040
16	2.750	.662	.000	.004	.007	.010	.015	.020	.028	-
20	2.750-3.0	.615	.000	.004	.006	.009	.014	.019	.025	-
28	2.875	.550	.000	.003	.005	.007	.012	.016	.022	-
*410	3.00	.410	.000	-	.004	-	.008	-	.017	-

+It is common for choke manufacturers to publish standards that vary slightly from this chart. Before buying aftermarket chokes and for a true precision fit, it is always wise to have your barrels measured with a micrometer. *Technically, the 410 is a bore size, not a "gauge." Except for custom manufacturing, the 10 gauge and 410-bore are not customarily provided with choke constrictions where data is missing.

SAAMI AND BARREL DATA

SAAMI, the Sporting Arms and Ammunition Manufacturers' Institute, is an association of America's leading manufacturers of sporting firearms, ammunition and components. Since it was founded in 1926, SAAMI has worked to develop industry-wide, but voluntary, standards, coordinate technical data, and promote safe and responsible firearms use. It is affiliated with the National Shooting Sports Foundation group in Newtown, Connecticut (www.saami.org).

The following chart presents bore and choke dimensions by gauge. The antique term "gauge," incidentally, used to identify most shotgun inner bore diameters, refers to the number of equal-size bore-diameter lead balls required to weigh 1 pound. Thus, from 1 pound of lead, you could fashion 12 balls for a 12-gauge shotgun.

UNDERSTANDING CHOKE

The principle behind using a choke to change pattern density has generally been known among gunsmiths for 150 years. The first patents, in the United States and Britain, date from the 1860s and screw-in chokes really took off when smokeless shotshells were invented.

Of course, by the middle of the 20th century, the WinChoke system was in general use and a gunsmith named Stan Baker in Seattle became perhaps the first person to install chokes as aftermarket accessories. Baker's method at that time was to flare the barrel ends, and this meant the barrels had to be separated. Jess Briley, who got his start working on Rottweil shotguns in the '50s, also experimented with developing an interchangeable choke system that would accommodate today's lightweight, thin-walled guns. Soon, Briley and others began machining tube sets for skeet shooting also, says Chuck Webb, the Briley General Manager.

The idea of a choke is that just a thousandth of an inch or two in constriction at the muzzle of a shotgun make a difference in your shooting. A standard Open or Cylinder choke is .729 inches across the bore of a 12 gauge; in essence, this is no choke at all. To go from Open to Improved Cylinder, you constrict or tighten the bore at the muzzle by only .009 inch, so that it is open only .720 inches. From that point to a Full choke is an additional 26 points or .026 inches, giving you an opening at the muzzle of just .694 inches. (Unless otherwise specified, we are talking about barrels and components firing lead-based shot rather than steel or other composite shot.)

Constricting the shot at the muzzle changes your shot pattern and your ability to shoot either close or long range effectively. A short, 15-yard shot at what is normally considered skeet range can effectively be

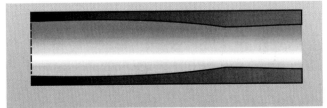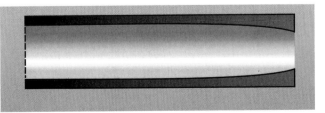

Your Choke – The choke that fits into your muzzle probably has one of the above two shapes. At left is a choke of "conical-parallel" design. Typically found on expensive shotguns, a conical-parallel fixed choke narrows gradually from the bore to a fixed diameter for Full or Modified designation. The last inch or so of barrel following the taper is a parallel section. The conical-choke style tapers later in the barrel and ends at the muzzle without a parallel section.

covered with an open bore or Cylinder choke that provides no constriction. To hit a 40-yard shot at an outgoing standard target, which may be a second shot in trap doubles, however, requires a pattern that does not begin to spread dramatically upon exiting your barrel. A more restrictive choke waits to spread to its maximum effective diameter well downrange. In this longer case, a Modified or even a Full choke might be appropriate.

Note that even though we equate a Cylinder or Open choke with having no choke in your shotgun at all, if you have a gun barrel that is threaded for a choke, you should never shoot without one in place. Two reasons. Hard shot can damage the delicate choke threading, which means that if you force a choke in past damaged threads you risk a "frozen choke" – one that you cannot easily remove – and "blow-by" or escaping gasses seeping between a choke and your barrel. You will have to take a frozen choke to a gunsmith to be repaired. Blow-by diminishes a shot's effectiveness, ruins your pattern and can, in a worst-case scenario, cause your choke to crack and deform.

Jerry Poe at Patternmaster Chokes and others have theorized that one of a choke's hidden functions and one of the reasons they work is their ability to help separate the shotcup from the shot. Because the shotcup holds the shot away from the powder and the steel of the bore, it too, along with the pellets, is blown out the muzzle of a shotgun. When the powder ignites, its heat expands the plastic wad and seals the barrel. As wad and shot travel down the barrel, they encounter a restrictive zone at the choke, which slows the wad, thereby separating it from the shot, but has essentially no effect on the shot itself.

Therefore, Poe suggests, the difference in little or no restriction at the muzzle and a great deal of restriction is what is responsible for your pattern and the length of a shot string. A Cylinder choke does not retard the shotcup, which proceeds to push the shot physically through the air – even outside the muzzle – because it is lighter than the shot and traveling faster (although air resistance almost immediately begins to slow it down much faster than the small, round shot). This causes your shot pattern to open right away.

A tighter Full choke at the muzzle retards the wad significantly. A restrictive choke separates the shotcup from the shot even before it exits your muzzle, and this allows a more concise pattern and shot string.

Patternmaster's particular solution is to machine exceptionally small studs in their ported chokes to physically retard the wad and this, they say, provides a shot pattern in which pellets are evenly distributed. By grouping the shot into a denser cloud, you have a shorter shot string. This also means their chokes are not labeled with the standard constrictions, as are, for instance, chokes from Trulock or Kick's.

Larry Nailon's Clearview Products in Oklahoma City specializes in barrels, recoil and shot-string testing;

The manager of the pro shop at any legitimate course or range can give you some pointers about keeping your barrel in top condition and direct you to competent gunsmiths in the area for specialized assistance.

Photo courtesy of Silverleaf Shotgun Sports.

custom-load development; and barrel modifications for high-performance shooting.

Nailon says there is no magic in shotgun chokes. "The amount of choke in a shotgun barrel is simply the difference in the barrel's bore diameter and the exit diameter at the muzzle. The best choke is the one that allows the pellets of your shot charge to exit the barrel with the least pellet deformation. Round pellets fly true to the point of aim, and with more velocity, than do deformed pellets. Deformed pellets lose velocity very quickly and patterns are poor and erratic."

From testing, he finds that pellets deformed even slightly during the firing process arrive in the rear of the shot cloud, significantly behind the round pellets from the same charge. "A shotgun's downrange performance," he says, "is determined by how near true to spherical the pellets are as they exit the muzzle. The value of a round pellet at muzzle exit just can't be overstated."

According to Nailon, the effect of any particular choke or constriction is highly variable. Such things as choke length, choke design (tapered versus parallel), shot charge velocity, porting, wad design and the actual flex of the barrel as the shot column passes play a part in pattern development. Hence, the importance of patterning your shotgun before you step into the shooter's cage!

Nailon says to remember that your shot charge passes through the choke constriction to be repositioned while it is at its highest velocity. Certainly, once they are outside the barrel, shot pellets immediately begin to slow down. Outside the barrel, they encounter air resistance and the shot engine, the burning powder, is used up. Pellets immediately begin to spread out.

Consequently, the amount of time a choke has to perform its important function is very small. Nailon has calculated that a 1-inch shot column traveling at a velocity of 1200 fps requires only 1/9600 second to pass through a 1 1/2-inch choke, and it has reached that velocity, from zero, in about 3 thousandths (.003) of a second.

"At 1200 feet per second," he says, "the shot is moving at 14,400 inches per second. Obviously, a longer choke gives your pellets greater time to reposition, but long chokes are difficult to machine and are therefore more expensive than shorter chokes. We find, by the way, that for most effective shooting, as load velocity increases, so should your choke length."

A choke does not perform in isolation from all other elements of a shot, though. Shot quality is terribly important in judging the effectiveness of a barrel-choke-load combination. Because hard or magnum shot deforms less than soft shot, its downrange efficiency is higher. Nailon has calculated the violence of the 1/2-millisecond explosion that is necessary to generate a 1200-fps pellet velocity in your 30-inch barrel at more than 10,000 psi is enough to deform any lead-based shot and some soft steel as well. Thus, he says, some shot deformation actually happens the instant you pull the trigger, even before the shot reaches the forcing cone and certainly before it reaches your choke.

His conclusion is that whether you are hunting or competing in sporting clays, harder and more expensive shot is well worth the additional cost, because its downrange performance in delivering a consistent pattern on target is going to be much better than softer promotional loads. "As the quality of your load improves," he says, "you will discover that the effectiveness of your choke also improves."

Not everyone is aware that the barrel of a gun flexes laterally when fired, Nailon says. Imagine the ball of burning powder and gas actually blowing the pellets down the barrel. Although this happens very fast, the amount of flex can be as much as .006 to .008 inches, even in a barrel made of high-grade steel. "This is not necessarily a problem, and something you certainly can't control," Nailon notes, "except to understand that the thickness of the barrel increases at the point you use a screw-in choke and, therefore, your 30-inch barrel flexes different amounts at different points along the bore."

Nailon illustrates his ideas about lateral force with a spent shotcup. The indentations caused by lead pellets are almost as severe in the side petals of the shotcup as they are in the base. An examination of thousands of shot cups has, therefore, led him to conclude that smaller pellets reposition more easily than larger pellets during barrel and choke passage. Thus, they are subject to less deformation as they pass through the barrel and choke. He concludes that smaller pellets usually give you better coverage and more efficient patterns. "Just like pellet quality and choke length, pellet size will affect how well a choke can redirect pellets towards your target."

Actually, the choke gets too much blame and too much credit for things that it cannot control, Nailon concludes: "The shotgun is a complex shooting instrument. I always recommend that shooters pattern chokes with all of the different styles of ammo they may shoot." This can obviously be a tedious process, the Clearview exec affirms, but the result will be a good understanding of how your gun barrel and your choke system perform with different loads of shot size and velocity.

At Briley, Cliff Moller agrees with the general assessment Nailon makes about the function and importance of choke. Moller says that nobody really

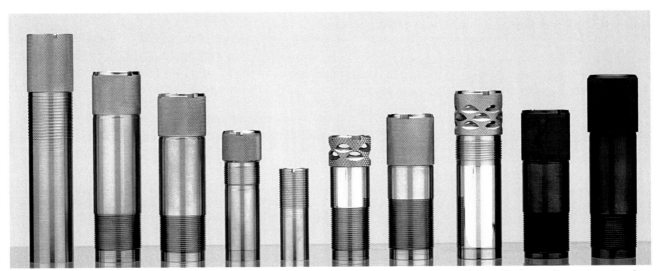

A lineup of Briley chokes illustrates the various styles and sizes available. A choke has two functions: retard the wad to keep it from interrupting the shot pattern and to shape the shot pattern.

scientifically understands how chokes work, but at Briley, they work from the ground up. They cut away metal in minute .002-inch increments, then shoot and then cut again and shoot different loads until they have a fairly empirical level of performance data. After all, he says, you are squeezing a lot of mass through a small area at ultra-high speed, and the mass is essentially made up of small droplets. All of the droplets, or pellets, are shoving and swirling around in a terribly confined space until they exit at the muzzle of a gun. Many engineers, therefore, apply the principles of fluid dynamics to the study of shotgun dynamics.

The folks at Briley say that selecting a choke is not a decision that you should make solely by estimating the distance to your target breakpoint. Three things need to be considered:

• First consider "Target Presentation" or how much surface area is being shown to the shooter. This means knowing, before you step into the shooting box, what type target is being thrown and at what angle.

• Second, "Target Vulnerability" or how easy is that surface to break with your load.

• The third and final consideration is "Target Distance." At what distance do you plan to break the target?

According to Briley, the easiest presentations to break are Belly-On and the Back-Lip where the shooter sees – and hence, shoots into – the cupped backside of a target. A standard size target will give you 14.19 square inches of cupped and vulnerable surface [Area = $(Pi)(r^2) = 3.14159 \times (2.125)^2 = 14.19$] with a Belly-On presentation. A Back-Lip presentation is tilted slightly backward at the shooter and there is not as much of the tender bottom surface area for your pellets to hit.

The most difficult shots are Edge-On and Dome-On where the shooter only sees the edge and/or top of a target. Briley rates the Edge-On as the least surface area to hit at 3.65 square inches, but claims that the Dome-On presentation is actually harder to break because most of the exposed surface area curves away from the shooter. This shoulder curve is the ribbed strength of a clay target.

In cooperation with Gil and Vicki Ash of OSP (Optimum Shotgun Performance) Shooting School, Briley has prepared a "Choke Chart," which is presented on the Internet at www.briley.com/choke_chart.html. The objective of this color chart (which you may print and study) is to give you a visual image to associate with learning about choke effectiveness on any given style or size target – standard, midi, mini, rabbit and battue – at yardage. Thus, by the chart, an Edge-On standard 108-mm bird at 30 yards is best taken with Improved Cylinder, but if the bird floats slightly to Dome-On, the recommendation would be to switch to a tighter, Light Modified choke. A thicker Battue at the same distance will probably require a more concentrated pattern and the chart suggests a Modified or even a Full choke. Conversely, a Belly-On target can probably be

taken effectively with Cylinder bore from the closest bird thrown out to 35 yards, and after that, only a small switch to Improved Cylinder is needed.

These days, most conventional chokes have conical and parallel sections. The conical section (sometimes referred to as the choke "ramp") connects the two parallel sections, the larger and longer bore, and the smaller and shorter choke. Briley says their testing indicates that the distance between the end of the bore parallel and the beginning of the choke parallel, and the amount of constriction between them, is so small that the best type of choke cone probably is a straight angle.

Briley works off a rough 3:1 ratio when building its chokes. Thus, a 12-gauge bore, which is .729 inches in diameter, could effectively use a 2.187-inch cone or ramp. Briley extends that to 2.75 inches on the theory that it is better to be a little long than too short at this critical juncture. Not only should the cone be longer rather than shorter, but according to Moller, the parallel section that follows the cone also needs to be at least 5/8 to 3/4 inch long to stabilize the moving pellets. Otherwise, inconsistent patterning results.

Chokes are so talked about in sporting clays because shot presentations are so variable. Station one may throw a 15-yard left-to-right crossing bird coupled with a springing teal, 25 yards and straight up. At station two, you may see a simultaneous pair, an incoming bird that you should take at 20 yards and an outgoing bird that you cannot engage until it is at 40 yards.

Screw-in chokes give the shooter a great deal of inexpensive flexibility. They are certainly better than carrying multiple fixed-choke guns from station to station. If they have a downside, it is at the junction between the end of the choke, its "skirt," and the point where the barrel threads end. It is almost impossible to fit a shotgun barrel with a choke tube and have a perfectly seamless transition there. Having a "lip," having the choke extend even by a thousandth of an inch, into the barrel can potentially be disastrous if pellets bombard that lip when you shoot. This can, at a minimum, result in a shattered choke and can permanently damage your barrel.

It is better if there is a minimal gap – think of it as a step down – from the smooth barrel to the point where the choke begins. Unfortunately, this can be a point of wad detritus build-up and should be cleaned often. A gap that is too large, from a choke that does not properly fit, will interfere with the moving shot, however.

The seating or fitting of a choke to a barrel must also be precise. A noticeable gap of any size between the butt of a choke's skirt and the barrel will ultimately cause damage to the barrel. This is why there is no one-size-fits-all approach to choke tubes with the many gun manufacturers from around the world.

"Blowback" can occur when gas pushes between the choke and the barrel. This means the choke was not properly installed or maybe not screwed in tight. A shot

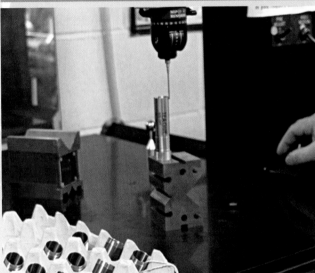

Steps In Machining A Choke Tube - *Chokes are milled from solid bar stock of steel or other metals such as the lighter, but more expensive, titanium. Computer patterns are programmed into CNC cutting machines, and bars are cut to length before they are drilled. Depending upon the type of choke - flush mount, extended, knurled - threads, knurled ends and perhaps choke ports will be separately machined. Sides are chamfered and smoothed to fit precisely in particular shotgun models. Finally, individual tubes are measured for exacting accuracy since tolerances must be tight to the thousandths of an inch.*

can rip a choke in half if this occurs. In a day of shooting, the wise shotgunner will occasionally check to be sure his choke is seated securely, as they can work loose. After all, a choke tube should normally only be screwed in finger tight and, yes, a very light oiling of the threads after cleaning will help it seat properly in the threads of the barrel (which you must also assiduously clean).

It needs to be mentioned that not all chokes will fit all guns. Although there has been a standardization movement in the industry, multiple thread patterns are still in existence. So before you take your WinChoke and try to screw it into a new shotgun, you would be advised to first check the manufacturer's specifications for chokes.

Cleaning out the plastic build-up in choke tubes, and especially ported choke tubes (as well as ported barrels), is critical to high-level shooting consistency. Plastic streaks affect concentricity and hence pattern density and alignment by slowing the wad unevenly. Clean your chokes thoroughly on occasion to prevent this.

A NOTE ABOUT STEEL SHOT

Not every choke will handle hard steel shot. A choke that is more than a few years old may or may not be hard enough, and even today, it is best to read a manufacturer's instructions and cautions before putting a load of steel shot or HeviShot through your barrel.

Early chokes were designed for lead shot only and when steel and other lead substitutes began coming on the scene in the early '80s, the fiercer passage of steel tended to weld some screw-in chokes destructively to their barrels. Waterfowl hunters soon learned that when they used steel, because it was much harder than lead, it was much lighter. Because it was, therefore, less susceptible to being deformed and it flew in a tighter pattern (unless there was a wind, but that is a separate issue), they needed to open their patterns at least one constriction.

THE "SHOT STRING"

Another question that Briley and Clearview address is shot string. While there is some question about whether the length of a string of shot is at all important, because the majority of pellets are bunched in an initial spread, a string of lead shot can be 10 to 12 feet long, including flyers. The length of a string of steel (or some of the hard substitutes for lead) will be much shorter and this means your configuration of target lead may need to be recalculated if you switch from one substance to another.

Although steel has become The Load for waterfowl, it is rarely required (and many would say, not desired) on sporting clays venues.

ADDITIONAL CHOKE SOLUTIONS

Anderson Custom Shotguns builds custom chokes designed to fit your gun's barrel. Each heat-treated stainless Anderson choke is clearly marked with points of constriction. No Anderson choke is ported. Keith Anderson says that "after ten years of extensive research, no significant recoil, muzzle jump or pattern improvement can be attributed to ported chokes. Non-ported chokes eliminate friction as well as plastic and powder residue build-up that can be a real problem with double-barrel guns. They are also easier to keep clean." (Anderson's Ballistic Specialties does offer ported chokes.)

Comp-N-Choke combines slot porting with CNC choke tube manufacturing. Escaping gases reduce recoil and the slots help grab the wad momentarily, which improves shot-pattern consistency by reducing flyers caused when the wad drives through the shot column. It also helps with muzzle rise to make your second shot easier. A more-dense pattern results, and this allows you to use a more-open choke (less

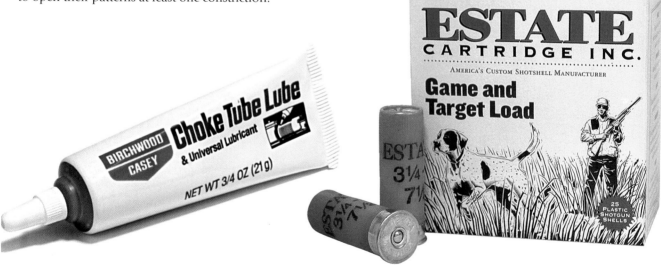

A very light application of Birchwood Casey's Choke Tube Lubricant applied to the threads of a choke after a thorough cleaning of the choke and the threads inside your shotgun will ensure a secure fit and will make the choke easier to remove.

In the middle of a shoot or a tournament, it may sometimes be wiser to change loads rather than to change chokes. It will depend on the time you have, the target presentations you see and the shells you have available.

Mini-tube-gauge reducers such as these Little Skeeters from Browning slip easily into the bore of your shotgun and allow you to shoot several gauges of ammunition in a 12 gauge. Bill Norton at Browning says they "do not affect the overall feel or swing of your gun" and may be used with any choke.

constriction) for a larger pattern. Extended chokes are conical-parallel in design with final constriction held to about 1-1/8 inches.

This same Georgia company also produces the Kick's line of directional, diagonally ported chokes. Kick's claims that its 135-degree ports, which directs the muzzle blast away from the shooter, reduces muzzle jump and felt recoil. The sharp angle of the inside forward lip of these chokes is designed to retard the wad for faster separation from your shot column. These chokes extend 1-3/4 inches forward of your shotgun's muzzle.

In business since the 1920s, Poly-Choke builds adjustable shotgun chokes with nine settings, from Extra Full to settings beyond or more open than Cylinder and including slug settings. "It operates like a garden hose and is like having nine separate shotguns," Poly-Choke says. "The average shooter uses four degrees of choke: Wide Open for skeet and up to 25-yard shots, Improved Cylinder for 20- to 30-yard shots, Modified for 30 to 35 yards and Full for 40 yards or more. Although these single-barrel chokes are available in ventilated or non-ventilated styles for 12-, 16-, 20- and 28-gauge shotguns, the author has never noticed one of these versatile chokes on a sporting clays course.

TruGlo sells several styles of screw-in choke tubes, some ported and some not, primarily advertised for hunting. Their Titan adjustable choke tube allows you to turn a graded collar to change choke settings without physically changing tubes. Choke settings are laser engraved and patterns are available in one choke from Cylinder to Extra Full. TruGlo says that in addition to lead shot, the Titan will handle all steel and HeviShot loads, too.

Teague chokes – extended, flush and ported – are manufactured from stainless steel in Great Britain. Teague believes in tapering the choke the full length of the tube, from skirt to muzzle. According to that company, this practice reduces recoil, results in fewer deformed pellets, and better maintains pattern density and pellet velocity.

Hastings, Cation and Briley have straight-rifled some of their chokes. They suggest that this helps stabilize shot patterns and eliminates wad spin. According to Cliff Moller at Briley, straight-rifling seems to pull some of the flyers into the outer edges of the pattern, which may result in an extra target or two over the course of a tournament. (While this works with lead shot, steel is still in the experimental stage.)

Briley says they "practically invented" sub-gauge tube sets. Their Companion sub-gauge tubes are weight graded, and at $400 to $600 a pair, cost substantially less than a quality sub-gauge gun.

SUB-GAUGE BARREL TUBES

Shotgunners are increasingly realizing that shooting sub-gauge for sporting clays, as well as other shotgun games, is both great fun and an additional challenge. The difficulty in the past has been the need to carry multiple guns to every shooting venue. Assuming that the 12 gauge has for many years been the bore of choice, versatile shooters needed to carry a 20 gauge or a separate 28-gauge gun to participate in additional shooting classes. But if you are going to travel to shotgun competitions, you want to get the most shooting possible during your visit.

If you are an over/under shooter, the way to travel today is with one gun (and perhaps a backup in case your Number One malfunctions) and a set of sub-gauge insert tubes. This gives you the greatest possible versatility at a reasonable cost, and they are legal on all shooting programs including NSCA and NSSA. There are two paths to achieve this versatility: full-length tubes and short tubes, or chamber inserts, that are designed to hold a sub-gauge shell in the chamber of your big 12, but makes use of the 12-gauge barrel. Tube sets, whether chamber-only or full-length, are not cheap, however. For the price of a top-of-the-line set, you can easily buy a low-end back-up shotgun.

Briley, who says they "practically invented" sub-gauge tube sets, has three grades of full-length tube sets. Their Matched Weight tubes guarantee a weight differential of no more than 1/4 ounce among all gauges. Their Ultra-Lite set guarantees a differential of no more than 2 ounces and features a titanium chamber in 410 and stainless chambers for 20 and 28. The Ultimate Ultra-Lite set comes with titanium chambers and tubes are weight-matched. A pair of Briley 28-gauge Sidekick chamber inserts cost $239 and weigh about 6.2 ounces.

A set of 20, 28 and 410 inserts is $600. A pair of full-length 28-gauge Companion tubes is $399 in Briley's Standard grade or $499 for Ultra-Lite tubes.

Chamber Mates from Seminole Gun Works are approximately the length of a fired shell and come with integral extractors that work in conjunction with the extractors of a gun. Seminole says the benefit of their short Chamber Mates is that they are so light – a couple ounces – that they do not alter the balance or "feel" of a gun. Unlike full-length tubes, which can add 1 to 2 pounds of weight inside your barrel, chamber inserts place their extra ounces between your hands for best possible balance. Seminole says they provide a 6-inch extension for their 410 Chamber Mate to allow slower-burning 410 powders to complete their burn before entering the larger chamber.

You would think a smaller gauge shotcup that does not seal a 12-gauge barrel effectively would cause pattern irregularities, but Seminole says, surprisingly, this is not so. According to them, sub-gauge shells pattern as well through a 12 gauge as they do through a specific sub-gauge barrel.

Seminole's sub-gauge inserts are held in place with a rubber O-ring and pattern effectively with all of your standard chokes. Sub-gauge inserts can be used with over/under, side-by-side or single-shot guns. Steel and other extremely heavy shot is not recommended for these lightweight stainless-steel inserts.

Rhino also builds full-length tube inserts. These tubes weigh approximately 3.75 ounces each, are 15 inches long and fit any 12-gauge side-by-side, over/under or single-barrel gun. They come standard with Skeet and Light Modified chokes and a cleaning kit.

12
Chapter

HANDLOADING
FOR SPORTING CLAYS
By John M. Taylor

Not only is reloading economical, allowing you to shoot more at less cost, but careful handloaders can assemble loads to enhance overall performance and tailor specific loads for special situations. Reloading in its purest form is simply the replacing of the components of a shotshell that are consumed when it is fired. The metal head of the shell is reformed to factory specifications to ensure proper chamber. The primer, powder, wad and shot are then replaced, in order, and finally the crimp is closed.

Shotshell reloading is easy, yet there are rules, and the most important is: *Obtain a good data manual and follow the data published therein without exception.* Handloaders who substitute components and otherwise alter published data are only kidding themselves. Not only can the resulting loads exceed safe pressures and be dangerous, but often the best this kind of load can offer is substandard and/or inefficient performance. Why waste our valuable time producing substandard loads to save a couple of bucks using up an old bag of wads, or a few primers? The wise reloader strives for quality and high performance, and if we follow a recipe from a manufacturer's manual, that is just what we will get.

GETTING STARTED

Unlike loading rifle ammo, the shotshell reloader does not need a vast array of equipment and accessories. A loading machine, a good data manual, several powder bushings that allow us to fine-tune the powder drop, a powder scale to verify the powder drop, some patience and willingness to learn are all that's needed. Loaders are available in two basic styles, single-stage and progressive, and in every size from 10 gauge to 410 bore. Because the cases become ever smaller, be aware that the smaller the gauge, the slower you should go to produce quality ammunition.

This MEC progressive uses a hydraulic system to cycle the tool as opposed to manually cycling it using a handle that is moved down and up to complete the reloading cycle. Other loaders using this system include the Spolar Gold and Ponsness/Warren.

Barry Reed loads a shell on a single-station MEC. This type loader is best for beginning handloaders, and most veterans keep one handy for specialized loading projects.

Normally, handloaders begin reloading 12s or 20s, and only later progress to the 28 gauge and even smaller 410 bore with some experience under their belt. Experienced handloaders consider the 28 gauge almost as easy to reload as the 12 and 20, but all agree that the 410 requires them to slow down and take their time in order to produce uniform loads. Nothing should dissuade anyone from learning to reload. It is fun, saves money and can greatly add to your enjoyment of shotgunning.

LOADERS

The most basic piece of equipment we need to handload shotshells is a loading machine or loader. They come in two styles: single-stage and progressive.

The single-stage loader moves a single hull or case from station to station around the loader, where each loading operation is performed individually until a single cartridge is loaded. The single-stage loader is without a doubt the best tool for the beginner, and the advanced reloader normally keeps one around for special projects such as loading buffered shot or just putting together a box or two of a new load he wants to try without converting his progressive loader.

Once the primers, powder and shot are loaded and the shell plate is full, progressive machines perform all of the loading operations at once, producing a loaded cartridge with each cycle of the handle. Built for speed and quantity production, progressive machines are hard to beat, but for the beginning and occasional reloader, the single-stage machine is the way to go.

A comprehensive list of currently available shotshell reloading machines is provided in Appendix III.

SINGLE-STAGE LOADERS

Beginners who want to learn the fundamentals of reloading and those who want to load only a few target and/or hunting loads should opt for a single-stage loader. Shells are loaded one at a time, showing novice reloaders how everything fits together, while providing a sufficiently large number of shells to satisfy all but the most ardent shooter. In operation, once the proper bushings that measure shot and powder are installed and verified with a scale, and the hoppers are filled with powder and shot, we are ready to load.

• A fired hull in good condition – split hulls and those with soft, tired crimps and other defects should be discarded – is placed under the first station. Here, the spent primer is removed and your machine resizes the metal head of the shell. During resizing, the metal is pressed back to factory specification, ensuring positive chambering.

• Moved to the next station, a fresh primer is placed on the re-prime station and then pressed into the primer pocket.

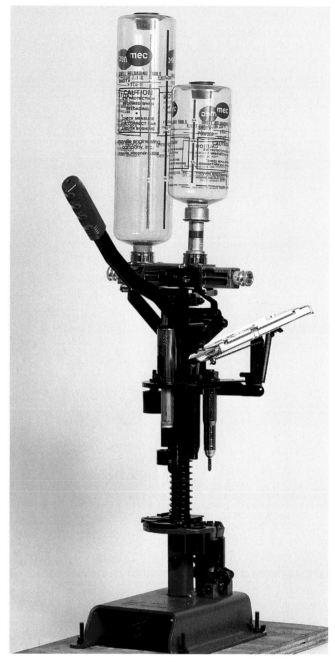

MEC's 700 Sizemaster single-station loader. This is a top-of-the-line single-station tool that provides excellent resizing of the shell's metal head and is easy to operate.

• At the next station, the powder is charged and frequently the wad is inserted and the shot also dropped while the hull is there; some loaders use two stations for these operations.

• Next, the crimp is started so that the original folds are pressed inward in order to form a good crimp.

• Lastly, the final crimp is formed and we are done.

The whole process takes less than a minute, and shells reloaded on a single-stage loader are of excellent quality. Once familiarity is developed, 100 rounds can be loaded in a few minutes.

Ponsness/Warren's latest accessory to speed loading is this case feeder that, when filled with empty hulls, drops a fresh hull on the platen each time the loader is cycled. A Dillon also incorporates this feature. Now, all you have to do is place a wad in the wad guide and cycle the tool.

Barry Reed operates an RCBS Grand. This new progressive loader provides features that prevent spilling of shot and powder and some other operator errors.

PROGRESSIVE LOADERS

Progressive loaders accomplish all of the tasks of a single-stage loader simultaneously with a single stroke of the loader's handle. Large quantities of ammunition can be produced quickly on a progressive loader, and for the passionate sporting clays enthusiast, a progressive machine is the best choice.

However, speed and quantity can come at the potential risk of quality. It is very easy for one of the components – primers, powder or shot – to become completely depleted and for several loads to come off the loader minus one of these components, providing numerous frustrating misfires. If the proper powder and shot bushings are installed and checked, and care is taken to ensure that the hoppers are kept full and primers move along their track, the same high-quality loads can be assembled as those that come off a single-stage loader.

Each loader is different, and it takes some time to become accustomed to its idiosyncrasies and what you need to watch while operating the tool. For example, I use a Spolar Power-Load that, in my opinion, is one of the best, albeit the most expensive, progressive tools on the market, and for all of its good points, it is necessary to watch the re-prime station on every stroke of the tool. If I do not, it is possible for a primer to be jostled sideways, or, if the primers hang up as they drop from the tray, I can end up with shells without primers. As *Music Man* Professor Harold Hill said, "You gotta' know the territory."

A further wrinkle with progressive machines is hydraulic operation. Instead of pulling a handle to cycle them, a touch of the toe activates the hydraulic drive, and the loader cycles; all that is necessary is to feed the cases and wads and keep the powder and shot hoppers and primer pan filled. Loaders such as the Ponsness/

147

The RCBS Grand progressive loader.

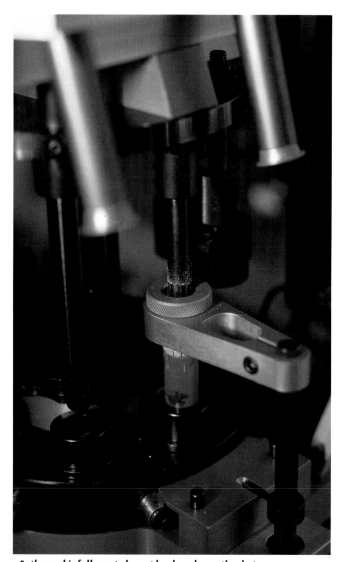

As the wad is fully seated, most loaders charge the shot.

Warren and Dillon even have case feeders, leaving the operator to only place a wad in the cup and cycle the machine to produce a load with every pull of the handle.

In terms of ease of loading, 12 and 20 gauges are the easiest. The cases are large, and components go in with little problem. The 28 gauge is not very difficult either, save the smaller wad that can sometimes not align properly. Still, I find 28-gauge loads no more difficult to assemble than 12s and 20s. The 410 presents the challenge of a very small case that if cocked only a trifle will make the wad miss the case mouth. Most reloaders I know eschew the progressive loader in the 410, and use a single-stage tool for these finicky shells. It should also be noted that 410 loaders are set up for 2 1/2-inch shells, and although most can be adjusted to load the 3-inch shell, they all come ready for the 2-1/2 case. I do not know a whole lot of shooters whose steady diet is the 410 anyway; hence, we really do not need buckets of them.

Earlier, I mentioned the need for a powder scale, a number of powder bushings and the care needed to ensure that the powder drop is exact. Bushings are cylindrical

tubes that fit into a bar located under the powder and shot reservoirs, which is moved back and forth to measure the powder and shot before dropping the charges into the waiting case. In a rifle load, a tenth of a grain can be the difference between an accurate load and one that is just average. Shotguns are more forgiving.

In general, we can accept powder drops that are within plus-or-minus three-tenths of a grain. Like the rifleman's powder measure, how we operate a shotshell loader affects the uniformity and accuracy of the powder drops. Those who cycle the tool gently will tend to drop lighter powder charges than one using a rougher technique. The vibration of the loader that results from the way the tool is operated causes more or less powder to settle into the bushing. Progressive loaders tend to drop more uniform charges because the powder remains in the bushing for only one up-and-down stroke of the operating handle. In single-stage loaders, the powder settles throughout the loading cycle, while the case visits the other stations, and hence a heavier charge normally results – and the potential for more variation exists.

The most critical part of obtaining a good crimp is the pre-crimp stage. Here, the original folds of the crimp are partially folded so that the crimper can completely fold and seal the finished shell.

A good final crimp will ensure proper ballistics, good performance and seal the shot within the finished shell.

Every loader leaves the factory with a chart showing what weight of powder a certain bushing will drop. These charts, which also appear in loading manuals, are only "ballpark" accurate. They do not take into consideration how the tool is operated, nor do they accommodate atmospheric conditions. All propellants or powders are hydrophilic, a big word that means that powders will absorb and release water depending on the relative humidity. On a day with low humidity, powder will weigh less than the same volume does on a humid day. Often the difference is negligible, but still, we need to check.

When beginning to load, regardless of the type of machine we are using, we need to insert the bushing the manufacturer states will provide the proper powder charge for our chosen load, partially fill the powder hopper, cycle the machine a few times to settle the powder, then drop a charge. Throw that charge back into the powder container and then, cycling the handle again using the same tempo as when loading, drop another and weigh it on our scale. Sometimes, the charge will be right on the money, but it is my guess it will not. Regardless, check a couple more drops to see if they are reasonably uniform. If the charge is within three-tenths of a grain or less for the load prescribed in the data, all is well; if not, it is necessary to drain the powder hopper and exchange the bushing for a larger or smaller one that will bring us to the desired powder charge.

It may take a little time to get the powder drop just right, but in terms of quality, it is time well spent. Commercial ammunition manufacturers go to extraordinary lengths to ensure that every powder drop is exact, even when machines are putting out 900 rounds a minute. It is what we expect, and we can expect the same uniformity from our handloads if we are careful and take the time to ensure we are following the load data to the letter.

Guard against the tendency, which I see all the time, to simply insert the next numbered bushing based on such evidence as how far an ejected round flies from a semi-auto, or the feel of the recoil. Every powder company – Hodgdon, Alliant, Accurate Arms, etc. – has a full-time laboratory that does nothing but develop and test loads in highly accurate, pressure-sensitive guns and across equally accurate chronographs. Because of the abundance of data their manuals provide, it is possible to select a load for nearly every occasion, from low-pressure loads of modest velocities to loads that are near the top of the usable pressure charts and that use about every component known. You just have to look.

While you are checking the powder drop, it is a good idea to check the shot bushing. Only one charge is necessary, but occasionally a bushing can be mis-stamped, so it is best to take a minute to double check.

Carter Spolar with his hydraulic Spolar Gold loader. Although this loader comes as a manually cycled reloader, by attaching the hydraulic system accessory, loading becomes effortless and fast.

Building a good load requires research and some common sense. Powders vary in their formulation, and some are better suited to sporting loads than others. In general, powders used for target loads are fast burning –Alliant e3, Red Dot, American Select, Green Dot; Hodgdon Clays, Universal, International, Longshot, TiteWad; Accurate Arms Solo, Winchester WST, and 231; and IMR 700X are some that come to mind. Because of the tiny capacity of the 410, spherical powders, often called ball powders, are the only choice, those being: Hodgdon Lil' Gun and H 110; Alliant 410; or Winchester 296. These powders are difficult to ignite and require that a hotter primer specifically designed to light these 410-specific powders be used.

That brings us to the subject of primers. When the firing pin strikes the primer, a shower of white-hot sparks is hurled forward into the powder charge, igniting it, and starting the process of firing the shell. These sparks actually penetrate the powder so that ignition is throughout the propellant and not only at the bottom where one would expect. Called brisance, primers vary in the amount and velocity of these sparks. Ron Reiber, chief ballistician at Hodgdon Powders, performed a series of tests for me regarding primers, and I believe the chart below will illustrate the need to use only the primer specified in published load data.

PRIMER COMPARISON TESTS

The following charts were created in Hodgdon's ballistic laboratory using Winchester [compression-formed] AA cases and Winchester AA wads. Cases were crimped excessively deep to create the highest pressure possible for a given load. Powder charges, wads and shot weight were the same throughout. As the tests reveal, not only do primer changes make drastic differences, but changing shot quantities also alters the way primers perform. Therefore, the always-present warning to reloaders - *use only those components listed and do not interchange components.*

Hornaday's 366 Auto Shotshell Reloading Press is the newest iteration of this classic progressive loader (formerly named the Pacific). By continuing to produce this excellent classic machine, Hornaday can supply repair parts for older Pacific tools.

As this chart shows, there are wide pressure swings, often with very modest changes in velocity, when primers are interchanged. Not only is safety an issue, so is performance. Hot weather can drive pressures even higher, and cold weather makes powders, especially spherical powders, harder to ignite.

1 1/8 oz. shot test			7/8 oz. shot test		
Primer	Velocity (fps)	Pressure (psi)	Primer	Velocity (fps)	Pressure (psi)
Win AATP	1,176	11,200	Win. 209	1,214	10,300
Fed. 209H	1,172	11,100	CCI 209M	1,217	10,200
Win. 209	1,173	10,900	Fed. 209	1,195	9,100
Fiocchi 616	1,171	10,800	Fiocchi 616	1,196	9,000
CCI 2069M	1,171	10,400	Win. AATP	1,191	8,400
Rem. 209P	1,156	8,500	Rem. 209P	1,187	8,200
CCI 209	1,162	8,400	CCI 209	1,180	7,700

Win. = Winchester, Fed. = Federal, Rem. = Remingto

The progressive RCBS Grand (left) and single-station Mini Grand (right) are displayed at the 2004 Grand American Trap Shoot in Vandalia, Ohio.

WADS

Because powder and shot are both granular, there must be some means of separating them, in addition to sealing the propellant gases behind the shot charge. Prior to the early 1960s, wads consisted of a 1/8-inch card wad that was placed atop the powder and then two or more felt wads of varying thickness completed the wad column. These wads cushioned the shot and took up space in the hull to ensure a good crimp.

Historically, shot was copper- or nickel-plated to help prevent it from melting and fusing when the white-hot propellant gases leaked around the inefficient card and felt wad columns. In 1945, Winchester-Western developed a fiber, over-powder cup wad that is still in use today in some Winchester field loads. By the early 1960s, Remington had produced the all-plastic Power-Piston wad that included an over-powder cup that would expand to seal the bore and keep the hot propellants gases behind the shot charge where they belong. Combined with this highly efficient gas seal was a cushioned section and a shot-protecting sleeve that largely prevented the deformation of shot, so long the enemy of downrange pattern performance.

Today, rare is the clays load that is not assembled using the familiar plastic one-piece wad. These excellent plastic wads make reloading easy, and

progressive loaders possible. However, just as with primers and powders, the proper wad must be used to ensure safety and performance.

The following test was performed using a 12-gauge Winchester AA hull (the old compression-formed hull), a Federal 209A primer, 16.0 grains of Hodgdon Clays powder and 1-1/8 ounces of lead shot. Only the wad was changed and the results are as follows:

Wad	Velocity (fps)	Pressure (psi)
Winchester WAA 12	1,145	10,800
Hornady Versalite	1,114	10,800
Remington Figure 8	1,113	9,300
Windjammer	1,112	8,500
Federal 12 S2	1,105	9,500
Pattern Control Red	1,050	8,100

It is interesting to note that when the Federal 12 S2 was substituted, the pressure actually rose as the velocity dropped.

CRIMP

The one aspect of our finished reload that is most visible is the crimp. Those crimps that emulate the original factory crimp of about .055 or just shy of 1/16 inch are the best. One may naively think that an extra-deep crimp is better, but unknown to many reloaders is that one of the quickest ways to run pressures into the unsafe or at least high range is to adjust the crimp die to over-crimp the finished shell. On the other hand, some reloaders feel that a shallower crimp extends hull life, but that comes at the cost of decreased velocity.

Hodgdon's Ron Reiber performed a second series of tests for me showing how crimp depth affects pressure. Note that as crimp increases, so does pressure, right into unsafe regions. Winchester 12-gauge AA (compression-formed) hulls, Winchester 209 primers, 20.0 grains Hodgdon Clays powder, and 7/8-ounce lead shot were used in this test.

On the left is a new, factory 20-gauge shell, while on the right is a reload produced on a Spolar Gold tool. Any of the currently available loaders will produce similar crimps. Along with proper assembly of the components, a good crimp will ensure maximum ballistic performance. Care should be exercised to re-crimp the shell to factory specifications, as too deep or too shallow a crimp can cause pressure and velocity problems.

Crimp Depth	Velocity (fps)	Pressure (psi)
0.030	1,308	9,300
0.050	1,329	10,500
0.070	1,351	11,900*
0.090	1,363	13,100*

* These loads are right at or exceed the service pressure and are unsafe.

PRESSURE

What is all this about pressure anyway? Modern propellants, more casually called powder, do not explode but rather burn at a controlled rate. When they do, they create an ever-expanding volume of gas that pushes the wad and shot out of the barrel. When shotguns are manufactured, they are "proof tested" by subjecting each firearm to an overload that generates about a third more pressure than the hottest commercially available load. However, the proof pressure is not the pressure used when shotshells are manufactured or reloading data generated. The top pressure that shotshells cannot exceed is called the "service pressure," and every load must be held below this threshold.

The following are the Sporting Arms and Ammunition Manufacturers Institute (SAAMI) service pressures used in the manufacture of ammunition to ensure that pressures remain within the safe limits of each particular gauge.

These pressures are the maximum allowable pressure for any round, and manufacturers and those who provide handloading data endeavor to keep pressures well below this level. Be aware, though, that high pressure is not necessarily good. In fact low-pressure loads often pattern better despite the velocities being similar. Certainly, a low-pressure load is better for the shotgun from which it is fired.

Reloading or handloading, done with care, is safe and fun. With some time at the patterning board and careful evaluation of results on clays, specific loads tailored to individual shooting styles and choking preferences can be developed. Provided the few and simple rules are followed, there is nothing dangerous about reloading. Furthermore, there is great reward in dropping a game bird, running a station or a 100 straight with shells you loaded.

Gauge/ Bore	Chamber Length (in.)	Maximum Service Pressure (psi)
10	3 1/2	11,000
12	3 1/2	14,000
12	3	11,500
12	2 3/4	11,500
16	2 3/4	11,500
20	3	12,000
20	2 3/4	12,000
28	2 3/4	12,500
410	3	13,500
410	2 1/2	12,500

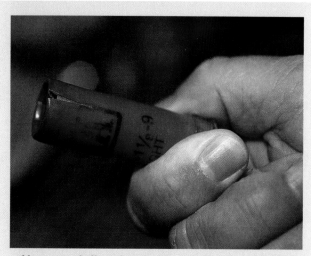

Old, worn-out hulls, such as this example, should be discarded before loading. Using them is a waste of time and good components.

SUGGESTED RELOAD DATA FOR SPORTING CLAYS

I asked Hodgdon Powder's ballistician Ron Reiber, who was the 2002 National AA Small-Bore High-Over-All Champion and the 2003 AA World Five-Stand Champion, to tell me about for his favorite loads.

Reiber prefers 1-ounce loads in the 12 gauge to reduce recoil and provide better patterns. Although the NSCA permits 1 1/8-ounce 12-gauge loads, FITASC now requires 1-ounce shot charges for their events. Reiber does not subscribe to the current high-velocity craze. "I primarily use 1200-fps loads. Recoil is less, patterns are superior to the higher velocity stuff and factory rounds that duplicate 1200 fps are easily obtainable when factory ammunition is required at some sporting clays shoots," he said.

Nonetheless, Reiber included three high-velocity loads, one each for the 12, 20 and 28 gauges:

12-gauge

Rem. STS Shell, Win. 209 primer, WAA12SL Wad, 1-oz hard #8 shot, 17.3 gr. Hodgdon Clays, 1200 fps
Win. AA Shell, Win. 209 primer, WAA12SL Wad, 1-oz hard #7-1/2 shot, 21.3 gr. Hodgdon International, 1300 fps

20-gauge

Win. AA Shell, Win. 209 primer, Rem. RXP20 Wad, 7/8-oz hard #8 shot, 15.0 gr. Hodgdon Universal, 1200 fps
Rem. STS Shell, Rem. 209P primer, WAA20 Wad, 7/8-oz hard #7-1/2 shot, 18.5 gr. Hodgdon Longshot, 1300 fps

28-gauge

Rem. STS Shell, Rem. 209P primer, Red Duster Wad, 3/4-oz hard #8 shot, 13.7 gr. Hodgdon Universal, 1200 fps
Rem. STS Shell, Rem. 209P primer, Red Duster Wad, 3/4-oz hard #8 shot, 15.3 gr. Hodgdon Longshot, 1275 fps

410-bore

Win. AAHS Shell, Win. 209 primer, Rem. SP410 Wad, 1/2-oz hard #8-1/2 shot, 13.3 gr. Hodgdon Lil' Gun, 1200 fps

SOURCES FOR LOADING TOOLS AND ACCESSORIES

Data Manuals

Ballistic Products, Inc. (various manuals), PO Box 293, Corcoran, MN 55340 (888) 273-5623

Hodgdon Shotshell Manual, Hodgdon Powder Co., P.O. Box 2932, Shawnee Mission, KS 66201 (913) 362-9455

Lyman 4th Edition Shotshell Manual, Lyman, 475 Smith St., Middletown, CT 06457 (800) 225-9626

Precision Reloading Shotshell Loading Manual, Precision Reloading, P.O. Box 122, Stafford Springs, CT 06076 (800) 223-0900

Reloading For Shotgunners, DBI Books/Krause Publications, 700 E. State St., Iola, WI 54990 (888) 457-2873

Single-Stage Loaders

Lee Precision, Inc., 4275 Highway U, Hartford, WI 53027 (262) 673-3075

Mayville Engineering Co., 715 South St., Mayville, WI 53050 (920) 387-4500

Ponsness/Warren, 768 Ohio St., Rathdrum, ID 83858 (800) 732-0706

RCBS, PO Box 605 Oro Dam Blvd., Oroville, CA 95965 (916) 533-5191

Progressive Loaders

Dillon Precision Products, 8009 E. Dillon's Way, Scottsdale, AZ 85260 (800) 223-4570

Hornady Mfg. Co., Box 1848, Grand Island, NE 68802 (800) 338-3220

Mayville Engineering Co., 715 South St., Mayville, WI 53050 (920) 387-4500

Ponsness/Warren, 768 Ohio St., Rathdrum, ID 83858 (800) 732-0706

RCBS, PO Box 605 Oro Dam Blvd., Oroville, CA 95965 (916) 533-5191

Spolar Power Load, 2273 S. Vista, B-2, Bloomington, CA 92316 (800) 227-9667

Powder Scales

Lyman, 475 Smith St., Middletown, CT 06457 (800) 225-9626

PACT, 2100 N. Highway 360, #1901, Grand Prairie, TX 75050

RCBS, PO Box 605 Oro Dam Blvd., Oroville, CA 95965 (916) 533-5191

13
Chapter

ACCESSORIZE FOR SAFETY

The theory behind any accessory is that it should help solve a particular shooting problem. Most accessories have an additional feature: they define and enhance your style. It is otherwise true, however, that you *demonstrate* style at the shooting stations around a course, and no one gets much respect until they begin to break more birds than they miss.

Sporting clays is a social game. It is as much about expressing who you are and how you approach life as it is about the busted disks you leave behind. Waiting your turn at a rabbit and teal station is not something you have to do. You have to earn a living. You have to obey the law. You do not have to shoot a shotgun. Therefore, how you play the game is a matter that carries your personal signature.

If you choose to shoot at flying disks in your spare time, there are some accessory items that you must have. Some are designed to protect you, and you will not be allowed on a course without them – eye and ear protection, for instance. Others, such as gloves and hats are optional, but often recommended. You must have a case to protect your equipment. Vests and shooting shirts are optional, although the rule of the '60s applies at most sporting clays courses: no shirt, no shoes, no service.

II.A.2. Mandatory Eye and Ear Protection: All persons, spectators, shooters, field judges, and trap personnel must wear eye and ear protection on the course at a tournament sanctioned by NSCA. [Official Rules of the National Sporting Clays Association]

The first rule of shooting is safety. Without an extreme emphasis on safety, there could not be any organized shooting games in America. You should spend as much time and money - relatively speaking - protecting your vision and your hearing as you do selecting your shotgun. In the safety category, the cheapest will definitely not be the best.

155

PROTECTING YOUR VISION

When you are shooting a shotgun, your eyes are probably your most valuable physical asset. People with other physical impairments shoot successfully from wheelchairs all the time. The truly sight challenged, vision impaired or completely blind, however, are extremely rare at a shotgun venue. The moral is to take care of your eyes.

An old adage says, "Youth is wasted on the young." It suggests that young people do not yet value the days they are given and that only as you lose your grasp on youth do you gain your perspective on life. Perhaps this is true. Nevertheless, the purpose of mandatory eye protection is to keep everyone's eyes, young and old, as safe as possible while engaging in regulated gunplay.

It may surprise you to learn that guns are nowhere near the statistical top of the list for eye injuries. That sad prominence belongs to ball sports: baseball, basketball and the other racquet sports. Perhaps this is true because shooting ranges, clay venues and other shooters strictly enforce the eyewear rule.

These JS410 Pro Sport Mirror Silver shooting glasses from DeGil have a lightweight, impact-resistant nylon frame, and the impact-resistant polycarbonate lenses have a scratch-resistant coating and provide 99.9 percent UV protection. In addition, their wrap-around style is both highly protective for the side of your eyes ... and ultra cool.

Still, everyone who lives long enough will eventually be vision impaired in some manner. It is a natural consequence of living. As we push our way into our 40s, our eyesight begins to deteriorate. The Association of Vision Science Librarians estimates that 15 million Americans over 40 years of age have "macular

Looking into the sun in a clear sky when you call for a bird is tough enough, but add the cold and glare of a snowy landscape and your visual acuity can be seriously degraded. Manufacturers of shooting glasses offer impact-resistant polycarbonate lenses in a variety of tints to help you acquire the bird. Find the one that is best for your shooting. This Canadian shooter has chosen "rose-colored glasses."

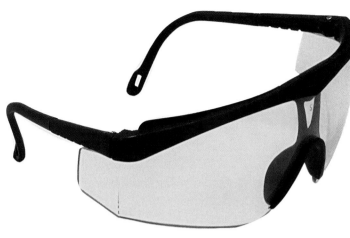

Slip on a pair of Silencio shooting glasses with yellow-tinted lenses on a gray day and the course will suddenly seem so bright that you will reach for the suntan lotion.

degeneration." This means that if you believe you are seeing spots, you probably are, either on the front (cornea) or back (retina) of your eyeball. It is the duty of shatterproof, impact-resistant eyewear to ensure that your vision does not deteriorate in one dramatic stroke of inexcusable misfortune.

If you are awake, your eyes are working, says Tommy Brown, a Florida optometrist and avid shooter. Because the average shooter is no longer young, and we often spend hours each day staring at a computer screen, our 21st-century eyes age more rapidly than did those of former generations.

Thus, we begin a lifelong struggle to protect and enhance our vision. If you wear prescription glasses, vision gets to be a three-ring circus because you eventually try contact lenses and then you graduate to bifocals and, soon enough, to bifocal contact lenses. Because truly superior shooting is the art of training a soft and undisciplined body to perform mechanically, all the changes your eyes go through as you pick up a few years can cause your shooting abilities to be haphazard and irregular.

Standard glasses with CR39 plastic lenses are not sufficiently protective for shooting. Polycarbonate lenses, which cost $50 to $60 more than CR39, are, however, designed to withstand frontal impact. Polycarbonate is the material used for safety lenses for sports and industrial activities, and it is certainly worth asking your optometrist about the lens qualities of your glasses.

Standard glasses are also wide open around their edges. You could wear goggles, and some people like them, but on a hot, humid day – or on a cold day when moisture from your breath fogs your lenses – they can be uncomfortable. Fortunately, options exist to standard frame glasses and goggles.

I do not have uncorrected 20-20 vision and my eyes compound that with a touch of astigmatism or depth perception difficulty. Therefore, I have gone through all of the vision enhancement phases. Today,

my eye protection preference is a pair of prescription contact lenses with impact-resistant sunglasses from HiDef Spex specifically made for shooting. This combination maximizes my protection and visual acuity.

Additionally, the combination of contact lenses – which provide no protection at all – with impact-resistant eyewear gives me the most versatility in lens tints for any kind of weather. As long as I keep my lenses clean and scratch-free, I can go a long way to developing shooting accuracy.

Recently, a friend recommended wearing one prescription contact lens on my right, dominant eye and not wearing a lens on the other eye. This system, she said, seemed to maximize her ability to both see at distance and to read maps and fill out forms. Well, this worked fine around the house, working in the office and even driving, but when it came to breaking clays, my score suffered. I believe the problem was that in this arrangement of lenses, my eyes found it difficult to triangulate speed and distance.

Shooting-specific eyewear is not designed to correct your vision (although you can order prescription shooting glasses), but to protect and enhance it. On the clay course, you want eyewear with lenses that will not shatter if a clay fragment or stray BB smacks them squarely in the center. You want a shape that will give you protection from shrapnel scratching your eyeball from the sides or even ricocheting up from the bottom. You want a comfortable, lightweight fit, especially over your nose, interchangeable lens tints and perhaps polarization as well, if you often shoot in bright conditions.

Before you walk away from any sales counter with a new pair of shooting glasses – and sales people tell you that this kind of purchase is often an *impulse buy* – you are going to be faced with a selection from a myriad of styles and lens colors. You would like to have them all, and some companies offer kits with multiple replaceable lenses that are designed to maximize your visual acuity in any weather. Perfect. The shape of the lens and frame are matters of personal choice, but most companies suggest lens tints based on guidelines that only you can interpret through your own eyes:

Clear: Use in low light where enhancement is needed. Allows maximum light transmission without changing the value of perceived colors. Blocks blue light and haze.

Yellow: For use in low light. Blocks blue haze and significantly enhances clarity.

Red: Improves detail and enhances depth perception in low or artificial light. Intensifies warm colors. (My personal favorite.)

Bronze/Brown: Improves visual definition and glare reduction in bright light. Sharpens and enhances ground level contours.

Slate/Gray: Maximum glare reduction without distorting colors.

Smoke Green: Excellent general-purpose use. Maximum glare reduction without distorting colors.

Mirror lenses: Diminishes glare by absorbing reflection across the mirror face.

Several companies offer goggle-style eyewear and these are excellent for true 100-percent eye protection. Unlike glasses, goggles literally encase your eyes. If you use goggles, make sure they have anti-fog protection because they are going to feel hot over your face, especially if their elastic strap holds them tight, and you sweat around your eyes. Because most of my shooting is done in the steamy southeast United States, I generally find goggles uncomfortable and do not like the heavy-framed, confined feeling they give my already imperfect vision.

Wiley X eyewear (www.wileyx.com) offers several styles of shatterproof eye protection. This California business says that military, law enforcement and sport shooters around the world use its eyewear.

All HVP eyewear models are certified to meet ANSI[1] (American National Standards Institute – www.ansi.org) high-velocity impact standard. According to Wiley X, every one of its lenses block 100 percent of UV rays and are made from "pure, shatterproof selenite polycarbonate that far exceed" ANSI standards. Wiley X frames are constructed from nearly indestructible "triloid nylon."

The Wiley X Internet site gives you a chance to view all eyewear and to mix and match tints. The #SG-1 ballistic eye-orbit sealing goggles, for instance, with an anti-fog coating on smoke green and clear lenses cost $100 and include a soft case. Wiley X recognizes that these low-profile goggles can become hot and so has developed the sealing foam with push-out notches to increase airflow. The #PT-1P ballistic wrap-around one-piece lens in "Pale Rose" tint costs $70 and extra lenses are $20 each.

HDS Performance Optics or HiDef Spex (www.hidefspex.com) is a new entry in the eyewear category and 12-time sporting clays world champion George Digweed endorses them. These are not wrap-around glasses, but are styled in classic aviator patterns. The cost of any style from their Internet site is $179 or, if lenses are ground to your prescription, $249.

HDS representative Carlo Pilla says their lenses are melanin-infused, as well as tinted, and incorporate a partial blue-blocker. "Sit in front of your television," Pilla suggests, "and it will seem like you have one of the expensive new high definition sets. This is because our lenses are melanin-infused."

What does it mean when lenses are "melanin-infused?" While the infusion process is both patented and protected, Pilla says, this lens treatment allows shooters to visually acquire targets faster and there is no color distortion. "Orange targets leap out of the background," he says, "and even black targets are better defined." Designed to provide optimal target vision under any light conditions, these lenses eliminate the

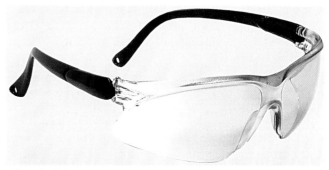

If you find that no tint helps you pick up a speeding clay or cuts the glare, or you are one of those shooters whom tints just seem to irritate, you will still need safety glasses. Clear polycarbonate wrap-around lenses from a company such as Silencio may be your ticket to high-level shooting.

need to search for the perfect color to cope with the weather. Additionally, melanin blocks harmful UV (ultraviolet) and HEV (high energy visible, blue and violet) rays that contribute to cataracts and "macular degeneration."

In mid 2004, HDS introduced a new plano (non-prescription) lens for shooters who need even more light available to their eyes than the standard HDS lens offers. The new lens (#HDS25) permits 60 percent more light transmission than the original lens (#HDS15). Night shooters and many seniors will like this.

If you have a favorite shooting frame, HDS will build lenses to the frames you select and will even build clip-on type lenses to fit your current clear-lens prescription glasses. HDS frames are "monel," a very hard, tarnish-resistant nickel/copper alloy used for machined parts exposed to wear and corrosive elements. "Monel is harder than stainless steel," Pilla says, "and more resistant to rust."

Canada's Degil Safety Products sells a variety of impact-resistant, UV-protective, scratch-resistant eyewear for sportsmen, everything from the stylish #JS410 Pro Sport Sliver ($9.90) to the #JD150 Metal Sport wrap-around ($23.90). (We will also mention Degil in the hearing protection section, and they sell a species of sunscreen called "CrocBloc.")

Degil's #J10 Sport Spec (www.degilsafety.com) deserves special mention. The clear, all-polycarbonate lens and frame of the #J10 are designed to fit over most prescription frames and lenses. It is available in clear, smoke or yellow lenses and matching frames. Like prescription drugs, the best deal available in eyewear today may be from our northern neighbor. The #J10 suggested retail price is only $4.58. The only drawback may be that wearing these "over-glasses" may feel awkward, as if you are wearing two pair of glasses – which you are.

BelOptix sunglass lenses (www.beloptix.com) use a photo-chromatic layer on the front surface that lightens and darkens according to the amount of UV light that is present. In the presence of UV rays, molecules in the layer turn inside-out. Celebrity spokesman Ray Eye says this quality is perfect for hunting and shooting: "It's like 3-D!"

"Polarized lenses reduce glare and are standard in sunglasses," BelOptix President Steve Wood says, "but they are often too dark for many ambient light conditions. We have combined polarization with photo-chromatic lens technologies to enhance vision in all outdoor daylight conditions."

Steve recommends their Target Orange lens, which darkens to Dark Brown in the most intense sunlight, for sporting clays shooting.

BelOptix eyewear is available with non-corrective lenses ($169) as well as single-vision ($295) and multi-focal or progressive ($495) prescriptions. Lenses are available in a multitude of tints and are coated for resistance to scratching, fogging and reflected sunlight. Wrap-around frames feature tinted side panels for protected peripheral vision and come in tortoise, camo and black. Each pair weighs one ounce.

Olympic Optical (www.olympicoptical.com), which markets both under its own name and for Smith &

Wesson (www.smith-wessonsafety.com), makes a variety of great-looking, lightweight safety glasses. Olympic even has a model with magnifying lens inserts in +1.5-, +2.0- and +2.5-power options.

The Smith & Wesson Ozone, Code 4 and Magnum 3G are all frameless, wrap-around styles with quick-change, no-screw, snap-fit lenses. At least 10 different tints are available. You can purchase Magnum 3G eyewear in regular and small sizes, to fit shooters from first gun to last shot fired. If you can see well, you can shoot well.

Impact resistant glasses from Decot Hy-Wyd (www.sportglasses.com) feature rimless frames with multi-tinted, interchangeable lenses for sport shooting. Bob Decot says his family's company will custom tint your lenses in 40 different shades and builds shooting glasses with regular or prescription lenses.

The term "Hy-Wyd" indicates that the lenses are set high and wide on a shooter's fact to enhance the corrected field of view where, except for the running rabbit, the clay targets are usually flying. An optional bridge allows you to adjust these glasses up or down on your face.

PROTECTING YOUR HEARING

What would it be like to live in a world of silence? If you knew no other world, hearing sound could be frightening. For a member of the hearing population, to suddenly go stone deaf would be just as dramatic. Even though hearing impairments almost never happen like that, the National Center for Health Statistics estimates that between 22 and 35 million people in the United States (between 10 and 15 percent of the population) have some form of hearing loss. If you mount a shotgun and pull the trigger without adequate hearing protection, you could soon be a member of that group. You could also develop tinnitus, a non-stop ringing in your ears, which could be worse.

The only hearing protection you can possibly afford is a style that protects you completely. Medical experts testify that two hours of exposure to 100 decibels (dB) of noise – a chain saw or pneumatic drill – can cause permanent hearing loss. An hour of 105 dB accomplishes the same thing, as does half an hour at 110 dB – motorcycle noise or a woodworking shop – or just 15 minutes at 115 dB. By the time you reach the higher ranges, 120 dB near an ambulance siren or amplified rock band, 130 dB for a jackhammer or 140 dB for a jet engine at takeoff, you are in danger of immediate and permanent damage … and pain.

Gunfire causes sharp flashes of noise at the very highest levels. Your first .22? Figure 140 dB. Your 12-gauge? Figure 152 to 165 dB, and that astonishing noise level is only inches from your ear. According to Elvex, a Connecticut manufacturer of eye, face and hearing protection, the generally accepted threshold of pain is around 120 dB while the loudest possible noise is 194 dB.

The Power Muff Quad earmuffs from Walker's Game Ear have a padded, adjustable head band and the cups are concave to help reduce interference with the shotgun comb. Independent volume controls and adjustable frequency tuning give you superb protection from the deafening blast of a shotgun but allow you to hear range commands spoken in a normal tone and volume.

Unlike the trapper, who appeared to stick his finger in his ear whenever someone shot (Had he forgotten his hearing protection or did he just not care?), the shotgunner on stand is wearing a set of earmuff-style hearing protectors. When you consider hearing protection, you must decide whether or not you will find muffs too irritating if they interfere with proper gun mount.

The ear is a delicate instrument made of thin, porous bones, specialized nerves and an array of canals and tubes that relay vibration and help us equalize pressure. To do anything that would carelessly allow damage to this amazing and intricate little miracle would be a terrible shame. It is appropriate to feel pity for the older members of your shooting club who have experienced hearing loss from shooting, the guys who have to turn their head so their "good ear" is toward the speaker. "Eh? What did you say?" It is neither appropriate nor macho to imitate them.

I have a love-hate relationship with hard-shell earmuffs. They unquestionably work very well and they are comfortable … until the day turns warm or I bump them with the stock of the shotgun. At that point, I want to take them off and switch to earplugs (although the best possible protection is a combination of plugs and muffs). With muffs, when I get a little tired or uncomfortable from the heat and bring the gun to my cheek, the stock sometimes bangs against the hard cup. I have had more than one joker "thunk" the hard outer shell with his fingertip. That sends a painfully loud noise through my ear and right through my eyeballs into my brain. It always causes me to wince.

Curiously, many inexpensive earplugs have NRR ratings higher than the larger, more complex and more expensive muffs. Silencio's NRR 32 soft foam Red-E-Fit Earplugs (#RFP-96) are as cheap as protection gets and their NRR is higher than the Hearsafe 2220 (#HSF-22) with an over-head NRR of only 22. The difference is squeezing something down your ear canal

These simple, soft foam Mul-T-Fit earplugs from DeGil have an amazing Noise Reduction Rating (NRR) of 28. The higher this rating, the greater the noise interruption hearing protection provides. The best combination for noise reduction is a pair of simple earplugs with a set of earmuffs that have a noise interruption circuit that silences the noise of a shot.

versus wearing the muffs over or behind your head. Some shooters are just not comfortable with plugs, and there is a perception they do not give you the protection afforded by muffs. That perception is wrong if inserted properly. Whatever you choose to wear, remember the very best hearing protection can be obtained by simultaneously using both plugs and muffs.

To spend time with your ear over the stock of a shotgun without some type of good quality decibel reducer (remember the 152 dB) is to tempt deafness. Fortunately, numerous companies, including Pro-Ears, which I do not specifically profile in this chapter, sell quality products to protect your ears while shooting.

You will usually see products listed with an NRR number. NRR means "noise reduction rating" and it is a curious, semi-scientific factor. The NRR is supposed to be the measure of protection you buy when you purchase earmuffs or plugs, but this number is actually self-determined by the manufacturer – following some loose government guidelines – and may vary a good bit between individuals. Everything is different, however, depending upon whether you hear continuous noise (a jackhammer) or impact noise (a gunshot). NRR is established in this rather general manner:

• First, 10 people are exposed to nine frequencies three times each. This establishes the lowest sound they can hear at each frequency.

• Next, they cover or plug their ears with some device, such as a set of lightweight, low-profile Elvex Silver muffs (NRR 25, $16.85 at www.elvex.com).

• The procedure with the range of frequencies is repeated.

• The difference between the two hearing thresholds – with and without protection – is determined at each frequency for each individual in the test. The total average reduction in the level of noise for all 10 people across all nine frequencies becomes the NRR.

• So, in a continuous noise environment of 140 dB, wearing the Elvex Silver muffs above would reduce the noise level to 115 dB [140 – 25 = 115]. Still loud, but far more acceptable. Silencio warns that this is different for impact noise, however, and reminds us that the very best possible hearing protection is earplugs and electronic earmuffs worn simultaneously.

Degil Safety Products (www.degilsafety.com) manufactures a variety of hearing protection products, from the cheapest, most basic earplugs to sophisticated earmuffs with noise reduction circuitry. Degil's disposable blaze orange DePlugs are made from either non-allergenic polyurethane foam or PVC. The DePlug comes in four styles: tapered, tapered with cord, cylindrical or Mul-T-Fit "beaded." These non-allergenic earplugs weigh next to nothing, but Degil insists that if they are inserted in the ear canal properly, they provide a surprisingly high level of noise reduction (NRR 28-29). Clubs and ranges buy these by the bucket (#7752050)

Here is a unique wrinkle for shooters who have a difficult time paying attention ... or perhaps for those who do not. The React Electronic combines Silencio's "active listening," which amplifies low-level sounds while limiting speaker output to a safe 82 decibels, with AM/FM stereo sound. One knob controls power, volume, frequency and AM/FM band selection. A second knob selects between active listening and radio mode.

and often hand them out free to visitors or sell them over the counter for a quarter.

The best value in the Degil line is probably the $7 DePlug Band-It (#7752100). This lightweight earplug band is worn under the chin and the suction-cast cushions are designed to trap air in the ear canal without actually entering it. Worn properly, Degil says, it offers a noise reduction rating of 17, which is significantly better than some of the higher-priced, non-electronic earmuffs.

Degil sells earmuffs in two categories, passive and electronic. The $29.90 Deluxe passive, foldable earmuff (#20010, NRR 25 dB) is designed to provide a comfortable and effective seal while reducing headband force. The sealing rings are ultra soft and have extra cushioning.

At the other end of the price range, the electronic $420 Supreme Pro (#75302) has an NRR of 18 dB. It requires two AAA batteries for operation. Degil describes these muffs as "a foldable level dependent earmuff developed to conform to international military specifications and extreme conditions." This high-quality earmuff limits hazardous impact noise to 82 dB, or well below the blast level of your shotgun. The Supreme Pro has five amplification settings and provides superior stereo-sound-quality reception. A special socket will connect to most radio handsets and dog tracking units. If the price seems a little steep, Degil's basic headband earmuff with impact protection and sound amplification (NRR 23 dB) costs only $178.

Bob Walker's original Game Ear (NRR 29 dB, www.walkersgameear.com) was developed for hunting and weighed less than 1/4 ounce. Walker says it increases your ability to hear up to five times by amplifying high frequency sounds with 46 dB of battery power.

Even the original design from about 1989 had a safety compression circuit or an impact filter to protect the user from loud sounds including muzzle blast. Such a circuit or filter is calibrated to close when noise reaches a certain decibel level and then reopen when it drops below that level. This all happens in micro-seconds.

The Game Ear for hunters morphed into a version for competitors called the Target Ear ($159.95). When the Game Ear/Target Ear II came out, it allowed users to tune their hearing device to match individual hearing needs. Consequently, you could hear range commands and still have muzzle blast hearing protection. The Game Ear/Target Ear III allowed for wireless voice communications when used with a "walkie talkie" such as a Motorola TalkAbout. The newest, digital version provides a clearer audio signature. Walker says it increases your hearing ability up to seven times while still incorporating the noise compression circuitry that keeps your ear from being smashed by muzzle blast.

Three sets of earmuffs are available through Walker's Game Ear. All three sets are nicely sculptured along the bottom to help prevent interference when shouldering your gun with proper shooting form. The Range Ear version has a noise reduction rating (NRR) of 24 dB. The electronic Power Muffs ($209) have two independent volume controls that allow for true stereo sound while wind-resistant high-frequency microphones make it easy to identify sound

and direction. The new Power Muff Quads ($259), which are my personal favorites, have 50 dB of battery power, four high-frequency directional, wind-resistant microphones and independent volume controls to decrease blast and noisy background chatter. Walker says the Quads (NRR 24) increase a user's hearing up to eight times. Both electronic models incorporate Sound Activated Compression circuits.

For shooters who prefer earmuffs, Olympic Optical has licensed the Smith & Wesson (www.smith-wessonsafety.com) name to sell their "Suppressor" earmuffs. The outer blue shells or cups are hard plastic and engraved with the S&W logo. Cups pivot on the plastic headband for a secure, comfortable fit and equal pressure distribution. According to Olympic, these earmuffs carry a noise reduction rating (NRR) of 25 dB.

Silencio (www.silencio.com) sells a wide variety of earmuffs and earplugs, many with contoured cups to minimize contact with your shotgun stock. From economical earmuffs such as their Original (#RBW-71) with foam-filled ear cups to the digital NightHawk Tactical (#NHT-21) with sound-suppression circuitry and the Regional 2 Communications Headset (#HLE-02) with both noise compression circuitry *and* a communications-enabled headset, Silencio has all the muffs. Their Relax Electronic (#HLE-04) includes an AM/FM stereo radio in the headset. This model is powered by a rechargeable nickel-metal hydride (NiMH) battery and comes with a battery charger. Silencio says it will play for 50 hours on a charge. A multi-function power inlet accepts input from portable audio devices or communications radios.

Muffs from Silencio are rated for three types of wear: over head, behind head or under chin. Their Original Earmuff (#LIQ-71) with liquid-filled cushions, for instance, is rated as follows: over head NRR 28, behind head NRR 23 and under chin NRR 21.

FOOTNOTES

[1] In order to receive the ANSI (American National Standards Institute) Z 87.1 rating, safety glasses must undergo extensive testing. According to the 1989 standard, they must be able to withstand the high mass impact of a 17.6-ounce ball dropped from 51.2 inches. Additionally, there must be zero penetration from high-velocity impact at 150 fps. All safety glasses receiving this rating have met the requirements for prism imbalance, refractive power, haze, transmittance and UV protection.

14
Chapter

ACCESSORIZE

We are infinitely fortunate in America to be able to own guns and shoot them with great latitude for style and ability, for hunting and target shooting, for fun and competition, in thousands of locations around our country. Whether you take your Mossberg pump chambered for 3-inch magnums or your engraved, hand-made Perazzi, you can find an open sporting clays course virtually any weekend – or even during the week – without the government interfering and requiring that we buy licenses or attend training courses or pay a special tax for the privilege of igniting a little gunpowder.

It is an interesting human phenomenon that after we have acquired a gun and the skill to use it effectively, we buy and spend more, not less. Perhaps that is the way of all hobbies. We try shooting in a cap, but our ears and neck sunburn, so we buy a wide-brim, crushable hat. We carry shells in our gym bag for a couple years, with the gun over our shoulder, and we are too strung out to drink more than one or two martinis at the end of the day. And that is too tired! Fortunately, there are dozens of accessories for purchase that promise to make our time with the guns more enjoyable. Here are a few ideas that may enhance your shooting experience.

THE SHOOTING VEST

At one time or another, most of us have worn an adjustable, padded harness to help us cope with our gun's recoil. In my experience, people rarely find these harnesses comfortable. Straps make a harness work, but they are irritating as well. In addition, the protection offered by the thinly padded section is minimal. Nevertheless, shooting harnesses are available from Boyt and Bob Allen. Bob Allen's adjustable $34 khaki Absorb-a-Coil Harness has a soft, visco-elastic polymer pad enclosed in a cotton pocket. This pad, the Bob Allen people say, absorbs up to 40 percent more recoil than the competition. It is faced with suede and available for right-hand or left-hand shooters.

A full shooting vest is superior to a harness because the cost is comparable, the recoil protection is comparable, its versatility is greater and the nuisance of the straps is eliminated.

Do not believe that because a shooter is young or small, he or she can be patronized. This small, redheaded shooter outshot everyone in his squad on Sunday at Turkey Run north of Gainesville, Florida. He was confident, fully equipped and well accessorized!

163

The best place to look for shooting accessories is a sporting goods retailer in your neighborhood. You may be able to buy some common items at a discount mart, but for true sales and service, you would be light years ahead getting to know the folks at an independent retail establishment.

With vests, your style of shooting, the place you shoot and time of year will help you determine what to buy. A vest is more than just a place to carry your shells. A vest is part of your shooting system, no less than your shells. It helps you achieve consistent gun mount and gun placement into the shoulder pocket. A vest is not necessary to good shooting, but it does help.

When selecting a shooting vest, consider the shotgun games you shoot. Trap and skeet shooters, who mount their gun on their shoulder before calling for the bird, get by with a small gun pad. A full front pad is virtually mandatory in low-gun games because the gun butt can catch on an abbreviated pad. Many shooters choose the international-style vest with full-length, vertical pad, because it works well in any shooting situation.

Sporting clay shooters should consider a vest with double divided shell pockets. This style allows one to keep track of up to four different loads. It is common to carry several different loads to the shooting stand and decide on the proper load when the first birds are tossed. Trap and skeet shooters, on the other hand, need just one big pocket for live shells and perhaps one for fired hulls if they reload.

Construction of your vest is important. In the hot, humid southeast, you rarely see a full-front and full-back cloth vest because they become too hot. They quickly become sweat-soaked and wind up several pounds heavier than when they started the day. That makes you uncomfortable and detracts from your concentration and confidence. Southern and hot-weather shooters favor mesh vests. Northern and cool-weather shooters generally prefer fuller vests for warmth, and because they sometimes compete during the winter.

For less than the suggested retail price of $49 you can wear a Bob Allen #102 Series shooting vest that has a breast pocket and two extra-large lower pockets for shells and empties. It is made from soft, tightly woven mesh poly-cotton twill and features a long, lightly stuffed gun pad. From this price point up to practically $150, you can purchase a vest with a variety of side tab adjustments, choke-tube pockets and interior security pockets with zippers. Vests in a range of colors, with towel loops and a gun pad, and trim made from leather are available. The more expensive your vest, the more extras it will have.

SHOOTING SHIRTS

We should be honest about apparel for sporting clays. Fewer than half the people on the course look like they stepped out of an LL Bean catalog. Some are actually wearing pajamas or old camo. Well, sporting clays is supposed to be a game. Even from a distance, however, the folks who look like they rolled out from under the truck where they were fixing a hole in the oil pan are usually men. And it is true that we men do take some perverse pleasure in looking like hell, but I nevertheless maintain that women have a better sense of themselves … or, and I am not sure of this, perhaps just better sense. Whatever side you come down on in this argument, there are some nicely distinctive (although a bit "bourgeoisie") shirts designed for shooters with nice little – although probably not supremely effective – recoil pads sewn into the shoulder pocket.

MizMac Designs (www.mizmac.com) offers "ladies shooting apparel designed by lady shooters for lady shooters." Their shirts, socks and visors are offered to fill a niche in the market – comfortable, functional and good-looking women's shooting apparel – that was not being served by other manufacturers or marketers. The short sleeve shirt ($65), which is 100-percent cotton, includes a collar and two pleats over the shoulder blades on the back for stretching and to prevent any constraining feel when you shoot. Shirts are available in sizes from small to extra-large, right-hand or left-hand (for the shooting patch) and four colors: flannel, natural, blue or red. MizMac also offers sleeveless shirts, a "hairdo saver" shooting visor and cushioned white shooting socks.

Most major firearms companies have clothing made for them that carries their logo. Beretta, for instance, offers a serious clothing section in their catalog: shirts, caps and even a few gloves, towels and jackets at www.berettausa.com. Even if you are not shooting for HOA, you will look good in Beretta's Big 5 Shooting Shirt and Blains Game Shorts (both $70 suggested retail).

HATS AND CAPS

Part of the sun's rays reaching us every day are ultraviolet rays, UVA and UVB. These invisible rays damage skin cells, causing visible and invisible injuries. Some immediately apparent injuries are sunburn and freckles. Other injuries, such as skin cancers, age spots and wrinkling of the skin can take years to appear.

An acrylic shooting sweater with shoulder patch from Boyt/Bob Allen will keep you warm on a cool or windy day, and it looks good, too.

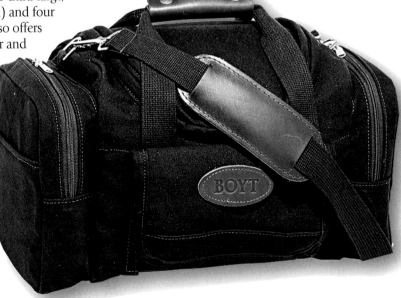

I find that a roomy shooting bag such as the SC25 Sporting Clays Bag from Boyt is extremely helpful in keeping my shooting gear organized for a trip to the course or range. This bag has a clamshell top for easy access and holds plenty of gear or eight boxes of shells. It's made of 22-ounce heavy-duty canvas with a retail price of $101.

A cap may be the most commonly seen headwear on a sporting clays course, but this shooter in Florida understands that a cap does not cover his ears and the back of his neck from the sun and its harmful UVA and UVB rays.

The standard headgear on a shooting course is a baseball-style cap. Every company, vacation destination and shooting venue sells them or gives them away with a purchase. At many angles of the sun during the middle of the day, a cap is fine for shading your face. It does nothing, however, for your ears or neck or for reflected sunlight.

Headgear is important for two reasons: first, the rate of skin cancer is increasing in North America and second, the age of the average sporting clays shooter is edging up. This means we are susceptible to sunburn in unusual places, like the top of our head!

A hat with a full, 180-degree brim is much better than a cap because it affords your face some protection from the sun no matter what direction you are facing. It gives you shade for your ears and neck, too.

New, crushable-style hats can be found in most shopping malls and sporting goods stores. I am surprised that Boyt Harness/Bob Allen do not carry a variety of hats in their catalog, but if you order from a cataloguer such as LL Bean (www.llbean.com), their imported $28 Tropicwear Outback Hat appears to be just right. Bean says this lightweight, woven-nylon hat has a sun protection factor (SPF) of 40 and that the polyester headband wicks moisture away from your face and head. Drop it in the water and it floats, or hold it by the adjustable keeper strap and dunk it in the water bucket before plopping it back on your head.

PROTECTING YOUR GUN

Hard-Sided Travel Cases

I am not shilling for any company, but whether or not you travel with your gun, I recommend you buy the best hard-sided case you can afford. I have bought inexpensive, plastic cases and ended a trip holding them together with duct tape. Of course, those were the days before 9-11. Today, for a variety of reasons, you must be more careful.

What do you look for in a hard-sided case? Check for such things as recessed hinges and locks that cannot be easily smashed by airport baggage handlers; steel-reinforced corners help prevent a cracked or damaged case if it is dropped; and when you think of carrying the case, a comfortable, sturdy, non-slip handle will make the difference between misery and misfortune. Check the locks and the seals because the case must be tamper-proof and moisture-proof.

Fortunately, there are plenty of superior cases available. Handsome models from T.Z. Case International (www.tzcase.com), high-performance carriers from Storm Case (www.stormcase.com), the rugged and well-known cases from Plano Molding (www.planomolding.com), padded cases and bags from SKB (www.skbcases.com) and the cases from other manufacturers are profiled below.

Although it is hard to beat Weatherby's custom, canvas-covered take-down shotgun case for presentation-style good looks – padded hunter green interior with leather corners – their heavy-gauge aluminum Magnum Take-Down case is an all-around better buy for storage and travel.

Dan Walter (www.danwaltercases.com) builds cases exclusively from 6061 T-6 extruded aluminum. Each corner is welded inside the case, leaving a perfectly mitered outside edge that is angled 30 degrees for aesthetics and strength. Top and bottom panels are aluminum, too. They lock into the extruded frame and are then welded in place. A center combination lock and two, heavy-duty key lockable draw latches keep the case tightly closed.

Inside, Walter begins with a sub-frame laminated to the extruded aluminum framework. Next, dense cross-link foam is laminated to the interior framework to cradle and cushion your firearm against damaging jolts during travel. Each interior piece is covered with velvet or an acrylic fabric that is not only beautiful but also adds more cushioning for your firearm.

Heavy-duty straps secure the barrel, forearm and stock/receiver. The rubber gasket ensures an airtight seal to keep dust and moisture out. "The competition uses a rolled piano hinge that can open over time and leave a weak joint," Walter says. "We machine our own full-length hinge and it will never open, even under the heavy abuse that can come with airline travel."

Although a "standard case" is not what you might think of ordering from a custom manufacturer, Walter's standard for an over/under breakdown runs about $446.

Doskosil is a high-end hard-plastic gun case manufacturer, which also manufactures under the name DoskoSport (www.doskosport.com). This company has a special case – sometimes several – for every shooting (and hunting) opportunity.

The inner dimensions of their black, AW Series Double Scoped Rifle/Shotgun Case are 52 x 13 x 5-1/4 inches. It conveniently carries two guns, but prevents them from bumping or scratching against each other. Doskocil says that its continuous overlapping seal ensures that you will have a watertight, airtight and dust-proof compartment.

To make handling this large case easy, it has two wide wheels and swivel handles. Holes drilled through the sturdy side rib allow you to fasten the case with your own padlock. The inside padding on top and bottom are thick layers of gray foam.

Vanguard (www.vanguardusa.com) markets Winchester cases for break-down shotguns. Their 7700 and 7800 series have lightweight black PVC panels, dark gray eggshell-foam padding and have both combination and key locks. The #7705 ($120) and #7805W ($135) have essentially the same inside dimensions in inches: 31-3/8 x 12-7/8 x 4. Because the 13 2/3-pound #7805W has steel-reinforced corners, it weighs about 3-3/4 pounds more than the #7705.

The brushed aluminum break-down shotgun cases from Winchester are the #WA-7048 ($160) and #WG-1151A ($170). Both styles offer full eggshell-foam padding, key locks and padlock receptacles. The WA case opens from both sides and weighs 16-3/4 pounds. The WG only weighs 9-1/2 pounds, but it only offers key locks. A universal Winchester (or some other brand) key will not open these locks.

Guardforce cases built by Vanguard are similar to those marketed by Winchester. They have four portable cases for break-down shotguns, which include those mentioned above, plus their #GDF-41000 series of molded, hard polyester cases. These lightweight cases have metal interior frames, carrying straps and handles. The #GDF-41833 weighs 6 pounds.

Ziegel Engineering (www.ziegeleng.com) in California is another custom case manufacturer. Of particular interest is Dean's 15-pound Model 75 (6-1/2 x 9 x 31 inches), which is designed primarily for over/under shotgun sets with 28-inch barrels. This heavy-duty aluminum case has reinforced corners and will accommodate four barrel sets and two receivers in a relatively compact format. It has four barrel compartments in the lower section and all dividers are covered with high-density foam. A built-in inner leaf separates barrels from receivers: receivers are held in place with Velcro fastening straps. The Model 75 is lined with a black polypropylene fabric. It has one handle on each side, plus two catches. This case can be padlocked through the stainless steel catches or with Dean's special AC16 Locking Rod. The suggested retail price is $301.95.

Perhaps no manufacturer has more carrying cases specifically dedicated to shotguns than Texas' Americase (www.americase.com). Their catalog shows photos and diagrams and gives exact dimensions of dozens of cases designed for specific carrying objectives such as a single stock and receiver with multiple barrels. Americase allows you to mix and match with #1008, the 25-pound Auto or Pump and Tubed Over-and-Under case for $419.

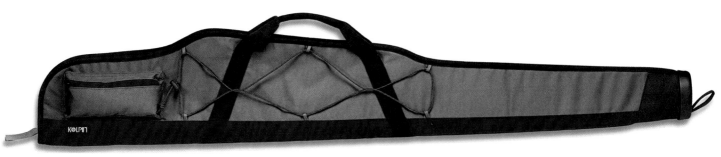

One of Kolpin's soft-sided shotgun cases would be an excellent carrier and temporary storage case for any shotgun.

If you are strictly a pump gun or semi-auto fan, #5043, the Ameri-Lite Two Take-down Pumps or Autos, weighs 14 pounds and costs $269.

Americase offers several custom accessories for its cases. Because most break-down shotgun cases are less than 38 inches long, an adjustable shoulder strap ($35) with a comfortable "Gel-Pad" for your carrying shoulder is available. When you order this accessory, D-rings for the strap will be attached to the case or case cover at the factory. Engraved name tags can be made and riveted to the case next to the handle or on the top side panel for a minimal fee and embroidery can be sewn onto any velvet interior case: game animals, your initials, the name of your favorite shotgun manufacturer, etc.

SOFT-SIDED CASES

Except for temporary storage and quick trips, soft-sided cases are not recommended for long-term storage of a firearm. While they are excellent when you want to reduce the bulk of a large, hard-sided case, they can trap moisture and induce rust and corrosion.

Kolpin (www.kolpin.com) is home to a wide variety of soft-sided shotgun cases. Their new Soft Armor Gun Boot 52 will protect scoped shotguns and rifles. This rugged case is attractive, with three-tone ballistic nylon and a swatch of Mossy Oak Breakup Camo over the exterior pocket. Additional protection is provided for the muzzle by an extra long rubber bumper. The case comes with a covered zipper, a removable, adjustable carrying sling and a separate wrap-around handle grip for the nylon handles. Kolpin says this $80 case will float … with the gun in it!

Boyt Harness and Bob Allen produce many very good looking and serviceable soft-sided cases. A soft-sided case is excellent on the day you are car-pooling to the range and there is not enough room for everyone's hard-sided case. The Boyt that will catch your eye right away is the $151 #GC36 Boundary Lakes with leather handles, saddle, tip and butt. This model has an outside choke tube/accessory pocket, a two-way brass zipper and removable, adjustable sling. Boyt cases (www.boytharness.com) are made with heavy 22-ounce canvas siding and soft 40-ounce cotton batting with flannel lining. They are available in green and khaki in lengths from 46 to 52 inches.

Boyt offers many specialty cases. Two-gun cases like their $114 green canvas #GS150 Two-Gun Canvas Sleeve open from the butt of the case with a strap rather than a zipper in 48-, 50- and 52-inch lengths. The #GC214 Take-Down Canvas Case is made with the same 22/40 materials with a heavy-duty padded suede divider to protect your stock from the barrel lugs. This $114 green case comes with an accessory pocket, brass zipper and leather sling in three lengths: 28, 30 and 34 inches.

The true beauty in the Boyt line-up has to be its

traditional leather case in lengths from 46 to 52 inches. For $433, you can own a heavy-duty, 9-ounce oil-tanned, hand-cut harness leather case with double brass zipper and fleece lining. It looks good and for just a few extra dollars you can have it personalized!

SHOOTING BAGS AND POUCHES

If you do not wear a shooting vest, you must have a bag or a pouch for shells. It doesn't matter what brand or color, just so you do not have to carry a box of shells in your hand or a fist-full jammed down in your pockets. That is awkward and it makes you look like a beginner: who needs that? Besides, we are not talking about much money for a shooting bag or pouch. What they add to your shooting day in comfort and convenience is well worth the cost.

The basic Shell Pouch #SC50 from Boyt (www.boytharness.com) comes with a heavy-duty web belt, zippered bottom and rugged but stylish green canvas

As we devoted shotgunners climb the ladder of years (God forbid!), a day of shooting sporting clays can be tiresome – not the shooting, but the waiting – and a lightweight, folding camp chair tucked onto your shooting cart will save lots of wear and tear on the body.

The Bob Allen 425T Deluxe Divided Pouch with Belt is backed with 1/4-inch foam for rigidity and has twin compartments that hold one box of shells each. It is made of heavy-duty nylon and comes with an adjustable web belt. For just $27 (suggested retail price), why carry shells in your pocket?

trimmed in leather. For $49, you can buy one with two interior compartments; perhaps one for "live" shells and one for "empties" in case you reload.

Bob Allen's $22 Classic Divided Pouch (#419L) comes with an adjustable, 2-inch web belt. It is made of water-repellent distressed synthetic leather. The twin compartments hold one box of 25 shells each. It is available in green, brown or black.

There is a very nice nylon-mesh combo-pouch (#437T) available from Bob Allen for just $25, and you see a lot of these at a shooting event. It holds a box of shells on top and 100 empties on bottom. The bottom compartment has a spring-top opening that makes it difficult to spill the shells destined to be reloads. This mesh pouch comes in navy, green or black.

On a big sporting clays venue, you may walk for miles and stand around for hours waiting your time on station to shoot. Depending on the target presentation, you may well want several types of shells, chokes, extra sunscreen and something cold to drink. Many shooter bags hold eight boxes of shells and have various pockets for miscellaneous necessary stuff, but do you really want to carry eight boxes of shells (200 rounds) by a strap over your shoulder? Just because a bag will hold eight

boxes does not mean you will or even ought to carry eight boxes!

Deluxe Sporting Clays Bag #500T from Bob Allen is made from heavy-duty nylon and has a central 14 x 8-inch inside compartment. It holds up to 12 boxes of shells and has a hard bottom and foam insert sides to add rigidity to your 25-pound load. The Deluxe has zippered front, back and side pockets. This bag is available in navy, green, black, or, for the competitor who is also a hunter, Advantage Timber camouflage for $67.

MTM (www.mtmcase-gard.com) makes a variation on the classic soft bag. Their hard-plastic 100-Round Shotshell Case (#SW-100) holds four boxes of shells and has a removable choke-tube holder that fastens to the top. Place open cartons of shells inside the case for quick retrieval. The see-through choke-tube case holds chokes, lube and most factory wrenches. The case measures 7 x 10.6 x 6 inches and is carried with a swiveling plastic handle.

ShootUK (www.shootuk.com) imports an interesting hard-sided bag (or perhaps it is a box?) for competitors. Their hard-sided Shoot Bag will, they say, "accommodate everything the serious shooter requires." The bag is black or green with an anodized aluminum lid. Inside, three compartments hold 200 shells plus hearing protection. Additional compartments allow you to separate miscellaneous items such as the bottle of sunscreen with the inevitable lost or broken cap. The Shoot Bag comes with a personalized plaque, self-balancing shoulder strap, bottle holder and clasp, fold-down rear compartment with a special box for choke tubes, side pockets for shooting glasses and personal belongings (kept safe in a "secret pocket"), a front compartment and a security lock!

SHOOTING CARS AND CARTS

At a major sporting clays event, you will see shooters zipping around in golf cars. So many, in fact, that you will probably check the map to see if you made a wrong turn and ended up in St. Petersburg.

Many tournaments – the final Seminole Cup held at the TM Ranch outside Orlando, Florida, in February 2004 was one – have dozens of golf cars on hand that you can rent for the weekend for a nominal fee. If the weather is hot or anyone in your group is even slightly incapacitated or just slow, renting a golf car makes good sense. On the other hand, if you object to paying $50 to rent a car every time you shoot a big sporting clays event, you could just buy one.

Yamaha's four-stroke #G22A gas golf car has an 11.4-hp, 357-cc engine and comes in a variety of colors. Why not order one of these? Most vendors will ship it free for about $4,378 (in ivory) or $4,601 (in metallic, candy apple red). For an extra $75, the folks at www.tntgolfcar.com (summer 2004) will attach a windshield and for $99 will install a floor-mounted gun holder. Light kits

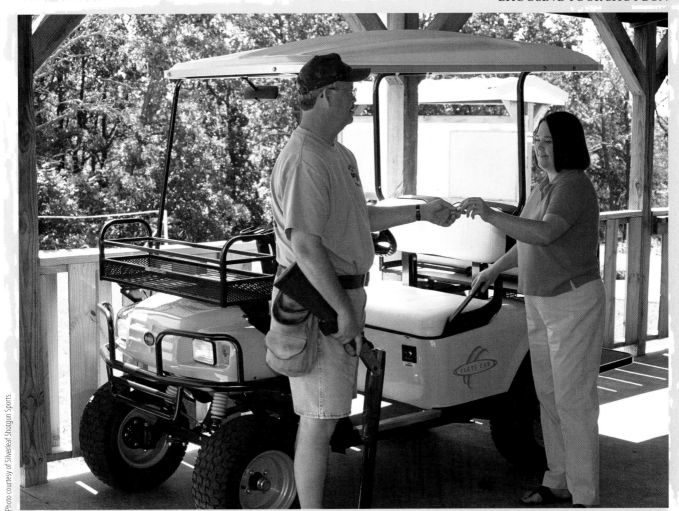

Renting a golf car, which is modified to carry shotguns, for a day of sporting clays shooting will be beneficial for an individual who may have difficulty walking the mile-plus distance around a course. Prices range from $10 to $25 per day, depending on availability.

cost $155 and three-sided curtain enclosures are $366. If you object to gas and do not feel the need for all that power and luxury, order the 48-volt rechargeable electric #G22E for only $4,501.

Stepping down ever so slightly to a more modest porter, and for those shooters who enjoy the exercise of walking from station to station, you can pull a golf cart (cart, not car) that is modified for shooters. There is no reason you cannot do this yourself, but if you choose a manufactured model, the basic, two-wheel folding Bag Boy #LT-450 with adjustable handle runs $69.99 (www. golfstockpile.com, summer 2004) while the deluxe Sun Mountain three-wheel Speed Cart is $178.99. The adjustable, folding Sun Mountain cart has pneumatic tires, a dual-tube frame and can be ordered in burgundy, blue or granite.

Dean Ziegel has designed an excellent field cart for sporting clays events where you often walk several miles while carrying your shotgun, shells, sunscreen, choke tubes and wrenches, a shell-whacker, water bottle and numerous other essential items. Even though you have shot most of your shells by the end of the day, this load can weigh as much as 100 pounds. Ziegel has named his

cart the Jackass Field Cart (www.ziegeleng.com). In price and versatility, it falls somewhere between riding and push/pull golf carts.

According to Ziegel, "The Jackass uses the same kind of high-quality machined aluminum materials you find on competition wheel chairs." The rear tires are 20 inches in diameter with 36 stainless steel spokes for stability over uneven ground. The 32-pound #J1-A Jackass ($549.95) disassembles and folds into a compact unit to fit into an automobile trunk (approximately 11 x 23 x 23 inches). It holds five shotguns in carpet-covered, foam-padded brackets and has a large aluminum front tray for shells and gear or perhaps to support a cooler. Gun butts rest on a 1-inch polypropylene high-density block covered with carpet to absorb shock. Casters and 4-inch, solid urethane wheels support the front. The upright handle of a Jackass resembles a standard hand truck, but the handle of the #J1-A is offset 30 degrees for easier pulling and is 42 inches above the centerline of the rear wheels. The #J3 economy Jackass ($150.95) is built on a heavy-duty 300-pound-capacity industrial hand truck so it is not very elegant. "Strong and simple," Ziegel says about the #J3.

A big clays shoot will often have long trails between stations, parking widely separated from registration, FITASC shooting far from the 5-Stand and sub-gauge shoots. Wise shooters will enjoy the walk, appreciate the exercise, and minimize the gear they carry in their hands. A pull cart for guns, ammo and accessories is the ticket.

CHEAP PRACTICE

If you want to get in a few shots on the weekend or after work without going to the club range, Champion (www.championtarget.com) has a couple traps to consider. The least complicated hand thrower you can buy is their lightweight and inexpensive Super Sport. Almost any *BoxMart* will have these on a rack. The Super Sport tosses one bird at a time and is adjustable for all size sporting clays targets, from standards to minis.

Do you want to throw a true pair? The EZ-Double Throw from family-owned and operated MTM Case-Gard (www.mtmcase-gard.com) gives you that option for practice. Its adjustability will allow you to throw "for countless horizontal and vertical separation choices," MTM says, and you can throw with your right or left hand. In red plastic, the total assembled length is 31 inches.

As you become more serious about practice and either do not live near a course or just want the convenience of shooting whenever you want to shoot, you will want to step up to a machine like Champion's High Fly string-release manual trap. The adjustable High Fly launches one or two birds with the pull of a cord. Its target clip ensures

secure bird placement and consistent flight path. You can stake this one in the ground or, Champion suggests, mount it on a tire so that it can easily change direction of the throw. The cost is less than $30.

Champion also sells orange clays: the 108-mm standard, 90-mm midi, 60-mm mini, and the sturdier, 108-mm rabbit. Champion suggests nesting a midi beneath a standard and throwing them together for a challenging doubles presentation.

If your shooting partner wants to sit down while he or she throws your birds, Champion, Trius (www.triustraps.com) and others have practice-style traps with seats attached … or you could take a lawn chair to the field. Anchored by the operator's weight, the Trius TrapMaster offers a padded orange plastic seat on one end of a string-activated trap. The trap and seat pivot so you can surprise the shooter with a varied shot presentation. The trap's large adjustment knobs allow you to change the aluminum arm's throwing angle without tools. Equipped with the Trius Trap, the TrapMaster costs $178.50 and weighs 36 pounds. It throws singles, doubles or piggyback (nested) doubles.

RECOIL TAMERS

After a full day on the sporting course and 100 or more 1 1/8-ounce rounds, your shoulder will almost certainly feel like it has taken a pounding. The resulting ache can make you resort to the Excedrin Migraine heavy-duty medicine.

There are several reasons your shoulder hurts. It is directly related, of course, to pulling the trigger on your shotgun. The resulting recoil of 100 rounds is like 100 punches in the shoulder. That many hits of recoil from a target load – Winchester #8-shot 2-3/4s (#AASCL12) for example – is going to be felt much differently, for instance, than a high-base game load such as Winchester's #2-shot 3-1/2s (#WEX12L). Nevertheless, *it is not* insignificant.

The other reason your shoulder hurts is poor shooting form. When you mount your gun, you must drive it into your shoulder and hold it there. If you relax the hold, the recoil impact will feel harsher because the moment arm is longer for the given force. The same is true with your cheek. If you lift your head, even slightly, before you fire, you will have a bruise in the morning.

Numerous companies make composite recoil pads to handle the microburst of a shot besides 100-Straight Products (Terminator) and Pachmayr (Decelerator), which are profiled below. These companies include Hogue, Galazan, Kick-EEZ, Old English, HiViz (Xcoil) and Sims (LimbSaver).

WHY BOTHER ABOUT RECOIL?

According to Krause Publications' **Gun Digest**, edited by Ken Ramage, a shotgun delivers quite a stroke of recoil. Perhaps more than you know. That is unusual because those of us who hardly think twice about tackling 100 sporting clays in a morning after splashing 25 birds warming up on the 5-Stand would certainly wince at the idea of putting 125 rounds through our hunting rifle in one day. Compared to many standard hunting rifles and loads, however, the 12-gauge delivers one heckuva lot of foot-pounds of free recoil. In fact, you need to shoot guns loaded for brown bear or deadly African game before you exceed the smoothbore's shoulder punch. The .458 Winchester Magnum with 600-grain bullet is a recommended load and caliber for

GUN	LOAD	FT-LBS RECOIL
6mm (.243 class)	100 gr.	8.5
.257 Roberts	120 gr.	9.9
.30-30 Winchester	170 gr.	12.4
.270 Roberts	150 gr.	16.0
7mm Remington Magnum	175 gr.	20.0
.30-06 Springfield	180 gr.	21.1
Average 20-gauge	3-inch, 1 5/16-oz. shot	27.2
.300 Weatherby Magnum	180 gr.	27.8
Average 12-gauge shotgun	3-inch, 1 1/4-oz. shot	30.4
.375 H&H Magnum	300 gr.	40.8
12-gauge pump shotgun	3-inch, 2 oz. shot	43.0
.458 Winchester Magnum	600 gr.	58.1
Mossberg 835 shotgun	3 1/2-inch, 2 1/4-oz. shot	60.3
.416 Rigby	400 gr.	61.7

If the "Rule of 96" still applies (and many would argue that it does not because of the advance in powders and firearms construction techniques), it is interesting to check your sporting clays loads and your turkey loads against your field and competition guns.

Let's say that for turkeys you are shooting a Beretta Urika Optima 12-gauge in Hardwoods HD camo. The gun weighs 7.4 pounds and is chambered for 3-inch shells. If you are shooting Remington premier Magnum Copper-Plated lead buffered turkey loads (P12XHM) with 2 ounces #4 shot, the formula suggests: 96 x 2 oz. = 192 oz. or 12 pounds. In this case, with a

elephant, by the way. So, here are a few statistics to think about:

An old rule of thumb for shotgun recoil was developed more than a century ago. In **The Gun and Its Development**, William Greener postulated that there was a "Rule of 96." Greener's book, which is still highly regarded by shotgun engineers, suggested that a shotgun needs to be at least 96 times heavier than the weight of the shot charge it fires to ensure:

- the shooter's shoulder is not battered unmercifully
- the tightest and most consistent patterns
- the gun is not destroyed by shock and vibration from recoil.

Specialized settings, such as south Florida for the Caribbean Cup, require specialized gear to get through a sporting clays range effectively and comfortably. In the Everglades, a good mosquito repellent would help.

difference of almost 5 pounds between the ideal calculated weight to handle recoil from this load effectively and the actual weight of your gun, you will want to consider some serious measures for buffering the bounce back.

Now, if you take that same gun to a sporting clays or 5-Stand course before turkey season and shoot a couple boxes of 2 3/4-inch Remington #8 Sport Loads with 1 ounce of shot, the formula results in a vastly different answer: 96 x 1 oz. = 96 oz or 6 pounds. For this load, your Beretta is 1.4 pounds to the positive and you should leave the course feeling fine.

100-Straight Products (www.100straight.com) advertises its $34.95 Terminator as the softest recoil pad available, softer than sorbothane. A closed-cell material means this pad is resistant to tearing and splitting. You can choose from black or brown with a flat or curved surface and four depths: 5/8, 3/4, 1 or 1-1/8 inches.

Coupled with 100-Straight's Polymer Buttstock Spacers, you can easily adjust your length of pull. These spacers are available in black or white. The plastic material is effortless to sand for a smooth, seamless fit on your gun and the slotted holes make it easy to adjust to any butt hole spacing or location. The cost varies from $4.50 for the 1/8-inch spacer to $8.55 for the 1/2-inch spacer.

Black buttstock pitch spacers are also available from 100-Straight. These are ideal for altering pitch without cutting your beautiful walnut stock. You can order positive pitch (thicker at top) or negative pitch (thicker at bottom). Quarter-inch spacers are $6.50 and 1/2-inch spacers are $9.

Pachmayr (www.pachmayr.com) offers a large line-up of its Decelerator pads in sporting clays or skeet with a straight to slightly convex face to prevent snagging on your clothes. (The trap version is concave from heel to toe to provide a positive, "hugging" grip on the shoulder.) Pads are offered in black or brown and one is available in red. Light face texturing (leather, lattice or ribbed) is designed to maximize mounting speed. Medium or field-shooting speeds are tied to line-checkered, screened or stippled faces; and heavy surfaces with basket-weave, pigeon or grooved faces are recommended for trap or live birds. The ultimate choice of face pattern depends on your personal preference for mounting ease. Thickness ranges from 0.6 to 1.1 inches and several pad faces can be purchased with a decorative white line.

The cost of a Decelerator depends on its thickness and face style, but the 1.1-inch Deluxe #S325 skeet-style ribbed face is $20.50. A do-it-yourself, pre-fit Decelerator pad for a Browning Citori, on the other hand, runs $36.98.

Pachmayr also makes two slip-on recoil pads in small, medium and large. The $32.98 brown leather slip-on is held in place with a hidden Velcro strip and includes a soft rubber insert. Also excellent for adjusting length of pull, these black or brown rubber slip-on pads cost $12.48.

There are at least two additional mechanisms for dampening recoil. The first is to shoot a lighter load or one of the newer "managed recoil" loads, which we will discuss elsewhere. The second is to install an after-market recoil reducer or recoil suppressor.

Recoil reducers come in two basic designs. The first is an adjustable buttplate mounted on a hydraulic piston in the buttstock. The hydraulic piston acts like a shock absorber. Your recoil pad attaches to the back of this buttplate. From Danuser or Breako, these cost about $165. (Danuser claims that its Counter Coil Recoil Reducer softens up to 52 percent of the actual [not "felt," but actual] recoil force!)

The second style of after-market recoil reducer is a permanently sealed, usually mercury-filled (a few are oil-filled or have springs and pistons inside) metal cylinder that can insert into the buttstock or perhaps the magazine tube or even attach to the barrel. Made by 100 Straight, Hirams, Edwards, C&H, Breako and others, these tubes are between 3 and 5 inches long. Most of them use the weight and inertia of mercury to help fight recoil because it is the heaviest, densest, liquid element. Mercury's viscosity varies only 1 percent from 0 to 90 degrees Fahrenheit. Thus, its recoil-fighting performance is consistent in almost any weather. Expect to pay about $50.

SIGHTS: PUT YOUR DOTS IN A ROW

A proper gun mount will line up the mid-point and front beads on your gun. Once you learn to tuck the gun tightly into your shoulder and hold it firmly against the same spot on your cheek each time, the steel beads on the rib will not be as important because with a shotgun, you are pointing, not aiming. Once you successfully learn to follow the leading edge of the speeding clay and either lead or swing through it smoothly, you may not care about the beads.

Until then, most novice shotgunners worry about bead alignment when they bring the gun to their cheek. They take their eye off the speeding target to double check bead alignment – not trusting their form and reflexes yet – and then must move the gun rapidly to reacquire the bird. As they work through this puzzle, the beads on the rib will be more important than for an experienced shooter. Until then, however, some inevitable visual confusion is going to cause missed shots.

Sporting clays began as a hunter's game. For a hunter, seeing the front bead sight is important in low light

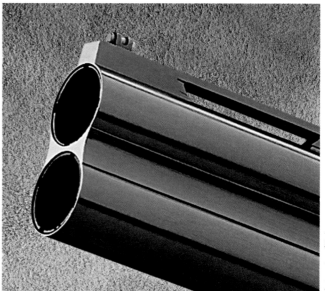

One of the fundamental teaching points in sporting clays instruction is to keep your eyes on the target, not on your sights. Nevertheless, for hunting and for patterning and perhaps other shooting situations, sights are useful and comforting.

conditions. For this reason, you may not find that the small, white BB bead typically mounted on the front of the rib by manufacturers is sufficient. They are easy to change and you do have options.

Beware of installing any fiber optic hunting sight that raises the bead or dot above the rib. Several of the popular fiber optic turkey sights, especially those which require you to center a single front fiber between two rear fibers, raise the aiming points by 1/8 to 1/4 inch and, while this may not seem like much, it is enough to change your point of impact for clay shooting. They are fine for turkey hunting because shots are typically close and the bird is usually standing or moving slowly.

Here are a few after-market sight options:

Pachmayr (www.pachmayr.com) makes a unique Uni-Dot fiber optic front sight (#P100) that is partially encased in a black, non-reflecting tube. In either bright red or fluorescent green, you can only see this 4-mm dot when the gun is properly mounted and aligned with your aiming eye. The Uni-Dot lets you aim with both eyes open and focused on the target. Pachmayr says its Uni-Dot promotes proper gun mounting and shooting technique, because if you mount the gun improperly or lift your head, the dot disappears. The carrier is made of high impact plastic and will snap on the rib anywhere along its length. No tapping, drilling or gluing is required. Seven sizes are available to fit most shotgun ribs ($23.98).

TruGlo (www.truglo.com), HiViz (www.northpass.com) and Williams Gun Sights (www.williamsgunsight.com) offer a series of fiber optic sights for sporting clay shooting that either snap over the rib of your shotgun without screws or tape, or they use a small piece of double-sided tape for extra mounting security.

The low-profile fiber optic pins in the TruGlo Glo-Dot series, with a composite base, are typically .060 inches in thickness and are available in four lengths – 1/4, 5/16, 3/8 inch or 6 mm – in red or green. The Bass Pro Shops (www.basspro.com) price is $14.99 for the Magnum Glo-Dot. TruGlo's Wing Stopper fiber optic is ideal for novice shooters because once it is properly positioned on the rib, it can only be seen if you are in perfect alignment for a shot.

HiViz FlashPoint series of fiber optic Light Pipes ($22.95) offer a unique triangular face. This, HiViz claims, is an aid to pointing your shotgun rather than aiming. The FlashPoint kit includes three triangular and one round red LightPipes, three triangular and one round green LightPipes, a clear guard and five screws for mounting on most shotgun brands without extra drilling and tapping for holes.

Williams' "fire yellow" low-profile FireSight Bead with aluminum base is comparable in brightness and color to the TruGlo green and snaps on the ventilated rib of a shotgun barrel. Williams offers three lengths – 1/4, 5/16 and 3/8 inch – for $16.95.

BARREL RESTORATION

If you have found an antique shotgun in the attic – say an early engraved Tipping and Lawden double-hammer 10 gauge – there is a good chance the barrels are pitted, scratched and have some moisture-related corrosion. Several manufacturers including Teague Precision Chokes (www.teaguechokes.co.uk) have developed a process for restoring the shooting characteristics of the gun, if not the barrel itself, to its original capabilities.

Teague virtually creates a new barrel by machining the inner barrel wall and affixing a permanent, ultra-thin wall liner from breech to muzzle. The liner restores the original bore dimensions, chamber length and shooting characteristics. And yes, if all other mechanical factors are in good shape, you can shoot the rejuvenated gun.

At the current 1.84 rate of exchange (U.S. dollars to British pounds sterling) and the current Ł 1,100 price (1,100 pounds), the cost for a double-barrel shotgun appears to be about $1900 plus taxes (Britain has a VAT or value added tax) and what Andrew Harvison at Teague called CIF: carriage, insurance and freight. Obviously, this service is intended only for very valuable and perhaps very old collector guns, because for this price, you could purchase new barrels for many fine quality guns and, indeed, quite a few fine-shooting over/unders – lock, stock AND barrel.

The old Tipping and Lawden mentioned above may or may not be a candidate for barrel restoration. Sentimental value may rule in this particular case, as this old and certainly handsome side-by-side was offered at auction by Old Town Station, Ltd. for $535 in the summer 2004 (www.armchairgunshow.com).

LITTLE EXTRAS

A toe rest can save your arms and back from endless strain. A shotgun only weighs 8 or 9 pounds, but most of us are chair-bound during our workweek, and after a day on a sporting clays course or even an hour or two at a trap shoot, the gun feels like it is pulling your arm down to about your knee. A toe rest looped into your shoelaces gives you a firm surface against which to rest your *unloaded* gun muzzle. Bob Allen's $10 toe rest is made from heavy leather with a tab and snap to fit over shoelaces.

At some time in your career, you will consider shooting with gloves. Perhaps on some winter day, the gun will just be too cold to handle effectively, or conversely, on a hot summer day, your hands will be sweaty and the gun will be hot. Some people like to wear gloves and some do not. It depends on the weather and on your body's individual mechanics – sweaty or nervous hands, for instance. For some, gloves protect their left hand from chafing on the roughness of the checkered grip. For others, a leather shooting glove tends to hang on the gun, sticky against its surface.

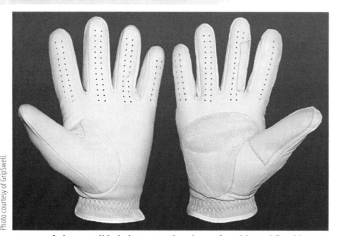

Photo courtesy of GripSwell.

A pair of gloves will help keep your hands comfortable and flexible on cold days, but on hot days, they can absorb sweat and hinder smooth movement on the stock and forend.

GripSwell ergonomic shooting gloves (www. gripswell.com) help absorb felt recoil and reduce fatigue. GripSwell's Tosh Ono says their padded goatskin gloves "provide a point of reference for a consistent mount" and act in the same manner as a palm swell on your shotgun stock. Look for gloves in un-dyed natural leather that will not stain or absorb heat, he suggests. GripSwell offers glove sizes from small through XXL at $34.95 per pair. Unlike golf gloves, which wear out quickly due to the extreme friction of your grip, these shooting gloves should last for years.

Finally, the person who carries a "wad knocker" in his or her pouch or tool kit will eventually become everyone's friend. From 100 Straight Products, the $6.50 solid-brass wad knocker is rounded on each end so that it will not scratch the inside of a shotgun barrel. The weight is approximately 4 ounces. You will rarely use a wad knocker, but experience proves that when you need it, you need it immediately.

15
Chapter

TOUR AMERICA AND BEYOND,
SPORTING CLAYS STYLE

Unlike trap or skeet shooters, it is not so easy for sporting gunners to slip into a rut. Every course is different; every shot presentation on a good course is changed at regular intervals. Nevertheless, when you are bitten by an urge to see the country, we invite you to use this guide as a reference for coast-to-coast shooting fun.

Sporting clays facilities abound in every section of the United States and in many foreign countries. Here are 50 courses that I believe are among the very best, or in some cases, the most unusual, in the world. Sometimes, they have been selected because they look friendly or are the kind of places the author would like to visit and shoot. Most of them can also be visited on the Internet, so we have included the most up-to-date information available about their facilities, opportunities for instruction and plenty of contact information.

Owning a business in America is risky. Unfortunately, more fail than succeed. Which is to say that by the time this book goes to press, several of the included telephone area codes will no doubt have changed, a couple of facilities will have changed their Internet domain names and one or two will have been bought and sold or just gone out of business. Our listing is accurate as of September 2004.

As we made the selection of clubs and courses for our travel directory, we looked for courses open to the public, at least on occasion, and that feature a diversity of clay offerings. Private clubs open only to members were not generally considered. Some of the clubs we profile offer plush, expensive accommodations; some are centered in high-profile family resort destinations; others have features or locations that make them unusual and interesting to visit, perhaps even fascinating. Most are one-of-a-kind and have their own character or personality.

A resort such as Nemacolin that includes sporting clays is a wonderful place for a family vacation and gives you a chance to introduce all members of the family to the shotgun sports. After that, you can ride the merry-go-round or go shopping or play paintball or go to the movies or relax in the spa or ... whatever!

After reviewing all of these wonderful places to shoot, we persist in believing that the best course for most of us, the one where we can find brothers and sisters of the gun and learn to shoot and reload, is at our local sporting clays station. For me, it was the TM Ranch in Orlando until they closed after the final Seminole Cup in early 2004. For gun writer John M. Taylor, it is J&P Hunting Lodge in Sudlersville, Maryland. Perhaps your local club is not as fancy as the Orvis-endorsed Wynfield Plantation in Albany, Georgia, as inclusive as the Busch Memorial Conservation Range Complex in St. Charles, Missouri, or as exotic as the Holland & Holland Shooting Grounds on Ducks Hill Road, Northwood, Middlesex, England, but it is home. Support it. Treasure it.

FIRST, A WORD FROM NASR

Occasionally, a facility will advertise that it is a "Five Star" range. It may surprise you to learn precisely what that means, since there is no national, independent rating service for shooting ranges.

A division of the National Shooting Sports Foundation, the National Association of Shooting Ranges (NASR), has developed a rating system for shooting ranges. Its system is "based on our vision of a well-managed, customer-oriented facility that is a strong competitor in the recreation marketplace."

Rather than being a public-relations gimmick to attract customers, the NASR 5-Star system is a three-dimensional checklist designed to help ranges "identify improvements." Acting on these, it is hoped, will give the range a higher, positive profile in their community and thereby help bring in new customers and new members.

No outside team swoops down on a hapless range, with clipboards and checklists in triplicate. The rating system is strictly for self-evaluation. Therefore, a range that advertises that it is a "NASR 5-Star" shooting facility has studied and responded positively to the challenges and opportunities posed by the rating system's six categories, each with 10 or more separate, challenging questions:

Appearance includes such questions as, "Do you have signage that clearly states basic range and/or firearm safety rules posted where everyone will see it, and it's readable and maintained?" (10 points)

A typical *Management* question is, "Is the entire staff trained to, and evaluated on, promptly greeting/welcoming visitors?" (10 points)

In *Customer/Member Focus*, the questionnaire asks, for example, "Is your firing line and target area brightly illuminated during hours of operation?" (5 points)

What makes a 5-Star NASR shooting range? Customer focus and customer development mean more than just making sure you wear safety glasses. A 5-Star range will have professional instruction available from certified instructors.

The *Customer/Member Development* section wants to know "Is rented safety glasses and/or hearing protection cleaned after <u>every</u> use?" (5 points)

Community Relations questions/suggestions include, for instance, "Are you or your manager(s) an active member of a local civic group (Rotary, Kiwanis, Lions, etc.?" (5 points)

In *Amenities,* NASR poses the challenge of food service and a pro shop: "Does your inventory include everything a target shooter could want, including firearms, ammunition, targets, optics, accessories, cleaning and reloading supplies, clothing, books/magazines/videos etc.?" (30 points)

So, as the NASR says, its rating system "isn't a test; it's a tool." For more information, you can write, call or check these sources on-line.

National Association Of Shooting Ranges
A division of National Shooting Sports Foundation
11 Mile Hill Rd.
Newtown, CT 06470-2359
Phone (203) 426-1320
www.rangeinfo.org

The USA is a big country and shooting opportunities abound in every environment. This may be the Golden Age of recreational shooting in America.

GET-IT-IN-GEAR TOUR OF AMERICA

ALABAMA: Limestone Hunting Preserve

Way up north in Alabama, 12 miles north of Huntsville and less than 5 miles from the Tennessee border, is a fine open-to-the-public sporting clays facility that is open every day from 8:00 a.m. until dusk, with the possible exception of major holidays. Nevertheless, to make sure there is someone to assist you with clay shooting, owner Wayne Mitchell recommends calling for a reservation before you show up on the doorstep.

Limestone has three sporting clays courses with 60 stations and everything you would find in a private, elite club, except a pro shop. Every kind of target gets tossed: standard clays, minis, midis and battue. There is a springing teal straight up, a running rabbit straight across and a dove tower for high incoming, outgoing and crossing shots. According to event coordinators George and Elizabeth Briscoe, Limestone hosts many shooting events including the National Rifle Association's Women on Target and Boy Scouts who want to earn their Shotgun Shooting Merit Badge (see www. usscouts.org/usscouts/meritbadges/asp for current Shotgun Shooting merit badge requirements).

Shooting is reasonably priced: 100 clays for $35, 50 for $25 and 25 for $15. In addition, there are two 5-Stand locations, two skeet fields, two trap fields and two FITASC *parcours*. A sporting clays membership is $1000 per year.

Hunting may initially have been the driving force behind Limestone. These days, during the season (generally October 1 through March 31), members may book guides for quail, dove, pheasant, chukar and whitetail deer.

Self-guided quail hunts for a member using his or her own dog (the membership is $500) and up to five guests (quail are $5 per bird, minimum 10 birds per hunter) are new options for memberships: "You asked for it, so ..." Limestone says.

Shooting lessons are available from Team USA member and Team USA FITASC captain Wendell Cherry, Peak Performance Hunting School, and Richard Patty. "My method has been developed through countless hours of study, practice, determination and experience," Cherry says at www.wendellcherry.net. "My coaching emphasizes the importance of discipline in these areas."

Limestone Hunting Preserve & Sporting Clays
Mailing address: 27393 Old Schoolhouse Rd.
Physical location: 28755 Coggins Rd.
Ardmore, AL 35739
Phone (256) 423-6029
Fax (256) 423-6395
www.limestonehunting.com

ALABAMA: White Oak Plantation

This full-service, year-round, hunting, shooting and recreational resort 20 miles southwest of Auburn celebrates its 22nd year in 2005. Located in south-central Alabama, along Opintlocco Creek, White Oak's 16,000 acres vary from low rolling hills covered by pine plantations and hardwood forests to croplands and dense, wooded bottomlands and swamps. This varied habitat is managed for whitetail deer and Eastern wild turkey, but also supports squirrels, rabbits, crows, bobcats, fox, beaver and coyote. Healthy, flight-conditioned quail are brought in for plantation-style quail hunts.

A shot past live oaks and yellow pines and over thick beds of palmettos characterizes sporting clays shooting stations in states bordering the Gulf of Mexico.

White Oak has a year-round program that offers something for every outdoor enthusiast. In addition to hunting, the summer program includes bird watching, hiking nature trails, fishing for largemouth bass and bream and sporting clays (competition, fun shooting and instruction). For shooters and hunters who also hit a golf ball, five courses lie within a 25-minute drive, including one in the Robert Trent Jones Trail guide.

"White Oak Plantation in Alabama hosts a number of national shoots. The Pittmans work hard to maintain a challenging series of presentations," says veteran, Florida-based outdoor writer Chris Christian. Christian, who is comfortable handling anything with fur, feathers or scales, says that some of the shots are "a bit too challenging for me. And it seems that when I finally do master one, they change it. I wouldn't say it's a conspiracy, but it does keep me coming back ... which is not a hardship, because it is a great place to spend a few days; whether you are busting clays or feathered game."

Besides functioning as an office and meeting facility, the main lodge is also a bed-and-breakfast destination, with prices ranging

Many sporting courses offer a 25-shot 5-Stand warm-up for $10 to $15 before your shooting group hits the 100-bird trail.

Dr. John Woods

Award-winning Mississippi outdoor writer, Dr. John J. Woods, says, "Of all the sporting clays courses I have had the pleasure of being embarrassed by, my all time favorite is the course at White Oak Plantation in Tuskegee, Alabama. I love the running rabbit stand most, but the high-altitude duck shots are a real humbling experience. Sporting clays action cannot be beat for fine tuning your shotgunning skills."

from $90 to $125 per night, depending on the season and room availability. A smaller, satellite lodge called Red Oak, is open for deer hunters only 5 weeks during the year, from after Christmas until January 31. Family-owned and family-operated, these lodges are furnished with antiques and personal curiosities and collections.

White Oak's hilly sporting clays course winds through lush woodlands and around a 13-acre lake. According to owner Robert Pittman, every effort is made to retain the area's natural and undisturbed beauty while still giving shooters, whether beginner or expert, a challenging experience. Pittman says that the 14 stations on his course use fully automatic traps and the layout is state-of-the-art. Shot profiles are re-configured monthly.

The White Oak 5-Stand and wobble trap setups are excellent for teaching beginners, for warming-up before a quail hunt or 100-bird sporting clays shoot, or just for fun.

Instruction by Matthew Pittman, an NSCA Level II teacher is available by prior arrangement at $75 per hour.

Memberships at White Oak are $140 per year for an individual and give the holder discounts on shooting, hunting packages and merchandise, plus invitations to member-only events and priority booking. Day memberships for travelers or guests are $25. Members pay $25 for a round of 100 clays; non-members with a day membership pay an additional $38. Wobble trap and 5-Stand are $6 and $10, respectively.

White Oak Plantation
5215 B Co. Rd. 10
Tuskegee, AL 36083
Phone (334) 727-9258/3411
www.whiteoakplantation.com

ARIZONA: Picacho Sporting Club

For your information, this is not the hottest sporting clays course in America. It is not the superb Ben Avery Target Center in Phoenix, either. There certainly must be some fine layouts in Central America, and our own Death Valley is just off the map to the left. Picacho does get hot, though, and that is part of what makes this course a challenge. All of the glorious sunshine in southern Arizona is why they open at 6 in the morning in the summer. Otherwise, normal Picacho hours are Friday through Sunday from 8:00 a.m. to 4:00 p.m. and Monday through Thursday by appointment. Otherwise, reservations are not required.

Picacho is located about halfway between Phoenix and Tucson, and just off Interstate 10. Its sporting clays, 5-Stand and wobble trap are fully automated. You can shoot 100 targets for $35 or 25 at their 5-Stand for $7.50. Although it is open for public shooting, members receive a substantial discount *and* can shoot all day for $50.

Membership is only $200 per year for an individual and $350 for the family, which makes it something of a bargain, even for its relatively Spartan dry-desert conditions. A membership card also entitles the bearer to discounts in the clubhouse, which Picacho's managers stock with products from Boyt and Bob Allen, and guns, ammo and clothing. Rental guns and carts are available, as is instruction from NSCA-certified instructors Steve Wacker and Wayne Bixenman.

If the car does not start or if it is just too blasted hot inside the cab of your pickup after an afternoon shoot, the Picacho clubhouse sleeps six. So, lean back with your favorite brew and enjoy the desert sunset and stars you may never see "back east." Picacho holds fun shoots and NSCA registered shoots the first Sunday of the month.

Picacho Sporting Club
PO Box 340
Picacho, AZ 85241
Phone (520) 705-8333/466-2906 • Fax (520) 466-6166
www.picachosportingclub.com

ARKANSAS: Bobwhite Hill Ranch

This 3200-acre facility just 15 miles north of Little Rock opens its shooting facilities to the public Thursday through Sunday from 8:00 a.m. until 6:00 p.m. Operated by Greg and Kathy Friday, members of the Friday family that owns the club, reservations are suggested to make sure guests have access to the shooting course, facility and activity they desire.

There are four sporting clays courses at Bobwhite Hill. Each is graded by level of difficulty: Fur & Feather (beginner), Wet & Wild (intermediate), Upland (intermediate) and Monster Duck Tower (advanced). Each course has six stations with fully automatic traps, and shot presentations are changed regularly. The tower is more than 100 feet high. Shooting a 50-target round costs $15 and you can purchase shells in the pro shop.

Bobwhite Hill has several other clay-popping options. Its 5-Stand ($7.50 for 25 birds) station uses seven traps in a semi-circle in front and one trap on a short tower behind the covered wooden shooting stand. Shooting skeet and wobble trap costs $5 for 25 targets.

The pro shop at Bobwhite Hill has rental guns ($15), carts and other shooting necessities. A rustic, but well-equipped cabin with kitchen and dining room on the ranch sleeps eight to 10 people in twin beds and rents for $200 per night. (New cabins are coming soon!)

Two NSCA-certified staff instructors are available for private or group lessons. Their ranch Level I instructor charges $20 per hour while instruction from their resident NSCA national champion is $60 per hour.

Shooting the Fur & Feather beginner course at Bobwhite Hill Ranch, North Little Rock, Arkansas. Bobwhite Hill has four sporting courses graded by level of difficulty, from easy to difficult.

Visitors can also fish, hunt for quail (in season) and ride horses on this ranch. A typical quail hunt, one of several packages, on the 800 dedicated acres lasts 2-1/2 hours after breakfast and includes 25 clays on the 5-Stand. This $150-per-person package includes a dozen quail, a guide, dogs and transportation. You can fish all day (six hours) for $15. Tackle, bait and small boats can be rented and lawn chairs are provided free for bank fishermen. And how about riding horseback to enjoy the country for $20 for the first hour or you can bring your own horse and use their facilities for much less.

Bobwhite Hill Ranch

64 Matt Abbott Dr.
North Little Rock, AR 72120
Phone (501) 835-6324 • Fax (501) 835-5693
www.bobwhitehillranch.com

CALIFORNIA: Birds Landing

Just down the road from the Terminator's new residence, Bird's Landing is a 1200-acre facility with sporting clays, 5-Stand and bird hunting. This club is 60 miles northeast of San Francisco and 45 miles southwest of Sacramento. A member of NSCA, Birds Landing hosts frequent competitive events, fun shoots and league shooting. The kitchen is open from 7:00 a.m. until 2:30 p.m. during hunting season, and otherwise from 9:00 a.m. until 2:30 p.m., serving breakfasts of pancakes and eggs and lunches of cheeseburgers, hotdogs and chili. A membership program is available, but shooting here is open to the public with a reservation.

Birds Landing is the closest sporting clays facility to Napa Valley. While the non-shooting spouse samples wine, you can bust clays.

According to the club's Internet site, the 15-station sporting clays course is "dynamic" with "target presentations varying from day to day. The speed, angle and size of the clays can be, and are, frequently changed. Traps are moved and even cover and terrain is modified to present 'new shooting challenges' every day."

Clay shooting hours between April 1 and September 30 are Wednesday through Sunday from 9:00 a.m. until 5:00 p.m. From October 11 to March 31, the hours are 10:00 a.m. to 3:00 p.m.

The cost for 100 targets is $40 and 50 targets are $22. To shoot the fully automated and professional 25-target 5-Stand course, expect to pay $8.

In the Birds Landing pro shop you can rent guns and buy shooting essentials like Fiocchi ammo, Bob Allen shooting vests and Browning Citori shotguns. You can also arrange for shotgunning instruction from NSCA-certified instructors who will give private lessons or work with groups. Nationally recognized shooting coaches often hold clinics at Birds Landing.

All hunting is by reservation. You may purchase a 10-bird card of pheasants from September 23 to March 13 for $360. Chukars are released from September 23 to April 25. A 15-bird release of chukar is $230. Quail hunting is also popular. Your birds can be shot, processed, smoked and even shipped direct from Birds Landing.

Birds Landing

2099 Collinsville Rd.
Birds Landing, CA 94512
Phone (707) 374-5092 • Fax (707) 374-2814
www.birdslanding.net

Birds Landing in California is a scenic, 1200-acre sporting clays course near Napa Valley.

CALIFORNIA: Oak Tree Gun Club

Only 10 miles north of Los Angeles, the 100-acre Oak Tree Gun Club has been open to the public since 1973. No memberships or reservations are required. This is unusual in such a heavily populated area on a course where you could run into a movie star or sports celebrity. Oak Tree's hours are Tuesdays 10:00 a.m. to 5:00 p.m.; Wednesday through Friday 10:00 a.m. to 11:00 p.m.; and Saturday and Sunday from 8:00 a.m. to 5:00 p.m.

This club operates two sporting clays courses with 21 stations, eight trap ranges (four double-trap and two of the more difficult bunker-trap or continental setups), three skeet ranges, one 5-Stand and wobble trap. In addition, there is a "duck canyon" fun station and a "Flush and Flurry" area.

At Oak Tree, sporting clays is designed as a walking course. The trail winds for a mile along scenic ridges and down through an old-oak forest. Because the course has a computer-activated, cord-operated trap system, you can even shoot it solo. The two-level 5-Stand venue has eight computer-controlled dedicated traps.

The "Duck Canyon" setup uses five stations to simulate the different flight patterns a waterfowl hunter will eventually encounter. Some targets are thrown as much as 60 feet overhead to simulate the high crossing shots.

Oak Tree's "Flush & Flurry" shoot is a combination of trap and skeet, and is designed to challenge shooters at all levels.

Because Oak Tree thinks of itself as a "full-service, all-in-one destination" for shotgun and pistol shooters, it has two fully stocked pro shops (one for shotgun and one for pistol) and a reloading center. Rental guns are available.

Shooting positions on the pistol range are covered, and downrange, the shooter is confronted with more than 170 moving targets. If you tire of blasting moving targets, duck into a shooting bay and bang away at the timed, falling targets. All targets are metal and give an instantaneous "ping" feedback from a hit. Oak Tree offers league shooting in pistol, skeet and trap.

Because its aim is to be a best-all-around shooting facility, a lot more is available at Oak Tree. Experienced shooting instructors are on hand for any skill level. An on-site booking

This mountainous shooting course in Colorado bears the unmistakable imprint of professional course designer and builder Mike Davey. Davey's magical, multi-layered structures are organized to give shooters opportunities at multiple levels and stations. They are built with natural materials – wood and stone.

agency will help arrange shooting, hunting and fishing destination travel. Young people can earn hunter education certification through club classes. The Oak Tree Bar & Grill is open for those who prefer that someone else cook and pop the top on their beer bottle. For those who do not, Oak Tree offers picnic facilities and RV hook-ups.

Oak Tree Gun Club
23121 N. Coltrane Ave.
Newhall, CA 91322
Phone (661) 259-7441 • Fax (661) 259-7738
www.oaktreegunclub.com

COLORADO: Scenic Mesa Ranch

After a few days of exposure to Colorado's mile-high open spaces, you may not want to go home to a thickly forested, densely inhabited eastern state. Instead, you will want to throw away your cap and buy a hat, trade your tennis shoes for boots and sell momma's Cadillac to buy an old pickup. After all, there are mountains in the distance and a billion stars overhead. A former cattle ranch, Scenic Mesa is the ideal place to let your imagination soar. Today, it is intensively managed to restore it to its "biological peak."

"The 8000-acre Scenic Mesa Ranch," its literature notes, "is a hunting preserve characterized by deep canyons, rocky draws, open meadows, irrigated grasslands and river bottoms rich in willows and fresh water springs. Populations of chukar, huns and pheasant are raised and released annually to supplement native populations." In addition, the ranch offers guided hunts for mule deer, elk and buffalo, fly-fishing expeditions to area rivers and canyons, and horseback riding. Its lodge is "Orvis endorsed."

Scenic Mesa has two NSCA-registered sporting clays courses. One is a challenging 12-station, 2-mile course, while the second, with 10 stations, is designed specifically for sub-gauge shooting. Views from each station are panoramic. The ranch has also installed an NSCA-registered 5-Stand setup with multiple shot possibilities at each station. Both 5-Stand and wobble trap can be shot day or night. Clay target hours are 8:00 a.m. until 10:30 p.m.

Scenic Mesa prefers that its hunters become members, but it allows – indeed it encourages – guests and visitors. Member prices for sporting clays are $12 for 50 birds and $25 for 100. The 25-round 5-Stand experience is $8; 12-round wobble trap is $6; and individual shooting instruction is $50 per hour. Non-member pricing is slightly more.

For such a remote operation, you would expect to need reservations, because staying overnight and dining at the ranch are certainly the way to experience the full flavor of western Colorado. Scenic Mesa has accommodations at its main lodge and clubhouse for $75 per night, at its "scenic lodge" for $55 and at its rustic bunk hose (kerosene lanterns and an outhouse with showers "down the road") for only $35.

Sit-down dining hours and costs are fixed. Breakfast ($15) is served at 8:00 a.m., lunch ($25) at noon and supper ($35) at 7:00 p.m.

For $125, someone from the ranch will pick you up at (and return you to) the airport.

Scenic Mesa Ranch
PO Box 370
7183 Scenic Mesa Rd.
Hotchkiss, CO 81419-0370
Phone (970) 872-3078/6031 • Fax (970) 921-3378
www.scenicmesa.com

DELAWARE: Owens Station Sporting Clays & Hunting Preserve

Bill Wolter, who founded this shooting and hunting preserve on family land 75 miles east of Washington, D.C., is a specialist in training dogs for outdoor work. He has numerous state, regional and national champions to his credit. Whether you want a retriever water-trained ($500 per month), a pointer trained for upland birds ($400 per month), or perhaps just want to board the family toy poodle overnight ($10), Owens Station can help.

Family owned for more than 100 years, Owens Station opened to the public in the early 1970s. Its year-round hours are Tuesday through Sunday from 9:00 a.m. to 5:30 p.m. Reservations are not required, but are appreciated. A trapper is available to pull birds at all times.

Owens Station hosted the 2004 Delaware State Sporting Clays Championship. It has five sporting clays courses with 40 stations covering 80 acres and a single, computerized 5-Stand with shots over water. The cost for 50 sporting targets is $17.

The clubhouse has a large meeting room and catering is available. Owens Station's bunkhouse will sleep four people and there are parking spaces for six campers with hookups for water and electricity. Of course, we have already mentioned the club's emphasis on dog breeding, training, sales and kennels.

Planted preserve fields are available for upland game hunting: quail ($7 each), chukar ($12.50), Huns and French red-legs ($15) and pheasant ($18.). The hunting dates are October 15 through March 31 except for the blindly medieval "Blue Law" that keeps hunters out of the woods and fields on Sundays. State licenses are required for dove, deer and waterfowl.

Owens Station Sporting Clays & Hunting Preserve

12613 Hunter's Cove Rd.
Greenwood, DE 19950
Phone (302) 349-4478/4334
Fax (302) 349-0860
www.owensstation.com

Photo courtesy of AYA.

Shotgunners traveling in Italy would certainly want to visit the Brescia region to see the outstanding gunmakers there - Perazzi and Bernardelli, for instance - with Beretta and Benelli within driving distance. Similarly, visitors to Spain will be fascinated by the rugged northern Basque country and the gunmakers clustered in the Eibar region such as AYA (Aguirre y Aranzabal).

FLORIDA: Indian River County Public Shooting Range

Indian River's far-sighted county commissioners created the $1.5 million Indian River public shooting complex, including sporting clays and 5-Stand, with the assistance of state and federal agencies such as the U.S. Fish & Wildlife Service and the Florida Fish & Wildlife Conservation Commission. We normally think of a public shooting range as a down-at-the-heel, poor-man's alternative to some terrifically cool private enclave, but that is not the case here! Indian River feels it has earned the National Association of Shooting Ranges' 5-Star rating for a "well-managed, customer-oriented facility that is a strong competitor in the recreation marketplace."

Indian River is about an hour south of the Cape Canaveral launching pad, so if a rocket goes up while you are on the range, you will both hear and see it. This also means that within a few miles of the shooting range there are thousands of motel rooms, hundreds of restaurants, beautiful beaches and plenty of putt-putt golf ranges if you take the kids.

In spite of the potential for distraction, Range Manager Kriss Holden says that if you shoot, Indian River has got you covered. For us shotgunners, a round of 100 clays on the sporting course costs $34, while 25 birds on the 5-Stand are only $6.25.

Indian River's covered pistol range has 35 firing stations and the covered rifle range has 29 stations. These ranges provide 25-, 50- and 100-yard targets, and two at 200 yards. Both ranges are lighted for nighttime use.

If you show up at Indian River without your gun or need instruction, county range officers at the handicap-accessible clubhouse can set you up. Loaner guns are available for all disciplines, and programs are routinely scheduled for women and young shooters. Some retail shooting needs are accommodated in the clubhouse.

That is not all, however. You can purchase food in the clubhouse or eat a picnic lunch and then shoot airguns and archery (3-D and target) at this course, which is just a couple miles east of Interstate 95. Hold a shell to your ear and you can hear the ocean. Cowboy action shooting is an occasional scheduled event, and an on-site, stocked fishing lake is reserved for kids: "Without a child, you may not fish." Of course, thoughtful as they are at Indian River, they will loan your kids a fishing pole.

It is worth going out of your way to see the Indian River public range – and then transplanting their ideas home! The hours are Wednesday and Thursday from 1:00 p.m. until 9:00 p.m. and Friday, Saturday and Sunday from 9:00 a.m. until 5:00 p.m.

Indian River County Public Shooting Range

10455 102nd Terr.
Sebastian, FL 32958
Phone (772) 581-4944
Fax (772) 581-4943
www.ircgov.com/Departments/General_Services/Shooting_Range/Index.htm

FLORIDA: Quail Creek Plantation

You could say that Quail Creek Plantation is in the middle of nowhere, but that is just the way many sportsmen like it. When guests are not shooting its sporting clays courses, they can fish or hunt bobwhite quail (October 1 through March 31). On a limited and seasonal basis, hunts for mourning dove, continental pheasant and Osceola turkey are also available.

Quail Creek opened on 110 acres of south Florida scrubland in 2002. Moderately canopied with pine and oak, it offers two sporting clays courses, with 14 two-position stations per course. One course is designed for beginner-to-intermediate shooters, and the second course, featuring longer shots and more acute angles, is for experts.

In May 2004, the fee for a round of 100 was $36 for non-members and $30 for members, although Quail Creek partner and live-in manager Fred Fanizzi said he expected the rate would increase during the next year. Electric cart rentals are $10 per round or $18 per day, while push-cart rentals are $10 per round. Quail Creek maintains a well-stocked clubhouse and both 12- and 20-gauge Beretta rental guns are available.

You may shoot one of the two covered 5-Stand courses for $8 (non-member) and $6 (member) for a round of 25.

A competitive "snooker" shoot, which requires competitors to tackle an increasingly difficult shooting regimen as they progress through the stations, is popular with Quail Creek guests.

Quail Creek's owners, Harris "Whit" Hudson, Fanizzi and others, developed the shooting facilities near the center of a 2700-acre wildlife preserve. From the beginning, they intended for the course, clubhouse and open-air pavilion to be first-class … and they are.

To reach Quail Creek, you could fly to Orlando (2 hours) or West Palm Beach (1-1/2 hours) and rent a car. If you fly into Ft. Pierce (1 hour from the lodge) or the small Okeechobee airport, Quail Creek will send a driver for a small charge. Motels are available within easy driving distance. The shooting-sports resort allowed self-contained camping, mostly recreational vehicles, Fanizzi says, when it hosted the April, 2004 Florida Sporting Clays Association state shoot. Hot showers and some 110-volt electrical hook-ups are available.

Normal operating hours for Quail Creek are 8:00 a.m. to 5:30 p.m. Wednesday through Sunday. (The last shooter goes out at 4:00 p.m.)

Quail Creek Plantation

12399 NE 224th St.
Okeechobee, FL 34974
Phone (863) 763-2529
Fax (863) 763-1414
www.quailcreekplantation.com

GEORGIA:
Callaway Gun Club at Callaway Gardens

Callaway Gardens opened in 1952 and today more than a million visitors a year attend a variety of events from car auctions to flower shows to marathon running. The Callaway Gun Club, with trap, skeet, 5-Stand and sporting clays venues, is sandwiched among 14,000 acres of world-famous lakes and gardens in the rolling hills 70 miles southwest of Atlanta.

The Gun Club is open between 1:00 and 7:00 p.m. Wednesday through Friday and Sunday, and 9:00 a.m. to 7:00 p.m. on Saturday. Although it is closed on Monday and Tuesday, shooting during closed hours may be made by reservation with a minimum of six shooters. Reservations are always required for sporting clays and are recommended for all shooting games.

According to the Callaway public relations people, shooting pros on the Gun Club staff can instruct at "all skill levels," so "whether you're a novice or a seasoned professional, you'll feel welcome." The club recently installed new traps on all four skeet fields, two new wobble traps, and one springing teal and one rabbit for the 11-station sporting clays course. Because Callaway operates some skeet events with tokens, you can shoot skeet at your own pace. Night shooting is available on the first and third Wednesday of each month at 7:00 p.m. Shells and rental guns are available. There is a complete pro shop on site.

Rates for shooting at Callaway Gun Club are, like most quality venues, lower for members, higher for non-members. A 50-target round of sporting clays is $23 and $35 for 100 targets. Shooting the 5-Stand is $10 for a 25-target round. Gun rental is $10 per round of 25 and ammo is $8 per box.

The Gun Club sponsors shooting schools and monthly fun shoots. For beginners, "Try It Out" classes cost $40 per person and include shells, targets, gun, safety equipment and instruction. Limited to six students, intermediate classes cost $40 to $120, depending on the number enrolled, but do not include targets, ammunition and gun rental. Intermediate classes teach the basics of breaking targets consistently: focus, hold-point, break-point and game plan. Finally, one-on-one classes are available for competitors who want to elevate their skills. One-on-ones, limited to three students per class, cost $60 to $120 per class, depending on the number enrolled.

Monthly fun shoots provide friendly competition among club members, Callaway guests and the general public in sporting clays ($35 per 100 targets) and in skeet, trap, wobble trap and 5-Stand ($10 per 25 targets).

Callaway Gun Club

4897 Salem Rd.
Pine Mountain, GA 31822
Phone (800) 225-5292/(706) 663-5129
Fax (706) 663-6724
www.callawaygardens.com

The Callaway Gun Club near Pine Mountain, Georgia, offers a 100-round of sporting clays for $35. Gun rental is $10 per round and a box of 25 shells is $8.

GEORGIA: Cherokee Rose

Cherokee Rose is owned and actively managed by Casey Atkinson, a Beretta shooter and one of the world's foremost shotgun champions. Atkinson won the 2004 World FITASC individual bronze medal and led the ladies team to the silver medal in France last year.

The Cherokee Rose is the Georgia state flower by the way, but it is also the name of a specific blossom with a peculiar relationship to suffering. According to legend, the rose came into being miraculously during the dispersal of the eastern Cherokee nation from the Carolinas and Georgia to Oklahoma in 1838-39, the famous "Trail of Tears" march. When a grieving mother's tears fell to the earth, this rose sprang up as a sign of the people's enduring strength and will to survive.

The only suffering you will experience at the outstanding Cherokee Rose sporting clays course today – unless you take their interesting "Star Shot," a separate game entirely, too lightly – is perhaps at the station named "The Ditch" (or more affectionately "The Bitch at The Ditch"). The Ditch is a ravine with 45-degree crossing targets flying at varying up or down angles 20 to 30 feet below the stand! It is absolutely "a bitch" to hit these birds as the author's guide, Gary Parker, demonstrated before allowing the author to similarly fail during the heat of a mid-July day.

Cherokee Rose is located half an hour south of the Atlanta airport and not far from the Atlanta Motor Speedway. Still, the twists and turns of the country roads leading to it may confound the first-timer unless you call for directions or, since Cherokee Rose does not at this time have an Internet site, try your luck with www.mapquest.com. Shooting here is well worth the effort. The sporting course, trap and skeet ranges are open Wednesday through Saturday from 9:00 a.m. to 7:00 p.m. and on Sunday from 1:00 to 7:00 p.m.

Cherokee Rose Resort
895 Baptist Camp Road
Griffin, GA 30223
Phone (770) 227-6569
Fax (770) 227-2565

HAWAII: Lana'i Pine

This course is a long way from the eastern United States, where most sporting clays shooters live, and this facility's Internet address is just too long to type without making a mistake. Nevertheless, a visit to Hawaii's Lana'i Pine Sporting Clays feels long overdue, especially after a cold, hard winter.

Lana'i is one of Hawaii's most secluded islands, measuring only 18 by 13 miles. The Lana'i Pine sporting clays field lies right in the middle of this small island, which is halfway down the Hawaiian island chain from Oahu to the Big Island of Hawaii. From the sporting clays course, manager Dennis Rapp says, you will enjoy viewing other Hawaiian islands and a vast stretch of the Pacific Ocean.

You can reach the shooting field easily from any hotel or lodge on the island, but shuttle service is available direct from the Lodge at Koele.

The Lana'i course has 14 shooting stations with 14 automated traps, six fully automated competition high towers and single-shooter delay circuitry for individual rounds. Except that reservations are required, this part is just like home. Hours are from 8:30 a.m. to 4:30 p.m. daily with the first shooters on the course at 9:00. The rate for 100 birds is $145 or $85 for 50. This includes a gun, ammo and eye and ear protection. Car rental is included for those who choose not to walk this fabulous course.

Lana'i Pine has a clubhouse and pro shop with shooting accessories available for purchase on site. Instructors are NSCA-trained and both private and group shooting lessons may be scheduled. Archery and air rifle shooting are also promoted at Lana'i Pine and, indeed, all of the gear you will need to enjoy these sports is provided. Air rifle takes place under a covered tent. There is a trap range, a skeet range, one 5-Stand and wobble trap.

You will probably not fly to Lana'i on a whim, but the "world-class" 102-room Lodge at Koele ("genteel luxury and Hawaiian hospitality") is just around the corner. With a daily bed-and-breakfast garden-room rate of $379 for two people (stay four and the fifth night is free), you will just have to suck it up and play the nearby "The Experience at Koele," which was rated the best golf course in the world by the readers of *Conde Nast Traveler* magazine. (Room rates can be as much as $2200 per night at this resort or $3500 per night just down the road at the Manele Bay Hotel.)

Incidentally, for clay shooters who are also big game hunters, Lana'i has a 3000-animal population of feral axis deer. Hawaii only charges non-residents $100 to hunt these beautiful, exotic creatures. The fee for a guided hunt, which includes a four-wheel drive vehicle to traverse the island's hot, rugged "out back," caping the trophy and packing the meat, is $750. The success rate is around 70 percent for antlered bucks.

If you are traveling all the way to Hawaii to shoot sporting clays, you might as well arrange to visit the 5-Stand station at the famous and hard-to-miss 175,000-acre Parker Ranch on the Big Island of Hawaii (www.parkerranch.com). And right next door to Lana'i, Maui Sporting Clays [808-879-4441] outside Kihei on the island of Maui also has a sporting course and 5-Stand.

Money-saving three-night-minimum sporting clay shooting packages for Lana'i Pine, Hawaii, can often be arranged through a travel agent or direct [800-321-4666: Reservation Code In-LSPC]. The double-occupancy package is $185 per person per night for the Lodge at Koele and includes accommodations for two, transportation to and from the hotel and 200 targets daily. For single occupancy, you will pay $285 per night and have 100 targets to bust each day. Such offers are often not valid during peak travel periods.

Lana'i Pine
PO Box 310
Lana'i City, HI 96763
Phone (808) 559-4600
www.lanai-activities.com/Koele
www.hawaiiweb.com/lanai/html/sites/lanai_pines.html

ILLINOIS: Rend Lake Shooting Complex

Rend Lake is the people's shooting complex. You cannot order a mint julep on the verandah here. Nevertheless, this is a superior complex in a large, public recreational area, and it is well worthwhile to spend time breaking clays there.

If you are driving, Rend Lake is on every roadmap because it is a huge recreational area in south-central Illinois near the Interstate 57 intersection with Interstate 64. The resort area offers a 27-hole golf course; boating, swimming and fishing on a 19,000-acre lake; horseback riding; plenty of accommodations and dining, plus a truly excellent shooting experience.

The center of the 400-acre shooting complex area is a comfortable clubhouse. Here, you can purchase ammo, buy souvenirs and shooting accessories, and rent Beretta 12- and 20-gauge semi-automatics. Private lessons from a certified instructor are available by appointment.

Trap, skeet, sporting clays, 5-Stand, wobble trap and guided bird hunts are all available at Rend Lake. And no one needs to make a reservation to shoot or spend thousands of dollars to become a member or worry about the name brand of gun they are shooting; just observe the hours, pay when asked and shoot responsibly, says manager Dennis Sneed! The hours are Wednesday through Sunday from 10:00 a.m. to 6:00 p.m. (On Thursdays, course hours are extended until 10:00 p.m.) Rend Lake is closed Mondays, Tuesdays and some holidays. There are lighted 5-Stand, trap and skeet ranges available for night shooting. This is one of few complexes that has ADA (Americans with Disabilities Act)-accessible facilities.

Rend Lake's two sporting clays courses feature 38 stations, three towers and all-electric traps. You can shoot sporting clays year-round. There are elevated stands, shots over water and an 8-foot concrete cart path. Shots are changed regularly and are reviewed to provide an appropriate challenge for both novice and expert shooters. The fees are $15 for 50 birds and $25 for 100 birds. You can purchase a five-round card for $112.50.

Other shooting charges are: $3.50 for 25 trap or skeet, and $4 for 25 shots at the 5-Stand station. You can purchase a five-round 5-Stand card for $18.75 and can shoot a round on the 30-target 3-D archery range for $6.

Rend Lake also has hunting packages with guides, dogs and a warm-up round of 25 clay targets. For $205, the hunter receives a round of 25 clay warm-up targets, two pheasants, two chukar, refreshments brought to the field, a night in the Seasons Lodge and a $25 meal voucher at the Seasons Restaurant. Your guides will clean your birds and pack them in ice inside coolers. (Hats, shells, gun rental, licenses and other necessities are available.)

Rend Lake Shooting Complex

PO Box 100
17738 Conservation Ln.
Whittington, IL 62897
Phone (618) 629-2368
Fax (618) 629-2125
www.rendlakeshooting.com

The shooting facilities at Rend Lake are handicap accessible and individuals with special needs are fully accommodated.

INDIANA: Oakwood Gun Club

Just a ways east of this club, the author's grandfather raised hunting dogs. He loved beagles so much that his local rod and gun club nicknamed him "Doggie." As a self-conscious teenager, this profoundly embarrassed the author, who was being raised on an island off the coast of Florida in a household that included No Dogs! Anyway, it took years to recognize what a compliment this was for the retired Hoosier Studebaker builder so, as a belated gesture of respect, the author has named his spaniel "Oscar." Turn about, as they say, is fair play.

Oakwood Gun Club is just an hour southeast of Chicago down Interstate 65. Its hours depend on your shooting discipline, but David Glissman says they are open every day except Mondays and Fridays. No memberships are required. Trap is shot on Wednesday evenings and Saturday/Sunday from 9:00 a.m. to 4:00 p.m. Skeet is shot during the same hours Saturday and Sunday. The cost for both of these and a warm-up of wobble trap is $3.50 for a round of 25.

Twelve sporting clays stands are dispersed along a wooded trail on club property. Clays are shot Saturdays and Sundays concurrently with skeet and trap, from 9:00 a.m. to 4:00 p.m. The 100-bird course costs $25 and can be shot at other times by appointment. Women and students shoot at half price.

Oakwood is an all-discipline facility. Certified instructors are available for skeet, trap and sporting clays. Leagues and shoots (competitive and fun) are scheduled regularly. In addition, the clubhouse sells a wide range of reloading supplies, ammo and shooting accessories.

Oakwood Gun Club

11388 N. State Rd. 49
Wheatfield, IN 46392
Phone (219) 956-4615
www.oakwoodgunclub.com

INDIANA: Quail Ridge Sportsman's Club

One thousand professionally managed acres of southeastern Indiana host a superb public/private facility that offers clay shooting, hunting and fishing. Only 45 minutes from downtown Cincinnati, Quail Ridge is open from Wednesday through Sunday, from 8:00 a.m. to 6:00 p.m. by appointment. Reservations are required here.

This club's two 15-station, 100-bird sporting clays courses are challenging and often changed. A 50-bird short course has recently been completed and Quail Ridge also hosts side-by-side shotgun events. There is a 5-Stand station with eight dedicated traps, FITASC shooting and a Make-A-Break station. Carts are available to rent if you prefer not to walk.

Novice to master, individual and group lessons are available from world champion shooter Jon Kruger. NSCA Level I and Level II instructors are on site, or if you prefer, you can bring your own instructor and call Quail Ridge home!

The hunting is diverse for whitetails and upland birds. No-limit upland bird shooting with professional guides and polished dogs is available for members. Hunters can have their birds cleaned and packaged on site. Quail Ridge offers continental-style driven shoots as well. Hunting is available from October 15 through April 1.

The comfortable, modern clubhouse has a dining room, member lounge, bedrooms, sauna and personal lockers. Family-style home cooking is the fare for Quail Ridge dining. The club has a well-stocked pro shop that sells licenses, shells, clothing, and is a Beretta Showcase Dealer.

Speaking of memberships, become a hunting member and you can experience no-limit bird hunting, fishing in 17 on-site lakes, reduced clay shooting costs, 10 percent off in the pro shop, priority bookings, member-only events, discounted cart rentals, and full use of the clubhouse, showers, locker room and sauna. This is a home-away-from-home … only better. A hunting membership is $1650 per year and there is a $1500 initiation fee. Clay target membership requires a $150 initiation fee and costs $300 per year with a $500 shooting card. What is a "punch?" The card gives you 80 punches: the 5-Stand costs one punch, for instance; a round of 100 sporting clays costs five, and there are 12 included days of "all you can shoot." Additional 80-punch cards are $400. Fishing is $300 per year with a $150 initiation fee.

Quail Ridge Sportsman's Club
21166 Quail Ridge Ln.
Sunman, IN 47041
Phone (812) 926-4999
Fax (812) 926-0534
www.quailridgeclub.com

IOWA: Steelclay Shooting Sports & Preserve

Steel & Clay is 60 miles southeast of Des Moines and, according to my *National Geographic Road Atlas,* is about the same distance southwest of the "Future Birthplace of Captain James T. Kirk." The irrepressible Captain Kirk commanded the original Federation starship Enterprise in television and movie versions of "Star Trek."

Give me all you got, Mister Scott! Warp factor eight.

Except for Little Switzerland in the northeast corner of the state, Iowa is flat and boring … at least its terrain is flat and boring. If you are a hunter of upland birds or big game, however, there is nothing boring about Iowa. In that case, Iowa can be a wonderful and exciting place filled with waterfowl and pheasants and big whitetails. Steelclay proves that Iowa is a great place to hunt clay pigeons and raise youngsters, too.

After banging away at pistol silhouettes for years, local corn and soybean farmer Larry Dunn opened a 10-station sporting clays course in May 1996. Larry shot sporting clays once and liked it, apparently a whole lot because the next thing he knew, he was hitting up the banker for additional seed money to grow a sporting clays course.

According to Larry and his wife Lisa, Steelclay is "Iowa's premier club for sporting clays fun. Bring your family and friends for a day," they say, "and shoot targets designed to fit your style and skill."

The Dunn's daughter, Haley, took to clay shooting as if she were a born champion. Her honors include a host of gold and silver medals in U.S. and international competition. In 2004, she was designated first alternate to the U.S. Olympic women's skeet team and has already traveled to a dozen foreign countries – Egypt, Brazil, Finland, Australia and others – to shoot competitively for the USA.

In addition to the obviously brilliant and accomplished Haley, the Dunns say Steelclay has been home course to nine state champions since 1999!

Steelclay has a particularly difficult shot called "the bridge." Dunn's trap sends a true pair in what appears to be a straightaway arc across a creek. In fact, because the trap arm is angled slightly to the left, the bird begins to slide to the left as it slows down. "It is a deceiving shot," Dunn admits. "If you break 10 in a row on this station, we'll give you a free cap. Only 11 people have done it since we opened in 1996."

Four years after opening the clays course, Larry and Lisa opened their hunting preserve. Now, from September to April, you can shoot clay targets and then have an exciting pheasant and quail hunt on the club's preserve. A fully stocked clubhouse sells guns and factory ammo. League shooting takes place throughout the year and an NSCA Level I instructor is available for private or group instruction.

Steelclay has a membership program, but it is open to the public on Saturday from noon until 6:00 p.m., Sunday from 10:00 a.m. to 6:00 p.m. and Tuesdays and Thursdays from 6:00 p.m. until 9:00 p.m. for shooting on the lighted 5-Stand or the lighted trap and skeet ranges. A 100-target round is $20 while the 25-bird 5-Stand is $5. Trap is $2.50, skeet is $3 and instruction is $50 per hour.

The relatively wide-open sporting clays courses include 20 stations. A call to book a reservation is recommended, but is not required before you turn into the driveway.

Annual memberships for shooting are $40. For hunting, the cost jumps to $100 and a combination membership is $125.

Steelclay Shooting Sports & Preserve
3353 Plymouth Ave.
Eddyville, IA 52553
Phone (641) 969-4387
www.steelclay.com

KANSAS: Flint Oak

There is no easy, convenient way to reach Flint Oak, which is 75 miles east of Wichita in the rolling Kansas countryside. It is a flight and a drive and perhaps a ride as well, for by paying a "reasonable fee," the lodge will send a driver to pick you up at one of the area airports.

Ray and Winona Walton began development of the 2800-acre Flint Oak in 1978 as a member-only bird-hunting club. Their $10 million went a long way to developing a magnificent shooting resort. After a major expansion in 2003, the facilities were opened to the public on a space-available basis between April 1 and September 30, but reservations are required. Bird and deer hunting are limited to Flint Oak members and guests.

According to their Internet site, Flint Oak is a five-star certified shooting complex based on criteria developed by the National Association of Shooting Ranges, an office of the National Shooting Sports Foundation. In spite of its relative remoteness, Flint Oak has hosted a number of quality events such as the 2004 Kansas State FITASC and 5-Stand championships. It has 10 sporting clays stations and a huge ("The world's tallest," Flint Oak says.) 157-foot tower; night-lighted trap, skeet and 5-Stand shooting plus FITASC events with 42 fully automated traps.

Flint Oak hosted the 2004 FITASC 5-Stand sporting championships and one of the setups was this unusual, but beautiful, setting on a down-slope toward a lake.

Shooting hours are Wednesday through Saturday 9:30 a.m. to dusk and Sunday 9:30 a.m. to 5:00 p.m. A 50-shot sporting clays round is $25 while a 25-shot 5-Stand round is $14. Skeet and trap are $8. Shotgun rental is $35 for the day; gun cleaning is $25 and lessons are $50 per hour.

Writing in *Gray's Sporting Journal* 10 years ago, Marty Fischer said, "Flint Oak probably features the prettiest 10 stations of any sporting clays course in America. There are elaborate decks, shrubs, flowers, manicured grass and bronze statues of the various game birds depicted by the targets at each shooting stand."

Flint Oak also has a complete pro shop and offers gun rentals for use on its clays ranges and courses. NSCA-certified instructors are available.

Accommodations are sparse in the immediate area, so if you shoot at Flint Oak, you will want to stay overnight in the 140-room, 30,000-square-foot lodge or the luxury motel on its grounds. A restaurant, cocktail lounge and swimming pool are also available.

Usually, businesses like Flint Oak style themselves as country clubs and offer multiple recreational opportunities with two price levels, one for members and one for non-members. Operations manager Jeff Oakes says a full hunting membership at Flint Oak is $3500 per year, but this includes a $1750 bird hunting credit and five free deer or turkey hunts. A half-year, April through September, social membership is only $100, however, with a $35 per month food and beverage minimum. Join as a social member and you may enjoy unlimited use of the pool and spa, the walking trails, bar, dining and lodging, plus discounted pro shop privileges.

Flint Oak

2639 Quail Road
Fall River, KS 67047
Phone (620) 658-4401 • Fax (620) 658-4806
www.flintoak.com

KANSAS: Ravenwood Lodge

At some destinations, the sporting clays course is the object; at others, it is something of a sideline. At Ken Corbet's Ravenwood Lodge near Topeka, 50 miles west of Kansas City, the 20 stations of his clays courses are admittedly something of a sideline. While Ravenwood specializes in hunting and shooting game, its rustic pioneer prairie flavor makes it worthy of a visit.

Sporting clays at Ravenwood are available to the public year-round by appointment, but Corbet says walk-ins are accommodated whenever possible. Like most lodges, there are two price levels, one for members and one for non-members. Non-member sporting clays prices are a reasonable $18 for 50-targets and $32 for 100-targets. Ravenwood also has a FITASC Tower Course, one 5-Stand and wobble trap. Shooting instruction is available.

Ravenwood makes accommodation for lodging, meals and RV hookups. The cost to spend the night in the 150-year old stone lodge is about $150, but you can stay in the bunkhouse for $25 to $45.

The hunting seasons in Kansas begin on September 1 and end March 31. You can put your sporting clays abilities to practice shooting quail, chukar and pheasants or hunting waterfowl. For men and women who primarily shoot clays to prepare for hunting, this is just fine. Deer and turkey hunting is also available on lodge grounds.

Ravenwood Lodge

10147 SW 61ˢᵗ St.
Topeka, KS 66610
Phone (800) 656-2454/(785) 256-6444
www.ravenwoodoutdoors.com

KENTUCKY: Elk Creek Hunt Club

Tennessee's sporting clays All-American Wendell Cherry learned to shoot clays on the Grinder's Switch sporting course near Nashville. Although Grinder's Switch is closed now, many people recall its "Little Switzerland" stations, which were built on the side slopes of a steep ravine and served by three remote-operated automatic traps, each with multiple settings. "Birds flew everywhere except behind you," Cherry remembers. "One of the courses I enjoy today is Elk Creek in Owenton, Kentucky. It's just a beautiful course. Very hilly with lots of towers, so you have plenty of up and down shooting. It's a terrific place to shoot."

Wendell Cherry

Your old Kentucky home was never this much fun. Elk Creek is a 2500-acre upland game hunting preserve and shooting complex in the middle of a triangle of meadow, forest and rolling hills with Cincinnati, Lexington and Louisville at the tips of the angles. It is an hour from any one of these cities, and although memberships are available and reservations are encouraged, this shooting preserve is open to the public.

Elk Creek has three "championship" sporting clays courses with two towers, one 40 feet high and one 65 feet. Its automatic, 50-clay mini-course is located on its own 150 acres and can be shot as a 50- or 100-target round. One course wanders through the woods with several shots over water and the other offers more open shooting situations. Thrown birds cost $17.50 for 50 and $35 for 100.

The two 5-Stand courses at Elk Creek are a bargain at 25 birds for $8.75 and 50 for $17. One of the 5-Stand venues can be shot as a "pro challenge," while the other features a 60-foot covered pavilion and mini-clubhouse for year-round shooting.

Elk Creek is open most of the hours you will want to shoot and offers lodging and meals on site. Its hours are Wednesday through Sunday from 9:00 a.m. until dark and Sunday from noon until dark. Luxury accommodations are available in the 8500-sq-ft lodge ($100 per night) and the 5000-sq-ft clubhouse has nine rooms ($60 per night). Elk Creek says its meals are "home-cooked:" breakfast and lunch are $7 and supper is $20.

The pro shop at Elk Creek carries a full line of sporting equipment and clothing. A gun cleaning station is open to guests and taxidermy can be arranged. Gun and cart rentals are available and shooting lessons can be arranged. To make your visit as comprehensive as possible, Elk Creek has a "Make-A-Break" fun shooting station and 3-D archery course.

The "other side" of Elk Creek is an 800-acre hunting preserve for shotgun, rifle and bow. Special package hunt and shoots are available such as "Sporting Clays & Archery" (50 targets $20, 100 targets $40). The 5-Stand costs $10 to shoot and cart rental is $10. A half-day unlimited quail hunt includes dogs and guides, lunch, cleaning and packaging birds: two-person minimum for $325 each and a third person costs $150.

Elk Creek Hunt Club

1860 Georgetown Rd.
Owenton, KY 40359
Phone (502) 484-4569
Fax (502) 484-2874
www.elkcreekhuntclub.com

LOUISIANA: High Point Shooting Grounds

If you are on your way to Jackson Square, Bourbon Street and the French Quarter, this club is not far out of the way – just 15 miles southeast – to High Point Shooting Grounds, where you can take aim at sporting clays and have some real fun.

High Point advertises two sporting courses with 28 stations, and it is only half an hour from downtown New Orleans. Although memberships are available, this shooting complex is open to the public, but Don Vallee at High Point recommends that you give them a call before getting in your car during the week.

For such a high-traffic urban area, the shooting cost is relatively reasonable. Sporting clays is $18 for 50 birds and $36 for 100. It costs $9 to shoot a 25-clay round of 5-Stand. Rental guns are available through the on-premises pro shop for $20 and carts are occasionally available.

The shooting hours are generous at High Point: Wednesday through Friday from 1:00 p.m. until dark, and Saturday and Sunday from 10:00 a.m. until dark.

A 5-Stand range and two FITASC shooting arrangements are available with wobble trap as a warm-up.

High Point Shooting Grounds

1637 Marengo St.
New Orleans, LA 70115
Phone (504) 891-6149
Fax (504) 899-4235

MAINE: Varney's Clay Sports

You are only a half hour from LL Bean's flagship store in Freeport when you are shooting on Brad Varney's Clay Sports course just up the road in Richmond. Unlike the famous and well-appointed retail outlet, this new course is not fancy, does not have a stupendously outfitted pro shop and the view – like much of Maine – is only of trees, with streaking orange disks.

Unless you have relatives there, the primary reason to visit Richmond is to shoot Varney's public course and perhaps to take advantage of a little shooting instruction from a man who *guarantees* that once you spend an hour or two with him one-on-one, you will be a better shooter. Putting his money where his mouth is, Varney offers to give you your money back if three conditions are not met: if you do not have fun, if you are not completely satisfied or if you do not feel he helped you become a better shooter.

Varney is now 62 years old. He has been shooting for 36 years and is certified as a coach by the NRA and NESCA. Primarily a wingshooter, when he goes to the field for grouse or woodcock, he usually takes home a limit he says.

Varney also says he has won many clay championships, but it is his "guarantee" that you will be a better shooter by taking instruction from him that is most interesting. Varney prefers a one-on-one instructor-student ratio and his charge per hour is a reasonable $40. For two or more students, the price is just $60.

Whether you take instruction at Varney's "Have Gun, Will Teach" Shooting School, his clay sports ranges are open on Thursday from 4:00 p.m. to dusk and Sunday from 10:00 a.m. until 4:00 p.m. You can shoot at other times by appointment, although a reservation is not normally required. Varney says he changes the 30 stations on his three sporting courses each week. In addition to the clays courses, there are two skeet ranges.

The cost to shoot Varney's is illustrated by his Sunday, August 15 "Sam's First Annual Fund Raiser." The main 50-bird event is $25. That day you can shoot a round of skeet for $5 or take part in the two-man, Duck Blind Flurry team event of 20-birds for only $6.

Even without a guarantee, Brad Varney's course packs a whole lot of value for your time and money.

Varney's Clay Sports

502 Langdon Rd.
Richmond, ME 04357
Phone (207) 737-4993
www.varneysclaysports.com

MARYLAND: Chesapeake Clays Bed & Breakfast

Every now and then, you bump into a small course that looks so inviting it makes you want to put the gun in the trunk and burn rubber. The vision of Chesapeake Clays' 150 acres, dining room and principal inn building did it for the author. I could picture myself slumping drowsily in a rocking chair while the 17-year locusts droned through the afternoon at this quiet country B&B – after busting a hundred birds, that is.

Chesapeake Clays is a public shooting course only 65 miles east of Washington, D.C., across the Chesapeake Bay Bridge on the Eastern Shore of Maryland. The hours are Monday and Wednesday through Saturday from 9:00 a.m. to 4:00 p.m., and Sunday from 10:00 a.m. until 4:00 p.m. It is closed Tuesday. Reservations are not required to shoot, but if you intend to spend the night, a phone call is obligatory.

Sporting shooting at Chesapeake Clays is a 47-station course with three towers; of course, rabbit, fox and many bird traps make the shooting fun and challenging. The cost is $15 for 50 targets, $20 for 75 and $30 for 100. On the last Sunday of every month, a shooter's first 50 clays are only $10. You can expect shots through the woods and over fields and ponds. A 5-Stand setup and wobble trap are also available.

The quality clubhouse and three-floor, 11-room bed and breakfast were built in 1986. The cost of $100 per night for a private room and bath includes a continental breakfast. Instruction can be arranged and factory ammo is available on site.

Chesapeake Clays Bed & Breakfast

16090 Oakland Rd.
Henderson, MD 21640
Phone (800) 787-4667/(410) 758-1824
Fax (410) 482-7189
www.chesapeakeclays.com

MICHIGAN: Brule Sporting Clays

Up here, it is Paul Bunyan country. Big-woods country. A resort in the middle of nowhere … well, Michigan's Upper Peninsula. Sounds perfect!

Brule Sporting Clays is one of those destinations – perhaps like Disney World or Six Flags – where you will probably go with the family, not alone. Thus, you will have an opportunity to sample shooting in a carnival atmosphere, like at The Dells in Wisconsin or Dollywood in Tennessee. After all, Brule Sporting Clays is a very small part of the Ski Brule resort complex. At this resort, the following activities are available: snow skiing, river rafting, horseback riding, canoe and raft rentals, mountain biking, hiking, golf, hunting, fishing … and, of course, sporting clays.

Nevertheless, this public shooting complex with a course of 60 clays stations packed into a half-mile course – a lot of shooting packed into a very small space – has stations with names like "Grouchy Grouse" and "60-Foot Tower" and "Road Reaction."

You have bought her a Mossberg 500 Field Bantam 20 gauge and she has done well. Now, take her to the range for a few lessons, but first make sure she has hearing and vision protection that fits as well as her shotgun.

If you left your gun and took your swimming trunks instead, the shooting clubhouse will rent you a gun for just $5. Depending on the quality of the gun, this is about the best price we have seen at shooting courses across the United States. It also sells ammo and other essentials. Shooting instruction can be arranged. Expect to pay $15 for 50 targets and $25 for 100.

Brule shooting hours are 9:00 a.m. to 5:00 p.m. every day. Reservations are not necessary but are certainly appreciated.

Unless you fly into Escanaba or Marquette, you will have to drive to Brule, but any road north through Wisconsin will be memorable for its wilderness, lodges and old European ethnic flavor. So much lodging is available in the area at so many price points that it is impossible to specify one or even two as typical. The Ski Brule Internet site lists dozens of options. There are plenty of camping and RV hookups in the area for any style rig.

Brule Sporting Clays
397 Brule Mt. Rd.
Iron River, MI 49935
Phone (800) 362-7853/(906) 265-6752
Fax (906) 265-6227
www.skibrule.com

MICHIGAN: Sugar Springs Sporting Clays and Hunting Preserve

Sugar Springs is 40 miles northwest of Bay City, in the middle of Michigan's "mitten." This means it is nicely situated so that its shooters can enjoy solitude without having complaining neighbors. So far, so good!

Open to the public on weekends from 10:00 a.m. to 3:00 p.m., this 440-acre course is available all year by reservation and hosts a mile and a half of sporting clays with 30 stations, a 5-Stand setup and wobble trap. Separate course presentations are designed to challenge novices, intermediates and even seasoned shotgunners. Target increments of 25 may be purchased with course completion times anticipated at 30 minutes to 2 hours depending on the size of the group. Numerous shotgun events are held at this Gladwin facility, and shooting instruction is always available during an event.

The computerized Sugar Springs 5-Stand operation consists of a combination of seven Remington Boss Sporters that will challenge even experienced shooters. Five targets are shot at each of the five stations. According to Lou Dallas at Sugar Springs, the 5-Stand has becomes the nucleus of winter league activity, allowing the course to preplan league programs. The winter league begins in mid-December and runs through May. "Lewis Class" scoring and an 80-percent handicap with NSCA rules apply.

Golf, tennis, camping, horseback riding, hunting, fishing and, yes, outlet malls are available in the local area. European-style tower hunts with released pheasants are scheduled during the summer. There are also hunting opportunities for pen-raised chukar, quail, huns and mallard ducks. The chest-high native grasses and thick pines provide excellent cover for the birds. Rental guns, food service and picnic areas are available.

Sugar Springs Sporting Clays and Hunting Preserve
1491 W. Sargent Rd.
Gladwin, MI 48624
Phone (989) 426-2645
Fax (989) 426-1608
www.sshpinc.com

MINNESOTA: Minnesota Horse & Hunt Club

The Minnesota Horse & Hunt Club advertises that you can "hunt, shoot, dine and meet friends all year 'round," which is saying something for Minnesota, where the native bird is the *Arctic Ice Mosquito*. This club shoots through the winter, however, including a "Frostbite Fun Shoot" in January when the temperatures can dip to 30 degrees below zero and a "Winter Freeze Fun Shoot" in February when howling winds out of Alberta can drive frozen pine needles through two-by-fours!

Randy Travalia's beautiful Horse & Hunt Club is located in Prior Lake, 25 minutes southwest of the Minneapolis/St. Paul metropolitan area. Because the international airport is also on the south side of Minneapolis (near the Mall of America) and the club is only 9 miles from Interstate 35, it is easy to reach. Thousands of motel rooms and plenty of restaurants are available in the area should the Lodge and the Inn on the club grounds be booked during your visit.

Sporting clays is a significant part of the Horse & Hunt layout. The course opened in 1985, one of the earliest in the United States. In the summer of 2002, it hosted the prestigious U.S. Open Sporting

Nick Sisley has been a full time gunwriter since 1969. He currently has magazine shotgun columns in the NRA's **Shooting Illustrated, Sporting Clays, the Skeet Shooting Review and Wildfowl.** *"One of my favorite sporting courses is The Willows in northwest Mississippi," he says. "The stations have a great deal of variation, and at each station the targets can be set anywhere from relatively easy to relatively hard. But my favorite place to shoot at The Willows is their* **Flurry.** *There are three shooting stands. At the proper signal, clays start flying – incomers and crossers – from seven or more traps. In only a few minutes, 50 to 100 birds can be thrown. The team of three doing the shooting must do their best to coordinate who takes what bird – if as many clays as possible are going to be broken – without many clays getting by without a shot fired, because no one has a shell in the gun. It's fast and furious action, and fun, fun, fun."*

Nick Sisley

Clays championship. Today, there are five courses with as many as 250 target presentations! There are also two trap fields, two skeet fields, two duck towers, FITASC, a pistol and rifle range (members only), wingshooting instruction and much more, including a fine dining room. The 5-Stand operation has eight dedicated, computer-controlled traps and includes both rabbit and tower shots.

The club's main lodge is reminiscent of real northwoods architecture celebrated by authors and environmentalists such as Sigurd Olson, with log wall construction and huge, handcrafted fieldstone fireplaces. Overnight lodging is available and 12-week sporting clays league shooting is encouraged.

The cost of shooting a 50-bird round of sporting clays as a non-member is $21. A 25-bird round of skeet, trap or duck tower is only $9 and 25 targets at the 5-Stand are $10. Gun rental is $8 and a box of target loads is $6.

Bob Fitzgerald, who learned shooting from master instructor Jack Mitchell in Cornwall, England, teaches shooting at Horse & Hunt. His lessons are $60 per hour or $75 per hour for two people.

A limited number of camping and RV facilities are available with showers, water and electricity for $25 to $32 per night.

One of the exciting options at Horse & Hunt is the ability to shoot quail, pigeons, pheasant, chukar, huns and turkeys.

Minnesota Horse & Hunt Club
2920 220th St.
Prior Lake, MN 55372
Phone (952) 447-2272
Fax (952) 447-2278
www.mnhorseandhunt.com

MISSISSIPPI: The Willows at Grand Casino Tunica

Anyone who likes a little roll of the dice between shooting rounds will definitely enjoy rolling into this sportsman's casino and shooting club just 15 miles south of Memphis. The Grand Casino Tunica invites sportsmen to "test all your skills" – two wobble trap stations, Make-A-Break, Duck Flush, some trap and skeet and a championship golf course – plus, of course, your skills with their dice and cards and slots. Why, melt me down a barrel and turn it into a putter, there is enough shooting variety at The Willows to satisfy the most hard-bitten skeptic.

Tunica is part of the Caesar's Entertainment division. Consequently, it is allied with the casinos in Gulfport and Biloxi. In Las Vegas, the same corporation operates Bally's and Caesar's Palace. These are not mom-and-pop operations, so you would expect the shooting to be First Class and, from what we hear, it is.

The Willows' sporting clays course has 14 automated stations, each with three levels of shooting difficulty. Guest shooters are accompanied by a certified trapper, too. Of course, if you have arrived without your shooting iron, the facility has Beretta loaner guns (eye and ear protection are provided), and should you need to brush up on your gun mount or follow-through, NRA-certified instructors are available for private or for group lessons.

The Willows offers 1/2-day quail hunts from October to March for $250, by reservation. You can stay overnight in the Grand Resort then for only an additional $35.

The Willows at Grand Casino Tunica
13615 Old Hwy. 61 North
Robinsville, MS 38664
Phone (662) 357-3154
Fax (662) 357-3218
www.grandcasinos.com

Alan Clemons is Outdoors Editor for **The Huntsville Times** *in Huntsville, Alabama. One of his favorite courses is The Willows at The Grand Casino in Tunica, Mississippi. "The Willows offers great shooting challenges including rabbits, flushing quail and crossing doves," he says. "Although it is not part of their outstanding clays course, my favorite shooting there is 'Duck Flush' in which three shooters attempt to hit as many targets in a 75-bird flurry as possible … within three minutes. Targets come in from the front, back, sides and going away, and it's a rush to compete while also working with other shooters to communicate about where a target is coming from and whether your gun is loaded and ready." For clays, Clemons shoots a Remington 300 Ideal over/under with Gamebore White Gold 7-1/2 shells or Winchester AA in the same size. If he is simply warming up before hunting season, he uncases his Remington 11-87 auto-loader rather than the over/under because the auto-loader is the gun he uses for doves and ducks.*

MISSOURI: Cedar Creek Rod and Gun Club

This is middle America at its finest … and its finest is apparently pretty good, because this club has everything, including reasonable prices and easy access.

Cedar Creek is a dozen miles east of Columbia and just north of Interstate 70. Although it encourages shooting memberships, it is open to the public. The hours are Tuesdays and Thursdays from noon to 8:00 p.m., Sundays from 10:00 a.m. to 8:00 p.m. and the second and third Saturdays between 10:00 a.m. and 5:00 p.m. If you want to shoot at other times, you should make an appointment. Otherwise, reservations are not required.

According to the Internet site, "We can challenge you or let you off easy, depending on whether you choose the 'No Whining' or the 'Whining' course. We have a wide range of target presentations with over 48 shooting stations on two separate courses. You can shoot over water, under a tower, from a variety of decks, in the woods, or in the meadow."

Cedar Creek also offers two 5-Stand setups and the owners make a point of mixing up the target presentations. "Our mini-clays present a unique shooting experience over a small lake with five shooting stations and 10-12 traps. This 25-bird course offers the convenience of 5-Stand with the variety of a sporting clays course. Both our 5-Stand and mini-clays are lighted for night shooting."

On the more traditional side, Cedar Creek offers both skeet and trap. Still, they do it right. The six skeet, six trap and wobble trap layouts are all lighted for night shooting. Skeet shooters can choose from American skeet, modern skeet or International skeet games. Trap shooters can shoot conventional trap, doubles or International.

Non-member (member) prices are: skeet and trap $5 ($3.35), International skeet $6 ($4.50), 5-Stand $8 ($6). A round of 50 sporting clays is just $18 or $13 for members. For the January 1 through December 31 membership year, individuals pay $75 and families pay $100. For full access to this club, that price sounds like a bargain.

A large clubhouse with full kitchen is available for breakfast, lunch or dinner. In addition, a limited number of overnight stays can be arranged in the clubhouse. Camping and RV hookups (eight) are also available on site.

Cedar Creek Rod and Gun Club
4251 N. Glendale Dr.
Columbia, MO 65202
Phone (573) 387-4747/474-5804 • Fax (573) 474-8609
www.cedarcreekrodandgunclub.com

MISSOURI:
Pin Oak Hill Game Management Area

"We are now serving food," Pin Oak's Internet site notes. "During regular hours of operation our snack bar is open for a variety of sandwiches and side items. We're also open Wednesday – Saturday evenings until 9 pm. Thursday night—ALL YOU CAN EAT HOT WINGS!! These spicy wings are Doug's specialty and he's sure to keep you coming back for more! Try our Pin Oak Hill House Steak, Prime Rib or Boiled Shrimp on Friday and Saturday nights."

Free hot wings! That is good enough for me.

Pin Oak is an hour or so northeast of Kansas City, depending on traffic. It opened in 1993 and is family owned and operated by brothers Scott and Doug Luetticke. The hours are currently set at: Wednesday through Friday 3:00 p.m. to 9:00 p.m., Saturday 10:00 a.m. to 9:00 p.m. and Sunday from 10:00 p.m. to 5:00 p.m. No reservations are required, but you can shoot almost anytime by appointment. The public is welcome for clay shooting and hunting.

Pin Oak has one 15-stand sporting clay course with fully automated traps, and shot presentations are routinely changed. Doug and Scott promote league shooting, fun shoots, classification shoots, fundraisers and sub-gauge events. A 52-foot tower has been built so that wingshooters can practice for doves. Your charge for 100 targets on the Luetticke's course will be $30.

There is a lighted trap range ($4 for 25 targets), a lighted 5-Stand station ($7.50 for 25 targets) and FITASC shooting.

Hunting is available for deer, turkey or upland birds. A 5-day firearm hunt is $3250 (archery $2500) and includes lodging, meals, a guide, field-dressing your deer and free does. Before you book, understand that Pin Oak charges an additional fee of $1500 – called a "fine" – if you harvest a buck that does not score at least 140.

Eastern turkey hunts (2-day bow or shotgun, $500 plus $100 shot fee) include a guide, meals and bird cleaning and meat packaging.

Upland birds are a Pin Oak specialty. Guides and dogs are available for quail, driven pheasant and chukar from October 1 through March 31. The cost is: pheasant $15, chukar $12 and quail $8, plus a $25 guide fee for the dog and handler.

The Pin Oak Mega European Driven Pheasant Shoot sounds like an event: 500 pheasants are released to 25 shooters in 25 blinds. For 3 hours (9:00 a.m. to noon), you can bang away at the birds. Following lunch, you shoot a 100-target sporting clays round while the guides clean and package your birds. The cost is $265 per gun.

Pin Oak has a clubhouse and pro shop. Meals, a dog kennel and dog training are available, as well as an NSCA Level I shooting instructor to train the dog's owner. With a paid adult, kids under 18 shoot for half price.

Scott and Doug can arrange airport pick-up and help you book an area motel.

Pin Oak Hill Game Management Area
RR1, Box 230B
Bogard, MO 64622
Phone (660) 745-3030 • Fax (660) 745-3070
www.pinoakhill.com

NEVADA: Desert Lake Country Club

Here is a totally new "country club" without a pool that was not designed for tennis moms and fat corporate execs. Well, not exclusively for fat corporate execs.

Desert Lake is situated in the El Dorado Valley 25 miles southeast of Las Vegas' famous casino strip. At Desert Lake, you can experience virtually any shooting venue while you breathe Nevada's clear, high desert air.

This shooting complex is just 10 minutes from the spectacular Hoover Dam and Lake Mead recreation area. PMC Ammunition, the "fourth largest ammo maker in the U.S.," owns Desert Lake. We refer to it as a "shooting complex" because within its 80 acres are multiple opportunities to have fun with almost any type of gun ... or even a bow.

Unless you are visiting on a 100-plus-degree day, sporting clays shooters will enjoy Desert Lake's mile-long, circular 20-station course. The paved trail meanders through scenic high desert country and, yes, golf car rentals are available. Two 5-Stand sporting clays stations are also up and running. One is situated on a hilltop with "a spectacular view" of desert and distant mountains; the other is next to the clubhouse.

For other shooting experiences, there is a five-station ATA trap range and an eight-station American skeet range. Of course, all traps are automatic. As a special enhancement to ensure that your shooting experience is complete, PMC has designed a rugged, mile-long 24-target archery range complete with a variety of 3-D targets including bears, deer and mountain lions. The 300-yard Desert Lake rifle range has five covered shooting stations, and the 50-yard pistol range uses metal reactive targets.

A 6500-square-foot lodge-style clubhouse, pro shop and restaurant offer visitors a 360-degree view of desert mountain scenery. Desert Lake has Verona shotguns for rent, sells PMC factory ammo and the pro shop is fully stocked with shooting accessories. Gunsmithing services and formal instruction from an NSCA Level III instructor are available.

David Shaw, president of Desert Lake and vice president/marketing of PMC, recommends that you call to make a shooting reservation. The country club is open Tuesday through Sunday from 8:00 a.m. until dusk, from August to June.

Desert Lake Country Club
PO Box 62308 (89006)
12801 US 95 S (89005)
Boulder City, NV
Phone (702) 294-0025 • Fax (702) 294-0121
www.desertlakecc.com or www.pmcammo.com

NEW JERSEY: M&M Hunting Preserve

M&M is only 20 miles south of Philadelphia, 60 miles from Baltimore and 120 miles south of the New York megalopolis. Just minutes from the Delaware River Bridge, this privately owned 2000-acre course is open to the public and offers memberships for both hunting and sporting clays shooting.

M&M owner Anthony Matarese says course hours are Tuesday through Sunday, 9:00 a.m. until 3:00 p.m. Reservations are recommended for weekday shooting, if you need a trap manager. Otherwise, the course is fully automated for people who prefer to pull their own targets.

The 40 stations on M&M's three clay courses are changed frequently to keep guests challenged. Matarese has two high towers for crossing doves (and driven pheasant hunting). One 5-Stand range is available. Prices are $18 for 50 birds, $35 for 100 birds and $8 for 25 shots on the 5-Stand range. Members pay $15, $30 and $7 respectively. "Shoot 10 rounds," Matarese says, "and number 11 is on the house!"

Numerous sporting events are held at M&M, including FITASC shoots and the club's own "Big Seafood Blast" and "Masters Cup." Because a clubhouse, dining room and outdoor pavilion are open on site and plenty of accommodations are available within a few minutes drive, the membership options here seem very reasonable: $100 per member (per year) or for a family membership, the cost is $100 per initial member and only $50 for additional members. RV hookups are available during an event.

For wingshooters who enjoy banging away at pheasants, chukar and ducks, M&M has hundreds of acres of prime upland and waterfowl hunting available. For hunting, a membership is encouraged.

Group and private shooting lessons are available from Anthony Matarese, Jr. a 4-year member of Team USA and a five-time All-American.

M&M Hunting Preserve
2 Winslow Rd.
Pennsville, NJ 08070
Phone (856) 935-1230 • Fax (856) 935-9356
www.mmhunting.com

NEW MEXICO: Creosote Flats Sporting Clays

You will be hundreds of miles from Area 51 and any possible shot manipulation by aliens who land there to communicate secretly with our government, so you will not have them to blame for a miss. Creosote Flats is an RV resort, but "resort" may be stretching the definition.

To reach Creosote Flats from Deming in southwest New Mexico, drive until the pavement ends, the road becomes gravel and finally dead-ends at the ranch. Suddenly, you find yourself in 7000 unfenced acres of howling coyotes, starry skies and solitude, with a few nearby RVs and perhaps some Lawrence Welk streaming out their windows. Actually, you will only be 15 minutes off the JAX-LAX, Interstate 10, and all around you will be an abundance of high desert scenery and ruins left by ancient cliff dwellers. In addition, you are only 30 minutes straight down Highway 11 from Old Mexico.

Creosote Flats' 10-stand sporting clays course is open to the public year-round, by appointment. Reservations are always required at this resort unless you are an RV guest. No guns or carts are rented and no ammo is available. Club policy is, "If you need it, you better bring it with you."

Mary Kay Gibbs hosts monthly fun shoots at Creosote Flats. Members pay $30 for 100 targets; non-members pay $40. If you live nearby, you should certainly join because individual member dues are only $50 a year. Normally, $36 will buy 100 birds for a non-member, non-guest. It is $30 for guests and $25 for members. For a small place, the options are astounding.

Chances are that you will not drive far out of your way to shoot this sporting clays course north of Deming, but perhaps you should. There are miles of hiking and biking trails and abundant bird-watching opportunities. The area is wonderful for photography, the cliff rocks still have undiscovered petroglyphs and you can ride your ATV throughout the ranch. A 30-target 3-D archery range ($10 for non-members or $2 for guests) winds through the mesquite-covered hills.

The recreation hall offers pool (not "a pool"), a video library and a paperback book exchange. There is a laundry, a driving range (Bring your own balls?) and modem hookup for your computer. In addition, you can play cards or bingo with other guests, and there is usually an ice cream social on the last Sunday of the month during the winter.

Standard RV lots have 30-amp service, water, sewer and electricity for $17 per night or $75 per week. Not bad rates since you have just spent $135,000 for a slightly used 2003 Monaco Diplomat diesel pusher. But it sleeps four!

In short, you must shoot Creosote Flats so that you can buy the tee shirt, for the ice cream social and because it is a lovely, lost slice of Americana … even if aliens are watching.

Creosote Flats Sporting Clays
12100 Hidden Valley Rd., NW
Deming, NM 88030
Phone (888) 546-3071/(505) 546-3071 • Fax (505) 544-2134
www.hiddenvalleyranchrv.com

NEW YORK: Orvis Sandanona

*Glenn Sapir is editorial director for the National Shooting Sports Foundation in Newtown, CT. He has served as an editor for several outdoor magazines and writes a weekly outdoor column for **The Journal News**. His professional travels have given him the opportunity to hunt and shoot all over the continent, but one of his favorite sporting clays courses, Orvis's Sandanona in Millbrook, New York, is close to home.*

"Sandanona was the first licensed preserve in the United States. Today, among its offerings is a challenging sporting clays course, and one of my favorite stations there is Fur and Feather, where a bouncing target darts from the underbrush on my right and scampers across my field of view. As soon as my gun barks, another target streaks through the air in front of the wooded hillside. It simulates rabbit hunting and wingshooting at their most challenging."

Orvis is hugely responsible for popularizing sporting clays shooting in the United States. Certainly, they were not alone, but the company founded in Manchester, Vermont, by Charles Orvis in 1856 is the world's oldest mail order company, and it still promotes the shooting sports.

The Orvis Sandanona shooting facility located 80 miles north of New York City in Millbrook is open 363 days a year from 9:00 a.m. to 5:00 p.m. It happily accepts memberships, but is open to the public. Reservations are required, and unless two people shoot together, a single shooter must shoot a double round. The maximum squad size is five.

The ever-changing, 30-stand sporting clay course at Orvis Sandanona is open to members for $50 per 100 clays and to non-members for $75. This is pricey, but Orvis says the grounds are meticulously maintained and that, after all, this is a very classy, almost haughty place to shoot. On the other hand, a sporting clays membership is only $150. Go figure!

There is a lot to see at the 19th-century shooting lodge after you shoot a round or two of clays. This venerable sporting institution is the oldest permitted shooting club in the country; so old in fact, that the main lodge was built during the presidency of Thomas Jefferson. You can sightsee or you can shoot a round of skeet ($15 members and $20 non-members) or wobble trap.

Orvis is famous for its quarter-century tradition of shooting and fly-fishing schools. The fundamentals of the Orvis shooting system include stance, footwork, gun handling, swing, visual concentration, proper gun mount and correct fit of the gunstock. Your tuition buys a complimentary gunfitting to establish and record individual stock dimensions, comprehensive instruction, all targets and ammunition, lunches each school day and a copy of the Orvis Wingshooting Handbook. You can use an Orvis shotgun at no additional charge if needed. One day of instruction is $495; two days are $990. Private instruction is $175 per hour.

Upland bird hunting is available to hunting members, but the cost of that membership is a little more than $150 per year. In fact, you must call them to personally discuss a hunting membership.

Orvis Sandanona
PO Box 450
311 Route 44A
Millbrook, NY 12545-0450
Phone (845) 677-9701 • Fax (845) 677-0092
www.orvis.com\sandanona

NEW YORK: Rochester Brooks Gun Club

Rochester Brooks is a private, member-only gun club that offers a full range of shooting sports, including skeet (14 fields; three are lighted for winter shooting), trap (14 fields; two are lighted), international skeet and trap, sporting clays, 5-Stand, pistol, rifle, archery and hunting for members. The current cost of a membership seems eminently reasonable for this amount of shooting potential: $225 buys a regular membership for yourself and your family. The $125 membership is for shooters who reside farther than 50 miles from the club, and the cheap $25 membership is for students. New members must be approved by the board and are required to go through the club's safety training before they can use the ranges. So, with more than 700 members, Rochester Brooks is private, but it is "openly private" to avoid liability problems says George Lehr, club president.

Only 15 miles south of Rochester, reservations are not required during normal shooing hours, which are Wednesday from 9:00 a.m. until 9:00 p.m. and Saturday/Sunday from 9:00 in the morning until 5:00 p.m.

The full-service Rochester Brooks clubhouse will accommodate up to 100 guests for dinner. The kitchen and bar are open for members whenever the club is open and on special occasions for private, member parties. Shooting instruction by qualified coaches can be arranged.

Three sporting clays courses wind their way around Rochester Brooks. A challenging, 100-target Field Course has all automatic machines in open terrain, and three towers. Most field stations have two traps and offer birds with speed, acute angles and curling patterns. The 50-bird woods course called Hickory Ridge requires a trapper: it is designed to appeal to new and small-gauge shooters because shots are shorter. The third course is open occasionally to offer shooting variety to the club's members. A 5-Stand is open year-round. At Rochester Brooks, the sporting clays season begins the last weekend in April.

Shooting costs are reasonable at Rochester Brooks, even if you are not a member. For 50 sporting clays targets, expect to pay $12 ($15 for non-members). Trap and skeet are $3 for a 25-bird round ($5 for non-members). Skeet and trap leagues and a traveling sporting clays league are offered to members. In addition, 200 acres are set aside for hunting and dog training when other activities are not scheduled.

This club has a BLAST. The acronym stands for "Brooks Ladies All-American Shooting Team," and, yes, it is only for women. In spite of the "All-American" designation, however, BLAST was formed by women and for women, to spread the word about the shooting sports, and so, even today, its members and activities are limited to women of any age, profession and skill level.

Rochester Brooks Gun Club offers shooters some of the premier facilities in New York. Rochester Brooks is "openly private," says club president George Lehr. A family membership is only $225 for a year or $125 for shooters who live farther than 5 miles from the club.

Rochester Brooks Gun Club
PO Box 289
962 Honeoye Falls Rd. #6
Rush, NY 14543
Phone (585) 533-9913
www.rochesterbrooks.org

Rabbit shooting at Rochester Brooks. Acquire the target visually, begin the gun mount and swing the muzzle. When the muzzle covers the running rabbit, trigger your shot.

NORTH CAROLINA: Deep River Sporting Clays

Here is a fine course in the center of the state that offers plenty of diverse shooting, excellent instructional opportunities and a well-stocked pro shop. It is convenient, and it is affordable for members and non-members. Already 16 years old, Deep River is 28 miles southwest of Raleigh. It occupies 65 acres of woods, fields and ponds.

Deep River is open Sunday through Friday from 1:00 to 6:00 p.m. and Saturday from 10:00 a.m. to 6:00 p.m. It is closed on Thanksgiving and Christmas. Reservations are only required if you want to shoot outside the normal hours.

The main sporting clays course offers a "pleasant walk through the woods" to 13 shooting stations. The 35-foot tower has a programmable international wobble trap on top for "exciting shooting" over a duck pond. The 10 stations surrounding the tower are reserved for members. Deep River has a compact clays course with 25 stations built around a wobble trap tower. There is also a pistol range at this Tar Heel facility.

The course offers ZZ Flyers and side-by-side shooting. Similar to Hélice, ZZ is a recent European imported shooting game, but the wing is steel and therefore reusable. This makes ZZ much less expensive to shoot than Hélice, which can cost more than $10 per flying target.

The pride of Deep River is its diverse shooting school offerings. Nine certified instructors are available including Bill Kempffer, who is at the NSCA Level III. Both individual and group coaching is available and try-gun fittings are a regular part of the classes. Concealed carry and pistol classes are in the curriculum also.

Although Deep River is open to the public, memberships are very reasonable. A family membership is $120 per year with a $50 initiation fee. Members receive shooting discounts, paying $6 for a 25-target compact sporting shoot and $12.50 for the 50-target sporting course, while non-members pay $9 and $19, respectively. Members can purchase shooting discount cards (buy nine rounds of 50 and get one round free) and may participate in club championships. They get an automatic 15-percent discount on shooting schools and purchases through the pro shop.

The Deep River clubhouse and full-service pro shop occupy 2300 square feet with restrooms. Rental guns ($3.00 per round of 50) and carts are available, too. Deep River offers NSCA-registered league shooting.

Deep River Sporting Clays

284 Cletus Hall Rd.
Sanford, NC 27330
Phone (919) 774-7080
Fax (919) 708-5052
www.deepriver.net

OHIO: Scioto River Hunting Club

A three-story Alpine-style log lodge distinguishes this 500-acre central Ohio hunting and shooting club. On its lower level are a snack bar, gun rental and a small shop for the purchase of ammo and safety gear. A huge stone fireplace dominates the main, mid-level room, which has access to a dining area, a fully equipped kitchen and wrap-around deck with gas grill. The upper level has three bedrooms and a full bath; it is sufficient for eight overnight guests (one to two people, $125 and three to eight, $250).

Scioto River is central to thousands of clay shooting enthusiasts. It is 75 miles to Columbus, 80 to Toledo and 60 to Dayton. Although Scioto River is open to the public, memberships are available and provide a number of discounts and admission to member-only events. Reservations are recommended, especially for holidays or for hunting.

From April 1 through October 31, Scioto River is open Thursday (noon to 6:00 p.m.) through Sunday (9:00 a.m. to 6:00 p.m.). From November 1 to March 31, the club closes an hour earlier.

Two different sporting clays courses, open field and woods, with 20 stations, trap (American and bunker), skeet ($4.50 for 25 clays) and wobble trap ($3 for 25) are available, as is pheasant hunting. For $12, you shoot 50 targets, or if you are under 15, you shoot for half price with a full-price adult.

Three hundred club acres are devoted strictly to pheasant hunting. Guests may bring their own dog or guides with dogs will be provided.

A sporting clays "fun shoot" is held on the second Sunday of every month. Shot presentations for the fun shoot are changed regularly to ensure that all participants are essentially shooting the course for the first time. When leagues are in progress, shots are changed weekly.

Shooting instruction can be arranged with an NSCA Level II instructor and the club often hosts Level I Instructor Schools.

Scioto River Hunting Club

17226 St. Rt. 235
Roundhead, OH 43346
Phone (419) 227-1661
Fax (937) 464-7464
www.srhuntclub.com

OKLAHOMA: Oklahoma Sporting Clays

"Located on the outskirts of Edmond, Oklahoma Sporting Clays [OSC] offers a unique shooting experience," says the OSC Internet site. "Surrounded by hills, trees, and lakes, shooters test their skills on clay targets that fly through the trees, over water, or bounce along the ground."

Open to public shooting, but accepting memberships, OSC is only 10 miles north of Oklahoma City. The year 2005 will be their 11th year in business. Hours are Wednesday through Sunday from 9:00 a.m. until dark. Reservations are recommended. Family memberships are only $150 per year and entitle members to reduced shooting fees, deep 25-percent discounts in the pro shop, fishing privileges in the 21-acre lake (12 to 27 feet deep) and use of other OSC facilities and services.

There are two sporting clays courses at OSC. The Green Course is a 50- or 100-bird championship course with a 10- to 13-station shooting experience. On this venue, clays move faster, distance to the target is greater and angles are more difficult. "Mini" clays are thrown at some stations, as are "double" traps and ground targets that resemble kangaroos more than rabbits.

With nine to 12 stations on line at any one time, the Red Course is less challenging for beginners and intermediate shotgunners. Each Red station has two shooting positions, "Easy" and "Advanced." Red stations are closer to the clubhouse too, so shooters do not have to walk as far and can shoot a round in less time. All paths are clearly marked and benches and water coolers are provided throughout the course. OSC has one 48-foot tower and a 19-foot portable tower for special, on-course surprises.

Member shooting costs for sporting clays are $22 for 100 targets and $11 for 50 targets.

In addition to the above opportunities, OSC has a covered and lighted 5-Stand pavilion ($5.50 for 25 targets) with bleachers and electronic traps. The 5-Stand pavilion is an excellent place to practice or to receive instruction. Two handgun ranges and one rifle range with 50- and 100-yard shooting lines are available to members. Travelers will enjoy the convenient on-site RV hookups.

The rustic log cabin-style clubhouse has a snack bar and a pro shop that sells reloading supplies, ammo and other shooting necessities, and rents carts for the sporting clays courses. A covered and lighted picnic pavilion is nearby.

Oklahoma Sporting Clays
PO Box 91
Arcadia, OK 73007
Phone (405) 396-2661
www.oksportingclays.com

OKLAHOMA: Silverleaf Shotgun Sports

David, Debbie and Dustin Rippetoe, proprietors of Silverleaf, are celebrating their 7th year in business in 2005. That certainly beats the small business average lifetime!

Located 25 miles north of Oklahoma City, the layout is open weekdays 9:00 a.m. until 7:00 p.m. and on weekends 7:00 a.m. until 7:00 p.m. Reservations are not required.

Dustin, who manages the shooting at Silverleaf, operates a primary and a secondary sporting clays course. Depending on the shooting event or the stage of change of target presentations, the main course has 10 to 14 stations. The smaller, north course is a five-station warm-up. Trails are graveled and rental carts are available.

In addition to sporting clays shooting, there are two skeet ranges, a trap range, a 5-Stand station and wobble trap.

The cost of shooting at Silverleaf is relatively reasonable. Sporting is $30 for 100 birds, $16 for 50 birds and on the small, north course, a 25-target mini round is $8. Trap, skeet and wobble trap cost just $6 for 25 targets. The 5-Stand and Snooker ranges are $8 for 25.

Silverleaf is open to the public, but does have a couple of membership options. A $250 annual fee allows individual members to shoot practice rounds for $12 per 50 targets. For $400 annually, a couple can buy a "Sweetheart Membership" that gives them the same privilege. A lifetime family membership is $2500, which gives your family half-price practice rounds and reduced league prices, presumably forever!

A clubhouse and pro shop are located on site and, through the club, you can arrange for certified NSCA shooting instruction.

Silverleaf Shotgun Sports
8513 S. Douglas Blvd.
Guthrie, OK 73044
Phone (405) 282-2787
www.silverleafshotgun.com

OREGON: Mitchell's Clay Target Sports

In 2001, Mitchell's was voted the NSCA and NSSA "Best All-Around" gun club. Operated by Dan and Patsy Mitchell, this club is located between Salem and Portland just off Interstate 5. The hours: Wednesday (noon to 8:00 p.m. in summer or to 6:00 p.m. in winter), Thursday (members only, noon to 6:00 p.m.), Friday (noon to 6:00 p.m.) and Saturday/Sunday (10:00 a.m. to 5:00 p.m.). Although this shooting club is open to the public, reservations are recommended and memberships are available that offer reduced shooting and pro-shop prices and the chance to participate in member-only events.

Mitchell's has one or more of everything. Winding through fields and trees, Mitchell's 10-15-station sporting clays course has four high towers and allows shotgunners to shoot a 50- or 100-bird ($30) round. There are 14 skeet and trap ranges ($4.50 for 25 targets), a single covered 5-Stand ($6 for 25 targets) and wobble trap.

Through the pro shop, one can purchase a variety of guns, clothing and shooting accessories. Mitchell's is a Beretta showcase pro shop and has rental guns ($10) and cart rentals. It also sells Verona shotguns, used guns and takes guns on consignment.

Dan, an NSSA and NSCA All-American who has been shooting competitively since 1967, is available for instruction at $50 per hour.

Food is available at the club on weekends, but the course is so centrally located that plenty of motel rooms and restaurants are within easy driving distance. RV hookups are on-site for campers and showers are available.

Mitchell's Clay Target Sports
6181 Concomly Rd. NE
Gervais, OR 97026
Phone (503) 792-3431
Fax (503) 792-3420
www.mitchellsclaytargetsports.com

Silverleaf Shotgun Sports in Guthrie, Oklahoma, has been in business 7 years and is owned and operated by the Rippetoe family.

PENNSYLVANIA:
Lehigh Valley Sporting Clays

Just up the street from the national Cement Industry Museum and wrapped around an abandoned limestone quarry, Lehigh Valley offers its private members and members of the public "one of the most unique courses you will ever shoot."

In east-central Pennsylvania only 4 miles north of Allentown, this course is readily available to millions of shotgunners and would-be shotgunners. An annual membership is only $125 for an individual or $225 for a family. These fees give you several hundred free targets, plus special discounts on shooting, ammo, instruction and purchases in the club's fully stocked pro shop.

Club hours are Wednesday through Sunday from 9:30 a.m. until at least 5:00 p.m. Bill Bachenberg, the owner, and Jason Hartshorn, the new club manager, allow shooting on Mondays and Tuesdays by appointment, but those days are typically reserved for corporate events.

The 17-station Lehigh sporting clays course has two stands at each station, an "A" stand for advanced shooters and a "B" stand for beginners. Stands are covered, traps are fully automated and target presentations are indicated at each station. At least three station presentations are changed each week. Shots on the clays course and at the covered 5-Stand include rabbits, teal, incomers, crossing, battue and minis. Lehigh has one high tower for high-flying duck and dove shots.

Although this popular course is situated in the midst of a heavily populated area, the cost of shooting at Lehigh is relatively modest: public prices are $9 for the 5-Stand and wobble trap; 50 sporting targets for $20 and 100 for $35. Golf cart and gun rental (Beretta and Krieghoff) is $15 per round and lessons are $45 per hour. NSCA-certified instructors at Levels I and II are on site and occasional guest instructors schedule clinics.

Lehigh hosts occasional novice and women-only events such as its annual "Golf with Gun Powder," Women-on-Target event each May 15. The emphasis in these get-togethers is to introduce first-timers to the fun of shooting a shotgun and breaking flying clay targets.

Lehigh Valley Sporting Clays
2750 Limestone St.
Coplay, PA 18037
Phone (610) 261-9616
Fax (610) 261-9618
www.lvsclays.com

New York-based gunwriter Dave Henderson travels extensively to hunt and shoot. The author of four books on shotgunning, he has hunted 25 states and seven Canadian provinces and shoots registered trap and sporting clays.

"My favorite sporting clays courses are White Oak Plantation in Tuskegee, Alabama, and Rock Mountain in Springville, Pennsylvania, both of which make ingenious use of the existing terrain," Dave says. "My all-time favorite station is No. 16 at Rock Mountain, called 'The Cliff Hanger,' where an incoming true pair is thrown from a cliff more than 200 feet above the shooter. The left bird courses with the wind and the right bird is actually a midi, which gives it the impression of being much farther away than it actually is."

PENNSYLVANIA:
Nemacolin Woodlands Resort & Spa

If you are shooting on a budget, do not expect to dine or sleep over at Nemacolin unless you bunk with a buddy or two. Ask how much it costs and you probably cannot afford it. When Nemacolin was founded in the 1930s, famed architect Frank Lloyd Wright designed the family lodge. Eventually, in the mid-1980s, the lodge was purchased at auction by "84 Lumber" founder Joe Hardy. Hardy has since built Nemacolin into a "world-class resort." It is plush by design!

This southwest Pennsylvania resort is expensive, but if you have an opportunity to attend any sponsored event at the Nemacolin "Shooting Academy," you should consider making the necessary sacrifice. Situated on 140 landscaped acres, the sporting clays course has 30 shooting stations and more than 80 automatic traps. Each station has a deck – many are split-level – which allows the course manager to vary shooting angles and positions, while spectators can observe in comfort. A paved road provides all-weather access to each station and golf carts rent for $10.

Nemacolin is designed to allow its guests to spend a great deal of money in beautiful and luxurious surroundings. Its shotgun opportunities are no different. A 25-target "Introduction to Sporting Clays" round with their equipment and ammo is $30. For $55 ($33 with your gear), you can shoot 50 targets. A round of 100 birds is $95 ($58 with your gear and ammo).

A 5-Stand pavilion for compact shooting stands near the lodge. It offers spectator seating on the main deck and multiple shooting decks at various heights. Shooters and spectators are completely sheltered from sun, rain and snow. A 25-clay round of 5-Stand is $14 or $24 with rental gear.

Nemacolin offers three "fun stations" set up with multiple traps, towers and European pheasant flush fields for tuning up before live bird hunts. These fun stations have large shooting decks with barbecue pits that groups of shooters may reserve for private parties.

The 7000-square-foot shooting lodge features a full-service pro shop and retail store. Meals are available throughout the day, and a bar is open to shooters who have completed their round. (No one is permitted to shoot after being served at the bar.)

Dave Henderson

The most beautiful shooting station on Joe Morales' Rhino course in Williston, Florida, is beneath an enormous live oak draped with Spanish moss.

Nemacolin has seven NSCA-certified instructors available year-round and visiting instructors offer clinics throughout the year. Individual shooting lessons are $92 per hour (their gear) or $60 (your own gun and ammo). Junior (under 16 years old) lessons are $72 per hour, but all gear is furnished. Contact Michael Mohr, shooting academy director, at 724-329-6770 for information or to inquire about their Saturday morning youth sporting clays clinics.

Nemacolin Woodlands Resort & Spa
1001 LaFayette Dr.
Farmington, PA 15437
Phone (800) 422-2736/(724) 329-8555 • Fax (724) 329-6694
www.nemacolin.com

RHODE ISLAND: Addieville East Farm

Rhode Island is a very small state, but just 20 miles north of Providence, its Addieville East Farm has a reputation as a superior, self-contained facility that is "suitable for shooters of any level." Guests and non-members are allowed to shoot there, but membership confers benefits in reduced prices, bird hunting and other club services.

Hours vary by day and season. Summer is April 15 to October 1: Monday (9:00 a.m. to 3:00 p.m.), Tuesday (closed to change the courses), Wednesday (10:00 a.m. to 5:00 p.m.), Thursday (10:00 to dark), Friday (10:00 a.m. to 5:00 p.m.), Saturday (9:00 a.m. to 6:00 p.m.) and Sunday (9:00 a.m. to 4:00 p.m.). During winter, October 1 to April 14, hours are 8:00 a.m. to dark every day except Tuesday. Reservations are recommended.

The Addieville East Shooting School, with renowned British shooting instructor Jack Mitchell and his American protégé, Russell Jette, is excellent for beginners as well as those who wish to take their shotgunning skills to a higher level. This is a comprehensive shooting program for everyone from the novice to the top competitor who needs to correct some minor problem, or wants supervised practice on a particular shot. Coaching focuses on sporting clays, driven game, upland hunting and waterfowl.

Addieville's two sporting clays courses and 55 stations are fully automated and stretch over 75 rolling acres of woods and fields. A 105-foot tower adds excitement to several of the shots. Rental guns and golf carts are available at the large, comfortable lodge, as is factory ammo. A $100-per-year sporting clays membership gives one a $5 discount on 50 clays (normally $20) and a $10 discount on 100 (normally $35).

5-Stand, FITASC and wobble trap are every-day shooting options (except Christmas). 5-Stand is $9 per round of 25 (members pay $7) and wobble trap costs $2.50 for 10 targets. Shooting the FITASC *parcour* is $10 (members pay $8).

Hunting at Addieville East Farm is by membership ($500 initiation fee and $700 per year), but there is currently a waiting list to hunt on the farm's 900 acres. Birds are released on 18 fields studded with patches of corn and surrounded by brushy thickets.

Farm owners, Geoff and Paula Gaebe, facilitate weeklong driven pheasant shooting trips to estates in England (Devon and Cornwall) with the cost running £6000, plus travel, tips and tax based on nine participating guns. Actual shooting lasts 5 days and as many as 12,500 pheasants will be released during the week. The tipping standard for the gamekeeper is usually £10 per 100 birds, East Addieville advises.

Addieville East Farm
200 Pheasant Dr.
Mapleville, RI 02839
Phone (401) 568-3185 • Fax (401) 568-3009
www.addieville.com

SOUTH CAROLINA: Broxton Bridge Plantation

If drenching in Civil War nostalgia interests you, a good many southern "plantations" like Broxton Bridge will allow you to imbibe the blue and the gray deeply. Owned and operated by Jerry Varn and family, the white, on-site settlement dates from the 1700s and has remained in the Varn family for nine generations. Today, it includes a five-bedroom bed-and-breakfast in a home originally built in the 1850s, a hunting lodge … and a good bit more.

The 7000-acre Broxton Bridge Plantation is open to the shooting public anytime by appointment. It is a half-hour north of Interstate 95, and an hour west of Charleston. If you have your own airplane, you can land next to the lodge on a 2600-foot (length) by 150-foot (width) sod airstrip.

As the south goes, Broxton Bridge is out in the country. Nevertheless, there is more on site than you might ever expect: sporting clays, 5-Stand and wobble trap; a 10-acre bass pond stocked with catfish and bream; an on-premises pro shop with loaner guns, factory ammo and rental carts; four Level I NSCA-certified instructors for shotgunning, fitting and wingshooting clinics; a pistol and rifle range; plenty of hunting and even league-shooting possibilities.

There are four sporting clays courses at Broxton Bridge, with 25 shot presentations each. The cost is $10 per 25 clays or $35 to shoot all four courses.

Hunting deer and game birds is a staple at the plantation. A 3-day deer hunt includes meals and lodging for $375 (August 15 through January 1). Bird hunting takes place between October 1 and March 31. Half-day duck hunts are $245, half-day quail hunts are $225 and both pheasants and chukar are raised for shooting. A 65-foot tower gives hunters many options for flinging lead at released birds.

The 100-year-old shooting lodge accommodates 15 to 20 overnight guests ($68 each) and has a separate dining room.

Of course, there was a Civil War battle on the grounds and guests can pack a picnic lunch for a tour. It is not obligatory, but it is encouraged.

Broxton Bridge Plantation
PO Box 97, Hwy. 601
Ehrhardt, SC 29081
Phone (800) 437-4868/(803) 267-3882 • Fax (803) 267-3241
www.broxtonbridge.com

SOUTH CAROLINA: Hermitage Farm Shooting Sports

Hermitage Farm Shooting Sports is located in deep woods just outside historic Camden, a half-hour east of Columbia. Open to the public, memberships are available and reservations are not required. Club president and resident professional instructor Joe Canty says it is "a place honoring its natural habitat and offering the opportunity to learn, hone your skills or simply enjoy superlative shooting sport."

The Hermitage sporting clays courses consist of natural stands with a mixture of manual and automatic traps placed along the crest of the 1500-acre tract's ridge. It offers a variety of challenging hillside and high-flying shots amid thickets of wild azalea and dogwood. Giant hickories and live oaks shadow the path and shooting stations.

The Camden facility includes South Carolina's first FITASC course, a more challenging European version of sporting clays than is commonly shot in the United States. Skeet shooting, 5-Stand and wobble trap are popular, as are the farm's rifle and pistol range. Loaner guns and factory ammo for all sports are available in the on-site pro shop.

The wobble trap is imaginatively placed below the deck of the 5-Stand platform overlooking a marsh pond. Several shooting stations offer alternative positions for highly challenging clay shots.

Shooting hours are Tuesday through Saturday from 10:00 a.m. until 8:00 p.m. and Sunday from noon until 8:00 p.m. At the end of the day, depending on the season, the clubhouse welcomes you to sit on its shady porches overlooking the forested hillside or at the hearth of the large fireplace. This is the perfect ending for a day of sharpening your gunning skills in the Deep South.

Hermitage Farm offers memberships that cut the cost of shooting. An individual membership is only $150 per year, and this reduces the cost of shooting a round of 100 sporting clays on the Cypress or Loblolly course from $34 to $25 and a round of 50 on the Cedar course from $20 to $15. Non-member prices are: FITASC $25, skeet and wobble trap $6, and 5-Stand $7. Gun rental is $6.50 and cart rental $10. Hermitage Farm is a member of the NSCA.

Hermitage Farm
PO Box 1258
2362 Tickle Hill Rd.
Camden, SC 29020
Phone (803) 432-0210
Fax (803) 425-7348
www.hermitage-farm.com

TENNESSEE: Heritage Meadows

Set on the western flank of the uncompromisingly beautiful Great Smoky Mountains, about halfway between Knoxville and Chattanooga, Heritage Meadows has three sporting clays courses with 45 shooting stations. The cost of shooting clays is $16 for 50 and $27 for 100 targets.

At Heritage Meadows, you can shoot clay year-round – depending on the severity of the weather – because it also has a skeet range ($4 for 25 birds) and a covered 5-Stand set-up ($8). Guests can choose to shoot FITASC *parcours* or hunt quail, chukar or pheasant "with eager, stylish dogs."

Laura and Gerald Hyde own Heritage Meadows and personally oversee the lodge, clubhouse and all shooting activities. A full kitchen and dining room are available to serve three meals a day. "Comfortable yet charmingly rustic rooms" can be reserved for a night or a week. Lodging is $85 per person per night and includes a breakfast of biscuits and gravy. Otherwise, meals begin at $10.

The club pro shop carries a long list of shooting items, many of which (guns and vests, for instance) can be rented if you forget, or choose not to travel with, your own.

Heritage Meadows hosts league shooting and instruction (by appointment). Its "Duck Flush" station ($8) allows from one to three shooters to receive 25 to 75 targets coming in over a simulated duck blind with average shots between 10 and 20 yards, all within 90 seconds! Shooters must work together to ensure that they break all the targets as well as not having more than one shooter aiming at the same target. Duck Flush is a fast-paced clay game that requires fast loading and accurate shooting.

At the wobble trap station ($8 for 25 birds), one to three shooters stand on a raised platform and shoot 25 targets, either fast-paced or slow, as they wish. Targets rise from beneath their feet, thrown from two traps that are moving right to left and up and down at the same time, hence the "wobbling."

By arrangement, hunts can be scheduled from October through April in a variety of packages. The full-day Premier Hunt for two people, with dog and handler is $975. It includes 100 quail or 35 pheasants or 50 chukar or Hungarian partridge. Lunch is included, as is bird cleaning. By contrast, the half-day Economy Hunt package for two, with dog and handler, is $275 and includes 20 quail, eight pheasants or 10 partridge. Bird cleaning is $20 minimum and the Internet site specifically notes that any hunting dogs shot by hunters will result in the decimal point moving to $2000.00.

Both memberships and shooting instruction can be arranged in advance. A member has numerous bargain opportunities in the pro shop and for shooting and hunts. Memberships begin at only $100 for an individual, and shooting instruction is $25 an hour.

Heritage Meadows
216 Ruralvale Rd.
Tellicao Plains, TN 37385
Phone (423) 253-2187
www.heritage-meadows.com

Texas' Greystone Castle is a bed-and-breakfast resort with a fully automated, 28-station sporting clays course and a unique, dual-level 5-Stand.

TEXAS: American Shooting Centers

Just 17 miles west of Houston, American Shooting Centers (ASC) has been open since 1989 on 563 acres in George Bush Park. If you like flat land and wide-open skies, you will love this course. The public is welcome to show up unannounced, individually or in groups. Reservations are not required to uncase your gun at this big course. From Wednesday through Friday, expect the hours to be noon to 7:00 p.m. On Saturday and Sunday, it is 9:00 a.m. to 7:00 p.m.

ASC notes that its three sporting clays routes have 45 fully automated stations and nine high towers, "the most in the US," to give shooters an ever-changing target presentation. If this were not enough, there are two 5-Stand clay events as well. ASC was host to the 2004 U.S. Open Sporting Clays Championship.

There are also seven skeet ranges, two trap ranges and one wobble trap station, plus a Make-A-Break fun station.

At ASC, a 50-target round of sporting clays is $23.50. The cost for 100 birds is $38. The fun, Make-A-Break shooting stand costs just $8.50.

The Outdoorsman Store is on site at the rifle and pistol range, and it carries rental shotguns in addition to selling new and used models, ammo and shooting accessories. It is set up to handle rifle and pistol shooters also.

ASC offers shooting instruction at $100 to $125, depending on the level of NSCA certification an instructor holds. This fee covers instruction, eye-ear protection and targets. Visiting pros like Gil & Vicki Ash of Optimum Shotgun Performance (OSP) Shooting School also hold shooting clinics.

American Shooting Centers

16500 Westheimer Pkwy.
Houston, TX 77082
Phone (281) 556-8199/8086/1597
Fax (281) 556-8403
www.amshootcenters.com

TEXAS: Greystone Castle Sporting Club

Only an hour west of the Dallas/Ft. Worth metroplex, Greystone Castle is an Orvis-endorsed wingshooting destination with 4000 acres of wildlife habitat surrounded by a high fence. This is a beautiful place, and it is open to the public from sunrise to sunset, seven days a week by appointment. Yes, reservations are required.

Two championship sporting clays courses – a valley course and a fully automated Castle course – let you shoot from 28 shooting stations. One hundred targets cost $40. There is a dual-level 5-Stand ($10 for 25 targets) and a "double wobble" trap setup ($10 for 24 targets). Customers shoot the "double-trap" setup from a shooting platform on the side of a hill. Views of the Texas countryside are panoramic. The Greystone Internet site says its "double-wobble" clays "fly like real birds in unpredictable speeds and angles."

Greystone Castle is a bed-and-breakfast resort with a pool and hot tub, nature hikes, clay shooting and hunting for game birds, resident whitetail deer and a herd of exotics. "Within the castle walls you will find five separate and unique 'lodges' each with four to five private suites with their own private bathroom facilities." The basic bed-and-breakfast package is $200 per night for two people. Unless you want to rent a car, ask about airport pick-up.

It would not be Texas if there were not numerous hunting options at Greystone. You can hunt quail, pheasant, chukar, huns and flighted mallards practically year-round, and doves and turkey are an option in the spring. A half-day "mixed-bag walk-up hunt" for pheasant, quail, chukar and huns is $975 and includes warm-up clays, guides, dogs, transportation to and from the field and bird processing. There is no bag limit.

Greystone's deer management program includes protein supplements, equalizing the buck-doe ratio and importing complementary genetic streams. Hunting whitetails between October 1 and January 31 requires a state license, as do turkey or dove hunting. A 3-day/2-night "management hunt" for bucks in the 110- to 130-range is $1500 and rates go up from there, depending on antler size. Hunt packages include castle lodging, gourmet meals, beverages, guide, transportation to and from the field, taxidermy preparation AND complimentary cigars.

You can hunt a variety of exotics at Greystone, including elk, red stag, sika and fallow deer, and oryx and black buck antelope. Trophy fees for an axis deer, for example, run between $1750 and $2000. A trophy elk can cost $7500. *A la carte* overnight lodging, meals and guide fee are $350 per day.

The walls of Greystone Castle are made of cinderblock, by the way. According to General Manager Doug Cannon, they are strong enough to prevent pass-through by a Comanche arrow, but an assault force of Crusaders will most certainly have their way with you … unless you shoot first and ask questions later.

Greystone Castle Sporting Club

P.O. Box 158
Mingus, TX 76463
Phone (800) 399-3006/(254) 672-5927
Fax (254) 672-5971
www.greystonecastle.com

VIRGINIA: The Homestead

"A few years ago, my wife and I shot The Homestead in Hot Springs, Virginia," says well-known gunwriter John M. Taylor. "That is one beautiful place. David Judah, the head shooting instructor, is wonderful. He does not try to force you to shoot a particular system or style, but works with what you bring him. David routinely takes people who have never shot a gun and teaches them to break birds. He and the sporting clays groundskeepers make excellent use of the area's rugged terrain to fashion an enjoyable, but challenging, shooting experience."

George Washington did sleep at The Homestead in Hot Springs, Virginia, as did 21 additional presidents.

Indeed, George Washington DID sleep here – as did 21 more presidents. The original 300 acres of this 15,000-acre resort were deeded to Virginia Militia Captain Thomas Bullett, who built the original lodge in 1766! The Homestead has been open as a resort practically from day one, when the good Captain's group went skinny-dipping in the hot mineral springs.

Only 75 miles north of Roanoke, The Homestead is one of the most diverse and, indeed, fanciest resorts in the Allegheny Mountains. There are 506 guest rooms and suites with prices starting at about $150 per night. Of course, the dining in multiple clubs, dining rooms and taverns on and around the grounds is equally wonderful … and pricey.

On your visit, expect seasonal offerings of golf, snow skiing, a spa, fine dining, horseback riding, carriage rides, hiking, paintball (!), caving and climbing, tennis, biking and fly fishing. Trap and skeet shooting venues were added in the '30s and two, 24-station sporting clays courses have been designed and built since then. All are open to the public year-round with a reservation. Today, there is one trap range, four skeet ranges, one 5-Stand and wobble trap.

The Homestead is proud of the shooting instruction available. No more than four students are accepted for a 2-day school. Quality guest instructors include World Ladies Champion Linda Joy-Sosebee, Sporting Clays National Champion Boo Dykes and National Champion Scott Robertson.

The Homestead
P.O. Box 2000, Main Street
Hot Springs, VA 24445
Phone (800) 838-1766
Fax (540) 839-7902
www.thehomestead.com

WISCONSIN: Milford Hills Hunt Club

Located between Madison and Milwaukee in southeast Wisconsin, Milford Hills is situated on forested rolling hills not far off Interstate 94. It is open to the public year-round. Summer hours (April through September 30) are Wednesday and Thursday from noon until dusk; Saturday and Sunday, 10:00 a.m. until 3:00 p.m. Winter hours (October through March) are Sunday from 10:00 a.m. until 3:00 p.m. Other shooting times may be accommodated by appointment.

Milford Hills has two sporting clays courses with eight to 14 stations, one 5-Stand and wobble trap on 400 acres of woods, water and fields. Developed in 1998, the sporting clays courses have two presentations each and automatic traps.

The 5-Stand shooting range is a superb, elevated hillside platform and may be the pride of the club's clay shooting experience. The 70-foot by 30-foot deck was built from Brazilian ironwood and cedar in 2000. Six automatic traps and three 40-foot towers will challenge you. The cost of shooting is $16 for 50 birds, $30 for 100 and only $7 for 25 shots on the 5-Stand. Gun rental is available in the lodge and pro shop.

Shooters can take part in sporting clays league shooting in both winter and summer. Summer leagues last 16 weeks and are shot on Saturday and Sunday from 10:00 a.m. to 3:00 p.m. and Thursday from 4:00 p.m. until dark.

The club hosted the 2004 Wisconsin State Sporting Clays Championship, and it is a member of the Wisconsin Sporting Clays Assn. and the NSCA. In 2002, Milford Hills was recognized by the NSCA as the "President's Outstanding Gun Club."

As well as its sporting shooting, Milford Hills also has upland game hunting of released pheasants, chukar and quail. Its nine fields are covered with switch grass and strips of sorghum for food and cover.

The handsome, rustic lodge has a full-service restaurant serving lunch and dinner, as well as a bar. The pro shop sells Browning, Fiocchi and other name-brand gear. Shooting instruction can be arranged.

Although it is open to the public, Milford Hills has membership options that offer discounted shooting and other amenities such as showers, a gun-cleaning station and a special dog-training field. Member-only social events and hunts are held throughout the year. A basic annual "Early Bird 25" membership paid by April 15 is $607 with tax. Membership prices go up from there with increasing numbers of game birds allowed on your card.

Milford Hills Hunt Club
W5670 French Rd.
Johnson Creek, WI 53038
Phone (920) 699-2249
Fax (920) 699-8919
www.milfordhills.com

WISCONSIN: Woods & Meadow Hunting Preserve and Sporting Clays

Warrens is 100 miles northwest of Madison and further than that from the Twin Cities. It is not close to anything much. Interstate 94 is just to the left and Necedah National Wildlife Refuge just to the right ... or vice versa, depending on your political orientation perhaps. So, this little burgh and its blue-collar hunting preserve and sporting clays courses are too far south to be thought of as a province of the Jack Pine Savage nation and too far north to be in touch with modern civilization. If you are in the area or only passing through, I believe this little sporting clays venue may be just right for a day or two of shooting, however.

Cancel that trip to a fancy resort in the northwoods and stay at the Woods & Meadow lodge. It bunks six and looks much like an old house set off the main farm area in the woods, perhaps to keep it out of sight. At the outrageous cost of $18 per night, you will still need to bring your own sleeping bag. Still, except for personal items, other linens and a full kitchen are available. The other overnight option is the club farmhouse, which sleeps seven in four bedrooms. It provides a large kitchen, living room and bathroom for guests, and for $20 a night, you do not need to bring a sleeping bag!

At Woods & Meadows, you can shoot sporting clays from Wednesday through Sunday between April and September, although events are held year-round and reservations are only required if you want to shoot at an unusual time or perhaps during the winter. Walk-ons are welcome.

Three course layouts have 40 shooting stations, and just like the fancy courses, all types of targets are thrown here in simulation of single and double flights of practically every game bird in North America, plus the bounding cottontail himself, Peter Rabbit. There is no waiting for a trapper because all traps are automatic. The cost of sporting clays at Woods & Meadow is $14 for 50 birds, $26 for 100 and $36 for 150. Team league shooting takes place in the spring and summer.

Private hunting on 1000 acres with no membership fees or bag limits is the Woods & Meadow specialty. Hunts can be booked for full or half days, and while reservations are not needed to shoot sporting clays, they are expected for hunting. Six separate zones are set aside on the club so that no hunter or stray dog ends up in anyone else's hunting area.

The hunting season begins in September and ends in March. Typical prices for a 2004-05 hunt are: huns $12 each, pheasant $16, dog and guide $12 per hour and bird cleaning $1.75 de-boned or $2.50 for whole-bird processing. Plenty of hunting options and packages are available.

Woods & Meadow Hunting Preserve and Sporting Clays
N4335 Potter Rd.
Warrens, WI 54666
Phone (608) 378-4223
Fax (608) 378-4223
www.woodsandmeadow.com

WYOMING: Canyon Ranch Gun Club

Canyon Ranch is a 3000-acre private reserve. It has been owned and operated by the Wallop family for more than a century. Located in Big Horn, just 15 miles south of Sheridan at the foot of the Bighorn Mountains, the ranch is the perfect spot for a unique vacation for a family or small group. The spectacular setting offers a variety of recreational opportunities for guests of all ages, including: fly-fishing; Merriam turkey hunting; sporting clays shooting; private driven shoots for pheasant, partridge and grouse; horseback riding at $50 per hour; nature walks and hiking; wildflower and wildlife viewing; therapeutic massage and many nearby historical sites.

Canyon Ranch is an Orvis-endorsed fly-fishing lodge, and other than the remote and spectacular scenery, fly-fishing in the area is its primary claim-to-fame. A full day of guided fly-fishing can be arranged for $300 for one to two people.

This ranch has been at the heart of the Wallop family since it was purchased in 1889. Today's hosts, Paul and Sandra Wallop, have preserved the beauty and diversity of the ranch. Their lodge sleeps 10 and the chef has earned a reputation for great meals. To stay in the lodge, you are required to book 3 nights at $150 per night, which is not bad if you consider that this includes three excellent meals.

Another accommodation option – and you will need to plan ahead for meals and accommodations if you drive to this ranch in Big Sky Country – is the old family cabin nestled in the foothills. This remote cabin does not have a telephone or electricity, but operates on gas appliances and will sleep six. It is close to the mule deer and whitetails, the elk and occasional moose, the mountain lions and great golden eagles. Expect to pay $300 per night and be required to book for at least 3 nights. A four-wheel drive vehicle will also be necessary to reach the cabin!

I did not forget sporting clays shooting although when you are sipping a beer on the verandah and are mesmerized by the Big Horn Mountains in the distance you may forget. Shooting Canyon Ranch's 14 sporting clays stations does require reservations, although you can shoot them in any order or even cross the three designated "courses" if you prefer. With reservations, anything is possible!

This area is so remote that if pulling the trigger on clay birds is a passion amid all the natural wonder of Wyoming, Clear Creek Hunting and Sporting Clays (307-737-2217, with skeet and 10 sporting stations) is half an hour to the east. Another facility that has received good reviews, Cody Shooting Complex (307-527-5546, with trap, skeet and, with 45 stations, plenty of sporting clays shooting) is about 3 hours straight west over the Big Horns.

Have I mentioned horseshoes and badminton on the Canyon Ranch lodge lawn? Prepare to enjoy.

Canyon Ranch Gun Club
PO Box 629
Big Horn, WY 82833
Phone (307) 674-6239
Fax (307) 672-2264
www.canyonranchbighorn.com

Photo courtesy of Bob Knopf.

Virtually anywhere you live in the United States, shooting instruction is available from NSCA-certified coaches. "Keep your head on the cheekpiece and your dominant eye centered down the gun's rib."

CANADA: Montreal Skeet Club

You can have the experience of shooting internationally by driving north only a few miles. Up there, "Samedi & Dimache 10h30 – 18h00" translates as Saturday and Sunday from 10:30 a.m. to 6:00 p.m. and "Mercredi 13h00 – 18h00" is Wednesday from 1:00 p.m. to 6:00 p.m. "Avril 21 a Octobre" of course means April 21 to October. It is French, but the translation is not difficult. If you understand the rules, etiquette and enjoy shooting, your visit to this gun club southwest of Montreal will be smooth and fun.

For the 2004 Quebec Open Sporting Clays Championships in May, the club used 20 stations with two automatic traps per station. Skeet, trap and 5-Stand are operating and a 15-machine bunker trap range is under construction.

Montreal Skeet Club has a membership option (a 1-year membership with initiation fees is valued at $2525), but most shooting events are open to the public.

Montreal Skeet Club

2070, Chemin du canal (route 338)
Les cedres, Quebec J7T 1L7
Phone (450) 452-2417
www.losttarget.com/montreal.html

The spacious shooting grounds of the Oshawa Skeet & Gun Club, Oshawa, Canada. Joe Potosky of The Lost Target at www.losttarget.com says Oshawa has the best course in eastern Canada.

Flint Oak Shooting Resort in Kansas boasts what they say is the world's tallest sporting clays tower. It is 157-feet high and topped with an American flag.

Sporting clays shooters testing their gear at La Roue du Roy in Hemmingford, Quebec.

CANADA: Oshawa Skeet & Gun Club

Joe Potosky, webmaster at The Lost Target (www.losttarget.com), says, "Oshawa in Ontario has the best course in eastern Canada." Joe sees a lot of courses, so that is a reliable endorsement.

Oshawa has a 5-Stand and a fully automated walk-around course. Marty Fischer, one of the premier course designers in North America, designed the walking course. It has 12 stations with 30 stands and 25 traps along with 70- and 80-foot towers with multiple trap capability.

Several major events including the Canadian National Championships are held at Oshawa each year. "We believe we have one of the finest shooting facilities in Canada," Oshawa's directors say on their Internet site, "and both encourage and welcome you to test your mettle at our club." The 5-Stand is $5 for 25 targets ($7 for non-members) while the 100-bird walk-around course is $26 ($30 non-members).

Five skeet fields with fully automatic, high-capacity traps and five trap fields with voice-activated trap release systems are open to member shooting. Skeet and trap shooting cost $5 for 25 targets, $7 for non-members.

The Oshawa club was founded in 1936 and is owned and operated by its members. About 30 minutes east of Toronto on 100 acres of rolling land, the shooter can see all the way to Lake Ontario. The clubhouse has a full kitchen and dining room. The hours are 9:30 a.m. to 3:30 p.m. on weekends and 11:00 a.m. to dusk on Wednesday. Oshawa also has a rifle range with 10 covered shooting stations.

Oshawa Skeet & Gun Club

5245 Wilson Rd. N.
Oshawa, Ontario L1H 8L7
Phone (905) 985-7763
www.gagnonsports.com/OSGC/index.htm

DOMINICAN REPUBLIC: Casa de Campo

Nine million Spanish-speaking residents of the Dominican Republic (DR) share the impoverished island of Hispaniola with eight million French-speaking people in Haiti. It is crowded. The CIA Factbook (www.cia.gov) says a representative democracy has recently sprung up in the DR, defying a "legacy of unsettled, mostly non-representative rule." But Sammy Sosa is from the DR, so the news cannot all be bad.

At the beautiful Casa de Campo resort on the southeast coast near La Romana and just a couple hours east of the capitol, Santo Domingo, *mi casa - su casa*. This resort is open to the public, but memberships are available. Indeed, their realtors will happily sell you a villa on site. Barring a devastating hurricane or social upheaval, you can shoot their 200-station sporting clays course year-round.

Sporting clays shooting at Casa de Camp began in 1986 on 245 acres that has been allowed to revert to natural vegetation. The course is open every day from 8:00 a.m. to 5:00 p.m. The feature attraction is a tri-level, 110-foot tower. The shooting facility also has American and Olympic trap, skeet, wobble trap and three 5-Stand pavilions. A round of golf at one of the championship courses cost $147 to $205, depending on the course and time of year, and a 100-target round of sporting clays is just as expensive, costing $146 with new factory ammo or $118 with reloads. Skeet and trap are relative bargains at $30 for new cartridges (25 targets) and $23 with reloads.

An "airy clubhouse" and dog-training facility are on site at the shooting range. Formal instruction with the assistant instructor is

$38 for skeet and $160 for sporting clays. With the shooting director himself, however, it is $174. Although you can bring your own gun into the country (not your own ammo though), these prices include rental gun and factory ammo. Rental carts will help people manage the rugged course layout.

Since this shooting facility is considered a world-class resort, plenty of lodging and meal opportunities are available. You can figure a round-trip flight via Dutch Caribbean Air from Miami for around $400 and a couple hundred dollars a night at Casa de Campo plus meals. Other activities include hand-manicured golf courses, tennis, trail riding, sport fishing, SCUBA diving, tours by land and sea plus special activities for kids.

Columbus should have discovered this!

Casa de Campo

PO Box 140
La Romana, Dominican Republic
Phone (800) 877-3643 / (809) 523-3333 • Fax (809) 523-8490
www.casadecampo.co

ENGLAND: West London Shooting School

The justifiably famous West London Shooting School ("Be Confident – Be Ready") is only 30 minutes (12 miles) west of London on 120 acres of parkland. While it is open to the public, it would not be considered "proper" to arrive without a reservation.

Instructors at West London have been teaching people how to shoot since 1901. "Our ethos is to make the lessons as enjoyable and simple as possible," their Internet site says, "yet to ensure you learn and improve your shooting."

Private and group lessons, gun fitting, and lessons for young people and women who have no gun experience can be arranged with staff or freelance instructors. In a typical lesson, all equipment

Not every sporting clays course is fancy, and while shooting a Perazzi is nice if you can afford it, sporting clays began as a hunter's game. If you want to shoot your turkey-choked Mossberg pump, you should go right ahead, because you will have as much fun as anyone on the course. Bradford Sporting Clays near Starke, Florida, has a bare-bones sporting course, plus skeet, a rifle range and a pistol range.

is provided. An hour of private instruction or gun fitting is £84, unless you are a lady or young person under 18, in which case the cost is £74; an hour of shooting instruction for two to three individuals is £56 per person.

The sporting clays course at West London, affectionately called the "100 Birder," requires that you bring your own gun and shoot only fiber wads (no plastic). A scoring guide accompanies each shooting group. To shoot the 100 Birder, expect to pay £35 or £32 during the week with a group of three or more. West End charges 20 pence per shell and 16 pence per clay.

Incidentally, the club's "Grouse Sequence," sponsored by James Purdy & Sons of old shotgun glory, is a "hugely exciting 26-bird challenge that realistically recreates the speed, variety and thrill of driven Grouse." It may be shot as part of a lesson or part of your 100 Birder. The top score on the Grouse Sequence to date (May, 2004) was shot by one Piers Methuen, who demolished "a very impressive" 23 out of 26 birds, so this must be tough.

Beginning in May 2004, the hours are Monday through Saturday from 8:00 a.m. until 6:00 p.m. The recently refurbished restaurant is open from 8:30 a.m. until 3:00 p.m. Its décor, the staff at West London say, creates "a distinct colonial club atmosphere."

("Our New Bothy: Last summer saw the completion of 'The Stanbury Bothy' (named after former Senior Instructor Percy Stanbury) in the back field of the shooting grounds. Built out of wood it will serve as a place to serve elevenses, shelter from the elements and act as unique luncheon venue for Corporate Events.")

NOTE: The Interbank rate of exchange in May 2004 listed a British Pound to be the equivalent of $1.78 US (www.oanda.com). Thus, it would cost approximately $62.30 to shoot the West London sporting course with the rather steep British 17.5 percent VAT (Value Added Tax) added.

West London Shooting School

Sharvel Lane, West End Road
Northolt, Middlesex UB5 6RA
United Kingdom
Phone (011) 44-20-8845-1377
　　　 (011) 44-07000-12-20-12
Fax (011) 44-20-8842-1493
www.shootingschool.co.uk

SCOTLAND: The Gleneagles Hotel

"Luxurious and impeccable though it is," notes the welcoming statement in Gleneagles literature, "you will find that Gleneagles has a refreshingly relaxed manner, unstarchy and unstiff, that is mirrored by the friendly courtesy of all the staff. From your first wholehearted Scottish welcome, you will be looked after warmly by the staff and the services offered. The avowed intention of the management is to create happiness."

Apparently, when Gleneagles opened in 1924, it was described as "a Riviera in the Highlands" and, perhaps with more than a little public relations flair, "the eighth wonder of the world." The hotel still revels in self-congratulatory adulation as the "glorious playground for people dedicated to leisure and pleasure in the most luxurious surroundings." Well, that certainly describes this author!

Okay, maybe not, but I would certainly be happy for Gleneagles to create some happiness in my household by drawing my name for the next "Room Competition Prize Draw" on the Home Page of its Internet site. Just one free night in a Classic Room for two with a full Scottish breakfast (a $600 value) might be worth the trip to this recreational shrine with ... lest we forget ... sporting clays!

Sporting clays at Gleneagles is only one of the shooting options with air rifle and archery. Sporting instruction is available at £60 per hour (approximately $110), which includes a gun and 25 shells. Thereafter, a box of shells is £6, which equates to about $45 per 100-target round. The clay course has one 40-foot tower for incoming pairs called "Gleneagles Pheasant," a 100-foot tower for singles or pairs that is naturally called "King's Pheasant" and a 50-foot tower for incoming driven pairs called "Queen's Pheasant." Springing teal, running rabbits, grouse and all the other clay presentations are detailed on the Gleneagles Internet site. Clay shooting is headquartered at a beautifully rustic lodge, and a shooting shop sells Gleneagles shooting clothing and accessories.

Now, if we can only win that free room and create some happiness!

The Gleneagles Hotel

Auchterarder, Perthshire, Scotland PH3 1NF
Phone (866) 881-9525 / 44 (0) 1764 662231
Fax 44 (0) 1764 662134
www.gleneagles.com

I
Appendix

SPORTING CLAYS OFFICIAL RULES
ORGANIZATION OF THE NATIONAL SPORTING CLAYS ASSOCIATION

The National Sporting Clays Association (NSCA) was formed in April of 1989, as a division of the National Skeet Shooting Association (NSSA), to promote sporting clays in the United States and other countries. The following is an informative summary of the organization of the NSCA, important official policies and rules that govern the NSCA, the shooting of registered targets, the conduct of shooters and the duties of shoot management. The NSCA has the responsibility for the formulation, regulation and enforcement of these rules. For any rules or policies not contained in this book, or in the official minutes of the NSCA Advisory Council meetings, refer to the bylaws of the NSSA. The NSCA reserves the right to make alterations in, or amendments to, these rules and policies at any time, when it deems it to be in the best interest of the National Sporting Clays Association and its members.

I. GENERAL INFORMATION

A. PURPOSE OF NSCA

The purpose of the National Sporting Clays Association is to promote and govern the sport of sporting clays throughout the United States and other countries, in a way that is beneficial to all who enjoy and participate in the game. The NSCA is dedicated to the development of the sport at all levels of participation. NSCA vows to create an atmosphere of healthy and safe competition and meaningful fellowship within its membership.

B. MEMBERSHIP

1. Individual

a. Annual membership dues for an individual are $40 and include a copy of the official magazine, *Sporting Clays Magazine,* beginning with the first issue available for mailing after dues received at headquarters. A $30 Associate membership is available to dependents of members but does not include magazine.

b. Six-year membership dues for an individual are $200 and include a copy of the official magazine, *Sporting Clays Magazine,* beginning with the first issue available for mailing after dues are received at headquarters. A Six Year Associate Membership is available to dependents of members for $150 but does not include the magazine.

c. Life membership for an individual is $500 and a Husband & Wife Life membership is $750.

d. The membership and shooting year begins on October 1 and ends on September 30 *of the following* year.

e. Annual membership may be applied for by filling out an application provided at an NSCA club/range or by contacting NSCA Headquarters for an application.

2. Clubs and Ranges

a. Annual membership dues for a club or range are $100 a year.

b. The membership and shooting year begins on October 1 and ends September 30 of the following year.

c. Annual Club/Range membership may be applied for by filling out an application provided by the NSCA.

3. Rules of Conduct

a. Each member and club will be furnished a copy of the Official NSCA rules, with the understanding that the member/member club will read and understand each rule. All members and member clubs are responsible to know these rules and abide by them, for their own benefit and safety, as well as that of other shooters.

b. By paying the membership fee, entering a competition or holding a competition, every member and member club agrees to abide by these rules and to accept all official decisions of the NSCA in interpreting and/or applying these rules.

c. It shall be a violation of these rules to:

1. Exhibit unsportsmanlike conduct of any kind, including but not limited to, falsifying scores or classification, cheating, swearing, verbal or physical abuse of any shooter, scorer, field judge, shoot official, or protest committee.

2. Disobey the order of any scorer, field judge or shoot official.

3. Violate any safety rules as set forth in Section II of these rules and regulations, or engage in any activity that is considered unsafe by the NSCA Executive Council.

4. Shoot at any place other than the designated station.

5. Interfere with the shoot management's procedures in conducting the shoot.

6. Violate any rule or regulation of a club or range.

7. Exhibit any conduct that is harmful to the NSCA, its membership, or the sport as a whole.

8. Failure to submit a written complaint to shoot management after witnessing the violation of one of the NSCA's rules or regulations.

9. Failure of shoot management to submit a written report to NSCA of written complaints received along with a report of action taken.

10. Violate any other rule or regulation of the NSCA as set forth in any other section or paragraph of the NSCA's rules and regulations.

4. Suspensions, Expulsions and Reinstatement

a. The Executive Council may, at any time at its discretion, suspend, expel or discipline any member or member club for the violation of any NSCA rule or regulation.

b. The procedure for suspension, expulsion or other disciplinary action is as follows:

1. Any member, shooter, scorer, field judge, shoot official or owner or member of management of a club or range who witnesses a violation of any NSCA rule shall submit to the NSCA Director or Executive Director a written complaint within thirty (30) days of the alleged violation which shall include:

i. the name of the alleged violator;

ii. the date and location of the alleged violation;

iii. a reasonably detailed description of the alleged violation;

iv. the names and addresses, if known, of all witnesses;

v. the name, address, phone number and signature of the complainant(s).

2. Upon receipt, the NSCA Director or Executive Director shall assign each complaint a complaint number consisting of the year of the receipt and consecutive number of receipt, i.e. 01-01, 01-02, etc.

3. The NSCA Director or Executive Director shall review the complaint and determine if it meets the requirements set forth above. Any complaint may be resubmitted so long as it is received within the requisite time period, described above. The NSCA Director or Executive Director has the discretion to consider and investigate or dismiss any complaint that does not meet the foregoing requirements.

4. Within ten (10) days of receipt of a complaint, the NSCA Director or Executive Director, or anyone acting pursuant to direction from the Director or Executive Director, shall serve written notice of the complaint and a copy of the complaint to the alleged violator, by certified mail, return receipt requested. The written notice shall instruct the alleged violator of his right to submit a written statement, which must be signed and should include the names, addresses and phone numbers of any witnesses not named in the complaint. Such written statement must be received by the NSCA Director or Executive Director within ten (10) days of the alleged violator's receipt of the notice and complaint. All statements received after such date shall not be considered.

5. The NSCA Director or Executive Director, or someone acting pursuant to direction from the Director or Executive Director, shall thoroughly investigate the allegations of the complaint by attempting to obtain written statements from all known witnesses. All witness statements must be in writing and signed by the witness.

6. After time for the alleged violator to respond expires, the NSCA Director or Executive Director shall review the complaint, the statement of the alleged violator, witness statements and any other relevant evidence. Upon such review, the NSCA Director or Executive Director shall recommend to the NSCA Executive Council a specific disciplinary action. The recommendation shall include:

i. all evidence that was considered, including the names of any witnesses who submitted statements;

ii. a determination of whether the alleged violation occurred; and

iii. the disciplinary action, if any, the NSCA Director or Executive Director recommends that the NSCA Executive Council impose.

7. The NSCA Director or Executive Director shall provide each member of the NSCA Executive Council with a copy of the complaint, the statement of the alleged violator, copies of any witness statements and a copy of the recommendation.

8. The NSCA Director or Executive Director shall schedule a conference call between the members of the NSCA Executive Council wherein the NSCA Executive Council shall review all information provided by the NSCA Director or Executive Director and issue a ruling on the matter by majority vote. The NSCA Executive Council's ruling shall include:

i. the date of issuance;

ii. all evidence that was considered, including the names of any witnesses who submitted statements;

iii. a determination of whether the alleged violation occurred; and

iv. the disciplinary action, if any, imposed by the NSCA Executive Council. The NSCA Executive Council shall have the discretion to suspend or expel a member or to impose any other disciplinary action it deems appropriate.

9. Upon issuance of a ruling, the NSCA Director or Executive Director shall serve the ruling on the violator by certified mail, return receipt requested. The ruling shall become effective on the date of issuance and continue until a hearing, if any, is held.

c. The violator shall have the right to appeal the NSCA Executive Council's ruling by notifying the NSCA Executive Council. Such notification of appeal must be in writing and must be postmarked no later than twenty (20) days from the date the ruling was issued.

1. Upon receipt of the notification of appeal, the NSCA Executive Council shall hold a hearing on the matter, which will take place at the next regularly scheduled quarterly meeting of the NSCA Executive Council.

2. At the hearing, the violator shall have the right to be present, the right to bring counsel, the right to testify and the right to present any evidence he so chooses. The violator does not have the right to cross-examine witnesses. The violator does not have the right to make a record and no transcript of the hearing will be made or allowed.

3. The NSCA Executive Council shall review the complaint, the written statement of the violator, and any other evidence it deems appropriate. The NSCA Executive Council may allow any and all witnesses to testify by telephone or in person.

4. At the conclusion of such hearing, the NSCA Executive Council shall have the authority to affirm, reverse or modify the disciplinary action imposed previously by majority vote. By paying the membership fee, entering a

competition or holding a competition, every member and member club agrees to abide by any decision of the NSCA Executive Council and further agrees and recognizes that as a voluntary amateur association, the NSCA has the right to impose, interpret and enforce its rules and regulations and that all decisions by the NSCA Executive Council following a hearing are final.

C. STRUCTURE

1. Advisory Council

The Advisory Council is comprised of NSCA members exhibiting the highest devotion to the sport, the members, and the Association. There are 45 available positions, divided equally between representatives of Industry, Range Owners and Shooters. The primary function of the Advisory Council is to promote and guide the Association.

a. Elections are held at the Annual *Advisory Council* meeting for terms to begin *at the end of the meeting.* Candidates must be present at this meeting in order to be considered for a council position and must receive a majority of votes in order to be elected.

b. Their term the first time elected is one year. For second and subsequent elections the term is two years. Term of office is from *Annual Meeting to Annual Meeting.*

c. An Advisory Council member must attend the annual meeting (date determined by Executive Council) each year and either the U.S. Open or the National Championship meeting or lose his/her position on the Advisory Council.

d. Advisory Council members are required to shoot the following minimums each year: Range Owners–500, Shooters–1,000. The Advisory Council will continue their present duties and responsibilities until such time as a new form of electing the Association management has been decided on. The NSCA Advisory Council will form a committee made up of Advisory Council members from all three categories, National Delegates and State Associations to make recommendations on how the NSCA can go forward with electing members to manage our Association.

2. Executive Council

The Executive Council is elected from and comprised of 6 members of the Advisory Council, 2 representing Industry, 2 representing Range Owners and 2 representing Shooters for a two-year term. These 6 members elected to the Executive Council must have served a minimum of three (3) cumulative years on the Advisory Council. The Executive Council election will always follow the annual meeting's Advisory Council election. The primary function of the Executive Council is to promote and guide the Advisory Council and act on behalf of the Advisory Council on matters needing immediate action.

3. National Delegate

National Delegates shall consist of members in good standing to hold office as follows: National Delegates shall be bona-fide residents of and be elected from the various states of the United States and from the provinces, territories or similar political subdivisions recognized by the Association in ratio of one National Delegate for a member population of 25 to 150; two National Delegates for a member population of 151 to 300; three National Delegates for a member population of 301 to 500; four National Delegates for a member population of 501 to 750; and five National Delegates for a member population over 750.

a. National Delegates must be nominated by five

(5) current NSCA members in their state and receive a minimum of five (5) votes from the state membership in order for the election to be valid. Write-in candidates are allowed but must receive five votes to be elected.

b. The term of office for all National Delegates shall be two (2) years and shall begin October 1 of the year elected and end September 30 two (2) years later.

c. All changes made in rules, regulations, classification and other issues will be decided by the National Delegates. If no state association exists, their responsibilities would also include the approval of NSCA-registered shoot dates and the location of the state shoot within that state; however, their primary duties will be on a national level governing our sport and the Association.

d. In the event that a National Delegate position is vacated before the end of the Delegate's term, the State Association (if one exists) will appoint a person to fill that position for the remainder of the current term. If no State Association exists, the Zone Delegate will make the appointment.

4. State Association

An association, recognized by the NSCA, comprised of NSCA members and NSCA member clubs within each individual state. The primary function of the State Association is to work with the National Delegate(s) and support the NSCA member clubs and NSCA members of their state through individual state bylaws, within the rules and parameters of the NSCA. Recognized NSCA State Associations will be responsible for the approval of shoot dates within the state.

5. Zones / Zone Delegates

Zones are groupings of states in a particular geographic area. There are seven zones. The Zone Map is located on a later page.

a. One Zone Delegate is elected from each of the seven zones *by vote of the National Delegates in that Zone.* Candidates for Zone Delegate must be currently elected National Delegates.

b. The Zone Delegate's duties and responsibilities are set forth in the NSCA Delegates Manual. The primary responsibility of the Zone Delegate is to organize and oversee the selection of the Zone Shoot host range.

II. SAFETY

A. SAFETY IS EVERYONE'S RESPONSIBILITY

1. It is everyone's responsibility to report any unsafe shooting condition or action immediately to Shoot Officials.

2. Mandatory Eye and Ear Protection—All persons, spectators, shooters, field judges and trap personnel must wear eye and ear protection on the course at a tournament sanctioned by NSCA.

3. Trap Personnel Protection—All trap personnel in front of the line of fire must be out of sight with screen protection able to withstand the charge of shot at the given distance.

4. All shooting stations must require the shooter (except wheelchair shooters) to engage all targets from the standing position.

5. Shooters must have the permission of a Field Judge to test fire any gun. Guns will be discharged only in attempt at competition targets.

6. The first person on every squad shall be allowed to view

a good presentation of targets from within the shoot station. This person is the only person permitted to mount their *unloaded* gun and track the targets being viewed.

7. It is the sole responsibility of the shooter to begin any event, station, and/or field with sufficient equipment, including safety equipment and ammunition. Failure to do so, which, in the opinion of the Field Judge will delay the shoot, will result in the loss of all targets as required to keep the shoot moving. Make-up targets will be provided only at the discretion of the Shoot Officials.

8. The shooting stations must be positioned in such a way that all shooters, trappers and spectators are protected from shot/target fall. Additionally, the shooting stations must be designed to restrict dangerous gun hold/ movement.

9. Target Drop Zones must be clear of ALL shooters and spectators.

10. Course Design Safety is the sole responsibility of the Range Owner/Shoot Officials.

11. The shooter must fire with his/her gun shouldered for all targets.

12. The use of any drug, legal or illegal and including alcohol, prior to or during an NSCA event by a registered competitor is prohibited with the exception of prescription medicine that does not impair a shooter's ability to perform safely.

13. Failure to comply with the NSCA Safety Rules may subject the Range Owner/Shoot Officials/Competitor to possible suspension.

14. Shotgun shooting safety is everyone's responsibility.

III. CLASSIFICATION

A. CLASSIFICATION SYSTEM

A shooter's classification carries over from one shooting year to the next. All new shooters will be assigned a class. During the current year, a shooter is subject to reclassify UPWARDS ONLY (with the exception of appeals). A classification card will be provided to all shooters. To maintain the integrity of the classification system, all NSCA members shooting on the course where a NSCA Registered Event is taking place must register their targets.

1. Determining Class

a. There are seven (7) classes a shooter can classify into: Master-AA-A-B-C-D-E. All registered events using the NSCA Classification system will offer all classes (including Master).

b. Non-Classified and New Members

1. A shooter who has never shot any registered clay targets will be assigned Class "D".

2. A shooter who has shot registered targets with any clay target organization other than a Sporting Clays Association (i.e., NSSA, ATA, NRA, International skeet or trap) will be assigned into Class "B" or one class lower than his/her highest class attained in that clay target organization, whichever is greater. Shooters, who are classed higher than "B", may use the "KNOWN ABILITY" appeal process should they think their classification is incorrect. (See III-A-6 Appeals.)

3. A shooter from another sporting clays organization, (i.e., USSCA/SCA, CPSA, F.I.T.A.S.C., Non-Registered Sporting Clay Events) will shoot their earned class or higher.

4. A shooter may be classified based on his/her "known ability". (See III-A-3 Reclassification/Known Ability.)

2. Moving up in Class

a. Shooters earn their way out of class by shooting the high score(s) or tying for the high score(s) in class.

1. NSCA Nationals and U.S. Open (main event only):

The top 5 scores and all ties in each class receive 4 punches; the sixth and seventh highest scores and all ties in each class receive 3 punches; the eighth and ninth highest scores and all ties in each class receive 2 punches; the tenth highest score and all ties in each class receive 1 punch.

2. In all events using the NSCA classification system, except the NSCA Nationals and U.S. Open main events, shooters will earn punches based on the number of entries in their respective class. Punches are awarded as follows:

Number of entries in class	Punches earned
0–4	No punch
5–9	One (1) punch for high score and all ties
10-14	Two (2) punches for high score and all ties
15-29	Four (4) punches for high score and all ties. Two (2) punches for second Highest score in all ties. One (1) punch for third Highest score and all ties.
30-44	Four (4) punches for high score and all ties. Four (4) punches for second highest score and ties. Two (2) punches for third highest score and ties. One (1) punch for fourth highest score and all ties.
45+	Four (4) punches to first, second, and third highest scores and all ties. Three (3) punches fourth highest score and all ties. Two (2) punches for fifth highest score and all ties. One (1) punch for sixth highest score and all ties.

b. It is the shooter's responsibility to determine these punches and move up one class after reaching the following number of punches:

E Class to D Class 4 punches
D Class to C Class 4 punches
C Class to B Class 6 punches
B Class to A Class 8 punches
A Class to AA Class 10 punches
AA Class to Master Class 16 punches

Note: Punches must be earned in Shooter's current class in order for them to be used in moving up in class. A person earning more than the necessary punches to move up in class enters the new class with no punches.

c. In events of 100+ entries, it is the responsibility of shoot management to notify all shooters of their move up in class or punches received. The shooter is also equally responsible to shoot in his/her proper class and to inquire and inform shoot management of any move up at the next tournament entered.

d. Upon entering a shoot with multiple events, a person will remain in the class he/she started in for all events held, and any punches he/she accrues will be awarded at the conclusion of all of the events at that shoot. A shooter cannot be moved up more than one class at the conclusion of the registered events based on punches; however, a shooter can be moved up more than one class based on "KNOWN ABILITY."

e. All punches, except Lewis Class, earned in a shooter's current class in *2003* will carry over into *2004*. Carry-over punches are for the target year just ended and the current year. Punches from prior target years *(2002 and before)* will not carry over.

f. *Registered Lewis Class events—All NSCA members must register their targets. No shooter will be moved out of class for having the high score at a registered Lewis Class event.*

g. All registered events of 50 targets or more, except Lewis Class Events (see III-A-2-g above), are subject to receive punches based on the number of participants and the number of shooters in class if the NSCA classification system is used. *Note: This will include sub-gauge events where the NSCA classification system is used.* (See III-A-2 Moving Up In Class)

h. The NSCA National Championship, U.S. Open, Zone Shoot and State Shoot must use the NSCA Classification system. NSCA strongly suggests that major shoots utilize the NSCA Classification system. (See IV-B-2 Major Shoot.)

3. Reclassification/Known Ability

a. A shooter may be reclassified based on their "KNOWN ABILITY."

b. An NSCA club, State Association, National Delegate, member (shooter) or member of the Advisory Council has the right to request a "known ability" review of a shooter's record if it appears that he/she is competing in a class other than his/her true level of ability. This request must be in writing. Upon review by the appropriate NSCA Committee, the shooter may be assigned a different class.

c. A shooter reclassified by NSCA will receive a new class card with the notice of the change from NSCA. The different class will become effective with the receipt of the class card. Should the shooter wish to appeal this different class, they must do so within 30 days from receipt of the NSCA notice. (See III-A-6 Appeals.)

d. A shooter may voluntarily declare into a class higher than assigned; however, the shooter must stay in that class or higher for the entire year. This applies to all classes except for Master, which must be earned and not declared. When the shooter so elects, they must (at a registered shoot) have their classification card marked before competing in the event in the class for which they are declaring. Their card shall be marked with the new classification by self-declaration in the class where they declared, and be entered on the Official Entry Form with notation "self-declared".

e. A shooter may also be reclassified *to a higher class* by Shoot Officials based on their "known ability". This reclassification will be for that event only and shooter will return to his/her original class, with one exception. If the shooter wins in the class they are placed in based on "known ability", depending on the shoot size (See III-A-2 Moving up in Class), they would then receive punches or be moved to the next higher class (one above the "known ability" class) for the remainder of the year.

f. Any person who has experienced a permanent medical impairment may request a review on their classification during the shooting year.

4. Classification Review

a. *A shooter's classification may be reviewed after each 1,000 registered targets. Shooters must request such a review in writing. The 1,000-target review may be used to move a shooter down in class.* An annual review will be done on each NSCA member with a minimum of 300 registered competition targets shot in their current class in the current shooting year.

b. A shooter who is assigned to a lower class may reject the class if the shooter wishes to remain in a higher class. To reject the assigned class, the shooter must sign the "refusal form," which will be at the bottom of the classification card, and return it to NSCA Headquarters.

5. Shooter's Responsibility

a. The shooter is responsible for presenting his/her classification card and/or additional documentation upon entry at any registered shoot and entering into the proper class. The classification card is intended for the purpose of providing Shoot Officials with up-to-date information regarding classification of each shooter entering a registered event.

b. The shooter is responsible for entering their scores with the date and score shot on the back of their classification card or, if more space is needed, on a supplemental record form, and to make certain that all placements and punches are properly recorded on their classification card at the conclusion of each NSCA registered tournament. Failure to accurately record scores and punches may lead to suspension from the NSCA.

c. A shooter who enters or allows themselves to be entered into a class lower than the one in which their record places them, unless the error is corrected prior to a specific time posted by shoot management, a time announced in the shoot program, completion of shoot-offs, and/or the awarding of trophies and/or monies, shall be subject to the following:

1. Forfeit all rights to all winnings he/she would have earned shooting in his/her proper class.

2. For the first offense, be disqualified and forfeit all winnings earned while shooting in the wrong class (See also IV-S-3). The shooter must return all winnings within 15 days after notification by the host club, National Delegates, State Association or NSCA Headquarters requesting the winnings be returned. Failure to return the winnings within the 15-day period shall subject the shooter to suspension and being PERMANENTLY barred from registered competition.

3. In the case of a second or subsequent offense of shooting in a lower class, the shooter will forfeit all winnings and also be barred from registered competition for a minimum of one year and/or suspended from NSCA.

6. Appeals

a. The shooter's appeal must be in writing and state specific reasons why they think they should not be moved up in class. Pending a determination of the appeal, all shoots entered by the shooter must be entered at the new higher class.

b. The NSCA Classification Committee has 30 days from the receipt of the appeal to respond. At the Committee's option, additional information may be requested from the Zone Coordinator, National Delegate(s), and/or State Association (if one exists) for additional input.

IV. RULES & REGULATIONS FOR REGISTERED TOURNAMENTS

A. PARTICIPATION

1. Club

a. Eligibility and Responsibility

1. Only clubs affiliated with NSCA with current fees paid and in good standing with NSCA as well as their State Association (if one exists) shall be eligible to conduct registered shoots. Evidence of club's status in this regard must be displayed in the form of an official NSCA membership certificate for the appropriate year.

2. In applying for and holding a registered shoot, it shall be deemed the responsibility of club owners, management and Shoot Officials to ensure that the shoot is conducted within NSCA official rules and safety regulations.

3. The club sponsoring a registered shoot shall check the NSCA membership card and classification card of each shooter before accepting his/her entry, and shall be responsible for the annual dues if they allow a participant to shoot when said participant's membership in NSCA has expired.

4. Shoot management may be billed by NSCA in all cases where expired members are allowed to shoot. Management may seek reimbursement from said shooters, but must first abide by IV-A-1-a-3 above.

5. Any club sponsoring a registered shoot accepts the responsibility for any clerical errors made throughout the shoot and shall correct those errors.

b. Applying for a Registered Shoot Date

1. The club should complete an NSCA registered shoot application and forward to the State Association (if one exists) or the National Delegate(s) for signature of approval at the state level.

2. The signed application should be forwarded immediately to the NSCA office for final approval. Shoot applications must be postmarked or received by NSCA at least 10 days prior to the shoot date.

3. A notice of the approval will be forwarded by NSCA to the club at the address on file.

4. Shoot dates may not be altered without prior approval at the state level and notification to headquarters.

2. Individual

a. Only members who have paid their annual dues and are in good standing with NSCA *as well as their State Association (if one exists)* may participate in registered NSCA shoots. It is the shooter's responsibility to provide their current year classification card to Shoot Officials when entering a registered shoot. This ensures that name, address and membership number are properly recorded so that errors in records and scores can be prevented.

b. It shall be the sole responsibility of the shooter, upon entering the shoot, to see that they are entered into all the events desired on the official NSCA cashier sheet/entry form. Once entered, clerical errors are the responsibility of shoot management.

c. Residency Requirements

1. An individual must be a bona-fide resident (permanent abode) of a state to be eligible for state championships or to shoot as a state team member, and must be a bona-fide resident of a state within the zone to be eligible for zone championships or to shoot as a zone team member.

a. Persons with residence in more than one state must declare their eligibility by writing their home state on the face of the current year membership card. Servicemen, by the same act, may choose their home state or place in which they are permanently assigned for duty, and declare the state on the current year membership card.

b. Persons who change their official abode shall become immediately eligible to shoot as an individual in the state or zone shoot of their new permanent address. They should contact NSCA for a new membership card reflecting change of address and present same before entering shoot.

c. No person shall be eligible for more than one closed state or zone competition during the NSCA shooting year.

B. TYPES OF TOURNAMENTS
Registered Shoot

A SHOOT WHERE TARGETS SHOT BY NSCA MEMBERS MUST BE REGISTERED. Non-members may participate, but in a separate category. *Any non-member participating in a registered event in a separate category shall not be eligible for any NSCA awards or monies. If offered by shoot management, the separate category may have its own separate awards and/or monies.* Shoot date(s) must be submitted to the appropriate State Association (if one exists) or the National Delegate for signature of approval at state level, who will then submit to NSCA Headquarters for final approval.

1. Registered Small-Gauge Events

Small-Gauge Events may be registered; *punches will be awarded and combined with punches earned in 12- gauge events for classification purposes.* Small Gauges are .410, 28 and 20. The member's 12-Gauge classification will be used for all Small-Gauge Event classes.

2. Major Shoot

A registered shoot where, by projection or past experience, 100 or more shooters are expected to attend. NSCA strongly suggests that these shoots utilize the NSCA Classification system.

3. State Shoot

An annual shoot held within each state, the location and dates of which are decided by the following process: Interested clubs (within the state) who are in good standing with the NSCA and the State Association (if one exists) should contact the State Association (if one exists), or the National Delegate(s).

a. The State Association and/or National Delegate(s) should then take a vote of (1) State Association members (if one exists) or (2) All NSCA clubs in good standing for a decision.

b. If the second method is used and the vote results in a tie, the National Delegate(s) shall cast a vote for the club they think should be awarded the tournament. This vote should break the tie; however, if there is still a tie, the Zone Delegate will be contacted. The Zone Delegate will in turn consult with the National Delegates Committee Chairman, and after discussing the situation, the Zone Delegate will cast a tie-breaking vote for the club they feel should host the state tournament.

c. All State Shoots must utilize the NSCA Classification system, and it is strongly recommended that the shoot be held before July 31 of each year.

d. To be eligible for class prizes, monies and/or awards at State Shoots, a shooter must have shot a minimum of 300 registered targets in the current year, prior to the shoot. If a shooter does not have a minimum of 300 targets, he/she may shoot the event and win prizes, monies and/or awards in a penalty class, one class above his/her current class.

e. Following the State Shoot, all shooters who were placed in a penalty class as a result of their failure to meet the 300 registered target requirement will return to their original class, with one exception. If the shooter wins the penalty class, depending on the shoot size (See III-A-2 Moving up in Class), they would then receive punches or be moved to the next higher class (one above the penalty class) for the remainder of the year.

4. Zone Shoot

One annual shoot held within each zone, the location and dates of which are decided as follows: NSCA clubs in good standing send a bid to either their State Association (if one exits) or National Delegate who will then submit the bid to the Zone Delegate. Zone Delegates then send a ballot to all National Delegates within the zone for a vote.

a. Zone Shoots must be conducted utilizing the NSCA Classification system, and it is strongly suggested that the shoot be held before August 31 of each year. The date and location for each Zone Championship is to be established before the end of the preceding Zone Championship.

b. To be eligible for class prizes, monies and/or awards at Zone Shoots, a shooter must have shot a minimum of 300 registered targets in the current year, prior to the shoot. If a shooter does not have a minimum of 300 targets, he/she may shoot the event and win prizes, monies and/or awards in a penalty class, one class above his/her current class.

c. Following the Zone Shoot, all shooters who were placed in a penalty class as a result of their failure to meet the 300 registered target requirement will return to their original class, with one exception. If the shooter wins the penalty class, depending on the shoot size (See III-A-2 Moving up in Class), they would then receive punches or be moved to the next higher class (one above the penalty class) for the remainder of the year.

5. U.S. Open

An annual shoot awarded by the NSCA Advisory Council according to the criteria set for the upcoming year.

a. To be eligible for class prizes, monies and/or awards a shooter must have shot a minimum of 500 registered targets in the current shoot year prior to the U.S. Open. If a shooter does not have a minimum of *500* targets, he/she may shoot events and win prizes, monies and /or awards in a penalty class, one class above his/her current class.

b. Following the U.S. Open, all shooters who were placed in a penalty class as a result of their failure to meet the 500 registered target requirement will return to their original class, with one exception. If the shooter wins the penalty class, depending on the shoot size (See III-A-2 Moving up in Class), they would then receive punches or be moved to the next higher class (one above the penalty class) for the remainder of the year.

6. National Championship

An annual shoot held by the National Sporting Clays Association on its Home Grounds.

a. To be eligible for open and/or concurrent prizes, monies and awards at the National Championship, a shooter must have shot a minimum of 500 registered targets in the current year, prior to the shoot. If a shooter does not have a minimum of 500 targets, he/she may shoot at the event and win prizes, monies and/or awards in a penalty class, one class above his/her current class.

b. Following the National Championship, all shooters who were placed in a penalty class as a result of their failure to meet the 500 registered target requirement, will return to their original class, with one exception. If the shooter wins the penalty class, depending on the shoot size (See III-A-2 Moving up in Class), they would then receive punches or be moved to the next higher class (one above the penalty class) for the remainder of the year.

c. A program will be published each year giving all details of the current year's tournament.

7. *Any NSCA registered target may be used to meet target minimums.*

C. GAUGE SPECIFICATIONS

1. Twelve-gauge events shall be open to all guns of 12 gauge or smaller, using shot loads not exceeding one and one-eighth (1-1/8) ounces.

2. Twenty-gauge events shall be open to all guns of 20 gauge or smaller, using shot loads not exceeding seven-eighths (7/8) of an ounce.

3. Twenty-eight gauge events shall be open to all guns of 28 gauge or smaller, using shot loads not exceeding three-quarters (3/4) of an ounce.

4. Four-ten events shall be open to all guns of .410 bore or smaller, using shot loads not exceeding one-half (1/2) of an ounce.

D. CONCURRENT EVENTS

These are events that are offered in concurrence with the seven (7) classes of shooters (Master, AA, A, B, C, D, E) that allow the participating shooters to compete and receive prizes or awards in these separate events in addition to their class. These events are based on age (Sub-Junior, Junior, Veteran and Super Veteran) or sex (Lady). Where shoot programs offer special concurrent events based upon age, a shooter entering such special events must be allowed to shoot in the one for which they are qualified for by age along with any other concurrent class for which they are eligible if such a concurrent class is available (i.e. Lady could also be a Veteran, Super Veteran, Junior or Sub-Junior).

1. A shooter's eligibility for concurrent events that are based on age is determined by the age of the shooter on the 1st day of the target year and shall determine their eligibility for the entire upcoming shooting year. No contestant shall be eligible for more than one individual concurrent event based on age.

Sub-Junior—Any person who has not reached their 14th birthday.

Junior—Any person who has not reached their 18th birthday.

Veteran—Any person 55 years of age and over who has not yet reached their 65th birthday.

Super Veteran—Any person 65 years of age and over.

For concurrent eligibility for F.I.T.A.S.C. (See Section VII-D.)

Lady—A female shooter of any age.

2. NSCA Nationals, U.S. Open, Zone, State and Major shoots must offer all Concurrent Events and provide some type of award.

3. Shooters are eligible to compete for both concurrent and class awards. Shoot Official(s) may specify in tournament program that a reduced fee is offered for concurrent events. At time of entry, the shooter has the option to pay the full entry fee and compete for both concurrent and class (open) titles or pay a reduced fee and compete for concurrent titles only. If the shooter elects to pay a reduced fee and compete for concurrent titles only, they are still subject to earning punches according to Rule III-A-2 Moving Up In Class.

4. No Junior or Sub-Junior shall be required to pay any part of entry fee that is to be returned to the shooter in the form of money.

5. Youth Teams

This is a concurrent category that can be offered at

the host club's discretion. If offered, this team event will be shot simultaneously with an already established tournament event.

a. Teams will consist of four or five members and are required to shoot as a group.

b. All team members must be in the Junior or Sub-Junior age group.

c. Each team must have a designated coach nearby.

d. For team competition, the lowest individual score will be dropped from a five-member team score even though there may be no four-member teams participating.

e. Even though the scores of all team members may not count toward the team's event score, all team members will be counted as participants in the shoot, and in their respective classes, and all individual scores will be registered.

E. EQUIPMENT

1. Targets

Targets thrown in any event may include any or all of the following:

a. Regulation SKEET or TRAP targets as specified by ATA, NSSA or NSCA.

b. Specialty targets—Mini, midi, battue, rocket, or rabbit targets as specified by NSCA.

c. Any sporting clays target approved by NSCA.

d. Poison Bird—Not Allowed.

e. Pairs

1. Report Pair—Two sequential targets where the second target is launched at the sound of the gun firing at the first target. Targets may be launched from one or more traps.

2. Following Pair—Two sequential targets where the second target is launched at the official's discretion after the first target. Targets may be launched from one or more traps.

3. Simultaneous Pair—Two targets launched simultaneously. Targets may be launched from one or more traps.

f. Target number, selection *and order of presentation* for any competition shall be at the discretion of the Shoot Officials, but must be the same for all shooters. It is recommended that 30% to 40% of targets for tournaments be specialty targets.

g. No less than 80% of all targets in a shoot shall be presented with a reasonably consistent trajectory, distance and velocity to all shooters (See IV-E-2-b).

2. Traps

a. Targets will be propelled by, and launched from, any of a number of commercially produced, modified, or handmade devices that will propel an approved target in a manner to approach the characteristics (in the opinion of the Shoot Officials) of a game bird or animal typically taken by a sporting shotgun.

b. Launching devices that provide for targets traveling at varying angles and distances to the competitors are acceptable (i.e. wobble traps). No more than 20% of the targets shall be presented from such devices.

c. Devices that provide for propelling multiple targets are permitted.

d. Devices propelling targets of more than one type and devices capable of providing targets at varying angles and distances shall be employed only as the varying aspects of these devices will be the same for all shooters and will be free of all human element of selection.

3. Shotguns

a. Shotguns of 12 gauge or smaller, in safe working order, and capable of firing two shots are to be used in attempting all targets. No more than two (2) shells may be loaded in the gun at one time.

b. Shotguns fitted for multiple barrels (of various chokes and/or lengths) are permitted. The shooter is allowed to change barrels only between stations. Failure to comply will result in all targets on that station attempted after the infraction being scored as "lost" or "missed".

c. Shotguns with interchangeable or adjustable chokes are permitted at the shooter's discretion. Chokes may be changed or adjusted only between stations. Failure to comply will result in all targets on that station attempted after the infraction being scored as "lost" or "missed".

d. Competitors may enter a shoot with various guns and attempt targets at various stations with different guns, or the gun of another competitor. Guns may be changed only between stations, except in the case of a malfunction (IV-L-1-b). Failure to comply will result in all targets on that station attempted after the infraction being scored as "lost" or "missed".

e. Guns with release-type triggers are allowed and must be clearly marked and Shoot Officials notified of their presence. Safety stickers designating "release trigger", with instructions on placement, are available at no charge from NSCA Headquarters. Please send your request in writing.

4. Ammunition

a. All shotshell ammunition, including reloads, may be used. Shoot Officials may limit the ammunition to commercially manufactured shot shells. The National Sporting Clays Association assumes no responsibility in connection with the use of reloads.

b. Maximum loads for any gauge EVENT may not exceed:

Gauge	Ounce Lead
12	1-1/8
20	7/8
28	3/4
.410 (2-1/2" Maximum)	1/2

c. No shot smaller than U.S. No. 9 (diameter 0.08) or larger than U.S. No. 7-1/2 (diameter 0.095) shall be used in any load. No steel shot smaller than U.S. No. 9 (a nominal diameter 0.080") or *larger than U.S. No. 6 (a nominal diameter 0.110)* shall be used in any load.

d. Shot shall be normal production spherical shot. Plated shot is permitted.

F. COURSE SETUP AND REQUIREMENTS

1. Station

A shooting position from which one or more targets are attempted.

2. Field

A station or group of stations from which targets are attempted sequentially. Once a squad or individual checks into a field, all stations and/or all targets on the field are attempted before moving to another field. NSCA 5-STAND is a group of stations considered to be one (1) field. The Shoot Officials will provide direction for execution of shooting at each field.

3. Registered events are required to throw a minimum of 25 targets. The course will provide for a predetermined

number of shooting fields from which each competitor will attempt various targets.

4. The number of Stations and the number and characteristics of targets from each station, on each field, will be determined by the Shoot Officials and will be the same for all shooters. Changes in target trajectory, distance and/or velocity due to wind, rain, time of day or any other natural cause does not constitute a violation of this rule.

G. SHOOT OFFICIALS AND PERSONNEL

1. Shoot Promoter

Individual(s) or entity that provides for the facilities and organization of the competition. Shoot Promoters may also act as Shoot Officials.

2. Shoot Official

Individual(s) appointed by the Shoot Promoter and responsible for course layout, target selection and appointment of Field Judges. Shoot Officials shall be responsible for both layout and testing of the course for safety. Shoot Officials are responsible for ensuring that competitors are not allowed to shoot the course prior to the competition.

a. Anyone who shoots the course prior to the competition is ineligible to compete in the tournament but may shoot for registered targets only.

b. Any person who sets or designs a course shall be allowed to shoot that course for registered targets only but will not be eligible for awards.

3. Field Judge (Referee)

An individual, who has integrity and knowledge of NSCA Rules, assigned by the Shoot Officials to enforce the rules and score targets at any NSCA event. This individual can be the chief referee, a certified referee or any individual appointed by the Shoot Official(s).

a. Field Judges will be required at each station in sufficient number to competently enforce all rules for the shooter, as well as to score the attempts accurately.

b. Numbers and positions for Field Judges shall be determined by the Shoot Officials.

4. Chief Referee

A person may be appointed by shoot management who is responsible for the general supervision over all other referees at a tournament and who shall be present throughout the shooting.

5. Certified Referee

A person who has completed and passed an NSCA Certified Referee Examination. Examination forms may be requested from NSCA Headquarters by recognized State Associations, National Delegate(s) and NSCA club owners/managers: all of whom may administer the test to an applicant in their presence. The completed examination should then be forwarded to NSCA Headquarters with a fee of $20.00 for processing. Certification will be for a period of 3 years, ending September 30 of the 3rd year. The applicant may refer to the NSCA Rule Book to complete the examination, however, ALL questions on the examination must be answered correctly in order to pass. NSCA will issue Certified Referee credentials (patch and card) to applicants who pass the examination. This is a voluntary program. All Certified Instructor courses will automatically include this examination.

H. SHOOTING ORDER / ROTATIONS

1. Format

Contestants shall proceed through the course and competition in one of the following formats:

a. European Rotation—Individual competitors or groups of 2 through 6 competitors will proceed to the various stations at random. Groups may shoot in any order of rotation selected by the shooters and may change the rotation from field to field. In European Rotation, a shoot start and shoot end time will be established. It will be the responsibility of each shooter to complete the entire event between these times.

b. Squadding—At the discretion of the Shoot Officials, groups of 3 to 6 shooters will be formed to proceed from field to field in a fixed sequence. Unless specified by Shoot Officials, squads may shoot in any order of rotation selected by the shooters and may change the rotation from field to field.

1. In squadding sequence, squads will be assigned a start time and it is the responsibility of each shooter to be ready on time, or within no more than 5 minutes of that time.

2. Time—Shots not attempted by the "shoot end time" (European Rotation), or shots not attempted by the shooter joining his squad after they have begun (squadding), will be scored as "lost". The Shoot Officials shall have the right to provide for make-up targets if sufficient justification can be presented. Make-up targets are provided solely at the discretion of the Shoot Officials.

I. ATTEMPTING TARGETS

1. It will be the responsibility of each shooter to be familiar with these rules. Ignorance of the rules will not be a cause to "re-attempt" targets lost because of rule violations.

2. It is the sole responsibility of the shooter to begin any event, station and/or field with sufficient equipment, including safety equipment and ammunition. Failure to do so, which in the opinion of the Field Judges will delay the shoot, will result in the loss of all targets as required to keep the shoot moving. Make-up targets will be provided only at the discretion of the Shoot Officials.

3. Call for Target—The target may be launched immediately or with a delay of up to 3 seconds.

4. Shotgun Mount and Position—The shooter may start with a low gun or a pre-mounted gun when calling for the target.

J. TARGET PRESENTATION AND SCORING

1. Targets will be presented for attempt by the shooter and scored at each station in one or more of the following formats.

a. Single Target

Two shots are allowed and the target will be scored "dead" if broken by either shot.

b. Pairs

Only two shots are allowed. Pairs may be presented as report, following or simultaneous.

1. In simultaneous pairs, the shooter has the right to shoot either of the targets first. If the shooter has missed the first target, he may fire the second cartridge at the same target.

2. When shooting report or following pairs, the shooter will have the right, if missing the first target, to fire the second cartridge at the same target (the result being scored on the first target and the second target being scored as "lost").

c. Scoring Pairs

1. Should the shooter break both targets with either the first or second shot then the result will be scored as two hits.

2. In the event of a "no bird" on a simultaneous or following pair, nothing can be established. Two good targets must be present to record the score. This will also apply for gun/ammunition malfunctions while shooting pairs. See IV-L-Malfunctions.

3. In the event of a "no bird" on the second target of a report pair, the first bird will be established as "dead" or "lost" and the shooter will repeat the pair to establish the result of the second target. When repeating the pair, the shooter must make a legitimate attempt at the first target.

4. In the event of a "shooter malfunction" on the first bird of a report pair, the first bird will be established as "lost" and the shooter will repeat the pair to establish the result of the second target. When repeating the pair, the shooter must make a legitimate attempt at the first target. The first target has already been established as "lost," and the result of the second target will be recorded. (See IV-L-2 "Shooter Malfunctions".)

d. Multiple Targets

Only 2 shots are allowed; 2 "hits" or "dead birds" maximum.

2. Time Reloads

Targets presented with set time periods for shooter to reload prior to the presentation of the subsequent targets are permitted. Five seconds is the normal reload time, but other intervals may be used at the discretion of the Shoot Official(s).

3. Shooters Viewing Targets

The first person on every squad shall be allowed to view a good presentation of targets from within the shooting station. *This person is the only person permitted to mount their unloaded gun and track the targets being viewed.*

K. SCORING PROCEDURE

1. Each shooter will be assigned a scorecard to be presented to the Field Judges at the various stations or fields. Field Judges will score each shooter's attempts on the individual's scorecard. The total shall be tallied, and the scores written in ink and initialed by the Field Judge.

2. Each shooter is responsible for his scorecard from assignment, at the start of the shoot, until the card is filed with the Shoot Officials at the end of each day's shooting.

3. Scores made on re-entry will not qualify for prizes.

4. Shooters are responsible for checking the Field Judge's totals of "hits and misses" at each station and/or field.

5. Field Judges may be assisted by markers to record scores on the shooter's scorecard.

6. Targets shall be scored as "hit" or "dead" and designated on scorecards by an (X) when, in the opinion of the Field Judge, a visible piece has been broken from the target. Targets not struck and broken by the shooters shot shall be called "lost" or "missed" and designated on scorecards by an (O).

7. The call of "lost" or "dead", "hit" or "miss" shall be announced by the Field Judge prior to recording the score on every target.

8. If the shooter disagrees with the Field Judge's call, he/she must protest before firing at another set of targets or before leaving that station. The Field Judge may poll the spectators and may reverse his/her original call. In all cases, the final decision of the Field Judge will stand.

9. During a registered event, each shooter must verify his/her score before leaving the station. Once the shooter has left the station, his/her score is final.

L. MALFUNCTIONS

The shooter shall be allowed a combined total of three (3) malfunctions per day, per event attributed to either the shooter's gun or ammunition. Targets not attempted on the three (3) allowed malfunctions shall be treated as "no birds". Targets not attempted due to the fourth or latter malfunctions shall be scored as "lost".

1. Gun Malfunctions

a. In the case of a gun malfunction, the shooter must remain in place, the gun pointed safely downrange, and must not open the gun or tamper with trigger, safety or barrel selector, until the field judge has determined the cause and made his/her ruling.

b. In the case of an inoperable gun, the shooter has the option to use another gun, if one is available, or he/she may drop out of competition until the gun is repaired. The shooter must, however, finish the event during the allotted scheduled shooting time.

2. Shooter Malfunctions

Targets shall be scored as "lost" if the shooter is unable to fire because of the following. Examples include but are not limited to:

a. Shooter has left the safety on.

b. Shooter has forgotten to load, load unfired shells, or properly cock the gun.

c. Shooter has forgotten to disengage the locking device from the magazine of a semi-automatic shotgun.

d. Shooter has not sufficiently released the trigger of a single-trigger gun having fired the first shot.

e. Shooter not seeing the target.

f. If the shooter fails to comply with item IV-L-1-a, the target or targets will be scored as "lost" or "missed".

3. Ammunition Malfunctions

In the case of an ammunition malfunction, the shooter must remain in place, the gun pointing safely downrange, and must not open the gun or tamper with the trigger, safety or barrel selector until the Field Judge has determined the cause and made his/her ruling. Examples include but are not limited to:

a. Failure to fire, providing firing pin indentation is clearly noticeable.

b. One in which the primer fires, but through failure of the shell or lack of components, and which, consequently, leaves part of or all of the charge of shot or wad in the gun. A soft load, in which the shot and wad leave the barrel, is not a misfire and shall be scored as "lost" or "missed".

c. Brass pulling off hull between shots on pairs.

d. Separation of brass from casing when gun is fired (usually accompanied by a "whistling" sound as the plastic sleeve leaves the barrel).

e. If the shooter fails to comply with item IV-L-3, the target or targets will be scored as "lost" or "missed".

4. Trap/Target Malfunctions

a. A target that breaks at launching shall be called a "no bird" and shooter will be provided a new target.

b. A target that is launched in an obviously different trajectory shall be called a "no bird" and the shooter will be provided a new target.

c. If a bad target or "no bird" is thrown during a timed reload sequence, the shooter will repeat the sequence beginning with the last target established. The shooter must make an attempt at the last established target before proceeding with the remaining sequence. If the last established target occurred before the timed reload, the shooter shall begin the sequence accordingly and proceed through the reloading again. The Field Judge shall enforce his/her judgment (either by implementing a suitable penalty or allowing a repeat of the reloading sequence) to prevent a "no bird" or "bad target" thrown after either a successful or an unsuccessful reloading attempt from changing the results of the initial sequence.

d. At a station of multiple targets (two or more – simultaneously launched), at least two good targets must be presented simultaneously or a "no bird" will be called and the multiple targets will be attempted again. Multiple targets shall be shot as "fair pair in the air"; two new shots will be attempted and scored. No scores from previous "no bird" attempts will stand.

M. WEATHER / MITIGATING CIRCUMSTANCES

In the event of extreme weather conditions, power failure, trap failure or unusually early darkness, the shoot management may elect to continue the event some other time (i.e., the next morning or the following weekend) but must immediately notify NSCA, with a full explanation, who will sanction the change, provided it is deemed in the best interest of sporting clays.

N. SHOOTOFFS

In all registered NSCA tournaments, all ties shall be shot off unless otherwise specified by shoot management and published in the program or posted at the registration table. Procedures for shootoffs and squads shall be posted prior to beginning of shoot. *If shootoffs are held, the shootoffs must be held on targets or positions not previously shot by any participating competitor.*

O. PROTESTS

1. A shooter may protest, if in his/her opinion, the rules as stated herein are improperly applied.

2. Any protest concerning calls or scoring of hits or misses must be made on the shooting station prior to leaving the station. The Field Judge's final decision will stand and no further protest allowed.

3. Protests shall be made immediately upon completion of the shooting at a given field with the Field Judge and with Shoot Official(s).

4. The Shoot Official(s) shall convene a predetermined "jury" of 3 to 5 Field Judges or competitors who are known to be representative of the shooters present and knowledgeable about these rules. The jury will decide on the validity of the protest and the resolution of the case. They will prescribe penalties or award bonuses as they determine to be fair and in the spirit of the competition.

P. CHECKS / PAYMENTS / OVERPAYMENTS

1. Anyone who presents a check at any shoot that is returned for insufficient funds, or other causes, must be notified by registered mail by the club to which it was presented and has fifteen (15) days to make full payment, plus penalty, to the club. Any club receiving such a check shall report name and address of the shooter issuing the check to the NSCA.

2. Any competitor at a registered shoot who, through error, has been overpaid on any purse, added money, optional or other prize money and who is notified of the overpayment by registered mail, must return the overpayment within fifteen days of notification. Failure to do so shall result in disbarment from all registered shoots until repayment is made.

3. See Section I-B-4 Suspension and Reinstatement.

Q. OFFICIAL SCORES

1. All scores or records, to be recognized as official, must be shot under all of the official NSCA rules.

2. Only the scores shot on scheduled dates, approved by NSCA, shall be registered. Scores made in shootoffs shall not be registered; however, all NSCA rules shall apply in shootoffs.

3. The scores of any NSCA member shooting on a course where a registered shoot is taking place shall be considered official and shall be registered with the NSCA even though the shooter had given notice that it was not his/her intention to have their score recorded.

4. The score of a contestant who voluntarily stops or withdraws (without just cause) or who is disqualified by shoot management from an event that the contestant has started will be reported to NSCA along with the other scores of the event. This contestant's partial score for the station in which he/she is shooting shall be entered as the score for that station even though the contestant may not have actually fired on all targets. However, the total score for this contestant will not include targets from any station where he/she did not actually fire on at least one target.

5. Scores for contestants who withdraw because of sickness or injury shall be based on and reported only on number of targets actually fired upon.

6. In the event that a station/stations must be eliminated from the competition and results must be determined on less than the original number of targets intended for the competition shoot officials must give all competitors (whether they shot the station/stations or not) credit for all targets planned for the eliminated station/stations and must report the total number of targets shot at as originally intended (i.e. 100, 150, 200, etc.) to NSCA Headquarters.

7. Scores in shoots on which complete records are not made by shoot management will not be recorded and the national association shall not be liable to refund fees received in such cases.

R. REGISTERED SHOOT REPORTS

1. Reporting Requirements

It is the duty of each club holding a registered shoot to fulfill the following obligations:

a. Make payments of all money, purses and options to the shooters. (See Section IX Nonpayment Penalties.)

b. All money collected for optional purses must be paid out 100% to the eligible shooter(s).

c. Range Owners are required to fulfill all registered shoot reporting requirements within 15 days of their event or a $25.00 delinquent fine will be imposed for all shoot reports, financial statements and fees not received at NSCA Headquarters within that period. NSCA Headquarters will also have 15 days from the date the registered shoot report is received to have all scores input or be faced with the same $25.00 fine to be returned to the club hosting the tournament. (See IX Nonpayment Penalties.)

d. Shoot report and financial form must be sent to NSCA on all registered shoots. Standard forms available from NSCA Headquarters must be used or any NSCA approved spreadsheet that includes all information in rules IV-R-2 and 3.

e. If an approved State Association exists, clubs within the state must submit all required documents to their State Association within 15 days.

2.Financial Report

a. Daily Fees

List number of targets shot each day of shoot and remit to NSCA the required daily registration fee (in U.S. Funds). Daily fees are $.03 per target.

b. NSCA dues collected—Remittance (in U.S. Funds) and original copies of receipts for all NSCA memberships sold at your shoot must be attached. Membership applications must be completely and legibly filled out with name and address.

3. Shoot Report

An individual entry form/cashier sheet must be submitted on every shooter unless the club is using an NSCA-approved spreadsheet. For every event (except Lewis events are not required to provide items "f" and "g"), these reports must include:

a. NSCA membership number

b. Member's full name

c. Member's complete address

d. Number of targets shot

e. Number of targets broken

f. Class in which member was entered (not required for Lewis Class shoots)

g. Awards won. Except for Lewis Class events, winners must be determined and reported under NSCA Classification system. This applies even if no awards are made. Do not list winners above class champions unless such awards were made.

h. Clubs are required to retain copies of scoreboard and/or field score sheet on file for 90 days after the end of the applicable shooting year. And for shooter's reference, keep an accurate record of the number of entries at each and every registered event.

i. It shall be the range owner's responsibility to keep on hand throughout the shoot year, a detailed list of shooters, scores and all monies paid out to shooters. If requested in writing by any participant in any event, it shall be the range owner's responsibility to provide the participant with a detailed list of all participants, their scores and all money and prizes paid out and presented to shooters no sooner than within fifteen (15) days of the shoot report due date. All requests for such information shall be in writing, accompanied by a stamped, self-addressed envelope. Clubs are required to retain this information on file for 90 days after the end of the applicable shooting year.

S. DISQUALIFICATION AND EXPULSION

The shoot management shall upon proper evidence:

1. Disqualify any shooter for the remainder of the shoot program for willful or repeated violation of gun safety precautions that endanger the safety of shooters, field personnel and/or spectators.

2. Elect to refuse the entry or cause the withdrawal of any contestant whose conduct, in the sole opinion of shoot management, is unsportsmanlike or whose participation is in any way detrimental to the best interests of the shoot.

3. Disqualify any shooter from a shoot for misrepresentation of his/her status under the eligibility rules (SANDBAGGING).

4. Expel or disqualify any shooter physically assaulting a Field Judge or any shooter using abusive language to a Field Judge upon sufficient evidence presented.

5. The shoot management shall report to NSCA all cases of disqualification and expulsion and the reasons for same. The circumstances under which any shooter is expelled from or disqualified from any NSCA function, event or club will be reviewed by the Executive Director after giving the shooter involved an opportunity to be heard. The Executive Council will direct the Executive Director to notify the shooter, in writing, of his/her membership status: A) No action taken B) Expulsion/loss of membership for a term to be determined by the Executive Council C) Probation for one (1) year and if any other mishaps, immediate expulsion and loss of membership for one (1) year. The Executive Council can amend the length of expulsion or probation. Members may be suspended for failing to pay for goods or services ordered from NSCA/NSCA Member Club or who give to NSCA/NSCA Member Club a check that is returned for insufficient funds or other cause. Members MAY BE reinstated upon receipt in full of the outstanding balance and any fees incurred, such as bank charges, as a result of the incident. The Executive Council can determine any penalties and/or suspensions as each case merits. (See I-B-3 Rules of Conduct.)

V. NSCA 5-STAND SPORTING™

NSCA 5-STAND Sporting events consist of targets shot in 25-bird increments from five shooting stands with each shooter rotating from station to station. The game offers several different skill levels and utilizes six or eight automatic traps to simulate game birds. Targets are released in a predetermined set sequence marked on a menu card in front of each shooting cage. Targets are registered separately under a special set of rules, however, utilize the NSCA Classification system, and all targets are included for total targets shot for the year. NSCA 5-STAND SPORTING rules must be followed at all times while conducting this event.

A. LAND

1. Minimum area 50 yards wide along Shooting Stand line.

2. Minimum 300 yards deep left and right of the center of Shooting Stand line creating an 80-degree arc for safe shot fall. (Game can be overlaid on a Skeet and or Trap field.)

B. EQUIPMENT

1. Six or eight automatic traps required.

2. Machines must include a rabbit trap and a vertical trap (minimum 60%).

3. Five Shooting Stands not less than seven feet tall and not more than 54 inches across the front opening.

4. One tower not less than 12 feet in height.

5. Controller (any NSCA approved).

6. Target sequence menu cards.

7. Trap location numbers.

8. Shooting Stand numbers.

9. Safety rules sign.

C. LAYOUT

1. Shooting Stands must be in a STRAIGHT LINE (for safety) not less than four yards apart or more than six yards apart (recommended five yards) center to center.

2. Trap placement and target flight paths must be arranged to include the following:

a. Left to right crossing and/or quartering away target.

b. Right to left crossing and/or quartering away target.

c. Vertical target (Springing Teal).

d. Rabbit target.

e. Tower target going away.

f. Incoming target.

3. For safety reasons, traps must be placed to prevent broken targets hitting the competitors or causing competitor's gun to be pointed in an unsafe direction. Traps placed parallel or too close to the Shooting Stand line can create a serious hazard. Recommended five-yard minimum for any traps placed in front of Shooting Stands. Tower placement must be a sufficient distance back or to the side of the Shooting Stand line to prevent broken targets from falling on the competitors. Traps placed to the side of the Shooting Stand line should be a sufficient distance forward or behind the Shooting Stands to prevent competitors from selecting a hold point too close to the Shooting Stand line when calling for the target.

D. RULES

1. Gun must be open and empty while changing stands.

2. Shooters may not leave their station until instructed to do so by the referee or until the last shooter has fired his last shot.

3. Only load gun while in Shooting Stand in ready position.

4. Shooter's feet must be behind the front opening of the Shooting Stand except when changing stands. Shooters will be warned, a "No-Bird" will be called, and continued disregard will result in losing a target or being disqualified.

5. No chokes may be changed after the round has begun. Failure to comply will result in loss of all targets attempted (in that round) after choke changed.

6. Target sequence menu cards must be posted.

VI. F.I.T.A.S.C.

F.I.T.A.S.C. (Federation Internationale de Tir aux Armes Sportives de Chasse), headquartered in Paris, France, has recognized the National Sporting Clays Association as the sole, exclusive association to govern Parcours de Chasse Sporting and Compak Sporting in the United States. F.I.T.A.S.C. targets will be registered separately and shot under F.I.T.A.S.C. rules. The F.I.T.A.S.C. gun mount rule applies in all F.I.T.A.S.C. events. The NSCA Classification system used and all targets will be included in the shooters total targets shot for the year. In case of controversial interpretation of the present regulation, the text written in French will make faith. NOTE: Chapters and numbers in parentheses correspond with official Federation rules.

A. GENERAL (Chapter 1)

1. (1.01) Shooting Stand—Taking into considerations the terrain, a sporting course must be equipped with a sufficient amount of traps so that the competitors will shoot under conditions as close as possible to game shooting: partridges, pheasants, ducks, rabbits, etc. in front, low and high, crossing and quartering in fields or in woods, hidden or not by trees and bushes.

2. (1.02) The course must have been approved by the National Federations, for the organization of national competitions and by the International Federation for the organization of international competitions.

3. (1.03) Traps—A minimum of 4 traps are required for each old system layout and a minimum of 3 traps for each new system shooting stand; that is 12 traps for each layout. Machines may be either manual, automatic or mixed, MARKED by alphabetical letters (A, B, C, D) from left to right of the shooting stand.

4. (1.04) Clays—The clays to be used are the standard targets and rabbit clays, as well as thinner clays and clays with a smaller diameter. They may also include midi, mini, battue, bourdon, flash and zz targets. The targets must be black or orange according to the layout background.

5. (1.05) Shooting Position—The shooter will adopt the ready position, i.e. standing with both feet within the limits of the shooting stand, WITH THE HEEL OF THE GUN TOUCHING THE BODY UNDER A HORIZONTAL LINE MARKED ON THE SHOOTER'S JACKET. THIS LINE WILL BE INDICATED BY A TAPE OF

CONTRASTING COLOR FIXED TO THE JACKET BY SOME PERMANENT MEANS. THE HORIZONTAL LINE SHALL BE LOCATED 25 cm (9.85″) BELOW

AN IMAGINARY LINE DRAWN OVER THE TOP OF THE SHOULDERS ALONG THEIR AXIS. The shooter will maintain this position with the gun not pre-mounted until the target(s) are in sight.

6. (1.06) In a double on report, simultaneous or rafale, the position of the gun is optional for the second target only.

7. (1.07) If the shooter is in a position NOT IN ACCORDANCE with (1.05) or if he aims his gun before the target appears, he will receive an initial WARNING.

8. (1.08) After *the first such occurrence* on the same layout, the target(s) will be declared:

a. Zero for a single target

b. Zero and NO BIRD for a double on report

c. Zero & Zero for a simultaneous double

d. Zero & Zero for a rafale double

9. (1.09) The shooter does not have the right to refuse a target unless he has not called for it. The referee alone shall decide on the regularity of a trajectory or on a NO BIRD.

10. (1.10) The shooting stands will be marked by a 1-meter square or by a circle of 1 meter in diameter.

11. (1.11) The shooter must fire with his gun shouldered for all targets.

12. (1.12) Under no circumstances, once the referee has clearly declared a target NO BIRD, may it be fired at. After the *first* warning, the shooter will be penalized:

a. Zero for a single target

b. Zero & NO BIRD for a double on report

c. Zero & Zero for a simultaneous double

d. Zero & Zero for a rafale double.

B. ORGANIZATION OF COMPETITION (Chapter 2)
JURY

1. (2.01) International events will be supervised by a jury consisting of a representative of each country participating *with a seniors team* with the representative of the organizing country as chairman.

2. (2.02) The jury shall make decisions by majority vote of members present. In the case of equal votes, the chairman's casting vote is final.

3. (2.03) The jury can only make valid decisions in the presence of its chairman or his representative accompanied by a quarter of the members of the jury.

4. (2.04) In urgent cases (example: the risk of cessation of shooting), two members of the jury, nominated by the chairman, may make a decision with the consent of the referee, provided that this decision is endorsed by the jury.

THE ROLE OF THE JURY IS:

5. (2.05) To verify, before the shooting begins, that the course conforms to regulations and that the preparatory arrangements are suitable and correct.

6. (2.06) To appoint a technical committee whose responsibility shall be to set, on the day before the competition, the various trajectories, the location of the shooting stands, the choice and speed of the targets that will be shot during the event.

7. (2.07) No practice will be permitted before the start of events over the layouts set by the technical committee.

8. (2.08) Before the beginning of the championships, the director of shooting will publish a list of the trajectories for each of the traps. Should these trajectories, established and calculated in calm conditions, be disturbed by the wind, they will still be considered regular.

9. (2.09) To require that, during the shooting, the rules are adhered to and to check the weapons, ammunition and targets by means of technical tests.

10. (2.10) To make the necessary decisions in cases of technical defects *if* these are not resolved by the referee.

11. (2.11) To deal with protests.

12. (2.12) To make decisions regarding penalties to be imposed on a shooter who does not adhere to the rules or behaves in an unsporting manner.

13. (2.13) To ensure that there are always at least two members of the jury present at the shooting ground.

APPEAL JURY

14. (2.14) An appeal jury will be set up for each international competition.

15. (2.15) In the case of a dispute concerning the decision of the jury by the shooters or by F.I.T.A.S.C., an appeal jury may be referred to. This appeal jury will consist of: the President of F.I.T.A.S.C. or his representative, the President of the Technical Committee or his representative, and the *President of the Organizing Federation*. This appeal jury will be formed at the same time as the jury. *If there is no Appeal Jury, the Jury's decision is definitive. All the disciplinary problems will be submitted to the F.I.T.A.S.C. Disciplinary Commission.*

16. (2.16) During international competitions, representatives of the same country shall be dispersed over the various squads. The organizing committee will announce the time and arrangements for a draw for the composition of the squads. Delegates from participating nations may be present.

17. (2.17) Shooting shall take place in squads of six shooters VI-B-8 (2.08) as drawn, with rotation of shooters not only at each stand but also for shooting doubles. At each stand, all six shooters of a squad will first fire at the single targets before any shoot at the doubles.

18. (2.18) All target trajectories will be presented at each stand to the first shooter of each group. This shooter must observe them from within the shooting stand.

19. (2.19) At the time of the presentation of the target, no shooting, aiming or pretense of firing is permitted (for penalty see article 1.07).

20. (2.20) "Report" pairs will not be shown, only targets of SIMULTANEOUS and RAFALE doubles will be shown to the first shooter of each group.

21. (2.21) Only targets having already been fired at as singles may be shot at as "report" pairs.

22. (2.22) In international competitions, shooting will be conducted in stages of 25 targets. However, exceptionally, the technical committee may change this if it is judged necessary.

23. (2.23) Shooters must take all precautions in order to be at the shooting stand on time. If a shooter is not present when his name is called, the referee must call the name and number of the shooter loudly 3 times during the period of one minute. If he has not missed his turn to shoot the singles on the first stand, he may rejoin the squad. If he has failed to join the squad before his turn, those targets not fired at, singles or doubles, will be scored zero. If the shooter presents himself at one of the following stands, ALL THE CLAYS NOT SHOT AT THE PREVIOUS STAND WILL BE SCORED ZERO. In no circumstances may the shooter shoot that layout in another squad. (See VI-B-24.)

24. (2.24) If the shooter feels that he has a valid excuse for his lateness, he MUST:

a. Not join his squad if it is in the process of shooting on that layout.

b. Put his case to the jury in writing.

c. Abide by the jury's decision.

d. Only the jury may authorize him to repeat the shoot of that layout in another squad.

e. If the jury decides that the reason put forward by the shooter is unacceptable, the latter will be scored 25 zeros, corresponding to the 25 clays not shot at.

25. (2.25) In the case of malfunction of a trap during the shoot, the referee will decide if the stage should be continued or interrupted because of mechanical troubles. After the trouble has been rectified, the shooter has the right to have the regular target(s) shown before continuing the shoot.

26. (2.26) During international competitions, the scores will be recorded by the referee or his delegate, who may be a shooter. The results of each stage will then be posted on a central notice board.

27. (2.27) On leaving each stand, the shooter must check that his correct score is recorded on the scorecard. If the shooter CONTESTS the result, HE MUST INFORM THE REFEREE IMMEDIATELY, BUT THE FINAL DECISION RESTS WITH THE REFEREE. However, the referee may seek information and advice before making his final decision. NO OBJECTION WILL BE ALLOWED AFTER THIS CHECK.

C. FIREARMS AND AMMUNITION (Chapter 3)

1. (3.01) All firearms, including semi-automatics, are permitted, providing their caliber does not exceed 12 bore, with a barrel length of 66 cm minimum.

2. (3.02) All firearms, even unloaded, must be handled with the greatest care at all times.

3. (3.03) Guns must be carried open; semi-automatic

guns must be carried WITH THE BREECH OPEN, and the muzzle pointing straight upward or downward.

4. (3.04) Straps or slings on guns are forbidden.

5. (3.05) When the shooter is not using a gun, it must be placed vertically in a gun rack or in a similar place as designated.

6. (3.06) It is forbidden to handle another shooter's gun without his specific permission.

7. (3.07) It is forbidden, during a competition or official championship, for two shooters of the same squad to use the same gun. (See 3.08.)

8. (3.08) In exceptional cases, owing to a malfunction of his gun, a shooter may be permitted to borrow the gun of another shooter with his permission.

9. (3.09) Complete or partial CHANGING OF A FIREARM, MOBILE CHOKE OR BARREL is allowed during the same round, between two stands or between single or double targets. However, no delay will be permitted for any of these reasons.

10. (3.10) Once the shooter is on the shooting stand, he will not be allowed to carry out any changes that are permitted in 3.09.

11. (3.11) A shooter is permitted a maximum time to ready himself between targets, whether singles or doubles, of 20 seconds. In a case where the shooter exceeds this time, the referee may, after two warnings to the shooter, apply article 1.08.

12. (3.12) In the case of a gun malfunction, verified by the referee, the shooter will twice only have the right to a new target in the course of the same round. The third and subsequent malfunction will be considered ZERO. Following the decision of the referee, the shooter will have the right to continue with his squad on condition that he obtains another weapon without delay (3.08). If this is not possible, he must leave his place in the squad and shoot his remaining birds when there is a free place in another squad and when the jury has given permission. If the gun is repaired before the sequence on that stand is finished by his squad, the shooter may retake his place in the squad with the referee's permission.

13. (3.13) Should both barrels fire simultaneously (double discharge) due to a gun malfunction and not the shooter's error, the target, whether a single or the first of a double will be declared NO BIRD with nothing established and Rule 3.12 will apply.

14. (3.14) The cartridge shot load must not exceed 36 grams. The shot will be SPHERICAL and of diameter between 2.0 and 2.5 mm.

15. (3.15) The use of dispersers or any other unusual loading device is strictly forbidden (spreader or duplex loads are not allowed). Reloaded cartridges are not permitted.

16. (3.16) The mixing of various qualities and diameters of shots is strictly forbidden.

17. (3.17) The use of blackpowder and tracers is forbidden.

18. (3.18) Two cartridges may be used on each single target, but the shooter will only be allowed two cartridges for each double.

19. (3.19) In a double, if the two targets are broken by one shot, they will be scored KILL AND KILL.

20. (3.20) The referee may, at any time, remove unused cartridges from a shooter's gun for inspection.

D. DRESS AND RULES OF CONDUCT (Chapter 4)

1. (4.01) Participants in competitions must be correctly dressed. *Diminutive shorts are not allowed; only long shorts (Bermuda style ending no higher than a maximum of 5 cm above the knee) are acceptable. Shirts must be worn and should have at least short sleeves and a collar (round neck tee-shirt style is permitted). The wearing of sandals is not allowed for reasons of safety.* The shooter's number must be worn in its entirety and the whole of the number must be visible. Any failure to comply with these rules of conduct will be penalized by A REFEREE'S FIRST WARNING, which may be followed by penalties up to exclusion from the competition, following the jury's decision.

2. (4.02) A shooter may only fire on his proper turn and only when a target has been thrown, except when permitted by the referee (test firing).

3. (4.03) It is forbidden to aim or shoot at other shooters' targets.

4. (4.04) It is also forbidden to aim or shoot intentionally at living animals.

5. (4.05) No pretense of shooting is permitted on the shooting stand or outside it.

6. (4.06) If a shooter, on the shooting stand, before saying READY, makes a pretense of shooting, or involuntarily fires a shot, the referee is obliged to issue a WARNING to the shooter. After two warnings, any further occurrence will be scored ZERO for the next target hit.

7. (4.07) When his name is called, the shooter must be ready to shoot immediately and he must have with him sufficient ammunition and equipment for that stand.

8. (4.08) In no case must a shooter move to a stand before the preceding shooter has left it, and it is his turn to shoot.

9. (4.09) The shooter is allowed to load his gun only when on the stand where he has taken his place, his gun always pointing down the range and only when the referee has authorized him to start shooting.

10. (4.10) Semi-automatic guns must only be loaded with a maximum of two cartridges.

11. (4.11) The shooter must not turn around or leave the shooting stand before he has broken his gun and removed the cartridges from the chambers, whether they have been fired or not.

12. (4.12) During the presentation of targets or when shooting is temporarily interrupted, the shooter must open and unload his gun. It shall only be closed when authorized by the referee.

13. (4.13) In the case of a misfire or any other malfunction of the gun or ammunition, the shooter must remain in his place, the gun pointing safely down the range, not broken, and without touching the safety catch until the referee has examined the gun.

14. (4.14) Shooting must proceed without interruption, shooters being allowed to pronounce only the necessary words of command READY, PULL, GO or another command and to answer the referee's questions.

15. (4.15) If a member of the jury observes anything that is not according to the rules, he must inform the referee. If the referee is unable to take the immediate necessary action, he must inform the jury.

E. REFEREE (Chapter 5)

1. (5.01) The referees must have been approved by the jury before the competition. In the case of a large number of referees not being fully qualified or experienced, they must be supervised by international referees.

2. (5.02) A referee must have a wide experience of clay shooting and must possess a valid F.I.T.A.S.C. Referee's Certificate and his National Association's License. If this is not the case, the jury must agree to accept assistant referees.

3. (5.03) The referees must ensure order and proper conduct on the shooting stand and during shoot-offs.

4. (5.04) The referee alone shall make decisions. If a shooter disagrees with the referee, the objection must be made immediately on the shooting stand by raising the arm and saying PROTEST or APPEAL. The referee must then interrupt the shooting and pronounce his final decision.

5. (5.05) The shooter may appeal against the referee's decision. The objection must be made in writing to the jury, accompanied by a deposit of a certain sum in operation on the day of the competition and which will be returned only if the objection is upheld. If the jury finds the objection justified, it may give instructions to the referee concerning future judgments or name a new referee or, finally, alter the referee's decision. No dispute shall be concerned with whether a clay was hit or missed, nor whether the thrown clay was defective - in these cases, no appeal may be made against the referee's decision.

6. (5.06) When the competitor is ready to shoot, he shall say READY to the referee and the target must be thrown during a period which may vary between 0 and 3 seconds after the referee has passed on the shooter's command to the pullers.

7. (5.07) The referee must pass on the shooter's command to the pullers in the shortest time possible.

8. (5.08) In exceptional circumstances, the referee may suspend the shooting if there is sudden heavy rain or a violent storm that appears to be of short duration. However, he must inform the jury if it looks likely that this interruption will last any length of time.

9. (5.09) In no circumstances is it permitted to pick up a target to see if it has been hit or not.

F. SINGLE BIRDS – HIT OR MISSED (Chapter 6)

THE TARGET IS DECLARED "KILLED" WHEN:

1. (6.01) It has been launched and the shooter has fired according to the rules and when at least one visible piece of it is broken off or is totally or partially destroyed. This applies equally to FLASH clays.

THE TARGET IS DECLARED "ZERO" (missed):

2. (6.02) If it is not hit and no piece is broken off or if only dust is raised (dusted bird).

3. (6.03) If the shooter is unable to fire because he has left the safety catch on, has forgotten to load or cock it, if the gun has not been sufficiently broken or closed or if the shooter has forgotten to take the necessary measures to load the cartridge into the chamber when he is using a semi-automatic gun.

4. (6.04) If there is a third malfunction of the gun during the same round: Article 3.12 will apply.

5. (6.05) If the shooter is unable to fire his SECOND shot because he has not loaded the second cartridge or he has not canceled the locking device of the loading chamber in a semi-automatic weapon or for any other reason.

6. (6.06) If the second shot cannot be fired because the shooter, using a single-trigger gun, has not released it sufficiently after firing the first shot.

7. (6.07) If the shooter, in the case of malfunction of his gun, opens it himself or touches the safety catch before the referee has examined the gun.

8. (6.08) If the shooter adopts a ready position that is not according to Articles 1.05, 1.07 and 1.11 and if he has already been warned once during the same round.

G. SINGLE CLAYS NO BIRD (Chapter 7)

1. (7.01) The target will be declared NO BIRD and a new target will be launched, whether the shooter has fired or not:

a. If the bird is thrown broken.

b. If the bird is thrown from the wrong trap.

c. If for a single bird two clays are launched from traps on the same shooting stand.

d. On a rabbit, if the clay breaks after being launched and missed by the first shot but before the second shot has been fired, the rabbit will be declared "NO BIRD". A new target will be launched, the shooter must miss with his first shot, and the result of the second shot scored. Although "rabbit" is specifically mentioned, this rule, in some instances, may apply to other targets that are prematurely terminated.

2. (7.02) If the target is definitely of another color from that of the other targets used on the same trajectory of the same stand.

3. (7.03) If the target is thrown before the shooter has called READY.

4. (7.04) If the target is thrown after a delay of more than 3 seconds after the referee's command.

5. (7.05) If the trajectory is judged irregular by the referee.

6. (7.06) If, when a semi-automatic gun is being used, the ejection of the first cartridge impedes the loading of the second cartridge (in this case, when the target is thrown again, the first shot shall be directed near the target but must not hit it, and the result of second shot only shall be scored).

7. (7.07) If there is a fault on the first shot as a result of failure of the cartridge or malfunction of the gun not attributable to the shooter and if the shooter does not fire his second shot. IF THE SHOOTER FIRES THE SECOND SHOT, THE RESULT WILL BE SCORED.

8. (7.08) The referee may also declare a target NO BIRD when the shooter has clearly been disturbed.

9. (7.09) When another competitor shoots at the same target.

10. (7.10) When the referee, for any reason, cannot decide if a target has been hit or missed.

11. (7.11) All targets NOT declared NO BIRD by the referee, must be shot at. However, the referee may declare NO BIRD after the target(s) have been shot at (as in the case of a fast or slow pull or irregular trajectory).

12. (7.12) In the case of a cartridge misfire or malfunction of the gun not attributable to the shooter, a target will be declared NO BIRD and a new clay will be thrown. After two misfires or two malfunctions of the weapon in the same stage (whether the shooter has changed his gun or not), further incident or incidents will be declared ZERO. (See article 3.12)

H. DOUBLE ON REPORT (Chapter 8)

DEFINITION OF DOUBLES "ON THE GUN" (Report Pairs)

1. (8.01) Two targets from one or two different traps, the second clay being launched within a period of 0 to 3 seconds after the first clay has been shot at.

NO BIRD SHALL BE DECLARED:

2. (8.02) If two targets are launched simultaneously.

3. (8.03) When a shooter does not fire, without legitimate reason, at his first target. The second target cannot be thrown (because there is no first shot); the double will be declared ZERO/NO BIRD, and a second double will be thrown to determine the result of the second shot only.

4. (8.04) If the clay is not thrown by the correct trap.

5. (8.05) If the first target is regular and the second irregular, (however, the result of the first target shall be scored KILL OR ZERO as the case may be).

6. (8.06) The double will be declared NO BIRD and the shooter will be asked to fire a second double to determine the scores of both shots:

a. Violation of article 1.05, ready position for the first target (1.07 & 1.08).

b. If during a double, the two shots are fired simultaneously due to a gun malfunction, even if the first bird was broken (See articles 3.12 & 3.13).

c. If the shooter fires his gun involuntarily on the shooting stand, whether whilst loading or because of a mishap before saying READY.

7. (8.07) In a double, when the second target is irregular, a NO BIRD shall be declared and the double must be attempted again, but the result of the first target will be recorded. The shooter will not have the chance to repeat the first target if it was declared ZERO but must still shoot at it.

a. If the shooter misses his first clay, and this clay hits the second one, before the second shot.

b. If pieces from the first clay hit and break the second one before the second shot.

c. If during a double, the second shot cannot be fired because of the malfunction of gun or ammunition, articles 3.12 & 3.13.

8. (8.08) If a malfunction of the gun or cartridge prevents the shooter from shooting his first bird, articles 3.12 & 3.13 will apply.

9. (8.09) If the shooter does not shoot in his proper turn, he will receive a WARNING; at the third incident on the same layout, the target will be declared ZERO FOR A SINGLE CLAY or ZERO/NO BIRD IF IT IS A DOUBLE ON REPORT or ZERO/ZERO IF IT IS A SIMULTANEOUS DOUBLE OR RAFALE DOUBLE.

10. (8.10) The rules of articles 6.01 to 7.12 ARE APPLICABLE TO THE FIRING OF DOUBLES ON REPORT.

I. DOUBLE ON REPORT - DECLARED KILL (Chapter 9)

ZERO AND ZERO/KILL OR ZERO/ZERO

1. (9.01) If the shooter, without legitimate reason, does not shoot at the second target of a regular double, the result of the first target shall be recorded and the second declared ZERO.

2. (9.02) The target will be declared ZERO on the third malfunction of the gun or cartridge in the same round – see articles 3.12 & 3.13.

3. (9.03) When a shooter in a double fires both shots at the same target. The result shall be scored, and the second target of the double be declared ZERO.

4. (9.04) The rules of articles 6.01 to 7.12 are applicable to the shooting of doubles.

J. SIMULTANEOUS DOUBLE (Chapter 10)

1. (10.01) There are two targets thrown at the same time by one or two traps.

2. (10.02) In a simultaneous double, NO SCORE shall be recorded if either target has been declared NO BIRD.

3. (10.03) May be broken by a single shot and scored KILL/KILL.

4. (10.04) The targets may be shot in any order.

5. (10.05) Without any legitimate reason, the shooter does not shoot a regular double, both clays will be ZERO (VI-H-3).

SIMULTANEOUS DOUBLE NO BIRD

6. (10.06) The double will be declared NO BIRD and the shooter will be asked to shoot a second double to determine the results of both shots:

a. If the target(s) break on being thrown;

b. If the target(s) are not thrown by the correct trap;

c. If the target(s) are clearly a different color from those used for the same double;

d. If the target(s) are thrown before the shooter has called READY;

e. If the double is thrown more than 3 seconds after the referee's command;

f. If one of the trajectories of the doubles is judged irregular by the referee;

g. If the shooter misses his first target and it collides with the second before the shooter has fired his second shot;

h. If the fragments of the first target breaks the second before the shooter has fired his second shot;

i. Violation of articles 1.05 & 1.06, ready position for the first target (1.07 & 1.08);

j. A malfunction of the gun or cartridge prevents the shooter from shooting his first target(s) (see also 3.12 & 3.13);

k. If in a double the second shot cannot be fired simultaneously due to gun malfunction, the double is NO BIRD and must be repeated (see also 3.12 & 3.13);

l. If, during a double, the two shots are fired simultaneously due to gun malfunction, the double is NO BIRD and must be repeated (see also 3.12 & 3.13);

m. If the shooter involuntarily fires his gun on the shooting stand, whether while loading or because of a mishap before calling READY.

7. (10.07) The rules of articles 6.02 to 6.08 ARE APPLICABLE TO THE SHOOTING OF SIMULTANEOUS DOUBLES.

K. RAFALE DOUBLES (Chapter 11)

DEFINITION OF A RAFALE DOUBLE (following pair)

1. (11.01) Two targets are thrown from the same trap on the same trajectory.

2. (11.02) Two cartridges may be fired at the same target.

3. (11.03) They may be fired at in any order by the shooter.

4. (11.04) In a rafale double, NO SCORE IS OBTAINED in the case of a NO BIRD on one of the targets.

5. (11.05) All the rules relating to a simultaneous double are applicable to a rafale double, that is articles 10.04 to 10.06.

6. (11.06) Also rules of articles 6.02 to 6.08 ARE APPLICABLE TO THE SHOOTING OF RAFALE DOUBLES.

L. PENALTIES (Chapter 12)

1. (12.01) All shooters are required to acquaint themselves with the current regulations that apply to shooting under PARCOURS DE CHASSE rules. By taking part in competitions, they accept the penalties and other consequences resulting from violation of the rules and referees' orders.

2. (12.02) Deliberate violation of the rules will, in the first place, incur a warning from the referee or jury. In the case of further or more serious offenses, the jury may penalize the shooter with a lost bird and, in more serious cases, exclude him from the round and or competition.

3. (12.03) In the case of a jury being aware that the competitor has intentionally delayed the shooting or that he has acted in a dishonorable manner, it may give him a warning or penalize him one bird or disqualify him from the competition.

M. SHOOT-OFF (Chapter 13)

1. (13.01) In the case of a shoot-off, if the time allows, a new layout may be set up by the jury.

2. (13.02) Shoot-offs for the first three places (Individual or National teams) will take place in a round of 25 targets. If a result has not been established, the shooters will shoot a second "zero eliminator" (sudden death) round, i.e. the first target on which scores differ, the shooter with a ZERO will be eliminated, until only the winner remains. Other shooters with the same score will show as "drawn".

3. (13.03) Shooting will be carried out in accordance with the preceding rules; the empty places in the squad will not be filled.

4. (13.04) When the shoot-off is not carried out at a previously announced time, the shooters concerned must remain in contact with the committee in order to be ready to shoot within 15 MINUTES after being called.

5. (13.05) Shooters not present at the start of the shoot-off will be declared "scratched".

6. (13.06) The jury may, in exceptional circumstances, decide that the shoot-off should be carried over to the following day. Shooters not present in this case shall be considered "scratched".

N. SCORE SHEET (Chapter 14)

1. (14.01) The score sheet will be held by the referee or under his responsibility to someone selected by himself. Every referee will use a different color pen on the same layout or on the same shooting line.

2. (14.02) Only clays ZERO will be notified on the score sheet. Every clay ZERO will be written down in order from left to right on the score sheet. Clays will be numbered in shooting order.

Example = station n°1

Clay n°1, n°2, n°3, n°4, Double n°5 and n°6

Example = station n°2

Clay n°1, n°2, n°3, Double n°4 and n°5, Double n°6 and n°7

To allow a further control, the number of the clay ZERO will be written in the corresponding space of the score sheet.

O. GLOSSARY

1. SQUAD: Group of 6 competitors shooting at the same time on the same layout.

2. ROUND: A round consists of 25 clays thrown from the same layout.

3. TRAP: Machine or device for throwing the clay.

4. SHOT: Firing of a cartridge.

5. CLAY: Clay pigeon or target.

6. TRAJECTORY: The line of flight of the clay through the air.

RULES APPROVED BY THE TECHNICAL COMMISSION SPORTING 2ND NOVEMBER 1996.

VII. AWARDS AND RECOGNITION

A. ALL-AMERICAN

1. NSCA annually recognizes up to three All-American teams in each of the six categories, depending upon the number of members who qualify based on the following criteria:

Open Team—Minimum 1200 registered targets.

Lady, Veteran and Super Veteran Teams—Minimum 1000 registered targets.

Junior and Sub-Junior Teams—Minimum 800 registered targets.

2. Mandatory attendance is a requirement at the National Sporting Clays Championship (participating in the Main Event) for all categories.

3. Performance in U.S. Open, Zone, State and Major shoots will be applied as additional criteria for All-American qualification.

4. To be eligible for the All-American team, you must be a citizen of the United States and be eligible for a U.S. passport.

B. NSCA ALL-STATE TEAM

NSCA will annually select an NSCA All-State Team for each state in order to recognize more shooters for their shooting ability. Selection is based on the following criteria:

1. Team consists of 17 All -State members as follows:

Five from Open = 5

One person from each class = 7

One person from each concurrent = 5

2. Persons who have been selected for an All-American Team would be ineligible in order to recognize an entire new category of shooters.

3. A minimum number of 500 registered targets must be shot annually within the home state by each individual.

4. Mandatory participation is required at the State Championship for all categories. If there was not a state championship, no team will be selected for that state.

5. NSCA All- State Teams may be in addition to any team that may have been selected by the State Association.

6. Team selection priority: Open, concurrent, then class.

7. Selection is based on wins, state-shoot score and total shoot performance.

8. Team selection for each class is based on a shooter's beginning year class.

9. To be eligible for the Open team, shooters must have attained "AA" classification by yearend.

10. End-of-year residence determines state status.

C. TARGET PARTICIPATION PIN

An annual target participation pin provided to recognize shooters who have shot 1000 or more targets during the year.

D. TEAM USA (F.I.T.A.S.C.)

Four teams will be selected for Team USA (F.I.T.A.S.C.) – Senior (Open), Lady, Junior* and Veteran*.

MINIMUM CRITERIA FOR ANNUAL TEAM USA SELECTION:

1. Must be a U.S. citizen. A U.S. citizen is defined as anyone who is eligible for a U.S. passport.

2. Must shoot a minimum of 500 registered F.I.T.A.S.C. targets.

3. Qualification tournaments, of which a shooter must attend five (5), will be printed in *Sporting Clays Magazine* in "Headlines From Headquarters".

4. F.I.T.A.S.C. experience and performance will be the deciding criteria.

5. Consideration will be given to international performance not captured by the NSCA system, provided that the results are submitted to NSCA Headquarters along with the appropriate daily fees.

*Concurrent Eligibility for Team USA (F.I.T.A.S.C.): The NSCA International Committee will select individuals to Team USA (F.I.T.A.S.C.) using international concurrent rules.

Junior—a shooter who is less than 21 years of age and who will not have their 21st birthday during the year of the competition.

Veteran—a shooter who had their 55th birthday the year before the competition and who is less than 66 years of age the year of the competition.

Super Veteran—a shooter who had their 65th birthday the year before the competition.

E. MASTERS PIN

A pin sent to those shooters who have "earned" their way into "Master Class," honoring their accomplishment.

VIII. CERTIFIED INSTRUCTORS PROGRAM

Members who have participated in and passed an NSCA Instructor Certification Course. There are *four* levels of Instructor Certification available: Youth Coach, Level I, II and III. Levels I-III must be taken in sequence. Youth Coach—teaching beginner and novice in organized youth programs.

Level I—teaching beginner to novice, Level II—teaching intermediates, and Level III—for advanced teachers. It takes a minimum of four (4) years and over 1700 hours of teaching to complete the certification program.

IX. NONPAYMENT PENALTIES

A. CLUBS

1. Failure to fulfill the reporting and payment requirements shall carry the following penalties:

a. Cancellation of all subsequent shoot dates for the offending club.

b. Denial of right to apply or reapply for any further registered shoot dates for a period of thirty (30) days in case of first offense, or ninety (90) days in case of second or subsequent offense or until obligations have been met.

c. Owners, officers and managers of any delinquent club may be barred from shooting registered targets and from all functions of the NSCA either certified, elected or appointed (for example but not limited to: Advisory Council positions, National Delegate positions, Zone Delegate, Certified Instructor) until which time as written verification is provided that all required obligations of said club are met to the shooters and NSCA.

2. Club membership may be suspended for any member club who fails to pay for goods or services ordered from NSCA or who gives to NSCA a check that is returned for insufficient funds or other cause. Membership may be reinstated upon receipt in full of the outstanding balance and any penalties incurred, such as bank charges, as a result of the incident.

3. Nothing in this section shall affect, modify or overrule the provisions in Section I-B-4 or the rights and powers of the NSCA as set forth therein.

B. INDIVIDUALS

1. Members may be suspended for failing to pay for goods or services ordered from NSCA or who give to NSCA a check that is returned for insufficient funds or other cause. Members may be reinstated upon receipt in full of the outstanding balance and any fees incurred, such as bank charges, as a result of the incident.

2. Nothing in this section shall affect, modify or overrule the provisions in Section I-B-4 or the rights and powers of the NSCA as set forth therein.

SHOTGUNS — Autoloaders

Includes a wide variety of sporting guns and guns suitable for various competitions.

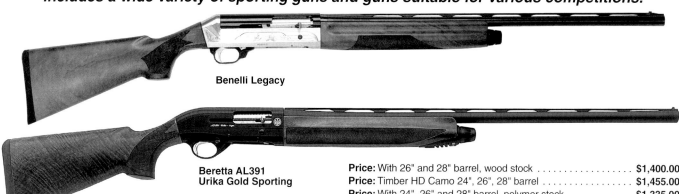

Benelli Legacy

Beretta AL391
Urika Gold Sporting

AYA MODEL 4/53 SHOTGUNS
Gauge: 12, 16, 20, 28, 410. **Barrel:** 27" (28 and 410) or 28". **Weight:** To customer specifications. **Length:** To customer specifications. **Features:** Hammerless boxlock action; double triggers; light scroll engraving; automatic safety; straight grip oil finish walnut stock; checkered butt.
Price: **$2,795.00**

BENELLI LEGACY SHOTGUN
Gauge: 12, 20, 2-3/4" and 3" chamber. **Barrel:** 24", 26", 28" (Full, Mod., Imp. Cyl., Imp. Mod., cylinder choke tubes). Mid-bead sight. **Weight:** 5.8 to 7.4 lbs. **Length:** 49-5/8" overall (28" barrel). **Stock:** Select European walnut with satin finish. **Features:** Uses the rotating bolt inertia recoil operating system with a two-piece steel/aluminum etched receiver (bright on lower, blue upper). Drop adjustment kit allows the stock to be custom fitted without modifying the stock. Introduced 1998. Imported from Italy by Benelli USA, Corp.
Price: **$1,435.00**

Benelli Sport II Shotgun
Similar to the Legacy model except has dual tone blue/silver receiver, two carbon fiber interchangeable vent ribs, adjustable butt pad, adjustable buttstock, and functions with ultra-light target loads. Walnut stock with satin finish. Introduced 1997. Imported from Italy by Benelli USA.
Price: **$1,470.00**

BENELLI M2 FIELD SHOTGUNS
Gauge: 12 ga. **Barrel:** 21", 24", 26", 28". **Weight:** 6 lbs., 9 oz. to 7 lbs., 2 oz. **Length:** 14-3/8" overall. **Stock:** Synthetic, Advantage® Max-4 HD™, Advantage® Timber HD™. **Sights:** Red bar. **Features:** Uses the Inertia Driven™ bolt mechanism. Vent rib. Comes with set of five choke tubes. Imported from Italy by Benelli USA.
Price: Timber HD **$1,165.00**
Price: 24" rifled barrel Synthetic **$1,165.00**
Price: 24" rifled barrel Timber HD **$1,165.00**

BENELLI MONTEFELTRO SHOTGUNS
Gauge: 12 and 20 ga. Full, Imp. Mod, Mod., Imp. Cyl. choke tubes. **Barrel:** 24", 26", 28". **Weight:** 6.8 to 7.1 lbs. **Stock:** Checkered walnut with satin finish. **Length:** 14-3/8" overall. **Features:** Uses the Montefeltro rotating bolt system with a simple inertia recoil design. Finish is blue. Introduced 1987.
Price: 24", 26", 28" **$1,070.00**
Price: Left-hand, 26" **$1,080.00**
Price: Grade I, 26" **$1,070.00**
Price: Short stock model **$1,080.00**

BENELLI SUPER BLACK EAGLE II SHOTGUNS
Gauge: 12, 3-1/2" chamber. **Barrel:** 24", 26", 28" (Cyl. Imp. Cyl., Mod., Imp. Mod., Full choke tubes). **Weight:** 7 lbs., 5 oz. **Length:** 49-5/8" overall (28" barrel). **Stock:** European walnut with satin finish, or polymer. Adjustable for drop. **Sights:** Red bar front. **Features:** Uses Montefeltro inertia recoil bolt system. Fires all 12 gauge shells from 2-3/4" to 3-1/2" magnums, vent rib. Introduced 1991. Imported from Italy by Benelli USA.

Price: With 26" and 28" barrel, wood stock **$1,400.00**
Price: Timber HD Camo 24", 26", 28" barrel **$1,455.00**
Price: With 24", 26" and 28" barrel, polymer stock **$1,335.00**
Price: Left-hand, 24", 26", 28", polymer stock **$1,455.00**
Price: Steadygrip Turkey Gun **$1,535.00**

Benelli Super Black Eagle Slug Guns
Similar to the Benelli Super Black Eagle except has 24" rifled barrel with 2-3/4" and 3" chamber, drilled and tapped for scope. Uses the inertia recoil bolt system. Matte finish receiver. Weight is 7.5 lbs., overall length 45.5". Wood or polymer stocks available. Introduced 1992. Imported from Italy by Benelli USA.
Price: With polymer stock **$1,465.00**
Price: 24" barrel, Timber HD camo **$1,585.00**
Price: W/ComforTech stock **$1,035.00**

BENELLI CORDOBA HIGH-VOLUME SHOTGUN
Gauge: 12; 5-round magazine. **Barrel:** 28" and 30", ported, 10mm sporting rib. **Weight:** 7.2 lbs. **Length:** 49.6". **Features:** Designed for high-volume sporting clays and Argentina dove shooting. Inertia-driven action, CrioChokes, ComfortTech stock reduces felt recoil by 49 percent.
Price: **$1,600.00**

BERETTA AL391 TEKNYS SHOTGUNS
Gauge: 12, 20 gauge; 3" chamber, semi-auto. **Barrel:** 26", 28". **Weight:** 5.9 lbs. (20 ga.), 7.3 lbs. (12 ga.). **Length:** NA. **Stock:** X-tra wood (special process wood enhancement). **Features:** Flat 1/4 rib, TruGlo Tru-Bead sight, recoil reducer, stock spacers, overbored bbls., flush choke tubes. Comes with fitted, lined case.
Price: **$1,295.00**
Price: Teknys Gold (green enamel inlays, oil-finished walnut) . . . **$1,595.00**
Price: Teknys Gold Sporting (blue inlays, select walnut) **$1,995.00**

BERETTA AL391 URIKA AUTO SHOTGUNS
Gauge: 12, 20 gauge; 3" chamber. **Barrel:** 22", 24", 26", 28", 30"; five Mobilchoke choke tubes. **Weight:** 5.95 to 7.28 lbs. **Length:** Varies by model. **Stock:** Walnut, black or camo synthetic; shims, spacers and interchangeable recoil pads allow custom fit. **Features:** Self-compensating gas operation handles full range of loads; recoil reducer in receiver; enlarged trigger guard; reduced-weight receiver, barrel and forend; hard-chromed bore. Introduced 2000. Imported from Italy by Beretta USA.
Price: AL391 Urika (12 ga., 26", 28", 30" barrels) **$1,095.00**
Price: AL391 Urika (20 ga., 24", 26", 28" barrels) **$1,095.00**
Price: AL391 Urika Synthetic
(12 ga., 24", 26", 28", 30" barrels) **$1,095.00**
Price: AL391 Urika Camo. (12 ga., Realtree Hardwoods
or Max 4-HD) **$1,195.00**

Beretta AL391 Urika Gold and Gold Sporting Auto Shotguns
Similar to AL391 Urika except features deluxe wood, jewelled bolt and carrier, gold-inlaid receiver with black or silver finish. Introduced 2000. Imported from Italy by Beretta USA.
Price: AL391 Urika Gold Sporting
(12 or 20, black receiver, engraving) **$1,395.00**
Price: AL391 Urika Gold Sporting
(12 ga., silver receiver, engraving **$1,395.00**

SHOTGUNS — Autoloaders

Beretta AL391 Urika Sporting

Beretta A391 Xtrema2 3.5

Browning
Gold Deer Hunter

Browning Gold Fusion

Beretta AL391 Urika Sporting Auto Shotguns
Similar to AL391 Urika except has competition sporting stock with rounded rubber recoil pad, wide vent rib with white front and mid-rib beads, satin-black receiver with silver markings. Available in 12 and 20 gauge. Introduced 2000. Imported from Italy by Beretta USA.
Price: AL391 Urika Sporting. **$1,195.00**

Beretta AL391 Urika Trap Auto Shotguns
Similar to AL391 Urika except in 12 ga. only, has wide vent rib with white front and mid-rib beads, Monte Carlo stock and special trap recoil pad. Gold Trap features highly figured walnut stock and forend, gold-filled Beretta logo and signature on receiver. Optima bore and Optima choke tubes. Introduced 2000. Imported from Italy by Beretta USA.
Price: AL391 Urika Trap **$1,195.00**

Beretta AL391 Urika Parallel Target RL and SL Auto Shotguns
Similar to AL391 Urika except has parallel comb, Monte Carlo stock with tighter grip radius and stepped vent rib. SL model has same features but with 13.5" length of pull stock. Introduced 2000. Imported from Italy by Beretta USA.
Price: AL391 Urika Parallel Target RL **$1,195.00**
Price: AL391 Urika Parallel Target SL **$1,195.00**

Beretta AL391 Urika Youth Shotgun
Similar to AL391 Urika except has a 24" or 26" barrel with 13.5" stock for youths and smaller shooters. Introduced 2000. From Beretta USA.
Price: **$1,035.00**

BERETTA A391 XTREMA2 3.5 AUTO SHOTGUNS
Gauge: 12 ga. 3-1/2" chamber. **Barrel:** 24", 26", 28". **Weight:** 7.8 lbs. **Stock:** Synthetic. **Features:** Semi-auto goes with two-lug rotating bolt and self-compensating gas valve, extended tang, cross bolt safety, self-cleaning, with case.
Price: Synthetic **$1,295.00**
Price: Realtree Hardwood HD Camo and Max 4-HD **$1,495.00**

BROWNING GOLD HUNTER AUTO SHOTGUN
Gauge: 12, 3" or 3-1/2" chamber; 20, 3" chamber. **Barrel:** 12 ga.-26", 28", 30", Invector Plus choke tubes; 20 ga.-26", 30", Invector choke tubes. **Weight:** 7 lbs., 9 oz. (12 ga.), 6 lbs., 12 oz. (20 ga.). **Length:** 46-1/4" overall (20 ga., 26" barrel). **Stock:** 14"x1-1/2"x2-1/3"; select walnut with gloss finish; palm swell grip. **Features:** Self-regulating, self-cleaning gas system shoots all loads; lightweight receiver with special non-glare deep black finish; large reversible safety button; large rounded trigger guard, gold trigger. The 20 gauge has slightly smaller dimensions; 12 gauge have back-bored barrels, Invector Plus tube system. Introduced 1994. Imported by Browning.
Price: 12 or 20 gauge, 3" chamber. **$894.00**
Price: 12 ga., 3-1/2" chamber **$1,038.00**
Price: Extra barrels . . . . **$336.00 to $415.00**

Browning Gold Rifled Deer Hunter Auto Shotgun
Similar to the Gold Hunter except 12 or 20 gauge, 22" rifled barrel with cantilever scope mount, walnut stock with extra-thick recoil pad. Weighs 7 lbs., 12 oz., overall length 42-1/2". Sling swivel studs fitted on the magazine cap and butt. Introduced 1997. Imported by Browning.
Price: 12 gauge **$1,131.00**
Price: With Mossy Oak® Break-up camouflage **$1,218.00**
Price: 20 ga. (satin-finish walnut stock, 3" chamber) **$1,131.00**

Browning Gold Deer Stalker Shotgun
Similar to the Gold Deer Hunter except has black composite stock and forend, fully rifled barrel, cantilever scope mount. Introduced 1999. Imported by Browning.
Price: 12 gauge **$1,131.00**

Browning Gold Fusion Auto Shotgun
Similar to the Gold Hunter, 12 and 20 gauge with 26", 28" or 30" barrel; front HiViz Pro-Comp and center bead on tapered vent rib; ported and back-bored Invector Plus barrel; 2-3/4" chamber; satin-finished stock with solid, radiused recoil pad with hard heel insert; non-glare black alloy receiver, shim-adj. stock. Introduced 1996. Imported from Japan by Browning.
Price:. **$2,095.00**

SHOTGUNS — Autoloaders

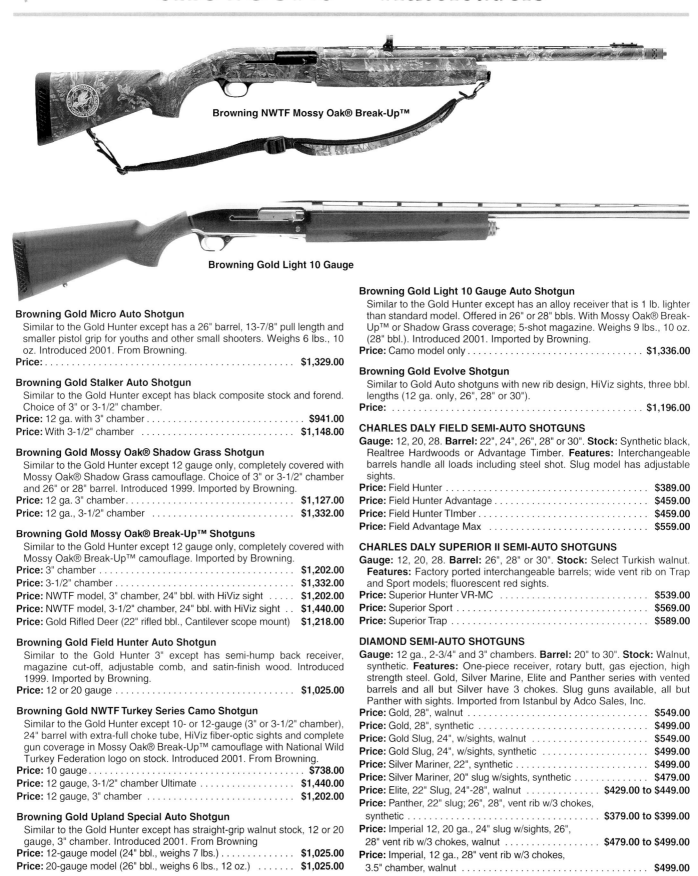

Browning NWTF Mossy Oak® Break-Up™

Browning Gold Light 10 Gauge

Browning Gold Micro Auto Shotgun

Similar to the Gold Hunter except has a 26" barrel, 13-7/8" pull length and smaller pistol grip for youths and other small shooters. Weighs 6 lbs., 10 oz. Introduced 2001. From Browning.
Price: **$1,329.00**

Browning Gold Stalker Auto Shotgun

Similar to the Gold Hunter except has black composite stock and forend. Choice of 3" or 3-1/2" chamber.
Price: 12 ga. with 3" chamber **$941.00**
Price: With 3-1/2" chamber **$1,148.00**

Browning Gold Mossy Oak® Shadow Grass Shotgun

Similar to the Gold Hunter except 12 gauge only, completely covered with Mossy Oak® Shadow Grass camouflage. Choice of 3" or 3-1/2" chamber and 26" or 28" barrel. Introduced 1999. Imported by Browning.
Price: 12 ga. 3" chamber **$1,127.00**
Price: 12 ga., 3-1/2" chamber **$1,332.00**

Browning Gold Mossy Oak® Break-Up™ Shotguns

Similar to the Gold Hunter except 12 gauge only, completely covered with Mossy Oak® Break-Up™ camouflage. Imported by Browning.
Price: 3" chamber **$1,202.00**
Price: 3-1/2" chamber **$1,332.00**
Price: NWTF model, 3" chamber, 24" bbl. with HiViz sight **$1,202.00**
Price: NWTF model, 3-1/2" chamber, 24" bbl. with HiViz sight .. **$1,440.00**
Price: Gold Rifled Deer (22" rifled bbl., Cantilever scope mount) **$1,218.00**

Browning Gold Field Hunter Auto Shotgun

Similar to the Gold Hunter 3" except has semi-hump back receiver, magazine cut-off, adjustable comb, and satin-finish wood. Introduced 1999. Imported by Browning.
Price: 12 or 20 gauge **$1,025.00**

Browning Gold NWTF Turkey Series Camo Shotgun

Similar to the Gold Hunter except 10- or 12-gauge (3" or 3-1/2" chamber), 24" barrel with extra-full choke tube, HiViz fiber-optic sights and complete gun coverage in Mossy Oak® Break-Up™ camouflage with National Wild Turkey Federation logo on stock. Introduced 2001. From Browning.
Price: 10 gauge **$738.00**
Price: 12 gauge, 3-1/2" chamber Ultimate **$1,440.00**
Price: 12 gauge, 3" chamber **$1,202.00**

Browning Gold Upland Special Auto Shotgun

Similar to the Gold Hunter except has straight-grip walnut stock, 12 or 20 gauge, 3" chamber. Introduced 2001. From Browning
Price: 12-gauge model (24" bbl., weighs 7 lbs.) **$1,025.00**
Price: 20-gauge model (26" bbl., weighs 6 lbs., 12 oz.) **$1,025.00**

Browning Gold Light 10 Gauge Auto Shotgun

Similar to the Gold Hunter except has an alloy receiver that is 1 lb. lighter than standard model. Offered in 26" or 28" bbls. With Mossy Oak® Break-Up™ or Shadow Grass coverage; 5-shot magazine. Weighs 9 lbs., 10 oz. (28" bbl.). Introduced 2001. Imported by Browning.
Price: Camo model only **$1,336.00**

Browning Gold Evolve Shotgun

Similar to Gold Auto shotguns with new rib design, HiViz sights, three bbl. lengths (12 ga. only, 26", 28" or 30").
Price: **$1,196.00**

CHARLES DALY FIELD SEMI-AUTO SHOTGUNS

Gauge: 12, 20, 28. **Barrel:** 22", 24", 26", 28" or 30". **Stock:** Synthetic black, Realtree Hardwoods or Advantage Timber. **Features:** Interchangeable barrels handle all loads including steel shot. Slug model has adjustable sights.
Price: Field Hunter **$389.00**
Price: Field Hunter Advantage **$459.00**
Price: Field Hunter TImber **$459.00**
Price: Field Advantage Max **$559.00**

CHARLES DALY SUPERIOR II SEMI-AUTO SHOTGUNS

Gauge: 12, 20, 28. **Barrel:** 26", 28" or 30". **Stock:** Select Turkish walnut. **Features:** Factory ported interchangeable barrels; wide vent rib on Trap and Sport models; fluorescent red sights.
Price: Superior Hunter VR-MC **$539.00**
Price: Superior Sport **$569.00**
Price: Superior Trap **$589.00**

DIAMOND SEMI-AUTO SHOTGUNS

Gauge: 12 ga., 2-3/4" and 3" chambers. **Barrel:** 20" to 30". **Stock:** Walnut, synthetic. **Features:** One-piece receiver, rotary butt, gas ejection, high strength steel. Gold, Silver Marine, Elite and Panther series with vented barrels and all but Silver have 3 chokes. Slug guns available, all but Panther with sights. Imported from Istanbul by Adco Sales, Inc.
Price: Gold, 28", walnut **$549.00**
Price: Gold, 28", synthetic **$499.00**
Price: Gold Slug, 24", w/sights, walnut **$549.00**
Price: Gold Slug, 24", w/sights, synthetic **$499.00**
Price: Silver Mariner, 22", synthetic **$499.00**
Price: Silver Mariner, 20" slug w/sights, synthetic **$479.00**
Price: Elite, 22" Slug, 24"-28", walnut .... **$429.00 to $449.00**
Price: Panther, 22" slug; 26", 28", vent rib w/3 chokes, synthetic .... **$379.00 to $399.00**
Price: Imperial 12, 20 ga., 24" slug w/sights, 26", 28" vent rib w/3 chokes, walnut .... **$479.00 to $499.00**
Price: Imperial, 12 ga., 28" vent rib w/3 chokes, 3.5" chamber, walnut **$499.00**

SHOTGUNS — Autoloaders

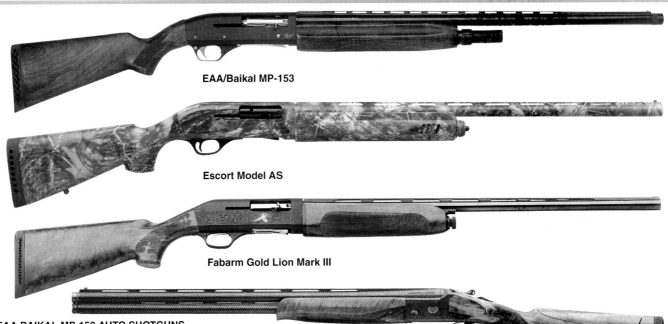

EAA/Baikal MP-153

Escort Model AS

Fabarm Gold Lion Mark III

Fabarm Sporting Clays Extra

EAA BAIKAL MP-153 AUTO SHOTGUNS
Gauge: 12, 3-1/2" chamber. **Barrel:** 24", 26", 28"; Imp., Mod. and Full choke tubes. **Weight:** 7.8 lbs. **Stock:** Walnut. **Features:** Gas-operated action with automatic gas-adjustment valve allows use of light and heavy loads interchangeably; 4-round magazine; rubber recoil pad. Introduced 2000. Imported by European American Armory.
Price: MP-153 (blued finish, walnut stock and forend) **$459.00**
Price: MP-153 (field grade, synthetic stock) **$349.00**

EAA SAIGA AUTO SHOTGUN
Gauge: 12, 20, .410, 3" chamber. **Barrel:** 19", 21", 24". **Weight:** 6.6 to 7.6 lbs. **Length:** 40" to 45". **Stock:** Synthetic. **Features:** Retains best features of the AK Rifle by Kalashnikov as the semi-auto shotgun. Magazine fed. Imported from Russia by EAA Corp.
Price: .410 ga. **$299.00**
Price: 20 ga. **$389.00**
Price: 12 ga. . . . . **$409.00 to $439.00**

ESCORT SEMI-AUTO SHOTGUNS
Gauge: 12, 20. **Barrel:** 22", 24", 26", 18" (AimGuard model); 3" chambers. **Weight:** 6 lbs, 4 0. to 7 lbs., 6 oz. **Stock:** Polymer, black, or camo finish; also Turkish walnut. **Features:** Black chrome finish; top of receiver dovetailed for sight mounting. Gold-plated trigger, trigger guard safety, magazine cut-off. Three choke tubes (IC, M, F — except AimGuard); 24" bbl. model comes with turkey choke tube. **Sights:** Optional HiViz Spark and TriViz fiber-optic sights. Introduced 2002. Camo model introduced 2003. Youth, Slug, Obsession Camo models introduced 2005. Imported from Turkey by Legacy Sports International.
Price: Model AS, walnut stock. **$421.00**
Price: Model PS, black polymer stock **$399.00**
Price: Camo polymer stock, Spark sight **$443.00**
Price: Camo, 24" bbl; 3.5 mag.; TriViz sight, turkey choke **$523.00**
Price: AimGuard, 18" bbl., black stock, cyl bore **$392.00**
Price: Waterfowl/turkey combo, camo, 2 bbls **$574.00**

FABARM GOLD LION MARK III AUTO SHOTGUN
Gauge: 12, 3" chamber. **Barrel:** 24", 26", 28", choke tubes. **Weight:** 7 lbs. **Length:** 45.5" overall. **Stock:** European walnut with gloss finish; olive wood grip cap. **Features:** TriBore barrel, reversible safety; gold-plated trigger and carrier release button; leather-covered rubber recoil pad. Introduced 1998. Imported from Italy by Heckler & Koch, Inc.
Price: **$939.00**

Fabarm Sporting Clays Extra Auto Shotgun
Similar to Gold Lion except 28" TriBore ported barrel with interchangeable colored front-sight beads, mid-rib bead, 10mm channeled vent rib, carbon-fiber finish, oil-finished walnut stock and forend with olive wood gripcap. Stock dimensions are 14.58"x1.58"x2.44". Distinctive gold-colored receiver logo. Available in 12 gauge only, 3" chamber. Introduced 1999. Imported from Italy by Heckler & Koch, Inc.
Price: **$1,249.00**

FRANCHI 48AL SHOTGUN
Gauge: 20 or 28, 2-3/4" chamber. **Barrel:** 24", 26", 28" (Full, Cyl., Mod., choke tubes). **Weight:** 5.5 lbs. (20 gauge). **Length:** 44" to 48". **Stock:** 14-1/4"x1-5/8"x2-1/2". Walnut with checkered grip and forend. **Features:** Long recoil-operated action. Chrome-lined bore; cross-bolt safety. Imported from Italy by Benelli USA.
Price: 20 ga. **$735.00**
Price: 28 ga. **$1,020.00**

Franchi 48AL Deluxe Shotgun
Similar to 48AL but with select walnut stock and forend and high-polish blue finish with gold trigger. Introduced 2000.
Price: (20 gauge, 26" barrel) **$970.00**
Price: (28 gauge, 26" barrel) **$990.00**

Franchi 48AL English Shotgun
Similar to 48AL Deluxe but with straight grip English-style stock. 20 ga., 28 ga., 26" bbl, ICMF tubes.
Price: 20 gauge **$970.00**
Price: 28 gauge **$1,020.00**

Franchi 48AL Short Stock Shotgun
Similar to 48AL but with stock shortened to 12-1/2" length of pull.
Price: (20 gauge, 26" barrel) **$735.00**

FRANCHI MODEL 912 SHOTGUNS
Gauge: 12. **Barrel:** 24", 26", 28", 30". **Weight:** 7.5 to 7.8 lbs. **Length:** 46" to 52". **Stock:** Satin walnut; synthetic. **Sights:** White bead front. **Features:** Chambered for 3-1/2" magnum shells with Dual-Recoil-Reduction-System, multi-lugged rotary bolt. Made in Italy and imported by Benelli USA.
Price: Walnut **$850.00**
Price: Synthetic **$790.00**
Price: Timber HD & Max-4 . . . . **$900.00**
Price: Steadygrip Timber HD **$850.00**

SHOTGUNS — Autoloaders

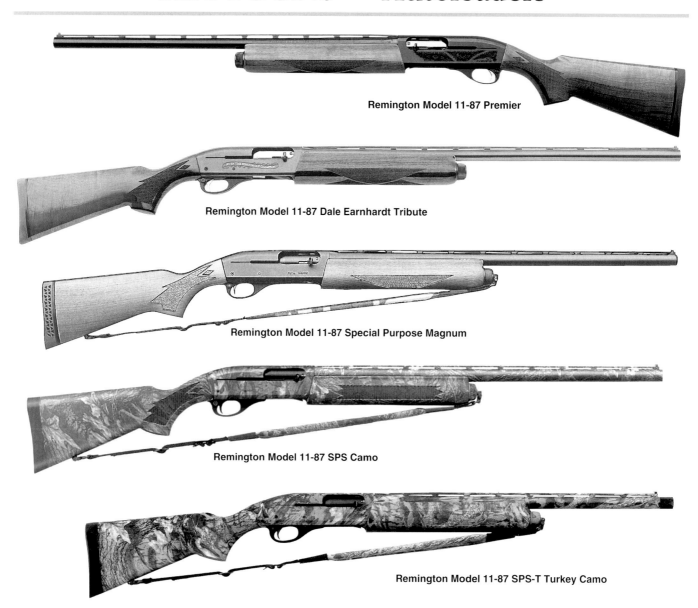

Remington Model 11-87 Premier

Remington Model 11-87 Dale Earnhardt Tribute

Remington Model 11-87 Special Purpose Magnum

Remington Model 11-87 SPS Camo

Remington Model 11-87 SPS-T Turkey Camo

FRANCHI RAPTOR SPORTING CLAYS SHOTGUN

Gauge: 12 and 20; 6-round capacity. **Barrel:** 30" (12 ga.) or 28" (20 ga.); ported; tapered target rib and bead front sight. **Weight:** 7.1 lbs. (Model 712) or 6.2 lbs. (Model 720). **Stock:** Walnut with WeatherCoat (impervious to weather). **Features:** Gas-operated, satin nickel receiver.
Price: $850.00

REMINGTON MODEL 11-87 PREMIER SHOTGUNS

Gauge: 12, 20, 3" chamber. **Barrel:** 26", 28", 30" RemChoke tubes. Light Contour barrel. **Weight:** About 7-3/4 lbs. **Length:** 46" overall (26" bbl.). **Stock:** Walnut with satin or high-gloss finish; cut checkering; solid brown buttpad; no white spacers. **Sights:** Bradley-type white-faced front, metal bead middle. **Features:** Pressure compensating gas system allows shooting 2-3/4" or 3" loads interchangeably with no adjustments. Stainless magazine tube; redesigned feed latch, barrel support ring on operating bars; pinned forend. Introduced 1987.
Price: Light contour barrel............................... $777.00
Price: Left-hand, 28" barrel $831.00
Price: Premier cantilever deer barrel, fully-rifled, 21" sling, swivels, Monte Carlo stock $859.00
Price: 3-1/2" Super Magnum, 28" barrel $865.00
Price: Dale Earnhardt Tribute, 12 ga., 28" barrel $972.00

Remington Model 11-87 Special Purpose Magnum

Similar to the 11-87 Premier except has dull stock finish, Parkerized exposed metal surfaces. Bolt and carrier have dull blackened coloring. Comes with 26" or 28" barrel with RemChokes, padded Cordura nylon sling and quick detachable swivels. Introduced 1987.
Price: With synthetic stock and forend (SPS) $791.00

Remington Model 11-87 SPS Special Purpose Synthetic Camo

Similar to the 11-87 Special Purpose Magnum except has synthetic stock and all metal (except bolt and trigger guard) and stock covered with Mossy Oak® Break-Up™ camo finish. In 12 gauge only, 26", RemChoke. Comes with camo sling, swivels. Introduced 1992.
Price: $925.00

Remington Model 11-87 SPS-T Turkey Camo

Similar to the 11-87 Special Purpose Magnum except with synthetic stock, 21" vent rib barrel with RemChoke tube. Completely covered with Mossy Oak® Break-Up™ Brown camouflage. Bolt body, trigger guard and recoil pad are non-reflective black.
Price:.. $905.00
Price: Model 11-87 SPS-T Camo CL cantilever................ $907.00

SHOTGUNS — Autoloaders

**Remington Model 11-87
SPS-T Synthetic Camo**

Remington Model 11-87 SPS-Deer

Remington Model 11-87 SPS Cantilever

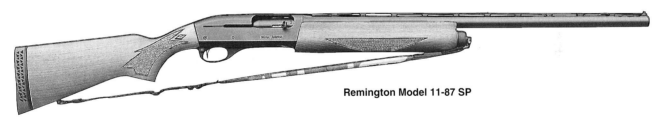

Remington Model 11-87 SP

Remington Model 11-87 SPS-T Super Magnum Synthetic Camo Shotguns
Similar to the 11-87 SPS-T Turkey Camo except has 23" vent rib barrel with Turkey Super full choke tube, chambered for 12 ga., 3-1/2", TruGlo rifle sights. Version available without TruGlo sights. Introduced 2001.
Price: **$963.00**

Remington Model 11-87 SPS-Deer Shotgun
Similar to the 11-87 Special Purpose Camo except has fully-rifled 21" barrel with rifle sights, black non-reflective, synthetic stock and forend, black carrying sling. Introduced 1993.
Price: **$824.00**
Price: With wood stock (Model 11-87 SP Deer Gun) RemChoke, 21" barrel w/rifle sights. **$756.00**

Remington Model 11-87 SPS Cantilever Shotgun
Similar to the 11-87 SPS except has fully rifled barrel; synthetic stock with Monte Carlo comb; cantilever scope mount deer barrel. Comes with sling and swivels. Introduced 1994.
Price: **$872.00**

Remington Model 11-87 SP and SPS Super Magnum Shotguns
Similar to Model 11-87 Special Purpose Magnum except has 3-1/2" chamber. Available in flat finish American walnut or black synthetic stock,

26" or 28" black matte finished barrel and receiver; Imp. Cyl., Modified and Full RemChoke tubes. Overall length 45-3/4", weighs 8 lbs., 2 oz. Introduced 2000. From Remington Arms Co.
Price: 11-87 SP Super Magnum (walnut stock) **$865.00**
Price: 11-87 SPS Super Magnum (synthetic stock) **$879.00**
Price: 11-87 SPS Super Magnum, 28" (camo) **$963.00**

Remington Model 11-87 Upland Special Shotgun
Similar to 11-87 Premier except has 23" vent rib barrel with straight grip, English-style walnut stock. Available in 12 or 20 gauge. Overall length 43-1/2", weighs 7-1/4 lbs. (6-1/2 lbs. in 20 ga.). Comes with Imp. Cyl., Modified and Full choke tubes. Introduced 2000.
Price: 12 or 20 gauge **$777.00**

REMINGTON MODEL 1100 SYNTHETIC LT-20 SHOTGUN
Gauge: 20. **Barrel:** 26" RemChokes. **Weight:** 6-3/4 lbs. **Stock:** 14"x1-1/2"x2-1/2". Black synthetic, checkered pistol grip and forend. **Features:** Matted receiver top with scroll work on both sides of receiver.
Price: **$549.00**
Price: Youth Gun LT-20 (21" RemChoke) **$549.00**
Price: Remington Model 1100 Synthetic, 12 gauge, black synthetic stock; vent rib 28" barrel, Mod. RemChoke tube. Weighs about 7-1/2 lbs. Introduced 1996 . . . . **$549.00**

SHOTGUNS — Autoloaders

Remington Model 1100 Youth Turkey Camo

Remington 1100 LT-20 Deer

Remington Model 1100 Sporting 28

Remington Model 1100 Classic Trap

Remington Model 1100 Sporting 12

Remington Model SP-10

Remington Model 1100 Youth Synthetic Turkey Camo Shotgun

Similar to the Model 1100 LT-20 except has 1" shorter stock, 21" vent rib barrel with Full RemChoke tube; 3" chamber; synthetic stock and forend are covered with Skyline Excel camo, and barrel and receiver have non-reflective, black matte finish. Introduced 2003.
Price: $612.00

Remington Model 1100 LT-20 Synthetic Deer Shotgun

Similar to the Model 1100 LT-20 except has 21" fully rifled barrel with rifle sights, 2-3/4" chamber, and fiberglass reinforced synthetic stock. Introduced 1997. Made in U.S. by Remington.
Price: $583.00

Remington Model 1100 Sporting 28 Shotgun

Similar to the 1100 LT-20 except in 28 gauge with 25" barrel; comes with skeet, Imp. Cyl., Light Mod., Mod. RemChoke tube. Semi-fancy walnut with gloss finish, Sporting rubber butt pad. Made in U.S. by Remington. Introduced 1996.
Price: $901.00

Remington Model 1100 Sporting 20 Shotgun

Similar to Model 1100 LT-20 except tournament-grade American walnut stock with gloss finish and sporting style recoil pad, 28" RemChoke barrel for skeet, Imp. Cyl., Light Modified and Modified. Introduced 1998.
Price: $868.00

Remington Model 1100 Classic Trap Shotgun

Similar to Standard Model 1100 except 12 gauge with 30", low-profile barrel, semi-fancy American walnut stock, high-polish blued receiver with engraving and gold eagle inlay. Singles, mid handicap and long handicap choke tubes. Overall length 50-1/2", weighs 8 lbs., 4 oz. Introduced 2000. From Remington Arms Co.
Price: $895.00

Remington Model 1100 Sporting 12 Shotgun

Similar to Model 1100 Sporting 20 Shotgun except in 12 gauge, 28" ventilated barrel with semi-fancy American walnut stock, gold-plated trigger. Overall length 49", weighs 8 lbs. Introduced 2000. From Remington Arms Co.
Price: $901.00

SHOTGUNS — Autoloaders

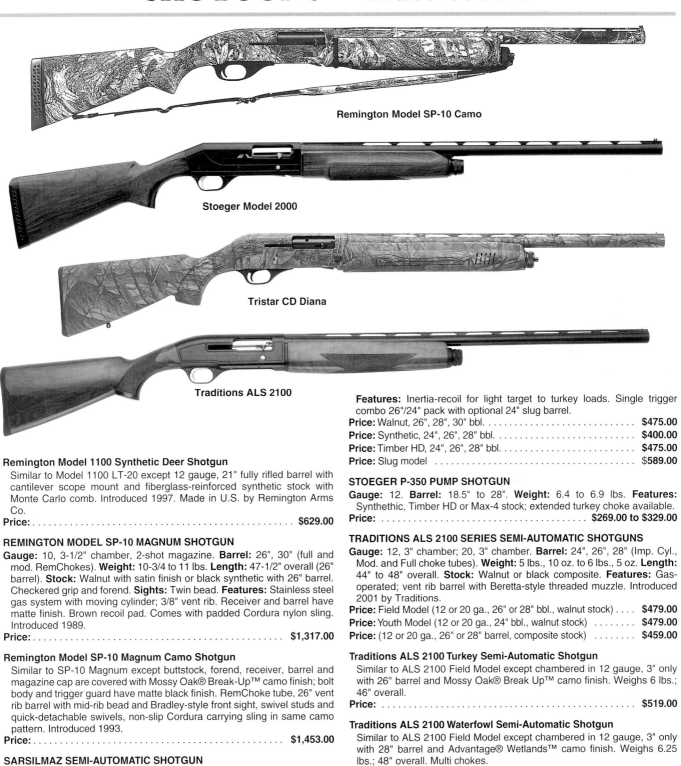

Remington Model SP-10 Camo

Stoeger Model 2000

Tristar CD Diana

Traditions ALS 2100

Remington Model 1100 Synthetic Deer Shotgun
Similar to Model 1100 LT-20 except 12 gauge, 21" fully rifled barrel with cantilever scope mount and fiberglass-reinforced synthetic stock with Monte Carlo comb. Introduced 1997. Made in U.S. by Remington Arms Co.
Price: **$629.00**

REMINGTON MODEL SP-10 MAGNUM SHOTGUN
Gauge: 10, 3-1/2" chamber, 2-shot magazine. **Barrel:** 26", 30" (full and mod. RemChokes). **Weight:** 10-3/4 to 11 lbs. **Length:** 47-1/2" overall (26" barrel). **Stock:** Walnut with satin finish or black synthetic with 26" barrel. Checkered grip and forend. **Sights:** Twin bead. **Features:** Stainless steel gas system with moving cylinder; 3/8" vent rib. Receiver and barrel have matte finish. Brown recoil pad. Comes with padded Cordura nylon sling. Introduced 1989.
Price: **$1,317.00**

Remington Model SP-10 Magnum Camo Shotgun
Similar to SP-10 Magnum except buttstock, forend, receiver, barrel and magazine cap are covered with Mossy Oak® Break-Up™ camo finish; bolt body and trigger guard have matte black finish. RemChoke tube, 26" vent rib barrel with mid-rib bead and Bradley-style front sight, swivel studs and quick-detachable swivels, non-slip Cordura carrying sling in same camo pattern. Introduced 1993.
Price: **$1,453.00**

SARSILMAZ SEMI-AUTOMATIC SHOTGUN
Gauge: 12, 3" chamber. **Barrel:** 26" or 28"; fixed chokes. **Stock:** Walnut or synthetic. **Features:** Handles 2-3/4" or 3" magnum loads. Introduced 2000. Imported from Turkey by Armsport Inc.
Price: With walnut stock **$969.95**
Price: With synthetic stock **$919.95**

STOEGER MODEL 2000 SHOTGUNS
Gauge: 12, 3" chamber, set of five choke tubes. **Barrel:** 24", 26", 28", 30". **Stock:** Walnut, deluxe, synthetic, and Timber HD. **Sights:** White bar.

Features: Inertia-recoil for light target to turkey loads. Single trigger combo 26"/24" pack with optional 24" slug barrel.
Price: Walnut, 26", 28", 30" bbl. **$475.00**
Price: Synthetic, 24", 26", 28" bbl. **$400.00**
Price: Timber HD, 24", 26", 28" bbl. **$475.00**
Price: Slug model **$589.00**

STOEGER P-350 PUMP SHOTGUN
Gauge: 12. **Barrel:** 18.5" to 28". **Weight:** 6.4 to 6.9 lbs. **Features:** Synthethic, Timber HD or Max-4 stock; extended turkey choke available.
Price: . . . . **$269.00 to $329.00**

TRADITIONS ALS 2100 SERIES SEMI-AUTOMATIC SHOTGUNS
Gauge: 12, 3" chamber; 20, 3" chamber. **Barrel:** 24", 26", 28" (Imp. Cyl., Mod. and Full choke tubes). **Weight:** 5 lbs., 10 oz. to 6 lbs., 5 oz. **Length:** 44" to 48" overall. **Stock:** Walnut or black composite. **Features:** Gas-operated; vent rib barrel with Beretta-style threaded muzzle. Introduced 2001 by Traditions.
Price: Field Model (12 or 20 ga., 26" or 28" bbl., walnut stock) **$479.00**
Price: Youth Model (12 or 20 ga., 24" bbl., walnut stock) **$479.00**
Price: (12 or 20 ga., 26" or 28" barrel, composite stock) **$459.00**

Traditions ALS 2100 Turkey Semi-Automatic Shotgun
Similar to ALS 2100 Field Model except chambered in 12 gauge, 3" only with 26" barrel and Mossy Oak® Break Up™ camo finish. Weighs 6 lbs.; 46" overall.
Price: **$519.00**

Traditions ALS 2100 Waterfowl Semi-Automatic Shotgun
Similar to ALS 2100 Field Model except chambered in 12 gauge, 3" only with 28" barrel and Advantage® Wetlands™ camo finish. Weighs 6.25 lbs.; 48" overall. Multi chokes.
Price: **$529.00**

Traditions ALS 2100 Hunter Combo
Similar to ALS 2100 Field Model except 2 barrels, 28" vent rib and 24" fully rifled deer. Weighs 6 to 6.5 lbs.; 48" overall. Choice TruGlo adj. sights or fixed cantilever mount on rifled barrel. Multi chokes.
Price: Walnut, rifle barrel **$609.00**
Price: Walnut, cantilever **$629.00**
Price: Synthetic **$579.00**

SHOTGUNS — Autoloaders

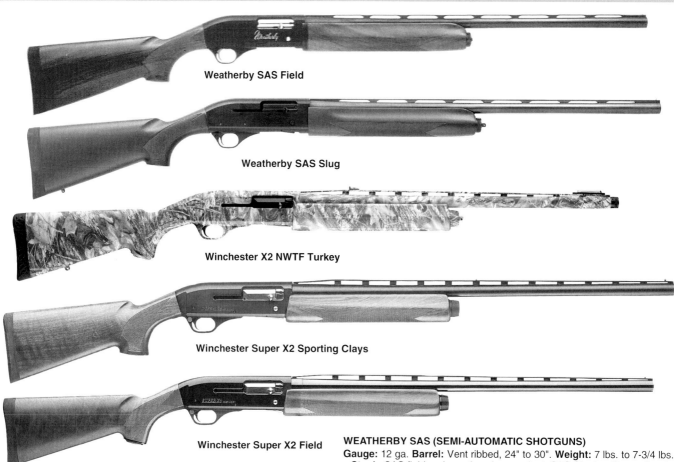

Weatherby SAS Field

Weatherby SAS Slug

Winchester X2 NWTF Turkey

Winchester Super X2 Sporting Clays

Winchester Super X2 Field

Traditions ALS 2100 Slug Hunter Shotgun

Similar to ALS 2100 Field Model, 12 ga., 24" barrel, overall length 44"; weighs 6.25 lbs. Designed specifically for the deer hunter. Rifled barrel has 1 in 36" twist. Fully adjustable fiber-optic sights.

Price: Walnut, rifle barrel **$529.00**
Price: Synthetic, rifle barrel **$499.00**
Price: Walnut, cantilever **$549.00**
Price: Synthetic, cantilever **$529.00**

Traditions ALS 2100 Home Security Shotgun

Similar to ALS 2100 Field Model, 12 ga., 20" barrel, overall length 40", weighs 6 lbs. Can be reloaded with one hand while shouldered and on-target. Swivel studs installed in stock.

Price: **$399.00**

TRISTAR CD DIANA AUTO SHOTGUNS

Gauge: 12, shoots 2-3/4" or 3" interchangeably. **Barrel:** 24", 26", 28" (Imp. Cyl., Mod., Full choke tubes). **Stock:** European walnut or black synthetic. **Features:** Gas-operated action; blued barrel; checkered pistol grip and forend; vent rib barrel. Available with synthetic and camo stock and in slug model. First introduced 1999 under the name "Tristar Phantom." Imported by Tristar Sporting Arms Ltd.

Price: . . . . **$399.00 to $535.00**

VERONA MODEL SX400 SEMI AUTO SHOTGUNS

Gauge: 12. **Barrel:** 26", 30". **Weight:** 6-1/2 lbs. **Stock:** Walnut, black composite. **Sights:** Red dot. **Features:** Aluminum receivers, gas-operated, 2-3/4" or 3" Magnum shells without adj. or Mod., 4 screw-in chokes and wrench included. Sling swivels, gold trigger. Blued barrel. Imported from Italy by B.C. Outdoors.

Price: 401S, 12 ga. **$398.40**
Price: 405SDS, 12 ga. **$610.00**
Price: 405L, 12 ga. **$331.20**

WEATHERBY SAS (SEMI-AUTOMATIC SHOTGUNS)

Gauge: 12 ga. **Barrel:** Vent ribbed, 24" to 30". **Weight:** 7 lbs. to 7-3/4 lbs. **Stock:** SAS field and sporting clays, walnut. SAS Shadow Grass, Break-Up™, Synthetic, composite. **Sights:** SAS sporting clays, brass front and mid-point rear. SAS Shadow Grass and Break-Up™, HiViz front and brass mid. Synthetic has brass front. **Features:** Easy to shoot, load, clean; lightweight, reduced recoil, IMC system includes 3 chrome-moly screw-in choke tubes. Slug gun has 22" rifled barrel with matte blue finish and cantilever base for scope mounting.

Price: Field, Sporting Clays, Shadow Grass, Break-Up™,
Synthetic, Slug Gun . . . . **$699.00 to $849.00**

WINCHESTER SUPER X2 AUTO SHOTGUNS

Gauge: 12, 3", 3-1/2" chamber. **Barrel:** Belgian, 24", 26", 28"; Invector Plus choke tubes. **Weight:** 7-1/4 to 7-1/2 lbs. **Stock:** 14-1/4"x1-3/4"x2". Walnut or black synthetic. **Features:** Gas-operated action shoots all loads without adjustment; vent rib barrels; 4-shot magazine. Introduced 1999. Assembled in Portugal by U.S. Repeating Arms Co.

Price: Magnum, 3-1/2", synthetic stock, 26" or 28" bbl. **$1,185.00**
Price: Camo Waterfowl, 3-1/2", Mossy Oak® Shadow Grass **$1,185.00**
Price: NWTF Turkey, 3-1/2", Mossy Oak® Break-Up™ camo . . . **$1,236.00**
Price: Universal Hunter Model **$1,252.00**

WINCHESTER SUPER X2 SPORTING CLAYS AUTO SHOTGUNS

Similar to the Super X2 except has two gas pistons (one for target loads, one for heavy 3" loads), adjustable comb system and high-post rib. Back-bored barrel with Invector Plus choke tubes. Offered in 28" and 30" barrels. Introduced 2001. From U.S. Repeating Arms Co.

Price: Super X2 sporting clays **$1,015.00**
Price: Signature red stock **$976.00**

Winchester Super X2 Field 3" Auto Shotgun

Similar to the Super X2 except 3" chamber, walnut stock and forearm and high-profile rib. Back-bored barrel and Invector Plus choke tubes. Introduced 2001. From U.S. Repeating Arms Co.

Price: Super X2 Field 3", 26" or 28" bbl. **$1,015.00**

SHOTGUNS — Slide & Lever Action

Includes a wide variety of sporting guns and guns suitable for competitive shooting.

Benelli Nova Pump

Benelli Nova Pump Slug

Browning BPS 10 gauge

Browning BPS 10 gauge
Mossy Oak® Shadow Grass

BENELLI NOVA PUMP SHOTGUNS

Gauge: 12, 20. **Barrel:** 24", 26", 28". **Stock:** Synthetic, Max-4 and Timber H-D (12 ga. and 20 ga). **Sights:** Red bar. **Features:** 2-3/4", 3" chamber (3-1/2" 12 ga. only). Montefeltro rotating bolt design with dual action bars, magazine cut-off, synthetic trigger assembly, 4-shot magazine. Introduced 1999. Imported from Italy by Benelli USA.

Price: Synthetic	$350.00
Price: Timber HD	$435.00
Price: Max-4	$425.00
Price: Youth Model	$440.00

Benelli Nova Pump Tactical Shotgun

Similar to the Nova except has 18.5" barrel with adjustable rifle-type or ghost ring sights; weighs 7.2 lbs.; black synthetic stock. Introduced 1999. Imported from Italy by Benelli USA.

Price: With rifle sights	$315.00
Price: With ghost-ring sights	$350.00

Benelli Nova Pump Rifled Slug Gun

Similar to Nova Pump Slug Gun except has 24" barrel and rifled bore; open rifle sights; synthetic stock; weighs 8.1 lbs.

Price: Synthetic	$525.00
Price: Timber HD	$600.00
Price: Field/Slug combo, synthetic	$545.00

BROWNING BPS PUMP SHOTGUNS

Gauge: 10, 12, 3-1/2" chamber; 12 or 20, 3" chamber (2-3/4" in target guns), 28, 2-3/4" chamber, 5-shot magazine, .410, 3" chamber. **Barrel:** 10 ga.-24" Buck Special, 28", 30", 32" Invector; 12, 20 ga.-22", 24", 26", 28", 30", 32" (Imp. Cyl., Mod. or Full), .410-26" barrel. (Imp. Cyl., Mod. and Full choke tubes.) Also available with Invector choke tubes, 12 or 20 ga.; Upland Special has 22" barrel with Invector tubes. BPS 3" and 3-1/2" have back-bored barrel. **Weight:** 7 lbs., 8 oz. (28" barrel). **Length:** 48-3/4" overall (28" barrel). **Stock:** 14-1/4"x1-1/2"x2-1/2". Select walnut, semi-beavertail forend, full pistol grip stock. **Features:** All 12 gauge 3" guns except Buck Special and game guns have back-bored barrels with Invector Plus choke tubes. Bottom feeding and ejection, receiver top safety, high post vent rib. Double action bars eliminate binding. Vent rib barrels only. All 12 and 20 gauge guns with 3" chamber available with fully engraved receiver flats at no extra cost. Each gauge has its own unique game scene. Introduced 1977. Imported from Japan by Browning.

Price: 12 ga., 3-1/2" Magnum Stalker (black syn. stock)	$688.00
Price: 12, 20 ga., Hunter, Invector Plus	$509.00
Price: 12 ga. Deer Hunter (22" rifled bbl., cantilever mount)	$624.00
Price: 28 ga., Hunter, Invector	$544.00
Price: .410, Hunter, Invector	$544.00

Browning BPS 10 Gauge Camo Pump Shotgun

Similar to the standard BPS except completely covered with Mossy Oak® Shadow Grass camouflage. Available with 24", 26", 28" barrel. Introduced 1999. Imported by Browning.

Price:	$688.00

Browning BPS Waterfowl Camo Pump Shotgun

Similar to the standard BPS except completely covered with Mossy Oak® Shadow Grass camouflage. Available in 12 gauge, with 24", 26" or 28" barrel, 3" chamber. Introduced 1999. Imported by Browning.

Price:	$688.00

Browning BPS Game Gun Deer Hunter

Similar to the standard BPS except has newly designed receiver/magazine tube/barrel mounting system to eliminate play, heavy 20.5" barrel with rifle-type sights with adjustable rear, solid receiver scope mount, "rifle" stock dimensions for scope or open sights, sling swivel studs. Gloss or matte finished wood with checkering, polished blue metal. Introduced 1992.

Price:	$624.00

Browning BPS Game Gun Turkey Special

Similar to the standard BPS except has satin-finished walnut stock and dull-finished barrel and receiver. Receiver is drilled and tapped for scope mounting. Rifle-style stock dimensions and swivel studs. Has Extra-Full Turkey choke tube. Introduced 1992.

Price:	$605.00

SHOTGUNS — Slide & Lever Action

EAA Baikal MP-133

Escort AimGuard

Escort Field Hunter

Price: Field Hunter $469.00
Price: Field Hunter Advantage $539.00
Price: Field Hunter Hardwoods $539.00
Price: Field Hunter Turkey $609.00

Browning BPS Stalker Pump Shotgun

Same gun as the standard BPS except all exposed metal parts have a matte blued finish and the stock has a durable black finish with a black recoil pad. Available in 10 ga. (3-1/2") and 12 ga. with 3" or 3-1/2" chamber, 22", 28", 30" barrel with Invector choke system. Introduced 1987.
Price: 12 ga., 3" chamber, Invector Plus $492.00
Price: 10, 12 ga., 3-1/2" chamber $579.00

Browning BPS NWTF Turkey Series Pump Shotgun

Similar to the BPS Stalker except has full coverage Mossy Oak® Break-Up™ camo finish on synthetic stock, forearm and exposed metal parts. Offered in 10 and 12 gauge, 3" or 3-1/2" chamber; 24" bbl. has extra-full choke tube and HiViz fiber-optic sights. Introduced 2001. From Browning.
Price: 10 ga., 3-1/2" chamber $738.00
Price: 12 ga., 3-1/2" chamber $674.00
Price: 12 ga., 3" chamber $738.00

Browning BPS Micro Pump Shotgun

Similar to the BPS Stalker except 20 ga. only, 22" Invector barrel, stock has pistol grip with recoil pad. Length of pull is 13-1/4"; weighs 6 lbs., 12 oz. Introduced 1986.
Price: $509.00

CHARLES DALY FIELD PUMP SHOTGUNS

Gauge: 12, 20. **Barrel:** Interchangeable 18-1/2", 24", 26", 28", 30" multi-choked. **Weight:** NA. **Stock:** Synthetic, various finishes, recoil pad. **Receiver:** Machined aluminum. **Features:** Field Tactical and Slug models come with adustable sights; Youth models may be upgraded to full size. Imported from Akkar, Turkey.
Price: Field Tactical $199.00
Price: Field Hunter $289.00
Price: Field Hunter, Realtree Hardwood $289.00
Price: Field Hunter Advantage $289.00

CHARLES DALY MAXI-MAG PUMP SHOTGUNS

Gauge: 12 gauge, 3-1/2". **Barrel:** 24", 26", 28"; multi-choke system. **Weight:** NA. **Stock:** Synthetic black, Realtree Hardwoods, or Advantage Timber receiver, aluminum alloy. **Features:** Handles 2-3/4", 3" and 3-1/2" loads. Interchangeable ported barrels; Turkey package includes sling, HiViz sights, XX Full choke. Imported from Akkar, Turkey.

DIAMOND 12 GA. PUMP SHOTGUNS

Gauge: 12, 2-3/4" and 3" chambers. **Barrel:** 18"-30". **Weight:** 7 lbs. **Stock:** Walnut, synthetic. **Features:** Aluminum one-piece receiver sculpted for lighter weight. Double locking on fixed bolt. Gold, Elite and Panther series with vented barrels and 3 chokes. All series slug guns available (Gold and Elite with sights). Imported from Istanbul by ADCO Sales.
Price: Gold, 28" vent rib w/3 chokes, walnut $359.00
Price: Gold, 28", synthetic $329.00
Price: Gold Slug, 24" w/sights, walnut or synthetic . . . . $329.00 to $359.00
Price: Silver Mariner 18.5" Slug, synthetic $399.00
Price: Silver Mariner 22" vent rib w/3 chokes $419.00
Price: Elite, 22" slug w/sights; 24", 28" vent rib w/3 chokes,
walnut . . . . $329.00 to $349.00
Price: Panther, 28", 30" vent rib w/3 chokes, synthetic $279.00
Price: Panther,18.5", 22" Slug, synthetic . . . . $209.00 to $265.00
Price: Imperial 12 ga., 28" vent rib w/3 chokes, 3.5" chamber,
walnut $399.00

EAA BAIKAL MP-133 PUMP SHOTGUN

Gauge: 12, 3-1/2" chamber. **Barrel:** 18-1/2", 20", 24", 26", 28"; Imp., Mod. and Full choke tubes. **Weight:** NA. **Stock:** Walnut; checkered grip and grooved forearm. **Features:** Hammer-forged, chrome-lined barrel with vent rib; machined steel parts; dual action bars; trigger-block safety; 4-shot magazine tube; handles 2-3/4" through 3-1/2" shells. Introduced 2000. Imported by European American Armory.
Price: MP-133 (blued finish, walnut stock and forend) $359.00

ESCORT PUMP SHOTGUNS

Gauge: 12, 20; 3" chamber. **Barrel:** 18" (AimGuard model); 22" (FH Slug model), 24", 26" and 28" (Field Hunter models), choke tubes (M, IC, F); turkey choke w/24" bbl. **Weight:** 6.4 to 7 lbs. **Stock:** Polymer, black chrome or camo finish. **Features:** Alloy receiver w/dovetail for sight mounting. Two stock adjusting spacers included. Introduced 2003. From Legacy Sports International.
Price: Field Hunter, black stock $247.00
Price: Field Hunter, camo stock $812.00
Price: Camo, 24" bbl. $363.00
Price: AimGuard, 20" bbl., black stock $211.00
Price: MarineGuard, nickel finish $254.00
Price: Combo (2 bbls.) $270.00

SHOTGUNS — Slide & Lever Action

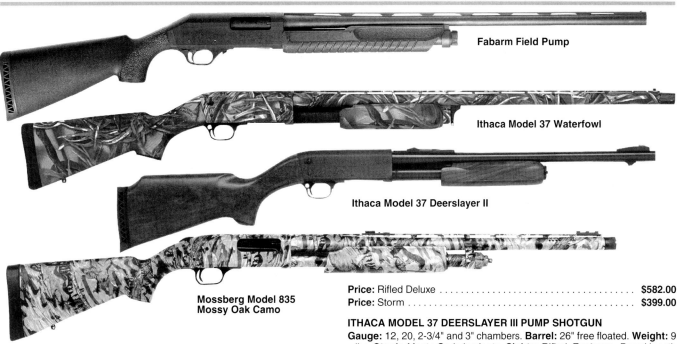

Fabarm Field Pump

Ithaca Model 37 Waterfowl

Ithaca Model 37 Deerslayer II

Mossberg Model 835
Mossy Oak Camo

FABARM FIELD PUMP SHOTGUN

Gauge: 12, 3" chamber. **Barrel:** 28" (24" rifled slug barrel available). **Weight:** 76.6 lbs. **Length:** 48.25" overall. **Stock:** Polymer. **Features:** Similar to Fabarm FP6 Pump Shotgun. Alloy receiver; twin action bars; available in black or Mossy Oak® Break-Up™ camo finish. Includes Cyl., Mod. and Full choke tubes. Introduced 2001. Imported from Italy by Heckler & Koch Inc.
Price: Matte black finish **$399.00**
Price: Mossy Oak® Break-Up™ finish **$469.00**

ITHACA MODEL 37 DELUXE PUMP SHOTGUNS

Gauge: 12, 16, 20, 3" chamber. **Barrel:** 26", 28", 30" (12 gauge), 26", 28" (16 and 20 gauge), choke tubes. **Weight:** 7 lbs. **Stock:** Walnut with cut-checkered grip and forend. **Features:** Steel receiver; bottom ejection; brushed blue finish, vent rib barrels. Reintroduced 1996. Made in U.S. by Ithaca Gun Co.
Price: **$633.00**
Price: With straight English-style stock **$803.00**
Price: Model 37 New Classic (ringtail forend, sunburst recoil pad, hand-finished walnut stock, 26" or 28" barrel) **$803.00**

Ithaca Model 37 Waterfowl Shotgun

Similar to Model 37 Deluxe except in 12 gauge only with 24", 26", or 30" barrel, special extended steel shot choke tube system. Complete coverage in Advantage Wetlands or Hardwoods camouflage. Storm models have synthetic stock. Introduced 1999. Made in U.S. by Ithaca Gun Co.
Price: . . . . **$499.00 to $549.00**

ITHACA MODEL 37 ULTRALIGHT DELUXE SHOTGUNS

Gauge: 16 ga. 2-3/4" chamber. **Barrel:** 24", 26", 28". **Weight:** 5.25 lbs. **Stock:** Standard deluxe. **Sights:** Raybar. **Features:** Vent rib, drilled and tapped, interchangeable barrel. F, M, IC choke tubes.
Price: Deluxe **$649.00**
Price: Classic/English **$824.00**
Price: Classic/Pistol **$824.00**

ITHACA MODEL 37 DEERSLAYER II PUMP SHOTGUNS

Gauge: 12, 16, 20; 3" chamber. **Barrel:** 24", 26", fully rifled. **Weight:** 11 lbs. **Stock:** Cut-checkered American walnut with Monte Carlo comb. **Sights:** Rifle-type. **Features:** Integral barrel and receiver. Bottom ejection. Brushed blue finish. Introduced 1999. Made in U.S. by Ithaca Gun Co. Reintroduced 1997. Made in U.S. by Ithaca Gun Co.
Price: **$633.00**
Price: Smooth Bore Deluxe **$582.00**

Price: Rifled Deluxe **$582.00**
Price: Storm **$399.00**

ITHACA MODEL 37 DEERSLAYER III PUMP SHOTGUN

Gauge: 12, 20, 2-3/4" and 3" chambers. **Barrel:** 26" free floated. **Weight:** 9 lbs. **Stock:** Monte Carlo laminate. **Sights:** Rifled. **Features:** Barrel length gives increased velocity. Trigger and sear set hand filed and stoned for creep-free operation. Weaver-style scope base. Swivel studs. Matte blue. Made in U.S. by Ithaca Gun Co.
Price: . . . . **Custom order only**

ITHACA MODEL 37 RUFFED GROUSE SPECIAL EDITION SHOTGUN

Gauge: 20 ga. **Barrel:** 22", 24", interchangeable choke tubes. **Weight:** 5.25 lbs. **Stock:** American black walnut. **Features:** Laser engraved stock with line art drawing. Bottom eject. Vent rib and English style. Right- or left-hand through simple safety change. Aluminum receiver. Made in U.S.A. by Ithaca Gun Co.
Price: **$840.00**

ITHACA TURKEYSLAYER STORM SHOTGUN

Gauge: 12 or 20 ga., 3" chamber. **Barrel:** 24" ported. **Stock:** Composite. **Sights:** TruGlo front and rear. **Features:** IthaChoke full turkey choke tube. Matte metal, Realtree Hardwoods pattern, swivel studs.
Price: Storm **$459.00**

MARLIN PARDNER PUMP SHOTGUN

Gauge: 12 ga., 3". **Barrel:** 28" vent rib, screw-in Modified choke tube. **Weight:** 7-1/2 lbs. **Length:** 48-1/2". **Stock:** American walnut, grooved forend, ventilated recoil pad. **Sights:** Bead front. **Features:** Machined steel receiver, double action bars, five-shot magazine.
Price: **$200.00**

MOSSBERG MODEL 835 ULTI-MAG PUMP SHOTGUNS

Gauge: 12, 3-1/2" chamber. **Barrel:** Ported 24" rifled bore, 24", 28", Accu-Mag choke tubes for steel or lead shot. **Weight:** 7-3/4 lbs. **Length:** 48-1/2" overall. **Stock:** 14"x1-1/2"x2-1/2". Dual Comb. Cut-checkered hardwood or camo synthetic; both have recoil pad. **Sights:** White bead front, brass mid-bead; fiber-optic rear. **Features:** Shoots 2-3/4", 3" or 3-1/2" shells. Back-bored and ported barrel to reduce recoil, improve patterns. Ambidextrous thumb safety, twin extractors, dual slide bars. Mossberg Cablelock included. Introduced 1988.
Price: 28" vent rib, hardwood stock **$394.00**
Price: Combos, 24" rifled or smooth bore, rifle sights, 24" vent rib Accu-Mag Ulti-Full choke tube, Mossy Oak® camo finish **$556.00**
Price: RealTree Camo Turkey, 24" vent rib, Accu-Mag extra-full tube, synthetic stock. **$460.00**
Price: Mossy Oak® Camo, 28" vent rib, Accu-Mag tubes, synthetic stock **$460.00**
Price: OFM Camo, 28" vent rib, Accu-Mag Mod. tube, synthetic stock **$438.00**

SHOTGUNS — Slide & Lever Action

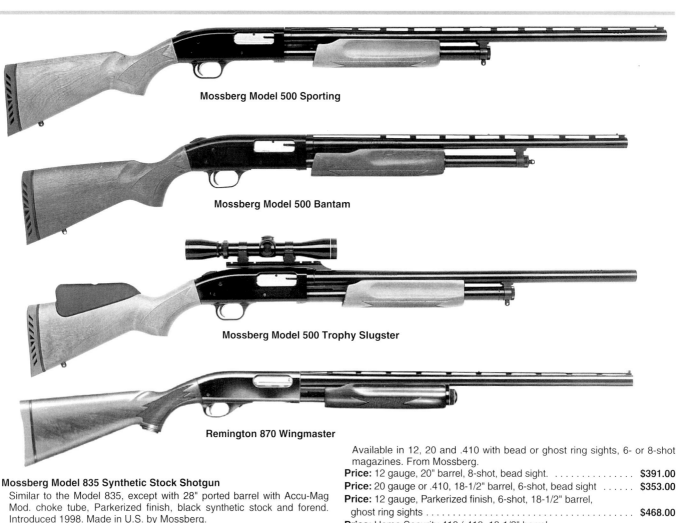

Mossberg Model 500 Sporting

Mossberg Model 500 Bantam

Mossberg Model 500 Trophy Slugster

Remington 870 Wingmaster

Mossberg Model 835 Synthetic Stock Shotgun

Similar to the Model 835, except with 28" ported barrel with Accu-Mag Mod. choke tube, Parkerized finish, black synthetic stock and forend. Introduced 1998. Made in U.S. by Mossberg.

Price: **$394.00**

MOSSBERG MODEL 500 SPORTING PUMP SHOTGUNS

Gauge: 12, 20, .410, 3" chamber. **Barrel:** 18-1/2" to 28" with fixed or Accu-Choke, plain or vent rib. **Weight:** 6-1/4 lbs. (.410), 7-1/4 lbs. (12). **Length:** 48" overall (28" barrel). **Stock:** 14"x1-1/2"x2-1/2". Walnut-stained hardwood. Cut-checkered grip and forend. **Sights:** White bead front, brass mid-bead; fiber-optic. **Features:** Ambidextrous thumb safety, twin extractors, disconnecting safety, dual action bars. Quiet Carry forend. Many barrels are ported. From Mossberg.

Price: . . . . From about **$316.00**
Price: Sporting Combos (field barrel and Slugster barrel) . . . From **$381.00**

Mossberg Model 500 Bantam Pump Shotgun

Same as the Model 500 Sporting Pump except 12 or 20 gauge, 22" vent rib Accu-Choke barrel with choke tube set; has 1" shorter stock, reduced length from pistol grip to trigger, reduced forend reach. Introduced 1992.

Price: **$316.00**
Price: With Realtree Hardwoods camouflage finish (20 ga. only) . . **$364.00**

Mossberg Model 500 Camo Pump Shotgun

Same as the Model 500 Sporting Pump except 12 gauge only and entire gun is covered with Mossy Oak® Advantage camouflage finish. Receiver drilled and tapped for scope mounting. Comes with quick detachable swivel studs, swivels, camouflage sling, Mossberg Cablelock.

Price: From about **$364.00**

MOSSBERG MODEL 500 PERSUADER/CRUISER SHOTGUNS

Similar to Mossberg Model 500 except has 18-1/2" or 20" barrel with cylinder bore choke, synthetic stock and blue or Parkerized finish.

Available in 12, 20 and .410 with bead or ghost ring sights, 6- or 8-shot magazines. From Mossberg.

Price: 12 gauge, 20" barrel, 8-shot, bead sight. **$391.00**
Price: 20 gauge or .410, 18-1/2" barrel, 6-shot, bead sight **$353.00**
Price: 12 gauge, Parkerized finish, 6-shot, 18-1/2" barrel,
ghost ring sights **$468.00**
Price: Home Security 410 (.410, 18-1/2" barrel
with spreader choke) **$335.00**

Mossberg Model 590 Special Purpose Shotgun

Similar to Model 500 except has Parkerized or Marinecote finish, 9-shot magazine and black synthetic stock (some models feature Speed Feed). Available in 12 gauge only with 20", cylinder bore barrel. Weighs 7-1/4 lbs. From Mossberg.

Price: Bead sight, heat shield over barrel **$417.00**
Price: Ghost ring sight, Speed Feed stock **$586.00**

MOSSBERG MODEL 500 SLUGSTER SHOTGUN

Gauge: 12, 20, 3" chamber. **Barrel:** 24", ported rifled bore. Integral scope mount. **Weight:** 7-1/4 lbs. **Length:** 44" overall. **Stock:** 14" pull, 1-3/8" drop at heel. Walnut. Dual Comb design for proper eye positioning with or without scoped barrels. Recoil pad and swivel studs. **Features:** Ambidextrous thumb safety, twin extractors, dual slide bars. Comes with scope mount. Mossberg Cablelock included. Introduced 1988.

Price: Rifled bore, integral scope mount, 12 or 20 ga. **$361.00**
Price: Fiber-optic, rifle sights **$361.00**
Price: Rifled bore, rifle sights **$338.00**
Price: 20 ga., Standard or Bantam . . . . From **$338.00**

REMINGTON MODEL 870 WINGMASTER SHOTGUNS

Gauge: 12 ga., 16 ga., 3" chamber. **Barrel:** 26", 28", 30" (RemChokes). **Weight:** 7-1/4 lbs. **Length:** 46", 48". **Stock:** Walnut, hardwood, synthetic. **Sights:** Single bead (Twin bead Wingmaster). **Features:** Light contour barrel. Double action bars, cross-bolt safety, blue finish.

Price: Wingmaster, walnut, blued, 26", 28", 30" **$584.00**
Price: 870 Wingmaster Super Magnum, 3-1/2" chamber, 28" **$665.00**

SHOTGUNS — Slide & Lever Action

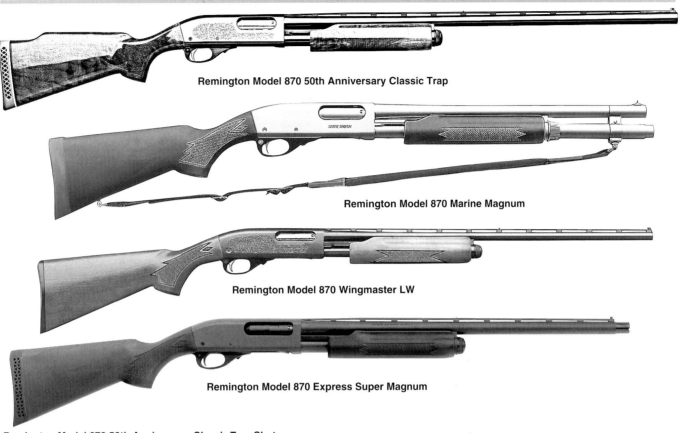

Remington Model 870 50th Anniversary Classic Trap

Remington Model 870 Marine Magnum

Remington Model 870 Wingmaster LW

Remington Model 870 Express Super Magnum

Remington Model 870 50th Anniversary Classic Trap Shotgun
Similar to Model 870 Wingmaster except has 30" vent rib, light contour barrel, singles, mid- and long-handicap choke tubes, semi-fancy American walnut stock, high-polish blued receiver with engraving. Chamber 2-1/2". From Remington Arms Co.
Price: **$792.00**

Remington Model 870 Marine Magnum Shotgun
Similar to 870 Wingmaster except all metal plated with electroless nickel, black synthetic stock and forend. Has 18" plain barrel (cyl.), bead front sight, 7-shot magazine. Introduced 1992.
Price: **$573.00**

Remington Model 870 Wingmaster LW Shotgun
Similar to Model 870 Wingmaster except in 20, 28 gauges and .410-bore only, 25" vent rib barrel with RemChoke tubes, high-gloss wood finish. 26" & 28" barrels 20 ga.
Price: 20 gauge **$584.00**
Price: .410-bore **$612.00**
Price: 28 gauge **$665.00**

Remington Model 870 Express Shotguns
Similar to Model 870 Wingmaster except walnut-toned hardwood stock with solid, black recoil pad and pressed checkering on grip and forend. Outside metal surfaces have black oxide finish. Comes with 26" or 28" vent rib barrel with mod. RemChoke tube.
Price: 12 ga., 20 ga., 16 ga. (28") **$332.00**
Price: Express Combo, 12 ga., 26" vent rib with mod. RemChoke and 20" fully rifled barrel with rifle sights, or RemChoke . . . . . **$443.00 to $476.00**
Price: Express L-H (left-hand), 12 ga., 28" vent rib with mod. RemChoke tube **$359.00**
Price: Express synthetic, 12-ga., 26" or 28" **$332.00**
Price: Express combo (20 ga.) with extra deer rifled barrel, fully rifled or RemChoke . . . . **$443.00 to $476.00**
Price: Express small bore 28 ga., 25" **$359.00**
Price: Express small bore .410, 25" **$359.00**

Remington Model 870 Express Super Magnum Shotgun
Similar to Model 870 Express except 28" vent rib barrel with 3-1/2" chamber, vented recoil pad. Introduced 1998.
Price: **$376.00**
Price: Super Magnum synthetic, 26" **$376.00**
Price: Super Magnum turkey camo (full-coverage RealTree Advantage camo), 23" **$500.00**
Price: Super Magnum combo (26" with Mod. RemChoke and 20" fully rifled deer barrel with 3" chamber and rifle sights; wood stock) **$523.00**
Price: Super Magnum synthetic turkey, 23" (black) **$389.00**

Remington Model 870 Wingmaster Super Magnum Shotgun
Similar to Model 870 Express Super Magnum except high-polish blued finish, 28" ventilated barrel with Imp. Cyl., Modified and Full choke tubes, checkered high-gloss walnut stock. Overall length 48", weighs 7-1/2 lbs. Introduced 2000.
Price: 3-1/2" chamber **$665.00**

Remington Model 870 SPS Super Slug Deer Gun Shotgun
Similar to the Model 870 Express synthetic except has 23" rifled, modified contour barrel with cantilever scope mount. Comes with black synthetic stock and forend with swivel studs, black Cordura nylon sling. Fully rifled centilever barrel. Introduced 1999.
Price: **$580.00**

Remington Model 870 SPS-T Synthetic Camo Shotguns
Similar to the Model 870 Express synthetic, chambered for 12 ga., 3" shells, has Mossy Oak® Break-Up™ synthetic stock and metal treatment, TruGlo fiber-optic sights. Introduced 2001.
Price: 20" RS, Rem. choke **$595.00**
Price: Youth version **$595.00**
Price: Super Magnum Camo, 23", CL Rem. Choke **$609.00**
Price: Super Magnum Camo 23", VT Rem. Choke **$591.00**
Price: 20 ga., Truglo sights, Rem. Choke, Mossy Oak® Break-Up™ Camo **$595.00**

SHOTGUNS — Slide & Lever Action

Remington Model 870 Express Deer Gun

Remington Model 870 Express Turkey

Remington Model 870 SPS Super Slug Deer Gun

Remington Model 870 SPS-T Camo

Winchester 1300 Walnut Field Pump

Remington Model 870 Express Youth Gun Shotgun
Same as Model 870 Express except 13" length of pull, 21" barrel with mod. RemChoke tube. Weighs 6.25 lbs. Hardwood stock with low-luster finish. Introduced 1991.
Price: 20 ga. Express Youth (1" shorter stock), from. **$332.00**
Price: 20 ga. Youth Deer 20" FR/RS **$365.00**
Price: 16 ga. Youth Synthetic **$332.00**

Remington Model 870 Express Rifle-Sighted Deer Gun Shotguns
Same as Model 870 Express except 20" barrel with fixed imp. cyl. choke, open iron sights, Monte Carlo stock. Introduced 1991.
Price: **$332.00**
Price: With fully rifled barrel **$365.00**
Price: Express Synthetic Deer
(black synthetic stock, black matte metal) **$372.00**

Remington Model 870 Express Turkey Shotguns
Same as Model 870 Express except 3" chamber, 21" vent rib turkey barrel and extra-full Rem. choke turkey tube; 12 ga. only. Introduced 1991.
Price: **$345.00**
Price: Express Turkey Camo stock has Skyline Excel
camo, matte black metal **$399.00**
Price: Express Youth Turkey camo (as above with 1" shorter
length of pull), 20 ga., Skyline Excel camo **$399.00**

Remington Model 870 Express Synthetic 18" Shotgun
Similar to Model 870 Express with 18" barrel except synthetic stock and forend; 7-shot. Introduced 1994.
Price: **$319.00**

REMINGTON MODEL 870 SPS SUPER MAGNUM CAMO SHOTGUN
Gauge: 12, 3-1/2" chamber. **Barrel:** 26", 28", vent rib, with Full, Mod., Imp. Cyl. RemChoke. **Weight:** 7-1/4 lbs. to 7-1/2 lbs. **Length:** 46" to 481/2" overall. **Stock:** Mossy Oak® Break-Up™ camo finish. **Sights:** Metal bead front. **Features:** Synthetic stock and all metal (except bolt and trigger guard) and stock covered with Mossy Oak® Break-Up™ camo finish. Comes with camo sling, swivels.
Price: **$637.00**

SARSILMAZ PUMP SHOTGUN
Gauge: 12, 3" chamber. **Barrel:** 26" or 28". **Stocks:** Oil-finished hardwood. **Features:** Includes extra pistol-grip stock. Introduced 2000. Imported from Turkey by Armsport Inc.
Price: With pistol-grip stock **$299.95**
Price: With metal stock **$349.95**

WINCHESTER MODEL 1300 WALNUT SPORTING/FIELD PUMP SHOTGUN
Gauge: 12, 20, 3" chamber, 5-shot capacity. **Barrel:** 26", 28", vent rib, with Full, Mod., Imp. Cyl. Winchoke tubes. **Weight:** 6-3/8 lbs. **Length:** 42-5/8" overall. **Stock:** American walnut with deep cut checkering on pistol grip, traditional ribbed forend; high luster finish. **Sights:** Metal bead front. **Features:** Twin action slide bars; front-locking rotary bolt; roll-engraved receiver; blued, highly polished metal; cross-bolt safety with red indicator. Introduced 1984. From U.S. Repeating Arms Co., Inc.
Price: **$439.00**

SHOTGUNS — Slide & Lever Action

Winchester 1300 Black Shadow Field Gun

Winchester 1300 Deer Black Shadow Gun

Winchester 1300 Ranger Compact

Winchester 9410

Winchester Model 1300 Upland Pump Shotgun
Similar to Model 1300 Walnut except straight-grip stock, 24" barrel. Introduced 1999. Made in U.S. by U.S. Repeating Arms Co.
Price: $438.00

Winchester Model 1300 Black Shadow Field Shotgun
Similar to Model 1300 Walnut except black composite stock and forend, matte black finish. Has vent rib 26" or 28" barrel, 3" chamber, Mod. Winchoke tube. Introduced 1995. From U.S. Repeating Arms Co., Inc.
Price: 12 or 20 gauge $351.00

Winchester Model 1300 Deer Black Shadow Shotguns
Similar to Model 1300 Black Shadow Turkey Gun except ramp-type front sight, fully adjustable rear, drilled and tapped for scope mounting. Black composite stock and forend, matte black metal. Smoothbore 22" barrel with one Imp. Cyl. Winchoke tube; 12 gauge only, 3" chamber. Weighs 6-3/4 lbs. Introduced 1994. From U.S. Repeating Arms Co., Inc.
Price: With rifled barrel $453.00
Price: Combo (22" rifled and 28" smoothbore bbls.) $453.00

WINCHESTER MODEL 1300 RANGER PUMP SHOTGUNS
Gauge: 12, 20, 3" chamber, 5-shot magazine. **Barrel:** 28" vent rib with Full, Mod., Imp. Cyl. Winchoke tubes. **Weight:** 7 to 7-1/4 lbs. **Length:** 48-5/8" to 50-5/8" overall. **Stock:** Walnut-finished hardwood with ribbed forend. **Sights:** Metal bead front. **Features:** Cross-bolt safety, black rubber recoil pad, twin action slide bars, front-locking rotating bolt. From U.S. Repeating Arms Co., Inc.

Price: Vent rib barrel, Winchoke $366.00
Price: Model 1300 Compact, 24" vent rib $366.00
Price: Compact wood model, 20 ga. $366.00

WINCHESTER MODEL 1300 UNIVERSAL HUNTER TURKEY SHOTGUN
Gauge: 12, 3". **Barrel:** 26" vent rib with Extra Long, Extra Full Extended, Full, Mod., Imp. Cyl. Winchoke tubes. **Weight:** 7 lbs. **Length:** 47" overall. **Stock:** Composite. **Sights:** Red dot. **Features:** Rotary bolt action. Durable Mossy Oak® break-up finish. TruGlo® 3-dot sights and stock sling studs also included. From U.S. Repeating Arms Co., Inc.
Price: Universal Hunter $509.00

WINCHESTER MODEL 9410 LEVER-ACTION SHOTGUN
Gauge: .410, 2-1/2" chamber. **Barrel:** 24" cyl. bore, also Invector choke system. **Weight:** 6-3/4 lbs. **Length:** 42-1/8" overall. **Stock:** Checkered walnut straight-grip; checkered walnut forearm. **Sights:** Adjustable "V" rear, TruGlo® front. **Features:** Model 94 rifle action (smoothbore) chambered for .410 shotgun. Angle Controlled Eject extractor/ejector; choke tubes; 9-shot tubular magazine; 13-1/2" length of pull. Introduced 2001. From U.S. Repeating Arms Co.
Price: 9410 fixed choke $626.00
Price: 9410 Packer w/chokes $647.00
Price: 9410 w/Invector, traditional model $626.00
Price: 9410 w/Invector, Packer model $647.00
Price: 9410 w/Invector, semi-fancy traditional $626.00

SHOTGUNS — Over/Under

Includes a variety of game guns and guns for competitive shooting.

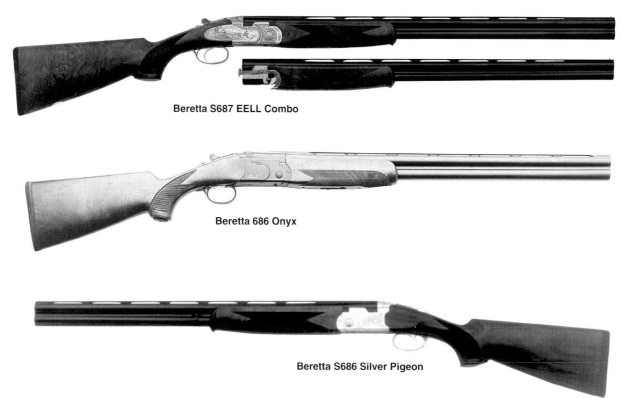

Beretta S687 EELL Combo

Beretta 686 Onyx

Beretta S686 Silver Pigeon

BERETTA DT10 TRIDENT SHOTGUNS

Gauge: 12, 2-3/4", 3" chambers. **Barrel:** 28", 30", 32", 34"; competition-style vent rib; fixed or Optima choke tubes. **Weight:** 7.9 to 9 lbs. **Stock:** High-grade walnut stock with oil finish; hand-checkered grip and forend, adjustable stocks available. **Features:** Detachable, adjustable trigger group, raised and thickened receiver, forend iron has adjustment nut to guarantee wood-to-metal fit. Introduced 2000. Imported from Italy by Beretta USA.

Price: DT10 Trident Trap (selective, lockable single trigger,
  adjustable stock). $6,995.00
Price: DT10 Trident Top Single $6,995.00
Price: DT10 Trident X Trap Combo
  (single and o/u barrels) $8,995.00
Price: DT10 Trident skeet (skeet stock with rounded recoil
  pad, tapered rib) $6,995.00
Price: DT10 Trident Sporting (sporting clays stock with
  rounded recoil pad) $6,495.00
Price: DT10L Sporting $7,995.00

BERETTA SERIES 682 GOLD E SKEET, TRAP, SPORTING O/U SHOTGUNS

Gauge: 12, 2-3/4" chambers. **Barrel:** skeet-28"; trap-30" and 32", Imp. Mod. & Full and Mobilchoke; trap mono shotguns-32" and 34" Mobilchoke; trap top single guns-32" and 34" Full and Mobilchoke; trap combo sets-from 30" O/U, to 32" O/U, 34" top single. **Stock:** Close-grained walnut, hand checkered. **Sights:** White Bradley bead front sight and center bead. **Features:** Receiver has Greystone gunmetal gray finish with gold accents. Trap Monte Carlo stock has deluxe trap recoil pad. Various grades available. Imported from Italy by Beretta USA.

Price: 682 Gold E Trap with adjustable stock $4,125.00
Price: 682 Gold E Trap Top Combo $5,295.00
Price: 682 Gold E Sporting $3,595.00
Price: 682 Gold E skeet, adjustable stock $3,905.00
Price: 687 EELL Diamond Pigeon Sporting $6,495.00

BERETTA 686 ONYX O/U SHOTGUNS

Gauge: 12, 3" chambers. **Barrel:** 28", 30" (Mobilchoke tubes). **Weight:** 7.7 lbs. **Stock:** Checkered American walnut. **Features:** Intended for the beginning sporting clays shooter. Has wide, vented target rib, radiused recoil pad. Polished black finish on receiver and barrels. Introduced 1993. Imported from Italy by Beretta U.S.A.

Price: White Onyx $1,795.00
Price: Onyx Pro $1,895.00
Price: Onyx Pro 3.5 . . . . $2,795.00

BERETTA 686 SILVER PIGEON O/U SHOTGUNS

Gauge: 12, 20, 28, 3" chambers (2-3/4" 28 ga.). **Barrel:** 26", 28". **Weight:** 6.8 lbs. **Stock:** Checkered walnut. **Features:** Interchangeable barrels (20 and 28 ga.), single selective gold-plated trigger, boxlock action, auto safety, Schnabel forend.

Price: Silver Pigeon S. $1,995.00
Price: Silver Pigeon S Combo $2,795.00

BERETTA ULTRALIGHT O/U SHOTGUNS

Gauge: 12, 2-3/4" chambers. **Barrel:** 26", 28", Mobilchoke tubes. **Weight:** About 5 lbs., 13 oz. **Stock:** Select American walnut with checkered grip and forend. **Features:** Low-profile aluminum alloy receiver with titanium breech face insert. Electroless nickel receiver with game scene engraving. Single selective trigger; automatic safety. Introduced 1992. Imported from Italy by Beretta U.S.A.

Price: $1,995.00
Price: Silver Pigeon II $2,395.00
Price: Silver Pigeon II Combo $3,295.00
Price: Silver Pigeon III $2,495.00
Price: Silver Pigeon IV $2,795.00
Price: Silver Pigeon V $3,295.00
Price: Ultralight Deluxe $2,495.00

SHOTGUNS — Over/Under

Beretta Over/Under Field Shotgun

Beretta SO9

Browning Citori White Lightning

Beretta Ultralight Deluxe O/U Shotgun
Similar to the Ultralight except has matte electroless nickel finish receiver with gold game scene engraving; matte oil-finished, select walnut stock and forend. Imported from Italy by Beretta U.S.A.
Price: **$2,495.00**

BERETTA COMPETITION SHOTGUNS
Gauge: 12, 20, 28, and .410 bore, 2-3/4", 3" and 3-1/2" chambers. **Barrel:** 26" and 28" (Mobilchoke tubes). **Stock:** Close-grained walnut. **Features:** Highly-figured, American walnut stocks and forends, and a unique, weather-resistant finish on barrels. Silver designates standard 686, 687 models with silver receivers; 686 Silver Pigeon has enhanced engraving pattern, Schnabel forend; Gold indicates higher grade 686EL, 687EL models with full sideplates; Diamond is for 687EELL models with highest grade wood, engraving. Case provided with Gold and Diamond grades. Imported from Italy by Beretta U.S.A.
Price: S687 EL Gold Pigeon II (deep relief engraving) **$4,795.00**
Price: S687 EEU Gold Pigeon Sporting (D.R. engraving) **$6,495.00**
Price: Gold Sporting Pigeon **$4,971.00**
Price: 28 and 410 combo **$5,520.00**

BERETTA MODEL SO5, SO6, SO9 SHOTGUNS
Gauge: 12, 2-3/4" chambers. **Barrel:** To customer specs. **Stock:** To customer specs. **Features:** SO5-trap, skeet and sporting clays models SO5; SO6-SO6 and SO6 EELL are field models. SO6 has a case-hardened or silver receiver with contour hand engraving. SO6 EELL has hand-engraved receiver in a fine floral or "fine English" pattern or game scene, with bas-relief chisel work and gold inlays. SO6 and SO6 EELL are available with sidelocks removable by hand. Imported from Italy by Beretta U.S.A.
Price: SO5 Trap, skeet, Sporting **$13,000.00**
Price: SO6 Trap, skeet, Sporting **$17,500.00**
Price: SO6 EELL Field, custom specs **$28,000.00**
Price: SO9 (12, 20, 28, .410, 26", 28", 30", any choke) **$31,000.00**

BRNO ZH 300 O/U SHOTGUNS
Gauge: 12, 2-3/4" chambers. **Barrel:** 26", 27-1/2", 29" (skeet, Imp. Cyl., Mod., Full). **Weight:** 7 lbs. **Length:** 44.4" overall. **Stock:** European walnut. **Features:** Double triggers; automatic safety; polished blue finish, engraved receiver. Announced 1998. Imported from the Czech Republic by Euro-Imports.
Price: ZH 301, field **$594.00**
Price: ZH 302, skeet **$608.00**
Price: ZH 303, 12 ga. trap **$608.00**
Price: ZH 321, 16 ga. **$595.00**

BRNO 501.2 O/U SHOTGUN
Gauge: 12, 2-3/4" chambers. **Barrel:** 27.5" (Full & Mod.). **Weight:** 7 lbs. **Length:** 44" overall. **Stock:** European walnut. **Features:** Boxlock action with double triggers, ejectors; automatic safety; hand-cut checkering. Announced 1998. Imported from the Czech Republic by Euro-Imports.
Price: **$850.00**

BROWNING CYNERGY O/U SHOTGUNS
Gauge: 12, 20, 28. **Barrel:** 26", 28", 30", 32". **Stock:** Walnut or composite. **Features:** Mono-Lock hinge, recoil-reducing Inflex recoil pad, silver nitride receiver; ported barrel option.
Price: Cynergy Field, 20 and 28 gauge **$2,062.00**
Price: Cynergy Sporting, 20 and 28 gauge **$3,080.00**
Price: Cynergy Field, 12 gauge **$2,048.00**
Price: Cynergy Field, composite stock **$1,890.00**
Price: Cynergy Sporting, 12 gauge **$3,046.00**
Price: Cynergy Sporting, composite stock **$2,846.00**

BROWNING CITORI O/U SHOTGUNS
Gauge: 12, 20, 28 and .410. **Barrel:** 26", 28" in 28 and .410. Offered with Invector choke tubes. All 12 and 20 gauge models have back-bored barrels and Invector Plus choke system. **Weight:** 6 lbs., 8 oz. (26" .410) to 7 lbs., 13 oz. (30" 12 ga.). **Length:** 43" overall (26" bbl.). **Stock:** Dense walnut, hand checkered, full pistol grip, beavertail forend. Field-type recoil pad on 12 ga. field guns and trap and skeet models. **Sights:** Medium raised beads, German nickel silver. **Features:** Barrel selector integral with safety, automatic ejectors, three-piece takedown. Imported from Japan by Browning.
Price: Lightning, 12 and 20 gauge **$1,645.00**
Price: Lightning, 28 and .410 .... **$1,709.00**
Price: White Lightning, 12 and 20 gauge **$1,714.00**
Price: White Lightning, 28 and .410 Lightning **$1,790.00**
Price: Lightning, 525 Field, 12, 20 .... **$1,981.00**
Price: Lightning, 525 Field, 28 and 410 .... **$2,010.00**
Price: Superlight Feather, 12, 20 .... **$1,938.00**
Price: Super Lightning, Grade I, 12 and 20 gauge **$1,866.00**
Price: Classic Lightning, Grade I, 12 and 20 gauge **$1,891.00**
Price: Classic Lightning Feather, Grade I, 12 and 20 gauge **$1,952.00**

Browning Citori High Grade Shotguns
Similar to standard Citori except has engraved hunting scenes and gold inlays, high-grade, hand-oiled walnut stock and forearm. Introduced 2000. From Browning.
Price: Citori VI Lightning blue or gray
(gold inlays of ducks and pheasants) From **$2,608.00**

SHOTGUNS — Over/Under

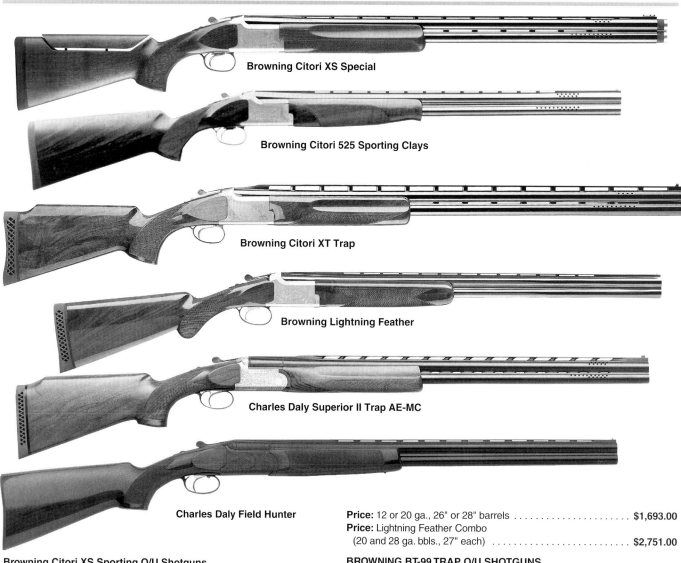

Browning Citori XS Special

Browning Citori 525 Sporting Clays

Browning Citori XT Trap

Browning Lightning Feather

Charles Daly Superior II Trap AE-MC

Charles Daly Field Hunter

Browning Citori XS Sporting O/U Shotguns
Similar to the standard Citori except available in 12, 20, 28 or .410 with, 26" or 28" barrels choked skeet, Cylinder, Imp. Cyl., Mod. and Imp. Mod. Has pistol grip stock, rounded or Schnabel forend. Weighs 7 lbs. 1 oz. to 8 lbs. 10 oz., 15 oz. Introduced 2005.
Price: Citori XS Special, 12 gauge **$2,727.00**
Price: Citori XS Sporting, 12 or 20 gauge **$2,472.00**
Price: Citori XS Skeet, 12 or 20 gauge **$2,434.00**
Price: Citori 525 Sporting, Grade I, 12 gauge **$2,319.00**
Price: Citori 525 Golden Clays, 12 or 20 gauge **$3,058.00**
Price: Citori 525 Golden Clays, 28 or .410 . . . . **$4,653.00**

Browning Citori XT Trap O/U Shotgun
Similar to the Citori XS Special except has engraved silver nitride receiver with gold highlights, vented side barrel rib. Available in 12 gauge with 30" or 32" barrels, Invector-Plus choke tubes, adjustable comb and buttplate. Introduced 1999. Imported by Browning.
Price: . . . . **$2,275.00 to $4,221.00**
Price: With adjustable-comb stock **$2,549.00**

Browning Citori Lightning Feather O/U Shotgun
Similar to the 12 gauge Citori Grade I except has 2-3/4" chambers, rounded pistol grip, lightning-style forend, and lightweight alloy receiver. Weighs 6 lbs. 15 oz. with 26" barrels (12 ga.); 6 lbs., 2 oz. (20 ga., 26" bbl.), silvered, engraved receiver. Introduced 1999. Imported by Browning.

Price: 12 or 20 ga., 26" or 28" barrels **$1,693.00**
Price: Lightning Feather Combo
(20 and 28 ga. bbls., 27" each) **$2,751.00**

BROWNING BT-99 TRAP O/U SHOTGUNS
GAUGE: 12. **Barrel:** 30", 32", 34". **Stock:** Walnut; standard or adjustable. **Weight:** 7 lbs. 11 oz. to 9 lbs. **Features:** Back-bored single barrel; interchangeable chokes; beavertail forearm; extractor only; high rib.
Price: BT-99, adj. comb **$1,329.00**
Price: BT-99, Golden Clays **$3,509.00**
Price: BT-99 Micro **$1,329.00**

CHARLES DALY SUPERIOR II TRAP AE-MC O/U SHOTGUN
Gauge: 12, 2-3/4" chambers. **Barrel:** 30" choke tubes. **Weight:** About 7 lbs. **Length:** 47-3/8". **Stock:** Checkered walnut; pistol grip, semi-beavertail forend. **Features:** Silver engraved receiver; gold single selective trigger; automatic safety, automatic ejectors; red bead front sight, metal bead center; recoil pad. Introduced 1997. Imported from Italy by K.B.I., Inc.
Price: **$1,699.00**

CHARLES DALY FIELD II HUNTER O/U SHOTGUN
Gauge: 12, 20, 28 and .410 bore (3" chambers, 28 ga. has 2-3/4"). **Barrel:** 28" Mod & Full, 26" Imp. Cyl. & Mod (.410 is Full & Full). **Weight:** About 7 lbs. **Length:** 42-3/4" to 44-3/4". **Stock:** Checkered walnut pistol grip and forend. **Features:** Blued engraved receiver, chrome-moly steel barrels; gold single selective trigger; automatic safety; gold bead front sight. Introduced 1997. Imported from Italy by K.B.I., Inc.
Price: 12 or 20 ga. **$1,029.00**
Price: 28 ga., .410 bore **$1,129.00**

SHOTGUNS — Over/Under

Charles Daly Superior Hunter

Charles Daly Empire II Mono Trap

Charles Daly Empire II EDL Hunter

Charles Daly
Empire Sporting O/U

Charles Daly Superior II Hunter AE O/U Shotgun

Similar to the Field Hunter AE except has silvered, engraved receiver. Introduced 1997. Imported from Italy by F.B.I., Inc.

Price: 28 ga., .410 bore **$1,449.00**

Charles Daly Field Hunter AE-MC O/U Shotgun

Similar to the Field Hunter except in 12 or 20 only, 26" or 28" barrels with five multi-choke tubes; automatic ejectors. Introduced 1997. Imported from Italy by K.B.I., Inc.

Price: 12 or 20 ga. **$1,279.00**

Charles Daly Superior II Sporting O/U Shotgun

Similar to the Field Hunter AE-MC except 28" or 30" barrels; silvered, engraved receiver; five choke tubes; ported barrels; red bead front sight. Introduced 1997. Imported from Italy by K.B.I., Inc.

Price: **$1,659.00**

CHARLES DALY EMPIRE II EDL HUNTER AE, AE-MC O/U SHOTGUNS

Gauge: 12, 20, .410, 3" chambers, 28 ga., 2-3/4". **Barrel:** 26", 28" (12, 20, choke tubes), 26" (Imp. Cyl. & Mod., 28 ga.), 26" (Full & Full, .410). **Weight:** About 7 lbs. **Stocks:** Checkered walnut pistol grip buttstock, semi-beavertail forend; recoil pad. **Features:** Silvered, engraved receiver; chrome-moly barrels; gold single selective trigger; automatic safety; automatic ejectors; red bead front sight, metal bead middle sight. Introduced 1997. Imported from Italy by K.B.I., Inc.

Price: Empire II EDL AE-MC (dummy sideplates) 12 or 20 . . . . . **$2,029.00**
Price: Empire II EDL AE, 28 . . . . **$2,019.00**
Price: Empire II EDL AE, .410 . . . . **$2,019.00**

Charles Daly Empire II Sporting AE-MC O/U Shotgun

Similar to the Empire II EDL Hunter except 12 or 20 gauge only, 28", 30" barrels with choke tubes; ported barrels; special stock dimensions. Introduced 1997. Imported from Italy by K.B.I., Inc.

Price: **$2,049.00**

CHARLES DALY EMPIRE II TRAP AE-MC O/U SHOTGUNS

Gauge: 12, 2-3/4" chambers. **Barrel:** 30" choke tubes. **Weight:** About 7 lbs. **Stock:** Checkered walnut; pistol grip, semi-beavertail forend. **Features:** Silvered, engraved, reinforced receiver; chrome-moly steel barrels; gold single selective trigger; automatic safety, automatic ejector; red bead front sight, metal bead center; recoil pad. Imported from Italy by K.B.I., Inc.

Price: **$2,099.00**
Price: Mono AE-MC, adj. comb **$2,999.00**
Price: AE-MC combo set, adj. comb **$3,919.00**

CHARLES DALY DIAMOND REGENT GTX DL HUNTER O/U SHOTGUNS

Gauge: 12, 20, .410, 3" chambers, 28, 2-3/4" chambers. **Barrel:** 26", 28", 30" (choke tubes), 26" (Imp. Cyl. & Mod. in 28, 26" (Full & Full) in .410. **Weight:** About 7 lbs. **Stock:** Extra select fancy European walnut with 24" hand checkering, hand rubbed oil finish. **Features:** Boss-type action with internal side lumps. Deep cut hand-engraved scrollwork and game scene set in full sideplates. GTX detachable single selective trigger system with coil springs; chrome-moly steel barrels; automatic safety; automatic ejectors, white bead front sight, metal bead center sight. Introduced 1997. Imported from Italy by K.B.I., Inc.

Price: 12 or 20 . . . . **Special order only**
Price: 28 . . . . **Special order only**
Price: .410 bore . . . . **Special order only**
Price: Diamond Regent GTX EDL Hunter (as above with engraved scroll
and birds, 10 gold inlays), 12 or 20 . . . . **Special order only**
Price: As above, 28 . . . . **Special order only**
Price: As above, .410 . . . . **Special order only**

CHARLES DALY DIAMOND GTX SPORTING O/U SHOTGUN

Gauge: 12, 20, 3" chambers. **Barrel:** 28", 30" with choke tubes. **Weight:** About 8.5 lbs. **Stock:** Checkered deluxe walnut; sporting clays dimensions. Pistol grip; semi-beavertail forend; hand rubbed oil finish. **Features:** Chromed, hand-engraved receiver; chrome-moly steel barrels; GTX detachable single selective trigger system with coil springs, automatic safety; automatic ejectors; red bead front sight; ported barrels. Introduced 1997. Imported from Italy by K.B.I., Inc.

Price: . . . . **Price on request**

CHARLES DALY DIAMOND GTX TRAP AE-MC O/U SHOTGUN

Gauge: 12, 2-3/4" chambers. **Barrel:** 30" (Full & Full). **Weight:** About 8.5 lbs. **Stock:** Checkered deluxe walnut; pistol grip; trap dimensions; semi-beavertail forend; hand-rubbed oil finish. **Features:** Silvered, hand-engraved receiver; chrome-moly steel barrels; GTX detachable single selective trigger system with coil springs, automatic safety, automatic ejectors, red bead front sight, metal bead middle; recoil pad. Imported from Italy by K.B.I., Inc.

Price: . . . . **Price on request**

SHOTGUNS — Over/Under

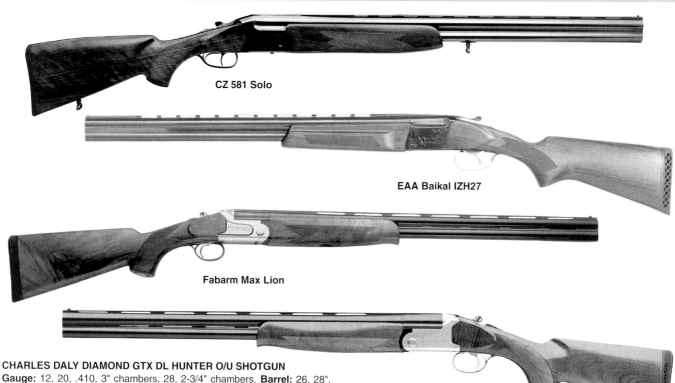

CZ 581 Solo

EAA Baikal IZH27

Fabarm Max Lion

Fabarm Silver Lion Youth

CHARLES DALY DIAMOND GTX DL HUNTER O/U SHOTGUN

Gauge: 12, 20, .410, 3" chambers, 28, 2-3/4" chambers. **Barrel:** 26, 28", choke tubes in 12 and 20 ga., 26" (Imp. Cyl. & Mod.), 26" (Full & Full) in .410-bore. **Weight:** About 8.5 lbs. **Stock:** Select fancy European walnut stock, with 24 lpi hand checkering; hand-rubbed oil finish. **Features:** Boss-type action with internal side lugs, hand-engraved scrollwork and game scene. GTX detachable single selective trigger system with coil springs; chrome-moly steel barrels, automatic safety, automatic ejectors, red bead front sight, recoil pad. Introduced 1997. Imported from Italy by K.B.I., Inc.

Price: . . . . **Special order only**

CZ 581 SOL O/U SHOTGUN

Gauge: 12, 2-3/4" chambers. **Barrel:** 27.6" (Mod. & Full). **Weight:** 7.37 lbs. **Length:** 44.5" overall. **Stock:** Circassian walnut. **Features:** Automatic ejectors; double triggers; Kersten-style double lump locking system. Imported from the Czech Republic by CZ-USA.

Price: $799.00

EAA BAIKAL IZH27 O/U SHOTGUN

Gauge: 12 (3" chambers), 16 (2-3/4" chambers), 20 (3" chambers), 28 (2-3/4" chambers), .410 (3"). **Barrel:** 26-1/2", 28-1/2" (imp., mod. and full choke tubes for 12 and 20 gauges; improved cylinder and modified for 16 and 28 gauges; Improved Modified and Full for .410; 16 also offered in Mod. and Full). **Weight:** NA. **Stock:** Walnut, checkered forearm and grip. Imported by European American Armory.

Price: IZH27 (12, 16 and 20 gauge) $509.00
Price: IZH27 (28 gauge and .410) $569.00

EAA Baikal IZH27 O/U Shotgun

Basic IZH27 with barrel porting, wide vent rib with double sight beads, engraved nickel receiver, checkered walnut stock and forend with palm swell and semi beavertail, 3 screw-in chokes, SS trigger, selectable ejectors, auto tang safety.

Price: 12 ga., 29" bbl. $589.00

EAA Baikal Nickel O/U Shotgun

Same as IZH27 but with polished nickel receiver.

Price: $529.00

FABARM MAX LION O/U SHOTGUN

Gauge: 12, 3" chambers, 20, 3" chambers. **Barrel:** 26", 28", 30" (12 ga.); 26", 28" (20 ga.), choke tubes. **Weight:** 7.4 lbs. **Length:** 47.5" overall (26"

barrel). **Stock:** European walnut; leather-covered recoil pad. **Features:** TriBore barrel, boxlock action with single selective trigger, manual safety, automatic ejectors; chrome-lined barrels; adjustable trigger. Silvered, engraved receiver. Comes with locking, fitted luggage case. Introduced 1998. Imported from Italy by Heckler & Koch, Inc.

Price: 12 or 20 . . . . $1,799.00

FABARM ULTRA CAMO MAG LION O/U SHOTGUN

Gauge: 12, 3-1/2" chambers. **Barrel:** 28" (Cyl., Imp. Cyl., Mod., Imp. Mod., Full, SS-mod., SS-full choke tubes). **Weight:** 7.9 lbs. **Length:** 50" overall. **Stock:** Camo-colored walnut. **Features:** TriBore barrel, Wetlands Camo finished metal surfaces, single selective trigger, non-auto ejectors, leather-covered recoil pad. Locking hard plastic case. Introduced 1998. Imported from Italy by Heckler & Koch, Inc.

Price: $1,229.00

FABARM MAX LION PARADOX O/U SHOTGUN

Gauge: 12, 20, 3" chambers. **Barrel:** 24". **Weight:** 7.6 lbs. **Length:** 44.5" overall. **Stock:** Walnut with special enhancing finish. **Features:** TriBore upper barrel, both wood and receiver are enhanced with special finishes, color case-hardened type finish.

Price: 12 or 20 . . . . $1,129.00

FABARM SILVER LION O/U SHOTGUN

Gauge: 12, 3" chambers, 20, 3" chambers. **Barrel:** 26", 28", 30" (12 ga.); 26", 28" (20 ga.), choke tubes. **Weight:** 7.2 lbs. **Length:** 47.5" overall (26" barrels). **Stock:** Walnut; leather-covered recoil pad. **Features:** TriBore barrel, boxlock action with single selective trigger; silvered receiver with engraving; automatic ejectors. Comes with locking hard plastic case. Introduced 1998. Imported from Italy by Heckler & Koch, Inc.

Price: 12 or 20 . . . . $1,229.00

Fabarm Silver Lion Youth Model O/U Shotgun

Similar to the Silver Lion except has 12.5" length of pull, 12 gauge only, comes with 24" TriBore barrel system. Weight is 6 lbs. Introduced 1999. Imported from Italy by Heckler & Koch, Inc.

Price: $1,229.00

SHOTGUNS — Over/Under

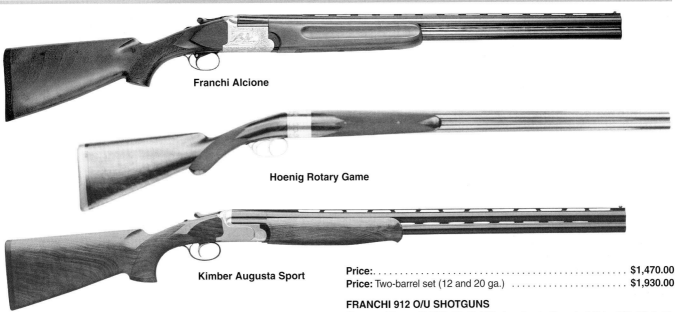

Franchi Alcione

Hoenig Rotary Game

Kimber Augusta Sport

FABARM CAMO TURKEY MAG O/U SHOTGUN
Gauge: 12, 3-1/2" chambers. **Barrel:** 20" TriBore (Ultra-Full ported tubes). **Weight:** 7.5 lbs. **Length:** 46" overall. **Stock:** 14.5"x1.5"x2.29". Walnut. **Sights:** Front bar, Picatinny rail scope base. **Features:** Completely covered with Xtra Brown camouflage finish. Unported barrels. Introduced 1999. Imported from Italy by Heckler & Koch, Inc.
Price: **$1,199.00**

FABARM SPORTING CLAYS COMPETITION EXTRA O/U SHOTGUN
Gauge: 12, 20, 3" chambers. **Barrel:** 12 ga. has 30", 20 ga. has 28"; ported TriBore barrel system with five tubes. **Weight:** 7 to 7.8 lbs. **Length:** 49.6" overall (20 ga.). **Stock:** 14.50"x1.38"x2.17" (20 ga.); deluxe walnut; leather-covered recoil pad. **Features:** Single selective trigger, auto ejectors; 10mm channeled rib; carbon fiber finish. Introduced 1999. Imported from Italy by Heckler & Koch, Inc.
Price: **$1,749.00**

FRANCHI ALCIONE FIELD O/U SHOTGUN
Gauge: 12, 20, 3" chambers. **Barrel:** 26", 28"; IC, M, F tubes. **Weight:** 7.5 lbs. **Length:** 43" overall with 26" barrels. **Stock:** European walnut. **Features:** Boxlock action with ejectors; barrel selector mounted on trigger; silvered, engraved receiver, vent center rib, automatic safety, interchangeable 20 ga. bbls., left-hand available. Imported from Italy by Benelli USA. Hard case included.
Price: **$1,310.00**
Price: (12 or 20 gauge barrel set) **$490.00**

Franchi Alcione SX O/U Shotgun
Similar to Alcione Field model with high grade walnut stock and forend. Gold engraved removeable sideplates, interchangeable barrels.
Price: **$1,855.00**
Price: (12 gauge barrel set) . . . . **$490.00 to $560.00**
Price: (20 gauge barrel set) **$490.00**

Franchi Alcione Sport SL O/U Shotgun
Similar to Alcione Field except 2-3/4" chambers, elongated forcing cones and porting for sporting clays shooting. 10mm vent rib, tightly curved pistol grip, manual safety, removeable sideplates. Imported from Italy by Benelli USA.
Price: **$1,700.00**

FRANCHI ALCIONE TITANIUM O/U SHOTGUN
Gauge: 12, 20, 3" chambers. **Barrel:** 26", 28"; IC, M, F tubes. **Weight:** 6.8 lbs. **Length:** 43", 45". **Stock:** Select walnut. **Sights:** Front/mid. **Features:** Receiver (titanium inserts) made of aluminum alloy. 7mm vent rib. Fast locking triggers. Left-hand available.

Price: **$1,470.00**
Price: Two-barrel set (12 and 20 ga.) **$1,930.00**

FRANCHI 912 O/U SHOTGUNS
Gauge: 12 ga., 2-3/4", 3", 3-1/2" chambers. **Barrel:** 24" to 30". **Weight:** Appx. 7.6 lbs. **Length:** 46" to 52". **Stock:** Walnut, synthetic, Timber HD, Max-4. **Sights:** White bead front. **Features:** Based on 612 design, magazine cut-off, stepped vent rib, dual-recoil-reduction system.
Price: Satin walnut **$850.00**
Price: Synthetic **$790.00**
Price: Timber HD & Max-4 . . . . **$900.00**
Price: Steadygrip Timber HD **$850.00**

FRANCHI VELOCE O/U SHOTGUN
Gauge: 20, 28. **Barrel:** 26", 28"; IC, M, F tubes. **Weight:** 5.5 to 5.8 lbs. **Length:** 43" to 45". **Stock:** High grade walnut. **Features:** Aluminum receiver with steel reinforcement scaled to 20 gauge for light weight. Pistol grip stock with slip recoil pad. Imported by Benelli USA. Hard case included.
Price: **$1,470.00**
Price: 28 ga. **$1,545.00**

Franchi Veloce English O/U Shotgun
Similar to Veloce standard model with straight grip English-style stock. Available with 26" barrels in 20 and 28 gauge. Hard case included.
Price: **$1,470.00**
Price: 28 ga. **$1,545.00**

HOENIG ROTARY ROUND ACTION GAME GUN O/U SHOTGUN
Gauge: 20, 28. **Barrel:** 26", 28", solid tapered rib. **Weight:** 6 lbs. and 6-1/4 lbs. **Stock:** English walnut to customer specifications. **Features:** Round action opens by rotating barrels, pulling forward. Inertia extraction system, rotary wing safety blocks strikers. Simple takedown without removing forend. Introduced 1997. Made in U.S.A. by George Hoenig.
Price: **$19,980.00**

KHAN ARTEMIS O/U SHOTGUN
Gauge: 12, 20, 28, 410. **Barrel:** 26", 28". **Stock:** Walnut. **Features:** Engraved receiver, single selective trigger, vent rib; choke tubes and extractors (Fixed IC, M choke on 410 models). Introduced 2005. Imported by Legacy Sports Int.
Price: . . . . **$617.00 to $791.00**
Price: Sporting clays model **$1,104.00**

KIMBER AUGUSTA O/U SHOTGUNS
Gauge: 12, 3". **Barrel:** 26" to 27-1/2". **Weight:** 7 lbs., 2 oz. **Length:** NA. **Stock:** Checkered AAA-grade European walnut. **Features:** Premium over/under, Boss-type action. Tri-alloy barrel with choke tubes. Back bored, long forcing cones. HiViz sight with center bead on vent rib. Satin or high gloss finish. Imported from Italy by Kimber Mfg., Inc.
Price: Field, Skeeet, Sporting, Trap **$6,000.00**

SHOTGUNS — Over/Under

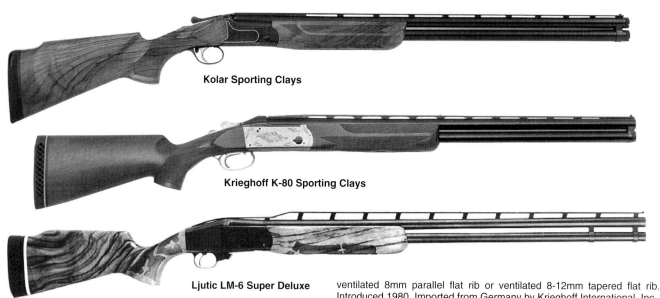

Kolar Sporting Clays

Krieghoff K-80 Sporting Clays

Ljutic LM-6 Super Deluxe

KOLAR SPORTING CLAYS O/U SHOTGUNS
Gauge: 12, 2-3/4" chambers. **Barrel:** 30", 32", 34"; extended choke tubes. **Stock:** 14-5/8"x2-1/2"x1-7/8"x1-3/8". French walnut. Four stock versions available. **Features:** Single selective trigger, detachable, adjustable for length; overbored barrels with long forcing cones; flat tramline rib; matte blue finish. Made in U.S. by Kolar.
Price: Standard **$7,995.00**
Price: Elite **$10,990.00**
Price: Elite Gold **$12,990.00**
Price: Legend **$13,990.00**
Price: Select **$15,990.00**
Price: Custom . . . . **Price on request**

Kolar AAA Competition Trap O/U Shotgun
Similar to the Sporting Clays gun except has 32" O/U /34" Unsingle or 30" O/U /34" Unsingle barrels as an over/under, unsingle, or combination set. Stock dimensions are 14-1/2"x2-1/2"x1-1/2"; American or French walnut; step parallel rib standard. Contact maker for full listings. Made in U.S.A. by Kolar.
Price: Over/under, choke tubes, standard. **$8,220.00**
Price: Unsingle, choke tubes, standard **$8,600.00**
Price: Combo (30"/34", 32"/34"), standard **$10,995.00**

Kolar AAA Competition Skeet O/U Shotgun
Similar to the Sporting Clays gun except has 28" or 30" barrels with Kolarite AAA sub gauge tubes; stock of American or French walnut with matte finish; flat tramline rib; under barrel adjustable for point of impact. Many options available. Contact maker for complete listing. Made in U.S.A. by Kolar.
Price: Standard, choke tubes **$8,645.00**
Price: Standard, choke tubes, two-barrel set **$10,995.00**

KRIEGHOFF K-80 SPORTING CLAYS O/U SHOTGUN
Gauge: 12. **Barrel:** 28", 30" or 32" with choke tubes. **Weight:** About 8 lbs. **Stock:** #3 Sporting stock designed for gun-down shooting. **Features:** Standard receiver with satin nickel finish and classic scroll engraving. Selective mechanical trigger adjustable for position. Choice of tapered flat or 8mm parallel flat barrel rib. Free-floating barrels. Aluminum case. Imported from Germany by Krieghoff International, Inc.
Price: Standard grade with five choke tubes, from **$9,395.00**

KRIEGHOFF K-80 SKEET O/U SHOTGUNS
Gauge: 12, 2-3/4" chambers. **Barrel:** 28", 30", (skeet & skeet), optional choke tubes). **Weight:** About 7-3/4 lbs. **Stock:** American skeet or straight skeet stocks, with palm-swell grips. Walnut. **Features:** Satin gray receiver finish. Selective mechanical trigger adjustable for position. Choice of ventilated 8mm parallel flat rib or ventilated 8-12mm tapered flat rib. Introduced 1980. Imported from Germany by Krieghoff International, Inc.
Price: Standard, skeet chokes **$8,220.00**
Price: Skeet Special (28" or 30", tapered flat rib, skeet & skeet choke tubes) **$8,920.00**

KRIEGHOFF K-80 TRAP O/U SHOTGUNS
Gauge: 12, 2-3/4" chambers. **Barrel:** 30", 32" (Imp. Mod. & Full or choke tubes). **Weight:** About 8-1/2 lbs. **Stock:** Four stock dimensions or adjustable stock available; all have palm-swell grips. Checkered European walnut. **Features:** Satin nickel receiver. Selective mechanical trigger, adjustable for position. Ventilated step rib. Introduced 1980. Imported from Germany by Krieghoff International, Inc.
Price: K-80 O/U (30", 32", Imp. Mod. & Full), from **$8,695.00**
Price: K-80 Unsingle (32", 34", Full), standard, from **$9,675.00**
Price: K-80 Combo (two-barrel set), standard, from **$13,990.00**

Krieghoff K-20 O/U Shotgun
Similar to the K-80 except built on a 20-gauge frame. Designed for skeet, sporting clays and field use. Offered in 20, 28 and .410; 28", 30" and 32" barrels. Imported from Germany by Krieghoff International Inc.
Price: K-20, 20 gauge, from **$9,395.00**
Price: K-20, 28 gauge, from **$9,545.00**
Price: K-20, .410, from **$9,545.00**

L. C. SMITH O/U SHOTGUN
Gauge: 12, 20. **Barrel:** 26", 28". **Stock:** Checkered walnut w/recoil pad. **Features:** 3" chambers; single selective trigger, selective automatic ejectors; vent rib; bead front sight. Imported from Italy by Marlin.
Price: **$1,394.00**

LEBEAU — COURALLY BOSS-VEREES O/U SHOTGUN
Gauge: 12, 20, 2-3/4" chambers. **Barrel:** 25" to 32". **Weight:** To customer specifications. **Stock:** Exhibition-quality French walnut. **Features:** Boss-type sidelock with automatic ejectors; single or double triggers; chopper lump barrels. A custom gun built to customer specifications. Imported from Belgium by Wm. Larkin Moore.
Price: From **$96,000.00**

LJUTIC LM-6 SUPER DELUXE O/U SHOTGUNS
Gauge: 12. **Barrel:** 28" to 34", choked to customer specs for live birds, trap, international trap. **Weight:** To customer specs. **Stock:** To customer specs. Oil finish, hand checkered. **Features:** Custom-made gun. Hollow-milled rib, pull or release trigger, push-button opener in front of trigger guard. From Ljutic Industries.
Price: Super Deluxe LM-6 O/U. **$19,995.00**
Price: Over/Under combo (interchangeable single barrel, two trigger guards, one for single trigger, one for doubles) **$27,995.00**
Price: Extra over/under barrel sets, 29"-32" **$6,995.00**

SHOTGUNS — Over/Under

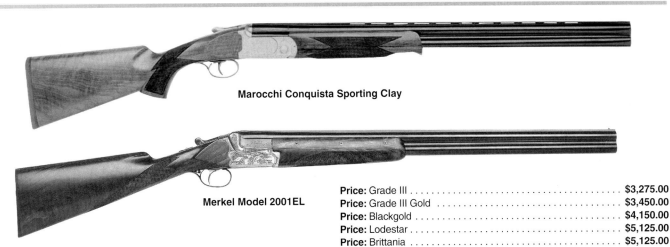

Marocchi Conquista Sporting Clay

Merkel Model 2001EL

LUGER CLASSIC O/U SHOTGUNS
Gauge: 12, 3" and 3-1/2" chambers. **Barrel:** 26", 28", 30"; Imp. Cyl. Mod. and Full choke tubes. **Weight:** 7-1/2 lbs. **Length:** 45" overall (28" barrel) **Stock:** Select-grade European walnut, hand-checkered grip and forend. **Features:** Gold, single selective trigger; automatic ejectors. Introduced 2000.
Price: Classic (26", 28" or 30" barrel; 3-1/2" chambers) $919.00
Price: Classic Sporting (30" barrel; 3" chambers) $964.00

MAROCCHI CONQUISTA SPORTING CLAYS O/U SHOTGUNS
Gauge: 12, 2-3/4" chambers. **Barrel:** 28", 30", 32" (ContreChoke tubes); 10mm concave vent rib. **Weight:** About 8 lbs. **Stock:** 14-1/2"-14-7/8"x2-3/16"x1-7/16"; American walnut with checkered grip and forend; sporting clays butt pad. **Sights:** 16mm luminescent front. **Features:** Lower mono-block and frame profile. Fast lock time. Ergonomically-shaped trigger adjustable for pull length. Automatic selective ejectors. Coin-finished receiver, blued barrels. Five choke tubes, hard case. Available as true left-hand model, opening lever operates from left to right; stock has left-hand cast. Introduced 1994. Imported from Italy by Precision Sales International.
Price: Grade I, right-hand $1,490.00
Price: Grade I, left-hand $1,615.00
Price: Grade II, right-hand $1,828.00
Price: Grade II, left-hand $2,180.00
Price: Grade III, right-hand, from $3,093.00
Price: Grade III, left-hand, from $3,093.00

Marocchi Conquista Trap O/U Shotguns
Similar to Conquista Sporting Clays model except 30" or 32" barrels choked Full & Full, stock dimensions of 14-1/2"-14-7/8"x1-11/16"x1-9/32"; weighs about 8-1/4 lbs. Introduced 1994. Imported from Italy by Precision Sales International.
Price: Grade I, right-hand $1,490.00
Price: Grade II, right-hand $1,828.00
Price: Grade III, right-hand, from $3,093.00

Marocchi Conquista Skeet O/U Shotguns
Similar to Conquista Sporting Clays model except 28" (skeet & skeet) barrels, stock dimensions of 14-3/8"-14-3/4"x2-3/16"x1-1/2". Weighs about 7-3/4 lbs. Introduced 1994. Imported from Italy by Precision Sales International.
Price: Grade I, right-hand $1,490.00
Price: Grade II, right-hand $1,828.00
Price: Grade III, right-hand, from $3,093.00

MAROCCHI MODEL 99 SPORTING TRAP AND SKEET O/U SHOTGUNS
Gauge: 12, 2-3/4", 3" chambers. **Barrel:** 28", 30", 32". **Stock:** French walnut. **Features:** Boss Locking system, screw-in chokes, low recoil, lightweight Monoblock barrels and ribs. Imported from Italy by Precision Sales International.
Price: Grade I $2,350.00
Price: Grade II $2,870.00
Price: Grade II Gold $3,025.00

Price: Grade III $3,275.00
Price: Grade III Gold $3,450.00
Price: Blackgold $4,150.00
Price: Lodestar $5,125.00
Price: Brittania $5,125.00
Price: Diana $6,350.00

MAROCCHI CONQUISTA USA MODEL 92 SPORTING CLAYS O/U SHOTGUN
Gauge: 12, 3" chambers. **Barrel:** 30"; back-bored, ported (ContreChoke Plus tubes); 10 mm concave ventilated top rib, ventilated middle rib. **Weight:** 8 lbs. 2 oz. **Stock:** 14-1/4"-14-5/8"x 2-1/8"x1-3/8"; American walnut with checkered grip and forend; sporting clays butt pad. **Features:** Low profile frame; fast lock time; automatic selective ejectors; blued receiver and barrels. Comes with three choke tubes. Ergonomically shaped trigger adjustable for pull length without tools. Barrels are back-bored and ported. Introduced 1996. Imported from Italy by Precision Sales International.
Price: $1,490.00

MERKEL MODEL 2001EL O/U SHOTGUN
Gauge: 12, 20, 3" chambers, 28, 2-3/4" chambers. **Barrel:** 12-28"; 20, 28 ga.-26-3/4". **Weight:** About 7 lbs. (12 ga.). **Stock:** Oil-finished walnut; English or pistol grip. **Features:** Self-cocking Blitz boxlock action with cocking indicators; Kersten double cross-bolt lock; silver-grayed receiver with engraved hunting scenes; coil spring ejectors; single selective or double triggers. Imported from Germany by GSI, Inc.
Price: 12, 20 . . . . $7,295.00
Price: 28 ga. $7,295.00
Price: Model 2000EL (scroll engraving, 12, 20 or 28) $5,795.00

MERKEL MODEL 303EL O/U Shotgun
Similar to Model 2001EL except Holland & Holland-style sidelock action with cocking indicators; English-style arabesque engraving. Available in 12, 20, 28 gauge. Imported from Germany by GSI, Inc.
Price: $19,995.00

Merkel Model 2002EL O/U Shotgun
Similar to Model 2001EL except dummy sideplates, arabesque engraving with hunting scenes; 12, 20, 28 gauge. Imported from Germany by GSI, Inc.
Price: $10,995.00

PERAZZI MX8/MX8 SPECIAL TRAP, SKEET O/U SHOTGUNS
Gauge: 12, 2-3/4" chambers. **Barrel:** Trap: 29-1/2" (Imp. Mod. & Extra Full), 31-1/2" (Full & Extra Full). Choke tubes optional. Skeet: 27-5/8" (skeet & skeet). **Weight:** About 8-1/2 lbs. (trap); 7 lbs., 15 oz. (skeet). **Stock:** Interchangeable and custom made to customer specs. **Features:** Has detachable and interchangeable trigger group with flat V springs. Flat 7/16" vent rib. Many options available. Imported from Italy by Perazzi U.S.A., Inc.
Price: From $12,756.00
Price: MX8 Special (adj. four-position trigger) From $11,476.00
Price: MX8 Special combo (o/u and single barrel sets) From . . . $15,127.00

Perazzi MX8 Special Skeet O/U Shotgun
Similar to the MX8 Skeet except has adjustable four-position trigger, skeet stock dimensions. Imported from Italy by Perazzi U.S.A., Inc.
Price: From $11,166.00

SHOTGUNS — Over/Under

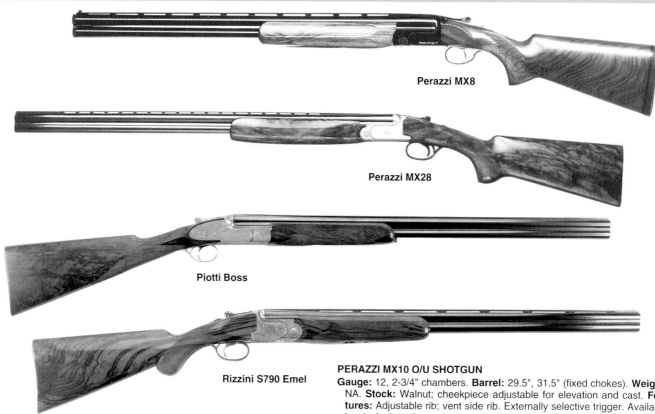

Perazzi MX8

Perazzi MX28

Piotti Boss

Rizzini S790 Emel

PERAZZI MX8 O/U SHOTGUNS

Gauge: 12, 2-3/4" chambers. **Barrel:** 28-3/8" (Imp. Mod. & Extra Full), 29-1/2" (choke tubes). **Weight:** 7 lbs., 12 oz. **Stock:** Special specifications. **Features:** Has single selective trigger; flat 7/16" x 5/16" vent rib. Many options available. Imported from Italy by Perazzi U.S.A., Inc.

Price: Standard **$12,532.00**
Price: Sporting **$11,166.00**
Price: Trap Double Trap (removable trigger group) **$15,581.00**
Price: Skeet **$12,756.00**
Price: SC3 grade (variety of engraving patterns) . . . . **$23,000.00+**
Price: SCO grade (more intricate engraving, gold inlays) . . . . **$39,199.00+**

Perazzi MX8/20 O/U Shotgun

Similar to the MX8 except has smaller frame and has a removable trigger mechanism. Available in trap, skeet, sporting or game models with fixed chokes or choke tubes. Stock is made to customer specifications. Introduced 1993. Imported from Italy by Perazzi U.S.A., Inc.

Price: From **$11,166.00**

PERAZZI MX12 HUNTING O/U SHOTGUNS

Gauge: 12, 2-3/4" chambers. **Barrel:** 26-3/4", 27-1/2", 28-3/8", 29-1/2" (Mod. & Full); choke tubes available in 27-5/8", 29-1/2" only (MX12C). **Weight:** 7 lbs., 4 oz. **Stock:** To customer specs; interchangeable. **Features:** Single selective trigger; coil springs used in action; Schnabel forend tip. Imported from Italy by Perazzi U.S.A., Inc.

Price: From **$11,166.00**
Price: MX12C (with choke tubes) From **$11,960.00**

Perazzi MX20 Hunting O/U Shotguns

Similar to the MX12 except 20 ga. frame size. Non-removable trigger group. Available in 20, 28, .410 with 2-3/4" or 3" chambers. 26" standard, and choked Mod. & Full. Weight is 6 lbs., 6 oz. Imported from Italy by Perazzi U.S.A., Inc.

Price: From **$11,166.00**
Price: MX20C (as above, 20 ga. only, choke tubes) From **$11,960.00**

PERAZZI MX10 O/U SHOTGUN

Gauge: 12, 2-3/4" chambers. **Barrel:** 29.5", 31.5" (fixed chokes). **Weight:** NA. **Stock:** Walnut; cheekpiece adjustable for elevation and cast. **Features:** Adjustable rib; vent side rib. Externally selective trigger. Available in single barrel, combo, over/under trap, skeet, pigeon and sporting models. Introduced 1993. Imported from Italy by Perazzi U.S.A., Inc.

Price: MX200410 . . . . **$18,007.00**

PERAZZI MX28, MX410 GAME O/U SHOTGUN

Gauge: 28, 2-3/4" chambers, .410, 3" chambers. **Barrel:** 26" (Imp. Cyl. & Full). **Weight:** NA. **Stock:** To customer specifications. **Features:** Made on scaled-down frames proportioned to the gauge. Introduced 1993. Imported from Italy by Perazzi U.S.A., Inc.

Price: From **$22,332.00**

PIOTTI BOSS O/U SHOTGUN

Gauge: 12, 20. **Barrel:** 26" to 32", chokes as specified. **Weight:** 6.5 to 8 lbs. **Stock:** Dimensions to customer specs. Best quality figured walnut. **Features:** Essentially a custom-made gun with many options. Introduced 1993. Imported from Italy by Wm. Larkin Moore.

Price: From **$48,000.00**

REMINGTON MODEL 332 O/U SHOTGUN

Gauge: 12, 3" chambers. **Barrel:** 26", 28", 30". **Weight:** 7.75 lbs. **Length:** 42" to 47". **Stock:** Satin-finished American walnut. **Sights:** Twin bead. **Features:** Light-contour, vent rib, RemChoke barrel, blued, traditional M-32 experience with M-300 Ideal performance, standard auto ejectors, set trigger. Proven boxlock action.

Price: **$1,624.00**

RIZZINI S790 EMEL O/U SHOTGUN

Gauge: 20, 28, .410. **Barrel:** 26", 27.5" (Imp. Cyl. & Imp. Mod.). **Weight:** About 6 lbs. **Stock:** 14"x1-1/2"x2-1/8". Extra fancy select walnut. **Features:** Boxlock action with profuse engraving; automatic ejectors; single selective trigger; silvered receiver. Comes with Nizzoli leather case. Introduced 1996. Imported from Italy by Wm. Larkin Moore & Co.

Price: From **$9,725.00**

Rizzini S792 EMEL O/U Shotgun

Similar to S790 EMEL except dummy sideplates with extensive engraving coverage. Nizzoli leather case. Introduced 1996. Imported from Italy by Wm. Larkin Moore & Co.

Price: From **$9,075.00**

SHOTGUNS — Over/Under

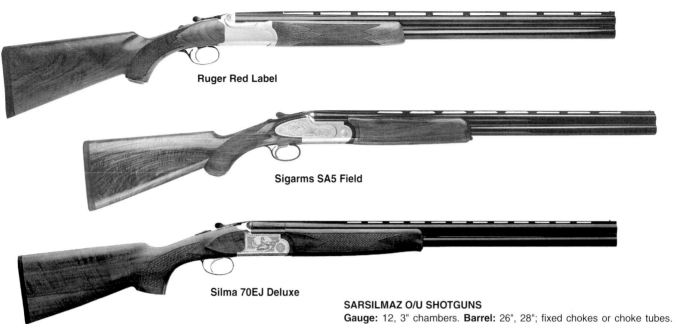

Ruger Red Label

Sigarms SA5 Field

Silma 70EJ Deluxe

RIZZINI UPLAND EL O/U SHOTGUN

Gauge: 12, 16, 20, 28, .410. **Barrel:** 26", 27-1/2", Mod. & Full, Imp. Cyl. & Imp. Mod. choke tubes. **Weight:** About 6.6 lbs. **Stock:** 14-1/2"x1-1/2"x2-1/4". **Features:** Boxlock action; single selective trigger; ejectors; profuse engraving on silvered receiver. Comes with fitted case. Introduced 1996. Imported from Italy by Wm. Larkin Moore & Co.
Price: From **$3,350.00**

Rizzini Artemis O/U Shotgun

Same as Upland EL model except dummy sideplates with extensive game scene engraving. Fancy European walnut stock. Fitted case. Introduced 1996. Imported from Italy by Wm. Larkin Moore & Co.
Price: From **$2,100.00**

RIZZINI S782 EMEL O/U SHOTGUN

Gauge: 12, 2-3/4" chambers. **Barrel:** 26", 27.5" (Imp. Cyl. & Imp. Mod.). **Weight:** About 6.75 lbs. **Stock:** 14-1/2"x1-1/2"x2-1/4". Extra fancy select walnut. **Features:** Boxlock action with dummy sideplates, extensive engraving with gold inlaid game birds, silvered receiver, automatic ejectors, single selective trigger. Nizzoli leather case. Introduced 1996. Imported from Italy by Wm. Larkin Moore & Co.
Price: From **$11,450.00**

RUGER RED LABEL O/U SHOTGUNS

Gauge: 12, 20, 3" chambers; 28 2-3/4" chambers. **Barrel:** 26", 28" (skeet [two], Imp. Cyl., Full, Mod. screw-in choke tubes). Proved for steel shot. **Weight:** About 7 lbs. (20 ga.); 7-1/2 lbs. (12 ga.). **Length:** 43" overall (26" barrels). **Stock:** 14"x1-1/2"x2-1/2". Straight grain American walnut or black synthetic. Checkered pistol grip and forend, rubber butt pad. **Features:** Stainless steel receiver. Single selective mechanical trigger, selective automatic ejectors; serrated free-floating vent rib. Comes with two skeet, one Imp. Cyl., one Mod., one Full choke tube and wrench. Made in U.S. by Sturm, Ruger & Co.
Price: Red Label with pistol grip stock **$1,622.00**
Price: English Field with straight-grip stock **$1,622.00**
Price: All-Weather Red Label with black synthetic stock **$1,622.00**
Price: Sporting clays (30" bbl.) **$1,622.00**

Ruger Engraved Red Label O/U Shotgun

Similar to Red Label except scroll engraved receiver with 24-carat gold game bird (pheasant in 12 gauge, grouse in 20 gauge, woodcock in 28 gauge, duck on All-Weather 12 gauge). Introduced 2000.
Price: Engraved Red Label
(12, 20 and 28 gauge in 26" and 28" barrels) **$1,811.00**

SARSILMAZ O/U SHOTGUNS

Gauge: 12, 3" chambers. **Barrel:** 26", 28"; fixed chokes or choke tubes. **Weight:** NA. **Length:** NA. **Stock:** Oil-finished hardwood. **Features:** Double or single selective trigger, wide vent rib, chrome-plated parts, blued finish. Introduced 2000. Imported from Turkey by Armsport Inc.
Price: Double triggers; mod. and full or imp. cyl.
and mod. fixed chokes **$499.95**
Price: Single selective trigger; imp. cyl. and mod. or mod.
and full fixed chokes **$575.00**
Price: Single selective trigger; five choke tubes and wrench **$695.00**

SIGARMS SA5 O/U SHOTGUNS

Gauge: 12, 20, 3" chamber. **Barrel:** 26-1/2", 27" (Full, Imp. Mod., Mod., Imp. Cyl., Cyl. choke tubes). **Weight:** 6.9 lbs. (12 gauge), 5.9 lbs. (20 gauge). **Stock:** 14-1/2" x 1-1/2" x 2-1/2". Select grade walnut; checkered 20 lpi at grip and forend. **Features:** Single selective trigger, automatic ejectors; hand engraved detachable side plate; matte nickel receiver, rest blued; tapered bolt lock-up. Introduced 1997. Imported by SIGARMS, Inc.
Price: Field, 12 gauge. **$2,670.00**
Price: Sporting clays **$2,800.00**
Price: Field 20 gauge **$2,670.00**

SILMA MODEL 70EJ DELUXE O/U SHOTGUNS

Gauge: 12 (3-1/2" chambers), 20, .410 (3" chambers), 28 (2-3/4" chambers). **Barrel:** 28" (12 and 20 gauge, fixed and tubed, 28 and .410 fixed), 26" (12 and 20 fixed). **Weight:** 7.6 lbs 12 gauge, 6.9 lbs, 20, 28 and .410. **Stock:** Checkered select European walnut, pistol grip, solid rubber recoil pad. **Features:** Monobloc construction, chrome-moly blued steel barrels, raised vent rib, automatic safety and ejectors, single selective trigger, gold plated, bead front sight. Brushed, engraved receiver. Introduced 2002. Clays models introduced 2003. Imported from Italy by Legacy Sports International.
Price: 12 gauge **$1,089.00**
Price: 20 gauge **$1,016.00**
Price: 28, .410 . . . . **$1,140.00**
Price: Sporting clays **$1,387.00**

Silma Model 70 EJ Superlight O/U Shotgun

Similar to Silma 70EJ Deluxe except 12 gauge, 3" chambers, alloy receiver, weighs 5.6 lbs.
Price: 12, 20 multi-chokes (IC, M, F) **$1,191.00**

Silma Model 70 EJ Standard O/U Shotgun

Similar to Silma 70EJ Deluxe except 12 and 20 gauge only, standard walnut stock, light engraving, silver-plated trigger.
Price: 12 gauge **$1,016.00**
Price: 20 gauge **$944.00**

SHOTGUNS — Over/Under

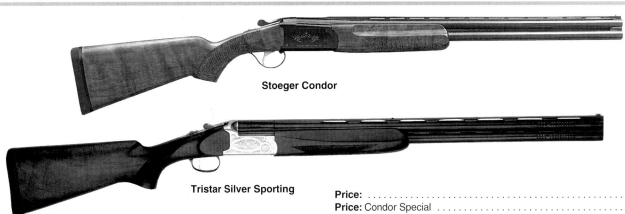

Stoeger Condor

Tristar Silver Sporting

SKB MODEL 85TSS O/U SHOTGUNS
Gauge: 12, 20, .410: 3"; 28, 2-3/4". **Barrel:** Chrome lined 26", 28", 30", 32" (w/choke tubes). **Weight:** 7 lbs., 7 oz. to 8 lbs., 14 oz. **Stock:** Hand-checkered American walnut with matte finish, Schnabel or grooved forend. Target stocks available in various styles. **Sights:** Metal bead front or HiViz competition sights. **Features:** Low profile boxlock action with Greener-style cross bolt; single selective trigger; manual safety. Back-bored barrels with lengthened forcing cones. Introduced 2004. Imported from Japan by G.U. Inc.
Price: Sporting clays, 12 or 20 . . . . **$1,949.00**
Price: Sporting clays, 28 . . . . **$1,949.00**
Price: Sporting clays set, 12 and 20 . . . . **$3,149.00**
Price: Skeet, 12 or 20 . . . . **$1,949.00**
Price: Skeet, 28 or .410 . . . . **$2,129.00 to $2,179.00**
Price: Skeet, three-barrel set, 20, 28, .410 . . . . **$4,679.00**
Price: Trap, standard or Monte Carlo **$1,499.00**
Price: Trap adjustable comb **$2,129.00**

SKB MODEL 585 O/U SHOTGUNS
Gauge: 12 or 20, 3"; 28, 2-3/4"; .410, 3". **Barrel:** 12 ga.-26", 28", 30", 32", 34" (InterChoke tubes); 20 ga.-26", 28" (InterChoke tubes); 28-26", 28" (InterChoke tubes); .410-26", 28" (InterChoke tubes). Ventilated side ribs. **Weight:** 6.6 to 8.5 lbs. **Length:** 43" to 51-3/8" overall. **Stock:** 14-1/8"x1-1/2"x2-3/16". Hand checkered walnut with high-gloss finish. Target stocks available in standard and Monte Carlo. **Sights:** Metal bead front (field), target style on skeet, trap, sporting clays. **Features:** Boxlock action; silver nitride finish with field or target pattern engraving; manual safety, automatic ejectors, single selective trigger. All 12 gauge barrels are back-bored, have lengthened forcing cones and longer choke tube system. Sporting clays models in 12 gauge with 28" or 30" barrels available with optional 3/8" step-up target-style rib, matte finish, nickel center bead, white front bead. Introduced 1992. Imported from Japan by G.U. Inc.
Price: Field. **$1,499.00**
Price: Two-barrel field set, 12 & 20 . . . . **$2,399.00**
Price: Two-barrel field set, 20 & 28 or 28 & .410 . . . . **$2,469.00**

SKB Model 585 Gold Package
Similar to Model 585 Field except gold-plated trigger, two gold-plated game inlays, Schnabel forend. Silver or blue receiver. Introduced 1998. Imported from Japan by G.U. Inc.
Price: 12, 20 ga. **$1,689.00**
Price: 28, .410 . . . . **$1,749.00**

SKB Model 505 O/U Shotgun
Similar to Model 585 except blued receiver, standard bore diameter, standard InterChoke system on 12, 20, 28, different receiver engraving. Imported from Japan by G.U. Inc.
Price: Field, 12 (26", 28"), 20 (26", 28") **$1,229.00**

STOEGER CONDOR SPECIAL O/U SHOTGUNS
Gauge: 12, 20, 2-3/4" 3" chambers. **Barrel:** 26", 28". **Weight:** 7.7 lbs. **Sights:** Brass bead. **Features:** IC and M screw-in choke tubes with each gun. Oil finished hardwood with pistol grip and forend. Auto safety, single trigger, automatic extractors.

Price: **$350.00**
Price: Condor Special **$415.00**
Price: Supreme Deluxe w/SS and red bar sights **$500.00**
Price: Youth Model **$350.00**
Price: Competition Model (w/ported bbls.) **$579.00**

TRADITIONS CLASSIC SERIES O/U SHOTGUNS
Gauge: 12, 3"; 20, 3"; 16, 2-3/4"; 28, 2-3/4"; .410, 3". **Barrel:** 26" and 28". **Weight:** 6 lbs., 5 oz. to 7 lbs., 6 oz. **Length:** 43" to 45" overall. **Stock:** Walnut. **Features:** Single-selective trigger; chrome-lined barrels with screw-in choke tubes; extractors (Field Hunter and Field I models) or automatic ejectors (Field II and Field III models); rubber butt pad; top tang safety. Imported from Fausti of Italy by Traditions.
Price: Field Hunter: Blued receiver; 12 or 20 ga.; 26" bbl. has IC and Mod. tubes, 28" has mod. and full tubes **$669.00**
Price: Field I: Blued receiver; 12, 20, 28 ga. or .410; fixed chokes (26" has I.C. and mod., 28" has mod. and full) **$619.00**
Price: Field II: Coin-finish receiver; 12, 16, 20, 28 ga. or .410; gold trigger; choke tubes **$789.00**
Price: Field III: Coin-finish receiver; gold engraving and trigger; 12 ga.; 26" or 28" bbl.; choke tubes **$999.00**
Price: Upland II: Blued receiver; 12 or 20 ga.; English-style straight walnut stock; choke tubes **$839.00**
Price: Upland III: Blued receiver, gold engraving; 20 ga.; high-grade pistol grip walnut stock; choke tubes **$1,059.00**
Price: Upland III: Blued, gold engraved receiver, 12 ga. Round pistol grip stock, choke tubes **$1,059.00**
Price: Sporting Clay II: Silver receiver; 12 ga.; ported barrels with skeet, i.c., mod. and full extended tubes **$959.00**
Price: Sporting Clay III: Engraved receivers, 12 and 20 ga., walnut stock, vent rib, extended choke tubes **$1,189.00**

TRADITIONS MAG 350 SERIES O/U SHOTGUNS
Gauge: 12, 3-1/2". **Barrel:** 24", 26" and 28". **Weight:** 7 lbs. to 7 lbs., 4 oz. **Length:** 41" to 45" overall. **Stock:** Walnut or composite with Mossy Oak® Break-Up™ or Advantage® Wetlands ™ camouflage. **Features:** Black matte, engraved receiver; vent rib; automatic ejectors; single-selective trigger; three screw-in choke tubes; rubber recoil pad; top tang safety. Imported from Fausti of Italy by Traditions.
Price: (Mag Hunter II: 28" black matte barrels, walnut stock, includes I.C., Mod. and Full tubes) **$799.00**
Price: (Turkey II: 24" or 26" camo barrels, Break-Up™ camo stock, includes Mod., Full and X-Full tubes) **$889.00**
Price: (Waterfowl II: 28" camo barrels, Advantage Wetlands camo stock, includes IC, Mod. and Full tubes) **$899.00**

TRISTAR SILVER SPORTING O/U SHOTGUN
Gauge: 12, 2-3/4" chambers, 20 3" chambers. **Barrel:** 28", 30" (skeet, Imp. Cyl., Mod., Full choke tubes). **Weight:** 7-3/8 lbs. **Length:** 45-1/2" overall. **Stock:** 14-3/8"x1-1/2"x2-3/8". Figured walnut, cut checkering; sporting clays quick-mount buttpad. **Sights:** Target bead front. **Features:** Boxlock action with single selective trigger, automatic selective ejectors; special broadway channeled rib; vented barrel rib; chrome bores. Chrome-nickel finish on frame, with engraving. Introduced 1990. Imported from Italy by Tristar Sporting Arms Ltd.
Price: **$799.00**

SHOTGUNS — Over/Under

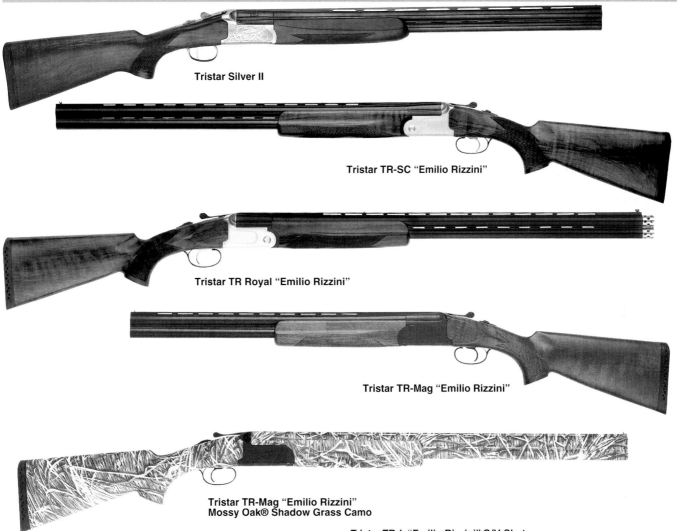

Tristar Silver II

Tristar TR-SC "Emilio Rizzini"

Tristar TR Royal "Emilio Rizzini"

Tristar TR-Mag "Emilio Rizzini"

Tristar TR-Mag "Emilio Rizzini"
Mossy Oak® Shadow Grass Camo

Tristar Silver II O/U Shotgun
Similar to the Silver except 26" barrel (Imp. Cyl., Mod., Full choke tubes, 12 and 20 ga.), 28" (Imp. Cyl., Mod., Full choke tubes, 12 ga. only), 26" (Imp. Cyl. & Mod. fixed chokes, 28 and .410), automatic selective ejectors. Weight is about 6 lbs., 15 oz. (12 ga., 26").
Price: **$669.00**

TRISTAR TR-SC "EMILIO RIZZINI" O/U SHOTGUN
Gauge: 12, 20, 3" chambers. **Barrel:** 28", 30" (Imp. Cyl., Mod., Full choke tubes). **Weight:** 7-1/2 lbs. **Length:** 46" overall (28" barrel). **Stock:** 1-1/2"x2-3/8"x14-3/8". Semi-fancy walnut; pistol grip with palm swell; semi-beavertail forend; black sporting clays recoil pad. **Features:** Silvered boxlock action with Four Locks locking system, auto ejectors, single selective (inertia) trigger, auto safety. Hard chrome bores. Vent 10mm rib with target-style front and mid-rib beads. Introduced 1998. Imported from Italy by Tristar Sporting Arms, Ltd.
Price: Sporting clay model **$1,047.00**
Price: 20 ga. **$1,127.00**

Tristar TR-Royal "Emilio Rizzini" O/U Shotgun
Similar to the TR-SC except has special parallel stock dimensions (1-1/2"x1-5/8"x14-3/8") to give low felt recoil; Rhino ported, extended choke tubes; solid barrel spacer; has "TR-Royal" gold engraved on the silvered receiver. Available in 12 gauge (28", 30") 20 and 28 gauge (28" only). Introduced 1999. Imported from Italy by Tristar Sporting Arms, Ltd.
Price: 12, 20, 28 ga. **$1,319.00**

Tristar TR-L "Emilio Rizzini" O/U Shotgun
Similar to the TR-SC except has stock dimensions designed for female shooters (1-1/2"x3"x13-1/2"). Standard grade walnut. Introduced 1998. Imported from Italy by Tristar Sporting Arms, Ltd.
Price: **$1,063.00**

TRISTAR TR-I, II "EMILIO RIZZINI" O/U SHOTGUNS
Gauge: 12, 20, 3" chambers (TR-I); 12, 16, 20, 28, .410 3" chambers. **Barrel:** 12 ga., 26" (Imp. Cyl. & Mod.), 28" (Mod. & Full); 20 ga., 26" (Imp. Cyl. & Mod.), fixed chokes. **Weight:** 7-1/2 lbs. **Stock:** 1-1/2"x2-3/8"x14-3/8". Walnut with palm swell pistol grip, hand checkering, semi-beavertail forend, black recoil pad. **Features:** Boxlock action with blued finish, Four Locks locking system, gold single selective (inertia) trigger system, automatic safety, extractors. Introduced 1998. Imported from Italy by Tristar Sporting Arms, Ltd.
Price: TR-I. **$779.00**
Price: TR-II (automatic ejectors, choke tubes) 12, 16 ga. **$919.00**
Price: 20, 28 ga., .410 . . . . **$969.00**

Tristar TR-Mag "Emilio Rizzini" O/U Shotguns
Similar to TR-I, 3-1/2" chambers; choke tubes; 24" or 28" barrels with three choke tubes; extractors; auto safety. Matte blue finish on all metal, non-reflective wood finish. Introduced 1998. Imported from Italy by Tristar Sporting Arms, Ltd.
Price: **$799.00**
Price: Mossy Oak® Break-Up™ camo **$969.00**
Price: Mossy Oak® Shadow Grass camo **$969.00**
Price: 10 ga., Mossy Oak® camo patterns **$1,132.10**

255

SHOTGUNS — Over/Under

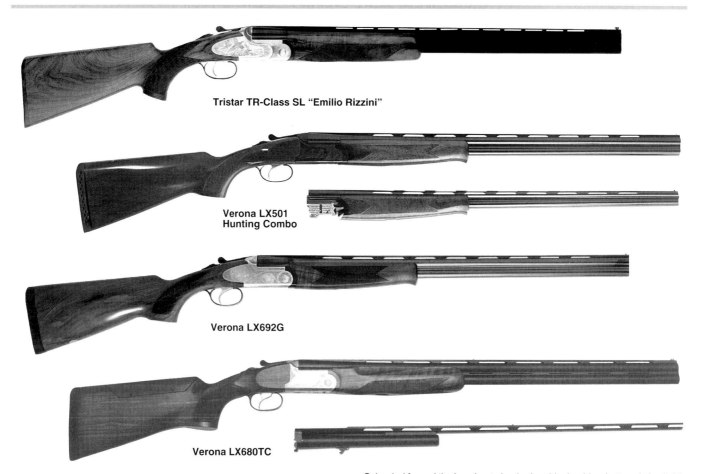

Tristar TR-Class SL "Emilio Rizzini"

Verona LX501
Hunting Combo

Verona LX692G

Verona LX680TC

TRISTAR TR-CLASS SL "EMILIO RIZZINI" O/U SHOTGUN

Gauge: 12, 2-3/4" chambers. **Barrel:** 28", 30". **Weight:** 7-3/4 lbs. **Stock:** Fancy walnut, hand checkering, semi-beavertail forend, black recoil pad, gloss finish. **Features:** Hand-fitted gun. Boxlock action with silvered, engraved sideplates; Four Lock locking system; automatic ejectors; hard chrome bores; vent tapered 7mm rib with target-style front bead. Introduced 1999. Imported from Italy by Tristar Sporting Arms, Ltd.
Price: **$1,775.00**

TRISTAR WS/OU 12 O/U SHOTGUN

Gauge: 12, 3-1/2" chambers. **Barrel:** 28" or 30" (Imp. Cyl., Mod., Full choke tubes). **Weight:** 6 lbs., 15 oz. **Length:** 46" overall. **Stock:** 14-1/8"x1-1/8"x2-3/8". European walnut with cut checkering, black vented recoil pad, matte finish. **Features:** Boxlock action with single selective trigger, automatic selective ejectors; chrome bores. Matte metal finish. Imported by Tristar Sporting Arms Ltd.
Price: **$645.00**

VERONA LX501 HUNTING O/U SHOTGUNS

Gauge: 12, 20, 28, .410 (2-3/4", 3" chambers). **Barrel:** 28"; 12, 20 ga. have Interchoke tubes, 28 ga. and .410 have fixed Full & Mod. **Weight:** 6-7 lbs. **Stock:** Matte-finished walnut with machine-cut checkering. **Features:** Gold-plated single-selective trigger; ejectors; engraved, blued receiver, non-automatic safety; coil spring-operated firing pins. Introduced 1999. Imported from Italy by B.C. Outdoors.
Price: 12 and 20 ga. **$878.08**
Price: 28 ga. and .410 . . . . **$926.72**
Price: .410 . . . . **$907.01**
Price: Combos 20/28, 28/.410 . . . . **$1,459.20**

Verona LX692 Gold Hunting O/U Shotguns

Similar to Verona LX501 except engraved, silvered receiver with false sideplates showing gold inlaid bird hunting scenes on three sides; Schnabel forend tip; hand-cut checkering; black rubber butt pad. Available in 12 and 20 gauge only, five Interchoke tubes. Introduced 1999. Imported from Italy by B.C. Outdoors.
Price: **$1,295.00**
Price: LX692G Combo 28/.410 . . . . **$2,192.40**

Verona LX680 Sporting O/U Shotgun

Similar to Verona LX501 except engraved, silvered receiver; ventilated middle rib; beavertail forend; hand-cut checkering; available in 12 or 20 gauge only with 2-3/4" chambers. Introduced 1999. Imported from Italy by B.C. Outdoors.
Price: **$1,159.68**

Verona LX680 Skeet/Sporting/Trap O/U Shotgun

Similar to Verona LX501 except skeet or trap stock dimensions; beavertail forend, palm swell on pistol grip; ventilated center barrel rib. Introduced 1999. Imported from Italy by B.C. Outdoors.
Price: **$1,736.96**

Verona LX692 Gold Sporting O/U Shotgun

Similar to Verona LX680 except false sideplates have gold-inlaid bird hunting scenes on three sides; red high-visibility front sight. Introduced 1999. Imported from Italy by B.C. Outdoors.
Price: Skeet/sporting **$1,765.12**
Price: Trap (32" barrel, 7-7/8 lbs.) **$1,594.80**

VERONA LX680 COMPETITION TRAP O/U SHOTGUNS

Gauge: 12. **Barrel:** 30" O/U, 32" single bbl. **Weight:** 8-3/8 lbs. combo, 7 lbs. single. **Stock:** Walnut. **Sights:** White front, mid-rib bead. **Features:** Interchangeable barrels switch from o/u to single configurations. 5 Briley chokes in combo, 4 in single bbl. extended forcing cones, ported barrels 32" with raised rib. By B.C. Outdoors.
Price: Trap Single (LX680TGTSB) **$1,736.96**
Price: Trap Combo (LX680TC) **$2,553.60**

SHOTGUNS — Over/Under

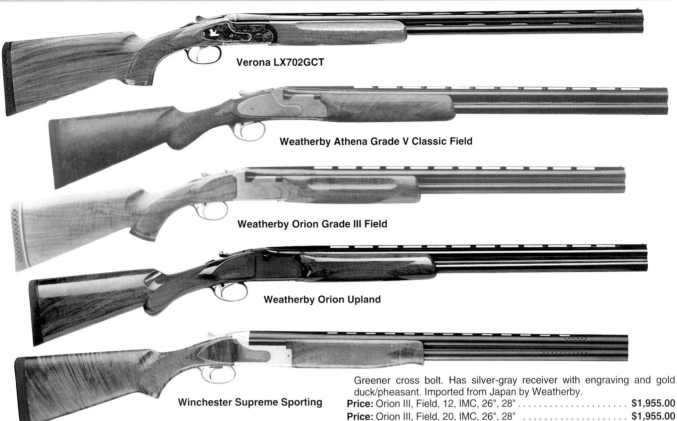

Verona LX702GCT

Weatherby Athena Grade V Classic Field

Weatherby Orion Grade III Field

Weatherby Orion Upland

Winchester Supreme Sporting

VERONA LX702 GOLD TRAP COMBO O/U SHOTGUNS
Gauge: 20/28, 2-3/4" chamber. **Barrel:** 30". **Weight:** 7 lbs. **Stock:** Turkish walnut with beavertail forearm. **Sights:** White front bead. **Features:** 2-barrel competition gun. Color case-hardened side plates and receiver with gold inlaid pheasant. Vent rib between barrels. 5 Interchokes. Imported from Italy by B.C. Outdoors.
Price: Combo **$2,467.84**
Price: 20 ga. **$1,829.12**

Verona LX702 Skeet/Trap O/U Shotguns
Similar to Verona LX702. Both are 12 gauge and 2-3/4" chamber. Skeet has 28" barrel and weighs 7-3/4 lbs. Trap has 32" barrel and weighs 7-7/8 lbs. By B.C. Outdoors.
Price: Skeet **$1,829.12**
Price: Trap **$1,829.12**

WEATHERBY ATHENA GRADE V CLASSIC FIELD O/U SHOTGUN
Gauge: 12, 20, 3" chambers. **Barrel:** 26", 28", IMC multi-choke tubes. **Weight:** 12 ga., 7-1/4 to 8 lbs.; 20 ga. 6-1/2 to 7-1/4 lbs. **Stock:** Oil-finished American Claro walnut with fine-line checkering, rounded pistol grip and slender forend. **Features:** Old English recoil pad. Sideplate receiver has rose and scroll engraving.
Price: **$3,037.00**

Weatherby Athena Grade III Classic Field O/U Shotgun
Similar to Athena Grade V, has Grade III Claro walnut with oil finish, rounded pistol grip, slender forend; silver nitride/gray receiver has rose and scroll engraving with gold-overlay upland game scenes. Introduced 1999. Imported from Japan by Weatherby.
Price: 12, 20, 28 ga. **$2,173.00**

WEATHERBY ORION GRADE III FIELD O/U SHOTGUNS
Gauge: 12, 20, 3" chambers. **Barrel:** 26", 28", IMC multi-choke tubes. **Weight:** 6-1/2 to 8 lbs. **Stock:** 14-1/4"x1-1/2"x2-1/2". American walnut, checkered grip and forend. Rubber recoil pad. **Features:** Selective automatic ejectors, single selective inertia trigger. Top tang safety, Greener cross bolt. Has silver-gray receiver with engraving and gold duck/pheasant. Imported from Japan by Weatherby.
Price: Orion III, Field, 12, IMC, 26", 28" **$1,955.00**
Price: Orion III, Field, 20, IMC, 26", 28" **$1,955.00**

Weatherby Orion Grade II Classic Field O/U Shotgun
Similar to Orion Grade III Field except stock has high-gloss finish, and bird on receiver is not gold. Available in 12 gauge, 26", 28", 30" barrels, 20 gauge, 26" 28", both with 3" chambers, 28 gauge, 26", 2-3/4" chambers. All have IMC choke tubes. Imported from Japan by Weatherby.
Price: **$1,622.00**

Weatherby Orion Upland O/U Shotgun
Similar to Orion Grade III Field. Plain blued receiver, gold W on trigger guard; rounded pistol grip, slender forend of Claro walnut with high-gloss finish; black butt pad. Available in 12 and 20 gauge with 26" and 28" barrels. Introduced 1999. Imported from Japan by Weatherby.
Price: **$1,299.00**

WEATHERBY ORION SSC O/U SHOTGUN
Gauge: 12, 3" chambers. **Barrel:** 28", 30", 32" (skeet, SC1, Imp. Cyl., SC2, Mod. IMC choke tubes). **Weight:** About 8 lbs. **Stock:** 14-3/4"x2-1/4"x1-1/2". Claro walnut with satin oil finish; Schnabel forend tip; sporter-style pistol grip; Pachmayr Decelerator recoil pad. **Features:** Designed for sporting clays competition. Has lengthened forcing cones and back-boring; ported barrels with 12mm grooved rib with mid-bead sight; mechanical trigger is adjustable for length of pull. Introduced 1998. Imported from Japan by Weatherby.
Price: SSC (Super Sporting Clays) **$2,059.00**

WINCHESTER SELECT O/U SHOTGUNS
Gauge: 12, 2-3/4", 3" chambers. **Barrel:** 28", 30", Invector Plus choke tubes. **Weight:** 7 lbs. 6 oz. to 7 lbs. 12. oz. **Length:** 45" overall (28" barrel). **Stock:** Checkered walnut stock. **Features:** Chrome-plated chambers; back-bored barrels; tang barrel selector/safety; deep-blued finish. Introduced 2000. From U.S. Repeating Arms. Co.
Price: Select Field (26" or 28" barrel, 6mm vent rib) **$1,498.00**
Price: Select Energy **$1,950.00**
Price: Select Elegance **$2,320.00**
Price: Select Energy Trap **$1,871.00**
Price: Select Energy Trap adjustable **$2,115.00**
Price: Select Energy Sporting adjustable **$2,115.00**

SHOTGUNS — Side-by-Side

Variety of models for utility and sporting use, including some competitive shooting.

Charles Daly Superior Hunter

Charles Daly Empire Hunter AE-MC

Charles Daly Diamond DL

Charles Daly Diamond Regent DL

ARRIETA SIDELOCK DOUBLE SHOTGUNS
Gauge: 12, 16, 20, 28, .410. **Barrel:** Length and chokes to customer specs. **Weight:** To customer specs. **Stock:** To customer specs. Straight English with checkered butt (standard), or pistol grip. Select European walnut with oil finish. **Features:** Essentially custom gun with myriad options. H&H pattern hand-detachable sidelocks, selective automatic ejectors, double triggers (hinged front) standard. Some have self-opening action. Finish and engraving to customer specs. Imported from Spain by Wingshooting Adventures.

Price: Model 557, auto ejectors . . . . From **$3,250.00**
Price: Model 570, auto ejectors . . . . From **$3,950.00**
Price: Model 578, auto ejectors . . . . From **$4,350.00**
Price: Model 600 Imperial, self-opening . . . . From **$6,050.00**
Price: Model 601 Imperial Tiro, self-opening . . . . From **$6,950.00**
Price: Model 801 . . . . From **$9,135.00**
Price: Model 802 . . . . From **$9,135.00**
Price: Model 803 . . . . From **$6,930.00**
Price: Model 871, auto ejectors . . . . From **$5,060.00**
Price: Model 872, self-opening . . . . From **$12,375.00**
Price: Model 873, self-opening . . . . From **$8,200.00**
Price: Model 874, self-opening . . . . From **$9,250.00**
Price: Model 875, self-opening . . . . From **$14,900.00**

CHARLES DALY SUPERIOR HUNTER AND SUPERIOR MC DOUBLE SHOTGUNS
Gauge: 12, 20, 3" chambers, 28, 2-3/4" chambers. **Barrel:** 28" (Mod. & Full) 26" (Imp. Cyl. & Mod.). **Weight:** About 7 lbs. **Stock:** Checkered walnut pistol grip buttstock, splinter forend. **Features:** Silvered, engraved receiver; chrome-lined barrels; gold single trigger; automatic safety; extractors; gold bead front sight. Introduced 1997. Imported from Italy by K.B.I., Inc.

Price: Superior Hunter, 28 gauge and .410 . . . . $1,659.00
Price: Superior Hunter MC 26"-28" $1,629.00

Charles Daly Empire Hunter AE-MC Double Shotgun
Similar to Superior Hunter except deluxe wood English-style stock, game scene engraving, automatic ejectors. Introduced 1997. Imported from Italy by K.B.I., Inc.
Price: 12 or 20 . . . . $2,119.00

CHARLES DALY DIAMOND DL DOUBLE SHOTGUN
Gauge: 12, 20, .410, 3" chambers, 28, 2-3/4" chambers. **Barrel:** 28" (Mod. & Full), 26" (Imp. Cyl. & Mod.), 26" (Full & Full, .410). **Weight:** From 5 lbs. to 7 lbs. **Stock:** Select fancy European walnut, English-style butt, beavertail forend; hand-checkered, hand-rubbed oil finish. **Features:** Drop-forged action with gas escape valves; demi-block barrels with concave rib; selective automatic ejectors; hand-detachable double safety sidelocks with hand-engraved rose and scrollwork. Hinged front trigger. Color case-hardened receiver. Introduced 1997. Imported from Spain by K.B.I., Inc.
Price: . . . . **Special order only**

CHARLES DALY DIAMOND REGENT DL DOUBLE SHOTGUN
Gauge: 12, 20, .410, 3" chambers, 28, 2-3/4" chambers. **Barrel:** 28" (Mod. & Full), 26" (Imp. Cyl. & Mod.), 26" (Full & Full, .410). **Weight:** About 5-7 lbs. **Stock:** Special select fancy European walnut, English-style butt, splinter forend; hand-checkered; hand-rubbed oil finish. **Features:** Drop-forged action with gas escape valves; demi-block barrels of chrome-nickel steel with concave rib; selective automatic-ejectors; hand-detachable, double-safety H&H sidelocks with demi-relief hand engraving; H&H pattern easy-opening feature; hinged trigger; coin finished action. Introduced 1997. Imported from Spain by K.B.I., Inc.
Price: Special Custom Order . . . . **NA**

DAKOTA PREMIER GRADE SHOTGUN
Gauge: 12, 16, 20, 28, .410. **Barrel:** 27". **Weight:** NA. **Length:** NA. **Stock:** Exhibition-grade English walnut, hand-rubbed oil finish with straight grip and splinter forend. **Features:** French grey finish; 50 percent coverage engraving; double triggers; selective ejectors. Finished to customer specifications. Made in U.S. by Dakota Arms.
Price: 12, 16, 20 gauge $13,950.00
Price: 28 gauge and .410 . . . . $15,345.00

SHOTGUNS — Side-by-Side

Charles Daly Field II Hunter

EAA Baikal IZH43K Bounty Hunter

EAA/Baikal MP-213

Fabarm Classic Lion

Fabarm Classic Lion Elite

Dakota Legend Shotgun
Similar to Premier Grade except has special selection English walnut, full-coverage scroll engraving, oak and leather case. Made in U.S. by Dakota Arms.
Price: 12, 16, 20 gauge **$18,000.00**
Price: 28 gauge and .410 .... **$19,800.00**

CHARLES DALY FIELD II, AE-MC HUNTER DOUBLE SHOTGUN
Gauge: 12, 20, 28, .410 (3" chambers; 28 has 2-3/4"). **Barrel:** 32" (Mod. & Mod.), 28, 30" (Mod. & Full), 26" (Imp. Cyl. & Mod.) .410 (Full & Full). **Weight:** 6 lbs. to 11.4 lbs. **Stock:** Checkered walnut pistol grip and forend. **Features:** Silvered, engraved receiver; gold single selective trigger in 10, 12, and 20 ga.; double triggers in 28 and .410; automatic safety; extractors; gold bead front sight. Introduced 1997. Imported from Spain by K.B.I., Inc.
Price: 28 ga., .410-bore................................ **$1,189.00**
Price: 12 or 20 AE-MC **$1,099.00**

EAA BAIKAL BOUNTY HUNTER IZH43K SHOTGUN
Gauge: 12, 3" chambers. **Barrel:** 18-1/2", 20", 24", 26", 28", three choke tubes. **Weight:** 7.28 lbs. **Overall length:** NA. **Stock:** Walnut, checkered forearm and grip. **Features:** Machined receiver; hammer-forged barrels with chrome-lined bores; external hammers; double triggers (single, selective trigger available); rifle barrel inserts optional. Imported by European American Armory.
Price: .... **$379.00 to 399.00**

EAA BAIKAL IZH43 BOUNTY HUNTER SHOTGUN
Gauge: 12, 3" chambers. **Barrel:** 20", 24", 26", 28"; imp., mod. and full choke tubes. **Stock:** Hardwood or walnut; checkered forend and grip. **Features:** Hammer forged barrel; internal hammers; extractors; engraved receiver; automatic tang safety; non-glare rib. Imported by European American Armory.
Price: IZH43 Bounty Hunter (12 gauge, 2-3/4" chambers, 20" brl., dbl. triggers, hardwood stock)............................ **$329.00**
Price: IZH43 Bounty Hunter (20 gauge, 3" chambers, 20" bbl., dbl. triggers, walnut stock) **$359.00**

E.M.F. HARTFORD MODEL COWBOY SHOTGUN
Gauge: 12. **Barrel:** 20". **Weight:** NA. **Length:** NA. **Stock:** Checkered walnut. **Sights:** Center bead. **Features:** Exposed hammers; color case-hardened receiver; blued barrel. Introduced 2001. Imported from Spain by E.M.F. Co. Inc.
Price: **$625.00**

FABARM CLASSIC LION DOUBLE SHOTGUNS
Gauge: 12, 3" chambers. **Barrel:** 26", 28", 30" (Cyl., Imp. Cyl., Mod., Imp. Mod., Full choke tubes). **Weight:** 7.2 lbs. **Length:** 44.5"-48.5. **Stock:** English-style or pistol grip oil-finished European walnut. **Features:** Boxlock action with double triggers, automatic ejectors, automatic safety. Introduced 1998. Imported from Italy by Heckler & Koch, Inc.
Price: Grade I **$1,499.00**
Price: Grade II **$2,099.00**
Price: Elite (color case-hardened type finish, 44.5") **$1,689.00**

SHOTGUNS — Side-by-Side

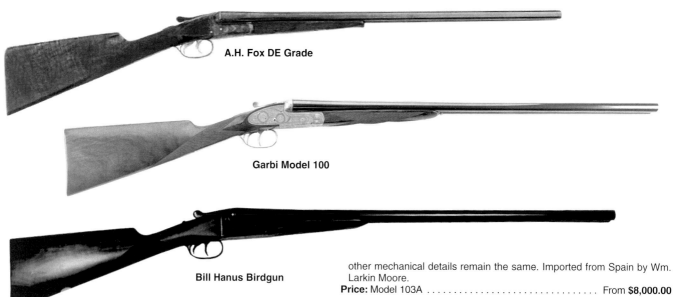

A.H. Fox DE Grade

Garbi Model 100

Bill Hanus Birdgun

FOX, A.H., SIDE-BY-SIDE SHOTGUNS

Gauge: 16, 20, 28, .410. **Barrel:** Length and chokes to customer specifications. Rust-blued Chromox or Krupp steel. **Weight:** 5-1/2 to 6-3/4 lbs. **Stock:** Dimensions to customer specifications. Hand-checkered Turkish Circassian walnut with hand-rubbed oil finish. Straight, semi or full pistol grip; splinter, Schnabel or beavertail forend; traditional pad, hard rubber buttplate or skeleton butt. **Features:** Boxlock action with automatic ejectors; double or Fox single selective trigger. Scalloped, rebated and color case-hardened receiver; hand finished and hand-engraved. Grades differ in engraving, inlays, grade of wood, amount of hand finishing. Introduced 1993. Made in U.S. by Connecticut Shotgun Mfg.

Price: CE Grade	$11,000.00
Price: XE Grade	$12,500.00
Price: DE Grade	$15,000.00
Price: FE Grade	$20,000.00
Price: Exhibition Grade	$30,000.00
Price: 28/.410 CE Grade	$12,500.00
Price: 28/.410 XE Grade	$14,000.00
Price: 28/.410 DE Grade	$16,500.00
Price: 28/.410 FE Grade	$21,500.00
Price: 28/.410 Exhibition Grade	$30,000.00
Price: 28 or .410-bore	$1,500.00

GARBI MODEL 100 DOUBLE SHOTGUN

Gauge: 12, 16, 20, 28. **Barrel:** 26", 28", choked to customer specs. **Weight:** 5-1/2 to 7-1/2 lbs. **Stock:** 14-1/2"x2-1/4"x1-1/2". European walnut. Straight grip, checkered butt, classic forend. **Features:** Sidelock action, automatic ejectors, double triggers standard. Color case-hardened action, coin finish optional. Single trigger; beavertail forend, etc. optional. Five additional models available. Imported from Spain by Wm. Larkin Moore.
Price: From **$4,850.00**

Garbi Model 101 Side-by-Side Shotgun

Similar to the Garbi Model 100 except hand engraved with scroll engraving; select walnut stock; better overall quality than the Model 100. Imported from Spain by Wm. Larkin Moore.
Price: . . . . From **$6,250.00**

Garbi Model 103 A & B Side-by-Side Shotguns

Similar to the Garbi Model 100 except has Purdey-type fine scroll and rosette engraving. Better overall quality than the Model 101. Model 103B has nickel-chrome steel barrels, H&H-type easy opening mechanism; other mechanical details remain the same. Imported from Spain by Wm. Larkin Moore.
Price: Model 103A . . . . From **$8,000.00**
Price: Model 103B . . . . From **11,800.00**

Garbi Model 200 Side-by-Side Shotgun

Similar to the Garbi Model 100 except has heavy-duty locks, magnum proofed. Very fine Continental-style floral and scroll engraving, well figured walnut stock. Other mechanical features remain the same. Imported from Spain by Wm. Larkin Moore.
Price: **$11,200.00**

HANUS BIRDGUN SHOTGUN

Gauge: 16, 20, 28. **Barrel:** 27", 20 and 28 ga.; 28", 16 ga. (skeet 1 & skeet 2). **Weight:** 5 lbs., 4 oz. to 6 lbs., 4 oz. **Stock:** 14-3/8"x1-1/2"x2-3/8", with 1/4" cast-off. Select walnut. **Features:** Boxlock action with ejectors; splinter forend, straight English grip; checkered butt; English leather-covered handguard and AyA snap caps included. Made by AyA. Introduced 1998. Imported from Spain by Bill Hanus Birdguns.
Price: **$2,795.00**

ITHACA CLASSIC DOUBLES SKEET GRADE SxS SHOTGUN

Gauge: 20, 28, 2-3/4" chambers, .410, 3". **Barrel:** 26", 28", 30", fixed chokes. **Weight:** 5 lbs., 14 oz. (20 gauge). **Stock:** 14-1/2"x2-1/4"x1-3/8". High-grade American black walnut, hand-rubbed oil finish; splinter or beavertail forend, straight or pistol grip. **Features:** Double triggers, ejectors; color case-hardened, engraved action body with matted top surfaces. Introduced 1999. Made in U.S. by Ithaca Classic Doubles.
Price: From **$5,999.00**

ITHACA CLASSIC DOUBLES GRADE 4E CLASSIC SXS SHOTGUN

Gauge: 10, 12, 16, 20, 28, .410 bore, 2-3/4" and 3" chambers. **Barrels:** 26", 28", 30". **Weight:** 5 lbs., 5 oz. to 6 lbs., 6 oz. **Features:** Gold-plated triggers, jewelled barrel flats and hand-turned locks. Feather crotch and flame-grained black walnut hand-checkered 28 lpi with fleur-de-lis pattern. Action body engraved with three game scenes and bank note scroll, color case-hardened. Introduced 1999. Made in U.S.A. by Ithaca Classic Doubles.
Price: From **$7,500.00**

ITHACA CLASSIC DOUBLES GRADE 5E SXS SHOTGUN

Gauge: 10, 12, 16, 20, 28, .410 bore, 2-3/4" and 3" chambers. **Barrels:** 26", 28", 30". **Weight:** 5 lbs., 5 oz. to 6 lbs., 6 oz. **Stock:** High-grade Turkish and American walnut and are hand-checkered. **Features:** Completely handmade, based on the early Ithaca engraving patterns of master engraver William McGraw. The hand engraving is at 90% coverage in deep chiseled floral scroll with game scenes in 24kt gold inlays. Available in 12, 16, 20, 28 gauges and .410 bore including two-barrel combination sets in 16/20 ga. and 28/.410 bore. Introduced 2003. Made in U.S.A. by Ithaca Classic Doubles.
Price: From **$8,500.00**

SHOTGUNS — Side-by-Side

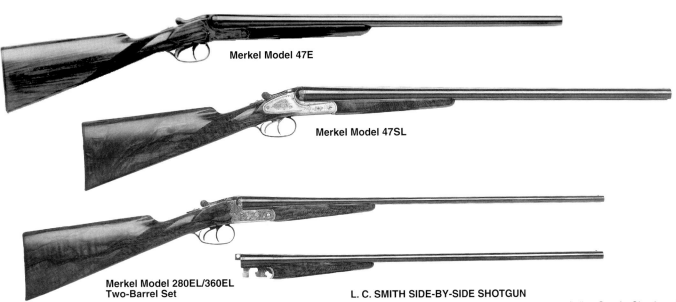

Merkel Model 47E

Merkel Model 47SL

Merkel Model 280EL/360EL
Two-Barrel Set

ITHACA CLASSIC DOUBLES GRADE 6E SIDE-BY-SIDE SHOTGUN
Gauge: 10, 12, 16, 20, 28, .410 bore, 2-3/4" and 3" chambers. **Barrels:** 26", 28", 30". **Weight:** 5 lbs., 5 oz. to 6 lbs., 6 oz. **Stock:** Handmade of best quality American, Turkish or English walnut with hand checkering. **Features:** Features hand engraving of fine English scroll coupled with game scenes and 24kt gold inlays. All metal work is finished in traditional bone and charcoal color case-hardening and deep rust blue. Available in 12, 16, 20, 28 gauges and .410 bore. Introduced 2003. Made in U.S.A. by Ithaca Classic Doubles.
Price: From **$10,000.00**

ITHACA CLASSIC DOUBLES GRADE 7E CLASSIC SXS SHOTGUN
Gauge: 10, 12, 16, 20, 28, .410 bore, 2-3/4" and 3" chambers. **Barrels:** 26", 28", 30". **Weight:** 5 lbs., 5 oz. to 6 lbs., 6 oz. **Stock:** Exhibition grade American black walnut stock and forend with eight-panel fleur-de-lis borders. **Features:** Engraved with banknote scroll and flat 24k gold game scenes: gold setter and gold pointer on opposite action sides, American bald eagle inlaid on bottom plate. Hand polished, jewelled ejectors and locks. Introduced 1999. Made in U.S.A. by Ithaca Classic Doubles.
Price: From **$11,000.00**

ITHACA CLASSIC DOUBLES SOUSA GRADE SIDE-BY-SIDE SHOTGUN
Gauge: 10, 12, 16, 20, 28, .410 bore, 3" chambers. **Barrels:** 26", 28", 30". **Weight:** 5 lbs., 5 oz. to 6 lbs., 6 oz. **Stock:** American black walnut, hand-carved and checkered. **Features:** Presentation grade hand-engraving with 24-karat gold inlays; tuned action and hand-applied finishes. Made in U.S.A. by Ithaca Classic Doubles.
Price: From **$18,000.00**

KIMBER VALIER GRADE I and II SHOTGUN
Gauge: 20, 3" chambers. **Barrels:** 26" or 28", IC and M. **Weight:** 6 lbs. 8 oz. **Stock:** Turkish walnut, English style. **Features:** Sidelock design, double triggers, 50-percent engraving; 24 lpi checkering; auto-ejectors (extractors only on Grade I). Color case-hardened sidelocks, rust blue barrels. Imported from Turkey by Kimber Mfg., Inc.
Price: Grade I **$3,879.00**
Price: Grade II **$4,480.00**

LEBEAU — COURALLY BOXLOCK SIDE-BY-SIDE SHOTGUN
Gauge: 12, 16, 20, 28, .410-bore. **Barrel:** 25" to 32". **Weight:** To customer specifications. **Stock:** French walnut. **Features:** Anson & Deely-type action with automatic ejectors; single or double triggers. Custom gun built to customer specifications. Imported from Belgium by Wm. Larkin Moore.
Price: From **$25,500.00**

L. C. SMITH SIDE-BY-SIDE SHOTGUN
Gauge: 12, 20. **Barrel:** 26", 28". **Weight:** 6 or 6-1/4 lbs. **Stock:** Checkered walnut w/recoil pad. **Features:** 3" chambers, single trigger, selective automatic ejectors; solid rib, bead front sight. Imported from Italy by Marlin.
Price: **$1,884.00**

LEBEAU — COURALLY SIDELOCK SIDE-BY-SIDE SHOTGUN
Gauge: 12, 16, 20, 28, .410-bore. **Barrel:** 25" to 32". **Weight:** To customer specifications. **Stock:** Fancy French walnut. **Features:** Holland & Holland-type action with automatic ejectors; single or double triggers. Custom gun built to customer specifications. Imported from Belgium by Wm. Larkin Moore.
Price: From **$56,000.00**

MERKEL MODEL 47E, 147E SIDE-BY-SIDE SHOTGUNS
Gauge: 12, 3" chambers, 16, 2-3/4" chambers, 20, 3" chambers. **Barrel:** 12, 16 ga.-28"; 20 ga.-26-3/4" (Imp. Cyl. & Mod., Mod. & Full). **Weight:** About 6-3/4 lbs. (12 ga.). **Stock:** Oil-finished walnut; straight English or pistol grip. **Features:** Anson & Deely-type boxlock action with single selective or double triggers, automatic safety, cocking indicators. Color case-hardened receiver with standard arabesque engraving. Imported from Germany by GSI.
Price: Model 47E (H&H ejectors) **$3,295.00**
Price: Model 147E (as above with ejectors) **$3,995.00**

Merkel Model 47SL, 147SL Side-by-Side Shotguns
Similar to Model 47E except H&H style sidelock action with cocking indicators, ejectors. Silver-grayed receiver and sideplates have arabesque engraving, engraved border and screws (Model 47S), or fine hunting scene engraving (Model 147S). Imported from Germany by GSI.
Price: Model 47SL **$5,995.00**
Price: Model 147SL **$7,995.00**
Price: Model 247SL (English-style engraving, large scrolls) **$7,995.00**
Price: Model 447SL (English-style engraving, small scrolls) **$9,995.00**

Merkel Model 280EL, 360EL Shotguns
Similar to Model 47E except smaller frame. Greener cross bolt with double under-barrel locking lugs, fine engraved hunting scenes on silver-grayed receiver, luxury-grade wood, Anson and Deely box-lock action. H&H ejectors, single-selective or double triggers. Introduced 2000. From Merkel.
Price: Model 280EL (28 gauge, 28" barrel, Imp. Cyl. and Mod. chokes) **$5,795.00**
Price: Model 360EL (.410, 28" barrel, Mod. and Full chokes) **$5,795.00**
Price: Model 280/360EL two-barrel set (28 and .410 gauge as above) **$8,295.00**

SHOTGUNS — Side-by-Side

Piotti Lunik

Rizzini Sidelock

Ruger Gold Label

Stoeger Uplander

Merkel Model 280SL and 360SL Shotguns

Similar to Model 280EL and 360EL except has sidelock action, double triggers, English-style arabesque engraving. Introduced 2000. From Merkel.

Price: Model 280SL (28 gauge, 28" barrel, Imp. Cyl. and
Mod. chokes) **$8,495.00**
Price: Model 360SL (.410, 28" barrel, Mod. and
Full chokes) **$8,495.00**
Price: Model 280/360SL two-barrel set **$11,995.00**

PIOTTI KING NO. 1 SIDE-BY-SIDE SHOTGUN

Gauge: 12, 16, 20, 28, .410. **Barrel:** 25" to 30" (12 ga.), 25" to 28" (16, 20, 28, .410). To customer specs. Chokes as specified. **Weight:** 6-1/2 lbs. to 8 lbs. (12 ga. to customer specs.). **Stock:** Dimensions to customer specs. Finely figured walnut; straight grip with checkered butt with classic splinter forend and hand-rubbed oil finish standard. Pistol grip, beavertail forend. **Features:** Holland & Holland pattern sidelock action, automatic ejectors. Double trigger; non-selective single trigger optional. Coin finish standard; color case-hardened optional. Top rib; level, file-cut; concave, ventilated optional. Very fine, full coverage scroll engraving with small floral bouquets. Imported from Italy by Wm. Larkin Moore.
Price: From **$29,600.00**

Piotti King Extra Side-by-Side Shotgun

Similar to the Piotti King No. 1 except with upgraded engraving. Choice of any type of engraving, including bulino game scene engraving and game scene engraving with gold inlays. Engraved and signed by a master engraver. Other mechanical specifications remain the same. Imported from Italy by Wm. Larkin Moore.
Price: From **$35,000.00**

Piotti Lunik Side-by-Side Shotgun

Similar to the Piotti King No. 1 in overall quality. Has Renaissance-style large scroll engraving in relief. Best quality Holland & Holland-pattern sidelock ejector double with chopper lump (demi-bloc) barrels. Other mechanical specifications remain the same. Imported from Italy by Wm. Larkin Moore.
Price: From **$30,900.00**

PIOTTI PIUMA SIDE-BY-SIDE SHOTGUN

Gauge: 12, 16, 20, 28, .410. **Barrel:** 25" to 30" (12 ga.), 25" to 28" (16, 20, 28, .410). **Weight:** 5-1/2 to 6-1/4 lbs. (20 ga.). **Stock:** Dimensions to customer specs. Straight grip stock with walnut checkered butt, classic splinter forend, hand-rubbed oil finish are standard; pistol grip, beavertail forend, satin luster finish optional. **Features:** Anson & Deeley boxlock ejector double with chopper lump barrels. Level, file-cut rib, light scroll and rosette engraving, scalloped frame. Double triggers; single non-selective optional. Coin finish standard, color case-hardened optional. Imported from Italy by Wm. Larkin Moore.
Price: From **$14,800.00**

RIZZINI SIDELOCK SIDE-BY-SIDE SHOTGUN

Gauge: 12, 16, 20, 28, .410. **Barrel:** 25" to 30" (12, 16, 20 ga.), 25" to 28" (28, .410). Chokes as specified. **Weight:** 6-1/2 lbs. to 8 lbs. (12 ga. to customer specs). **Stock:** Dimensions to customer specs. Finely figured walnut; straight grip with checkered butt with classic splinter forend and hand-rubbed oil finish standard. Pistol grip, beavertail forend. **Features:** Sidelock action, auto ejectors. Double triggers or non-selective single trigger standard. Coin finish standard. Imported from Italy by Wm. Larkin Moore.
Price: 12, 20 ga. From **$66,900.00**
Price: 28, .410 bore. From **$75,500.00**

RUGER GOLD LABEL SIDE-BY-SIDE SHOTGUN

Gauge: 12, 3" chambers. **Barrel:** 28" with skeet tubes. **Weight:** 6-1/2 lbs. **Length:** 45". **Stock:** American walnut straight or pistol grip. **Sights:** Gold bead front, full length rib, serrated top. **Features:** Spring-assisted break-open, SS trigger, auto eject. Five interchangeable screw-in choke tubes, combination safety/barrel selector with auto safety reset.
Price: **$2,000.00**

STOEGER UPLANDER SIDE-BY-SIDE SHOTGUNS

Gauge: 16, 28, 2-3/4 chambers. 12, 20, .410, 3" chambers. **Barrel:** 26", 28". **Weight:** 7.3 lbs. **Sights:** Brass bead. **Features:** Double trigger, IC & M fixed choke tubes with gun.
Price: With fixed chokes **$335.00**
Price: With screw-in chokes) **$350.00**
Price: With English stock . . . . **$335.00 to $350.00**
Price: Upland Special **$375.00**
Price: Upland Supreme with SST, red bar sights **$445.00**
Price: Upland Short Stock (Youth) **$335.00**

SHOTGUNS — Side-by-Side

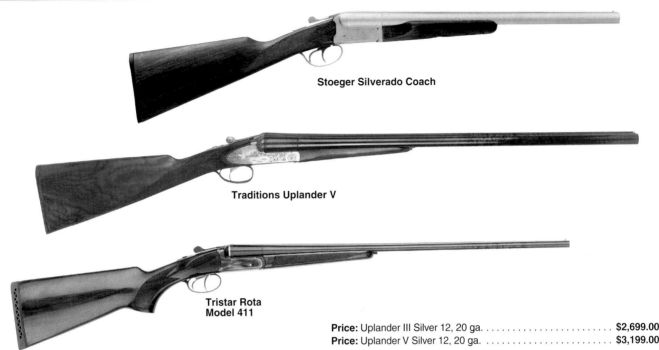

Stoeger Silverado Coach

Traditions Uplander V

Tristar Rota Model 411

STOEGER COACH GUN SIDE-BY-SIDE SHOTGUNS
Gauge: 12, 20, .410, 2-3/4", 3" chambers. **Barrel:** 20". **Weight:** 6-1/2 lbs. **Stock:** Brown hardwood, classic beavertail forend. **Sights:** Brass bead. **Features:** IC & M fixed chokes, tang auto safety, auto extractors, black plastic buttplate. 12 ga. and 20 ga. also with English style stock.
Price: $320.00
Price: Nickel $375.00
Price: Silverado $375.00
Price: With English stock $375.00

TRADITIONS ELITE SERIES SIDE-BY-SIDE SHOTGUNS
Gauge: 12, 3"; 20, 3"; 28, 2-3/4"; .410, 3". **Barrel:** 26". **Weight:** 5 lbs., 12 oz. to 6-1/2 lbs. **Length:** 43" overall. **Stock:** Walnut. **Features:** Chrome-lined barrels; fixed chokes (Elite Field III ST, Field I DT and Field I ST) or choke tubes (Elite Hunter ST); extractors (Hunter ST and Field I models) or automatic ejectors (Field III ST); top tang safety. Imported from Fausti of Italy by Traditions.
Price: Elite Field I DT — 12, 20, 28 ga. or .410; IC and Mod. fixed chokes (F and F on .410); double triggers .... **$789.00 to $969.00**
Price: Elite Field I ST — 12, 20, 28 ga. or .410; same as DT but with single trigger .... **$969.00 to $1,169.00**
Price: Elite Field III ST — 28 ga. or .410; gold-engraved receiver; high-grade walnut stock **$2,099.00**
Price: Elite Hunter ST — 12 or 20 ga.; blued receiver; IC and Mod. choke tubes **$999.00**

TRADITIONS UPLANDER SERIES SIDE-BY-SIDE SHOTGUNS
Gauge: 12, 3"; 20, 3". **Barrel:** 26", 28". **Weight:** 6-1/4 lbs. to 6-1/2 lbs. **Length:** 43" to 45" overall. **Stock:** Walnut. **Features:** Barrels threaded for choke tubes (Improved Cylinder, Modified and Full); top tang safety, extended trigger guard. Engraved silver receiver with side plates and lavish gold inlays. Imported from Fausti of Italy by Traditions.

Price: Uplander III Silver 12, 20 ga. $2,699.00
Price: Uplander V Silver 12, 20 ga. $3,199.00

TRISTAR ROTA MODEL 411 SIDE-BY-SIDE SHOTGUN
Gauge: 12, 16, 20, .410, 3" chambers; 28, 2-3/4". **Barrel:** 12 ga., 26", 28"; 16, 20, 28 ga., .410-bore, 26"; 12 and 20 ga. have three choke tubes, 16, 28 (Imp. Cyl. & Mod.), .410 (Mod. & Full) fixed chokes. **Weight:** 6-1/2 to 7-1/4 lbs. **Stock:** 14-3/8" l.o.p. Standard walnut with pistol grip, splinter-style forend; hand checkered. **Features:** Engraved, color case-hardened boxlock action; double triggers, extractors; solid barrel rib. Introduced 1998. Imported from Italy by Tristar Sporting Arms, Ltd.
Price: $849.00

Tristar Rota Model 411D Side-by-Side Shotgun
Similar to Model 411 except automatic ejectors, straight English-style stock, single trigger. Solid barrel rib with matted surface; chrome bores; color case-hardened frame; splinter forend. Introduced 1999. Imported from Italy by Tristar Sporting Arms, Ltd.
Price: $1,110.00

Tristar Rota Model 411R Coach Gun Side-by-Side Shotgun
Similar to Model 411 except in 12 or 20 gauge only with 20" barrels and fixed chokes (Cyl. & Cyl.). Double triggers, extractors, choke tubes. Introduced 1999. Imported from Italy by Tristar Sporting Arms, Ltd.
Price: $745.00

Tristar Rota Model 411F Side-by-Side Shotgun
Similar to Model 411 except silver, engraved receiver, ejectors, IC, M and F choke tubes, English-style stock, single gold trigger, cut checkering. Imported from Italy by Tristar Sporting Arms Ltd.
Price: $1,608.00

TRISTAR DERBY CLASSIC SIDE-BY-SIDE SHOTGUN
Gauge: 12. **Barrel:** 28" Mod. & Full fixed chokes. **Features:** Sidelock action, engraved, double trigger, auto ejectors, English straight stock. Made in Europe for Tristar Sporting Arms Ltd.
Price: $1,059.00

SHOTGUNS — Military & Police

Designs for utility, suitable for and adaptable to competitions and other sporting purposes.

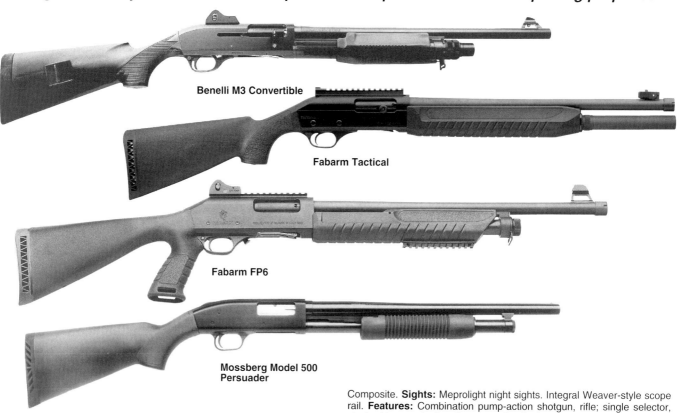

Benelli M3 Convertible

Fabarm Tactical

Fabarm FP6

Mossberg Model 500 Persuader

BENELLI M3 CONVERTIBLE SHOTGUN

Gauge: 12, 2-3/4", 3" chambers, 5-shot magazine. **Barrel:** 19-3/4" (Cyl.). **Weight:** 7 lbs., 4oz. **Length:** 41" overall. **Stock:** High-impact polymer with sling loop in side of butt; rubberized pistol grip on stock. **Sights:** Open rifle, fully adjustable. Ghost ring and rifle type. **Features:** Combination pump/auto action. Alloy receiver with inertia recoil rotating locking lug bolt; matte finish; automatic shell release lever. Introduced 1989. Imported by Benelli USA. Price with pistol grip, open rifle sights.

Price: With standard stock, open rifle sights $1,235.00
Price: With ghost ring sight system, standard stock $1,185.00
Price: With ghost ring sights, pistol grip stock $1,165.00

BENELLI M2 TACTICAL SHOTGUN

Gauge: 12, 2-3/4", 3" chambers, 5-shot magazine. **Barrel:** 18.5" IC, M, F choke tubes. **Weight:** 6.7 lbs. **Length:** 39.75" overall. **Stock:** Black polymer. **Sights:** Rifle type with ghost ring system, tritium night sights optional. **Features:** Semi-auto intertia recoil action. Cross-bolt safety; bolt release button; matte-finish metal. Introduced 1993. Imported from Italy by Benelli USA.

Price: With rifle sights, standard stock $1,000.00
Price: With ghost ring rifle sights, standard stock $1,065.00
Price: With ghost ring sights, pistol grip stock $1,065.00
Price: With rifle sights, pistol grip stock $1,000.00
Price: ComforTech stock, rifle sights $1,135.00
Price: Comfortech Stock, Ghost-Ring $1,185.00

Benelli M2 Practical Shotgun

Similar to M2 Tactical shotgun, Picatinny receiver rail for scope mounting, nine-round magazine, 26" compensated barrel and ghost ring sights. Designed for IPSC competition.

Price: $1,335.00

CROSSFIRE SHOTGUN/RIFLE

Gauge/Caliber: 12, 2-3/4" Chamber: 4-shot/223 Rem. (5-shot). **Barrel:** 20" (shotgun), 18" (rifle). **Weight:** About 8.6 lbs. **Length:** 40" overall. **Stock:**

Composite. **Sights:** Meprolight night sights. Integral Weaver-style scope rail. **Features:** Combination pump-action shotgun, rifle; single selector, single trigger; dual action bars for both upper and lower actions; ambidextrous selector and safety. Introduced 1997. Made in U.S. From Hesco.

Price: About $1,895.00
Price: With camo finish $1,995.00

FABARM TACTICAL SEMI-AUTOMATIC SHOTGUN

Gauge: 12, 3" chamber. **Barrel:** 20". **Weight:** 6.6 lbs. **Length:** 41.2" overall. **Stock:** Polymer or folding. **Sights:** Ghost ring (tritium night sights optional). **Features:** Gas operated; matte receiver; twin forged action bars; over-sized bolt handle and safety button; Picatinny rail; includes cylinder bore choke tube. New features include polymer pistol grip stock. Introduced 2001. Imported from Italy by Heckler & Koch Inc.

Price: $999.00

FABARM FP6 PUMP SHOTGUN

Gauge: 12, 3" chamber. **Barrel:** 20" (Cyl.); accepts choke tubes. **Weight:** 6.6 lbs. **Length:** 41.25" overall. **Stock:** Black polymer with textured grip, grooved slide handle. **Sights:** Blade front. **Features:** Twin action bars; anodized finish; free carrier for smooth reloading. Introduced 1998. New features include ghost-ring sighting system, low profile Picatinny rail, and pistol grip stock. Imported from Italy by Heckler & Koch, Inc.

Price: (Carbon fiber finish) $499.00
Price: With flip-up front sight, Picatinny rail with rear sight, oversize safety button $499.00

MOSSBERG MODEL 500 PERSUADER SECURITY SHOTGUNS

Gauge: 12, 20, .410, 3" chamber. **Barrel:** 18-1/2", 20" (Cyl.). **Weight:** 7 lbs. **Stock:** Walnut-finished hardwood or black synthetic. **Sights:** Metal bead front. **Features:** Available in 6- or 8-shot models. Top-mounted safety, double action slide bars, swivel studs, rubber recoil pad. Blue, Parkerized, Marinecote finishes. Mossberg Cablelock included. From Mossberg.

Price: 12 ga., 18-1/2", blue, wood or synthetic stock, 6-shot $353.00
Price: Cruiser, 12 ga., 18-1/2", blue, pistol grip, heat shield $357.00
Price: As above, 20 ga. or .410 bore $345.00

SHOTGUNS — Military & Police

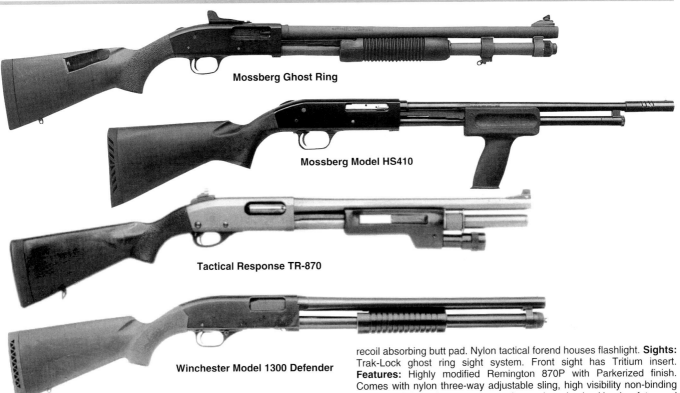

Mossberg Ghost Ring

Mossberg Model HS410

Tactical Response TR-870

Winchester Model 1300 Defender

Mossberg Model 500, 590 Mariner Pump Shotgun
Similar to the Model 500 or 590 Persuader except all metal parts finished with Marinecote metal finish to resist rust and corrosion. Synthetic field stock; pistol grip kit included. Mossberg Cablelock included.
Price: 6-shot, 18-1/2" barrel **$497.00**
Price: 9-shot, 20" barrel **$513.00**

Mossberg Model 500, 590 Ghost-Ring Shotgun
Similar to the Model 500 Persuader except has adjustable blade front, adjustable Ghost-Ring rear sight with protective "ears." Model 500 has 18.5" (Cyl.) barrel, 6-shot capacity; Model 590 has 20" (Cyl.) barrel, 9-shot capacity. Both have synthetic field stock. Mossberg Cablelock included. Introduced 1990. From Mossberg.
Price: 500 Parkerized **$468.00**
Price: 590 Parkerized **$543.00**
Price: 590 Parkerized Speedfeed stock **$586.00**

Mossberg Model HS410 Shotgun
Similar to the Model 500 Persuader pump except chambered for 20 gauge or .410 with 3" chamber; has pistol grip forend, thick recoil pad, muzzle brake and has special spreader choke on the 18.5" barrel. Overall length is 37.5", weight is 6.25 lbs. Blue finish; synthetic field stock. Mossberg Cablelock and video included. Introduced 1990.
Price: HS 410 .... **$355.00**

MOSSBERG MODEL 590 SHOTGUN
Gauge: 12, 3" chamber. **Barrel:** 20" (Cyl.). **Weight:** 7-1/4 lbs. **Stock:** Synthetic field or Speedfeed. **Sights:** Metal bead front. **Features:** Top-mounted safety, double slide action bars. Comes with heat shield, bayonet lug, swivel studs, rubber recoil pad. Blue, Parkerized or Marinecote finish. Mossberg Cablelock included. From Mossberg.
Price: Blue, synthetic stock **$417.00**
Price: Parkerized, synthetic stock **$476.00**
Price: Parkerized, Speedfeed stock **$519.00**

TACTICAL RESPONSE TR-870 STANDARD MODEL SHOTGUNS
Gauge: 12, 3" chamber, 7-shot magazine. **Barrel:** 18" (Cyl.). **Weight:** 9 lbs. **Length:** 38" overall. **Stock:** Fiberglass-filled polypropolene with non-snag recoil absorbing butt pad. Nylon tactical forend houses flashlight. **Sights:** Trak-Lock ghost ring sight system. Front sight has Tritium insert. **Features:** Highly modified Remington 870P with Parkerized finish. Comes with nylon three-way adjustable sling, high visibility non-binding follower, high performance magazine spring, Jumbo Head safety, and Side Saddle extended 6-shot shell carrier on left side of receiver. Introduced 1991. From Scattergun Technologies, Inc.
Price: Standard model **$815.00**
Price: FBI model **$770.00**
Price: Patrol model **$595.00**
Price: Border Patrol model **$605.00**
Price: K-9 model (Rem. 11-87 action) **$995.00**
Price: Urban Sniper, Rem. 11-87 action **$1,290.00**
Price: Louis Awerbuck model **$705.00**
Price: Practical Turkey model **$725.00**
Price: Expert model **$1,350.00**
Price: Professional model **$815.00**
Price: Entry model **$840.00**
Price: Compact model **$635.00**
Price: SWAT model **$1,195.00**

WINCHESTER MODEL 1300 DEFENDER PUMP GUN SHOTGUNS
Gauge: 12, 20, 3" chamber, 5- or 8-shot capacity. **Barrel:** 18" (Cyl.). **Weight:** 6-3/4 lbs. **Length:** 38-5/8" overall. **Stock:** Walnut-finished hardwood stock and ribbed forend, synthetic or pistol grip. **Sights:** Metal bead front or TruGlo® fiber-optic. **Features:** Cross-bolt safety, front-locking rotary bolt, twin action slide bars. Black rubber butt pad. From U.S. Repeating Arms Co.
Price: Practical Defender **$392.00**
Price: 8-Shot Pistol Grip (pistol grip synthetic stock) **$354.00**

Winchester Model 1300 Coastal Pump Gun Shotgun
Same as the Defender 8-Shot except has bright chrome finish, nickel-plated barrel, bead front sight. Phosphate coated receiver for corrosion resistance.
Price: **$575.00**

Winchester Model 1300 Camp Defender® Shotgun
Same as the Defender 8-Shot except has hardwood stock and forearm, fully adjustable open sights and 22" barrel with WinChoke® choke tube system (cylinder choke tube included). Weighs 6-7/8 lbs. Introduced 2001. From U.S. Repeating Arms Co.
Price: Camp Defender® **$392.00**

SHOTSHELL RELOADING PRESSES

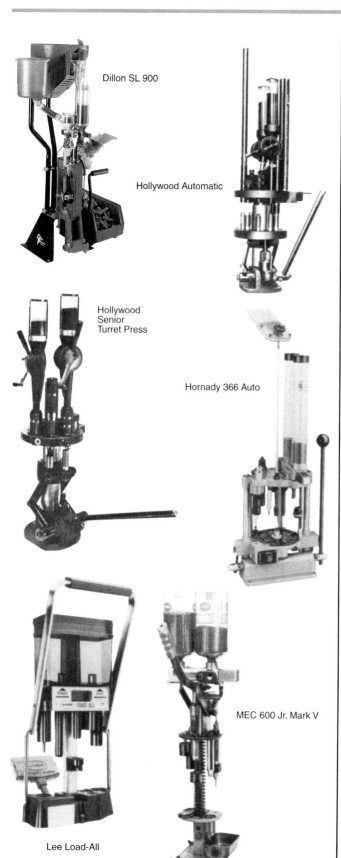

Dillon SL 900

Hollywood Automatic

Hollywood Senior Turret Press

Hornady 366 Auto

MEC 600 Jr. Mark V

Lee Load-All

DILLON SL 900

Press Type: Progressive
Avg. Rounds Per Hour: 700-900
Weight: 51 lbs.
Features: 12-ga. only; factory adjusted to load AA hulls; extra large 25-pound capacity shot hopper; fully-adjustable case-activated shot system; hardened steel starter crimp die; dual-action final crimp and taper die; tilt-out wad guide; auto prime; auto index; strong mount machine stand. From Dillon Precision Products.
    Price: **$844.90**

HOLLYWOOD Automatic Shotshell Press

Press Type: Progressive
Avg. Rounds Per Hour: 1,800
Weight: 100 lbs.
Features: Ductile iron frame; fully automated press with shell pickup and ejector; comes completely set up for one gauge; one starter crimp; one finish crimp; wad guide for plastic wads; decap and powder dispenser unit; one wrench for inside die lock screw; one medium and one large spanner wrench for spanner nuts; one shellholder; powder and shot measures. Available for 10, 12, 20, 28 or 410. From Hollywood Engineering.
    Price: **$3,600.00**

HOLLYWOOD Senior Turret Press

Press Type: Turret
Avg. Rounds Per Hour: 200
Weight: 50 lbs.
Features: Multi-stage press constructed of ductile iron comes completely equipped to reload one gauge; one starter crimp; one finish crimp; wad guide for plastic wads; decap and powder dispenser unit; one wrench for inside die lock screw; one medium and one large spanner wrench for spanner nuts; one shellholder; powder and shot measures. Available for 10, 12, 16, 20, 28 or 410. From Hollywood Engineering.
    Price: Press only **$700.00**
    Price: Dies **$195.00**

HORNADY 366 Auto

Press Type: Progressive
Avg. Rounds Per Hour: NA
Weight: 25 lbs.
Features: Heavy-duty die cast and machined steel body and components; auto primer feed system; large capacity shot and powder tubes; adjustable for right- or left-hand use; automatic charge bar with shutoff; swing-out wad guide; primer catcher at base of press; interchangeable shot and powder bushings; life-time warranty. Available for 12, 20, 28 2-3/4" and 410 2-1/2". From Hornady Mfg. Co.
    Price: **$434.95**
    Price: Die set, 12, 20, 28 . . . . **$196.86**
    Price: Magnum conversion dies, 12, 20 . . . . **$43.25**

LEE Load-All II

Press Type: Single stage
Avg. Rounds Per Hour: 100
Weight: 3 lbs. 3 oz.
Features: Loads steel or lead shot; built-in primer catcher at base with door in front for emptying; recesses at each station for shell positioning; optional primer feed. Comes with safety charge bar with 24 shot and powder bushings. Available for 12-, 16- or 20-gauge. From Lee Precision, Inc.
    Price: **$49.98**

MEC 600 Jr. Mark V

Press Type: Single stage
Avg. Rounds Per Hour: 200
Weight: 10 lbs.
Features: Spindex crimp starter for shell alignment during crimping; a cam-action crimp die; Pro-Check to keep charge bar properly positioned; adjustable for three shells. Available in 10, 12, 16, 20, 28 gauges and 410 bore. Die set not included. From Mayville Engineering Company, Inc.
    Price: **$120.50**
    Price: Die set **$61.16**

SHOTSHELL RELOADING PRESSES

MEC 650N

Press Type: Progressive
Avg. Rounds Per Hour: 400
Weight: 19 lbs.
Features: Six-station press; does not resize except as separate operation; auto primer feed standard; three crimping stations for starting, closing and tapering crimp. Die sets not available. Available in 12, 16, 20, 28 and 410. From Mayville Engineering Company, Inc.
Price: **$240.00**

MEC 8567N Grabber

Press Type: Progressive
Avg. Rounds Per Hour: 400
Weight: 22 lbs.
Features: Six-station press; auto primer feed; auto-cycle charging; three-stage crimp; power ring resizer returns base to factory specs; resizes high and low base shells; optional kits to reload three shells and steel shot. Available in 12, 16, 20, 28 gauge and 410 bore. From Mayville Engineering Company, Inc.
Price: **$338.05**
Price: 3" kit, 12-ga. **$70.70**
Price: 3" kit, 20-ga. **$40.40**
Price: Steel shot kit **$35.35**

MEC 9000GN

Press Type: Progressive
Avg. Rounds Per Hour: 400
Weight: 26 lbs.
Features: All same features as the MEC Grabber but with auto-indexing and auto-eject. Finished shells automatically ejected from shell carrier to drop chute for boxing. Available in 12, 16, 20, 28 and 410. From Mayville Engineering Company, Inc.
Price: **$407.70**

MEC 9000HN

Press Type: Progressive
Avg. Rounds Per Hour: 400
Weight: 30 lbs.
Features: Same features as 9000GN with addition of foot pedal-operated hydraulic system for complete automation. Operates on standard 110V household current. Comes with bushing-type charge bar and three bushings. Available in 12, 16, 20, 28 gauge and 410 bore. From Mayville Engineering Company, Inc.
Price: **$958.00**

MEC 8120 Sizemaster

Press Type: Single stage
Avg. Rounds Per Hour: 150
Weight: 20 lbs.
Features: Power ring eight-fingered collet resizer returns base to factory specs; handles brass or steel, high or low base heads; auto primer feed; adjustable for three shells. Available in 10, 12, 16, 20, 28 gauges and 410 bore. From Mayville Engineering Company, Inc.
Price: **$196.79**
Price: Die set, 12, 16, 20, 28, 410 . . . . **$72.11**
Price: Die set, 10-ga. **$88.59**

MEC Steelmaster

Press Type: Single stage
Avg. Rounds Per Hour: 150
Weight: 20 lbs.
Features: Same features as Sizemaster except can load steel shot. Press is available for 3-1/2" 10-ga. and 12-ga. 2-3/4", 3" or 3-1/2". For loading lead shot, die sets available in 10, 12, 16, 20, 28 and 410. From Mayville Engineering Company, Inc.
Price: **$196.79**
Price: 12 ga. 3-1/2" **$220.41**

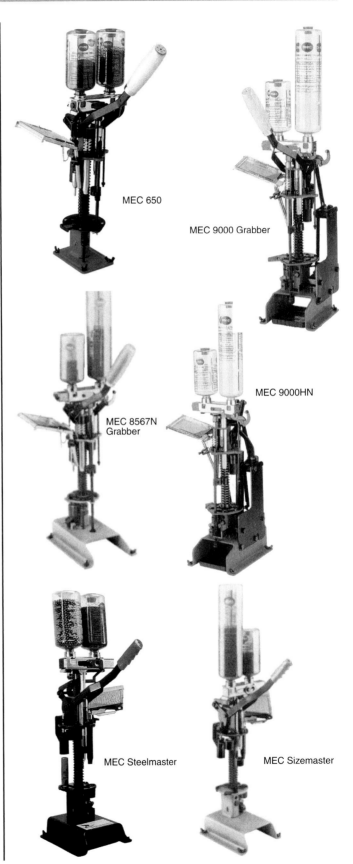

MEC 650

MEC 9000 Grabber

MEC 9000HN

MEC 8567N Grabber

MEC Steelmaster

MEC Sizemaster

SHOTSHELL RELOADING PRESSES

Ponsness/Warren
Du-O-Matic 375C

Ponsness/Warren
Hydro-Multispeed

Ponsness/Warren
Size-O-Matic
900 Elite

Ponsness/Warren
Platinum 2000

RCBS The Grand

PONSNESS/WARREN Du-O-Matic 375C

Press Type: Progressive
Avg. Rounds Per Hour: NA
Weight: 31 lbs.
Features: Steel or lead shot reloader; large shot and powder reservoirs; bushing access plug for dropping in shot buffer or buckshot; positive lock charging ring to prevent accidental flow of powder; double-post construction for greater leverage; removable spent primer box; spring-loaded ball check for centering size die at each station; tip-out wad guide; two-gauge capacity tool head. Available in 10 (extra charge), 12, 16, 20, 28 and 410 with case lengths of 2-1/2", 2-3/4", 3" and 3-1/2". From Ponsness/ Warren.
Price: 12-, 20-, and 28-ga., 2-3/4" and 410, 2-1/2" **$289.00**
Price: 12-ga. 3-1/2"; 3" 12, 20, 410 . . . . **$305.00**
Price: 12, 20 2-3/4" **$383.95**
Price: 10-ga. press **$315.00**

PONSNESS/WARREN Hydro-Multispeed

Hydraulic system developed for Ponsness/Warren L/S-1000. Usable for the 950, 900 and 800 series presses. Three reloading speed settings operated with variable foot pedal control. Features stop/reverse at any station; automatic shutdown with pedal control release; fully adjustable hydraulic cylinder rod to prevent racking or bending of machine; quick disconnect hoses for ease of installation. Preassembled with step-by-step instructions. From Ponsness/Warren.
Price: **$879.00**
Price: Cylinder kit **$399.95**

PONSNESS/WARREN L/S-1000

Frame: Die cast aluminum
Avg. Rounds Per Hour: NA
Weight: 55 lbs.
Features: Fully progressive press to reload steel, bismuth or lead shot. Equipped with new Uni-Drop shot measuring and dispensing system which allows the use of all makes of shot in any size. Shells automatically resized and deprimed with new Auto-Size and De-Primer system. Loaded rounds drop out of shellholders when completed. Each shell pre-crimped and final crimped with Tru-Crimp system. Available in 10-gauge 3-1/2" or 12-gauge 2-3/4" and 3". 12-gauge 3-1/2" conversion kit also available. 20-gauge 2-3/4" and 3" special order only. From Ponsness/Warren.
Price: 12 ga. **$849.00**
Price: 10 ga. **$895.00**
Price: Conversion kit **$199.00**

PONSNESS/WARREN Size-O-Matic 900 Elite

Press Type: Progressive
Avg. Rounds Per Hour: 500-800
Weight: 49 lbs.
Features: Progressive eight-station press; frame of die-cast aluminum; center post design index system ensures positive indexing; timing factory set, drilled and pinned. Automatic features include index, deprime, reprime, powder and shot drop, crimp start, tapered final crimp, finished shell ejection. Available in 12, 20, 28 and 410. 16-ga. special order. Kit includes new shellholders, seating port, resize/primer knockout assembly, new crimp assembly. From Ponsness/Warren.
Price: **$749.00**
Price: Conversion tooling, 12, 20, 28, 410 . . . . **$189.00**

PONSNESS/WARREN Platinum 2000

Press Type: Progressive
Avg. Rounds Per Hour: 500-800
Weight: 52 lbs.
Features: Progressive eight-station press, similar to 900 and 950 except has die removal system that allows removal of any die component during reloading cycle. Comes standard with 25-lb. shot tube, 19" powder tube, brass adjustable priming feed allows adjustment of primer seating depth. From Ponsness/Warren.
Price: **$889.00**

RCBS The Grand

Press Type: Progressive
Avg. Rounds Per Hour: NA
Weight: NA
Features: Constructed from a high-grade aluminum casting, allows complete resizing of high and low base hulls. Available for 12 and 20 gauge.
Price: **$688.95**

MANUFACTURER'S DIRECTORY

A

A Zone Bullets, 2039 Walter Rd., Billings, MT 59105 / 800-252-3111; FAX: 406-248-1961

A&W Repair, 2930 Schneider Dr., Arnold, MO 63010 / 617-287-3725

A.A. Arms, Inc., 4811 Persimmont Ct., Monroe, NC 28110 / 704-289-5356; or 800-935-1119; FAX: 704-289-5859

A.B.S. III, 9238 St. Morritz Dr., Fern Creek, KY 40291

A.G. Russell Knives, Inc., 1920 North 26th Street, Lowell, AR 72745-8489 / 800-255-9034; FAX: 479-636-8493 ag@agrussell.com agrussell.com

A.R.M.S., Inc., 230 W. Center St., West Bridgewater, MA 02379-1620 / 508-584-7816; FAX: 508-588-8045

A.W. Peterson Gun Shop, Inc., 4255 W. Old U.S. 441, Mt. Dora, FL 32757-3299 / 352-383-4258; FAX: 352-735-1001

A.W. Peterson Gun Shop, Inc., The, 4255 West Old U.S. 441, Mount Dora, FL 32757-3299 / 352-383-4258

AC Dyna-tite Corp., 155 Kelly St., P.O. Box 0984, Elk Grove Village, IL 60007 / 847-593-5566; FAX: 847-593-1304

Acadian Ballistic Specialties, P.O. Box 787, Folsom, LA 70437 / 504-796-0078 gunsmith@neasolft.com

Accuracy Den, The, 25 Bitterbrush Rd., Reno, NV 89523 / 702-345-0225

Accuracy International, Foster, P.O. Box 111, Wilsall, MT 59086 / 406-587-7922; FAX: 406-585-9434

Accuracy Internationl Precision Rifles (See U.S.)

Accuracy Int'l. North America, Inc., P.O. Box 5267, Oak Ridge, TN 37831 / 423-482-0330; FAX: 423-482-0336

Accuracy Unlimited, 7479 S. DePew St., Littleton, CO 80123

Accuracy Unlimited, 16036 N. 49 Ave., Glendale, AZ 85306 / 602-978-9089; FAX: 602-978-9089 fglenn@cox.net www.glenncustom.com

Accura-Site (See All's, The Jim Tembelis Co., Inc.)

Accurate Arms Co., Inc., 5891 Hwy. 230 West, McEwen, TN 37101 / 931-729-4207; FAX: 931-729-4211 burrensburg@aac-ca.com www.accuratepowder.com

Accu-Tek, 4510 Carter Ct., Chino, CA 91710

Ackerman & Co., Box 133 U.S. Highway Rt. 7, Pownal, VT 05261 / 802-823-9874 muskets@togsther.net

Ackerman, Bill (See Optical Services Co.)

Acra-Bond Laminates, 134 Zimmerman Rd., Kalispell, MT 59901 / 406-257-9003; FAX: 406-257-9003 merlins@digisys.net www.acrabondlaminates.com

Action Bullets & Alloy Inc., RR 1, P.O. Box 189, Quinter, KS 67752 / 785-754-3609; FAX: 785-754-3629 bullets@ruraltel.net

Action Direct, Inc., P.O. Box 770400, Miami, FL 33177 / 305-969-0056; FAX: 305-256-3541 www.action-direct.com

Action Products, Inc., 22 N. Mulberry St., Hagerstown, MD 21740 / 301-797-1414; FAX: 301-733-2073

Action Target, Inc., P.O. Box 636, Provo, UT 84603 / 801-377-8033; FAX: 801-377-8096 www.actiontarget.com

Actions by "T" Teddy Jacobson, 16315 Redwood Forest Ct., Sugar Land, TX 77478 / 281-277-4008; FAX: 281-277-9112 tjacobson@houston.rr.com www.actionsbyt.us

AcuSport Corporation, 1 Hunter Place, Bellefontaine, OH 43311-3001 / 513-593-7010; FAX: 513-592-5625

Ad Hominem, 3130 Gun Club Lane, RR #3, Orillia, ON L3V 6H3 CANADA / 705-689-5303; FAX: 705-689-5303

Adair Custom Shop, Bill, 2886 Westridge, Carrollton, TX 75006

ADCO Sales, Inc., 4 Draper St. #A, Woburn, MA 01801 / 781-935-1799; FAX: 781-935-1011

Adkins, Luther, 1292 E. McKay Rd., Shelbyville, IN 46176-8706 / 317-392-3795

Advance Car Mover Co., Rowell Div., P.O. Box 1, 240 N. Depot St., Juneau, WI 53039 / 414-386-4464; FAX: 414-386-4416

Advantage Arms, Inc., 25163 W. Ave. Stanford, Valencia, CA 91355 / 661-257-2290

Adventure 16, Inc., 4620 Alvarado Canyon Rd., San Diego, CA 92120 / 619-283-6314

Aero Peltor, 90 Mechanic St., Southbridge, MA 01550 / 508-764-5500; FAX: 508-764-0188

African Import Co., 22 Goodwin Rd., Plymouth, MA 02360 / 508-746-8552; FAX: 508-746-0404 africanimport@aol.com

AFSCO Ammunition, 731 W. Third St., P.O. Box L, Owen, WI 54460 / 715-229-2516 sailers@webtv.net

Ahlman Guns, 9525 W. 230th St., Morristown, MN 55052 / 507-685-4243; FAX: 507-685-4280 www.ahlmans.com

Ahrends Grips, Box 203, Clarion, IA 50525 / 515-532-3449; FAX: 515-532-3926 ahrends@goldfieldaccess.net

Ahrends, Kim, Box 203, Clarion, IA 50525 / 515-532-3449; FAX: 515-532-3926

Aimtech Mount Systems, P.O. Box 223, Thomasville, GA 31799 / 229-226-4313; FAX: 229-227-0222 mail@aimtech-mounts.com www.aimtech-mounts.com

Air Arms, Hailsham Industrial Park, Diplocks Way, Hailsham, E. Sussex, BN27 3JF ENGLAND / 011-0323-845853; FAX: 1323 440573 general.air-arms.co.uk. www.air-arms.co.uk.

Air Rifle Specialists, P.O. Box 138, 130 Holden Rd., Pine City, NY 14871-0138 / 607-734-7340; FAX: 607-733-3261 ars@stny.rr.com www.air-rifles.com

Air Venture Airguns, 9752 E. Flower St., Bellflower, CA 90706 / 562-867-6355

AirForce Airguns, P.O. Box 2478, Fort Worth, TX 76113 / 817-451-8966; FAX: 817-451-1613 www.airforceairguns.com

Airrow, 11 Monitor Hill Rd., Newtown, CT 06470 / 203-270-6343

Aitor-Cuchilleria Del Norte S.A., Izelaieta, 17, 48260, Ermua, SPAIN / 43-17-08-50 info@aitor.com www.ailor.com

Ajax Custom Grips, Inc., 9130 Viscount Row, Dallas, TX 75247 / 214-630-8893; FAX: 214-630-4942

Aker International, Inc., 2248 Main St., Suite 6, Chula Vista, CA 91911 / 619-423-5182; FAX: 619-423-1363 aker@akerleather.com www.akerleather.com

AKJ Concealco, P.O. Box 871596, Vancouver, WA 98687-1596 / 360-891-8222; FAX: 360-891-8221 Concealco@aol.com www.greatholsters.com

Alana Cupp Custom Engraver, P.O. Box 207, Annabella, UT 84711 / 801-896-4834

Alaska Bullet Works, Inc., 9978 Crazy Horse Drive, Juneau, AK 99801 / 907-789-3834; FAX: 907-789-3433

Alaskan Silversmith, The, 2145 Wagner Hollow Rd., Fort Plain, NY 13339 / 518-993-3983 sidbell@capital.net www.sidbell.cizland.com

Aldis Gunsmithing & Shooting Supply, 502 S. Montezuma St., Prescott, AZ 86303 / 602-445-6723; FAX: 602-445-6763

Alessi Holsters, Inc., 2465 Niagara Falls Blvd., Amherst, NY 14228-3527 / 716-691-5615

Alex, Inc., 3420 Cameron Bridge Rd., Manhattan, MT 59741-8523 / 406-282-7396; FAX: 406-282-7396

Alfano, Sam, 36180 Henry Gaines Rd., Pearl River, LA 70452 / 504-863-3364; FAX: 504-863-7715

All American Lead Shot Corp., P.O. Box 224566, Dallas, TX 75062

All Rite Products, Inc., 9554 Wells Circle, Suite D, West Jordan, UT 84088-6226 / 800-771-8471; FAX: 801-280-8302 info@allriteproducts.com www.allriteproducts.com

Allard, Gary/Creek Side Metal & Woodcrafters, Fishers Hill, VA 22626 / 540-465-3903

Allen Co., Inc., 525 Burbank St., Broomfield, CO 80020 / 303-469-1857; or 800-876-8600; FAX: 303-466-7437

Allen Firearm Engraving, P.O. Box 155, Camp Verde, AZ 86322 / 928-567-6711 rosebudmulgco@netzero.com rosebudmulgco@netzero.com

Allen Mfg., 6449 Hodgson Rd., Circle Pines, MN 55014 / 612-429-8231

Alley Supply Co., P.O. Box 848, Gardnerville, NV 89410 / 775-782-3800; FAX: 775-782-3827 jetalley@aol.com www.alleysupplyco.com

Alliant Techsystems, Smokeless Powder Group, P.O. Box 6, Rt. 114, Bldg. 229, Radford, VA 24141-0096 www.alliantpowder.com

Allred Bullet Co., 932 Evergreen Drive, Logan, UT 84321 / 435-752-6983; FAX: 435-752-6983

All's, The Jim J. Tembelis Co., Inc., 216 Loper Ct., Neenah, WI 54956 / 920-725-5251; FAX: 920-725-5251

Alpec Team, Inc., 201 Ricken Backer Cir., Livermore, CA 94550 / 510-606-8245; FAX: 510-606-4279

Alpha 1 Drop Zone, 2121 N. Tyler, Wichita, KS 67212 / 316-729-0800; FAX: 316-729-4262 www.alpha1dropzone.com

Alpha LaFranck Enterprises, P.O. Box 81072, Lincoln, NE 68501 / 402-466-3193

Alpha Precision, Inc., 3238 Della Slaton Rd., Comer, GA 30629-2212 / 706-783-2131 jim@alphaprecisioninc.com www.alphaprecisioninc.com

Alpine Indoor Shooting Range, 2401 Government Way, Coeur d'Alene, ID 83814 / 208-676-8824; FAX: 208-676-8824

Altamont Co., 901 N. Church St., P.O. Box 309, Thomasboro, IL 61878 / 217-643-3125; or 800-626-5774; FAX: 217-643-7973

Alumna Sport by Dee Zee, 1572 NE 58th Ave., P.O. Box 3090, Des Moines, IA 50316 / 800-798-9899

Amadeo Rossi S.A., Rua: Amadeo Rossi, 143, Sao Leopoldo, RS 93030-220 BRAZIL / 051-592-5566 rossi.firearms@pnet.com.br

Amato, Jeff. See: J&M PRECISION MACHINING

AmBr Software Group Ltd., P.O. Box 301, Reistertown, MD 21136-0301 / 800-888-1917; FAX: 410-526-7212

American Ammunition, 3545 NW 71st St., Miami, FL 33147 / 305-835-7400; FAX: 305-694-0037

American Derringer Corp., 127 N. Lacy Dr., Waco, TX 76705 / 800-642-7817; or 254-799-9111; FAX: 254-799-7935

American Display Co., 55 Cromwell St., Providence, RI 02907 / 401-331-2464; FAX: 401-421-1264

American Gas & Chemical Co., Ltd.,, 220 Pegasus Ave., Northvale, NJ 07647 / 201-767-7300

American Gunsmithing Institute, 1325 Imola Ave. #504, Napa, CA 94559 / 707-253-0462; FAX: 707-253-7149 www.americangunsmith.com

American Handgunner Magazine, 12345 World Trade Dr., San Diego, CA 92128 / 800-537-3006; FAX: 858-605-0204 www.americanhandgunner.com

American Pioneer Video, P.O. Box 50049, Bowling Green, KY 42102-2649 / 800-743-4675

American Products, Inc., 14729 Spring Valley Road, Morrison, IL 61270 / 815-772-3336; FAX: 815-772-8046

American Safe Arms, Inc., 1240 Riverview Dr., Garland, UT 84312 / 801-257-7472; FAX: 801-785-8156

American Security Products Co., 11925 Pacific Ave., Fontana, CA 92337 / 909-685-9680; or 800-421-6142; FAX: 909-685-9685

American Small Arms Academy, P.O. Box 12111, Prescott, AZ 86304 / 602-778-5623

American Target, 1328 S. Jason St., Denver, CO 80223 / 303-733-0433; FAX: 303-777-0311

American Target Knives, 1030 Brownwood NW, Grand Rapids, MI 49504 / 616-453-1998

Americase, P.O. Box 271, 1610 E. Main, Waxahachie, TX 75165 / 800-880-3629; FAX: 214-937-8373

Ames Metal Products, 4323 S. Western Blvd., Chicago, IL 60609 / 773-523-3230; or 800-255-6937; FAX: 773-523-3854

Amherst Arms, P.O. Box 1457, Englewood, FL 34295 / 941-475-2020; Fax: 941-473-1212

Ammo Load Worldwide, Inc., 815 D St., Lewiston, ID 83501 / 208-743-7418; FAX: 208-746-1703 ammoload@microwavedsl.com

Ammo Load, Inc., 1560 E. Edinger, Suite G, Santa Ana, CA 92705 / 714-558-8858; FAX: 714-569-0319

Amrine's Gun Shop, 937 La Luna, Ojai, CA 93023 / 805-646-2376

Amsec, 11925 Pacific Ave., Fontana, CA 92337

Analog Devices, Box 9106, Norwood, MA 02062

Andela Tool & Machine, Inc., RD3, Box 246, Richfield Springs, NY 13439

Anderson Manufacturing Co., Inc., 22602 53rd Ave. SE, Bothell, WA 98021 / 206-481-1858; FAX: 206-481-7839

Andres & Dworsky KG, Bergstrasse 4, A-3822 Karlstein, Thaya, AUSTRIA / 0 28 44-285; FAX: 0 28 44-28619 andres.dnorsky@wvnet.as

Angelo & Little Custom Gun Stock Blanks, P.O. Box 240046, Dell, MT 59724-0046

Answer Products Co., 1519 Westbury Drive, Davison, MI 48423 / 810-653-2911

Antique American Firearms, P.O. Box 71035, Dept. GD, Des Moines, IA 50325 / 515-224-6552

Antique Arms Co., 1110 Cleveland Ave., Monett, MO 65708 / 417-235-6501

AO Sight Systems, 2401 Ludelle St., Fort Worth, TX 76105 / 888-744-4880; or 817-536-0136; FAX: 817-536-3517

Apel GmbH, Ernst, Am Kirschberg 3, D-97218, Gerbrunn, GERMANY / 0 (931) 707192 info@eaw.de www.eaw.de

Aplan Antiques & Art, James O., HC 80, Box 793-25, Piedmont, SD 57769 / 605-347-5016

AR-7 Industries, LLC, 998 N. Colony Rd., Meriden, CT 06450 / 203-630-3536; FAX: 203-630-3637

Arizona Ammunition, Inc., 21421 No. 14th Ave., Suite E, Phoenix, AZ 85027 / 623-516-9004; FAX: 623-516-9012 www.azammo.com

ArmaLite, Inc., P.O. Box 299, Geneseo, IL 61254 / 800-336-0184; or 309-944-6939; FAX: 309-944-6949

Armament Gunsmithing Co., Inc., 525 Rt. 22, Hillside, NJ 07205 / 908-686-0960; FAX: 718-738-5019 armamentgunsmithing@worldnet.att.net

Armas Garbi, S.A., 12-14 20.600 Urki, 12, Eibar (Guipuzcoa), SPAIN / 943 20 3873; FAX: 943 20 3873 armosgarbi@euskalnet.n

Armas Kemen S. A. (See U.S. Importers)

Armfield Custom Bullets, 10584 County Road 100, Carthage, MO 64836 / 417-359-8480; FAX: 417-359-8497

Armi Perazzi S.P.A., Via Fontanelle 1/3, I-25080, Botticino Mattina, ITALY / 030-2692591; FAX: 030-2692594

Armi San Marco (See Taylor's & Co.)

Armi San Paolo, 172-A, I-25062, via Europa, ITALY / 030-2751725

Armi Sport (See Cape Outfitters)

269

MANUFACTURER'S DIRECTORY

Armite Laboratories, 1560 Superior Ave., Costa Mesa, CA 92627 / 213-587-7768; FAX: 213-587-5075

Armoloy Co. of Ft. Worth, 204 E. Daggett St., Fort Worth, TX 76104 / 817-332-5604; FAX: 817-335-6517

Armor (See Buck Stop Lure Co.)

Armor Metal Products, P.O. Box 4609, Helena, MT 59604 / 406-442-5560; FAX: 406-442-5650

Armory Publications, 2120 S. Reserve St., PMB 253, Missoula, MT 59801 / 406-549-7670; FAX: 406-728-0597 armorypub@aol.com www.armorypub.com

Armoury, Inc., The, Rt. 202, Box 2340, New Preston, CT 06777 / 860-868-0001; FAX: 860-868-2919

Arms & Armour Press, Wellington House, 125 Strand, London, WC2R 0BB ENGLAND / 0171-420-5555; FAX: 0171-240-7265

Arms Corporation of the Philippines, Bo. Parang Marikina, Metro Manila, PHILIPPINES / 632-941-6243; or 632-941-6244; FAX: 632-942-0682

Arms Craft Gunsmithing, 1106 Linda Dr., Arroyo Grande, CA 93420 / 805-481-2830

Arms Software, 4851 SW Madrona St., Lake Oswego, OR 97035 / 800-366-5559; or 503-697-0533; FAX: 503-697-3337

Arms, Programming Solutions (See Arms Software)

Armscor Precision, 5740 S. Arville St. #219, Las Vegas, NV 89118 / 702-362-7750

Armscorp USA, Inc., 4424 John Ave., Baltimore, MD 21227 / 410-247-6200; FAX: 410-247-6205 info@armscorpusa.com www.armscorpusa.com

Arratoonian, Andy (See Horseshoe Leather Products)

Arrieta S.L., Morkaiko 5, 20870, Elgoibar, SPAIN / 34-43-743150; FAX: 34-43-743154

Art Jewel Enterprises Ltd., Eagle Business Ctr., 460 Randy Rd., Carol Stream, IL 60188 / 708-260-0400

Artistry in Wood, 134 Zimmerman Rd., Kalispell, MT 59901 / 406-257-9003; FAX: 406-257-9167 merlins@digisys.net www.acrabondlaminates.com

Art's Gun & Sport Shop, Inc., 6008 Hwy. Y, Hillsboro, MO 63050

Arundel Arms & Ammunition, Inc., A., 24A Defense St., Annapolis, MD 21401 / 410-224-8683

Aspen Outfitting Co., Jon Hollinger, 9 Dean St., Aspen, CO 81611 / 970-925-3406

A-Square Co., 205 Fairfield Ave., Jeffersonville, IN 47130 / 812-283-0577; FAX: 812-283-0375

Astra Sport, S.A., Apartado 3, 48300 Guernica, Espagne, SPAIN / 34-4-6250100; FAX: 34-4-6255186

Atamec-Bretton, 19 rue Victor Grignard, F-42026, St.-Etienne (Cedex 1, FRANCE / 33-77-93-54-69; FAX: 33-77-93-57-98

Atlanta Cutlery Corp., 2143 Gees Mill Rd., Box 839 CIS, Conyers, GA 30207 / 800-883-0300; FAX: 404-388-0246

Atlantic Mills, Inc., 1295 Towbin Ave., Lakewood, NJ 08701-5934 / 800-242-7374

Atsko/Sno-Seal, Inc., 2664 Russell St., Orangeburg, SC 29115 / 803-531-1820; FAX: 803-531-2139 info@atsko.com www.atsko.com

Auguste Francotte & Cie S.A., rue du Trois Juin 109, 4400 Herstal-Liege, BELGIUM / 32-4-248-13-18; FAX: 32-4-948-11-79

Austin & Halleck, Inc., 2150 South 950 East, Provo, UT 84606-6285 / 877-543-3256; or 801-374-9990; FAX: 801-374-9998 www.austinhallek.com

Austin Sheridan USA, Inc., P.O. Box 577, 36 Haddam Quarter Rd., Durham, CT 06422 / 860-349-1772; FAX: 860-349-1771 swalzer@palm.net

Autauga Arms, Inc., Pratt Plaza Mall No. 13, Prattville, AL 36067 / 800-262-9563; FAX: 334-361-2961

Auto Arms, 738 Clearview, San Antonio, TX 78228 / 512-434-5450

Auto-Ordnance Corp., P.O. Box 220, Blauvelt, NY 10913 / 914-353-7770

Autumn Sales, Inc. (Blaser), 1320 Lake St., Fort Worth, TX 76102 / 817-335-1634; FAX: 817-338-0119

Avnda Otaola Norica, 16 Apartado 68, 20600, Eibar, SPAIN

AWC Systems Technology, P.O. Box 41938, Phoenix, AZ 85080-1938 / 623-780-1050; FAX: 623-780-2967 awc@awcsystech.com www.awcsystech.com

Axtell Rifle Co., 353 Mill Creek Road, Sheridan, MT 59749 / 406-842-5814

AYA (See U.S. Importer-New England Custom Gun Serv

B

B&D Trading Co., Inc., 3935 Fair Hill Rd., Fair Oaks, CA 95628 / 800-334-3790; or 916-967-9366; FAX: 916-967-4873

B&P America, 12321 Brittany Cir., Dallas, TX 75230 / 972-726-9069

B.A.C., 17101 Los Modelos St., Fountain Valley, CA 92708 / 435-586-3286

B.B. Walker Co., P.O. Box 1167, 414 E Dixie Dr., Asheboro, NC 27204 / 910-625-1380; FAX: 910-625-8125

B.C. Outdoors, Larry McGhee, PO Box 61497, Boulder City, NV 89006 / 702-294-3056; FAX: 702-294-0413 jdalton@pmcammo.com www.pmcammo.com

B.M.F. Activator, Inc., 12145 Mill Creek Run, Plantersville, TX 77363 / 936-894-2397; FAX: 936-894-2397 bmf25years@aol.com

Baelder, Harry, Alte Goennebeker Strasse 5, 24635, Rickling, GERMANY / 04328-722732; FAX: 04328-722733

Baer's Hollows, P.O. Box 603, Taft, CA 93268 / 719-438-5718

Bagmaster Mfg., Inc., 2731 Sutton Ave., St. Louis, MO 63143 / 314-781-8002; FAX: 314-781-3363 sales@bagmaster.com www.bagmaster.com

Bain & Davis, Inc., 307 E. Valley Blvd., San Gabriel, CA 91776-3522 / 626-573-4241; FAX: 323-283-7449 baindavis@aol.com

Baker, Stan. See: STAN BAKER SPORTS

Baker's Leather Goods, Roy, P.O. Box 893, Magnolia, AR 71754 / 870-234-0344 pholsters@ipa.net

Bald Eagle Precision Machine Co., 101-A Allison St., Lock Haven, PA 17745 / 570-748-6772; FAX: 570-748-4443 bepmachine@aol.com baldeaglemachine.com

Balickie, Joe, 408 Trelawney Lane, Apex, NC 27502 / 919-362-5185

Ballard, Donald. See: BALLARD INDUSTRIES

Ballard Industries, Donald Ballard Sr., P.O. Box 2035, Arnold, CA 95223 / 408-996-0957; FAX: 408-257-6828

Ballard Rifle & Cartridge Co., LLC, 113 W. Yellowstone Ave., Cody, WY 82414 / 307-587-4914; FAX: 307-527-6097 ballard@wyoming.com www.ballardrifles.com

Ballistic Products, Inc., 20015 75th Ave. North, Corcoran, MN 55340-9456 / 763-494-9237; FAX: 763-494-9236 info@ballisticproducts.com www.ballisticproducts.com

Ballistic Program Co., Inc., The, 2417 N. Patterson St., Thomasville, GA 31792 / 912-228-5739 or 800-368-0835

Ballistic Research, 1108 W. May Ave., McHenry, IL 60050 / 815-385-0037

Ballisti-Cast, Inc., P.O. Box 1057, Minot, ND 58702-1057 / 701-497-3333; FAX: 701-497-3335

Bandcor Industries, Div. of Man-Sew Corp., 6108 Sherwin Dr., Port Richey, FL 34668 / 813-848-0432

Bang-Bang Boutique (See Holster Shop, The)

Bansner's Ultimate Rifles, LLC, P.O. Box 839, 261 E. Main St., Adamstown, PA 19501 / 717-484-2370; FAX: 717-484-0523 bansner@aol.com www.bansnersrifle.com

Barbour, Inc., 55 Meadowbrook Dr., Milford, NH 03055 / 603-673-1313; FAX: 603-673-6510

Barnes, 4347 Tweed Dr., Eau Claire, WI 54703-6302

Barnes Bullets, Inc., P.O. Box 215, American Fork, UT 84003 / 801-756-4222; or 800-574-9200; FAX: 801-756-2465 email@barnesbullets.com www.barnesbullets.com

Baron Technology, 62 Spring Hill Rd., Trumbull, CT 06611 / 203-452-0515; FAX: 203-452-0663 dbaron@baronengraving.com www.baronengraving.com

Barraclough, John K., 55 Merit Park Dr., Gardena, CA 90247 / 310-324-2574 johnbar120@aol.com

Barramundi Corp., P.O. Drawer 4259, Homosassa Springs, FL 32687 / 904-628-0200

Barrel & Gunworks, 2601 Lake Valley Rd., Prescott Valley, AZ 86314 / 928-772-4060 www.cutrifle.com

Barrett Firearms Manufacturer, Inc., P.O. Box 1077, Murfreesboro, TN 37133 / 615-896-2938; FAX: 615-896-7313

Bar-Sto Precision Machine, 73377 Sullivan Rd., P.O. Box 1838, Twentynine Palms, CA 92277 / 760-367-2747; FAX: 760-367-2407 barsto@eee.org www.barsto.com

Barta's Gunsmithing, 10231 U.S. Hwy. 10, Cato, WI 54230 / 920-732-4472

Barteaux Machete, 1916 SE 50th Ave., Portland, OR 97215-3238 / 503-233-5880

Bartlett Engineering, 40 South 200 East, Smithfield, UT 84335-1645 / 801-563-5910

Bates Engraving, Billy, 2302 Winthrop Dr. SW, Decatur, AL 35603 / 256-355-3690 bbrn@aol.com www.angelfire.com/al/billybates

Battenfeld Technologies, Inc., 5885 W. Van Horn Tavern Rd., Columbia, MO 65203 / 573-445-9200; FAX: 573-447-4158 battenfeldtechnologies.com

Bauer, Eddie, 15010 NE 36th St., Redmond, WA 98052

Baumgartner Bullets, 3011 S. Alane St., W. Valley City, UT 84120

Bauska Barrels, 105 9th Ave. W., Kalispell, MT 59901 / 406-752-7706

Bear Archery, RR 4, 4600 Southwest 41st Blvd., Gainesville, FL 32601 / 904-376-2327

Bear Arms, 374-A Carson Rd., St. Mathews, SC 29135

Bear Mountain Gun & Tool, 120 N. Plymouth, New Plymouth, ID 83655 / 208-278-5221; FAX: 208-278-5221

Beartooth Bullets, P.O. Box 491, Dept. HLD, Dover, ID 83825-0491 / 208-448-1865 bullets@beartoothbullets.com beartoothbullets.com

Beaver Park Product, Inc., 840 J St., Penrose, CO 81240 / 719-372-6744

BEC, Inc., 1227 W. Valley Blvd., Suite 204, Alhambra, CA 91803 / 626-281-5751; FAX: 626-293-7073

Beeks, Mike. See: GRAYBACK WILDCATS

Beeman Precision Airguns, 5454 Argosy Dr., Huntington Beach, CA 92649 / 714-890-4808; FAX: 714-890-4808

Behlert Precision, Inc., P.O. Box 288, 7067 Easton Rd., Pipersville, PA 18947 / 215-766-8681; or 215-766-7301; FAX: 215-766-8681

Beitzinger, George, 116-20 Atlantic Ave., Richmond Hill, NY 11419 / 718-847-7661

Belding's Custom Gun Shop, 10691 Sayers Rd., Munith, MI 49259 / 517-596-2388

Bell & Carlson, Inc., Dodge City Industrial Park, 101 Allen Rd., Dodge City, KS 67801 / 800-634-8586; or 620-225-6688; FAX: 620-225-6688 email@bellandcarlson.com www.bellandcarlson.com

Bell Reloading, Inc., 1725 Harlin Lane Rd., Villa Rica, GA 30180

Bell's Gun & Sport Shop, 3309-19 Mannheim Rd., Franklin Park, IL 60131

Bell's Legendary Country Wear, 22 Circle Dr., Bellmore, NY 11710 / 516-679-1158

Benchmark Knives (See Gerber Legendary Blades)

Benelli Armi S.P.A., Via della Stazione, 61029, Urbino, ITALY / 39-722-307-1; FAX: 39-722-327427

Benelli USA Corp., 17603 Indian Head Hwy., Accokeek, MD 20607 / 301-283-6981; FAX: 301-283-6988 benelliusa.com

Bengtson Arms Co., L., 6345-B E. Akron St., Mesa, AZ 85205 / 602-981-6375

Benjamin/Sheridan Co., Crosman, Rts. 5 and 20, E. Bloomfield, NY 14443 / 716-657-6161; FAX: 716-657-5405 www.crosman.com

Bentley, John, 128-D Watson Dr., Turtle Creek, PA 15145

Beretta S.P.A., Pietro, Via Beretta, 18, 25063, Gardone Vae Trompia, ITALY / 39-30-8341-1 info@benetta.com www.benetta.com

Beretta U.S.A. Corp., 17601 Beretta Dr., Accokeek, MD 20607 / 301-283-2191; FAX: 301-283-0435

Berger Bullets Ltd., 5443 W. Westwind Dr., Glendale, AZ 85310 / 602-842-4001; FAX: 602-934-9083

Bernardelli, Vincenzo, P.O. Box 460243, Houston, TX 77056-8243 www.bernardelli.com

Bernardelli, Vincenzo, Via Grande, 10, Sede Legale Torbole Casaglia, Brescia, ITALY / 39-30-8912851-2-3; FAX: 39-030-2150963 bernardelli@bernardelli.com www.bernardelli.com

Berry's Mfg., Inc., 401 North 3050 East St., St. George, UT 84770 / 435-634-1682; FAX: 435-634-1683 sales@berrysmfg.com www.berrysmfg.com

Bersa S.A., Benso Bonadimani, Magallanes 775 B1704 FLC, Ramos Mejia, ARGENTINA / 011-4656-2377; FAX: 011-4656-2093+ info@bersa-sa.com.dr www.bersa-sa.com.ar

Bert Johanssons Vapentillbehor, S-430 20 Veddige, SWEDEN,

Bertuzzi (See U.S. Importer-New England Arms Co.)

Better Concepts Co., 663 New Castle Rd., Butler, PA 16001 / 412-285-9000

Beverly, Mary, 3201 Horseshoe Trail, Tallahassee, FL 32312

Bianchi International, Inc., 100 Calle Cortez, Temecula, CA 92590 / 909-676-5621; FAX: 909-676-6777

Big Bear Arms & Sporting Goods, Inc., 1112 Milam Way, Carrollton, TX 75006 / 972-416-8051; or 800-400-BEAR; FAX: 972-416-0771

Big Bore Bullets of Alaska, P.O. Box 521455, Big Lake, AK 99652 / 907-373-2673; FAX: 907-373-2673 doug@mtaonline.net ww.awloo/bbb/index.

Big Bore Express, 2316 E. Railroad St., Nampa, ID 83651 / 800-376-4010 FAX: 208-466-6927 info@powerbeltbullets.com bigbore.com

Big Spring Enterprises "Bore Stores", P.O. Box 1115, Big Spring Rd., Yellville, AR 72687 / 870-449-5297; FAX: 870-449-4446

Bilal, Mustafa. See: TURK'S HEAD PRODUCTIONS

Bilinski, Bryan. See: FIELDSPORT LTD.

Bill Adair Custom Shop, 2886 Westridge, Carrollton, TX 75006 / 972-418-0950

Bill Austin's Calls, Box 284, Kaycee, WY 82639 / 307-738-2552

Bill Hanus Birdguns, LLC, P.O. Box 533, Newport, OR 97365 / 541-265-7433; FAX: 541-265-7400 www.billhanusbirdguns.com

Bill Russ Trading Post, William A. Russ, 25 William St., Addison, NY 14801-1326 / 607-359-3896

MANUFACTURER'S DIRECTORY

Bill Wiseman and Co., P.O. Box 3427, Bryan, TX 77805 / 409-690-3456; FAX: 409-690-0156
Billeb, Stephen. See: QUALITY CUSTOM FIREARMS
Billings Gunsmiths, 1841 Grand Ave., Billings, MT 59102 / 406-256-8390; FAX: 406-256-6530 blgsgunsmiths@msn.com www.billingsgunsmiths.net
Billingsley & Brownell, P.O. Box 25, Dayton, WY 82836 / 307-655-9344
Bill's Gun Repair, 1007 Burlington St., Mendota, IL 61342 / 815-539-5786
Billy Bates Engraving, 2302 Winthrop Dr. SW, Decatur, AL 35603 / 256-355-3690 bbrn@aol.com www.angelfire.com/al/billybates
Birchwood Casey, 7900 Fuller Rd., Eden Prairie, MN 55344 / 800-328-6156; or 612-937-7933; FAX: 612-937-7979
Birdsong & Assoc., W. E., 1435 Monterey Rd., Florence, MS 39073-9748 / 601-366-8270
Bismuth Cartridge Co., 3500 Maple Ave., Suite 1650, Dallas, TX 75219 / 214-521-5880; FAX: 214-521-9035
Bison Studios, 1409 South Commerce St., Las Vegas, NV 89102 / 702-388-2891; FAX: 702-383-9967
Bitterroot Bullet Co., 2001 Cedar Ave., Lewiston, ID 83501-0412 / 208-743-5635 brootbil@lewiston.com
BKL Technologies, P.O. Box 5237, Brownsville, TX 78523
Black Belt Bullets (See Big Bore Express)
Black Hills Ammunition, Inc., P.O. Box 3090, Rapid City, SD 57709-3090 / 605-348-5150; FAX: 605-348-9827
Black Hills Shooters Supply, P.O. Box 4220, Rapid City, SD 57709 / 800-289-2506
Black Powder Products, 67 Township Rd. 1411, Chesapeake, OH 45619 / 614-867-8047
Black Sheep Brand, 3220 W. Gentry Pkwy., Tyler, TX 75702 / 903-592-3853; FAX: 903-592-0527
Blacksmith Corp., P.O. Box 280, North Hampton, OH 45349 / 937-969-8389; FAX: 937-969-8399 sales@blacksmithcorp.com www.blacksmithcorp.com
BlackStar AccuMax Barrels, 11501 Brittmoore Park Drive, Houston, TX 77041 / 281-721-6040; FAX: 281-721-6041
BlackStar Barrel Accurizing (See BlackStar AccuMax)
Blacktail Mountain Books, 42 First Ave. W., Kalispell, MT 59901 / 406-257-5573
Blammo Ammo, P.O. Box 1677, Seneca, SC 29679 / 803-882-1768
Blaser Jagdwaffen GmbH, D-88316, Isny Im Allgau, GERMANY
Blount, Inc., Sporting Equipment Div., 2299 Snake River Ave., P.O. Box 856, Lewiston, ID 83501 / 800-627-3640; or 208-746-2351; FAX: 208-799-3904
Blount/Outers ATK, P.O. Box 39, Onalaska, WI 54650 / 608-781-5800; FAX: 608-781-0368
Blue and Gray Products Inc. (See Ox-Yoke Originals)
Blue Book Publications, Inc., 8009 34th Ave. S., Ste. 175, Minneapolis, MN 55425 / 952-854-5229; FAX: 952-853-1486 bluebook@bluebookinc.com www.bluebookinc.com
Blue Mountain Bullets, 64146 Quail Ln., Box 231, John Day, OR 97845 / 541-820-4594; FAX: 541-820-4594
Blue Ridge Machinery & Tools, Inc., P.O. Box 536-GD, Hurricane, WV 25526 / 800-872-6500; FAX: 304-562-5311 blueridgemachine@worldnet.att.net www.blueridgemachinery.com
BMC Supply, Inc., 26051 - 179th Ave. SE, Kent, WA 98042
Bob Allen Co., P.O. Box 477, 214 SW Jackson, Des Moines, IA 50315 / 800-685-7020; FAX: 515-283-0779
Bob Allen Sportswear, 220 S. Main St., Osceola, IA 50213 / 210-344-8531; FAX: 210-342-2703 sales@bob-allen.com www.bob-allen.com
Bob Rogers Gunsmithing, P.O. Box 305, 344 S. Walnut St., Franklin Grove, IL 61031 / 815-456-2685; FAX: 815-456-2685
Bob's Gun Shop, P.O. Box 200, Royal, AR 71968 / 501-767-1970; FAX: 501-767-1970 gunparts@hsnp.com www.gun-parts.com
Bob's Tactical Indoor Shooting Range & Gun Shop, 90 Lafayette Rd., Salisbury, MA 01952 / 508-465-5561
Boessler, Erich, Am Vogeltal 3, 97702, Munnerstadt, GERMANY
Boker USA, Inc., 1550 Balsam Street, Lakewood, CO 80214 / 303-462-0662; FAX: 303-462-0668 sales@bokerusa.com bokerusa.com
Boltin, John M., P.O. Box 644, Estill, SC 29918 / 803-625-2185
Bo-Mar Tool & Mfg. Co., 6136 State Hwy. 300, Longview, TX 75604 / 903-759-4784; FAX: 903-759-9141 marykor@earthlink.net bo-mar.com
Bonadimani, Benso. See: BERSA S.A.
Bonanza (See Forster Products), 310 E. Lanark Ave., Lanark, IL 61046 / 815-493-6360; FAX: 815-493-2371
Bond Arms, Inc., P.O. Box 1296, Granbury, TX 76048 / 817-573-4445; FAX: 817-573-5636

Bond Custom Firearms, 8954 N. Lewis Ln., Bloomington, IN 47408 / 812-332-4519
Bonham's & Butterfields, 220 San Bruno Ave., San Francisco, CA 94103 / 415-861-7500; FAX: 415-861-0183 arms@butterfields.com www.butterfields.com
Boone Trading Co., Inc., P.O. Box 669, Brinnon, WA 98320 / 800-423-1945; or 360-796-4330; FAX: 360-796-4511 sales@boonetrading.com boonetrading.com
Boone's Custom Ivory Grips, Inc., 562 Coyote Rd., Brinnon, WA 98320 / 206-796-4330
Boonie Packer Products, P.O. Box 12517, Salem, OR 97309-0517 / 800-477-3244; or 503-581-3244; FAX: 503-581-3191 customerservice@booniepacker.com www.booniepacker.com
Borden Ridges Rimrock Stocks, RR 1 Box 250 BC, Springville, PA 18844 / 570-965-2505; FAX: 570-965-2328
Borden Rifles Inc., RD 1, Box 250 #BC, Springville, PA 18844 / 717-965-2505; FAX: 717-965-2328
Border Barrels Ltd., Riccarton Farm, Newcastleton, SCOTLAND UK
Borovnik K.G., Ludwig, 9170 Ferlach, Bahnhofstrasse 7, AUSTRIA / 042 27 24 42; FAX: 042 26 43 49
Bosis (See U.S. Importer-New England Arms Co.)
Boss Manufacturing Co., 221 W. First St., Kewanee, IL 61443 / 309-852-2131; or 800-447-4581; FAX: 309-852-0848
Bostick Wildlife Calls, Inc., P.O. Box 728, Estill, SC 29918 / 803-625-2210; or 803-625-4512
Bowen Classic Arms Corp., P.O. Box 67, Louisville, TN 37777 / 865-984-3583 www.bowenclassicarms.com
Bowen Knife Co., Inc., P.O. Box 590, Blackshear, GA 31516 / 912-449-4794
Bowerly, Kent, 710 Golden Pheasant Dr., Redmond, OR 97756 / 541-923-3501 jkbowerly@aol.com
Boyds' Gunstock Industries, Inc., 25376 403 Rd. Ave., Mitchell, SD 57301 / 605-996-5011; FAX: 605-996-9878 www.boydsgunstocks.com
Brace, Larry D., 771 Blackfoot Ave., Eugene, OR 97404 / 541-688-1278; FAX: 541-607-5833
Brauer Bros., 1520 Washington Ave., St. Louis, MO 63103 / 314-231-2864; FAX: 314-249-4952 www.brauerbros.com
Break-Free, Inc., 13386 International Pkwy., Jacksonville, FL 32218 / 800-428-0588; FAX: 904-741-5407 contactus@armorholdings.com www.break-free.com
Brenneke GmbH, P.O. Box 1646, 30837, Langenhagen, GERMANY / +49-511-97262-0; FAX: +49-511-97262-62 info@brenneke.de brenneke.com
Bridgeman Products, Harry Jaffin, 153 B Cross Slope Ct., Englishtown, NJ 07726 / 732-536-3604; FAX: 732-972-1004
Bridgers Best, P.O. Box 1410, Berthoud, CO 80513
Briese Bullet Co., Inc., 3442 42nd Ave. SE, Tappen, ND 58487 / 701-327-4578; FAX: 701-327-4579
Brigade Quartermasters, 1025 Cobb International Blvd., Dept. VH, Kennesaw, GA 30144-4300 / 404-428-1248; or 800-241-3125; FAX: 404-426-7726
Briganti, A.J. See: BRIGANTI CUSTOM GUNSMITH
Briganti Custom Gunsmith, A.J. Briganti, 512 Rt. 32, Highland Mills, NY 10930 / 845-928-9513
Briley Mfg. Inc., 1230 Lumpkin, Houston, TX 77043 / 800-331-5718; or 713-932-6995; FAX: 713-932-1043
Brill, R. See: ROYAL ARMS INTERNATIONAL
British Sporting Arms, RR 1, Box 130, Millbrook, NY 12545 / 914-677-8303
Broad Creek Rifle Works, Ltd., 120 Horsey Ave., Laurel, DE 19956 / 302-875-5446; FAX: 302-875-1448 bcrw4guns@aol.com
Brockman's Custom Gunsmithing, P.O. Box 357, Gooding, ID 83330 / 208-934-5050
Broken Gun Ranch, 10739 126 Rd., Spearville, KS 67876 / 316-385-2587; FAX: 316-385-2597 nbowlin@ucom.net www.brokengunranch
Brooker, Dennis, Rt. 1, Box 12A, Derby, IA 50068 / 515-533-2103
Brooks Tactical Systems-Agrip, 279-C Shorewood Ct., Fox Island, WA 98333 / 253-549-2866 FAX: 253-549-2703 brooks@brookstactical.com www.brookstactical.com
Brown Dog Ent., 2200 Calle Camelia, 1000 Oaks, CA 91360 / 805-497-2318; FAX: 805-497-1618
Brown Precision, Inc., 7786 Molinos Ave., Los Molinos, CA 96055 / 530-384-2506; FAX: 916-384-1638 www.brownprecision.com
Brown Products, Inc., Ed, 43825 Muldrow Trl., Perry, MO 63462 / 573-565-3261; FAX: 573-565-2791 edbrown@edbrown.com www.edbrown.com
Brownells, Inc., 200 S. Front St., Montezuma, IA 50171 / 800-741-0015; FAX: 800-264-3068 orderdesk@brownells.com www.brownells.com
Browning Arms Co., One Browning Place, Morgan, UT 84050 / 801-876-2711; FAX: 801-876-3331 www.browning.com

Browning Arms Co. (Parts & Service), 3005 Arnold Tenbrook Rd., Arnold, MO 63010 / 617-287-6800; FAX: 617-287-9751
BRP, Inc. High Performance Cast Bullets, 1210 Alexander Rd., Colorado Springs, CO 80909 / 719-633-0658
Brunton U.S.A., 620 E. Monroe Ave., Riverton, WY 82501 / 307-856-6559; FAX: 307-857-4702 info@brunton.com www.brunton.com
Bryan & Assoc., R. D. Sauls, P.O. Box 5772, Anderson, SC 29623-5772 / 864-261-6810 bryanandac@aol.com www.huntersweb.com/bryanandac
Brynin, Milton, P.O. Box 383, Yonkers, NY 10710 / 914-779-4333
BSA Guns Ltd., Armoury Rd. Small Heath, Birmingham B11 2PP, ENGLAND / 011-021-772-8543; FAX: 011-021-773-0845 sales@bsagun.com www.bsagun.com
BSA Optics, 3911 SW 47th Ave., Ste. 914, Ft. Lauderdale, FL 33314 / 954-581-2144; FAX: 954-581-3165 4info@basaoptics.com www.bsaoptics.com
B-Square Company, Inc., P.O. Box 11281, 2708 St. Louis Ave., Ft. Worth, TX 76110 / 817-923-0964 or 800-433-2909; FAX: 817-926-7012
Buchsenmachermeister, Peter Hofer Jagdwaffen, A-9170 Ferlach, Kirchgasse 24, Kirchgasse, AUSTRIA / 43 4227 3683; or 43 664 3200216; FAX: 43 4227 368330 peterhofer@hoferwaffen.com www.hoferwaffen.com
Buck Knives, Inc., 1900 Weld Blvd., P.O. Box 1267, El Cajon, CA 92020 / 619-449-1100; or 800-326-2825; FAX: 619-562-5774
Buck Stix-SOS Products Co., Box 3, Neenah, WI 54956
Buck Stop Lure Co., Inc., 3600 Grow Rd. NW, P.O. Box 636, Stanton, MI 48888 / 989-762-5091; FAX: 989-762-5124 buckstop@nethawk.com www.buckstopscents.com
Buckeye Custom Bullets, 6490 Stewart Rd., Elida, OH 45807 / 419-641-4463
Buckhorn Gun Works, 8109 Woodland Dr., Black Hawk, SD 57718 / 605-787-6472
Buckskin Bullet Co., P.O. Box 1893, Cedar City, UT 84721 / 435-586-3286
Budin, Dave, 817 Main St., P.O. Box 685, Margaretville, NY 12455 / 914-568-4103; FAX: 914-586-4105
Budin, Dave. See: DEL-SPORTS, INC.
Buenger Enterprises/Goldenrod Dehumidifier, 3600 S. Harbor Blvd., Oxnard, CA 93035 / 800-451-6797; or 805-985-5828; FAX: 805-985-1534
Buffalo Arms Co., 660 Vermeer Ct., Ponderay, ID 83852 / 208-263-6953; FAX: 208-265-2096 www.buffaloarms.com
Buffalo Bullet Co., Inc., 12637 Los Nietos Rd., Unit A, Santa Fe Springs, CA 90670 / 800-423-8069; FAX: 562-944-5054
Buffalo Gun Center, 3385 Harlem Rd., Buffalo, NY 14225 / 716-833-2581; FAX: 716-833-2265 www.buffaloguncenter.com
Buffalo Rock Shooters Supply, R.R. 1, Ottawa, IL 61350 / 815-433-2471
Buffer Technologies, P.O. Box 104930, Jefferson City, MO 65110 / 573-634-8529; FAX: 573-634-8522
Bull Mountain Rifle Co., 6327 Golden West Terrace, Billings, MT 59106 / 406-656-0778
Bullberry Barrel Works, Ltd., 2430 W. Bullberry Ln., Hurricane, UT 84737 / 435-635-9866; FAX: 435-635-0348 fred@bullberry.com www.bullberry.com
Bullet Metals, Bill Ferguson, P.O. Box 1238, Sierra Vista, AZ 85636 / 520-458-5321; FAX: 520-458-1421 info@theantimonyman.com www.bullet-metals.com
Bullet N Press, 1210 Jones St., Gastonia, NC 28052 / 704-853-0265 bnpress@quik.com www.oldwestgunsmith.com
Bullet Swaging Supply, Inc., P.O. Box 1056, 303 McMillan Rd., West Monroe, LA 71291 / 318-387-3266; FAX: 318-387-7779 leblackmon@colla.com
Bull-X, Inc., 411 E. Water St., Farmer City, IL 61842-1556 / 309-928-2574 or 800-248-3845; FAX: 309-928-2130
Burkhart Gunsmithing, Don, P.O. Box 852, Rawlins, WY 82301 / 307-324-6007
Burnham Bros., P.O. Box 1148, Menard, TX 78659 / 915-396-4572; FAX: 915-396-4574
Burris Co., Inc., P.O. Box 1747, 331 E. 8th St., Greeley, CO 80631 / 970-356-1670; FAX: 970-356-8702
Bushmaster Firearms, Inc., 999 Roosevelt Trail, Windham, ME 04062 / 800-998-7928; FAX: 207-892-8068 info@bushmaster.com www.bushmaster.com
Bushmaster Hunting & Fishing, 451 Alliance Ave., Toronto, ON M6N 2J1 CANADA / 416-763-4040; FAX: 416-763-0623
Bushnell Sports Optics Worldwide, 9200 Cody, Overland Park, KS 66214 / 913-752-3400 or 800-423-3537; FAX: 913-752-3550

MANUFACTURER'S DIRECTORY

Buster's Custom Knives, P.O. Box 214, Richfield, UT 84701 / 435-896-5319; FAX: 435-896-8333 www.warenskiknives.com

Butler Creek Corp., 2100 S. Silverstone Way, Meridian, ID 83642-8151 / 800-423-8327 or 406-388-1356; FAX: 406-388-7204

Butler Enterprises, 834 Oberting Rd., Lawrenceburg, IN 47025 / 812-537-3584

Buzz Fletcher Custom Stockmaker, 117 Silver Road, P.O. Box 189, Taos, NM 87571 / 505-758-3486

C

C&D Special Products (See Claybuster Wads & Harvester Bullets)

C&H Research, 115 Sunnyside Dr., Box 351, Lewis, KS 67552 / 316-324-5445; or 888-324-5445; FAX: 620-324-5984 info@mercuryrecoil.com www.mercuryrecoil.com

C. Palmer Manufacturing Co., Inc., P.O. Box 220, West Newton, PA 15089 / 412-872-8200; FAX: 412-872-8302

C. Sharps Arms Co. Inc./Montana Armory, 100 Centennial Dr., P.O. Box 885, Big Timber, MT 59011 / 406-932-4353; FAX: 406-932-4443

C.S. Van Gorden & Son, Inc., 1815 Main St., Bloomer, WI 54724 / 715-568-2612 vangorden@bloomer.net

C.W. Erickson's L.L.C., 530 Garrison Ave. NE, P.O. Box 522, Buffalo, MN 55313 / 763-682-3665; FAX: 763-682-4328 www.archerhunter.com

Cabanas (See U.S. Importer-Mandall Shooting Supply

Cabela's, One Cabela Drive, Sidney, NE 69160 / 308-254-5505; FAX: 308-254-8420

Cabinet Mtn. Outfitters Scents & Lures, P.O. Box 766, Plains, MT 59859 / 406-826-3970

Cache La Poudre Rifleworks, 140 N. College, Ft. Collins, CO 80524 / 920-482-6913

Cain's Outdoors, Inc., 1832 Williams Hwy., Williamstown, WV 26187 / 304-375-7842; FAX: 304-375-7842 muzzleloading@cainsoutdoor.com www.cainsoutdoor.com

Calhoon Mfg., 4343 U.S. Highway 87, Havre, MT 59501 / 406-395-4079 www.jamescalhoon.com

Cali'co Hardwoods, Inc., 3580 Westwind Blvd., Santa Rosa, CA 95403 / 707-546-4045; FAX: 707-546-4027 calicohardwoods@msn.com

Calico Light Weapon Systems, 1489 Greg St., Sparks, NV 89431

California Sights (See Fautheree, Andy)

Cambos Outdoorsman, 532 E. Idaho Ave., Ontario, OR 97914 / 541-889-3135; FAX: 541-889-2633

Cambos Outdoorsman, Fritz Hallberg, 532 E. Idaho Ave., Ontario, OR 97914 / 541-889-3135; FAX: 541-889-2633

Camdex, Inc., 2330 Alger, Troy, MI 48083 / 810-528-2300; FAX: 810-528-0989

Cameron's, 16690 W. 11th Ave., Golden, CO 80401 / 303-279-7365; FAX: 303-568-1009 ncnoremac@aol.com

Camillus Cutlery Co., 54 Main St., Camillus, NY 13031 / 315-672-8111; FAX: 315-672-8832

Campbell, Dick, 196 Garden Homes Dr., Colville, WA 99114 / 509-684-6080; FAX: 509-684-6080 dicksknives@aol.com

Camp-Cap Products, P.O. Box 3805, Chesterfield, MO 63006 / 866-212-4639; FAX: 636-536-6320 www.langenberghats.com

Cannon Safe, Inc., 216 S. 2nd Ave. #BLD-932, San Bernardino, CA 92400 / 310-692-0636; or 800-242-1055; FAX: 310-692-7252

Canyon Cartridge Corp., P.O. Box 152, Albertson, NY 11507 FAX: 516-294-8946

Cape Outfitters, 599 County Rd. 206, Cape Girardeau, MO 63701 / 573-335-4103; FAX: 573-335-1555

Caraville Manufacturing, P.O. Box 4545, Thousand Oaks, CA 91359 / 805-499-1234

Carbide Checkering Tools (See J&R Engineering)

Carhartt, Inc., P.O. Box 600, 3 Parklane Blvd., Dearborn, MI 48121 / 800-358-3825; or 313-271-8460; FAX: 313-271-3455

Carl Walther GmbH, B.P. 4325, D-89033, Ulm, GERMANY

Carl Zeiss Inc., 13005 N. Kingston Ave., Chester, VA 23836 / 800-441-3005; FAX: 804-530-8481

Carolina Precision Rifles, 1200 Old Jackson Hwy., Jackson, SC 29831 / 803-827-2069

Carrell, William. See: CARRELL'S PRECISION FIREARMS

Carrell's Precision Firearms, William Carrell, 1952 W.Silver Falls Ct., Meridian, ID 83642-3837

Carry-Lite, Inc., P.O. Box 1587, Fort Smith, AR 72902 / 479-782-8971; FAX: 479-783-0234

Carter's Gun Shop, 225 G St., Penrose, CO 81240 / 719-372-6240 rlewiscarter@msn.com

Cascade Bullet Co., Inc., 2355 South 6th St., Klamath Falls, OR 97601 / 503-884-9316

Cascade Shooters, 2155 N.W. 12th St., Redwood, OR 97756

Case & Sons Cutlery Co., W R, Owens Way, Bradford, PA 16701 / 814-368-4123; or 800-523-6350; FAX: 814-768-5369

Case Sorting System, 12695 Cobblestone Creek Rd., Poway, CA 92064 / 619-486-9340

Cash Mfg. Co., Inc., P.O. Box 130, 201 S. Klein Dr., Waunakee, WI 53597-0130 / 608-849-5664; FAX: 608-849-5664

Caspian Arms, Ltd., 14 North Main St., Hardwick, VT 05843 / 802-472-6454; FAX: 802-472-6709

Cast Bullet Association, The, 12857 S. Road, Hoyt, KS 66440-9116 cbamemdir@castbulletassoc.org www.castbulletassoc.org

Cast Performance Bullet Company, P.O. Box 153, Riverton, WY 82501 / 307-857-2940; FAX: 307-857-3132 castperform@wyoming.com castperformance.com

Casull Arms Corp., P.O. Box 1629, Afton, WY 83110 / 307-886-0200

Caswell International, 720 Industrial Dr. No. 112, Cary, IL 60013 / 847-639-7666; FAX: 847-639-7694 www.caswellintl.com

Cathey Enterprises, Inc., P.O. Box 2202, Brownwood, TX 76804 / 915-643-2553; FAX: 915-643-3653

Cation, 2341 Alger St., Troy, MI 48083 / 810-689-0658; FAX: 810-689-7558

Caywood, Shane J., P.O. Box 321, Minocqua, WI 54548 / 715-277-3866

Caywood Gunmakers, 18 Kings Hill Estates, Berryville, AR 72616 / 870-423-4741 www.caywoodguns.com

CBC, Avenida Humberto de Campos 3220, 09400-000, Ribeirao Pires, SP, BRAZIL / 55 11 4822 8378; FAX: 55 11 4822 8323 export@cbc.com.bc www.cbc.com.bc

CBC-BRAZIL, 3 Cuckoo Lane, Honley, Yorkshire HD7 2BR, ENGLAND / 44-1484-661062; FAX: 44-1484-663709

CCG Enterprises, 5217 E. Belknap St., Halton City, TX 76117 / 800-819-7464

CCI/Speer Div of ATK, P.O. Box 856, 2299 Snake River Ave., Lewiston, ID 83501 / 800-627-3640 or 208-746-2351

CCL Security Products, 199 Whiting St., New Britain, CT 06051 / 800-733-8588

Cedar Hill Game Calls, LLC, 238 Vic Allen Rd., Downsville, LA 71234 / 318-982-5632; FAX: 318-982-2031

Centaur Systems, Inc., 1602 Foothill Rd., Kalispell, MT 59901 / 406-755-8609; FAX: 406-755-8609

Center Lock Scope Rings, 9901 France Ct., Lakeville, MN 55044 / 952-461-2114; FAX: 952-461-2194 marklee55044@usfamily.net

Central Specialties Ltd. (See Trigger Lock Division)

Century Gun Dist. Inc., 1467 Jason Rd., Greenfield, IN 46140 / 317-462-4524

Century International Arms, Inc., 430 S. Congress Ave. Ste. 1, Delray Beach, FL 33445-4701 / 800-527-1252; FAX: 561-998-1993 support@centuryarms.com www.centuryarms.com

CFVentures, 509 Harvey Dr., Bloomington, IN 47403-1715 paladinwilltravel@yahoo.com www.caversam16.freeserve.co.uk

CH Tool & Die Co. (See 4-D Custom Die Co.), 711 N Sandusky St., P.O. Box 889, Mt. Vernon, OH 43050-0889 / 740-397-7214; FAX: 740-397-6600

Chace Leather Products, 507 Alden St., Fall River, MA 02722 / 508-678-7556; FAX: 508-675-9666 chacelea@aol.com www.chaceleather.com

Chadick's Ltd., P.O. Box 100, Terrell, TX 75160 / 214-563-7577

Chambers Flintlocks Ltd., Jim, 116 Sams Branch Rd., Candler, NC 28715 / 828-667-8361; FAX: 828-665-0852 www.flintlocks.com

Champion Shooters' Supply, P.O. Box 303, New Albany, OH 43054 / 614-855-1603; FAX: 614-855-1209

Champion Target Co., 232 Industrial Parkway, Richmond, IN 47374 / 800-441-4971

Champion's Choice, Inc., 201 International Blvd., LaVergne, TN 37086 / 615-793-4066; FAX: 615-793-4070 champ.choice@earthlink.net www.champchoice.com

Champlin Firearms, Inc., P.O. Box 3191, Woodring Airport, Enid, OK 73701 / 580-237-7388; FAX: 580-242-6922 info@champlinarms.com www.champlinarms.com

Chapman Academy of Practical Shooting, 4350 Academy Rd., Hallsville, MO 65255 / 573-696-5544; FAX: 573-696-2266 hq@chapmanacademy.com chapmanacademy.com

Chapman, J. Ken. See: OLD WEST BULLET MOULDS

Chapman Manufacturing Co., 471 New Haven Rd., P.O. Box 250, Durham, CT 06422 / 860-349-9228; FAX: 860-349-0084 sales@chapmanmfg.com www.chapmanmfg.com

Chapuis Armes, Z1 La Gravoux, BP15, 42380 P.O. Box 15, St. Bonnet-le-Chatea, FRANCE / (33)477.50.06.96; FAX: (33)477 50 10 70 info@chapuis.armes.com www.chapuis-armes.com

Charter 2000, 273 Canal St., Shelton, CT 06484 / 203-922-1652

Checkmate Refinishing, 370 Champion Dr., Brooksville, FL 34601 / 352-799-5774; FAX: 352-799-2986 checkmatecustom.com

Cheddite, France S.A., 99 Route de Lyon, F-26501, Bourg-les-Valence, FRANCE / 33-75-56-4545; FAX: 33-75-56-3587 export@cheddite.com

Chelsea Gun Club of New York City Inc., 237 Ovington Ave., Apt. D53, Brooklyn, NY 11209 / 718-836-9422; or 718-833-2704

Cherry Creek State Park Shooting Center, 12500 E. Belleview Ave., Englewood, CO 80111 / 303-693-1765

CheVron Bullets, RR1, Ottawa, IL 61350 / 815-433-2471

Cheyenne Pioneer Products, P.O. Box 28425, Kansas City, MO 64188 / 816-413-9196; FAX: 816-455-2859 cheyennepp@aol.com www.cartridgeboxes.com

Chicago Cutlery Co., 1536 Beech St., Terre Haute, IN 47804 / 800-457-2665

Chicasaw Gun Works, 4 Mi. Mkr., Pluto Rd., Box 868, Shady Spring, WV 25918-0868 / 304-763-2848; FAX: 304-763-3725

Chip McCormick Corp., P.O. Box 1560, Manchaca, TX 78652 / 800-328-2447; FAX: 512-280-4282 www.chipmccormick.com

Chipmunk (See Oregon Arms, Inc.)

Choate Machine & Tool Co., Inc., P.O. Box 218, 116 Lovers Ln., Bald Knob, AR 72010 / 501-724-6193; or 800-972-6390; FAX: 501-724-5873

Christensen Arms, 192 East 100 North, Fayette, UT 84630 / 435-528-7999; FAX: 435-528-7494 www.christensenarms.com

Christie's East, 20 Rockefeller Plz., New York, NY 10020-1902 / 212-606-0406 christics.com

Chu Tani Ind., Inc., P.O. Box 2064, Cody, WY 82414-2064

Chuck's Gun Shop, P.O. Box 597, Waldo, FL 32694 / 904-468-2264

Churchill (See U.S. Importer-Ellett Bros.)

Churchill, Winston G., 2838 20 Mile Stream Rd., Proctorville, VT 05153 / 802-226-7772

Churchill Glove Co., James, P.O. Box 298, Centralia, WA 98531 / 360-736-2816; FAX: 360-330-0151

CIDCO, 21480 Pacific Blvd., Sterling, VA 22170 / 703-444-5353

Cimarron F.A. Co., P.O. Box 906, Fredericksburg, TX 78624-0906 / 830-997-9090; FAX: 830-997-0802 cimgraph@koc.com www.cimarron-firearms.com

Cincinnati Swaging, 2605 Marlington Ave., Cincinnati, OH 45208

Clark Custom Guns, Inc., 336 Shootout Lane, Princeton, LA 71067 / 318-949-9884; FAX: 318-949-9829

Clark Firearms Engraving, 6347 Avon Ave., San Gabriel, CA 91775-1801 / 818-287-1652

Clarkfield Enterprises, Inc., 1032 10th Ave., Clarkfield, MN 56223 / 612-669-7140

Claro Walnut Gunstock Co., 1235 Stanley Ave., Chico, CA 95928 / 530-342-5188; FAX: 530-342-5199 wally@clarowalnutgunstocks.com www.clarowalnutgunstocks.com

Classic Arms Company, Rt 1 Box 120F, Burnet, TX 78611 / 512-756-4001

Classic Arms Corp., P.O. Box 106, Dunsmuir, CA 96025-0106 / 530-235-2000

Classic Old West Styles, 1060 Doniphan Park Circle C, El Paso, TX 79936 / 915-587-0684

Claybuster Wads & Harvester Bullets, 309 Sequoya Dr., Hopkinsville, KY 42240 / 800-922-6287; or 800-284-1746; FAX: 502-885-8088

Clean Shot Technologies, 21218 St. Andrews Blvd. Ste 504, Boca Raton, FL 33433 / 888-866-2532

Clearview Mfg. Co., Inc., 413 S. Oakley St., Fordyce, AR 71742 / 501-352-8557; FAX: 501-352-7120

Clearview Products, 3021 N. Portland, Oklahoma City, OK 73107

Cleland's Outdoor World, Inc., 10306 Airport Hwy., Swanton, OH 43558 / 419-865-4713; FAX: 419-865-5865 mail@clelands.com www.clelands.com

Clements' Custom Leathercraft, Chas, 1741 Dallas St., Aurora, CO 80010-2018 / 303-364-0403; FAX: 303-739-9824 gryphons@home.com kuntaoslcat.com

Clenzoil Worldwide Corp., Jack Fitzgerald, 25670 1st St., Westlake, OH 44145-1430 / 440-899-0482; FAX: 440-899-0483

Clift Mfg., L. R., 3821 Hammonton Rd., Marysville, CA 95901 / 916-755-3390; FAX: 916-755-3393

Clymer Mfg. Co., 1645 W. Hamlin Rd., Rochester Hills, MI 48309-3312 / 248-853-5555; FAX: 248-853-1530

C-More Systems, P.O. Box 1750, 7553 Gary Rd., Manassas, VA 20108 / 703-361-2663; FAX: 703-361-5881

MANUFACTURER'S DIRECTORY

Cobra Enterprises, Inc., 1960 S. Milestone Drive, Suite F, Salt Lake City, UT 84104 FAX: 801-908-8301 www.cobrapistols@networld.com

Cobra Sport S.R.I., Via Caduti Nei Lager No. 1, 56020 San Romano, Montopoli v/Arno Pi, ITALY / 0039-571-450490; FAX: 0039-571-450492

Coffin, Charles H., 3719 Scarlet Ave., Odessa, TX 79762 / 915-366-4729; FAX: 915-366-4729

Cogar's Gunsmithing, 206 Redwine Dr., Houghton Lake, MI 48629 / 517-422-4591

Coghlan's Ltd., 121 Irene St., Winnipeg, MB R3T 4C7 CANADA / 204-284-9550; FAX: 204-475-4127

Cold Steel Inc., 3036 Seaborg Ave. Ste. A, Ventura, CA 93003 / 800-255-4716; or 800-624-2363; FAX: 805-642-9727

Cole-Grip, 16135 Cohasset St., Van Nuys, CA 91406 / 818-782-4424

Coleman Co., Inc., 3600 N. Hydraulic, Wichita, KS 67219 / 800-835-3278; www.coleman.com

Cole's Gun Works, Old Bank Building, Rt. 4 Box 250, Moyock, NC 27958 / 919-435-2345

Collector's Armoury, Ltd., Tom Nelson, 9404 Gunston Cove Rd., Lorton, VA 22079 / 703-493-9120; FAX: 703-493-9424 www.collectorsarmoury.com

Collings, Ronald, 1006 Cielta Linda, Vista, CA 92083

Colonial Arms, Inc., P.O. Box 636, Selma, AL 36702-0636 / 334-872-9455; FAX: 334-872-9540 colonialarms@mindspring.com www.colonialarms.com

Colonial Repair, 47 Navarre St., Roslindale, MA 02131-4725 / 617-469-4951

Colorado Gunsmithing Academy, RR 3 Box 79B, El Campo, TX 77437 / 719-336-4099; or 800-754-2046; FAX: 719-336-9642

Colorado School of Trades, 1575 Hoyt St., Lakewood, CO 80215 / 800-234-4594; FAX: 303-233-4723

Colt Blackpowder Arms Co., 110 8th Street, Brooklyn, NY 11215 / 718-499-4678; FAX: 718-768-8056

Colt's Mfg. Co., Inc., P.O. Box 1868, Hartford, CT 06144-1868 / 800-962-COLT; or 860-236-6311; FAX: 860-244-1449

Compass Industries, Inc., 104 East 25th St., New York, NY 10010 / 212-473-2614 or 800-221-9904; FAX: 212-353-0826

Compasseco, Ltd., 151 Atkinson Hill Ave., Bardtown, KY 40004 / 502-349-0910

Competition Electronics, Inc., 3469 Precision Dr., Rockford, IL 61109 / 815-874-8001; FAX: 815-874-8181

Competitive Pistol Shop, The, 5233 Palmer Dr., Fort Worth, TX 76117-2433 / 817-834-8479

Competitor Corp., Inc., 26 Knight St. Unit 3, P.O. Box 352, Jaffrey, NH 03452 / 603-532-9483; FAX: 603-532-8209 competitorcorp@aol.com competitor-pistol.com

Component Concepts, Inc., 530 S. Springbrook Road, Newberg, OR 97132 / 503-554-8095; FAX: 503-554-9370 cci@cybcon.com www.phantomonline.com

Concealment Shop, Inc., The, 3550 E. Hwy. 80, Mesquite, TX 75149 / 972-289-8997; or 800-444-7090; FAX: 972-289-4410 info@theconcealmentshop.com www.theconcealmentshop.com

Concept Development Corp., 16610 E. Laser Drive, Suite 5, Fountain Hills, AZ 85268-6644

Conetrol Scope Mounts, 10225 Hwy. 123 S., Seguin, TX 78155 / 830-379-3030; or 800-CONETROL; FAX: 830-379-3030 email@conetrol.com www.conetrol.com

Connecticut Shotgun Mfg. Co., P.O. Box 1692, 35 Woodland St., New Britain, CT 06051 / 860-225-6581; FAX: 860-832-8707

Connecticut Valley Classics (See CVC, BPI)

Conrad, C. A., 3964 Ebert St., Winston-Salem, NC 27127 / 919-788-5469

Cook Engineering Service, 891 Highbury Rd., Vict 3133, 3133 AUSTRALIA

Cooper Arms, P.O. Box 114, Stevensville, MT 59870 / 406-777-0373; FAX: 406-777-5228

Cooper-Woodward Perfect Lube, 4120 Oesterle Rd., Helena, MT 59602 / 406-459-2287 cwperfectlube@mt.net cwperfectlube.com

Corbin Mfg. & Supply, Inc., 600 Industrial Circle, P.O. Box 2659, White City, OR 97503 / 541-826-5211; FAX: 541-826-8669 sales@corbins.com www.corbins.com

Cor-Bon Inc./Glaser LLC, P.O. Box 173, 1311 Industry Rd., Sturgis, SD 57785 / 605-347-4544; or 800-221-3489; FAX: 605-347-5055 email@corbon.com www.corbon.com

Corkys Gun Clinic, 4401 Hot Springs Dr., Greeley, CO 80634-9226 / 970-330-0516

Corry, John, 861 Princeton Ct., Neshanic Station, NJ 08853 / 908-369-8019

Cosmi Americo & Figlio S.N.C., Via Flaminia 307, Ancona, ITALY / 071-888208; FAX: 39-071-887008

Coulston Products, Inc., P.O. Box 30, 201 Ferry St. Suite 212, Easton, PA 18044-0030 / 215-253-0167; or 800-445-9927; FAX: 215-252-1511

Counter Assault, 120 Industrial Court, Kalispell, MT 59901 / 406-257-4740; FAX: 406-257-6674

Country Armourer, The, P.O. Box 308, Ashby, MA 01431-0308 / 508-827-6797; FAX: 508-827-4845

Cousin Bob's Mountain Products, 7119 Ohio River Blvd., Ben Avon, PA 15202 / 412-766-5114; FAX: 412-766-9354

CP Bullets, 1310 Industrial Hwy #5-6, South Hampton, PA 18966 / 215-953-7264; FAX: 215-953-7275

CQB Training, P.O. Box 1739, Manchester, MO 63011

Craftguard, 3624 Logan Ave., Waterloo, IA 50703 / 319-232-2959; FAX: 319-234-0804

Crandall Tool & Machine Co., 19163 21 Mile Rd., Tustin, MI 49688 / 616-829-4430

Creative Craftsman, Inc., The, 95 Highway 29 N., P.O. Box 331, Lawrenceville, GA 30246 / 404-963-2112; FAX: 404-513-9488

Creedmoor Sports, Inc., 3052 Industry St. #103, Oceanside, CA 92054 / 767-757-5529; FAX: 760-757-5558 shoot@creedmorsports.com www.creedmorsports.com

Creek Side Metal & Woodcrafters, Fishers Hill, VA 22626 / 703-465-3903

Creighton Audette, 19 Highland Circle, Springfield, VT 05156 / 802-885-2331

Crimson Trace Lasers, 8090 S.W. Cirrus Dr., Beverton, OR 97008 / 800-442-2406; FAX: 503-627-0166 www.crimsontrace.com

Crit'R Call (See Rocky Mountain Wildlife Products)

Crosman Airguns, Rts. 5 and 20, E. Bloomfield, NY 14443 / 716-657-6161; FAX: 716-657-5405

Crosman Blades (See Coleman Co., Inc.)

Crouse's Country Cover, P.O. Box 160, Storrs, CT 06268 / 860-423-8736

CRR, Inc./Marble's Inc., 420 Industrial Park, P.O. Box 111, Gladstone, MI 49837 / 906-428-3710; FAX: 906-428-3711

Crucelegui, Hermanos (See U.S. Importer-Mandall)

Cubic Shot Shell Co., Inc., 98 Fatima Dr., Campbell, OH 44405 / 330-755-0349

Cullity Restoration, 209 Old Country Rd., East Sandwich, MA 02537 / 508-888-1147

Cumberland Arms, 514 Shafer Road, Manchester, TN 37355 / 800-797-8414

Cumberland Mountain Arms, P.O. Box 710, Winchester, TN 37398 / 615-967-8414; FAX: 615-967-9199

Cummings Bullets, 1417 Esperanza Way, Escondido, CA 92027

Cupp, Alana, Custom Engraver, P.O. Box 207, Annabella, UT 84711 / 801-896-4834

Curly Maple Stock Blanks (See Tiger-Hunt)

Curtis Cast Bullets, 527 W. Babcock St., Bozeman, MT 59715 / 406-587-8117; FAX: 406-587-8117

Curtis Gun Shop (See Curtis Cast Bullets)

Custom Bullets by Hoffman, 2604 Peconic Ave., Seaford, NY 11783

Custom Calls, 607 N. 5th St., Burlington, IA 52601 / 319-752-4465

Custom Checkering Service, Kathy Forster, 2124 S.E. Yamhill St., Portland, OR 97214 / 503-236-5874

Custom Firearms (See Ahrends, Kim)

Custom Products (See Jones Custom Products)

Custom Shop, The, 890 Cochrane Crescent, Peterborough, ON K9H 5N3 CANADA / 705-742-6693

Custom Single Shot Rifles, 9651 Meadows Lane, Guthrie, OK 73044 / 405-282-3634

Custom Tackle and Ammo, P.O. Box 1886, Farmington, NM 87499 / 505-632-3539

Cutco Cutlery, P.O. Box 810, Olean, NY 14760 / 716-372-3111

CVA, 5988 Peachtree Corners East, Norcross, GA 30071 / 770-449-4687; FAX: 770-242-8546 info@cva.com www.cva.com

Cylinder & Slide, Inc., William R. Laughridge, 245 E. 4th St., Fremont, NE 68025 / 402-721-4277; FAX: 402-721-0263 bill@cylinder-slide.com www.clinder-slide.com

CZ USA, P.O. Box 171073, Kansas City, KS 66117 / 913-321-1811; FAX: 913-321-4901

D

D&D Gunsmiths, Ltd., 363 E. Elmwood, Troy, MI 48083 / 248-583-1512; FAX: 248-583-1524

D&G Precision Duplicators (See Greenwood Precision)

D&H Precision Tooling, 7522 Barnard Mill Rd., Ringwood, IL 60072 / 815-653-4011

D&L Industries (See D.J. Marketing)

D&L Sports, P.O. Box 651, Gillette, WY 82717 / 307-686-4008

D.C.C. Enterprises, 259 Wynburn Ave., Athens, GA 30601

D.J. Marketing, 10602 Horton Ave., Downey, CA 90241 / 310-806-0891; FAX: 310-806-6231

D.L. Unmussig Bullets, 7862 Brentford Dr., Richmond, VA 23225 / 804-320-1165; FAX: 804-320-4587

Dade Screw Machine Products, 2319 N.W. 7th Ave., Miami, FL 33127 / 305-573-5050

Daisy Outdoor Products, P.O. Box 220, Rogers, AR 72757 / 479-636-1200; FAX: 479-636-0573 www.daisy.com

Dakota (See U.S. Importer-EMF Co., Inc.)

Dakota Arms, Inc., 130 Industry Road, Sturgis, SD 57785 / 605-347-4686; FAX: 605-347-4459 info@dakotaarms.com www.dakotaarms.com

Dakota Corp., 77 Wales St., P.O. Box 543, Rutland, VT 05701 / 802-775-6062; or 800-451-4167; FAX: 802-773-3919

Daly, Charles/KBI, P.O. Box 6625, Harrisburg, PA 17112 / 866-DALY GUN

Da-Mar Gunsmith's, Inc., 102 1st St., Solvay, NY 13209

damascususa@inteliport.com, 149 Deans Farm Rd., Tyner, NC 27980 / 252-221-2010; FAX: 252-221-2010 damascususa@inteliport.com www.damascususa.com

Dan Wesson Firearms, 5169 Rt. 12 South, Norwich, NY 13815 / 607-336-1174; FAX: 607-336-2730 danwessonfirearms@citlink.net danwessonfirearms.com

Dangler, Homer L., 2870 Lee Marie Dr., Adrian, MI 49221 / 517-266-1997

Danner Shoe Mfg. Co., 12722 N.E. Airport Way, Portland, OR 97230 / 503-251-1100; or 800-345-0430; FAX: 503-251-1119

Dan's Whetstone Co., Inc., 418 Hilltop Rd., Pearcy, AR 71964 / 501-767-1616; FAX: 501-767-9598 questions@danswhetstone.com www.danswhetstone.com

Danuser Machine Co., 550 E. Third St., P.O. Box 368, Fulton, MO 65251 / 573-642-2246; FAX: 573-642-2240 sales@danuser.com www.danuser.com

Dara-Nes, Inc. (See Nesci Enterprises, Inc.)

D'Arcy Echols & Co., P.O. Box 421, Millville, UT 84326 / 435-755-6842

Darlington Gun Works, Inc., P.O. Box 698, 516 S. 52 Bypass, Darlington, SC 29532 / 803-393-3931

Dart Bell/Brass (See MAST Technology Inc.)

Darwin Hensley Gunmaker, P.O. Box 329, Brightwood, OR 97011 / 503-622-5411

Data Tech Software Systems, 19312 East Eldorado Drive, Aurora, CO 80013

Dave Norin Schrank's Smoke & Gun, 2010 Washington St., Waukegan, IL 60085 / 708-662-4034

Dave's Gun Shop, P.O. Box 2824, Casper, WY 82602-2824 / 307-754-9724

David Clark Co., Inc., P.O. Box 15054, Worcester, MA 01615 / 508-756-6216; FAX: 508-753-5827 sales@davidclark.com www.davidclark.com

David Condon, Inc., 109 E. Washington St., Middleburg, VA 22117 / 703-687-5642

David Miller Co., 3131 E. Greenlee Rd., Tucson, AZ 85716 / 520-326-3117

David R. Chicoine, 1210 Jones Street, Gastonia, NC 28052 / 704-853-0265 bnpress@quik.com www.oldwestgunsmith.com

David W. Schwartz Custom Guns, 2505 Waller St., Eau Claire, WI 54703 / 715-832-1735

Davide Pedersoli and Co., Via Artigiani 57, Gardone VT, Brescia 25063, ITALY / 030-8915000; FAX: 030-8911019 info@davidepedersoli.com www.davide_pedersoli.com

Davis, Don, 1619 Heights, Katy, TX 77493 / 713-391-3090

Davis Industries (See Cobra Enterprises, Inc.)

Davis Products, Mike, 643 Loop Dr., Moses Lake, WA 98837 / 509-765-6178; or 509-766-7281

Daystate Ltd., Birch House Lanee, Cotes Heath Staffs, ST15.022, ENGLAND / 01782-791755; FAX: 01782-791617

Dayton Traister, 4778 N. Monkey Hill Rd., P.O. Box 593, Oak Harbor, WA 98277 / 360-679-4657; FAX: 360-675-1114

D-Boone Ent., Inc., 5900 Colwyn Dr., Harrisburg, PA 17109

Dead Eye's Sport Center, 76 Baer Rd., Shickshinny, PA 18655 / 570-256-7432 deadeyeprizz@aol.com

Deepeeka Exports Pvt. Ltd., D-78, Saket, Meerut-250-006, INDIA / 011-91-121-640363 or ; FAX: 011-91-121-640988 deepeeka@poboxes.com www.deepeeka.com

Defense Training International, Inc., 749 S. Lemay, Ste. A3-337, Ft. Collins, CO 80524 / 303-482-2520; FAX: 303-482-0548

deHaas Barrels, 20049 W. State Hwy. Z, Ridgeway, MO 64481 / 660-872-6308

Del Rey Products, P.O. Box 5134, Playa Del Rey, CA 90296-5134 / 213-823-0494

MANUFACTURER'S DIRECTORY

Delhi Gun House, 1374 Kashmere Gate, New Delhi 110 006, INDIA / 2940974; or 394-0974; FAX: 2917344 dgh@vsnl.com

Delorge, Ed, 6734 W. Main, Houma, LA 70360 / 985-223-0206 delorge@triparish.net www.eddelorge.com

Del-Sports, Inc., Dave Budin, P.O. Box 685, 817 Main St., Margaretville, NY 12455 / 845-586-4103; FAX: 845-586-4105

Delta Arms Ltd., P.O. Box 1000, Delta, VT 84624-1000

Delta Enterprises, 284 Hagemann Drive, Livermore, CA 94550

Delta Frangible Ammunition LLC, P.O. Box 2350, Stafford, VA 22555-2350 / 540-720-5778; or 800-339-1933; FAX: 540-720-5667 dfa@dfanet.com www.dfanet.com

Dem-Bart Checkering Tools, Inc., 1825 Bickford Ave., Snohomish, WA 98290 / 360-568-7356 walt@dembartco.com www.dembartco.com

Denver Instrument Co., 6542 Fig St., Arvada, CO 80004 / 800-321-1135; or 303-431-7255; FAX: 303-423-4831

DeSantis Holster & Leather Goods, Inc., 431 Bayview Ave., Amityville, NY 11701 / 631-841-6300; FAX: 631-841-6320 www.desantisholster.com

Desert Mountain Mfg., P.O. Box 130184, Coram, MT 59913 / 800-477-0762; or 406-387-5361; FAX: 406-387-5361

Detonics USA, 53 Perimeter Center East #200, Atlanta, GA 30346 / 866-759-1169

DGR Custom Rifles, 4191 37th Ave. SE, Tappen, ND 58487 / 701-327-8135

DGS, Inc., Dale A. Storey, 1117 E. 12th, Casper, WY 82601 / 307-237-2414; FAX: 307-237-2414 dalest@trib.com www.dgsrifle.com

DHB Products, 336 River View Dr., Verona, VA 24482-2547 / 703-836-2648

Diamond Machining Technology Inc. (See DMT)

Diamond Mfg. Co., P.O. Box 174, Wyoming, PA 18644 / 800-233-9601

Dibble, Derek A., 555 John Downey Dr., New Britain, CT 06051 / 203-224-2630

Dietz Gun Shop & Range, Inc., 421 Range Rd., New Braunfels, TX 78132 / 210-885-4662

Dilliott Gunsmithing, Inc., 657 Scarlett Rd., Dandridge, TN 37725 / 865-397-9204 gunsmithd@aol.com dilliottgunsmithing.com

Dillon Precision Products, Inc., 8009 East Dillon's Way, Scottsdale, AZ 85260 / 480-948-8009; or 800-762-3845; FAX: 480-998-2786 sales@dillonprecision.com www.dillonprecision.com

Dina Arms Corporation, P.O. Box 46, Royersford, PA 19468 / 610-287-0266; FAX: 610-287-0266

Dixie Gun Works, P.O. Box 130, Union City, TN 38281 / 731-885-0700; FAX: 731-885-0440 info@dixiegunworks.com www.dixiegunworks.com

Dixon Muzzleloading Shop, Inc., 9952 Kunkels Mill Rd., Kempton, PA 19529 / 610-756-6271 dixonmuzzleloading.com

DKT, Inc., 14623 Vera Dr., Union, MI 49130-9744 / 800-741-7083 orders; FAX: 616-641-2015

DLO Mfg., 10807 SE Foster Ave., Arcadia, FL 33821-7304

DMT-Diamond Machining Technology, Inc., 85 Hayes Memorial Dr., Marlborough, MA 01752 FAX: 508-485-3924

Dohring Bullets, 100 W. 8 Mile Rd., Ferndale, MI 48220

Dolbare, Elizabeth, P.O. Box 502, Dubois, WY 82513-0502 / 307-450-7500 edolbare@hotmail.com www.scrimshaw-engraving.com

Domino, P.O. Box 108, 20019 Settimo Milanese, Milano, ITALY / 1-39-2-33512040; FAX: 1-39-2-33511587

Don Klein Custom Guns, 433 Murray Park Dr., Ripon, WI 54971 / 920-748-2931 daklein@charter.net www.donkleincustomguns.com

Donnelly, C. P., 405 Kubli Rd., Grants Pass, OR 97527 / 541-846-6604

Doskocil Mfg. Co., Inc., P.O. Box 1246, 4209 Barnett, Arlington, TX 76017 / 817-467-5116; FAX: 817-472-9810

Douglas Barrels, Inc., 5504 Big Tyler Rd., Charleston, WV 25313-1398 / 304-776-1341; FAX: 304-776-8560 www.benchrest.com/douglas

Downsizer Corp., P.O. Box 710316, Santee, CA 92072-0316 / 619-448-5510 www.downsizer.com

DPMS (Defense Procurement Manufacturing Services, Inc.), 13983 Industry Ave., Becker, MN 55308 / 800-578-DPMS; or 763-261-5600; FAX: 763-261-5599

Dr. O's Products Ltd., P.O. Box 111, Niverville, NY 12130 / 518-784-3333; FAX: 518-784-2800

Drain, Mark, SE 3211 Kamilche Point Rd., Shelton, WA 98584 / 206-426-5452

Dremel Mfg. Co., 4915-21st St., Racine, WI 53406

Dri-Slide, Inc., 411 N. Darling, Fremont, MI 49412 / 616-924-3950

Dropkick, 1460 Washington Blvd., Williamsport, PA 17701 / 717-326-6561; FAX: 717-326-4950

DS Arms, Inc., P.O. Box 370, 27 West 990 Industrial Ave., Barrington, IL 60010 / 847-277-7258; FAX: 847-277-7259 www.dsarms.com

DTM International, Inc., 40 Joslyn Rd., P.O. Box 5, Lake Orion, MI 48362 / 313-693-6670

Duane A. Hobbie Gunsmithing, 2412 Pattie Ave., Wichita, KS 67216 / 316-264-8266

Duane's Gun Repair (See DGR Custom Rifles)

Dubber, Michael W., P.O. Box 312, Evansville, IN 47702 / 812-424-9000; FAX: 812-424-6551

Duffy, Charles E. (See Guns Antique & Modern DBA), Williams Ln., P.O. Box 2, West Hurley, NY 12491 / 914-679-2997

Du-Lite Corp., 171 River Rd., Middletown, CT 06457 / 203-347-2505; FAX: 203-347-9404

Dumoulin, Ernest, Rue Florent Boclinville 8-10, 13-4041, Votten, BELGIUM / 41 27 78 92

Duncan's Gun Works, Inc., 1619 Grand Ave., San Marcos, CA 92069 / 760-727-0515

DunLyon R&D, Inc., 52151 E. U.S. Hwy. 60, Miami, AZ 85539 / 928-473-9027

Duofold, Inc., RD 3 Rt. 309, Valley Square Mall, Tamaqua, PA 18252 / 717-386-2666; FAX: 717-386-3652

Dybala Gun Shop, P.O. Box 1024, FM 3156, Bay City, TX 77414 / 409-245-0866

Dykstra, Doug, 411 N. Darling, Fremont, MI 49412 / 616-924-3950

Dynalite Products, Inc., 215 S. Washington St., Greenfield, OH 45123 / 513-981-2124

Dynamit Nobel-RWS, Inc., 81 Ruckman Rd., Closter, NJ 07624 / 201-767-7971; FAX: 201-767-1589

E

E&L Mfg., Inc., 4177 Riddle Bypass Rd., Riddle, OR 97469 / 541-874-2137; FAX: 541-874-3107

E. Arthur Brown Co. Inc., 4353 Hwy. 27 E., Alexandria, MN 56308 / 320-762-8847; FAX: 320-763-4310 www.eabco.com

E.A.A. Corp., P.O. Box 1299, Sharpes, FL 32959 / 407-639-4842; or 800-536-4442; FAX: 407-639-7006

Eagan, Donald V., P.O. Box 196, Benton, PA 17814 / 717-925-6134

Eagle Arms, Inc. (See ArmaLite, Inc.)

Eagle Grips, Eagle Business Center, 460 Randy Rd., Carol Stream, IL 60188 / 800-323-6144; or 708-260-0400; FAX: 708-260-0486

Eagle Imports, Inc., 1750 Brielle Ave., Unit B1, Wanamassa, NJ 07712 / 732-493-0333; FAX: 732-493-0301 gsodini@aol.com www.bersa-llama.com

E-A-R, Inc., Div. of Cabot Safety Corp., 5457 W. 79th St., Indianapolis, IN 46268 / 800-327-3431; FAX: 800-488-8007

EAW (See U.S. Importer-New England Custom Gun Serv

Eckelman Gunsmithing, 3125 133rd St. SW, Fort Ripley, MN 56449 / 218-829-3176

Ed Brown Products, Inc., P.O. Box 492, Perry, MO 63462 / 573-565-3261; FAX: 573-565-2791 edbrown@edbrown.com www.edbrown.com

Edenpine, Inc. c/o Six Enterprises, Inc., 320 D Turtle Creek Ct., San Jose, CA 95125 / 408-999-0201; FAX: 408-999-0216

EdgeCraft Corp., S. Weiner, 825 Southwood Rd., Avondale, PA 19311 / 610-268-0500; or 800-342-3255; FAX: 610-268-3545 www.edgecraft.com

Edmisten Co., P.O. Box 1293, Boone, NC 28607

Edmund Scientific Co., 101 E. Gloucester Pike, Barrington, NJ 08033 / 609-543-6250

Ed's Gun House, Ed Kukowski, P.O. Box 62, Minnesota City, MN 55959 / 507-689-2925

Effebi SNC-Dr. Franco Beretta, via Rossa, 4, 25062, ITALY / 030-2751955; FAX: 030-2180414

Eggleston, Jere D., 400 Saluda Ave., Columbia, SC 29205 / 803-799-3402

Eichelberger Bullets, Wm., 158 Crossfield Rd., King Of Prussia, PA 19406

Ekol Leather Care, P.O. Box 2652, West Lafayette, IN 47906 / 317-463-2250; FAX: 317-463-7004

El Paso Saddlery Co., P.O. Box 27194, El Paso, TX 79926 / 915-544-2233; FAX: 915-544-2535 info@epsaddlery.com www.epsaddlery.com

Electro Prismatic Collimators, Inc., 1441 Manatt St., Lincoln, NE 68521

Electronic Shooters Protection, Inc., 15290 Gadsden Ct., Brighton, CO 80603 / 800-797-7791; FAX: 303-659-8668 esp@usa.net espamerican.com

Eley Ltd., Selco Way Minworth Industrial Estate, Minworth Sutton Coldfield, West Midlands, B76 1BA ENGLAND / 44 0 121-313-4567; FAX: 44 0 121-313-4568 www.eley.co.uk

Elite Ammunition, P.O. Box 3251, Oakbrook, IL 60522 / 708-366-9006

Ellett Bros., 267 Columbia Ave., P.O. Box 128, Chapin, SC 29036 / 803-345-3751; or 800-845-3711; FAX: 803-345-1820 www.ellettbrothers.com

Ellicott Arms, Inc. / Woods Pistolsmithing, 8390 Sunset Dr., Ellicott City, MD 21043 / 410-465-7979

EMAP USA, 6420 Wilshire Blvd., Los Angeles, CA 90048 / 213-782-2000; FAX: 213-782-2867

Emerging Technologies, Inc. (See Laseraim Technologies, Inc.)

EMF Co. Inc., 1900 E. Warner Ave., Suite 1-D, Santa Ana, CA 92705 / 949-261-6611; FAX: 949-756-0133

Empire Cutlery Corp., 12 Kruger Ct., Clifton, NJ 07013 / 201-472-5155; FAX: 201-779-0759

Empire Rifles, P.O. Box 406, Meriden, NH 03770 info@empirerifles.com www.empirerifles.com

English, Inc., A.G., 708 S. 12th St., Broken Arrow, OK 74012 / 918-251-3399 www.agenglish.com

Engraving Artistry, 36 Alto Rd., Burlington, CT 06013 / 860-673-6837 bobburt44@hotmail.com

Enguix Import-Export, Alpujarras 58, Alzira, Valencia, SPAIN / (96) 241 43 95; FAX: (96) 241 43 95

Enhanced Presentations, Inc., 5929 Market St., Wilmington, NC 28405 / 910-799-1622; FAX: 910-799-5004

Enlow, Charles, Box 895, Beaver, OK 73932 / 405-625-4487

Ensign-Bickford Co., The, 660 Hopmeadow St., Simsbury, CT 06070

Entreprise Arms, Inc., 5321 Irwindale Ave., Irwindale, CA 91706-2025 / 626-962-8712; FAX: 626-962-4692 www.entreprise.com

EPC, 1441 Manatt St., Lincoln, NE 68521 / 402-476-3946

Erhardt, Dennis, 4508 N. Montana Ave., Helena, MT 59602 / 406-442-4533

Essex Arms, P.O. Box 363, Island Pond, VT 05846 / 802-723-6203; FAX: 802-723-6203

Estate Cartridge, Inc., 900 Bob Ehlen Dr., Anoka, MN 55303-7502 / 409-856-7277; FAX: 409-856-5486

Euber Bullets, No. Orwell Rd., Orwell, VT 05760 / 802-948-2621

Euroarms of America, Inc., P.O. Box 3277, Winchester, VA 22604 / 540-662-1863; FAX: 540-662-4464 www.euroarms.net

Euro-Imports, 2221 Upland Ave. S., Pahrump, NV 89048 / 775-751-6671; FAX: 775-751-6671

European American Armory Corp. (See E.A.A. Corp.)

Eversull Co., Inc., 1 Tracemont, Boyce, LA 71409 / 318-793-8728; FAX: 318-793-5483 bestguns@aol.com

Evolution Gun Works, Inc., 48 Belmont Ave., Quakertown, PA 18951-1347 www.egw-guns.com

Excalibur Electro Optics, Inc., P.O. Box 400, Fogelsville, PA 18051-0400 / 610-391-9105; FAX: 610-391-9220

Excalibur Publications, P.O. Box 89667, Tucson, AZ 85752 / 520-575-9057 excalibureditor@earthlink.net

Excel Industries, Inc., 4510 Carter Ct., Chino, CA 91710 / 909-627-2404; FAX: 909-627-7817

Executive Protection Institute, P.O. Box 802, Berryville, VA 22611 / 540-554-2540; FAX: 540-554-2558 ruk@crosslink.net www.personalprotecion.com

Eze-Lap Diamond Prods., P.O. Box 2229, 15164 W. State St., Westminster, CA 92683 / 714-847-1555; FAX: 714-897-0280

E-Z-Way Systems, P.O. Box 4310, Newark, OH 43058-4310 / 614-345-6645; or 800-848-2072; FAX: 614-345-6600

F

F&W Publications, Inc., 700 E. State St., Iola, WI 54990 / 715-445-2214; FAX: 715-445-4087

F.A.I.R., Via Gitti, 41, 25060 Marcheno Bresc, ITALY / 030 861162-8610344; FAX: 030 8610179 info@fair.it www.fair.it

Fabarm S.p.A., Via Averolda 31, 25039 Travagliato, Brescia, ITALY / 030-6863629; FAX: 030-6863684 info@fabarm.com www.fabarm.com

Fagan Arms, 22952 15 Mile Rd., Clinton Township, MI 48035 / 810-465-4637; FAX: 810-792-6996

Faith Associates, P.O. Box 549, Flat Rock, NC 28731-0549 FAX: 828-697-6827

Falcon Industries, Inc., P.O. Box 1690, Edgewood, NM 87015 / 505-281-3783; FAX: 505-281-3991 shines@ergogrips.net www.ergogrips.net

Far North Outfitters, Box 1252, Bethel, AK 99559

Farm Form Decoys, Inc., 1602 Biovu, P.O. Box 748, Galveston, TX 77553 / 409-744-0762; or 409-765-6361; FAX: 409-765-8513

Farr Studio, Inc., 17149 Bournbrook Ln., Jeffersonton, VA 22724-1796 / 615-638-8825

Farrar Tool Co., Inc., 11855 Cog Hill Dr., Whittier, CA 90601-1902 / 310-863-4367; FAX: 310-863-5123

MANUFACTURER'S DIRECTORY

Faulhaber Wildlocker, Dipl.-Ing. Norbert Wittasek, Seilergasse 2, A-1010 Wien, AUSTRIA / 43-1-5137001; FAX: 43-1-5137001 faulhaber1@utanet.at

Faulk's Game Call Co., Inc., 616 18th St., Lake Charles, LA 70601 / 337-436-9726; FAX: 337-494-7205

Faust Inc., T. G., 544 Minor St., Reading, PA 19602 / 610-375-8549; FAX: 610-375-4488

Fautheree, Andy, P.O. Box 4607, Pagosa Springs, CO 81157 / 970-731-5003; FAX: 970-731-5009

Feather, Flex Decoys, 4500 Doniphan Dr., Neosho, MO 64850 / 318-746-8596; FAX: 318-742-4815

Federal Cartridge Co., 900 Ehlen Dr., Anoka, MN 55303 / 612-323-2300; FAX: 612-323-2506

Federal Champion Target Co., 232 Industrial Pkwy., Richmond, IN 47374 / 800-441-4971; FAX: 317-966-7747

Federated-Fry (See Fry Metals)

FEG, Budapest, Soroksariut 158, H-1095, HUNGARY

Feinwerkbau Westinger & Altenburger, Neckarstrasse 43, 78727, Oberndorf a. N., GERMANY / 07423-814-0; FAX: 07423-814-200 info@feinwerkbau.de www.feinwerkbau.de

Felk Pistols, Inc., P.O. Box 33, Bracey, VA 23919 / 434-636-2537; FAX: 208-988-4834

Ferguson, Bill, P.O. Box 1238, Sierra Vista, AZ 85636 / 520-458-5321; FAX: 520-458-9125

Ferguson, Bill. See: BULLET METALS

FERLIB, Via Parte 33 Marcheno/BS, Marcheno/BS, ITALY / 00390308610191; FAX: 00390308966882 info@ferlib.com www.ferlib.com

Ferris Firearms, 7110 F.M. 1863, Bulverde, TX 78163 / 210-980-4424

Fibron Products, Inc., P.O. Box 430, Buffalo, NY 14209-0430 / 716-886-2378; FAX: 716-886-2394

Fieldsport Ltd., Bryan Bilinski, 3313 W. South Airport Rd., Traverse City, MI 49684 / 616-933-0767

Fiocchi Munizioni S.A. (See U.S. Importer-Fiocch

Fiocchi of America, Inc., 5030 Fremont Rd., Ozark, MO 65721 / 417-725-4118; or 800-721-2666; FAX: 417-725-1039

Firearm Brokers, 4143 Taylor Blvd., Louisville, KY 40215 / 502-366-0555 firearmbrokers@aol.com www.firearmbrokers.com

Firearm Training Center, The, 9555 Blandville Rd., West Paducah, KY 42086 / 502-554-5886

Firearms Co. Ltd. / Alpine (See U.S. Importer-Mandall

Firearms Engraver's Guild of America, 3011 E. Pine Dr., Flagstaff, AZ 86004 / 928-527-8427 fegainfo@fega.com

Fisher, Jerry A., 631 Crane Mt. Rd., Big Fork, MT 59911 / 406-837-2722

Fisher Custom Firearms, 2199 S. Kittredge Way, Aurora, CO 80013 / 303-755-3710

Fitzgerald, Jack. See: CLENZOIL WORLDWIDE CORP.

Flambeau, Inc., 15981 Valplast Rd., Middlefield, OH 44062 / 216-632-1631; FAX: 216-632-1581 www.flambeau.com

Flayderman & Co., Inc., P.O. Box 2446, Fort Lauderdale, FL 33303 / 954-761-8855 www.flayderman.com

Fleming Firearms, 7720 E. 126th St. N., Collinsville, OK 74021-7016 / 918-665-3624

Fletcher-Bidwell, LLC, 305 E. Terhune St., Viroqua, WI 54665-1631 / 866-637-1860 fbguns@netscape.net

Flintlocks, Etc., 160 Rossiter Rd., Box 181, Richmond, MA 01254 / 413-698-3822; FAX: 413-698-3866 flintetc@berkshire.rr.com

Flitz International Ltd., 821 Mohr Ave., Waterford, WI 53185 / 414-534-5898; FAX: 414-534-2991

Fluoramics, Inc., 18 Industrial Ave., Mahwah, NJ 07430 / 800-922-0075; FAX: 201-825-7035

Flynn's Custom Guns, P.O. Box 7461, Alexandria, LA 71306 / 318-455-7130

FN Manufacturing, P.O. Box 24257, Columbia, SC 29224 / 803-736-0522

Folks, Donald E., 205 W. Lincoln St., Pontiac, IL 61764 / 815-844-7901

Foothills Video Productions, Inc., P.O. Box 651, Spartanburg, SC 29304 / 803-573-7023; or 800-782-5358

Foredom Electric Co., Rt. 6, 16 Stony Hill Rd., Bethel, CT 06801 / 203-792-8622

Forgett, Valmore. See: NAVY ARMS COMPANY

Forgreens Tool & Mfg., Inc., P.O. Box 955, Robert Lee, TX 76945 / 915-453-2800; FAX: 915-453-2460

Forkin Custom Classics, 205 10th Ave. S.W., White Sulphur Spring, MT 59645 / 406-547-2344

Forrest Tool Co., P.O. Box 768, 44380 Gordon Ln., Mendocino, CA 95460 / 707-937-2141; FAX: 717-937-1817

Forster, Kathy (See Custom Checkering)

Forster, Larry L., Box 212, 216 Hwy. 13 E., Gwinner, ND 58040-0212 / 701-678-2475

Forster Products, Inc., 310 E. Lanark Ave., Lanark, IL 61046 / 815-493-6360; FAX: 815-493-2371 info@forsterproducts.com www.forsterproductscom

Fort Hill Gunstocks, 12807 Fort Hill Rd., Hillsboro, OH 45133 / 513-466-2763

Fort Knox Security Products, 1051 N. Industrial Park Rd., Orem, UT 84057 / 801-224-7233; or 800-821-5216; FAX: 801-226-5493

Forthofer's Gunsmithing & Knifemaking, 5535 U.S. Hwy. 93S, Whitefish, MT 59937-8411 / 406-862-2674

Fortune Products, Inc., 205 Hickory Creek Rd., Marble Falls, TX 78654 / 210-693-6111; FAX: 210-693-6394 randy@accusharp.com

Forty-Five Ranch Enterprises, Box 1080, Miami, OK 74355-1080 / 918-542-5875

Foster, . See: ACCURACY INTERNATIONAL

Fountain Products, 492 Prospect Ave., West Springfield, MA 01089 / 413-781-4651; FAX: 413-733-8217

Fowler Bullets, 806 Dogwood Dr., Gastonia, NC 28054 / 704-867-3259

Fowler, Bob (See Black Powder Products)

Fox River Mills, Inc., P.O. Box 298, 227 Poplar St., Osage, IA 50461 / 515-732-3798; FAX: 515-732-5128

Frank Knives, 13868 NW Keleka Pl., Seal Rock, OR 97376 / 541-563-3041; FAX: 541-563-3041

Frank Mittermeier, Inc., P.O. Box 1, Bronx, NY 10465

Franzen International, Inc. (See U.S. Importer-Importer Co.)

Fred F. Wells/Wells Sport Store, 110 N. Summit St., Prescott, AZ 86301 / 928-445-3655 www.wellssportstore@cableone.net

Freedom Arms, Inc., P.O. Box 150, Freedom, WY 83120 / 307-883-2468; FAX: 307-883-2005

Fremont Tool Works, 1214 Prairie, Ford, KS 67842 / 316-369-2327

Front Sight Firearms Training Institute, P.O. Box 2619, Aptos, CA 95001 / 800-987-7719; FAX: 408-684-2137

Frontier, 2910 San Bernardo, Laredo, TX 78040 / 956-723-5409; FAX: 956-723-1774

Frontier Arms Co., Inc., 401 W. Rio Santa Cruz, Green Valley, AZ 85614-3932

Frontier Products Co., 2401 Walker Rd., Roswell, NM 88201-8950 / 614-262-9357

Frontier Safe Co., 3201 S. Clinton St., Fort Wayne, IN 46806 / 219-744-7233; FAX: 219-744-6678

Frost Cutlery Co., P.O. Box 22636, Chattanooga, TN 37422 / 615-894-6079; FAX: 615-894-9576

Fry Metals, 4100 6th Ave., Altoona, PA 16602 / 814-946-1611

Fujinon, Inc., 10 High Point Dr., Wayne, NJ 07470 / 201-633-5600; FAX: 201-633-5216

Fullmer, Geo. M., 2499 Mavis St., Oakland, CA 94601 / 510-533-4193

Fulton Armory, 8725 Bollman Place No. 1, Savage, MD 20763 / 301-490-9485; FAX: 301-490-9547 www.fulton.armory.com

Furr Arms, 91 N. 970 West, Orem, UT 84057 / 801-226-3877; FAX: 801-226-3877

G

G&H Decoys, Inc., P.O. Box 1208, Hwy. 75 North, Henryetta, OK 74437 / 918-652-3314; FAX: 918-652-3400

G.C. Bullet Co., Inc., 40 Mokelumne River Dr., Lodi, CA 95240 / 513-466-2763

G.G. & G., 3602 E. 42nd Stravenue, Tucson, AZ 85713 / 520-748-7167; FAX: 520-748-7583 ggg&3@aol.com www.ggg&3.com

G.H. Enterprises Ltd., Bag 10, Okotoks, AB T0L 1T0 CANADA / 403-938-6070

G.U., Inc. (See U.S. Importer-New SKB Arms Co.)

G96 Products Co., Inc., 85 5th Ave., Bldg. #6, Paterson, NJ 07544 / 973-684-4050; FAX: 973-684-3848 g96prod@aol

Gage Manufacturing, 663 W. 7th St., A, San Pedro, CA 90731 / 310-832-3546

Gaillard Barrels, Box 68, St. Brieux, SK S0K 3V0 CANADA / 306-752-3769; FAX: 306-752-5969

Galati International, P.O. Box 10, 616 Burley Ridge Rd., Wesco, MO 65586 / 636-584-0785; FAX: 573-775-4308 support@galatiinternational.com www.galatiinternational.com

Galaxy Imports Ltd., Inc., P.O. Box 3361, Victoria, TX 77903 / 361-573-4867; FAX: 361-576-9622 galaxy@cox-internet.com

GALCO International Ltd., 2019 W. Quail Ave., Phoenix, AZ 85027 / 623-474-7070; FAX: 623-582-6854 customerservice@usgalco.com www.usgalco.com

Galena Industries AMT, 5463 Diaz St., Irwindale, CA 91706 / 626-856-8883; FAX: 626-856-8878

Gamba S.p.A. Societa Armi Bresciane Srl, Renato, Via Artigiani 93, ITALY / 30-8911640; FAX: 30-8911648

Gamba, USA, P.O. Box 60452, Colorado Springs, CO 80960 / 719-578-1145; FAX: 719-444-0731

Game Haven Gunstocks, 13750 Shire Rd., Wolverine, MI 49799 / 616-525-8257

Gamebore Division, Polywad, Inc., P.O. Box 7916, Macon, GA 31209 / 478-477-0669; or 800-998-0669

Gamo (See U.S. Importers-Arms United Corp., Daisy M

Gamo USA, Inc., 3911 SW 47th Ave., Suite 914, Fort Lauderdale, FL 33314 / 954-581-5822; FAX: 954-581-3165 gamousa@gate.net www.gamo.com

Gander Mountain, Inc., 12400 Fox River Rd., Wilmont, WI 53192 / 414-862-6848

GAR, 590 McBride Ave., West Paterson, NJ 07424 / 973-754-1114; FAX: 973-754-1114 garreloading@aol.com www.garreloading.com

Garcia National Gun Traders, Inc., 225 SW 22nd Ave., Miami, FL 33135 / 305-642-2355

Garrett Cartridges, Inc., P.O. Box 178, Chehalis, WA 98532 / 360-736-0702 www.garrettcartridges.com

Garthwaite Pistolsmith, Inc., Jim, 12130 State Route 405, Watsontown, PA 17777 / 570-538-1566; FAX: 570-538-2965 www.garthwaite.com

Gary Goudy Classic Stocks, 1512 S. 5th St., Dayton, WA 99328 / 509-382-2726 goudy@innw.net

Gary Reeder Custom Guns, 2601 7th Ave. E., Flagstaff, AZ 86004 / 928-526-3313; FAX: 928-527-0840 gary@reedercustomguns.com www.reedercustomguns.com

Gator Guns & Repair, 7952 Kenai Spur Hwy., Kenai, AK 99611-8311

Gaucher Armes, S.A., 46 rue Desjoyaux, 42000, Saint-Etienne, FRANCE / 04-77-33-38-92; FAX: 04-77-61-95-72

GDL Enterprises, 409 Le Gardeur, Slidell, LA 70460 / 504-649-0693

Gehmann, Walter (See Huntington Die Specialties)

Genco, P.O. Box 5704, Asheville, NC 28803

Genecco Gun Works, 10512 Lower Sacramento Rd., Stockton, CA 95210 / 209-951-0706; FAX: 209-931-3872

Gene's Custom Guns, P.O. Box 10534, White Bear Lake, MN 55110 / 651-429-5105; FAX: 651-429-7365

Gentex Corp., 5 Tinkham Ave., Derry, NH 03038 / 603-434-0311; FAX: 603-434-3002 sales@derry.gentexcorp.com www.derry.gentexcorp.com

Gentner Bullets, 109 Woodlawn Ave., Upper Darby, PA 19082 / 610-352-9396 dongentner@rcn.com www.gentnerbullets.com

Gentry Custom LLC, 314 N. Hoffman, Belgrade, MT 59714 / 406-388-GUNS gentryshop@earthlink.net www.gentrycustom.com

George & Roy's, P.O. Box 2125, Sisters, OR 97759-2125 / 503-228-5424; or 800-553-3022; FAX: 503-225-9409

George Hoenig, Inc., 6521 Morton Dr., Boise, ID 83704 / 208-375-1116; FAX: 208-375-1116

George Ibberson (Sheffield) Ltd., 25-31 Allen St., Sheffield, S3 7AW ENGLAND / 0114-2766123; FAX: 0114-2738465 sales@eggintongroupco.uk www.eggintongroup.co.uk

Gerber Legendary Blades, 14200 SW 72nd Ave., Portland, OR 97223 / 503-639-6161; or 800-950-6161; FAX: 503-684-7008

Gervais, Mike, 3804 S. Cruise Dr., Salt Lake City, UT 84109 / 801-277-7729

Getz Barrel Company, P.O. Box 88, 426 E. Market St., Beavertown, PA 17813 / 570-658-7263; FAX: 570-658-4110 www.getzbrl.com

Giacomo Sporting USA, 6234 Stokes Lee Center Rd., Lee Center, NY 13363

Gibbs Rifle Co., Inc., 219 Lawn St., Martinsburg, WV 25401 / 304-262-1651; FAX: 304-262-1658 support@gibbsrifle.com www.gibbsrifle.com

Gil Hebard Guns, Inc., 125 Public Square, Knoxville, IL 61448 / 309-289-2700; FAX: 309-289-2233

Gilbert Equipment Co., Inc., 960 Downtowner Rd., Mobile, AL 36609 / 205-344-3322

Gillmann, Edwin, 33 Valley View Dr., Hanover, PA 17331 / 717-632-1662 gillmaned@superpa.net

Gilmore Sports Concepts, Inc., 5949 S. Garnett Rd., Tulsa, OK 74146 / 918-250-3810; FAX: 918-250-3845 info@gilmoresports.com www.gilmoresports.com

Glacier Glove, 4890 Aircenter Circle, Suite 210, Reno, NV 89502 / 702-825-8225; FAX: 702-825-6544

Glaser LLC, P.O. Box 173, Sturgis, SD 57785 / 605-347-4544; or 800-221-3489; FAX: 605-347-5055 email@corbon.com www.safetyslug.com

Glaser Safety Slug, Inc., P.O. Box 8223, Foster City, CA 94404 / 800-221-3489; FAX: 510-785-6685 safetyslug.com

Glass, Herb, P.O. Box 25, Bullville, NY 10915 / 914-361-3021

Glimm, Jerome. See: GLIMM'S CUSTOM GUN ENGRAVING

Glimm's Custom Gun Engraving, Jerome C. Glimm, 19 S. Maryland, Conrad, MT 59425 / 406-278-3574 jandlglimm@mcn.net www.gunengraver.biz

MANUFACTURER'S DIRECTORY

Glock GmbH, P.O. Box 50, A-2232, Deutsch, Wagram, AUSTRIA

Glock, Inc., P.O. Box 369, Smyrna, GA 30081 / 770-432-1202; FAX: 770-433-8719

Glynn Scobey Duck & Goose Calls, Rt. 3, Box 37, Newbern, TN 38059 / 731-643-6128

GML Products, Inc., 394 Laredo Dr., Birmingham, AL 35226 / 205-979-4867

Goens, Dale W., P.O. Box 224, Cedar Crest, NM 87008 / 505-281-5419

Goergen's Gun Shop, Inc., 17985 538th Ave., Austin, MN 55912 / 507-433-9280

GOEX, Inc., P.O. Box 659, Doyline, LA 71023-0659 / 318-382-9300; FAX: 318-382-9303 mfahringer@goexpowder.com www.goexpowder.com

Golden Age Arms Co., 115 E. High St., Ashley, OH 43003 / 614-747-2488

Golden Bear Bullets, 3065 Fairfax Ave., San Jose, CA 95148 / 408-238-9515

Gonic Arms North American Arms, Inc., 134 Flagg Rd., Gonic, NH 03839 / 603-332-8456; or 603-332-8457

Goodling's Gunsmithing, 1950 Stoverstown Rd., Spring Grove, PA 17362 / 717-225-3350

Goodwin, Fred. See: GOODWIN'S GUNS

Goodwin's Guns, Fred Goodwin, Silver Ridge, ME 04776 / 207-365-4451

Gotz Bullets, 11426 Edgemere Ter., Roscoe, IL 61073-8232

Gould & Goodrich Leather, Inc., 709 E. McNeil St., Lillington, NC 27546 / 910-893-2071; FAX: 910-893-4742 info@gouldusa.com www.gouldusa.com

Gournet Artistic Engraving, Geoffroy Gournet, 820 Paxinosa Ave., Easton, PA 18042 / 610-559-0710 www.geoffroygournet.com

Gournet, Geoffroy. See: GOURNET ARTISTIC ENGRAVING

Grace, Charles E., 718 E. 2nd, Trinidad, CO 81082 / 719-846-9435 chuckgrace@sensonics.org

Grace Metal Products, P.O. Box 67, Elk Rapids, MI 49629 / 616-264-8133

Graf & Sons, 4050 S. Clark St., Mexico, MO 65265 / 573-581-2266; FAX: 573-581-2875 customerservice@grafs.com www.grafs.com

Grand Slam Hunting Products, Box 121, 25454 Military Rd., Cascade, MD 21719 / 301-241-4900; FAX: 301-241-4900 rlj6call@aol.com

Granite Mountain Arms, Inc., 3145 W. Hidden Acres Trail, Prescott, AZ 86305 / 520-541-9758; FAX: 520-445-6826

Grant, Howard V., Hiawatha 15, Woodruff, WI 54568 / 715-356-7146

Graphics Direct, P.O. Box 372421, Reseda, CA 91337-2421 / 818-344-9002

Graves Co., 1800 Andrews Ave., Pompano Beach, FL 33069 / 800-327-9103; FAX: 305-960-0301

Grayback Wildcats, Mike Beeks, 5306 Bryant Ave., Klamath Falls, OR 97603 / 541-884-1072; FAX: 541-884-1072 graybackwildcats@aol.com

Graybill's Gun Shop, 1035 Ironville Pike, Columbia, PA 17512 / 717-684-2739

Great American Gunstock Co., 3420 Industrial Drive, Yuba City, CA 95993 / 800-784-4867; FAX: 530-671-3906 gunstox@hotmail.com www.gunstocks.com

Great Lakes Airguns, 6175 S. Park Ave., Hamburg, NY 14075 / 716-648-6666; FAX: 716-648-6666 www.greatlakesairguns.com

Green, Arthur S., 485 S. Robertson Blvd., Beverly Hills, CA 90211 / 310-274-1283

Green, Roger M., P.O. Box 984, 435 E. Birch, Glenrock, WY 82637 / 307-436-9804

Green Head Game Call Co., RR 1, Box 33, Lacon, IL 61540 / 309-246-2155

Green Mountain Rifle Barrel Co., Inc., P.O. Box 2670, 153 W. Main St., Conway, NH 03818 / 603-447-1095; FAX: 603-447-1099 info@gmriflebarrel.com www.gmriflebarrel.com

Greenwood Precision, P.O. Box 407, Rogersville, MO 65742 / 417-725-2330

Greg Gunsmithing Repair, 3732 26th Ave. N., Robbinsdale, MN 55422 / 612-529-8103

Greg's Superior Products, P.O. Box 46219, Seattle, WA 98146

Greider Precision, 431 Santa Marina Ct., Escondido, CA 92029 / 760-480-8892; FAX: 760-480-9800 greider@msn.com

Gre-Tan Rifles, 29742 W.C.R. 50, Kersey, CO 80644 / 970-353-6176; FAX: 970-356-5940 www.gtrtooling.com

Grier Hard Cast Bullets, P.O. Box 41, Tillamook, OR 97141-0041 / 503-963-8796

Grier's Hard Cast Bullets, 1107 11th St., LaGrande, OR 97850 / 503-963-8796

Griffin & Howe, Inc., 340 W. Putnam Ave., Greenwich, CT 06830 / 203-618-0270 info@griffinhowe.com www.griffinhowe.com

Griffin & Howe, Inc., 33 Claremont Rd., Bernardsville, NJ 07924 / 908-766-2287; FAX: 908-766-1068 info@griffinhowe.com www.griffinhowe.com

Grifon, Inc., 58 Guinam St., Waltham, MS 02154

Groenewold, John. See: JG AIRGUNS, LLC

GRS/Glendo Corp., P.O. Box 1153, 900 Overlander St., Emporia, KS 66801 / 620-343-1084; or 800-836-3519; FAX: 620-343-9640 glendo@glendo.com www.glendo.com

Grulla Armes, Apartado 453, Avda Otaloa 12, Eiber, SPAIN

Gruning Precision, Inc., 7101 Jurupa Ave., No. 12, Riverside, CA 92504 / 909-289-4371; FAX: 909-689-7791 gruningprecision@earthlink.net www.gruningprecision.com

GSI, Inc., 7661 Commerce Ln., Trussville, AL 35173 / 205-655-8299

GTB-Custom Bullets, 482 Comerwood Court, S. San Francisco, CA 94080 / 650-583-1550

Guarasi, Robert. See: WILCOX INDUSTRIES CORP.

Guardsman Products, 411 N. Darling, Fremont, MI 49412 / 616-924-3950

Gun City, 212 W. Main Ave., Bismarck, ND 58501 / 701-223-2304

Gun Doc, Inc., 5405 NW 82nd Ave., Miami, FL 33166 / 305-477-2777; FAX: 305-477-2778 www.gundoc.com

Gun Doctor, The, 435 E. Maple, Roselle, IL 60172 / 708-894-0668

Gun Hunter Books (See Gun Hunter Trading Co.), 5075 Heisig St., Beaumont, TX 77705 / 409-835-3006; FAX: 409-838-2266 gunhuntertrading@hotmail.com

Gun Hunter Trading Co., 5075 Heisig St., Beaumont, TX 77705 / 409-835-3006; FAX: 409-838-2266 gunhuntertrading@hotmail.com

Gun Leather Limited, 116 Lipscomb, Fort Worth, TX 76104 / 817-334-0225; FAX: 800-247-0609

Gun List (See F&W Publications), 700 E. State St., Iola, WI 54990 / 715-445-2214; FAX: 715-445-4087

Gun Room Press, The, 127 Raritan Ave., Highland Park, NJ 08904 / 732-545-4344; FAX: 732-545-6686 gunbooks@rutgersgunbooks.com www.rutgersgunbooks.com

Gun Room, The, 1121 Burlington, Muncie, IN 47302 / 765-282-9073; FAX: 765-282-5270 bshstleguns@aol.com

Gun Shop, The, 62778 Spring Creek Rd., Montrose, CO 81401

Gun Shop, The, 5550 S. 900 East, Salt Lake City, UT 84117 / 801-263-3633

Gun South, Inc. (See GSI, Inc.)

Gun Vault, 7339 E. Acoma Dr., Ste. 7, Scottsdale, AZ 85260 / 602-951-6855

Gun Works, The, 247 S. 2nd St., Springfield, OR 97477 / 541-741-4118; FAX: 541-988-1097 gunworks@worldnet.att.net www.thegunworks.com

Gun-Alert, 1010 N. Maclay Ave., San Fernando, CA 91340 / 818-365-0864; FAX: 818-365-1308

Guncraft Books (See Guncraft Sports, Inc.), 10737 Dutchtown Rd., Knoxville, TN 37932 / 865-966-4545; FAX: 865-966-4500 findit@guncraft.com www.guncraft.com

Guncraft Sports, Inc., 10737 Dutchtown Rd., Knoxville, TN 37932 / 865-966-4545; FAX: 865-966-4500 findit@guncraft.com www.usit.net/guncraft

Guncraft Sports, Inc., Marie C. Wiest, 10737 Dutchtown Rd., Knoxville, TN 37932 / 865-966-4545; FAX: 865-966-4500 findit@guncraft.com www.guncraft.com

Guncrafter Industries, 171 Madison 1510, Huntsville, AR 72740 / 479-665-2466 www.guncrafterindustries.com

Gun-Ho Sports Cases, 110 E. 10th St., St. Paul, MN 55101 / 612-224-9491

Gunline Tools, 2950 Saturn St., "O", Brea, CA 92821 / 714-993-5100; FAX: 714-572-4128

Gunnerman Books, P.O. Box 81697, Rochester Hills, MI 48308 / 248-608-2856 gunnermanbks@att.net

Guns Antique & Modern DBA / Charles E. Duffy, Williams Lane, West Hurley, NY 12491 / 914-679-2997

Guns Div. of D.C. Engineering, Inc., 8633 Southfield Fwy., Detroit, MI 48228 / 313-271-7111; or 800-886-7623; FAX: 313-271-7112 guns@rifletech.com www.rifletech.com

GUNS Magazine, 12345 World Trade Dr., San Diego, CA 92128-3743 / 619-297-5350; FAX: 619-297-5353

Gunsight, The, 1712 N. Placentia Ave., Fullerton, CA 92631

Gunsite Training Center, P.O. Box 700, Paulden, AZ 86334 / 520-636-4565; FAX: 520-636-1236

Gunsmithing Ltd., 57 Unquowa Rd., Fairfield, CT 06824 / 203-254-0436; FAX: 203-254-1535

Gunsmithing, Inc., 30 W. Buchanan St., Colorado Springs, CO 80907 / 719-632-3795; FAX: 719-632-3493 www.nealsguns.com

Gurney, F. R., Box 13, Sooke, BC V0S 1N0 CANADA / 604-642-5282; FAX: 604-642-7859

H

H&B Forge Co., Rt. 2, Geisinger Rd., Shiloh, OH 44878 / 419-895-1856

H&P Publishing, 7174 Hoffman Rd., San Angelo, TX 76905 / 915-655-5953

H&R 1871.LLC, 60 Industrial Rowe, Gardner, MA 01440 / 508-632-9393; FAX: 508-632-2300 hr1871@hr1871.com www.hr1871.com

H. Krieghoff Gun Co., Boschstrasse 22, D-89079, Ulm, GERMANY / 731-401820; FAX: 731-4018270

H.K.S. Products, 7841 Founion Dr., Florence, KY 41042 / 606-342-7841; or 800-354-9814; FAX: 606-342-5865

H.P. White Laboratory, Inc., 3114 Scarboro Rd., Street, MD 21154 / 410-838-6550; FAX: 410-838-2802 info@hpwhite.com www.hpwhite.com

Hafner World Wide, Inc., P.O. Box 1987, Lake City, FL 32055 / 904-755-6481; FAX: 904-755-6595 hafner@isgroupe.net

Hakko Co. Ltd., 1-13-12, Narimasu, Itabashiku Tokyo, JAPAN / 03-5997-7870/2; FAX: 81-3-5997-7840

Half Moon Rifle Shop, 490 Halfmoon Rd., Columbia Falls, MT 59912 / 406-892-4409 halfmoonrs@centurytel.net

Hall Manufacturing, 142 CR 406, Clanton, AL 35045 / 205-755-4094

Hall Plastics, Inc., John, P.O. Box 1526, Alvin, TX 77512 / 713-489-8709

Hallberg, Fritz. See: CAMBOS OUTDOORSMAN

Hallowell & Co., P.O. Box 1445, Livingston, MT 59047 / 406-222-4770; FAX: 406-222-4792 morris@hallowellco.com www.hallowellco.com

Hally Caller, 443 Wells Rd., Doylestown, PA 18901 / 215-345-6354; FAX: 215-345-6354 info@hallycaller.com www.hallycaller.com

Hamilton, Alex B. (See Ten-Ring Precision, Inc.)

Hammans, Charles E., P.O. Box 788, 2022 McCracken, Stuttgart, AR 72160-0788 / 870-673-1388

Hammerli AG, Industrieplaz, a/Rheinpall, CH-8212 Neuhausen, SWITZERLAND info@hammerli.com www.haemmerliich.com

Hammerli Service-Precision Mac, Rudolf Marent, 9711 Tiltree St., Houston, TX 77075 / 713-946-7028 rmarent@webtv.net

Hammerli USA, 19296 Oak Grove Circle, Groveland, CA 95321 FAX: 209-962-5311

Hammond Custom Guns Ltd., 619 S. Pandora, Gilbert, AZ 85234 / 602-892-3437

HandCrafts Unltd. (See Clements' Custom Leathercraft), 1741 Dallas St., Aurora, CO 80010-2018 / 303-364-0403; FAX: 303-739-9824 gryphons@home.com kuntaoslcat.com

Handgun Press, P.O. Box 406, Glenview, IL 60025 / 847-657-6500; FAX: 847-724-8831 handgunpress@comcast.net

Hank's Gun Shop, Box 370, 50 W. 100 South, Monroe, UT 84754 / 435-527-4456 hanksgs@compuvision.com

Hanned Line, The, 4463 Madoc Way, San Jose, CA 95130 smith@hanned.com www.hanned.com

Hanned Precision (See The Hanned Line)

Hansen & Co., 244-246 Old Post Rd., Southport, CT 06490 / 203-259-6222; FAX: 203-254-3832

Hanson's Gun Center, Dick, 233 Everett Dr., Colorado Springs, CO 80911

Harford (See U.S. Importer-EMF Co., Inc.)

Harper's Custom Stocks, 928 Lombrano St., San Antonio, TX 78207 / 210-732-7174

Harrell's Precision, 5756 Hickory Dr., Salem, VA 24153 / 540-380-2683

Harrington & Richardson (See H&R 1871, Inc.)

Harris Engineering Inc., Dept. GD54, 999 Broadway, Barlow, KY 42024 / 270-334-3633; FAX: 270-334-3000

Harris Enterprises, P.O. Box 105, Bly, OR 97622 / 503-353-2625

Harris Hand Engraving, Paul A., 113 Rusty Ln., Boerne, TX 78006-5746 / 512-391-5121

Harris Publications, 1115 Broadway, New York, NY 10010 / 212-807-7100; FAX: 212-627-4678

Harrison Bullets, 6437 E. Hobart St., Mesa, AZ 85205

Harry Lawson Co., 3328 N. Richey Blvd., Tucson, AZ 85716 / 520-326-1117; FAX: 520-326-1117

Hart & Son, Inc., Robert W., 401 Montgomery St., Nescopeck, PA 18635 / 717-752-3655; FAX: 717-752-1088

Hart Rifle Barrels, Inc., P.O. Box 182, 1690 Apulia Rd., Lafayette, NY 13084 / 315-677-9841; FAX: 315-677-9610 hartrb@aol.com hartbarrels.com

Hartford (See U.S. Importer-EMF Co. Inc.)

Hartmann & Weiss GmbH, Rahlstedter Bahnhofstr. 47, 22143, Hamburg, GERMANY / (40) 677 55 85; FAX: (40) 677 55 92 hartmannundweiss@t-online.de

MANUFACTURER'S DIRECTORY

Harvey, Frank, 218 Nightfall, Terrace, NV 89015 / 702-558-6998

Hastings, P.O. Box 135, Clay Center, KS 67432 / 785-632-3169; FAX: 785-632-6554

Hatfield Gun, 224 N. 4th St., St. Joseph, MO 64501

Hawk Laboratories, Inc. (See Hawk, Inc.), 849 Hawks Bridge Rd., Salem, NJ 08079 / 609-299-2700; FAX: 609-299-2800

Hawk, Inc., 849 Hawks Bridge Rd., Salem, NJ 08079 / 609-299-2700; FAX: 609-299-2800 info@hawkbullets.com www.hawkbullets.com

Hawken Shop, The, P.O. Box 593, Oak Harbor, WA 98277 / 206-679-4657; FAX: 206-675-1114

Hawken Shop, The (See Dayton Traister)

Haydel's Game Calls, Inc., 5018 Hazel Jones Rd., Bossier City, LA 71111 / 318-746-3586; FAX: 318-746-3711 www.haydels.com

Hecht, Hubert J., Waffen-Hecht, P.O. Box 2635, Fair Oaks, CA 95628 / 916-966-1020

Heckler & Koch GmbH, P.O. Box 1329, 78722 Oberndorf, Neckar, GERMANY / 49-7423179-0; FAX: 49-7423179-2406

Heckler & Koch, Inc., 21480 Pacific Blvd., Sterling, VA 20166-8900 / 703-450-1900; FAX: 703-450-8160 www.hecklerkoch-usa.com

Hege Jagd-u. Sporthandels GmbH, P.O. Box 101461, W-7770, Ueberlingen a. Boden, GERMANY

Heidenstrom Bullets, Dalghte 86-3660 Rjukan, 35091818, NORWAY, olau.joh@online.tuo

Heilmann, Stephen, P.O. Box 657, Grass Valley, CA 95945 / 530-272-8758; FAX: 530-274-0285 sheilmann@jps.net www.metalwood.com

Heinie Specialty Products, 301 Oak St., Quincy, IL 62301-2500 / 217-228-9500; FAX: 217-228-9502 rheinie@heinie.com www.heinie.com

Helwan (See U.S. Importer-Interarms)

Henigson & Associates, Steve, P.O. Box 2726, Culver City, CA 90231 / 310-305-8288; FAX: 310-305-1905

Henriksen Tool Co., Inc., 8515 Wagner Creek Rd., Talent, OR 97540 / 541-535-2309; FAX: 541-535-2309

Henry Repeating Arms Co., 110 8th St., Brooklyn, NY 11215 / 718-499-5600; FAX: 718-768-8056 info@henryrepeating.com www.henryrepeating.com

Hensley, Gunmaker, Darwin, P.O. Box 329, Brightwood, OR 97011 / 503-622-5411

Heppler, Keith. See: KEITH'S CUSTOM GUNSTOCKS

Hercules, Inc. (See Alliant Techsystems Smokeless Powder Group)

Heritage Firearms (See Heritage Mfg., Inc.)

Heritage Manufacturing, Inc., 4600 NW 135th St., Opa Locka, FL 33054 / 305-685-5966; FAX: 305-687-6721 infohmi@heritagemfg.com www.heritagemfg.com

Heritage/VSP Gun Books, P.O. Box 887, McCall, ID 83638 / 208-634-4104; FAX: 208-634-3101 heritage@gunbooks.com www.gunbooks.com

Herrett's Stocks, Inc., P.O. Box 741, Twin Falls, ID 83303 / 208-733-1498

Herter's Manufacturing Inc., 111 E. Burnett St., P.O. Box 518, Beaver Dam, WI 53916-1811 / 414-887-1765; FAX: 414-887-8444

Hesco-Meprolight, 2139 Greenville Rd., LaGrange, GA 30241 / 706-884-7967; FAX: 706-882-4683

Hesse Arms, Robert Hesse, 1126 70th St. E., Inver Grove Heights, MN 55077-2416 / 651-455-5760; FAX: 612-455-5760

Hesse, Robert. See: HESSE ARMS

Heydenberk, Warren R., 1059 W. Sawmill Rd., Quakertown, PA 18951 / 215-538-2682

Hickman, Jaclyn, Box 1900, Glenrock, WY 82637

Hidalgo, Tony, 12701 SW 9th Pl., Davie, FL 33325 / 954-476-7645

High Bridge Arms, Inc., 3185 Mission St., San Francisco, CA 94110 / 415-282-8358

High North Products, Inc., P.O. Box 2, Antigo, WI 54409 / 715-627-2331; FAX: 715-623-5451

High Performance International, 5734 W. Florist Ave., Milwaukee, WI 53218 / 414-466-9040; FAX: 414-466-7050 mike@hpirifles.com hpirifles.com

High Precision, Bud Welsh, 80 New Road, E. Amherst, NY 14051 / 716-688-6344; FAX: 716-688-0425 welsh5168@aol.com www.high-precision.com

High Standard Mfg. Co./F.I., Inc., 5200 Mitchelldale St., Ste. E17, Houston, TX 77092-7222 / 713-462-4200; or 800-272-7816; FAX: 713-681-5665 info@highstandard.com www.highstandard.com

High Tech Specialties, Inc., P.O. Box 839, 293 E Main St., Rear, Adamstown, PA 19501 / 717-484-0405; FAX: 717-484-0523 bansner@aol.com www.bansmersrifle.com/hightech

Highline Machine Co., Randall Thompson, Randall Thompson, 654 Lela Place, Grand Junction, CO 81504 / 970-434-4971

Highwood Special Products, 1531 E. Highwood, Pontiac, MI 48340

Hill, Loring F., 304 Cedar Rd., Elkins Park, PA 19027

Hill Speed Leather, Ernie, 4507 N 195th Ave., Litchfield Park, AZ 85340 / 602-853-9222; FAX: 602-853-9235

Hinman Outfitters, Bob, 107 N Sanderson Ave., Bartonville, IL 61607-1839 / 309-691-8132

Hi-Performance Ammunition Company, 484 State Route 366, Apollo, PA 15613 / 304-674-9000; FAX: 304-675-6700

HIP-GRIP Barami Corp., P.O. Box 252224, West Bloomfield, MI 48325-2224 / 248-738-0462; FAX: 248-738-2542 hipgripja@aol.com www.hipgrip.com

Hi-Point Firearms/MKS Supply, 8611-A North Dixie Dr., Dayton, OH 45414 / 877-425-4867; FAX: 937-454-0503 www.hi-pointfirearms.com

Hiptmayer, Armurier, RR 112 750, P.O. Box 136, Eastman, PQ JOE 1P0 CANADA / 514-297-2492

Hiptmayer, Heidemarie, RR 112 750, P.O. Box 136, Eastman, PQ JOE 1P0 CANADA / 514-297-2492

Hiptmayer, Klaus, RR 112 750, P.O. Box 136, Eastman, PQ JOE 1P0 CANADA / 514-297-2492

Hirtenberger AG, Leobersdorferstrasse 31, A-2552, Hirtenberg, AUSTRIA / 43(0)2256 81184; FAX: 43(0)2256 81808 www.hirtenberger.ot

HJS Arms, Inc., P.O. Box 3711, Brownsville, TX 78523-3711 / 956-542-2767; FAX: 956-542-2767

Hoag, James W., 8523 Canoga Ave., Suite C, Canoga Park, CA 91304 / 818-998-1510

Hobson Precision Mfg. Co., 210 Big Oak Ln., Brent, AL 35034 / 205-926-4662; FAX: 205-926-3193 cahobbob@dbtech.net

Hodgdon Powder Co., 6231 Robinson, Shawnee Mission, KS 66202 / 913-362-9455; FAX: 913-362-1307

Hodgman, Inc., 1750 Orchard Rd., Montgomery, IL 60538 / 708-897-7555; FAX: 708-897-7558

Hodgson, Richard, 9081 Tahoe Lane, Boulder, CO 80301

Hoehn Sales, Inc., 2045 Kohn Road, Wright City, MO 63390 / 636-745-8144; FAX: 636-745-7868 hoehnsal@usmo.com

Hofer Jagdwaffen, P., A9170 Ferlach, Kirchgasse 24, Kirchgasse, AUSTRIA / 43 4227 3683; or 43 664 3200216; FAX: 43 4227 368330 peterhofer@hoferwaffen.com www.hoferwaffen.com

Hoffman New Ideas, 821 Northmoor Rd., Lake Forest, IL 60045 / 312-234-4075

Hogue Grips, P.O. Box 1138, Paso Robles, CA 93447 / 800-438-4747 or 805-239-1440; FAX: 805-239-2553

Holland & Holland Ltd., 33 Bruton St., London, ENGLAND / 44-171-499-4411; FAX: 44-171-408-7962

Holland's Gunsmithing, P.O. Box 69, Powers, OR 97466 / 541-439-5155; FAX: 541-439-5155

Hollinger, Jon. See: ASPEN OUTFITTING CO.

Hollywood Engineering, 10642 Arminta St., Sun Valley, CA 91352 / 818-842-8376; FAX: 818-504-4168 cadqueenel1@aol.com

Homak, 350 N. La Salle Dr. Ste. 1100, Chicago, IL 60610-4731 / 312-523-3100; FAX: 312-523-9455

Hoppe's Div. Penguin Industries, Inc., P.O. Box 1690, Oregon City, OR 97045-0690 / 610-384-6000

Horizons Unlimited, P.O. Box 426, Warm Springs, GA 31830 / 706-655-3603; FAX: 706-655-3603

Hornady Mfg. Co., P.O. Box 1848, Grand Island, NE 68802 / 800-338-3220 or 308-382-1390; FAX: 308-382-5761

Horseshoe Leather Products, Andy Arratoonian, The Cottage Sharow, Ripon, ENGLAND U.K. / 44-1765-605858 andy@horseshoe.co.uk www.holsters.org

House of Muskets, Inc., The, PO Box 4640, Pagosa Springs, CO 81157 / 970-731-2295

Houtz & Barwick, P.O. Box 435, W. Church St., Elizabeth City, NC 27909 / 800-775-0337; or 919-335-4191; FAX: 919-335-1152

Howa Machinery, Ltd., Sukaguchi, Shinkawa-cho Nishikasugai-gun, Aichi 452-8601, JAPAN / 81-52-408-1231; FAX: 81-52-401-4999 howa@howa.co.jp http://www.howa.cojp

Howell Machine, Inc., 815 D St., Lewiston, ID 83501 / 208-743-7418; FAX: 208-746-1703

H-S Precision, Inc., 1301 Turbine Dr., Rapid City, SD 57701 / 605-341-3006; FAX: 605-342-8964

HT Bullets, 244 Belleville Rd., New Bedford, MA 02745 / 508-999-3338

Hubert J. Hecht Waffen-Hecht, P.O. Box 2635, Fair Oaks, CA 95628 / 916-966-1020

Huebner, Corey O., P.O. Box 564, Frenchtown, MT 59834 / 406-721-7168 bugsboys@hotmail.com

Huey Gun Cases, 820 Indiana St., Lawrence, KS 66044-2645 / 785-842-0062; FAX: 785-842-0062 hueycases@aol.com www.hueycases.com

Hume, Don, P.O. Box 351, Miami, OK 74355 / 800-331-2686; FAX: 918-542-4340 info@donhume.com www.donhume.com

Hunkeler, A. (See Buckskin Machine Works), 3235 S 358th St., Auburn, WA 98001 / 206-927-5412

Hunter Co., Inc., 3300 W. 71st Ave., Westminster, CO 80030 / 303-427-4626; FAX: 303-428-3980 debbiet@huntercompany.com www.huntercompany.com

Hunterjohn, P.O. Box 771457, St. Louis, MO 63177 / 314-531-7250 www.hunterjohn.com

Hunter's Specialties Inc., 6000 Huntington Ct. NE, Cedar Rapids, IA 52402-1268 / 319-395-0321; FAX: 319-395-0326

Hunters Supply, Inc., P.O. Box 313, Tioga, TX 76271 / 940-437-2458; FAX: 940-437-2228 hunterssupply@hotmail.com www.hunterssupply.net

Huntington Die Specialties, 601 Oro Dam Blvd., Oroville, CA 95965 / 530-534-1210; FAX: 530-534-1212 buy@huntingtons.com www.huntingtons.com

Hutton Rifle Ranch, P.O. Box 170317, Boise, ID 83717 / 208-345-8781 www.martinbrevik@aol.com

Hydrosorbent Products, P.O. Box 437, Ashley Falls, MA 01222 / 800-448-7903; FAX: 413-229-8743 orders@dehumidify.com www.dehumidify.com

I

I.A.B. (See U.S. Importer-Taylor's & Co., Inc.)

I.D.S.A. Books, 1324 Stratford Drive, Piqua, OH 45356 / 937-773-4203; FAX: 937-778-1922

I.N.C. Inc. (See Kickeez I.N.C., Inc.)

I.S.W., 106 E. Cairo Dr., Tempe, AZ 85282

IAR Inc., 33171 Camino Capistrano, San Juan Capistrano, CA 92675 / 949-443-3642; FAX: 949-443-3647 sales@iar-arms.com iar-arms.com

Ide, Ken. See: STURGEON VALLEY SPORTERS

IGA (See U.S. Importer-Stoeger Industries)

Image Ind. Inc., 11220 E. Main St., Huntley, IL 60142-7369 / 630-766-2402; FAX: 630-766-7373

Impact Case & Container, Inc., P.O. Box 1129, Rathdrum, ID 83858 / 877-687-2452; FAX: 208-687-0632 bradk@icc-case.com www.icc-case.com

Imperial (See E-Z-Way Systems), P.O. Box 4310, Newark, OH 43058-4310 / 614-345-6645; FAX: 614-345-6600 ezway@infinet.com www.jcunald.com

Imperial Magnum Corp., P.O. Box 249, Oroville, WA 98844 / 604-495-3131; FAX: 604-495-2816

Imperial Miniature Armory, 1115 FM 359, Houston, TX 77035-3305 / 800-646-4288; FAX: 832-595-8787 miniguns@houston.rr.com www.1800miniature.com

Imperial Schrade Corp., 7 Schrade Ct., Box 7000, Ellenville, NY 12428 / 914-647-7601; FAX: 914-647-8701 csc@schradeknives.com www.schradeknives.com

Import Sports Inc., 1750 Brielle Ave., Unit B1, Wanamassa, NJ 07712 / 732-493-0302; FAX: 732-493-0301 gsodini@aol.com www.bersa-llama.com

IMR Powder Co., 1080 Military Turnpike, Suite 2, Plattsburgh, NY 12901 / 518-563-2253; FAX: 518-563-6916

Info-Arm, P.O. Box 1262, Champlain, NY 12919 / 514-955-0355; FAX: 514-955-0357 infoarm@qc.aira.com

Innovative Weaponry Inc., 2513 E. Loop 820 N., Fort Worth, TX 76118 / 817-284-0099 or 800-334-3573

INTEC International, Inc., P.O. Box 5708, Scottsdale, AZ 85261 / 602-483-1708

Inter Ordnance of America LP, 3305 Westwood Industrial Dr., Monroe, NC 28110-5204 / 704-821-8337; FAX: 704-821-8523

Intercontinental Distributors, Ltd., P.O. Box 815, Beulah, ND 58523

International Shooters Service, P.O. Box 185234, Ft. Worth, TX 76181 / 817-595-2090; FAX: 817-595-2090 is_s_@sbcglobal.net

Intrac Arms International, 5005 Chapman Hwy., Knoxville, TN 37920

Ion Industries, Inc., 3508 E Allerton Ave., Cudahy, WI 53110 / 414-486-2007; FAX: 414-486-2017

Iosso Products, 1485 Lively Blvd., Elk Grove Village, IL 60007 / 847-437-8400; FAX: 847-437-8478

Iron Bench, 12619 Bailey Rd., Redding, CA 96003 / 916-241-4623

Ironside International Publishers, Inc., P.O. Box 1050, Lorton, VA 22199

Ironsighter Co., P.O. Box 85070, Westland, MI 48185 / 734-326-8731; FAX: 734-326-3378 www.ironsighter.com

Irwin, Campbell H., 140 Hartland Blvd., East Hartland, CT 06027 / 203-653-3901

Israel Arms Inc., 5625 Star Ln. #B, Houston, TX 77057 / 713-789-0745; FAX: 713-914-9515 www.israelarms.com

MANUFACTURER'S DIRECTORY

Ithaca Classic Doubles, Stephen Lamboy, No. 5 Railroad St., Victor, NY 14564 / 716-924-2710; FAX: 716-924-2737 ithacadoubles.com

Ithaca Gun Company LLC, 901 Rt. 34 B, King Ferry, NY 13081 / 315-364-7171; FAX: 315-364-5134 info@ithacagun.com

Ivanoff, Thomas G. (See Tom's Gun Repair)

J

J J Roberts Firearm Engraver, 7808 Lake Dr., Manassas, VA 20111 / 703-330-0448; FAX: 703-264-8600 james.roberts@angelfire.com www.angelfire.com/va2/engraver

J&D Components, 75 East 350 North, Orem, UT 84057-4719 / 801-225-7007 www.jdcomponents.com

J&J Products, Inc., 9240 Whitmore, El Monte, CA 91731 / 818-571-5228; FAX: 800-927-8361

J&J Sales, 1501 21st Ave. S., Great Falls, MT 59405 / 406-727-9789 mtshootingbench@yahoo.com www.j&jsales.us

J&L Superior Bullets (See Huntington Die Specialties)

J&M Precision Machining, Jeff Amato, RR 1 Box 91, Bloomfield, IN 47424

J&R Engineering, P.O. Box 77, 200 Lyons Hill Rd., Athol, MA 01331 / 508-249-9241

J&R Enterprises, 4550 Scotts Valley Rd., Lakeport, CA 95453

J&S Heat Treat, 803 S. 16th St., Blue Springs, MO 64015 / 816-229-2149; FAX: 816-228-1135

J. Dewey Mfg. Co., Inc., P.O. Box 2014, Southbury, CT 06488 / 203-264-3064; FAX: 203-262-6907 deweyrods@worldnet.att.net www.deweyrods.com

J. Korzinek Riflesmith, RD 2, Box 73D, Canton, PA 17724 / 717-673-8512

J.A. Blades, Inc. (See Christopher Firearms Co.)

J.A. Henckels Zwillingswerk Inc., 9 Skyline Dr., Hawthorne, NY 10532 / 914-592-7370

J.G. Anschutz GmbH & Co. KG, Daimlerstr. 12, D-89079 Ulm, Ulm, GERMANY / 49 731 40120; FAX: 49 731 4012700 JGA-info@anschuetz-sport.com www.anschuetz-sport.com

J.G. Dapkus Co., Inc., Commerce Circle, P.O. Box 293, Durham, CT 06422 www.explodingtargets.com

J.I.T. Ltd., P.O. Box 230, Freedom, WY 83120 / 708-494-0937

J.J. Roberts / Engraver, 7808 Lake Dr., Manassas, VA 20111 / 703-330-0448 jjrengraver@aol.com www.angelfire.com/va2/engraver

J.R. Williams Bullet Co., 2008 Tucker Rd., Perry, GA 31069 / 912-987-0274

J.W. Morrison Custom Rifles, 4015 W. Sharon, Phoenix, AZ 85029 / 602-978-3754

Jack A. Rosenberg & Sons, 12229 Cox Ln., Dallas, TX 75234 / 214-241-6302

Jack Dever Co., 8520 NW 90th St., Oklahoma City, OK 73132 / 405-721-6393 jbdever1@home.com

Jack First, Inc., 1201 Turbine Dr., Rapid City, SD 57703 / 605-343-8481; FAX: 605-343-9420

Jack Jonas Appraisals & Taki, 13952 E. Marina Dr., #604, Aurora, CO 80014

Jackalope Gun Shop, 1048 S. 5th St., Douglas, WY 82633 / 307-358-3441

Jaffin, Harry. See: BRIDGEMAN PRODUCTS

Jagdwaffen, Peter. See: BUCHSENMACHERMEISTER

James Churchill Glove Co., PO Box 298, Centralia, WA 98531 / 360-736-2816; FAX: 360-330-0151 churchillglove@localaccess.com

James Wayne Firearms for Collectors and Investors, 2608 N. Laurent, Victoria, TX 77901 / 361-578-1258; FAX: 361-578-3559

Jamison International, Marc Jamison, 3551 Mayer Ave., Sturgis, SD 57785 / 605-347-5090; FAX: 605-347-4704 jbell2@masttechnology.com

Jamison, Marc. See: JAMISON INTERNATIONAL

Jamison's Forge Works, 4527 Rd. 6.5 NE, Moses Lake, WA 98837 / 509-762-2659

Jantz Supply, 309 West Main Dept HD, Davis, OK 73030-0584 / 580-369-2316; FAX: 580-369-3082 jantz@brightok.net www.knifemaking.com

Jarrett Rifles, Inc., 383 Brown Rd., Jackson, SC 29831 / 803-471-3616 www.jarrettrifles.com

Jarvis, Inc., 1123 Cherry Orchard Lane, Hamilton, MT 59840 / 406-961-4392

Javelina Lube Products, P.O. Box 337, San Bernardino, CA 92402 / 909-350-9556; FAX: 909-429-1211

Jay McCament Custom Gunmaker, Jay McCament, 1730-134th St. Ct. S., Tacoma, WA 98444 / 253-531-8832

JB Custom, P.O. Box 6912, Leawood, KS 66206 / 913-381-2329

Jeff Flannery Engraving, 11034 Riddles Run Rd., Union, KY 41091 / 859-384-3127; FAX: 859-384-2222 engraving@fuse.net http://home.fuse.net/engraving/

Jeffredo Gunsight, P.O. Box 669, San Marcos, CA 92079 / 760-728-2695

Jena Eur, P.O. Box 319, Dunmore, PA 18512

Jenco Sales, Inc., P.O. Box 1000, Manchaca, TX 78652 / 800-531-5301; FAX: 800-266-2373 jencosales@sbcglobal.net

Jenkins Recoil Pads, 5438 E. Frontage Ln., Olney, IL 62450 / 618-395-3416

Jensen Bullets, RR 1 Box 187, Arco, ID 83213 / 208-785-5590

Jensen's Custom Ammunition, 5146 E. Pima, Tucson, AZ 85712 / 602-325-3346; FAX: 602-322-5704

Jensen's Firearms Academy, 1280 W. Prince, Tucson, AZ 85705 / 602-293-8516

Jericho Tool & Die Co., Inc., 121 W. Keech Rd., Bainbridge, NY 13733-3248 / 607-563-8222; FAX: 607-563-8560 jerichotool.com www.jerichotool.com

Jerry Phillips Optics, P.O. Box L632, Langhorne, PA 19047 / 215-757-5037; FAX: 215-757-7097

Jesse W. Smith Saddlery, 0499 County Road J, Pritchett, CO 81064 / 509-325-0622

Jester Bullets, Rt. 1 Box 27, Orienta, OK 73737

Jewell Triggers, Inc., 3620 Hwy. 123, San Marcos, TX 78666 / 512-353-2999; FAX: 512-392-0543

JG Airguns, LLC, John Groenewold, P.O. Box 830, Mundelein, IL 60060 / 847-566-2365; FAX: 847-566-4065 jgairguns@jgairguns www.jgairguns.com

JGS Precision Tool Mfg., LLC, 60819 Selander Rd., Coos Bay, OR 97420 / 541-267-4331; FAX: 541-267-5996 jgstools@harborside.com www.jgstools.com

Jim Blair Engraving, P.O. Box 64, Glenrock, WY 82637 / 307-436-8115 jblairengrav@msn.com

Jim Noble Co., 204 W. 5th St., Vancouver, WA 98660 / 360-695-1309; FAX: 360-695-6835 jnobleco@aol.com

Jim Norman Custom Gunstocks, 14281 Cane Rd., Valley Center, CA 92082 / 619-749-6252

Jim's Precision, Jim Ketchum, 1725 Moclips Dr., Petaluma, CA 94952 / 707-762-3014

JLK Bullets, 414 Turner Rd., Dover, AR 72837 / 501-331-4194

Johanssons Vapentillbehor, Bert, S-430 20, Veddige, SWEDEN

John Hall Plastics, Inc., P.O. Box 1526, Alvin, TX 77512 / 713-489-8709

John J. Adams & Son Engravers, 7040 VT Rt 113, Vershire, VT 05079 / 802-685-0019

John Masen Co. Inc., 1305 Jelmak, Grand Prairie, TX 75050 / 817-430-8732; FAX: 817-430-1715

John Partridge Sales Ltd., Trent Meadows Rugeley, Staffordshire, WS15 2HS ENGLAND

John Rigby & Co., 500 Linne Rd. Ste. D, Paso Robles, CA 93446 / 805-227-4236; FAX: 805-227-4723 jrigby@calinet www.johnrigbyandco.com

John's Custom Leather, 523 S. Liberty St., Blairsville, PA 15717 / 724-459-6802; FAX: 724-459-5996

Johnson Wood Products, 34897 Crystal Road, Strawberry Point, IA 52076 / 563-933-6504 johnsonwoodproducts@yahoo.com

Jonad Corp., 2091 Lakeland Ave., Lakewood, OH 44107 / 216-226-3161

Jonathan Arthur Ciener, Inc., 8700 Commerce St., Cape Canaveral, FL 32920 / 321-868-2200; FAX: 321-868-2201 www.22lrconversions.com

Jones Co., Dale, 680 Hoffman Draw, Kila, MT 59920 / 406-755-4684

Jones Custom Products, Neil A., 17217 Brookhouser Rd., Saegertown, PA 16433 / 814-763-2769; FAX: 814-763-4228 njones@mdul.net neiljones.com

Jones, J. See: SSK INDUSTRIES

Jones Moulds, Paul, 4901 Telegraph Rd., Los Angeles, CA 90022 / 213-262-1510

JP Enterprises, Inc., P.O. Box 378, Hugo, MN 55038 / 651-426-9196; FAX: 651-426-2472 www.jprifles.com

JP Sales, Box 307, Anderson, TX 77830

JRP Custom Bullets, RR2 2233 Carlton Rd., Whitehall, NY 12887 / 518-282-0084 or 802-438-5548

JSL Ltd. (See U.S. Importer-Specialty Shooters Supply)

Juenke, Vern, 25 Bitterbush Rd., Reno, NV 89523 / 702-345-0225

Jungkind, Reeves C., 509 E. Granite St., Llano, TX 78643-3055 / 325-247-1151

Jurras, L. See: L. E. JURRAS & ASSOC.

Justin Phillippi Custom Bullets, P.O. Box 773, Ligonier, PA 15658 / 412-238-9671

K

K&M Industries, Inc., Box 66, 510 S. Main, Troy, ID 83871 / 208-835-2281; FAX: 208-835-5211

K&M Services, 5430 Salmon Run Rd., Dover, PA 17315 / 717-292-3175; FAX: 717-292-3175

K. Eversull Co., Inc., 1 Tracemont, Boyce, LA 71409 / 318-793-8728; FAX: 318-793-5483 bestguns@aol.com

K.B.I. Inc., P.O. Box 6625, Harrisburg, PA 17112 / 717-540-8500; FAX: 717-540-8567

Ka Pu Kapili, P.O. Box 745, Honokaa, HI 96727 / 808-776-1644; FAX: 808-776-1731

KA-BAR Knives, 200 Homer St., Olean, NY 14760 / 800-282-0130; FAX: 716-790-7188 info@ka-bar.com www.ka-bar.com

Kahles A. Swarovski Company, 2 Slater Rd., Cranston, RI 02920 / 401-946-2220; FAX: 401-946-2587

Kahr Arms, P.O. Box 220, 630 Route 303, Blauvelt, NY 10913 / 845-353-7770; FAX: 845-353-7833 www.kahr.com

Kailua Custom Guns Inc., 51 N. Dean Street, Coquille, OR 97423 / 541-396-5413 kailuacustom@aol.com www.kailuacustom.com

Kalispel Case Line, P.O. Box 267, Cusick, WA 99119 / 509-445-1121

Kamik Outdoor Footwear, 554 Montee de Liesse, Montreal, PQ H4T 1P1 CANADA / 514-341-3950; FAX: 514-341-1861

Kane, Edward, P.O. Box 385, Ukiah, CA 95482 / 707-462-2937

Kapro Mfg. Co. Inc. (See R.E.I.)

Kasenit Co., Inc., 39 Park Ave., Highland Mills, NY 10930 / 845-928-9595; FAX: 845-986-8038

Kaswer Custom, Inc., 13 Surrey Drive, Brookfield, CT 06804 / 203-775-0564; FAX: 203-775-6872

KDF, Inc., 2485 Hwy. 46 N., Seguin, TX 78155 / 830-379-8141; FAX: 830-379-5420

KeeCo Impressions, Inc., 346 Wood Ave., North Brunswick, NJ 08902 / 800-468-0546

Kehr, Roger, 2131 Agate Ct. SE, Lacy, WA 98503 / 360-491-0691

Keith's Bullets, 942 Twisted Oak, Algonquin, IL 60102 / 708-658-3520

Keith's Custom Gunstocks, Keith M. Heppler, 540 Banyan Circle, Walnut Creek, CA 94598 / 925-934-3509; FAX: 925-934-3143 kmheppler@hotmail.com

Kelbly, Inc., 7222 Dalton Fox Lake Rd., North Lawrence, OH 44666 / 216-683-4674; FAX: 216-683-7349

Keller Co., The, P.O. Box 4057, Port Angeles, WA 98363-0997 / 214-770-8585

Kelley's, P.O. Box 125, Woburn, MA 01801-0125 / 800-879-7273; FAX: 781-272-7077 kels@star.net www.kelsmilitary.com

Kellogg's Professional Products, 325 Pearl St., Sandusky, OH 44870 / 419-625-6551; FAX: 419-625-6167 skwigton@aol.com

Kelly, Lance, 1723 Willow Oak Dr., Edgewater, FL 32132 / 904-423-4933

Kel-Tec CNC Industries, Inc., P.O. Box 236009, Cocoa, FL 32923 / 407-631-0068; FAX: 407-631-1169

Kemen America, 2550 Hwy. 23, Wrenshall, MN 55797 / 218-384-3670 patrickl@midwestshootingschool.com midwestshootingschool.com

Ken Eyster Heritage Gunsmiths, Inc., 6441 Bisop Rd., Centerburg, OH 43011 / 740-625-6131; FAX: 740-625-7811

Ken Starnes Gunmaker, 15940 SW Holly Hill Rd., Hillsboro, OR 97123-9033 / 503-628-0705; FAX: 503-443-2096 kstarnes@kdsa.com

Keng's Firearms Specialty, Inc./US Tactical Systems, 875 Wharton Dr., P.O. Box 44405, Atlanta, GA 30336-1405 / 404-691-7611; FAX: 404-505-8445

Kennebec Journal, 274 Western Ave., Augusta, ME 04330 / 207-622-6288

Kennedy Firearms, 10 N. Market St., Muncy, PA 17756 / 717-546-6695

Kenneth W. Warren Engraver, P.O. Box 2842, Wenatchee, WA 98807 / 509-663-6123; FAX: 509-665-6123

Ken's Kustom Kartridges, 331 Jacobs Rd., Hubbard, OH 44425 / 216-534-4595

Kent Cartridge America, Inc., P.O. Box 849, 1000 Zigor Rd., Kearneysville, WV 25430

Keowee Game Calls, 608 Hwy. 25 North, Travelers Rest, SC 29690 / 864-834-7204; FAX: 864-834-7831

Kershaw Knives, 18600 SW Teton Ave., Tualatin, OR 97062 / 503-682-1966; or 800-325-2891; FAX: 503-682-7168

Kesselring Gun Shop, 4024 Old Hwy. 99N, Burlington, WA 98233 / 360-724-3113; FAX: 360-724-7003 info@kesselrings.com www.kesselrings.com

Ketchum, Jim (See Jim's Precision)

Keystone Sporting Arms, Inc. (Crickett Rifles), 8920 State Route 405, Milton, PA 17847 / 800-742-2777; FAX: 570-742-1455

Kickeez I.N.C., Inc., 301 Industrial Dr., Carl Junction, MO 64834-8806 / 419-649-2100; FAX: 417-649-2200 kickeez@gbronline.com www.kickeez.net

MANUFACTURER'S DIRECTORY

Kilham & Co., Main St., P.O. Box 37, Lyme, NH 03768 / 603-795-4112

Kimar (See U.S. Importer-IAR, Inc.)

Kimber of America, Inc., 1 Lawton St., Yonkers, NY 10705 / 800-880-2418; FAX: 914-964-9340

King & Co., P.O. Box 1242, Bloomington, IL 61702 / 309-473-3964; or 800-914-5464; FAX: 309-473-2161

King's Gun Works, 1837 W. Glenoaks Blvd., Glendale, CA 91201 / 818-956-6010; FAX: 818-548-8606

Kirkpatrick Leather Co., P.O. Box 677, Laredo, TX 78040 / 956-723-6631; FAX: 956-725-0672
mike@kirkpatrickleather.com
www.kirkpatrickleather.com

KK Air International (See Impact Case & Container Co., Inc.)

Kleen-Bore, Inc., 16 Industrial Pkwy., Easthampton, MA 01027 / 413-527-0300; FAX: 413-527-2522
info@kleen-bore.com www.kleen-bore.com

Kleinendorst, K. W., RR 1, Box 1500, Hop Bottom, PA 18824 / 717-289-4687

Klingler Woodcarving, P.O. Box 141, Thistle Hill, Cabot, VT 05647 / 802-426-3811 www.vermartcrafts.com

Knifeware, Inc., P.O. Box 3, Greenville, WV 24945 / 304-832-6878

Knight Rifles, 21852 Hwy. J46, P.O. Box 130, Centerville, IA 52544 / 515-856-2626; FAX: 515-856-2628
www.knightrifles.com

Knight Rifles (See Modern Muzzleloading, Inc.)

Knight's Manufacturing Co., 701 Columbia Blvd., Titusville, FL 32780 / 321-607-9900; FAX: 321-268-1498
civiliansales@knightarmco.com www.knightarmco.com

Knock on Wood Antiques, 355 Post Rd., Darien, CT 06820 / 203-655-9031

Knoell, Doug, 9737 McCardle Way, Santee, CA 92071 / 619-449-5189

Knopp, Gary. See: SUPER 6 LLC

Koevenig's Engraving Service, Box 55 Rabbit Gulch, Hill City, SD 57745 / 605-574-2239 ekoevenig@msn.com

KOGOT, 410 College, Trinidad, CO 81082 / 719-846-9406; FAX: 719-846-9406

Kolar, 1925 Roosevelt Ave., Racine, WI 53406 / 414-554-0800; FAX: 414-554-9093

Kolpin Outdoors, Inc., P.O. Box 107, 205 Depot St., Fox Lake, WI 53933 / 414-928-3118; FAX: 414-928-3687
cdutton@kolpin.com www.kolpin.com

Korth Germany GmbH, Robert Bosch Strasse, 11, D-23909, 23909 Ratzeburg, GERMANY / 4541-840363; FAX: 4541-84 05 35 info@korthwaffen.de
www.korthwaffen.de

Korth USA, 437R Chandler St., Tewksbury, MA 01876 / 978-851-8656; FAX: 978-851-9462 info@kortusa.com
www.korthusa.com

Korzinek Riflesmith, J., RD 2 Box 73D, Canton, PA 17724 / 717-673-8512

Koval Knives, 5819 Zarley St., Suite A, New Albany, OH 43054 / 614-855-0777; FAX: 614-855-0945
koval@kovalknives.com www.kovalknives.com

Kowa Optimed, Inc., 20001 S. Vermont Ave., Torrance, CA 90502 / 310-327-1913; FAX: 310-327-4177
scopekowa@kowa.com www.kowascope.com

KP Books Division of F&W Publications, 700 E. State St., Iola, WI 54990-0001 / 715-445-2214

Kramer Designs, P.O. Box 129, Clancy, MT 59634 / 406-933-8658; FAX: 406-933-8658

Kramer Handgun Leather, P.O. Box 112154, Tacoma, WA 98411 / 800-510-2666; FAX: 253-564-1214
www.kramerleather.com

Krico Deutschland GmbH, Nurnbergerstrasse 6, D-90602, Pyrbaum, GERMANY / 09180-2780; FAX: 09180-2661

Krieger Barrels, Inc., 2024 Mayfield Rd, Richfield, WI 53076 / 262-628-8558; FAX: 262-628-8748

Krieghoff Gun Co., H., Boschstrasse 22, D-89079 Elm, GERMANY / 731-4018270

Krieghoff International,Inc., 7528 Easton Rd., Ottsville, PA 18942 / 610-847-5173; FAX: 610-847-8691

Kukowski, Ed. See: ED'S GUN HOUSE

Kulis Freeze Dry Taxidermy, 725 Broadway Ave., Bedford, OH 44146 / 216-232-8352; FAX: 216-232-7305
jkulis@kastaway.com kastaway.com

KVH Industries, Inc., 110 Enterprise Center, Middletown, RI 02842 / 401-847-3327; FAX: 401-849-0045

Kwik-Site Co., 5555 Treadwell St., Wayne, MI 48184 / 734-326-1500; FAX: 734-326-4120 kwiksiteco@aol.com

L

L&R Lock Co., 2328 Cains Mill Rd., Sumter, SC 29154 / 803-481-5790; FAX: 803-481-5795

L&S Technologies Inc. (See Aimtech Mount Systems)

L. Bengtson Arms Co., 6345-B E. Akron St., Mesa, AZ 85205 / 602-981-6375

L. E. Jurras & Assoc., L. E. Jurras, P.O. Box 680, Washington, IN 47501 / 812-254-6170; FAX: 812-254-6170
jurras@sbcglobal.net www.leejurras.com

L.A.R. Mfg., Inc., 4133 W. Farm Rd., West Jordan, UT 84088 / 801-280-3505; FAX: 801-280-1972

L.B.T., Judy Smith, HCR 62, Box 145, Moyie Springs, ID 83845 / 208-267-3588

L.E. Wilson, Inc., Box 324, 404 Pioneer Ave., Cashmere, WA 98815 / 509-782-1328; FAX: 509-782-7200

L.L. Bean, Inc., Freeport, ME 04032 / 207-865-4761; FAX: 207-552-2802

L.P.A. Inc., Via Alfieri 26, Gardone V.T., Brescia, ITALY / 30-891-14-81; FAX: 30-891-09-51

L.R. Clift Mfg., 3821 Hammonton Rd., Marysville, CA 95901 / 916-755-3390; FAX: 916-755-3393

La Clinique du .45, 1432 Rougemont, Chambly, PQ J3L 2L8 CANADA / 514-658-1144

Labanu Inc., 2201-F Fifth Ave., Ronkonkoma, NY 11779 / 516-467-6197; FAX: 516-981-4112

LaBoone, Pat. See: MIDWEST SHOOTING SCHOOL, THE

LaBounty Precision Reboring, Inc, 7968 Silver Lake Rd., PO Box 186, Maple Falls, WA 98266 / 360-599-2047; FAX: 360-599-3018

LaCrosse Footwear Inc., 18550 NE Riverside Parkway, Portland, OR 97230 / 503-766-1010; or 800-323-2668; FAX: 503-766-1015

LaFrance Specialties, P.O. Box 87933, San Diego, CA 92138 / 619-293-3373; FAX: 619-293-0819 timlafrance@att.net
lafrancespecialties.com

Lake Center Marina, P.O. Box 670, St. Charles, MO 63302 / 314-946-7500

Lakefield Arms Ltd. (See Savage Arms, Inc.)

Lakewood Products LLC, 275 June St., Berlin, WI 54923 / 800-872-8458; FAX: 920-361-7719
lakewood@centurytel.net www.lakewoodproducts.com

Lamboy, Stephen. See: ITHACA CLASSIC DOUBLES

Lampert, Ron, Rt. 1, 44857 Schoolcraft Trl., Guthrie, MN 56461 / 218-854-7345

Lamson & Goodnow Mfg. Co., 45 Conway St., Shelburne Falls, MA 03170 / 413-625-6564; or 800-872-6564; FAX: 413-625-9816 www.lamsonsharp.com

Lansky Levine, Arthur. See: LANSKY SHARPENERS

Lansky Sharpeners, Arthur Lansky Levine, P.O. Box 50830, Las Vegas, NV 89016 / 702-361-7511; FAX: 702-896-9511

LaPrade, P.O. Box 250, Ewing, VA 24248 / 423-733-2615

LaRocca Gun Works, 51 Union Place, Worcester, MA 01608 / 508-754-2887; FAX: 508-754-2887
www.laroccagunworks.com

Larry Lyons Gunworks, 110 Hamilton St., Dowagiac, MI 49047 / 616-782-9478

Laser Devices, Inc., 2 Harris Ct. A-4, Monterey, CA 93940 / 831-373-0701; FAX: 831-373-0903
sales@laserdevices.com www.laserdevices.com

Laseraim Technologies, Inc., P.O. Box 3548, Little Rock, AR 72203 / 501-375-2227

Laserlyte, 2201 Amapola Ct., Torrance, CA 90501

LaserMax, Inc., 3495 Winton Place, Bldg. B, Rochester, NY 14623-2807 / 800-527-3703; FAX: 716-272-5427
customerservice@lasermax-inc.com www.lasermax.com

Lassen Community College, Gunsmithing Dept., P.O. Box 3000, Hwy. 139, Susanville, CA 96130 / 916-251-8800; FAX: 916-251-8838 staylor@lassencollege.com
www.lassencommunitycollege.edu

Lathrop's, Inc., 5146 E. Pima, Tucson, AZ 85712 / 520-881-0266; or 800-875-4867; FAX: 520-322-5704

Laughridge, William R. (See Cylinder & Slide, Inc.)

Laurel Mountain Forge, P.O. Box 52, Crown Point, IN 46308 / 219-548-2950; FAX: 219-548-2950

Laurona Armas Eibar, S.A.L., Avenida de Otaola 25, P.O. Box 260, Eibar 20600, SPAIN / 34-43-700600; FAX: 34-43-700616

Lawrence Brand Shot (See Precision Reloading, Inc.)

Lawrence Leather Co., P.O. Box 1479, Lillington, NC 27546 / 910-893-2071; FAX: 910-893-4742

Lawson Co., Harry, 3328 N Richey Blvd., Tucson, AZ 85716 / 520-326-1117; FAX: 520-326-1117

Lawson, John. See: SIGHT SHOP, THE

Lawson, John G. (See Sight Shop, The)

Lazzeroni Arms Co., P.O. Box 26696, Tucson, AZ 85726 / 888-492-7247; FAX: 520-624-4250

Le Clear Industries (See E-Z-Way Systems)

Leapers, Inc., 7675 Five Mile Rd., Northville, MI 48167 / 248-486-1231; FAX: 248-486-1430

Leatherman Tool Group, Inc., 12106 NE Ainsworth Cir., P.O. Box 20595, Portland, OR 97294 / 503-253-7826; FAX: 503-253-7830

Lebeau-Courally, Rue St. Gilles, 386 4000, Liege, BELGIUM / 042-52-48-43; FAX: 32-4-252-2008
info@lebeau-courally.com www.lebeau-courally.com

Leckie Professional Gunsmithing, 546 Quarry Rd., Ottsville, PA 18942 / 215-847-8594

Ledbetter Airguns, Riley, 1804 E Sprague St., Winston Salem, NC 27107-3521 / 919-784-0676

Lee Precision, Inc., 4275 Hwy. U, Hartford, WI 53027 / 262-673-3075; FAX: 262-673-9273
info@leeprecision.com www.leeprecision.com

Lee Supplies, Mark, 9901 France Ct., Lakeville, MN 55044 / 612-461-2114

LeFever Arms Co., Inc., 6234 Stokes, Lee Center Rd., Lee Center, NY 13363 / 315-337-6722; FAX: 315-337-1543

Legacy Sports International, 206 S. Union St., Alexandria, VA 22314 / 703-548-4837 www.legacysports.com

Leica USA, Inc., 156 Ludlow Ave., Northvale, NJ 07647 / 201-767-7500; FAX: 201-767-8666

Leonard Day, 3 Kings Hwy., West Hatfield, MA 01027-9506 / 413-337-8369

Les Baer Custom, Inc., 29601 34th Ave., Hillsdale, IL 61257 / 309-658-2716; FAX: 309-658-2610 www.lesbaer.com

LesMerises, Felix. See: ROCKY MOUNTAIN ARMOURY

Lethal Force Institute (See Police Bookshelf), P.O. Box 122, Concord, NH 03301 / 603-224-6814; FAX: 603-226-3554

Lett Custom Grips, 672 Currier Rd., Hopkinton, NH 03229-2652 / 800-421-5388; FAX: 603-226-4580
info@lettgrips.com www.lettgrips.com

Leupold & Stevens, Inc., 14400 NW Greenbrier Pky., Beaverton, OR 97006 / 503-646-9171; FAX: 503-526-1455

Lever Arms Service Ltd., 2131 Burrard St., Vancouver, BC V6J 3H7 CANADA / 604-736-2711; FAX: 604-738-3503
leverarms@leverarms.com www.leverarms.com

Lew Horton Dist. Co., Inc., 15 Walkup Dr., Westboro, MA 01581 / 508-366-7400; FAX: 508-366-5332

Lewis Lead Remover, The (See Brownells, Inc.)

Liberty Metals, 2233 East 16th St., Los Angeles, CA 90021 / 213-581-9171; FAX: 213-581-9351
libertymfgsolder@hotmail.com

Liberty Safe, 999 W. Utah Ave., Payson, UT 84651-1744 / 800-247-5625; FAX: 801-489-6409

Liberty Shooting Supplies, P.O. Box 357, Hillsboro, OR 97123 / 503-640-5518; FAX: 503-640-5518
info@libertyshootingsupplies.com
www.libertyshootingsupplies.com

Lightning Performance Innovations, Inc., RD1 Box 555, Mohawk, NY 13407 / 315-866-8819; FAX: 315-867-5701

Lilja Precision Rifle Barrels, P.O. Box 372, Plains, MT 59859 / 406-826-3084; FAX: 406-826-3083 lilja@riflebarrels.com
www.riflebarrels.com

Lincoln, Dean, Box 1886, Farmington, NM 87401

Linder Solingen Knives, 4401 Sentry Dr. #B, Tucker, GA 30084 / 770-939-6915; FAX: 770-939-6738

Lindsay Engraving & Tools, Steve Lindsay, 3714 W. Cedar Hills, Kearney, NE 68845 / 308-236-7885
steve@lindsayengraving.com www.handgravers.com

Lindsay, Steve. See: LINDSAY ENGRAVING & TOOLS

Lindsley Arms Cartridge Co., P.O. Box 757, 20 College Hill Rd., Henniker, NH 03242 / 603-428-3127

Linebaugh Custom Sixguns, P.O. Box 455, Cody, WY 82414 / 307-645-3332 www.sixgunner.com

Lion Country Supply, P.O. Box 480, Port Matilda, PA 16870

List Precision Engineering, Unit 1 Ingley Works, 13 River Road, Barking, ENGLAND / 011-081-594-1686

Lithi Bee Bullet Lube, 1728 Carr Rd., Muskegon, MI 49442 / 616-788-4479 lithibee@att.net

"Little John's" Antique Arms, 1740 W. Laveta, Orange, CA 92668

Littler Sales Co., 20815 W. Chicago, Detroit, MI 48228 / 313-273-6889; FAX: 313-273-1099 littlersales@aol.com

Littleton, J. F., 275 Pinedale Ave., Oroville, CA 95966 / 916-533-6084

Ljutic Industries, Inc., 732 N. 16th Ave., Suite 22, Yakima, WA 98902 / 509-248-0476; FAX: 509-576-8233
ljuticgun@earthlink.net www.ljuticgun.com

Llama Gabilondo Y Cia, Apartado 290, E-01080, Victoria, SPAIN

Lock's Philadelphia Gun Exchange, 6700 Rowland Ave., Philadelphia, PA 19149 / 215-332-6225; FAX: 215-332-4800 locks.gunshop@verizon.net

Lodewick, Walter H., 2816 NE Halsey St., Portland, OR 97232 / 503-284-2554 wlodewick@aol.com

Lodgewood Mfg., P.O. Box 611, Whitewater, WI 53190 / 262-473-5444; FAX: 262-473-6448 lodgewd@idcnet.com
lodgewood.com

Log Cabin Sport Shop, 8010 Lafayette Rd., Lodi, OH 44254 / 330-948-1082; FAX: 330-948-4307
logcabin@logcabinshop.com www.logcabinshop.com

Logan, Harry M., Box 745, Honokaa, HI 96727 / 808-776-1644

279

MANUFACTURER'S DIRECTORY

Logdewood Mfg., P.O. Box 611, Whitewater, WI 53190 / 262-473-5444; FAX: 262-473-6448 lodgewd@idcnet.com www.lodgewood.com

Lohman Mfg. Co., Inc., 4500 Doniphan Dr., P.O. Box 220, Neosho, MO 64850 / 417-451-4438; FAX: 417-451-2576

Lomont Precision Bullets, 278 Sandy Creek Rd., Salmon, ID 83467 / 208-756-6819; FAX: 208-756-6824 www.klomont.com

London Guns Ltd., Box 3750, Santa Barbara, CA 93130 / 805-683-4141; FAX: 805-683-1712

Lone Star Gunleather, 1301 Brushy Bend Dr., Round Rock, TX 78681 / 512-255-1805

Lone Star Rifle Company, 11231 Rose Road, Conroe, TX 77303 / 936-856-3363; FAX: 936-856-3363 dave@lonestar.com

Long, George F., 1402 Kokanee Ln., Grants Pass, OR 97527 / 541-476-0836

Lortone Inc., 2856 NW Market St., Seattle, WA 98107

Lothar Walther Precision Tool Inc., 3425 Hutchinson Rd., Cumming, GA 30040 / 770-889-9998; FAX: 770-889-4919 lotharwalther@mindspring.com www.lothar-walther.com

LPS Laboratories, Inc., 4647 Hugh Howell Rd., P.O. Box 3050, Tucker, GA 30084 / 404-934-7800

Lucas, Edward E, 32 Garfield Ave., East Brunswick, NJ 08816 / 201-251-5526

Lupton, Keith. See: PAWLING MOUNTAIN CLUB

Lyman Instant Targets, Inc. (See Lyman Products Corp.)

Lyman Products Corp., 475 Smith St., Middletown, CT 06457-1541 / 800-423-9704; FAX: 860-632-1699 lymansales@cshore.com www.lymanproducts.com

M

M.H. Canjar Co., 6510 Raleigh St., Arvada, CO 80003 / 303-295-2638; FAX: 303-295-2638

MA Systems, Inc., P.O. Box 894, Pryor, OK 74362-0894 / 918-824-3705; FAX: 918-824-3710

Mac-1 Airgun Distributors, 13974 Van Ness Ave., Gardena, CA 90249-2900 / 310-327-3581; FAX: 310-327-0238 mac1@maclairgun.com www.mac1airgun.com

Machinist's Workshop-Village Press, P.O. Box 1810, Traverse City, MI 49685 / 800-447-7367; FAX: 616-946-3289

Madis Books, 2453 West Five Mile Pkwy., Dallas, TX 75233 / 214-330-7168

Madis, George. See: WINCHESTER CONSULTANTS

MAG Instrument, Inc., 1635 S. Sacramento Ave., Ontario, CA 91761 / 909-947-1006; FAX: 909-947-3116

Magma Engineering Co., P.O. Box 161, 20955 E. Ocotillo Rd., Queen Creek, AZ 85242 / 602-987-9008; FAX: 602-987-0148

Mag-Na-Port International, Inc., 41302 Executive Dr., Harrison Twp., MI 48045-1306 / 586-469-6727; FAX: 586-469-0425 email@magnaport.com www.magnaport.com

Magnum Power Products, Inc., P.O. Box 17768, Fountain Hills, AZ 85268

Magnum Research, Inc., 7110 University Ave. NE, Minneapolis, MN 55432 / 800-772-6168 or 763-574-1868; FAX: 763-574-0109 info@magnumresearch.com

Magnus Bullets, P.O. Box 239, Toney, AL 35773 / 256-420-8359; FAX: 256-420-8360 bulletman@mchsi.com www.magnusbullets.com

Mag-Pack Corp., P.O. Box 846, Chesterland, OH 44026 / 440-285-9480 magpack@hotmail.com

MagSafe Ammo Co., 4700 S US Highway 17/92, Casselberry, FL 32707-3814 / 407-834-9966; FAX: 407-834-8185 www.magsafeonline.com

Magtech Ammunition Co. Inc., 6845 20th Ave. S., Ste. 120, Centerville, MN 55038 / 651-762-8500; FAX: 651-429-9485 www.magtechammunition.com

Mahony, Philip Bruce, 67 White Hollow Rd., Lime Rock, CT 06039-2418 / 860-435-9341 filbalony-redbeard@snet.net

Mahovsky's Metalife, R.D. 1, Box 149a Eureka Road, Grand Valley, PA 16420 / 814-436-7747

Makinson, Nicholas, RR 3, Komoka, ON N0L 1R0 CANADA / 519-471-5462

Mallardtone Game Calls, 10406 96th St., Court West, Taylor Ridge, IL 61284 / 309-798-2481; FAX: 309-798-2501

Mandall Shooting Supply Inc., 5442 E. Cambridge Ave., Phoenix, AZ 85008-1721 / 602-952-0097; FAX: 480-949-0734

Marble Arms (See CRR, Inc./Marble's Inc.)

Marchmon Bullets, 6502 Riverdale Rd., Whitmore Lake, MI 48189

Marent, Rudolf. See: HAMMERLI SERVICE-PRECISION MAC

Mark Lee Supplies, 9901 France Ct., Lakeville, MN 55044 / 952-461-2114; FAX: 952-461-2194 marklee55044@usfamily.net

Markell, Inc., 422 Larkfield Center 235, Santa Rosa, CA 95403 / 707-573-0792; FAX: 707-573-9867

Markesbery Muzzle Loaders, Inc., 7785 Foundation Dr., Ste. 6, Florence, KY 41042 / 606-342-5553 or 606-342-2380

Marksman Products, 5482 Argosy Dr., Huntington Beach, CA 92649 / 714-898-7535; or 800-822-8005; FAX: 714-891-0782

Marlin Firearms Co., 100 Kenna Dr., North Haven, CT 06473 / 203-239-5621; FAX: 203-234-7991 www.marlinfirearms.com

Marocchi F.lli S.p.A, Via Galileo Galilei 8, I-25068 Zanano, ITALY

Marsh, Mike, Croft Cottage, Main St., Derbyshire, DE4 2BY ENGLAND / 01629 650 669

Marshall Enterprises, 792 Canyon Rd., Redwood City, CA 94062

Marshall Fish Mfg. Gunsmith Sptg. Co., 87 Champlain Ave., Westport, NY 12993 / 518-962-4897; FAX: 518-962-4897

Martin B. Retting Inc., 11029 Washington, Culver City, CA 90232 / 213-837-2412 retting@retting.com

Martini & Hagn, 1264 Jimsmith Lake Rd., Cranbrook, BC V1C 6V6 CANADA / 250-417-2926; FAX: 250-417-2928

Martin's Gun Shop, 937 S. Sheridan Blvd., Lakewood, CO 80226 / 303-922-2184

Martz, John V., 8060 Lakeview Lane, Lincoln, CA 95648 FAX: 916-645-3815

Marvel, Alan, 3922 Madonna Rd., Jarretsville, MD 21084 / 301-557-6545

Marx, Harry (See U.S. Importer for FERLIB)

Maryland Paintball Supply, 8507 Harford Rd., Parkville, MD 21234 / 410-882-5607

MAST Technology, Inc., 14555 US Hwy. 95 S., P.O. Box 60969, Boulder City, NV 89006 / 702-293-6969; FAX: 702-293-7255 info@masttechnology.com www.bellammo.com

Master Lock Co., 2600 N. 32nd St., Milwaukee, WI 53245 / 414-444-2800

Match Prep-Doyle Gracey, P.O. Box 155, Tehachapi, CA 93581 / 661-822-5383; FAX: 661-823-8680 gracenotes@csurpers.net www.matchprep.com

Mathews Gun Shop & Gunsmithing, Inc., 10224 S. Paramount Blvd., Downey, CA 90241 / 562-928-2129; FAX: 562-928-8629

Matthews Cutlery, 4401 Sentry Dr. #B, Tucker, GA 30084 / 770-939-6915

Mauser Werke Oberndorf Waffensysteme GmbH, Postfach 1349, 78722, Oberndorf/N., GERMANY

Maverick Arms, Inc., 7 Grasso Ave., P.O. Box 497, North Haven, CT 06473 / 203-230-5300; FAX: 203-230-5420

Maxi-Mount Inc., P.O. Box 291, Willoughby Hills, OH 44096-0291 / 440-944-9456; FAX: 440-944-9456 maximount454@yahoo.com

Mayville Engineering Co. (See MEC, Inc.)

Mazur Restoration, Pete, 13083 Drummer Way, Grass Valley, CA 95949 / 530-268-2412

McCament, Jay. See: JAY MCCAMENT CUSTOM GUNMAKER

McCann, Tom, 14 Walton Dr., New Hope, PA 18938 / 215-862-2728

McCann Industries, P.O. Box 641, Spanaway, WA 98387 / 253-537-6919; FAX: 253-537-6919 mccann.machine@worldnet.att.net www.mccannindustries.com

McCluskey Precision Rifles, 10502 14th Ave. NW, Seattle, WA 98177 / 206-781-2776

McCombs, Leo, 1862 White Cemetery Rd., Patriot, OH 45658 / 740-256-1714

McDonald, Dennis, 8359 Brady St., Peosta, IA 52068 / 319-556-7940

McFarland, Stan, 2221 Idella Ct., Grand Junction, CO 81505 / 970-243-4704

McGhee, Larry. See: B.C. OUTDOORS

McGowen Rifle Barrels, 5961 Spruce Lane, St. Anne, IL 60964 / 815-937-9816; FAX: 815-937-4024

Mchalik, Gary. See: ROSSI FIREARMS

McKenzie, Lynton, 6940 N. Alvernon Way, Tucson, AZ 85718 / 520-299-5090

McMillan Fiberglass Stocks, Inc., 1638 W. Knudsen Dr. #102, Phoenix, AZ 85027 / 623-582-9635; FAX: 623-581-3825 mfsinc@mcmfamily.com www.mcmfamily.com

McMillan Optical Gunsight Co., 28638 N. 42nd St., Cave Creek, AZ 85331 / 602-585-7868; FAX: 602-585-7872

McMillan Rifle Barrels, P.O. Box 3427, Bryan, TX 77805 / 409-690-3456; FAX: 409-690-0156

McMurdo, Lynn, P.O. Box 404, Afton, WY 83110 / 307-886-5535

MCS, Inc., 166 Pocono Rd., Brookfield, CT 06804-2023 / 203-775-1013; FAX: 203-775-9462

McWelco Products, 6730 Santa Fe Ave., Hesperia, CA 92345 / 619-244-8876; FAX: 619-244-9398 products@mcwelco.com www.mcwelco.com

MDS, P.O. Box 1441, Brandon, FL 33509-1441 / 813-653-1180; FAX: 813-684-5953

Meacham Tool & Hardware Co., Inc., 37052 Eberhardt Rd., Peck, ID 83545 / 208-486-7171 smeacham@clearwater.net www.meachamrifles.com

Measurement Group Inc., Box 27777, Raleigh, NC 27611

Measures, Leon. See: SHOOT WHERE YOU LOOK

MEC, Inc., 715 South St., Mayville, WI 53050 reloaders@mayvl.com www.mecreloaders.com

MEC-Gar S.R.L., Via Madonnina 64, Gardone V.T. Brescia, ITALY / 39-030-3733668; FAX: 39-030-3733687 info@mec-gar.it www.mec-gar.it

MEC-Gar U.S.A., Inc., Hurley Farms Industr. Park, 115, Hurley Road 6G, Oxford, CT 06478 / 203-262-1525; FAX: 203-262-1719 mecgar@aol.com www.mec-gar.com

Mech-Tech Systems, Inc., 1602 Foothill Rd., Kalispell, MT 59901 / 406-755-8055

Meister Bullets (See Gander Mountain)

Mele, Frank, 201 S. Wellow Ave., Cookeville, TN 38501 / 615-526-4860

Menck, Gunsmith Inc., T.W., 5703 S 77th St., Ralston, NE 68127

Mendez, John A., 1309 Continental Dr., Daytona Beach, FL 32117-3807 / 407-344-2791

Men-Metallwerk Elisenhuette GmbH, P.O. Box 1263, Nassau/Lahn, D-56372 GERMANY / 2604-7819

Meprolight (See Hesco-Meprolight)

Mercer Custom Guns, 216 S. Whitewater Ave., Jefferson, WI 53549 / 920-674-3839

Merit Corp., P.O. Box 9044, Schenectady, NY 12309 / 518-346-1420 sales@meritcorporation.com www.meritcorporation.com

Merkel, Schutzenstrasse 26, D-98527 Suhl, Suhl, GERMANY FAX: 011-49-3681-854-203 www.merkel-waffen.de

Metal Merchants, P.O. Box 186, Walled Lake, MI 48390-0186

Metalife Industries (See Mahovsky's Metalife)

Michael's Antiques, Box 591, Waldoboro, ME 04572

Michaels of Oregon Co., P.O. Box 1690, Oregon City, OR 97045 www.michaels-oregon.com

Micro Sight Co., 242 Harbor Blvd., Belmont, CA 94002 / 415-591-0769; FAX: 415-591-7531

Microfusion Alfa S.A., Paseo San Andres N8, P.O. Box 271, Eibar 20600, 20600 SPAIN / 34-43-11-89-16; FAX: 34-43-11-40-38

Mid-America Recreation, Inc., 1328 5th Ave., Moline, IL 61265 / 309-764-5089; FAX: 309-764-5089 fmilcusguns@aol.com www.midamericarecreation.com

Middlebrooks Custom Shop, 7366 Colonial Trail East, Surry, VA 23883 / 757-357-0881; FAX: 757-365-0442

Midway Arms, Inc., 5875 W. Van Horn Tavern Rd., Columbia, MO 65203 / 800-243-3220; FAX: 800-992-8312 www.midwayusa.com

Midwest Gun Sport, 1108 Herbert Dr., Zebulon, NC 27597 / 919-269-5570

Midwest Shooting School, The, Pat LaBoone, 2550 Hwy. 23, Wrenshall, MN 55797 / 218-384-3670 shootingschool@starband.net

Midwest Sport Distributors, Box 129, Fayette, MO 65248

Mike Davis Products, 643 Loop Dr., Moses Lake, WA 98837 / 509-765-6178; or 509-766-7281

Mike Yee Custom Stocking, 29927 56 Pl. S., Auburn, WA 98001 / 253-839-3991

Military Armament Corp., P.O. Box 120, Mt. Zion Rd., Lingleville, TX 76461 / 817-965-3253

Millennium Designed Muzzleloaders, P.O. Box 536, Routes 11 & 25, Limington, ME 04049 / 207-637-2316

Miller Arms, Inc., P.O. Box 260 Purl St., St. Onge, SD 57779 / 605-642-5160; FAX: 605-642-5160

Miller Custom, 210 E. Julia, Clinton, IL 61727 / 217-935-9362

Miller Single Trigger Mfg. Co., 6680 Rt. 5-20, P.O. Box 471, Bloomfield, NY 14469 / 585-657-6338

Millett Sights, 7275 Murdy Circle, Adm. Office, Huntington Beach, CA 92647 / 714-842-5575 or 800-645-5388; FAX: 714-843-5707

Mills Jr., Hugh B., 3615 Canterbury Rd., New Bern, NC 28560 / 919-637-4631

Milstor Corp., 80-975 Indio Blvd. C-7, Indio, CA 92201 / 760-775-9998; FAX: 760-775-5229 milstor@webtv.net

Minute Man High Tech Industries, 10611 Canyon Rd. E., Suite 151, Puyallup, WA 98373 / 800-233-2734

Mirador Optical Corp., P.O. Box 11614, Marina Del Rey, CA 90295-7614 / 310-821-5587; FAX: 310-305-0386

Mitchell, Jack, c/o Geoff Gaebe, Addieville East Farm, 200 Pheasant Dr., Mapleville, RI 02839 / 401-568-3185

Mitchell Bullets, R.F., 430 Walnut St., Westernport, MD 21562

Mitchell Mfg. Corp., P.O. Box 9295, Fountain Valley, CA 92728 / 714-444-2220

MANUFACTURER'S DIRECTORY

Mitchell Optics, Inc., 2072 CR 1100 N, Sidney, IL 61877 / 217-688-2219; or 217-621-3018; FAX: 217-688-2505 mitchell@attglobal.net
Mitchell's Accuracy Shop, 68 Greenridge Dr., Stafford, VA 22554 / 703-659-0165
Mitchell's Mauser, P.O. Box 9295, Fountain Valley, CA 92728 / 714-979-7663; FAX: 714-899-3660
MI-TE Bullets, 1396 Ave. K, Ellsworth, KS 67439 / 785-472-4575; FAX: 785-472-5579
Mittleman, William, P.O. Box 65, Etna, CA 96027
Mixson Corp., 7635 W. 28th Ave., Hialeah, FL 33016 / 305-821-5190; or 800-327-0078; FAX: 305-558-9318
MJK Gunsmithing, Inc., 417 N. Huber Ct., E. Wenatchee, WA 98802 / 509-884-7683
MKS Supply, Inc. (See Hi-Point Firearms)
MMC, 2700 W. Sahara Ave. 440, Las Vegas, NV 89102-1703 / 817-831-9557; FAX: 817-834-5508
MOA Corporation, 2451 Old Camden Pike, Eaton, OH 45320 / 937-456-3669 www.moaguns.com
Mobile Area Networks, Inc., 2772 Depot St., Sanford, FL 32773 / 407-333-2350; FAX: 407-333-9903 georgew@mobilan.com
Modern Gun Repair School, P.O. Box 846, Saint Albans, VT 05478 / 802-524-2223; FAX: 802-524-2053 jfwp@dlilearn.com www.mgsinfoadlifearn.com
Modern Muzzleloading, Inc., P.O. Box 130, Centerville, IA 52544 / 515-856-2626
Moeller, Steve, 1213 4th St., Fulton, IL 61252 / 815-589-2300
Mogul Co./Life Jacket, 500 N. Kimball Rd., Ste. 109, South Lake, TX 76092
Monell Custom Guns, 228 Red Mills Rd., Pine Bush, NY 12566 / 914-744-3021
Moneymaker Guncraft Corp., 1420 Military Ave., Omaha, NE 68131 / 402-556-0226
Montana Armory, Inc., 100 Centennial Dr., P.O. Box 885, Big Timber, MT 59011 / 406-932-4353; FAX: 406-932-4443
Montana Outfitters, Lewis E. Yearout, 308 Riverview Dr. E., Great Falls, MT 59404 / 406-761-0859; or 406-727-4560
Montana Precision Swaging, P.O. Box 4746, Butte, MT 59702 / 406-494-0600; FAX: 406-494-0600
Montana Rifleman, Inc., 2593A Hwy. 2 East, Kalispell, MT 59901 / 406-755-4867
Montana Vintage Arms, 2354 Bear Canyon Rd., Bozeman, MT 59715
Morini (See U.S. Importers-Mandall Shooting Supplies, Inc.)
Morrison Custom Rifles, J. W., 4015 W Sharon, Phoenix, AZ 85029 / 602-978-3754
Morrison Precision, 6719 Calle Mango, Hereford, AZ 85615 / 520-378-6207 morprec@c2i2.com
Morrow, Bud, 11 Hillside Lane, Sheridan, WY 82801-9729 / 307-674-8360
Morton Booth Co., P.O. Box 123, Joplin, MO 64802 / 417-673-1962; FAX: 417-673-3642
Mo's Competitor Supplies (See MCS, Inc.)
Moss Double Tone, Inc., P.O. Box 1112, 2101 S. Kentucky, Sedalia, MO 65301 / 816-827-0827
Mountain Plains Industries, 3720 Otter Place, Lynchburg, VA 24503 / 800-687-3000; FAX: 434-845-6594 MPItargets@verizon.net
Mowrey Gun Works, P.O. Box 246, Waldron, IN 46182 / 317-525-6181; FAX: 317-525-9595
Mowrey's Guns & Gunsmithing, 119 Fredericks St., Canajoharie, NY 13317 / 518-673-3483
MPC, P.O. Box 450, McMinnville, TN 37110-0450 / 615-473-5513; FAX: 615-473-5516 thebox@blomand.net www.mpc-thebox.com
MPI Stocks, P.O. Box 83266, Portland, OR 97283 / 503-226-1215; FAX: 503-226-2661
MSR Targets, P.O. Box 1042, West Covina, CA 91793 / 818-331-7840
MTM Molded Products Co., Inc., 3370 Obco Ct., Dayton, OH 45414 / 937-890-7461; FAX: 937-890-1747
Mulberry House Publishing, P.O. Box 2180, Apache Junction, AZ 85217 / 888-738-1567; FAX: 480-671-1015
Mulhern, Rick, Rt. 5, Box 152, Rayville, LA 71269 / 318-728-2688
Mullins Ammunition, Rt. 2 Box 304N, Clintwood, VA 24228 / 276-926-6772; FAX: 276-926-6092 mammo@extremeshockusa.com www.extremeshockusa.com
Mullis Guncraft, 3523 Lawyers Road E., Monroe, NC 28110 / 704-283-6683
Multiplex International, 26 S. Main St., Concord, NH 03301 FAX: 603-796-2223
Multipropulseurs, La Bertrandiere, 42580, FRANCE / 77 74 01 30; FAX: 77 93 19 34
Mundy, Thomas A., 69 Robbins Road, Somerville, NJ 08876 / 201-722-2199
Murmur Corp., 2823 N. Westmoreland Ave., Dallas, TX 75222 / 214-630-5400

Murphy, R.R. Murphy Co., Inc. See: MURPHY, R.R. CO., INC.
Murphy, R.R. Co., Inc., R.R. Murphy Co., Inc. Murphy, P.O. Box 102, Ripley, TN 38063 / 901-635-4003; FAX: 901-635-2320
Murray State College, 1 Murray Campus St., Tishomingo, OK 73460 / 508-371-2371 darnold@mscol.edu
Muscle Products Corp., 112 Fennell Dr., Butler, PA 16002 / 800-227-7049; or 724-283-0567; FAX: 724-283-8310 mpc@mpc_home.com www.mpc_home.com
Muzzleloaders Etcetera, Inc., 9901 Lyndale Ave. S., Bloomington, MN 55420 / 952-884-1161 www.muzzleloaders-etcetera.com
MWG Co., P.O. Box 971202, Miami, FL 33197 / 800-428-9394; or 305-253-8393; FAX: 305-232-1247

N

N.B.B., Inc., 24 Elliot Rd., Sterling, MA 01564 / 508-422-7538; or 800-942-9444
N.C. Ordnance Co., P.O. Box 3254, Wilson, NC 27895 / 919-237-2440; FAX: 919-243-9845
Nagel's Custom Bullets, 100 Scott St., Baytown, TX 77520-2849
Nalpak, 1937-C Friendship Drive, El Cajon, CA 92020 / 619-258-1200
Nammo Lapua Oy, P.O. Box 5, Lapua, FINLAND / 358-6-4310111; FAX: 358-6-4310317 info@nammo.ti www.lapua.com
Nastoff, Steve. See: NASTOFFS 45 SHOP, INC.
Nastoffs 45 Shop, Inc., Steve Nastoff, 1057 Laverne Dr., Youngstown, OH 44511
National Bullet Co., 1585 E. 361 St., Eastlake, OH 44095 / 216-951-1854; FAX: 216-951-7761
National Target Co., 3958-D Dartmouth Ct., Frederick, MD 21703 / 800-827-7060; FAX: 301-874-4764
Nationwide Airgun Repair, 2310 Windsor Forest Dr., Louisville, KY 40272 / 502-937-2614; FAX: 812-637-1463 shortshoestring@insightbb.com
Naval Ordnance Works, 467 Knott Rd., Sheperdstown, WV 25443 / 304-876-0998; FAX: 304-876-0998 nvordfdy@earthlink.net
Navy Arms Co., 219 Lawn St., Martinsburg, WV 25401 / 304-262-9870; FAX: 304-262-1658
Navy Arms Company, Valmore J. Forgett Jr., 815 22nd Street, Union City, NJ 07087 / 201-863-7100; FAX: 201-863-8770 info@navyarms.com www.navyarms.com
NCP Products, Inc., 3500 12th St. N.W., Canton, OH 44708 / 330-456-5130; FAX: 330-456-5234
Necessary Concepts, Inc., P.O. Box 571, Deer Park, NY 11729 / 516-667-8509; FAX: 516-667-8588
NEI Handtools, Inc., 10960 Gary Player Dr., El Paso, TX 79935
Neil A. Jones Custom Products, 17217 Brookhouser Road, Saegertown, PA 16433 / 814-763-2769; FAX: 814-763-4228
Nelson, Gary K., 975 Terrace Dr., Oakdale, CA 95361 / 209-847-4590
Nelson, Stephen. See: NELSON'S CUSTOM GUNS, INC.
Nelson's Custom Guns, Inc., Stephen Nelson, 7430 Valley View Dr. N.W., Corvallis, OR 97330 / 541-745-5232 nelsons-custom@attbi.com
Nesci Enterprises Inc., P.O. Box 119, Summit St., East Hampton, CT 06424 / 203-267-2588
Nesika Bay Precision, 22239 Big Valley Rd., Poulsbo, WA 98370 / 206-697-3830
Nettestad Gun Works, 38962 160th Avenue, Pelican Rapids, MN 56572 / 218-863-1338
Neumann GmbH, Am Galgenberg 6, 90575, GERMANY / 09101/8258; FAX: 09101/6356
New England Ammunition Co., 1771 Post Rd. East, Suite 223, Westport, CT 06880 / 203-254-8048
New England Arms Co., Box 278, Lawrence Lane, Kittery Point, ME 03905 / 207-439-0593; FAX: 207-439-0525 info@newenglandarms.com www.newenglandarms.com
New England Custom Gun Service, 438 Willow Brook Rd., Plainfield, NH 03781 / 603-469-3450; FAX: 603-469-3471 bestguns@adelphia.net www.newenglandcustom.com
New Orleans Jewelers Supply Co., 206 Charters St., New Orleans, LA 70130 / 504-523-3839; FAX: 504-523-3836
New SKB Arms Co., C.P.O. Box 1401, Tokyo, JAPAN / 81-3-3943-9550; FAX: 81-3-3943-0695
New Ultra Light Arms, LLC, P.O. Box 340, Granville, WV 26534
Newark Electronics, 4801 N. Ravenswood Ave., Chicago, IL 60640
Newell, Robert H., 55 Coyote, Los Alamos, NM 87544 / 505-662-7135
Newman Gunshop, 2035 Chester Ave. #411, Ottumwa, IA 52501-3715 / 515-937-5775
NgraveR Co., The, 67 Wawecus Hill Rd., Bozrah, CT 06334 / 860-823-1533; FAX: 860-887-6252 ngraver98@aol.com www.ngraver.com

Nicholson Custom, 17285 Thornlay Road, Hughesville, MO 65334 / 816-826-8746
Nickels, Paul R., 4328 Seville St., Las Vegas, NV 89121 / 702-435-5318
Niemi Engineering, W. B., Box 126 Center Rd., Greensboro, VT 05841 / 802-533-7180; FAX: 802-533-7141
Nikon, Inc., 1300 Walt Whitman Rd., Melville, NY 11747 / 516-547-8623; FAX: 516-547-0309
Noreen, Peter H., 5075 Buena Vista Dr., Belgrade, MT 59714 / 406-586-7383
Norica, Avnda Otaola, 16 Apartado 68, Eibar, SPAIN
Norinco, 7A Yun Tan N, Beijing, CHINA
Norincoptics (See BEC, Inc.)
Norma Precision AB (See U.S. Importers-Dynamit)
Normark Corp., 10395 Yellow Circle Dr., Minnetonka, MN 55343-9101 / 612-933-7060; FAX: 612-933-0046
North American Arms, Inc., 2150 South 950 East, Provo, UT 84606-6285 / 800-821-5783; or 801-374-9990; FAX: 801-374-9998
North American Correspondence Schools, The Gun Pro, Oak & Pawney St., Scranton, PA 18515 / 717-342-7701
North American Shooting Systems, P.O. Box 306, Osoyoos, BC V0H 1V0 CANADA / 250-495-3131; FAX: 250-495-3131 rifle@cablerocket.com
North Devon Firearms Services, 3 North St., Braunton, EX33 1AJ ENGLAND / 01271 813624; FAX: 01271 813624
North Mountain Pine Training Center (See Executive Protection Institute)
North Star West, P.O. Box 488, Glencoe, CA 95232 / 209-293-7010 northstarwest.com
Northern Precision, 329 S. James St., Carthage, NY 13619 / 315-493-1711
Northside Gun Shop, 2725 NW 109th, Oklahoma City, OK 73120 / 405-840-2353
Northwest Arms, 26884 Pearl Rd., Parma, ID 83660 / 208-722-6771; FAX: 208-722-1062
Northwest Custom Projectile, P.O. Box 127, Butte, MT 59703-0127 www.customprojectile.com
No-Sho Mfg. Co., 10727 Glenfield Ct., Houston, TX 77096 / 713-723-5332
Nosler, Inc., P.O. Box 671, Bend, OR 97709 / 800-285-3701; or 541-382-3921; FAX: 541-388-4667 www.nosler.com
Novak's, Inc., 1206 1/2 30th St., P.O. Box 4045, Parkersburg, WV 26101 / 304-485-9295; FAX: 304-428-6722 www.novaksights.com
Nowlin Mfg. Co., 20622 S 4092 Rd., Claremore, OK 74017 / 918-342-0689; FAX: 918-342-0624 nowlinguns@msn.com nowlinguns.com
NRI Gunsmith School, P.O. Box 182968, Columbus, OH 43218-2968
Nu Line Guns, 8150 CR 4055, Rhineland, MO 65069 / 573-676-5500; FAX: 314-447-5018 nlg@ktis.net
Null Holsters Ltd. K.L., 161 School St. N.W., Resaca, GA 30735 / 706-625-5643; FAX: 706-625-9392 ken@klnullholsters.com www.klnullholsters.com
Numrich Gun Parts Corporation, 226 Williams Lane, P.O. Box 299, West Hurley, NY 12491 / 866-686-7424; FAX: 877-GUNPART info@gunpartscorp.com www.e-gunparts.com
Nygord Precision Products, Inc., P.O. Box 12578, Prescott, AZ 86304 / 928-717-2315; FAX: 928-717-2198 nygords@northlink.com www.nygordprecision.com

O

O.F. Mossberg & Sons, Inc., 7 Grasso Ave., North Haven, CT 06473 / 203-230-5300; FAX: 203-230-5420
Oakman Turkey Calls, RD 1, Box 825, Harrisonville, PA 17228 / 717-485-4620
Obermeyer Rifled Barrels, 23122 60th St., Bristol, WI 53104 / 262-843-3537; FAX: 262-843-2129 www.obermeyerbarrels.com
October Country Muzzleloading, P.O. Box 969, Dept. GD, Hayden, ID 83835 / 208-772-2068; FAX: 208-772-9230 ocinfo@octobercountry.com www.octobercountry.com
Oehler Research, Inc., P.O. Box 9135, Austin, TX 78766 / 512-327-6900; or 800-531-5125; FAX: 512-327-6903 www.oehler-research.com
Oil Rod and Gun Shop, 69 Oak St., East Douglas, MA 01516 / 508-476-3687
OK Weber, Inc., P.O. Box 7485, Eugene, OR 97401 / 541-747-0458; FAX: 541-747-5927 okweber@pacinfo www.okweber.com
Oker's Engraving, P.O. Box 126, Shawnee, CO 80475 / 303-838-6042
Oklahoma Ammunition Co., 3701A S. Harvard Ave., No. 367, Tulsa, OK 74135-2265 / 918-396-3187; FAX: 918-396-4270
Oklahoma Leather Products, Inc., 500 26th NW, Miami, OK 74354 / 918-542-6651; FAX: 918-542-6653

MANUFACTURER'S DIRECTORY

Olathe Gun Shop, 716-A South Rogers Road, Olathe, KS 66062 / 913-782-6900; FAX: 913-782-6902 info@olathegunshop.com www.olathegunshop.com
Old Wagon Bullets, 32 Old Wagon Rd., Wilton, CT 06897
Old West Bullet Moulds, J. Ken Chapman, P.O. Box 519, Flora Vista, NM 87415 / 505-334-6970
Old West Reproductions, Inc. R.M. Bachman, 446 Florence S. Loop, Florence, MT 59833 / 406-273-2615; FAX: 406-273-2615 rick@oldwestreproductions.com www.oldwestreproductions.com
Old Western Scrounger Ammunition Inc., 50 Industrial Parkway, Carson City, NV 89706 / 775-246-2091; FAX: 775-246-2095 www.ows-ammunition.com
Old World Gunsmithing, 2901 SE 122nd St., Portland, OR 97236 / 503-760-7681
Ole Frontier Gunsmith Shop, 2617 Hwy. 29 S., Cantonment, FL 32533 / 904-477-8074
Olson, Myron, 989 W. Kemp, Watertown, SD 57201 / 605-886-9787
Olson, Vic, 5002 Countryside Dr., Imperial, MO 63052 / 314-296-8086
Olympic Arms Inc., 620-626 Old Pacific Hwy. SE, Olympia, WA 98513 / 360-456-3471; FAX: 360-491-3447 info@olyarms.com www.olyarms.com
Olympic Optical Co., P.O. Box 752377, Memphis, TN 38175-2377 / 901-794-3890; or 800-238-7120; FAX: 901-794-0676
Omega Sales, P.O. Box 1066, Mt. Clemens, MI 48043 / 810-469-7323; FAX: 810-469-0425
One Of A Kind, 15610 Purple Sage, San Antonio, TX 78255 / 512-695-3364
One Ragged Hole, P.O. Box 13624, Tallahassee, FL 32317-3624
Op-Tec, P.O. Box L632, Langhorn, PA 19047 / 215-757-5037; FAX: 215-757-7097
Optical Services Co., P.O. Box 1174, Santa Teresa, NM 88008-1174 / 505-589-3833
Orchard Park Enterprise, P.O. Box 563, Orchard Park, NY 14127 / 616-656-0356
Ordnance Works, The, 2969 Pigeon Point Rd., Eureka, CA 95501 / 707-443-3252
Oregon Arms, Inc. (See Rogue Rifle Co., Inc.)
Oregon Trail Bullet Company, P.O. Box 529, Dept. P, Baker City, OR 97814 / 800-811-0548; FAX: 514-523-1803
Original Box, Inc., 700 Linden Ave., York, PA 17404 / 717-854-2897; FAX: 717-845-4276
Original Deer Formula Co., The, P.O. Box 1705, Dickson, TN 37056 / 800-874-6965; FAX: 615-446-0646 deerformula1@aol.com www.deerformula.com
Orion Rifle Barrel Co., RR2, 137 Cobler Village, Kalispell, MT 59901 / 406-257-5649
Orvis Co., The, Rt. 7, Manchester, VT 05254 / 802-362-3622; FAX: 802-362-3525
Otis Technology, Inc., RR 1 Box 84, Boonville, NY 13309 / 315-942-3320
Ottmar, Maurice, Box 657, 113 E. Fir, Coulee City, WA 99115 / 509-632-5717
Outa-Site Gun Carriers, 219 Market St., Laredo, TX 78040 / 210-722-4678; or 800-880-9715; FAX: 210-726-4858
Outdoor Connection, Inc., The, 7901 Panther Way, Waco, TX 76712-6556 / 800-533-6076; FAX: 254-776-3553 info@outdoorconnection.com www.outdoorconnection.com
Outdoor Edge Cutlery Corp., 4699 Nautilus Ct. S. Ste. 503, Boulder, CO 80301-5310 / 303-530-7667; FAX: 303-530-7020 www.outdooredge.com
Outdoor Enthusiast, 3784 W. Woodland, Springfield, MO 65807 / 417-883-9841
Outdoor Sports Headquarters, Inc., 967 Watertower Ln., West Carrollton, OH 45449 / 513-865-5855; FAX: 513-865-5962
Outers Laboratories Div. of ATK, Route 2, P.O. Box 39, Onalaska, WI 54650 / 608-781-5800; FAX: 608-781-0368
Ox-Yoke Originals, Inc., 34 Main St., Milo, ME 04463 / 800-231-8313; or 207-943-7351; FAX: 207-943-2416
Ozark Gun Works, 11830 Cemetery Rd., Rogers, AR 72756 / 479-631-1024; FAX: 479-631-1024 ozarkgunworks@cox.net www.geocities.com

P

P&M Sales & Services, LLC, 4697 Tote Rd. Bldg. H-B, Comins, MI 48619 / 989-848-8364; FAX: 989-848-8364 info@pmsales-online.com
P.S.M.G. Gun Co., 10 Park Ave., Arlington, MA 02174 / 781-646-1699; FAX: 781-643-7212 psmg2@aol.com
Pachmayr Div. Lyman Products, 475 Smith St., Middletown, CT 06457 / 860-632-2020; or 800-225-9626; FAX: 860-632-1699 lymansales@cshore.com www.pachmayr.com

Pacific Armament Corp, 4813 Enterprise Way, Unit K, Modesto, CA 95356 / 209-545-2800 gunsparts@att.net
Pacific Rifle Co., P.O. Box 841, Carlton, OR 97111 / 503-852-6276 pacificrifle@aol.com
PAC-NOR Barreling, 99299 Overlook Rd., P.O. Box 6188, Brookings, OR 97415 / 503-469-7330; FAX: 503-469-7331 info@pac-nor.com www.pac-nor.com
PACT, Inc., P.O. Box 535025, Grand Prairie, TX 75053 / 972-641-0049; FAX: 972-641-2641
Page Custom Bullets, P.O. Box 25, Port Moresby, NEW GUINEA
Pagel Gun Works, Inc., 2 SE 1st St., Grand Rapids, MN 55744
Pager Pal, 200 W Pleasantview, Hurst, TX 76054 / 800-561-1603; FAX: 817-285-8769 www.pagerpal.com
Paintball Games International Magazine Aceville, Castle House 97 High St., Essex, ENGLAND / 011-44-206-564840
Palsa Outdoor Products, P.O. Box 81336, Lincoln, NE 68501 / 402-488-5288; FAX: 402-488-2321
Pansch, Robert F, 1004 Main St. #10, Neenah, WI 54956 / 920-725-8175
Paragon Sales & Services, Inc., 2501 Theodore St., Crest Hill, IL 60435-1613 / 815-725-9212; FAX: 815-725-8974
Para-Ordnance Mfg., Inc., 980 Tapscott Rd., Scarborough, ON M1X 1E7 CANADA / 416-297-7855; FAX: 416-297-1289
Para-Ordnance, Inc., 1919 NE 45th St., Ste 215, Ft. Lauderdale, FL 33308 info@paraord.com www.paraord.com
Pardini Armi Srl, Via Italica 154, 55043, Lido Di Camaiore Lu, ITALY / 584-90121; FAX: 584-90122
Paris, Frank J., 17417 Pershing St., Livonia, MI 48152-3822
Park Rifle Co., Ltd., The, Unit 6a Dartford Trade Park, Power Mill Lane, Dartford DA7 7NX, ENGLAND / 011-0322-222512
Parker & Sons Shooting Supply, 9337 Smoky Row Road, Strawberry Plains, TN 37871 / 865-933-3286; FAX: 865-932-8586
Parker Gun Finishes, 9337 Smokey Row Rd., Strawberry Plains, TN 37871 / 865-933-3286; FAX: 865-932-8586 parcraft7838@netzero.com
Parsons Optical Mfg. Co., PO Box 192, Ross, OH 45061 / 513-867-0820; FAX: 513-867-8380 psscopes@concentric.net
Partridge Sales Ltd., John, Trent Meadows, Rugeley, ENGLAND
Pasadena Gun Center, 206 E. Shaw, Pasadena, TX 77506 / 713-472-0417; FAX: 713-472-1322
Passive Bullet Traps, Inc. (See Savage Range Systems, Inc.)
Paterson Gunsmithing, 438 Main St., Paterson, NJ 07502 / 201-345-4100
Pathfinder Sports Leather, 2920 E. Chambers St., Phoenix, AZ 85040 / 602-276-0016
Patrick W. Price Bullets, 16520 Worthley Drive, San Lorenzo, CA 94580 / 510-278-1547
Pattern Control, 114 N. Third St., P.O. Box 462105, Garland, TX 75046 / 214-494-3551; FAX: 214-272-8447
Paul A. Harris Hand Engraving, 113 Rusty Lane, Boerne, TX 78006-5746 / 512-391-5121
Paul and Sharon Dressel, 209 N. 92nd Ave., Yakima, WA 98908 / 509-966-9233; FAX: 509-966-3365 dressels@nwinfo.net www.dressels.com
Paul Co., The, 27385 Pressonville Rd., Wellsville, KS 66092 / 785-883-4444; FAX: 785-883-2525
Paul D. Hillmer Custom Gunstocks, 7251 Hudson Heights, Hudson, IA 50643 / 319-988-3941
Paul Jones Moulds, 4901 Telegraph Rd., Los Angeles, CA 90022 / 213-262-1510
Paulsen Gunstocks, Rt. 71, Box 11, Chinook, MT 59523 / 406-357-3403
Pawling Mountain Club, Keith Lupton, P.O. Box 573, Pawling, NY 12564 / 914-855-3825
Paxton Quigley's Personal Protection Strategies, 9903 Santa Monica Blvd., 300, Beverly Hills, CA 90212 / 310-281-1762 www.defend-net.com/paxton
Payne Photography, Robert, Robert, P.O. Box 141471, Austin, TX 78714 / 512-272-4554
Peacemaker Specialists, P.O. Box 157, Whitmore, CA 96096 / 530-472-3438 www.peacemakerspecialists.com
Pearce Grip, Inc., P.O. Box 40367, Fort Worth, TX 76140 / 817-568-9704; FAX: 817-568-9707 info@pearcegrip.com www.pearcegrip.com
PECAR Herbert Schwarz GmbH, Kreuzbergstrasse 6, 10965, Berlin, GERMANY / 004930-785-7383; FAX: 004930-785-1934 michael.schwart@pecar-berlin.de www.pecar-berlin.de
Pecatonica River Longrifle, 5205 Nottingham Dr., Rockford, IL 61111 / 815-968-1995; FAX: 815-968-1996
Pedersen, C. R., 2717 S. Pere Marquette Hwy., Ludington, MI 49431 / 231-843-2061; FAX: 231-845-7695 fega@fega.com

Pedersen, Rex C., 2717 S. Pere Marquette Hwy., Ludington, MI 49431 / 231-843-2061; FAX: 231-845-7695 fega@fega.com
Peifer Rifle Co., P.O. Box 220, Nokomis, IL 62075
Pejsa Ballistics, 1314 Marquette Ave., Apt 906, Minneapolis, MN 55403 / 612-332-5073; FAX: 612-332-5204 pejsa@sprintmail.com pejsa
Peltor, Inc. (See Aero Peltor)
PEM's Mfg. Co., 5063 Waterloo Rd., Atwater, OH 44201 / 216-947-3721
Pence Precision Barrels, 7567 E. 900 S., S. Whitley, IN 46787 / 219-839-4745
Pendleton Royal, c/o Swingler Buckland Ltd., 4/7 Highgate St., Birmingham, ENGLAND / 44 121 440 3060; or 44 121 446 5898; FAX: 44 121 446 4165
Pendleton Woolen Mills, P.O. Box 3030, 220 N.W. Broadway, Portland, OR 97208 / 503-226-4801
Penn Bullets, P.O. Box 756, Indianola, PA 15051
Pennsylvania Gun Parts Inc., RR 7 Box 150, Mount Pleasant, PA 15666
Pennsylvania Gunsmith School, 812 Ohio River Blvd., Avalon, Pittsburgh, PA 15202 / 412-766-1812; FAX: 412-766-0855 pgs@pagunsmith.com www.pagunsmith.com
Penrod, Mark. See: PENROD PRECISION
Penrod Precision, Mark Penrod, 312 College Ave., P.O. Box 307, N. Manchester, IN 46962 / 260-982-8385; FAX: 260-982-1819 markpenrod@kconline.com
Pentax U.S.A. Inc., 600 12th St. Ste. 300, Golden, CO 80401 / 303-799-8000; FAX: 303-460-1628 www.pentaxlightseeker.com
Pentheny de Pentheny, c/o H.P. Okelly, 321 S. Main St., Sebastopol, CA 95472 / 707-824-1637; FAX: 707-824-1637
Perazone-Gunsmith, Brian, Cold Spring Rd., Roxbury, NY 12474 / 607-326-4088; FAX: 607-326-3140 bpgunsmith@catskill.net www.bpgunsmith.catskill.net
Perazzi U.S.A. Inc., 1010 West Tenth, Azusa, CA 91702 / 626-334-1234; FAX: 626-334-0344 perazziusa@aol.com
Performance Specialists, 308 Eanes School Rd., Austin, TX 78746 / 512-327-0119
Perugini Visini & Co. S.r.l., Via Camprelle, 126, 25080 Nuvolera, ITALY / 30-6897535; FAX: 30-6897821 peruvisi@virgilia.it
Pete de Coux Auction House, 14940 Brenda Dr., Prescott, AZ 86305-7447 / 928-776-8285; FAX: 928-776-8276 pdbullets@commspeed.net
Pete Mazur Restoration, 13083 Drummer Way, Grass Valley, CA 95949 / 530-268-2412; FAX: 530-268-2412
Pete Rickard, Inc., 115 Roy Walsh Rd, Cobleskill, NY 12043 / 518-234-2731: FAX: 518-234-2454 rickard@telenet.net www.peterickard.com
Peter Dyson & Son Ltd., 3 Cuckoo Lane, Honley, Holmfirth, West Yorkshire, HD9 6AS ENGLAND / 44-1484-661062; FAX: 44-1484-663709 peter@peterdyson.co.uk www.peterdyson.co.uk
Peter Hale/Engraver, 997 Maple Dr., Spanish Fork, UT 84660-2524 / 801-798-8215
Peters Stahl GmbH, Stettiner Strasse 42, D-33106, Paderborn, GERMANY / 05251-750025; FAX: 05251-75611
Peterson Gun Shop, Inc., A.W., 4255 W. Old U.S. 441, Mt. Dora, FL 32757-3299 / 352-383-4258; FAX: 352-735-1001
Petro-Explo Inc., 7650 U.S. Hwy. 287, Suite 100, Arlington, TX 76017 / 817-478-8888
Pettinger Books, Gerald, 47827 300th Ave., Russell, IA 50238 / 641-535-2239 gpettinger@lisco.com
Pflumm Mfg. Co., 10662 Widmer Rd., Lenexa, KS 66215 / 800-888-4867; FAX: 913-451-7857
PFRB Co., P.O. Box 1242, Bloomington, IL 61702 / 309-473-3964; or 800-914-5464; FAX: 309-473-2161
Philip S. Olt Co., P.O. Box 550, 12662 Fifth St., Pekin, IL 61554 / 309-348-3633; FAX: 309-348-3300
Phillippi Custom Bullets, Justin, P.O. Box 773, Ligonier, PA 15658 / 724-238-2962; FAX: 724-238-9671 jrp@wpa.net http://www.wpa.net~jrphil
Phillips & Rogers, Inc., 852 FM 980 Rd., Conroe, TX 77320 / 409-435-0011
Phoenix Arms, 4231 Brickell St., Ontario, CA 91761 / 909-937-6900; FAX: 909-937-0060
Piedmont Community College, P.O. Box 1197, Roxboro, NC 27573 / 336-599-1181; FAX: 336-597-3817 www.piedmont.cc.nc.us
Pietta (See U.S. Importers-Navy Arms Co, Taylor's
Pine Technical College, 1100 4th St., Pine City, MN 55063 / 800-521-7463; FAX: 612-629-6766
Pinetree Bullets, 133 Skeena St., Kitimat, BC V8C 1Z1 CANADA / 604-632-3768; FAX: 604-632-3768
Pioneer Arms Co., 355 Lawrence Rd., Broomall, PA 19008 / 215-356-5203

MANUFACTURER'S DIRECTORY

Piotti (See U.S. Importer-Moore & Co., Wm. Larkin)

Piquette, Paul. See: PIQUETTE'S CUSTOM ENGRAVING

Piquette's Custom Engraving, Paul R. Piquette, 511 Southwick St., Feeding Hills, MA 01030 / 413-789-4582 ppiquette@comcast.net www.pistoldynamics.com

Plaza Cutlery, Inc., 3333 Bristol, 161 South Coast Plaza, Costa Mesa, CA 92626 / 714-549-3932

Plum City Ballistic Range, N2162 80th St., Plum City, WI 54761 / 715-647-2539

PlumFire Press, Inc., 30-A Grove Ave., Patchogue, NY 11772-4112 / 800-695-7246; FAX: 516-758-4071

PMC/Eldorado Cartridge Corp., P.O. Box 62508, 12801 U.S. Hwy. 95 S., Boulder City, NV 89005 / 702-294-0025; FAX: 702-294-0121 kbauer@pmcammo.com www.pmcammo.com

Poburka, Philip (See Bison Studios)

Pointing Dog Journal, Village Press Publications, P.O. Box 968, Dept. PGD, Traverse City, MI 49685 / 800-272-3246; FAX: 616-946-3289

Police Bookshelf, P.O. Box 122, Concord, NH 03301 / 603-224-6814; FAX: 603-226-3554

Polywad, Inc., P.O. Box 7916, Macon, GA 31209 / 478-477-0669; or 800-998-0669 FAX: 478-477-0666 polywadmpb@aol.com www.polywad.com

Ponsness, Warren, 7634 W. Ohio St., Rathdrum, ID 83858 / 800-732-0706; FAX: 208-687-2233 www.reloaders.com

Pony Express Reloaders, 608 E. Co. Rd. D, Suite 3, St. Paul, MN 55117 / 612-483-9406; FAX: 612-483-9884

Pony Express Sport Shop, 23404 Lyons Ave., PMB 448, Newhall, CA 91321-2511 / 818-895-1231

Potts, Wayne E., 1580 Meade St. Apt. A, Denver, CO 80204-5930 / 303-355-5462

Powder Horn Ltd., P.O. Box 565, Glenview, IL 60025 / 305-565-6060

Powell & Son (Gunmakers) Ltd., William, 35-37 Carrs Lane, Birmingham, B4 7SX ENGLAND / 121-643-0689; FAX: 121-631-3504 sales@william-powell.co.uk www.william-powell.co.uk

Powell Agency, William, 22 Circle Dr., Bellmore, NY 11710 / 516-679-1158

Power Custom, Inc., 29739 Hwy. J, Gravois Mills, MO 65037 / 573-372-5684; FAX: 573-372-5799 rwpowers@laurie.net www.powercustom.com

Power Plus Enterprises, Inc., P.O. Box 38, Warm Springs, GA 31830 / 706-655-2132

Powley Computer (See Hutton Rifle Ranch)

Practical Tools, Inc., 7067 Easton Rd., P.O. Box 133, Pipersville, PA 18947 / 215-766-7301; FAX: 215-766-8681

Prairie Gun Works, 1-761 Marion St., Winnipeg, MB R2J 0K6 CANADA / 204-231-2976; FAX: 204-231-8566

Prairie Rifle Co., 1220 N. Sixth St., Princeton, IL 61356 / 815-875-1616; or 800-445-1541; FAX: 815-875-1402

Pranger, Ed G., 1414 7th St., Anacortes, WA 98221 / 206-293-3488

Precision Airgun Sales, Inc., 5247 Warrensville Ctr Rd., Maple Hts., OH 44137 / 216-587-5005; FAX: 216-587-5005

Precision Cast Bullets, 101 Mud Creek Lane, Ronan, MT 59864 / 406-676-5135

Precision Delta Corp., P.O. Box 128, Ruleville, MS 38771 / 662-756-2810; FAX: 662-756-2590

Precision Firearm Finishing, 25 N.W. 44th Avenue, Des Moines, IA 50313 / 515-288-8680; FAX: 515-244-3925

Precision Gun Works, 104 Sierra Rd., Dept. GD, Kerrville, TX 78028 / 830-367-4587

Precision Reloading, Inc., P.O. Box 122, Stafford Springs, CT 06076 / 860-684-7979; FAX: 860-684-6788 info@precisionreloading.com www.precisionreloading.com

Precision Shooting, Inc., 222 McKee St., Manchester, CT 06040 / 860-645-8776; FAX: 860-643-8215 www.theaccuraterifle.com or precisionshooting.com

Precision Small Arms Inc., 9272 Jeronimo Rd., Ste. 121, Irvine, CA 92618 / 800-554-5515; or 949-768-3530; FAX: 949-768-4808 www.tcbebe.com

Precision Sport Optics, 15571 Producer Lane, Unit G, Huntington Beach, CA 92649 / 714-891-1309; FAX: 714-892-6920

Premier Reticles, 920 Breckinridge Lane, Winchester, VA 22601-6707 / 540-722-0601; FAX: 540-722-3522

Prescott Projectile Co., 1808 Meadowbrook Road, Prescott, AZ 86303

Preslik's Gunstocks, 4245 Keith Ln., Chico, CA 95926 / 916-891-8236

Price Bullets, Patrick W., 16520 Worthley Dr., San Lorenzo, CA 94580 / 510-278-1547

Prime Reloading, 30 Chiswick End, Meldreth, ROYSTON UK / 0763-260636

Primedia Publishing Co., 6420 Wilshire Blvd., Los Angeles, CA 90048 / 213-782-2000; FAX: 213-782-2867

Primos Hunting Calls, 604 First St., Flora, MS 39071 / 601-879-9323; FAX: 601-879-9324 www.primos.com

PRL Bullets, c/o Blackburn Enterprises, 114 Stuart Rd., Ste. 110, Cleveland, TN 37312 / 423-559-0340

Pro Load Ammunition, Inc., 5180 E. Seltice Way, Post Falls, ID 83854 / 208-773-9444; FAX: 208-773-9441

Professional Gunsmiths of America, Rt 1 Box 224, Lexington, MO 64067 / 660-259-2636

Professional Hunter Supplies, P.O. Box 608, 468 Main St., Ferndale, CA 95536 / 707-786-9140; FAX: 707-786-9117 wmebride@humboldt.com

PrOlixr Lubricants, P.O. Box 1348, Victorville, CA 92393 / 760-243-3129; FAX: 760-241-0148 prolix@accex.net www.prolixlubricant.com

Pro-Mark Div. of Wells Lamont, 6640 W. Touhy, Chicago, IL 60648 / 312-647-8200

Proofmark Corp., P.O. Box 357, Burgess, VA 22432 / 804-453-4337; FAX: 804-453-4337 proofmark@direzway.com www.proofmarkbullets.com

Pro-Port Ltd., 41302 Executive Dr., Harrison Twp., MI 48045-1306 / 586-469-6727; FAX: 586-469-0425 e-mail@magnaport.com www.magnaport.com

Pro-Shot Products, Inc., P.O. Box 763, Taylorville, IL 62568 / 217-824-9133; FAX: 217-824-8861 www.proshotproducts.com

Protector Mfg. Co., Inc., The, 443 Ashwood Pl., Boca Raton, FL 33431 / 407-394-6011

Protektor Model, 1-11 Bridge St., Galeton, PA 16922 / 814-435-2442 mail@protektormodel.com www.protektormodel.com

Prototech Industries, Inc., 10532 E Road, Delia, KS 66418 / 785-771-3571 prototec@grapevine.net

ProWare, Inc., 15847 NE Hancock St., Portland, OR 97230 / 503-239-0159

PWL Gunleather, P.O. Box 450432, Atlanta, GA 31145 / 800-960-4072; FAX: 770-822-1704 covert@pwlusa.com www.pwlusa.com

PWM Sales Ltd., N.D.F.S., Gowdall Lane, Pollington DN14 0AU, ENGLAND / 01405862688; FAX: 01405862622 Paulwelburn9@aol.com

Pyramyd Stone Inter. Corp., 2447 Suffolk Lane, Pepper Pike, OH 44124-4540

Q

Quack Decoy & Sporting Clays, 4 Ann & Hope Way, P.O. Box 98, Cumberland, RI 02864 / 401-723-8202; FAX: 401-722-5910

Quaker Boy, Inc., 5455 Webster Rd., Orchard Parks, NY 14127 / 716-662-3979; FAX: 716-662-9426

Quality Arms, Inc., Box 19477, Dept. GD, Houston, TX 77224 / 281-870-8377 arrieta2@excite.com www.arrieta.com

Quality Cartridge, P.O. Box 445, Hollywood, MD 20636 / 301-373-3719 www.qual-cart.com

Quality Custom Firearms, Stephen Billeb, 22 Vista View Dr., Cody, WY 82414 / 307-587-4278; FAX: 307-587-4297 stevebilleb@wyoming.com

Quarton Beamshot, 4538 Centerview Dr., Ste. 149, San Antonio, TX 78228 / 800-520-8435; FAX: 210-735-1326 www.beamshot.com

Que Industries, Inc., P.O. Box 2471, Everett, WA 98203 / 425-303-9088; FAX: 206-514-3266 queinfo@queindustries.com

Queen Cutlery Co., P.O. Box 500, Franklinville, NY 14737 / 800-222-5233; FAX: 800-299-2618

R

R&C Knives & Such, 2136 CANDY CANE WALK, Manteca, CA 95336-9501 / 209-239-3722; FAX: 209-825-6947

R&D Gun Repair, Kenny Howell, RR1 Box 283, Beloit, WI 53511

R&J Gun Shop, 337 S. Humbolt St., Canyon City, OR 97820 / 541-575-2130 rjgunshop@highdesertnet.com

R&S Industries Corp., 8255 Brentwood Industrial Dr., St. Louis, MO 63144 / 314-781-5169 ron@miraclepolishingcloth.com www.miraclepolishingcloth.com

R. Murphy Co., Inc., 13 Groton-Harvard Rd., P.O. Box 376, Ayer, MA 01432 / 617-772-3481 www.r.murphyknives.com

R.A. Wells Custom Gunsmith, 3452 1st Ave., Racine, WI 53402 / 414-639-5223

R.E. Seebeck Assoc., P.O. Box 59752, Dallas, TX 75229

R.E.I., P.O. Box 88, Tallevast, FL 34270 / 813-755-0085

R.E.T. Enterprises, 2608 S. Chestnut, Broken Arrow, OK 74012 / 918-251-GUNS; FAX: 918-251-0587

R.F. Mitchell Bullets, 430 Walnut St., Westernport, MD 21562

R.T. Eastman Products, P.O. Box 1531, Jackson, WY 83001 / 307-733-3217; or 800-624-4311

Rabeno, Martin, 530 The Eagle Pass, Durango, CO 81301 / 970-382-0353 fancygun@aol.com

Radack Photography, Lauren, 21140 Jib Court L-12, Aventura, FL 33180 / 305-931-3110

Radiator Specialty Co., 1900 Wilkinson Blvd., P.O. Box 34689, Charlotte, NC 28234 / 800-438-6947; FAX: 800-421-9525 tkrossell@gunk.com www.gunk.com

Radical Concepts, P.O. Box 1473, Lake Grove, OR 97035 / 503-538-7437

Rainier Ballistics, 4500 15th St. East, Tacoma, WA 98424 / 800-638-8722; FAX: 253-922-7854 sales@rainierballistics.com www.rainierballistics.com

Ralph Bone Engraving, 718 N. Atlanta St., Owasso, OK 74055 / 918-272-9745

Ram-Line ATK, P.O. Box 39, Onalaska, WI 54650

Ramon B. Gonzalez Guns, P.O. Box 370, Monticello, NY 12701 / 914-794-4515; FAX: 914-794-4515

Rampart International, 2781 W. MacArthur Blvd., B-283, Santa Ana, CA 92704 / 800-976-7240 or 714-557-6405

Ranch Products, P.O. Box 145, Malinta, OH 43535 / 313-277-3118; FAX: 313-565-8536

Randall-Made Knives, P.O. Box 1988, Orlando, FL 32802 / 407-855-8075

Randco UK, 286 Gipsy Rd., Welling, DA16 1JJ ENGLAND / 44 81 303 4118

Randolph Engineering, Inc., Ranger Shooting Glasses, 26 Thomas Patten Dr., Randolph, MA 02368 / 800-541-1405; FAX: 781-986-0337 sales@randolphusa.com www.randolphusa.com

Randy Duane Custom Stocks, 7822 Church St., Middletown, VA 22645-9521

Range Brass Products Company, P.O. Box 218, Rockport, TX 78381

Ransom International Corp., 1027 Spire Dr., Prescott, AZ 86305 / 928-778-7899; FAX: 928-778-7993 ransom@cableone.net www.ransomrest.com

Rapine Bullet Mould Mfg. Co., 9503 Landis Lane, East Greenville, PA 18041 / 215-679-5413; FAX: 215-679-9795

Ravell Ltd., 289 Diputacion St., 08009, Barcelona, SPAIN / 34(3) 4874486; FAX: 34(3) 4881394

Ray Riling Arms Books Co., 6844 Gorsten St., Philadelphia, PA 19119 / 215-438-2456; FAX: 215-438-5395 sales@rayrilingarmsbooks.com www.rayrilingarmsbooks.com

Ray's Gunsmith Shop, 3199 Elm Ave., Grand Junction, CO 81504 / 970-434-6162; FAX: 970-434-6162

Raytech Div. of Lyman Products Corp., 475 Smith Street, Middletown, CT 06457-1541 / 860-632-2020 or 800-225-9626; FAX: 860-632-1699 raysales@cshore.com www.raytech-ind.com

RCBS Operations/ATK, 605 Oro Dam Blvd., Oroville, CA 95965 / 530-533-5191 or 800-533-5000; FAX: 530-533-1647 www.rcbs.com

RCBS/ATK, 605 Oro Dam Blvd., Oroville, CA 95965 / 800-533-5000; FAX: 916-533-1647

Reardon Products, P.O. Box 126, Morrison, IL 61270 / 815-772-3155

Red Diamond Dist. Co., 1304 Snowdon Dr., Knoxville, TN 37912

Redding Reloading Equipment, 1089 Starr Rd., Cortland, NY 13045 / 607-753-3331; FAX: 607-756-8445 techline@redding-reloading.com www.redding-reloading.com

Redfield Media Resource Center, 4607 N.E. Cedar Creek Rd., Woodland, WA 98674 / 360-225-5000; FAX: 360-225-7616

Redman's Rifling & Reboring, 189 Nichols Rd., Omak, WA 98841 / 509-826-5512

Redwood Bullet Works, 3559 Bay Rd., Redwood City, CA 94063 / 415-367-6741

Reed, Dave, Rt. 1, Box 374, Minnesota City, MN 55959 / 507-689-2944

Reimer Johannsen, Inc., 438 Willow Brook Rd., Plainfield, NH 03781 / 603-469-3450; FAX: 603-469-3471

Reloaders Equipment Co., 4680 High St., Ecorse, MI 48229

Reloading Specialties, Inc., Box 1130, Pine Island, MN 55463 / 507-356-8500; FAX: 507-356-8800

Remington Arms Co., Inc., 870 Remington Drive, P.O. Box 700, Madison, NC 27025-0700 / 800-243-9700; FAX: 910-548-8700

Remington Double Shotguns, 7885 Cyd Dr., Denver, CO 80221 / 303-429-6947

Renato Gamba S.p.A.-Societa Armi Bresciane Srl., Via Artigiani 93, 25063 Gardone, Val Trompia (BS), ITALY / 30-8911640; FAX: 30-8911648

Renegade, P.O. Box 31546, Phoenix, AZ 85046 / 602-482-6777; FAX: 602-482-1952

MANUFACTURER'S DIRECTORY

Renfrew Guns & Supplies, R.R. 4, Renfrew, ON K7V 3Z7 CANADA / 613-432-7080

Reno, Wayne, 2808 Stagestop Road, Jefferson, CO 80456

Republic Arms, Inc. (See Cobra Enterprises, Inc.)

Retting, Inc., Martin B., 11029 Washington, Culver City, CA 90232 / 213-837-2412

RG-G, Inc., P.O. Box 935, Trinidad, CO 81082 / 719-845-1436

RH Machine & Consulting Inc., P.O. Box 394, Pacific, MO 63069 / 314-271-8465

Rhino, P.O. Box 787, Locust, NC 28097 / 704-753-2198

Rhodeside, Inc., 1704 Commerce Dr., Piqua, OH 45356 / 513-773-5781

Rice, Keith (See White Rock Tool & Die)

Richards MicroFit Stocks, Inc., P.O. Box 1066, Sun Valley, CA 91352 / 800-895-7420; FAX: 818-771-1242 sales@rifle-stocks.com www.rifle-stocks.com

Ridgeline, Inc., Bruce Sheldon, P.O. Box 930, Dewey, AZ 86327-0930 / 800-632-5900; FAX: 520-632-5900

Ridgetop Sporting Goods, P.O. Box 306, 42907 Hilligoss Ln. East, Eatonville, WA 98328 / 360-832-6422; FAX: 360-832-6422

Ries, Chuck, 415 Ridgecrest Dr., Grants Pass, OR 97527 / 503-476-5623

Rifles, Inc., 3580 Leal Rd., Pleasanton, TX 78064 / 830-569-2055; FAX: 830-569-2297

Riggs, Jim, 206 Azalea, Boerne, TX 78006 / 210-249-8567

Riley Ledbetter Airguns, 1804 E. Sprague St., Winston Salem, NC 27107-3521 / 919-784-0676

Rim Pac Sports, Inc., 1034 N. Soldano Ave., Azusa, CA 91702-2135

Ringler Custom Leather Co., 31 Shining Mtn. Rd., Powell, WY 82435 / 307-645-3255

Ripley Rifles, 42 Fletcher Street, Ripley, Derbyshire, DE5 3LP ENGLAND / 011-0773-748353

Rizzini F.lli (See U.S. Importers-Wm. Larkin Moore & Co., N.E. Arms Corp.)

Rizzini SNC, Via 2 Giugno, 7/7Bis-25060, Marcheno (Brescia), ITALY

RLCM Enterprises, 110 Hill Crest Drive, Burleson, TX 76028

RMS Custom Gunsmithing, 4120 N. Bitterwell, Prescott Valley, AZ 86314 / 520-772-7626 www.customstockmaker.com

Robar Co., Inc., The, 21438 N. 7th Ave., Suite B, Phoenix, AZ 85027 / 623-581-2648; FAX: 623-582-0059 info@robarguns.com www.robarguns.com

Robert Evans Engraving, 332 Vine St., Oregon City, OR 97045 / 503-656-5693

Robert Valade Engraving, 931 3rd Ave., Seaside, OR 97138 / 503-738-7672

Robinett, R. G., P.O. Box 72, Madrid, IA 50156 / 515-795-2906

Robinson, Don, Pennsylvania Hse, 36 Fairfax Crescent, W Yorkshire, ENGLAND / 0422-364458 donrobinsonuk@yahoo.co.uk www.guns4u2.co.uk

Robinson Armament Co., P.O. Box 16776, Salt Lake City, UT 84116 / 801-355-0401; FAX: 801-355-0402 zdf@robarm.com www.robarm.com

Robinson Firearms Mfg. Ltd., 1699 Blondeaux Crescent, Kelowna, BC V1Y 4J8 CANADA / 604-868-9596

Robinson H.V. Bullets, 3145 Church St., Zachary, LA 70791 / 504-654-4029

Rochester Lead Works, 76 Anderson Ave., Rochester, NY 14607 / 716-442-8500; FAX: 716-442-4712

Rock River Arms, 101 Noble St., Cleveland, IL 61241

Rockwood Corp., Speedwell Division, 136 Lincoln Blvd., Middlesex, NJ 08846 / 800-243-8274; FAX: 980-560-7475

Rocky Mountain Armoury, Mr. Felix LesMerises, 610 Main Street, P.O. Box 691, Frisco, CO 80443-0691 / 970-668-0136; FAX: 970-668-4484 felix@rockymountainarmoury.com

Rocky Mountain Arms, Inc., 1813 Sunset Pl., Unit D, Longmont, CO 80501 / 800-375-0846; FAX: 303-678-8766

Rocky Mountain Target Co., 3 Aloe Way, Leesburg, FL 34788 / 352-365-9598

Rocky Mountain Wildlife Products, P.O. Box 999, La Porte, CO 80535 / 970-484-2768; FAX: 970-484-0807 critrcall@larinet.net www.critrcall.com

Rocky Shoes & Boots, 294 Harper St., Nelsonville, OH 45764 / 800-848-9452; or 614-753-1951; FAX: 614-753-4024

Rogue Rifle Co., Inc., 1140 36th St. N., Ste. B, Lewiston, ID 83501 / 208-743-4355; FAX: 208-743-4163

Rogue River Rifleworks, 500 Linne Road #D, Paso Robles, CA 93446 / 805-227-4706; FAX: 805-227-4723 rrrifles@calinet.com

Rohner, Hans, 1148 Twin Sisters Ranch Rd., Nederland, CO 80466-9600

Rohner, John, 186 Virginia Ave., Asheville, NC 28806 / 828-281-3704

Rohrbaugh, P.O. Box 785, Bayport, NY 11705 / 631-363-2843; FAX: 631-363-2681 API380@aol.com

Romain's Custom Guns, Inc., RD 1, Whetstone Rd., Brockport, PA 15823 / 814-265-1948 romwhetstone@penn.com

Ron Frank Custom Classic Arms, 7131 Richland Rd., Ft. Worth, TX 76118 / 817-284-9300; FAX: 817-284-9300 rfrank3974@aol.com

Rooster Laboratories, P.O. Box 414605, Kansas City, MO 64141 / 816-474-1622; FAX: 816-474-7622

Rorschach Precision Products, 417 Keats Cir., Irving, TX 75061 / 214-790-3487

Rosenberg & Son, Jack A., 12229 Cox Ln., Dallas, TX 75234 / 214-241-6302

Ross, Don, 12813 West 83 Terrace, Lenexa, KS 66215 / 913-492-6982

Rosser, Bob, 2809 Crescent Ave., Suite 20, Homewood, AL 35209 / 205-870-4422; FAX: 205-870-4421 www.hand-engravers.com

Rossi Firearms, Gary Mchalik, 16175 NW 49th Ave., Miami, FL 33014-6314 / 305-474-0401; FAX: 305-623-7506

Rottweil Compe, 1330 Glassell, Orange, CA 92667

Roy Baker's Leather Goods, P.O. Box 893, Magnolia, AR 71754 / 870-234-0344

Royal Arms Gunstocks, 919 8th Ave. NW, Great Falls, MT 59404 / 406-453-1149 royalarms@lmt.net www.lmt.net/~royalarms

Royal Arms International, R J Brill, P.O. Box 6083, Woodland Hills, CA 91365 / 818-704-5110; FAX: 818-887-2059 royalarms.com

Roy's Custom Grips, 793 Mt. Olivet Church Rd., Lynchburg, VA 24504 / 434-993-3470

RPM, 15481 N. Twin Lakes Dr., Tucson, AZ 85739 / 520-825-1233; FAX: 520-825-3333

Rubright Bullets, 1008 S. Quince Rd., Walnutport, PA 18088 / 215-767-1339

Rucker Dist. Inc., P.O. Box 479, Terrell, TX 75160 / 214-563-2094

Ruger (See Sturm Ruger & Co., Inc.)

Ruger, Chris. See: RUGER'S CUSTOM GUNS

Ruger's Custom Guns, Chris Ruger, 1050 Morton Blvd., Kingston, NY 12401 / 845-336-7106; FAX: 845-336-7106 rugerscustom@outdrs.net rugergunsmith.com

Rundell's Gun Shop, 6198 Frances Rd., Clio, MI 48420 / 313-687-0559

Rupert's Gun Shop, 2202 Dick Rd., Suite B, Fenwick, MI 48834 / 517-248-3252 17rupert@pathwaynet.com

Russ Haydon's Shooters' Supply, 15018 Goodrich Dr. NW, Gig Harbor, WA 98329 / 877-663-6249; FAX: 253-857-7884 info@shooters-supply.com www.shooters-supply.com

Russ, William. See: BILL RUSS TRADING POST

Rusteprufe Laboratories, 1319 Jefferson Ave., Sparta, WI 54656 / 608-269-4144; FAX: 608-366-1972 rusteprufe@centurytel.net www.rusteprufe.com

Rusty Duck Premium Gun Care Products, 7785 Foundation Dr., Suite 6, Florence, KY 41042 / 606-342-5553; FAX: 606-342-5556

Rutgers Book Center, 127 Raritan Ave., Highland Park, NJ 08904 / 732-545-4344; FAX: 732-545-5686 gunbooks@rutgersgunbooks.com www.rutgersgunbooks.com

Rutten (See U.S. Importer-Labanu Inc.)

RWS (See U.S. Importer-Dynamit Nobel-RWS, Inc.), 81 Ruckman Rd., Closter, NJ 07624 / 201-767-7971; FAX: 201-767-1589

S

S&K Scope Mounts, RD 2 Box 21C, Sugar Grove, PA 16350 / 814-489-3091; or 800-578-9862; FAX: 814-489-5466 comments@scopemounts.com www.scopemounts.com

S&S Firearms, 74-11 Myrtle Ave., Glendale, NY 11385 / 718-497-1100; FAX: 718-497-1105 info@ssfirearms.com ssfirearms.com

S.A.R.L. G. Granger, 66 cours Fauriel, 42100, Saint Etienne, FRANCE / 04 77 25 14 73; FAX: 04 77 38 66 99

S.C.R.C., P.O. Box 660, Katy, TX 77492-0660 FAX: 281-492-6332

S.D. Meacham, 1070 Angel Ridge, Peck, ID 83545

S.I.A.C.E. (See U.S. Importer-IAR Inc.)

Sabatti SPA, Via A Volta 90, 25063 Gandome V.T.(BS), Brescia, ITALY / 030-8912207-831312; FAX: 030-8912059 info@sabatti.it www.sabatti.com

SAECO (See Redding Reloading Equipment)

Safari Arms/Schuetzen Pistol Works, 620-626 Old Pacific Hwy. SE, Olympia, WA 98513 / 360-459-3471; FAX: 360-491-3447 info@olyarms.com www.olyarms.com

Safari Press, Inc., 15621 Chemical Lane B, Huntington Beach, CA 92649 / 714-894-9080; FAX: 714-894-4949 info@safaripress.com www.safaripress.com

Safariland Ltd., Inc., 3120 E. Mission Blvd., P.O. Box 51478, Ontario, CA 91761 / 909-923-7300; FAX: 909-923-7400

SAFE, P.O. Box 864, Post Falls, ID 83877 / 208-773-3624; FAX: 208-773-6819 staysafe@safe-llc.com www.safe-llc.com

Sako Ltd. (See U.S. Importer-Stoeger Industries)

Sam Welch Gun Engraving, Sam Welch, HC 64 Box 2110, Moab, UT 84532 / 435-259-8131

Samco Global Arms, Inc., 6995 NW 43rd St., Miami, FL 33166 / 305-593-9782; FAX: 305-593-1014 samco@samcoglobal.com www.samcoglobal.com

Sampson, Roger, 2316 Mahogany St., Mora, MN 55051 / 612-679-4868

San Marco (See U.S. Importers-Cape Outfitters-EMF Co., Inc.

Sandia Die & Cartridge Co., 37 Atancacio Rd. NE, Albuquerque, NM 87123 / 505-298-5729

Sarco, Inc., 323 Union St., Stirling, NJ 07980 / 908-647-3800; FAX: 908-647-9413

Sarsilmaz Shotguns-Turkey (see B.C. Outdoors)

Sauer (See U.S. Importers-Paul Co., The Sigarms Inc.)

Sauls, R. See: BRYAN & ASSOC.

Saunders Gun & Machine Shop, 145 Delhi Rd., Manchester, IA 52057 / 563-927-4026

Savage Arms (Canada), Inc., 248 Water St., P.O. Box 1240, Lakefield, ON K0L 2H0 CANADA / 705-652-8000; FAX: 705-652-8431 www.savagearms.com

Savage Arms, Inc., 100 Springdale Rd., Westfield, MA 01085 / 413-568-7001; FAX: 413-562-7764

Savage Range Systems, Inc., 100 Springdale Rd., Westfield, MA 01085 / 413-568-7001; FAX: 413-562-1152 snailtraps@savagearms.com www.snailtraps.com

Saville Iron Co. (See Greenwood Precision)

Scansport, Inc., P.O. Box 700, Enfield, NH 03748 / 603-632-7654

Sceery Game Calls, P.O. Box 6520, Sante Fe, NM 87502 / 505-471-9110; FAX: 505-471-3476

Schaefer Shooting Sports, P.O. Box 1515, Melville, NY 11747-0515 / 516-643-5466; FAX: 516-643-2426 robert@robertschaefer.com www.schaefershooting.com

Scharch Mfg., Inc.-Top Brass, 10325 Co. Rd. 120, Salida, CO 81201 / 800-836-4683; FAX: 719-539-3021 topbrass@scharch.com www.handgun-brass.com

Scherer, Liz. See: SCHERER SUPPLIES

Scherer Supplies, Liz Scherer, Box 250, Ewing, VA 24248 FAX: 423-733-2073

Schiffman, Mike, 8233 S. Crystal Springs, McCammon, ID 83250 / 208-254-9114

Schmidt & Bender, Inc., P.O. Box 134, Meriden, NH 03770 / 603-469-3565; FAX: 603-469-3471 scopes@adelphia.net www.schmidtbender.com

Schmidtke Group, 17050 W. Salentine Dr., New Berlin, WI 53151-7349

Schneider Bullets, 3655 West 214th St., Fairview Park, OH 44126

Schneider Rifle Barrels, Inc., 1403 W. Red Baron Rd., Payson, AZ 85541 / 602-948-2525

School of Gunsmithing, The, 6065 Roswell Rd., Atlanta, GA 30328 / 800-223-4542

Schroeder Bullets, 1421 Thermal Ave., San Diego, CA 92154 / 619-423-3523; FAX: 619-423-8124

Schulz Industries, 16247 Minnesota Ave., Paramount, CA 90723 / 213-439-5903

Schumakers Gun Shop, 512 Prouty Corner Lp. A, Colville, WA 99114 / 509-684-4848

Scope Control, Inc., 5775 Co. Rd. 23 SE, Alexandria, MN 56308 / 612-762-7295

Score High Gunsmithing, 9812-A, Cochiti SE, Albuquerque, NM 87123 / 800-326-5632; or 505-292-5532; FAX: 505-292-2592 scorehi@scorehi.com www.probed2000.com

Scot Powder, Rt. 1 Box 167, McEwen, TN 37101 / 800-416-3006; FAX: 615-729-4211

Scott Fine Guns Inc., Thad, P.O. Box 412, Indianola, MS 38751 / 601-887-5929

Searcy Enterprises, P.O. Box 584, Boron, CA 93596 / 760-762-6771; FAX: 760-762-0191

Second Chance Body Armor, P.O. Box 578, Central Lake, MI 49622 / 616-544-5721; FAX: 616-544-9824

Seebeck Assoc., R.E., P.O. Box 59752, Dallas, TX 75229

Segway Industries, P.O. Box 783, Suffern, NY 10901-0783 / 914-357-5510

Seligman Shooting Products, Box 133, Seligman, AZ 86337 / 602-422-3607 shootssp@yahoo.com

Sellier & Bellot, USA, Inc., P.O. Box 27006, Shawnee Mission, KS 66225 / 913-685-0916; FAX: 913-685-0917

Selsi Co., Inc., P.O. Box 10, Midland Park, NJ 07432-0010 / 201-935-0388; FAX: 201-935-5851

MANUFACTURER'S DIRECTORY

Semmer, Charles (See Remington Double Shotguns), 7885 Cyd Dr., Denver, CO 80221 / 303-429-6947

Sentinel Arms, P.O. Box 57, Detroit, MI 48231 / 313-331-1951; FAX: 313-331-1456

Servus Footwear Co., 1136 2nd St., Rock Island, IL 61204 / 309-786-7741; FAX: 309-786-9808

Shappy Bullets, 76 Milldale Ave., Plantsville, CT 06479 / 203-621-3704

Sharp Shooter Supply, 4970 Lehman Road, Delphos, OH 45833 / 419-695-3179

Sharps Arms Co., Inc., C., 100 Centennial, Box 885, Big Timber, MT 59011 / 406-932-4353

Shaw, Inc., E. R. (See Small Arms Mfg. Co.)

Shay's Gunsmithing, 931 Marvin Ave., Lebanon, PA 17042

Sheffield Knifemakers Supply, Inc., P.O. Box 741107, Orange City, FL 32774-1107 / 386-775-6453; FAX: 386-774-5754

Sheldon, Bruce. See: RIDGELINE, INC.

Shepherd Enterprises, Inc., Box 189, Waterloo, NE 68069 / 402-779-2424; FAX: 402-779-4010 sshepherd@shepherdscopes.com www.shepherdscopes.com

Sherwood, George, 46 N. River Dr., Roseburg, OR 97470 / 541-672-3159

Shilen, Inc., 205 Metro Park Blvd., Ennis, TX 75119 / 972-875-5318; FAX: 972-875-5402

Shiloh Rifle Mfg., P.O. Box 279, Big Timber, MT 59011

Shockley, Harold H., 204 E. Farmington Rd., Hanna City, IL 61536 / 309-565-4524

Shoot Where You Look, Leon Measures, Dept GD, 408 Fair, Livingston, TX 77351

Shooters Arms Manufacturing, Inc., Rivergate Mall, Gen. Maxilom Ave., Cebu City 6000, PHILIPPINES / 6332-254-8478 www.shootersarms.com.ph

Shooter's Choice Gun Care, 15050 Berkshire Ind. Pkwy., Middlefield, OH 44062 / 440-834-8888; FAX: 440-834-3388 www.shooterschoice.com

Shooter's Edge Inc., 3313 Creekstone Dr., Fort Collins, CO 80525

Shooters Supply, 1120 Tieton Dr., Yakima, WA 98902 / 509-452-1181

Shooter's World, 3828 N. 28th Ave., Phoenix, AZ 85017 / 602-266-0170

Shooters, Inc., 5139 Stanart St., Norfolk, VA 23502 / 757-461-9152; FAX: 757-461-9155 gflocker@aol.com

Shootin' Shack, 357 Cypress Drive, No. 10, Tequesta, FL 33469 / 561-842-0990; FAX: 561-545-4861

Shooting Gallery, The, 8070 Southern Blvd., Boardman, OH 44512 / 216-726-7788

Shoot-N-C Targets (See Birchwood Casey)

Shotgun Sports, P.O. Box 6810, Auburn, CA 95604 / 530-889-2220; FAX: 530-889-9106 custsrv@shotgunsportsmagazine.com shotgunsportsmagazine.com

Shotgun Sports Magazine, dba Shootin' Accessories Ltd., P.O. Box 6810, Auburn, CA 95604 / 916-889-2220 custsrv@shotgunsportsmagazine.com shotgunsportsmagazine.com

Shotguns Unlimited, 2307 Fon Du Lac Rd., Richmond, VA 23229 / 804-752-7115

Siegrist Gun Shop, 8752 Turtle Road, Whittemore, MI 48770 / 989-873-3929

Sierra Bullets, 1400 W. Henry St., Sedalia, MO 65301 / 816-827-6300; FAX: 816-827-6300

Sierra Specialty Prod. Co., 1344 Oakhurst Ave., Los Altos, CA 94024 FAX: 415-965-1536

SIG, CH-8212 Neuhausen, SWITZERLAND

Sigarms Inc., 18 Industrial Dr., Exeter, NH 03833 / 603-772-2302; FAX: 603-772-9082 www.sigarms.com

Sight Shop, The, John G. Lawson, 1802 E. Columbia Ave., Tacoma, WA 98404 / 253-474-5456 parahellum9@aol.com www.thesightshop.org

Sightron, Inc., 1672B Hwy. 96, Franklinton, NC 27525 / 919-528-8783; FAX: 919-528-0995 info@sightron.com www.sightron.com

SIG-Sauer (See U.S. Importer-Sigarms, Inc.)

Silencio/Safety Direct, 56 Coney Island Dr., Sparks, NV 89431 / 800-648-1812; or 702-354-4451; FAX: 702-359-1074

Silent Hunter, 1100 Newton Ave., W. Collingswood, NJ 08107 / 609-854-3276

Silhouette Leathers, 8598 Hwy. 51 N. #4, Millington, TN 38053 silhouetteleathers@yahoo.com silhouetteleathers.com

Silver Eagle Machining, 18007 N. 69th Ave., Glendale, AZ 85308

Silver Ridge Gun Shop (See Goodwin Guns)

Simmons, Jerry, 715 Middlebury St., Goshen, IN 46528-2717 / 574-533-8546

Simmons Gun Repair, Inc., 700 S. Rogers Rd., Olathe, KS 66062 / 913-782-3131; FAX: 913-782-4189

Simmons Outdoor Corp., 6001 Oak Canyon, Irvine, CA 92618 / 949-451-1450; FAX: 949-451-1460 www.meade.com

Sinclair International, Inc., 2330 Wayne Haven St., Fort Wayne, IN 46803 / 260-493-1858; or 800-717-8211; FAX: 260-493-2530 sales@sinclairintl.com www.sinclairintl.com

Singletary, Kent, 4538 W. Carol Ave., Glendale, AZ 85302 / 602-526-6836 kent@kscustom www.kscustom.com

Siskiyou Gun Works (See Donnelly, C. P.)

Six Enterprises, 320-D Turtle Creek Ct., San Jose, CA 95125 / 408-999-0201; FAX: 408-999-0216

SKB Shotguns, 4325 S. 120th St., Omaha, NE 68137 / 800-752-2767; FAX: 402-330-8040 skb@skbshotguns.com www.skbshotguns.com

Skeoch, Brian R., P.O. Box 279, Glenrock, WY 82637 / 307-436-9655 skeochbrian@netzero.com

Skip's Machine, 364 29 Road, Grand Junction, CO 81501 / 303-245-5417

Sklany's Machine Shop, 566 Birch Grove Dr., Kalispell, MT 59901 / 406-755-4257

Slug Site, Ozark Wilds, 21300 Hwy. 5, Versailles, MO 65084 / 573-378-6430 john@ebeling.com john.ebeling.com

Small Arms Mfg. Co., 5312 Thoms Run Rd., Bridgeville, PA 15017 / 412-221-4343; FAX: 412-221-4303

Small Arms Specialists, 443 Firchburg Rd., Mason, NH 03048 / 603-878-0427; FAX: 603-878-3905 miniguns@empire.net miniguns.com

Smires, C. L., 5222 Windmill Lane, Columbia, MD 21044-1328

Smith & Wesson, 2100 Roosevelt Ave., Springfield, MA 01104 / 413-781-8300; FAX: 413-731-8980

Smith, Art, P.O. Box 645, Park Rapids, MN 56470 / 218-732-5333

Smith, Mark A., P.O. Box 182, Sinclair, WY 82334 / 307-324-7929

Smith, Michael, 2612 Ashmore Ave., Red Bank, TN 37415 / 615-267-8341

Smith, Ron, 5869 Straley, Fort Worth, TX 76114 / 817-732-6768

Smith, Sharmon, 4545 Speas Rd., Fruitland, ID 83619 / 208-452-6329 sharmon@fmtc.com

Smith Abrasives, Inc., 1700 Sleepy Valley Rd., Hot Springs, AR 71902-5095 / 501-321-2244; FAX: 501-321-9232 www.smithabrasives.com

Smith, Judy. See: L.B.T.

Smith Saddlery, Jesse W., 0499 County Road J, Pritchett, CO 81064 / 509-325-0622

Smokey Valley Rifles, E1976 Smokey Valley Rd., Scandinavia, WI 54977 / 715-467-2674

Snapp's Gunshop, 6911 E. Washington Rd., Clare, MI 48617 / 989-386-9226 snapp@glccomputers.com

Sno-Seal, Inc. (See Atsko/Sno-Seal, Inc.)

Societa Armi Bresciane Srl (See U.S. Importer-Cape Outfitters)

SOS Products Co. (See Buck Stix-SOS Products Co.), Box 3, Neenah, WI 54956

Sotheby's, 1334 York Ave. at 72nd St., New York, NY 10021 / 212-606-7260

Sound Tech Silencers, Box 391, Pelham, AL 35124 / 205-664-5860 silenceio@wmconnect.com www.soundtechsilencers.com

South Bend Replicas, Inc., 61650 Oak Rd., South Bend, IN 46614 / 219-289-4500

Southeastern Community College, 1015 S. Gear Ave., West Burlington, IA 52655 / 319-752-2731

Southern Ammunition Co., Inc., 4232 Meadow St., Loris, SC 29569-3124 / 803-756-3262; FAX: 803-756-3583

Southern Armory, The, 25 Millstone Rd., Woodlawn, VA 24381 / 703-238-1343; FAX: 703-238-1453

Southern Bloomer Mfg. Co., P.O. Box 1621, Bristol, TN 37620 / 615-878-6660; FAX: 615-878-8761

Southern Security, 1700 Oak Hills Dr., Kingston, TN 37763 / 423-376-6297; FAX: 800-251-9992

Sparks, Milt, 605 E. 44th St. No. 2, Boise, ID 83714-4800

Spartan-Realtree Products, Inc., 1390 Box Circle, Columbus, GA 31907 / 706-569-9101; FAX: 706-569-0042

Specialty Gunsmithing, Lynn McMurdo, P.O. Box 404, Afton, WY 83110 / 307-886-5535

Specialty Shooters Supply, Inc., 3325 Griffin Rd., Suite 9mm, Fort Lauderdale, FL 33317

Speer Bullets, P.O. Box 856, Lewiston, ID 83501 / 208-746-2351 www.speer-bullets.com

Spegel, Craig, P.O. Box 387, Nehalem, OR 97131 / 503-368-5653

Speiser, Fred D., 2229 Dearborn, Missoula, MT 59801 / 406-549-8133

Spencer Reblue Service, 1820 Tupelo Trail, Holt, MI 48842 / 517-694-7474

Spencer's Rifle Barrels, Inc., 4107 Jacobs Creek Dr., Scottsville, VA 24590 / 804-293-6836; FAX: 804-293-6836 www.spencersriflebarrels.com

SPG LLC, P.O. Box 1625, Cody, WY 82414 / 307-587-7621; FAX: 307-587-7695 spg@cody.wtp.net www.blackpowderspg.com

Sphinx Systems Ltd., Gesteigtstrasse 12, CH-3800, Matten, BRNE, SWITZERLAND

Splitfire Sporting Goods, L.L.C., P.O. Box 1044, Orem, UT 84059-1044 / 801-932-7950; FAX: 801-932-7959 www.splitfireguns.com

Spolar Power Load, Inc., 17376 Filbert, Fontana, CA 92335 / 800-227-9667

Sport Flite Manufacturing Co., 637 Kingsley Trl., Bloomfield Hills, MI 48304-2320 / 248-647-3747

Sporting Clays Of America, 9257 Bluckeye Rd., Sugar Grove, OH 43155-9632 / 740-746-8334; FAX: 740-746-8605

Sports Afield Magazine, 15621 Chemical Lane B, Huntington Beach, CA 92649 / 714-894-9080; FAX: 714-894-4949 info@sportsafield.com www.sportsafield.com

Sports Innovations, Inc., P.O. Box 5181, 8505 Jacksboro Hwy., Wichita Falls, TX 76307 / 817-723-6015

Sportsman Safe Mfg. Co., 6309-6311 Paramount Blvd., Long Beach, CA 90805 / 800-266-7150; or 310-984-5445

Sportsman's Communicators, 588 Radcliffe Ave., Pacific Palisades, CA 90272 / 800-538-3752

Sportsmatch U.K. Ltd., 16 Summer St. Leighton, Buzzard Beds, Bedfordshire, LU7 1HT ENGLAND / 4401525-381638; FAX: 4401525-851236 info@sportsmatch-uk.com www.sportsmatch-uk.com

Sportsmen's Exchange & Western Gun Traders, Inc., 813 Doris Ave., Oxnard, CA 93030 / 805-483-1917

Spradlin's, 457 Shannon Rd., Texas Creek Cotopaxi, CO 81223 / 719-275-7105; FAX: 719-275-3852 spradlins@prodigy.net www.spradlins.net

Springfield Armory, 420 W. Main St., Geneseo, IL 61254 / 309-944-5631; FAX: 309-944-3676 sales@springfield-armory.com www.springfieldarmory.com

Springfield Sporters, Inc., RD 1, Penn Run, PA 15765 / 412-254-2626; FAX: 412-254-9173

Springfield, Inc., 420 W. Main St., Geneseo, IL 61254 / 309-944-5631; FAX: 309-944-3676

Spyderco, Inc., 820 Spyderco Way, Golden, CO 80403 / 800-525-7770; or 800-525-7770; FAX: 303-278-2229 sales@spyderco.com www.spyderco.com

SSK Industries, J. D. Jones, 590 Woodvue Lane, Wintersville, OH 43953 / 740-264-0176; FAX: 740-264-2257 www.sskindustries.com

Stackpole Books, 5067 Ritter Rd., Mechanicsburg, PA 17055-6921 / 717-796-0411; or 800-732-3669; FAX: 717-796-0412 tmanney@stackpolebooks.com www.stackpolebooks.com

Stalker, Inc., P.O. Box 21, Fishermans Wharf Rd., Malakoff, TX 75148 / 903-489-1010

Stalwart Corporation, P.O. Box 46, Evanston, WY 82931 / 307-789-7687; FAX: 307-789-7688

Stan Baker Sports, Stan Baker, 10000 Lake City Way, Seattle, WA 98125 / 206-522-4575

Stan De Treville & Co., 4129 Normal St., San Diego, CA 92103 / 619-298-3393

Stanley Bullets, 2085 Heatheridge Ln., Reno, NV 89509

Star Ammunition, Inc., 5520 Rock Hampton Ct., Indianapolis, IN 46268 / 800-221-5927; FAX: 317-872-5847

Star Custom Bullets, P.O. Box 608, 468 Main St., Ferndale, CA 95536 / 707-786-9140; FAX: 707-786-9117 wmebridge@humboldt.com

Star Machine Works, P.O. Box 1872, Pioneer, CA 95666 / 209-295-5000

Starke Bullet Company, P.O. Box 400, 605 6th St. NW, Cooperstown, ND 58425 / 888-797-3431

Starkey Labs, 6700 Washington Ave. S., Eden Prairie, MN 55344

Starkey's Gun Shop, 9430 McCombs, El Paso, TX 79924 / 915-751-3030

Starlight Training Center, Inc., Rt. 1, P.O. Box 88, Bronaugh, MO 64728 / 417-843-3555

Starline, Inc., 1300 W. Henry St., Sedalia, MO 65301 / 660-827-6640; FAX: 660-827-6650 info@starlinebrass.com http://www.starlinebrass.com

Starr Trading Co., Jedediah, P.O. Box 2007, Farmington Hills, MI 48333 / 810-683-4343; FAX: 810-683-3282

Starrett Co., L. S., 121 Crescent St., Athol, MA 01331 / 978-249-3551; FAX: 978-249-8495

Steelman's Gun Shop, 10465 Beers Rd., Swartz Creek, MI 48473 / 810-735-4884

Steffens, Ron, 18396 Mariposa Creek Rd., Willits, CA 95490 / 707-485-0873

Stegall, James B., 26 Forest Rd., Wallkill, NY 12589

Steve Henigson & Associates, P.O. Box 2726, Culver City, CA 90231 / 310-305-8288; FAX: 310-305-1905

Steve Kamyk Engraver, 9 Grandview Dr., Westfield, MA 01085-1810 / 413-568-0457 stevek201@comcast.net

Steven Dodd Hughes, P.O. Box 545, Livingston, MT 59047 / 406-222-9377; FAX: 406-222-9377

MANUFACTURER'S DIRECTORY

Steves House of Guns, Rt. 1, Minnesota City, MN 55959 / 507-689-2573

Stewart Game Calls, Inc., Johnny, P.O. Box 7954, 5100 Fort Ave., Waco, TX 76714 / 817-772-3261; FAX: 817-772-3670

Stewart's Gunsmithing, P.O. Box 5854, Pietersburg North 0750, Transvaal, SOUTH AFRICA / 01521-89401

Steyr Mannlicher GmbH & Co. KG, Mannlicherstrasse 1, 4400 Steyr, Steyr, AUSTRIA / 0043-7252-896-0; FAX: 0043-7252-78620 office@steyr-mannlicher.com www.steyr-mannlicher.com

STI International, 114 Halmar Cove, Georgetown, TX 78628 / 800-959-8201; FAX: 512-819-0465 www.stiguns.com

Stiles Custom Guns, 76 Cherry Run Rd., Box 1605, Homer City, PA 15748 / 712-479-9945 glstiles@yourinter.net www.yourinter.net/glstiles

Stillwell, Robert, 421 Judith Ann Dr., Schertz, TX 78154

Stoeger Industries, 17603 Indian Head Hwy., Suite 200, Accokeek, MD 20607-2501 / 301-283-6300; FAX: 301-283-6986 www.stoegerindustries.com

Stoeger Publishing Co. (See Stoeger Industries)

Stone Enterprises Ltd., 426 Harveys Neck Rd., P.O. Box 335, Wicomico Church, VA 22579 / 804-580-5114; FAX: 804-580-8421

Stone Mountain Arms, 5988 Peachtree Corners E., Norcross, GA 30071 / 800-251-9412

Stoney Point Products, Inc., P.O. Box 234, 1822 N. Minnesota St., New Ulm, MN 56073-0234 / 507-354-3360; FAX: 507-354-7236 stoney@newulmtel.net www.stoneypoint.com

Storm, Gary, P.O. Box 5211, Richardson, TX 75083 / 214-385-0862

Stott's Creek Armory, Inc., 2526 S. 475W, Morgantown, IN 46160 / 317-878-5489; FAX: 317-878-9489 sccalendar@aol.com www.Sccalendar.aol.com

Stratco, Inc., P.O. Box 2270, Kalispell, MT 59901 / 406-755-1221; FAX: 406-755-1226

Strayer, Sandy. See: STRAYER-VOIGT, INC.

Strayer-Voigt, Inc., Sandy Strayer, 3435 Ray Orr Blvd., Grand Prairie, TX 75050 / 972-513-0575

Strong Holster Co., 39 Grove St., Gloucester, MA 01930 / 508-281-3300; FAX: 508-281-6321

Strutz Rifle Barrels, Inc., W. C., P.O. Box 611, Eagle River, WI 54521 / 715-479-4766

Stuart, V. Pat, Rt. 1, Box 447-S, Greenville, VA 24440 / 804-556-3845

Sturgeon Valley Sporters, Ken Ide, P.O. Box 283, Vanderbilt, MI 49795 / 989-983-4338 k.ide@mail.com

Sturm Ruger & Co. Inc., 200 Ruger Rd., Prescott, AZ 86301 / 928-541-8820; FAX: 520-541-8850 www.ruger.com

Sullivan, David S. (See Westwind Rifles, Inc.)

"Su-Press-On", Inc., P.O. Box 09161, Detroit, MI 48209 / 313-842-4222

Sun Welding Safe Co., 290 Easy St. No. 3, Simi Valley, CA 93065 / 805-584-6678; or 800-729-SAFE; FAX: 805-584-6169 sunwelding.com

Sunny Hill Enterprises, Inc., W1790 Cty. HHH, Malone, WI 53049 / 920-795-4722; FAX: 920-795-4822

Super 6 LLC, Gary Knopp, 3806 W. Lisbon Ave., Milwaukee, WI 53208 / 414-344-3343; FAX: 414-344-0304

Surecase Co., The, 233 Wilshire Blvd., Ste. 900, Santa Monica, CA 90401 / 800-92ARMLOC

Sure-Shot Game Calls, Inc., P.O. Box 816, 6835 Capitol, Groves, TX 77619 / 409-962-1636; FAX: 409-962-5465

Svon Corp., 2107 W. Blue Heron Blvd., Riviera Beach, FL 33404 / 508-881-8852

Swampfire Shop, The (See Peterson Gun Shop, Inc., A.W.)

Swann, D. J., 5 Orsova Close, Eltham North Vic., 3095 AUSTRALIA / 03-431-0323

Swanndri New Zealand, 152 Elm Ave., Burlingame, CA 94010 / 415-347-6158

Swanson, Mark, 975 Heap Avenue, Prescott, AZ 86301 / 928-778-4423

Swarovski Optik North America Ltd., 2 Slater Rd., Cranston, RI 02920 / 401-946-2220; or 800-426-3089; FAX: 401-946-2587

Sweet Home, Inc., P.O. Box 900, Orrville, OH 44667-0900

Swenson's 45 Shop, A. D., 3839 Ladera Vista Rd., Fallbrook, CA 92028-9431

Swift Bullet Co., P.O. Box 27, 201 Main St., Quinter, KS 67752 / 913-754-3959; FAX: 913-754-2359

Swift Instruments, Inc., 952 Dorchester Ave., Boston, MA 02125 / 617-436-2960; FAX: 617-436-3232

Swift River Gunworks, 450 State St., Belchertown, MA 01007 / 413-323-4052

Szweda, Robert (See RMS Custom Gunsmithing)

T

T&S Industries, Inc., 1027 Skyview Dr., W. Carrollton, OH 45449 / 513-859-8414; FAX: 937-859-8404 keith.tomlinson@tandsshellcatcher.com www.tandsshellcatcher.com

T.F.C. S.p.A., Via G. Marconi 118, B, Villa Carcina 25069, ITALY / 030-881271; FAX: 030-881826

T.G. Faust, Inc., 544 Minor St., Reading, PA 19602 / 610-375-8549; FAX: 610-375-4488

T.K. Lee Co., 1282 Branchwater Ln., Birmingham, AL 35216 / 205-913-5222 odonmich@aol.com www.scopedot.com

T.W. Menck Gunsmith, Inc., 5703 S. 77th St., Ralston, NE 68127 guntools@cox.net http://llwww.members.cox.net/guntools

Tabler Marketing, 2554 Lincoln Blvd., Suite 555, Marina Del Rey, CA 90291 / 818-386-0373; FAX: 818-386-0373

Taconic Firearms Ltd., Perry Lane, P.O. Box 553, Cambridge, NY 12816 / 518-677-2704; FAX: 518-677-5974

Tactical Defense Institute, 2174 Bethany Ridges, West Union, OH 45693 / 937-544-7228; FAX: 937-544-2887 tdiohio@dragonbbs.com www.tdiohio.com

Talley, Dave, P.O. Box 369, Santee, SC 29142 / 803-854-5700; or 307-436-9315; FAX: 803-854-9315 talley@diretway www.talleyrings.com

Talon Industries Inc. (See Cobra Enterprises, Inc.)

Tamarack Products, Inc., P.O. Box 625, Wauconda, IL 60084 / 708-526-9333; FAX: 708-526-9353

Tanfoglio Fratelli S.r.l., via Valtrompia 39, 41, Brescia, ITALY / 011-39-030-8910361; FAX: 011-39-030-8910183 info@tanfoglio.it www.tanfoglio.it

Tanglefree Industries, 1261 Heavenly Dr., Martinez, CA 94553 / 800-982-4868; FAX: 510-825-3874

Tank's Rifle Shop, P.O. Box 474, Fremont, NE 68026-0474 / 402-727-1317 jtank@tanksrifleshop.com www.tanksrifleshop.com

Tanner (See U.S. Importer-Mandall Shooting Supplies, Inc.)

Taracorp Industries, Inc., 1200 Sixteenth St., Granite City, IL 62040 / 618-451-4400

Target Shooting, Inc., P.O. Box 773, Watertown, SD 57201 / 605-882-6955; FAX: 605-882-8840

Tar-Hunt Custom Rifles, Inc., 101 Dogtown Rd., Bloomsburg, PA 17815 / 570-784-6368; FAX: 570-389-9150 www.tar-hunt.com

Tarnhelm Supply Co., Inc., 431 High St., Boscawen, NH 03303 / 603-796-2551; FAX: 603-796-2918 info@tarnhelm.com www.tarnhelm.com

Tasco Sales, Inc., 2889 Commerce Pkwy., Miramar, FL 33025

Taurus Firearms, Inc., 16175 NW 49th Ave., Miami, FL 33014 / 305-624-1115; FAX: 305-623-7506

Taurus International Firearms (See U.S. Importer Taurus Firearms, Inc.)

Taurus S.A. Forjas, Avenida Do Forte 511, Porto Alegre, RS BRAZIL 91360 / 55-51-347-4050; FAX: 55-51-347-3065

Taylor & Robbins, P.O. Box 164, Rixford, PA 16745 / 814-966-3233

Taylor's & Co., Inc., 304 Lenoir Dr., Winchester, VA 22603 / 540-722-2017; FAX: 540-722-2018 info@taylorsfirearms.com www.taylorsfirearms.com

TCCI, P.O. Box 302, Phoenix, AZ 85001 / 602-237-3823; FAX: 602-237-3858

TCSR, 3998 Hoffman Rd., White Bear Lake, MN 55110-4626 / 800-328-5323; FAX: 612-429-0526

TDP Industries, Inc., P.O. Box 249, Ottsville, PA 18942-0249 / 215-345-8687; FAX: 215-345-6057

Techno Arms (See U.S. Importer- Auto-Ordnance Corp.)

Tecnolegno S.p.A., Via A. Locatelli, 6 10, 24019 Zogno, ITALY / 0345-55111; FAX: 0345-55155

Ted Blocker Holsters, Inc., 9396 S.W. Tigard St., Tigard, OR 97223 / 800-650-9742; FAX: 503-670-9692 www.tedblocker.com

Tele-Optics, 630 E. Rockland Rd., P.O. Box 6313, Libertyville, IL 60048 / 847-362-7757; FAX: 847-362-7757

Tennessee Valley Mfg., 14 County Road 521, Corinth, MS 38834 / 601-286-5014 tvm@avsia.com www.avsia.com/tvm

Ten-Ring Precision, Inc., Alex B. Hamilton, 1449 Blue Crest Lane, San Antonio, TX 78232 / 210-494-3063; FAX: 210-494-3066

TEN-X Products Group, 1905 N. Main St., Suite 133, Cleburne, TX 76031-1305 / 972-243-4016; or 800-433-2225; FAX: 972-243-4112

Tepeco, P.O. Box 342, Friendswood, TX 77546 / 713-482-2702

Terry K. Kopp Professional Gunsmithing, Rt 1 Box 224, Lexington, MO 64067 / 816-259-2636

Testing Systems, Inc., 220 Pegasus Ave., Northvale, NJ 07647

Tetra Gun Care, 8 Vreeland Rd., Florham Park, NJ 07932 / 973-443-0004; FAX: 973-443-0263

Tex Shoemaker & Sons, Inc., 714 W. Cienega Ave., San Dimas, CA 91773 / 909-592-2071; FAX: 909-592-2378 texshoemaker@texshoemaker.com www.texshoemaker.com

Texas Armory (See Bond Arms, Inc.)

Texas Platers Supply Co., 2453 W. Five Mile Parkway, Dallas, TX 75233 / 214-330-7168

Thad Rybka Custom Leather Equipment, 2050 Canoe Creek Rd., Springvale, AL 35146-6709

Thad Scott Fine Guns, Inc., P.O. Box 412, Indianola, MS 38751 / 601-887-5929

Theis, Terry, 21452 FM 2093, Harper, TX 78631 / 830-864-4438

Thiewes, George W., 14329 W. Parada Dr., Sun City West, AZ 85375

Things Unlimited, 235 N. Kimbau, Casper, WY 82601 / 307-234-5277

Thirion Gun Engraving, Denise, P.O. Box 408, Graton, CA 95444 / 707-829-1876

Thomas, Charles C., 2600 S. First St., Springfield, IL 62704 / 217-789-8980; FAX: 217-789-9130 books@ccthomas.com www.ccthomas.com

Thompson Bullet Lube Co., P.O. Box 409, Wills Point, TX 75169 / 866-476-1500; FAX: 866-476-1500 thompsonbulletlube.com www.thompsonbulletlube.com

Thompson Precision, 110 Mary St., P.O. Box 251, Warren, IL 61087 / 815-745-3625

Thompson, Randall. See: HIGHLINE MACHINE CO.

Thompson Target Technology, 4804 Sherman Church Ave. S.W., Canton, OH 44710 / 330-484-6480; FAX: 330-491-1087 www.thompsontarget.com

Thompson Tool Mount, 1550 Solomon Rd., Santa Maria, CA 93455 / 805-934-1281 ttm@pronet.net www.thompsontoolmount.com

Thompson/Center Arms, P.O. Box 5002, Rochester, NH 03866 / 603-332-2394; FAX: 603-332-5133 tech@tcarms.com www.tcarms.com

Thunden Ranch, HCR 1, Box 53, Mountain Home, TX 78058 / 830-640-3138

Tiger-Hunt Longrifle Gunstocks, Box 379, Beaverdale, PA 15921 / 814-472-5161 tigerhunt4@aol.com www.gunstockwood.com

Tikka (See U.S. Importer-Stoeger Industries)

Time Precision, 4 Nicholas Sq., New Milford, CT 06776-3506 / 860-350-8343; FAX: 860-350-6343 timeprecision@aol.com

Tinks & Ben Lee Hunting Products (See Wellington Outdoors)

Tink's Safariland Hunting Corp., P.O. Box 244, 1140 Monticello Rd., Madison, GA 30650 / 706-342-4915; FAX: 706-342-7568

Tioga Engineering Co., Inc., P.O. Box 913, 13 Cone St., Wellsboro, PA 16901 / 570-724-3533; FAX: 570-724-3895 tiogaeng@epix.net

Tippman Pneumatics, Inc., 2955 Adams Center Rd., Fort Wayne, IN 46803

Tirelli, Snc Di Tirelli Primo E.C., Via Matteotti No. 359, Gardone V.T. Brescia, ITALY / 0039-030-8912819; FAX: 0039-030-832240 tirelli@tirelli.it www.tirelli.it

TM Stockworks, 6355 Maplecrest Rd., Fort Wayne, IN 46835 / 219-485-5389

Tom Forrest, Inc., P.O. Box 326, Lakeside, CA 92040 / 619-561-5800; FAX: 888-GUN-CLIP info@gunmag.com www.gunmags.com

Tombstone Smoke`n' Deals, PO Box 31298, Phoenix, AZ 85046 / 602-905-7013; FAX: 602-443-1998

Tom's Gun Repair, Thomas G. Ivanoff, 76-6 Rt. Southfork Rd., Cody, WY 82414 / 307-587-6949

Tom's Gunshop, 3601 Central Ave., Hot Springs, AR 71913 / 501-624-3856

Tonoloway Tack Drives, HCR 81, Box 100, Needmore, PA 17238

Torel, Inc./Tandy Brands Outdoors/AA & E, 208 Industrial Loop, Yoakum, TX 77995 / 361-293-6366; FAX: 361-293-9127

TOZ (See U.S. Importer-Nygord Precision Products, Inc.)

Track of the Wolf, Inc., 18308 Joplin St. NW, Elk River, MN 55330-1773 / 763-633-2500; FAX: 763-633-2550

Traditions Performance Firearms, P.O. Box 776, 1375 Boston Post Rd., Old Saybrook, CT 06475 / 860-388-4656; FAX: 860-388-4657 info@traditionsfirearms.com www.traditionsfirearms.com

Trafalgar Square, P.O. Box 257, N. Pomfret, VT 05053 / 802-457-1911

Trail Visions, 5800 N. Ames Terrace, Glendale, WI 53209 / 414-228-1328

Trax America, Inc., P.O. Box 898, 1150 Eldridge, Forrest City, AR 72335 / 870-633-0410; or 800-232-2327; FAX: 870-633-4788 trax@ipa.net www.traxamerica.com

MANUFACTURER'S DIRECTORY

Treadlok Gun Safe, Inc., 1764 Granby St. NE, Roanoke, VA 24012 / 800-729-8732; or 703-982-6881; FAX: 703-982-1059

Treebone Carving, P.O. Box 551, Cimarron, NJ 87714 / 505-376-2145 treebonecarving.com

Treemaster, P.O. Box 247, Guntersville, AL 35976 / 205-878-3597

Trevallion Gunstocks, 9 Old Mountain Rd., Cape Neddick, ME 03902 / 207-361-1130

Trico Plastics, 28061 Diaz Rd., Temecula, CA 92590 / 909-676-7714; FAX: 909-676-0267 ustinfo@ustplastics.com www.tricoplastics.com

Trigger Lock Division / Central Specialties Ltd., 220-D Exchange Dr., Crystal Lake, IL 60014 / 847-639-3900; FAX: 847-639-3972

Trijicon, Inc., 49385 Shafer Ave., P.O. Box 930059, Wixom, MI 48393-0059 / 248-960-7700; or 800-338-0563

Trilby Sport Shop, 1623 Hagley Rd., Toledo, OH 43612-2024 / 419-472-6222

Trilux, Inc., P.O. Box 24608, Winston-Salem, NC 27114 / 910-659-9438; FAX: 910-768-7720

Trinidad St. Jr. Col. Gunsmith Dept., 600 Prospect St., Trinidad, CO 81082 / 719-846-5631; FAX: 719-846-5667

Triple-K Mfg. Co., Inc., 2222 Commercial St., San Diego, CA 92113 / 619-232-2066; FAX: 619-232-7675 sales@triplek.com www.triplek.com

Tristar Sporting Arms, Ltd., 1814 Linn St. #16, N. Kansas City, MO 64116-3627 / 816-421-1400; FAX: 816-421-4182 tristar@blitz-it.net www.tristarsportingarms

Trius Traps, Inc., P.O. Box 25, 221 S. Miami Ave., Cleves, OH 45002 / 513-941-5682; FAX: 513-941-7970 triustraps@fuse.net www.triustraps.com

Trooper Walsh, 2393 N. Edgewood St., Arlington, VA 22207

Trotman, Ken, 135 Ditton Walk, Unit 11, Cambridge, CB5 8PY ENGLAND / 01223-211030; FAX: 01223-212317 www.kentrolman.com

Tru-Balance Knife Co., P.O. Box 140555, Grand Rapids, MI 49514 / 616-647-1215

True Flight Bullet Co., 5581 Roosevelt St., Whitehall, PA 18052 / 610-262-7630; FAX: 610-262-7806

Truglo, Inc., P.O. Box 1612, McKinna, TX 75070 / 972-774-0300; FAX: 972-774-0323 www.truglosights.com

Trulock Tool, P.O. Box 530, Whigham, GA 31797 / 229-762-4678; FAX: 229-762-4050 trulockchokes@hotmail.com trulockchokes.com

Tru-Nord Compass, 1504 Erick Lane, Brainerd, MN 56401 / 218-829-2870; FAX: 218-829-2870 www.trunord.com

Tru-Square Metal Products, Inc., 640 First St. SW, P.O. Box 585, Auburn, WA 98071 / 253-833-2310; or 800-225-1017; FAX: 253-833-2349 t-tumbler@qwest.net

Tucker, James C., P.O. Box 366, Medford, OR 97501 / 541-664-9160 jctstocker@yahoo.com

Tucson Mold, Inc., 930 S. Plumer Ave., Tucson, AZ 85719 / 520-792-1075; FAX: 520-792-1075

Turk's Head Productions, Mustafa Bilal, 908 NW 50th St., Seattle, WA 98107-3634 / 206-782-4164; FAX: 206-783-5677 info@turkshead.com www.turkshead.com

Turnbull Restoration, Doug, 6680 Rts. 5 & 20, P.O. Box 471, Bloomfield, NY 14469 / 585-657-6338; FAX: 585-657-6338 turnbullrest@mindspring.com www.turnbullrestoration.com

Tuttle, Dale, 4046 Russell Rd., Muskegon, MI 49445 / 616-766-2250

U

U.S. Importer-Wm. Larkin Moore, 8430 E. Raintree Ste. B-7, Scottsdale, AZ 85260

U.S. Optics, A Division of Zeitz Optics U.S.A., 5900 Dale St., Buena Park, CA 90621 / 714-994-4901; FAX: 714-994-4904 www.usoptics.com

U.S. Repeating Arms Co., Inc., 275 Winchester Ave., Morgan, UT 84050-9333 / 801-876-3440; FAX: 801-876-3737 www.winchester-guns.com

U.S. Tactical Systems (See Keng's Firearms Specialty, Inc.)

Ugartechea S. A., Ignacio, Chonta 26, Eibar, SPAIN / 43-121257; FAX: 43-121669

Ultra Dot Distribution, P.O. Box 362, 6304 Riverside Dr., Yankeetown, FL 34498 / 352-447-2255; FAX: 352-447-2266

Ultralux (See U.S. Importer-Keng's Firearms Specialty, Inc.)

UltraSport Arms, Inc., 1955 Norwood Ct., Racine, WI 53403 / 414-554-3237; FAX: 414-554-9731

Uncle Bud's, HCR 81, Box 100, Needmore, PA 17238 / 717-294-6000; FAX: 717-294-6005

Uncle Mike's (See Michaels of Oregon, Co.)

Unertl Optical Co., Inc., 103 Grand Avenue, P.O. Box 895, Mars, PA 16046-0895 / 724-625-3810; FAX:

724-625-3819 unertl@nauticom.net www.unertloptics.net

UniTec, 1250 Bedford SW, Canton, OH 44710 / 216-452-4017

United Binocular Co., 9043 S. Western Ave., Chicago, IL 60620

United Cutlery Corp., 1425 United Blvd., Sevierville, TN 37876 / 865-428-2532; or 800-548-0835; FAX: 865-428-2267 www.unitedcutlery.com

United States Products Co., 518 Melwood Ave., Pittsburgh, PA 15213-1136 / 412-621-2130; FAX: 412-621-8740 sales@us-products.com www.usporepaste.com

Universal Sports, P.O. Box 532, Vincennes, IN 47591 / 812-882-8680; FAX: 812-882-8680

Upper Missouri Trading Co., P.O. Box 100, 304 Harold St., Crofton, NE 68730-0100 / 402-388-4844 www.uppermotradingco.com

USAC, 4500-15th St. East, Tacoma, WA 98424 / 206-922-7589

Uselton/Arms, Inc., 842 Conference Dr., Goodlettsville, TN 37072 / 615-851-4919

Utica Cutlery Co., 820 Noyes St., Utica, NY 13503 / 315-733-4663; FAX: 315-733-6602

V

V. H. Blackinton & Co., Inc., 221 John L. Dietsch, Attleboro Falls, MA 02763-0300 / 508-699-4436; FAX: 508-695-5349

Valdada Enterprises, P.O. Box 773122, 31733 County Road 35, Steamboat Springs, CO 80477 / 970-879-2983; FAX: 970-879-0851 www.valdada.com

Valtro USA, Inc., 1281 Andersen Dr., San Rafael, CA 94901 / 415-256-2575; FAX: 415-256-2576

VAM Distribution Co. LLC, 1141-B Mechanicsburg Rd., Wooster, OH 44691 www.rex10.com

Van Gorden & Son Inc., C. S., 1815 Main St., Bloomer, WI 54724 / 715-568-2612

Van Horn, Gil, P.O. Box 207, Llano, CA 93544

Van Patten, J. W., P.O. Box 145, Foster Hill, Milford, PA 18337 / 717-296-7069

Vann Custom Bullets, 2766 N. Willowside Way, Meridian, ID 83642

Van's Gunsmith Service, 224 Route 69-A, Parish, NY 13131 / 315-625-7251

Varmint Masters, LLC, Rick Vecqueray, P.O. Box 6724, Bend, OR 97708 / 541-318-7306; FAX: 541-318-7306 varmintmasters@bendcable.com www.varmintmasters.net

Vecqueray, Rick. See: VARMINT MASTERS, LLC

Vector Arms, Inc., 270 W. 500 N., North Salt Lake, UT 84054 / 801-295-1917; FAX: 801-295-9316 vectorarms@bbscmail.com www.vectorarms.com

Vega Tool Co., c/o T. R. Ross, 4865 Tanglewood Ct., Boulder, CO 80301 / 303-530-0174 clanlaird@aol.com www.vegatool.com

Venco Industries, Inc. (See Shooter's Choice Gun Care)

Venus Industries, P.O. Box 246, Sialkot-1, PAKISTAN FAX: 92 432 85579

Verney-Carron, 54 Boulevard Thiers-B.P. 72, 42002 St. Etienne Cedex 1, St. Etienne Cedex 1, FRANCE / 33-477791500; FAX: 33-477790702 email@verney-carron.com www.verney-carron.com

Vest, John, 1923 NE 7th St., Redmond, OR 97756 / 541-923-8898

VibraShine, Inc., P.O. Box 577, Taylorsville, MS 39168 / 601-785-9854; FAX: 601-785-9874 rdbeke@vibrashine.com www.vibrashine.com

Vibra-Tek Co., 1844 Arroya Rd., Colorado Springs, CO 80906 / 719-634-8611; FAX: 719-634-6886

Vic's Gun Refinishing, 6 Pineview Dr., Dover, NH 03820-6422 / 603-742-0013

Victory Ammunition, P.O. Box 1022, Milford, PA 18337 / 717-296-5768; FAX: 717-296-9298

Victory USA, P.O. Box 1021, Pine Bush, NY 12566 / 914-744-2060; FAX: 914-744-5181

Vihtavuori Oy, FIN-41330 Vihtavuori, FINLAND, / 358-41-3779211; FAX: 358-41-3771643

Vihtavuori Oy/Kaltron-Pettibone, 1241 Ellis St., Bensenville, IL 60106 / 708-350-1116; FAX: 708-350-1606

Viking Video Productions, P.O. Box 251, Roseburg, OR 97470

Village Restorations & Consulting, Inc., P.O. Box 569, Claysburg, PA 16625 / 814-239-8200; FAX: 814-239-2165 www.villagerestoration@yahoo.com

Vincent's Shop, 210 Antoinette, Fairbanks, AK 99701

Viper Bullet and Brass Works, 11 Brock St., Box 582, Norwich, ON N0J 1P0 CANADA

Viramontez Engraving, Ray Viramontez, 601 Springfield Dr., Albany, GA 31721 / 229-432-9683 sgtvira@aol.com

Viramontez, Ray. See: VIRAMONTEZ ENGRAVING

Virgin Valley Custom Guns, 450 E 800 N. #20, Hurricane, UT 84737 / 435-635-8941; FAX: 435-635-8943 vvcguns@infowest.com www.virginvalleyguns.com

Visible Impact Targets, Rts. 5 & 20, E. Bloomfield, NY 14443 / 716-657-6161; FAX: 716-657-5405

Vitt/Boos, 1195 Buck Hill Rd., Townshend, VT 05353 / 802-365-9232

Voere-KGH GmbH, Untere Sparchen 56, A-6330 Kufstein, Tirol, AUSTRIA / 0043-5372-62547; FAX: 0043-5372-65752 voere@aon.com www.voere.com

Volquartsen Custom Ltd., 24276 240th Street, P.O. Box 397, Carroll, IA 51401 / 712-792-4238; FAX: 712-792-2542 vcl@netins.net www.volquartsen.com

Vorhes, David, 3042 Beecham St., Napa, CA 94558 / 707-226-9116; FAX: 707-253-7334

VSP Publishers (See Heritage/VSP Gun Books), P.O. Box 887, McCall, ID 83638 / 208-634-4104; FAX: 208-634-3101 heritage@gunbooks.com www.gunbooks.com

VTI Gun Parts, P.O. Box 509, Lakeville, CT 06039 / 860-435-8068; FAX: 860-435-8146 mail@vtigunparts.com www.vtigunparts.com

Vulpes Ventures, Inc., Fox Cartridge Division, P.O. Box 1363, Bolingbrook, IL 60440-7363 / 630-759-1229

W

W. Square Enterprises, 9826 Sagedale Dr., Houston, TX 77089 / 281-484-0935; FAX: 281-464-9940 lfdw@pdq.net www.loadammo.com

W. Waller & Son, Inc., 2221 Stoney Brook Rd., Grantham, NH 03753-7706 / 603-863-4177 www.wallerandson.com

W.B. Niemi Engineering, Box 126 Center Road, Greensboro, VT 05841 / 802-533-7180; or 802-533-7141

W.C. Wolff Co., P.O. Box 458, Newtown Square, PA 19073 / 610-359-9600; or 800-545-0077 mail@gunsprings.com www.gunsprings.com

W.E. Birdsong & Assoc., 1435 Monterey Rd., Florence, MS 39073-9748 / 601-366-8270

W.E. Brownell Checkering Tools, 9390 Twin Mountain Cir., San Diego, AZ 92126 / 858-695-2479; FAX: 858-695-2479

W.J. Riebe Co., 3434 Tucker Rd., Boise, ID 83703

W.R. Case & Sons Cutlery Co., Owens Way, Bradford, PA 16701 / 814-368-4123; or 800-523-6350; FAX: 814-368-1736 jsullivan@wrcase.com www.wrcase.com

Wagoner, Vernon G., 2325 E. Encanto St., Mesa, AZ 85213-5917 / 480-835-1307

Waldron, Herman, Box 475, 80 N. 17th St., Pomeroy, WA 99347 / 509-843-1404

Walker Arms Co., Inc., 499 County Rd. 820, Selma, AL 36701 / 334-872-6231; FAX: 334-872-6262

Wallace, Terry, 385 San Marino, Vallejo, CA 94589 / 707-642-7041

Walls Industries, Inc., P.O. Box 98, 1905 N. Main, Cleburne, TX 76033 / 817-645-4366; FAX: 817-645-7946 www.wallsoutdoors.com

Walters Industries, 6226 Park Lane, Dallas, TX 75225 / 214-691-6973

Walters, John. See: WALTERS WADS

Walters Wads, John Walters, 500 N. Avery Dr., Moore, OK 73160 / 405-799-0376; FAX: 405-799-7727 www.tinwadman@cs.com

Walther America, P.O. Box 22, Springfield, MA 01102 / 413-747-3443 www.walther-usa.com

Walther GmbH, Carl, B.P. 4325, D-89033 Ulm, GERMANY

Walt's Custom Leather, Walt Whinnery, 1947 Meadow Creek Dr., Louisville, KY 40218 / 502-458-4361

WAMCO-New Mexico, P.O. Box 205, Peralta, NM 87042-0205 / 505-869-0826

Ward & Van Valkenburg, 114 32nd Ave. N., Fargo, ND 58102 / 701-232-2351

Ward Machine, 5620 Lexington Rd., Corpus Christi, TX 78412 / 512-992-1221

Wardell Precision Handguns Ltd., P.O. Box 391, Clyde, AZ 79510-0391 / 602-465-7995

Warenski Engraving, Julie Warenski, 590 E. 500 N., Richfield, UT 84701 / 435-896-5319; FAX: 435-896-8333 julie@warenskiknives.com

Warenski, Julie. See: WARENSKI ENGRAVING

Warne Manufacturing Co., 9057 SE Jannsen Rd., Clackamas, OR 97015 / 503-657-5590; or 800-683-5590; FAX: 503-657-5695 info@warnescopemounts.com www.warnescopemounts.com

Warren Muzzleloading Co., Inc., Hwy. 21 North, P.O. Box 100, Ozone, AR 72854 / 501-292-3268

Washita Mountain Whetstone Co., P.O. Box 20378, Hot Springs, AR 71903 / 501-525-3914 www.@hsnp.com

Wasmundt, Jim, P.O. Box 130, Powers, OR 97466-0130

Watson Bros., 39 Redcross Way, London Bridge SE1 1H6, London, ENGLAND FAX: 44-171-403-336

MANUFACTURER'S DIRECTORY

Watson Bullets, 231 Allies Pass, Frostproof, FL 33843 / 863-635-7948 cbestbullet@aol.com

Wayne Specialty Services, 260 Waterford Drive, Florissant, MO 63033 / 413-831-7083

WD-40 Co., 1061 Cudahy Pl., San Diego, CA 92110 / 619-275-1400; FAX: 619-275-5823

Weatherby, Inc., 3100 El Camino Real, Atascadero, CA 93422 / 805-466-1767; FAX: 805-466-2527 www.weatherby.com

Weaver Products ATK, P.O. Box 39, Onalaska, WI 54650 / 800-648-9624; or 608-781-5800; FAX: 608-781-0368

Weaver Scope Repair Service, 1121 Larry Mahan Dr., Suite B, El Paso, TX 79925 / 915-593-1005

Webb, Bill, 6504 North Bellefontaine, Kansas City, MO 64119 / 816-453-7431

Weber & Markin Custom Gunsmiths, 4-1691 Powick Rd., Kelowna, BC V1X 4L1 CANADA / 250-762-7575; FAX: 250-861-3655 www.weberandmarkinguns.com

Webley and Scott Ltd., Frankley Industrial Park, Tay Rd., Birmingham, B45 0PA ENGLAND / 011-021-453-1864; FAX: 0121-457-7846 guns@webley.co.uk www.webley.co.uk

Webster Scale Mfg. Co., P.O. Box 188, Sebring, FL 33870 / 813-385-6362

Weems, Cecil, 510 W. Hubbard St., Mineral Wells, TX 76067-4847 / 817-325-1462

Weigand Combat Handguns, Inc., 1057 South Main Rd., Mountain Top, PA 18707 / 570-868-8358; FAX: 570-868-5218 sales@jackweigand.com www.jackweigand.com

Weihrauch KG, Hermann, Industriestrasse 11, 8744 Mellrichstadt, Mellrichstadt, GERMANY

Welch, Sam. See: SAM WELCH GUN ENGRAVING

Wellington Outdoors, P.O. Box 244, 1140 Monticello Rd., Madison, GA 30650 / 706-342-4915; FAX: 706-342-7568

Wells, Rachel, 110 N. Summit St., Prescott, AZ 86301 / 928-445-3655 wellssportstore@cableone.net

Wells Creek Knife & Gun Works, 32956 State Hwy. 38, Scottsburg, OR 97473 / 541-587-4202; FAX: 541-587-4223

Welsh, Bud. See: HIGH PRECISION

Wenger North America/Precise Int'l., 15 Corporate Dr., Orangeburg, NY 10962 / 800-431-2996; FAX: 914-425-4700

Wenig Custom Gunstocks, 103 N. Market St., P.O. Box 249, Lincoln, MO 65338 / 660-547-3334; FAX: 660-547-2881 gustock@wenig.com www.wenig.com

Werth, T. W., 1203 Woodlawn Rd., Lincoln, IL 62656 / 217-732-1300

Wescombe, Bill (See North Star West)

Wessinger Custom Guns & Engraving, 268 Limestone Rd., Chapin, SC 29036 / 803-345-5677

West, Jack L., 1220 W. Fifth, P.O. Box 427, Arlington, OR 97812

Western Cutlery (See Camillus Cutlery Co.)

Western Mfg. Co., 550 Valencia School Rd., Aptos, CA 95003 / 831-688-5884 lotsabears@eathlink.net

Western Missouri Shooters Alliance, P.O. Box 11144, Kansas City, MO 64119 / 816-597-3950; FAX: 816-229-7350

Western Nevada West Coast Bullets, P.O. BOX 2270, DAYTON, NV 89403-2270 / 702-246-3941; FAX: 702-246-0836

Westley Richards & Co. Ltd., 40 Grange Rd., Birmingham, ENGLAND / 010-214722953; FAX: 010-214141138 sales@westleyrichards.com www.westleyrichards.com

Westley Richards Agency USA (See U.S. Importer

Westwind Rifles, Inc., David S. Sullivan, P.O. Box 261, 640 Briggs St., Erie, CO 80516 / 303-828-3823

Weyer International, 2740 Nebraska Ave., Toledo, OH 43607 / 419-534-2020; FAX: 419-534-2697

Whildin & Sons Ltd., E.H., RR 2 Box 119, Tamaqua, PA 18252 / 717-668-6743; FAX: 717-668-6745

Whinnery, Walt (See Walt's Custom Leather)

White Barn Wor, 431 County Road, Broadlands, IL 61816

White Pine Photographic Services, Hwy. 60, General Delivery, Wilno, ON K0J 2N0 CANADA / 613-756-3452

White Rifles, Inc., 234 S. 1250 W., Linden, UT 84042 / 801-932-7950 www.whiterifles.com

White Rock Tool & Die, 6400 N. Brighton Ave., Kansas City, MO 64119 / 816-454-0478

Whitestone Lumber Corp., 148-02 14th Ave., Whitestone, NY 11357 / 718-746-4400; FAX: 718-767-1748 whstco@aol.com

Wichita Arms, Inc., 923 E. Gilbert, Wichita, KS 67211 / 316-265-0661; FAX: 316-265-0760 sales@wichitaarms.com www.wichitaarms.com

Wick, David E., 1504 Michigan Ave., Columbus, IN 47201 / 812-376-6960

Widener's Reloading & Shooting Supply, Inc., P.O. Box 3009 CRS, Johnson City, TN 37602 / 615-282-6786; FAX: 615-282-6651

Wideview Scope Mount Corp., 13535 S. Hwy. 16, Rapid City, SD 57702 / 605-341-3220; FAX: 605-341-9142 wvdon@rapidnet.com www.wideviewscopemount.com

Wiebe, Duane, 5300 Merchant Cir. #2, Placerville, CA 95667 / 530-344-1357; FAX: 530-344-1357 wiebe@d-wdb.com

Wiest, Marie. See: GUNCRAFT SPORTS, INC.

Wilcox All-Pro Tools & Supply, 4880 147th St., Montezuma, IA 50171 / 515-623-3138; FAX: 515-623-3104

Wilcox Industries Corp., Robert F. Guarasi, 53 Durham St., Portsmouth, NH 03801 / 603-431-1331; FAX: 603-431-1221

Wild Bill's Originals, P.O. Box 13037, Burton, WA 98013 / 206-463-5738; FAX: 206-465-5925 wildbill@halcyon.com billcleaver@centurytel.net

Wild West Guns, 7521 Old Seward Hwy., Unit A, Anchorage, AK 99518 / 800-992-4570; or 907-344-4500; FAX: 907-344-4005 wwguns@ak.net www.wildwestguns.com

Wilderness Sound Products Ltd., 4015 Main St. A, Springfield, OR 97478

Wildey F. A., Inc., 45 Angevin Rd., Warren, CT 06754-1818 / 860-355-9000; FAX: 860-354-7759 wildeyfa@optonline.net www.wildeyguns.com

Wildlife Research Center, Inc., 1050 McKinley St., Anoka, MN 55303 / 763-427-3350; or 800-USE-LURE; FAX: 763-427-8354 www.wildlife.com

Will-Burt Co., 169 S. Main, Orrville, OH 44667

William E. Phillips Firearms, 38 Avondale Rd., Wigston, Leicester, ENGLAND / 0116 2886334; FAX: 0116 2810644 william.phillips2@tesco.net

William Powell Agency, 22 Circle Dr., Bellmore, NY 11710 / 516-679-1158

Williams Gun Sight Co., 7389 Lapeer Rd., Box 329, Davison, MI 48423 / 810-653-2131; or 800-530-9028; FAX: 810-658-2140 williamsgunsight.com

Williams Mfg. of Oregon, 110 East B St., Drain, OR 97435 / 503-836-7461; FAX: 503-836-7245

Williams Shootin' Iron Service, The Lynx-Line, Rt. 2 Box 223A, Mountain Grove, MO 65711 / 417-948-0902; FAX: 417-948-0902

Williamson Precision Gunsmithing, 117 W. Pipeline, Hurst, TX 76053 / 817-285-0064; FAX: 817-280-0044

Willow Bend, P.O. Box 203, Chelmsford, MA 01824 / 978-256-8508; FAX: 978-256-8508

Wilsom Combat, 2234 CR 719, Berryville, AR 72616-4573 / 800-955-4856; FAX: 870-545-3310

Wilson Arms Co., The, 63 Leetes Island Rd., Branford, CT 06405 / 203-488-7297; FAX: 203-488-0135

Wilson Case, Inc., P.O. Box 1106, Hastings, NE 68902-1106 / 800-322-5493; FAX: 402-463-5276 sales@wilsoncase.com www.wilsoncase.com

Wilson Combat, 2234 CR 719, Berryville, AR 72616-4573 / 800-955-4856

Winchester Consultants, George Madis, P.O. Box 545, Brownsboro, TX 75756 / 903-852-6480; FAX: 903-852-5486 gmadis@earthlink.com www.georgemadis.com

Winchester Div. Olin Corp., 427 N. Shamrock, E. Alton, IL 62024 / 618-258-3566; FAX: 618-258-3599

Winchester Sutler, Inc., The, 270 Shadow Brook Lane, Winchester, VA 22603 / 540-888-3595; FAX: 540-888-4632

Windish, Jim, 2510 Dawn Dr., Alexandria, VA 22306 / 703-765-1994

Winfield Galleries LLC, 748 Hanley Industrial Ct., St. Louis, MO 63144 / 314-645-7636; FAX: 314-781-0224 info@winfieldgalleries.com www.winfieldgalleries.com

Wingshooting Adventures, 0-1845 W. Leonard, Grand Rapids, MI 49544 / 616-677-1980; FAX: 616-677-1986

Winter, Robert M., P.O. Box 484, 42975-287th St., Menno, SD 57045 / 605-387-5322

Wise Custom Guns, 1402 Blanco Rd., San Antonio, TX 78212-2716 / 210-828-3388

Wise Guns, Dale, 1402 Blanco Rd., San Antonio, TX 78212 / 210-734-9999

Wiseman and Co., Bill, P.O. Box 3427, Bryan, TX 77805 / 409-690-3456; FAX: 409-690-0156

Wisners, Inc., P.O. Box 58, Adna, WA 98522 / 360-748-4590; FAX: 360-748-6028 parts@wisnersinc.com www.wisnersinc.com

Wolf Performance Ammunition, 2201 E. Winston Rd., Ste. K, Anaheim, CA 92806-5537 / 702-837-8506; FAX: 702-837-9250

Wolfe Publishing Co., 2625 Stearman Rd., Ste. A, Prescott, AZ 86301 / 928-445-7810; or 800-899-7810; FAX: 928-778-5124

Wolverine Footwear Group, 9341 Courtland Dr. NE, Rockford, MI 49351 / 616-866-5500; FAX: 616-866-5658

Woodleigh (See Huntington Die Specialties)

Woods Wise Products, P.O. Box 681552, Franklin, TN 37068 / 800-735-8182; FAX: 615-726-2637

Woodstream, P.O. Box 327, Lititz, PA 17543 / 717-626-2125; FAX: 717-626-1912

Woodworker's Supply, 1108 North Glenn Rd., Casper, WY 82601 / 307-237-5354

Woolrich, Inc., Mill St., Woolrich, PA 17701 / 800-995-1299; FAX: 717-769-6234/6259

World of Targets (See Birchwood Casey)

World Trek, Inc., 7170 Turkey Creek Rd., Pueblo, CO 81007-1046 / 719-546-2121; FAX: 719-543-6886

Worthy Products, Inc., RR 1, P.O. Box 213, Martville, NY 13111 / 315-324-5298

Wright's Gunstock Blanks, 8540 SE Kane Rd., Gresham, OR 97080 / 503-666-1705 doyal@wrightsguns.com www.wrightsguns.com

WTA Manufacturing, P.O. Box 164, Kit Carson, CO 80825 / 719-962-3570; or 719-962-3570 wta@rebeltec.net http://www.members.aol.com/ductman249/wta.html

Wyant Bullets, Gen. Del., Swan Lake, MT 59911

Wyoming Custom Bullets, 1626 21st St., Cody, WY 82414

Wyoming Knife Corp., 101 Commerce Dr., Fort Collins, CO 80524 / 303-224-3454

X

XS Sight Systems, 2401 Ludelle St., Fort Worth, TX 76105 / 888-744-4880; FAX: 800-734-7939

X-Spand Target Systems, 26-10th St. SE, Medicine Hat, AB T1A 1P7 CANADA / 403-526-7997; FAX: 403-528-2362

Y

Yankee Gunsmith "Just Glocks", 2901 Deer Flat Dr., Copperas Cove, TX 76522 / 817-547-8433; FAX: 254-547-8887 ed@justglocks.com www.justglocks.com

Yavapai College, 1100 E. Sheldon St., Prescott, AZ 86301 / 520-776-2353; FAX: 520-776-2355

Yavapai Firearms Academy Ltd., P.O. Box 27290, Prescott Valley, AZ 86312 / 928-772-8262; FAX: 928-772-0062 info@yfainc.com www.yfainc.com

Yearout, Lewis E. (See Montana Outfitters)

Yellowstone Wilderness Supply, P.O. Box 129, West Yellowstone, MT 59758 / 406-646-7613

Yesteryear Armory & Supply, P.O. Box 408, Carthage, TN 37030

York M-1 Conversion, 12145 Mill Creek Run, Plantersville, TX 77363 / 936-894-2397; FAX: 936-894-2397 bmf25years@aol.com

Young Country Arms, William, 1409 Kuehner Dr. #13, Simi Valley, CA 93063-4478

Z

Zabala Hermanos S.A., P.O. Box 97, Elbar Lasao, 6, Elgueta, Guipuzcoa, 20600 SPAIN / 34-943-768076; FAX: 34-943-768201 imanol@zabalahermanos.com www.zabalahermanos.com

Zander's Sporting Goods, 7525 Hwy. 154 West, Baldwin, IL 62217-9706 / 800-851-4373; FAX: 618-785-2320

Zanotti Armor, Inc., 123 W. Lone Tree Rd., Cedar Falls, IA 50613 / 319-232-9650 www.zanottiarmor.com

Zeeryp, Russ, 1601 Foard Dr., Lynn Ross Manor, Morristown, TN 37814 / 615-586-2357

Zero Ammunition Co., Inc., 1601 22nd St. SE, P.O. Box 1188, Cullman, AL 35056-1188 / 800-545-9376; FAX: 205-739-4683 zerobulletco@aoz.com www.zerobullets.com

Ziegel Engineering, 1390 E. Bunnett St. "F", Signal Hill, CA 90755 / 562-596-9481; FAX: 562-598-4734 ziegel@aol.com www.ziegeleng.com

Zim's, Inc., 4370 S. 3rd West, Salt Lake City, UT 84107 / 801-268-2505

Z-M Weapons, 203 South St., Bernardston, MA 01337 / 413-648-9501; FAX: 413-648-0219

Numbers

100 Straight Products, Inc., P.O. Box 6148, Omaha, NE 68106 / 402-556-1055; FAX: 402-556-1055

3-Ten Corp., P.O. Box 269, Feeding Hills, MA 01030 / 413-789-2086; FAX: 413-789-1549 www.3-ten.com

4-D Custom Die Co., 711 N. Sandusky St., P.O. Box 889, Mt. Vernon, OH 43050-0889 / 740-397-7214; FAX: 740-397-6600 info@ch4d.com ch4d.com